FOUNDATIONS OF INFORMATION TECHNOLOGY

FOUNDATIONS OF INFORMATION TECHNOLOGY

THIRD EDITION

D.S. YADAV
Assistant Professor
Department of Computer Science & Engineering
Institute of Engineering & Technology
Lucknow

PUBLISHING FOR ONE WORLD

NEW AGE INTERNATIONAL (P) LIMITED, PUBLISHERS
New Delhi • Bangalore • Chennai •Cochin • Guwahati • Hyderabad
Jalandhar • Kolkata • Lucknow • Mumbai • Ranchi
Visit us at **www.newagepublishers.com**

Published by New Age International (P) Ltd., Publishers
First Edition: 2001
Third Edition: 2006
Reprint: 2011

Branches:

- No. 37/10, 8th Cross (Near Hanuman Temple), Azad Nagar, Chamrajpet, **Bangalore** - 560 018. Tel.: (080) 26756823, Telefax: 26756820, E-mail: bangalore@newagepublishers.com
- 26, Damodaran Street, T. Nagar, **Chennai** - 600 017. Tel.: (044) 24353401, Telefax: 24351463 E-mail: chennai@newagepublishers.com
- CC-39/1016, Carrier Station Road, Ernakulam South, **Cochin** - 682 016. Tel.: (0484) 2377004, Telefax: 4051303 E-mail: cochin@newagepublishers.com
- Hemsen Complex, Mohd. Shah Road, Paltan Bazar, Near Starline Hotel, **Guwahati** - 781 008.Tel.: (0361) 2513881 Telefax: 2543669, E-mail: guwahati@newagepublishers.com
- No. 105, 1st Floor, Madhiray Kaveri Tower, 3-2-19, Azam Jahi Road, Nimboliadda, **Hyderabad** - 500 027. Tel.: (040) 24652456, Telefax: 24652457, E-mail:hyderabad@newagepublishers.com
- RDB Chambers (Formerly Lotus Cinema)106A, 1st Floor, S.N. Banerjee Road, **Kolkata** - 700 014. Tel.: (033) 22273773, Telefax: 22275247, E-mail:kolkata@newagepublishers.com
- 16-A, Jopling Road, **Lucknow** - 226 001. Tel.: (0522) 2209578, 4045297, Telefax: 2204098 E-mail: lucknow@newagepublishers.com
- 142C, Victor House, Ground Floor, N.M. Joshi Marg, Lower Parel, **Mumbai** - 400 013.Tel.: (022) 24927869 Telefax: 24915415, E-mail: mumbai@newagepublishers.com
- 22, Golden House, Daryaganj, **New Delhi** - 110 002. Tel.: (011) 23262370, 23262368, Telefax: 43551305 E-mail: sales@newagepublishers.com

---

ISBN (10) : 81-224-1762-0
ISBN (13) : 978-81-224-1762-3

₹ 295.00

C-11-06-5669

Printed in India at Saras Ghraphics, Rai, Haryana.
Typeset at Goswami Associates, Delhi

PUBLISHING FOR ONE WORLD
NEW AGE INTERNATIONAL (P) LIMITED, PUBLISHERS
4835/24, Ansari Road, Daryaganj, New Delhi-110002
Visit us at **www.newagepublishers.com**

PREFACE TO THE THIRD EDITION

The earlier edition of book was adopted by several universities as a reference to introduce the subject to the beginners in the field. The revision of book became necessary to include some topics which were either not dealt in previous edition or an explanatory note was required to increase the readability of certain topics. It was also a long standing demand of readers mainly from faculty members to include an introductory note on operating system. Therefore, in this edition we decided to add **a new chapter on *Operating System*** which deals with the fundamental concepts in operating system. Layout of the book and organization of chapters and topic is similar to previous editions. All attempt has been made to improve the readability of the text in this edition.

This book is the outcome of my several years of teaching information technology courses at Institute of Engineering and Technology, Lucknow and other universities. The book is intended to provide basic foundation to the students starting their university level studies especially in engineering subjects. The book also caters to the need of professional beginners in the field. Therefore, rather than describing the design and structure of various concepts relating information technology, the book emphasizes fundamental concepts which forms the basis of the subject. We decided the content of book after surveying the existing curriculum of several universities in India and abroad. It has been in demand to subject the book for minor revisions so that it can address to the need of wider audience. Following topics have been explained in several chapters of the book.

Information Concepts and Processing

Information Concepts, Entropy of Information, Value and Quality of Information, Data Compression and Compression Techniques , Shannon Fano Codes, Huffman Code, Extended Huffman Codes, LZ & LZW Compression.

Computer Appreciation and Program Development

Program Development, Object Oriented Programming, Software Development, Life Cycles, Data Flow Diagrams, Storage Devices, Fourth Generation Languages, Memory and Memory Hierarchy, Software Quality Assurance, ISO, CMM Standards.

Operating System and Digital Fundamentals

Principles of Operating System, Evolution, Functions, Resource Management, Classifications, Case Studies including Windows, Unix and Future Trends in Operating System, Boolean Algebra, Logic Gates, Flip Flops Digital Circuits, Sequential and Combinational Circuit, Counters and Registers.

Data Communication and Computer Networks

Model of Communication, Modulation, Amplitude, Frequency Modulation, PAM, PDM, PCM, Digital Modulation, ASK, FSK, Multiplexing of Signals, Computer Networks, ISO OSI Layers, ISDN, ATM.

MS Windows, MS Office, Internet and Web Technologies

Windows, Object and Functions of Windows, Managing Files and Folders in Windows, Introductory Note on MS Word , MS Excel and MS Access.

Fundamental Concepts in Internet and Protocols, WWW, E-Mail, Browsing, how to Use Mail Services, HTML, Search Engines, Managing E-Mails in Windows and Using PINE.

E-Commerce and Internet Security

Security threats to E-Commerce, E-Commerce Advantages, Virtual Organizations, Business Transaction on Web, Infrastructure Requirement for E-Commerce, E-Governance, Electronic Data Interchange, Electronic Payment System, Payment Instruments in E-Commerce, Cryptography, Digital Signatures, System of Keys for Encryption and Decryption, Finger Prints, Firewall.

Data Management and SQL

A Basic Introduction to Database Management, Data Abstraction, Schema, Relational Database, System of Keys, Primary and Super Keys, Querying a Database, Structured Query Language, Some Operations on Database Using SQL.

Website Development, Web Technologies and IT Applications

E-Commerce Application Development, Characteristics of E-Commerce Projects, Introduction to Java, Applets and Other Technologies HTML, WAP, WML, VBscripts etc.

We continued with the short introduction to 'C' programming language in this edition. This will help students to develop 'C' program in laboratory sessions. Best effort has been taken to incorporate the suggestions received on mails. I thank all those readers of book who took pain in mailing several critical and constructive suggestions to me in last few years. I thank Mr. Saumya Gupta and Mr. L N Misra for their persuasions, efforts and involvement in bringing out this text. I also thank all staff at New Age Publishers who worked hard to bring this edition in print form.

I shall greatly appreciate the omissions, comments and suggestion reported from the readers at divakar_yadav@rediffmail.com <mailto:divakar_yadav@rediffmail.com>.

D S Yadav

05 August 2005
Southampton
U.K.

PREFACE TO THE FIRST EDITION

In the past few years, several universities have taken the initiative to start undergraduate and postgraduate programs in Information Technology. The subject is also being offered to all branches of engineering and technology, management, pharmacy, and science students. It has been noticed that the students have to refer to the number of books for their course of study. This book has been designed strictly according to the syllabus of UP Technical University, Lucknow for the core subject offered to B.Tech (all branches of engineering) and MBA. It is an attempt to provide the basic learning material to the beginners in the field of Information Technology. It provides the systematic presentation of information technology, principles and practices and caters to the requirements of a first course on the subject.

This book is the outcome of the continuous persuasion of my friends, and colleagues from different engineering colleges/institutions to develop basic course material for this subject. I have tried to incorporate the suggestions of my colleagues and teachers. I have tried my best to organize the contents of this book with sufficient examples and diagrams. I hope this book would be helpful to both academicians and students.

I shall greatly appreciate the comments and suggestions from the readers at *divakar_yadav@rediffmail.com.*

D S Yadav

ACKNOWLEDGEMENTS

I would like to acknowledge my deep sense of gratitude to Prof. D S Chauhan, a man of spiritual personality, for his soft words, continuous encouragement, efforts towards achieving academic excellence in the UP Technical University. I consider privileged and fortunate enough to retain the affection of following distinguished personalities.

Prof. G N Pandey, who has always motivated me to achieve high academic values, Prof. A K Majumdar, my guide and teacher at IIT Kharagpur, has always been my source of inspiration. Prof. R C Sarswat for his constant encouragement, and Prof. S K Bajpai for his valuable suggestions and help during preparation of this text.

I would like to thank Dr. A N Pathak, Council of Science & Technology, Lucknow for acknowledging the work on the subject, his encouragement and critical suggestions. I have been deeply inspired with his attitude and approach towards academics. I thank Er. S K Shukla, Registrar, IET, Lucknow for his efforts towards enrichment of academics at this Institute and providing necessary help whenever required.

I wish to put on record Dr. B N Mishra, Dr. D S Kushwaha, Dr. Sanjay Singh, Prof. Arun Mittal, Prof. Vikram Bisen, Prof. Girish Chandra, Prof. Manik Chandra, Mrs. Dipali Awasthi of IET Lucknow; Dr. Vikram Singh of BIET, Jhansi for their constructive suggestions. I am very thankful to my colleagues, Mr. Pavan Tripathi Mr. Manoj Waria, Dr. Rajiv Srivatsava, Mr. Yash Pal Singh, Prof. Vinay Pathak, Prof. Rajiv Mishra, Dr. O P Singhal, Prof. M H Khan and Mr. S S Soam who have helped and kept me motivated for writing this text.

I thank the staff at New Age International especially Mr. L N Misra for his deep involvement in this project and bringing this text in a presentable form.

I would like to thank my wife Gayatri, daughters Ankita and Surbhi for their patience and continuing support to make this task complete with pleasure, and parents for their blessings. At last, I thank every one who has directly or indirectly contributed something to this work.

D S Yadav

CONTENTS

1

CONCEPTS IN INFORMATION AND PROCESSING

Contents

1 CONCEPTS IN INFORMATION AND PROCESSING

1.1 INFORMATION TECHNOLOGY

The last decade in the global arena has witnessed a tremendous growth in the area of information technology. Rapid advances in the technologies for communication media like television, computer, internet, printing and publishing has enabled us to get prompt access to required information. The computer is the most versatile machine man has ever made. The use of computer at home has become a reality and the use of computers at work is very common. Now almost all the government departments and commercial organizations have accepted the computer as a major tool to renovate their function. Computers are being used in multiple areas ranging from solving intricate scientific problems to art, cultural, historical, accounting, financial, medical and even domestic sectors. Truly, with Information Technology, the computers has made a significant impact on all dimensions of our day to day life, e.g. reservation of air and railway tickets, buying and selling items on Internet, electronic market, bank transaction on net, entertainment, education, communication, hotel reservations and so on. Information Technology has replaced the conventional methods to solve technical and operational problem by introducing a much faster and more convenient method which is based on its ability to access large and complex pools of data.

Initially computer could process information contained in the form of text only. A text is written with letters, digits and other characters which you can read. Later it was also realized that the information contained in form of images, animation, audio, video can also be processed. Imagine, if you have to create a database of your friends for future references, you will have to create the database using attributes like Name, Date of Birth, Father Name, Telephone No., Street, City, Pin Code etc. Just think, how good it would be if you could store the image of your friend, his voice or video clip in which he is seen to your database. The pressing demand for storage and retrieval of data represented in multiple forms like Text, Image, Animation, Graphics, Audio, Video has given a new direction to computer scientists and technologists to process information stored in multiple formats. All this has revolutionized information technology.

Information Technology is a generic name for the following functions:

1. Information/Data Representation
2. Information/Data Storage
3. Information/Data Retrieval and Processing
4. Information/Data Communication

The computer is as a tool to do the above mentioned tasks effectively, efficiently and extremely quickly.

1.2 AN OVERVIEW OF CURRENT INFORMATION TECHNOLOGY APPLICATIONS

Among the fundamental computer applications are processing, storage and retrieval of information and developing effective technologies for communicating the information represented in various formats. The information may be contained in form of text, image, graphics, audio, video or animations. An important application is Video on Demand. The video on demand is very common now-a-days. The cable TV operator provides services to watch any video clipping, movie or any favorite TV program. The channel is established from the computer at home and the cable operator. You may surf the TV program and select any program of your choice by selecting the appropriate program on your computer. In such cases, the compressed video is transmitted over the communication channel, usually the cable, and is decompressed on your computer while playing. All video cassette player functions are provided at your computer to record, play, forward or rewind. Another important application is multimedia conferencing. It is now possible to arrange meeting between several executives when they are not physically present at one place. Using current technologies, a group of persons can talk and discuss with each other as though they were present in one room. Anybody who will speak will be listened by everybody. This is achieved using a underlying high bandwidth channel which is able to transmit the video data at an extremely fast rate.

Applications like home shopping or shopping on web, knowing the details of the items to be purchased in the form of images, graphics or video are very common today. All healthcare systems using Telemedicine or Geographic Information System require a high bandwidth as in all such cases it is necessary to communicate video or graphics. The information contained in any format other than text requires high storage capacity. Storage, retrieval and processing of such information is a costly affair because of two reason, namely, lack of bandwidth and lack of effective tools and technologies to handle such large information.

Apart from the applications described above, the Information Technology concepts are being used in business applications ranging from inventory control, preparation of various business documents like invoices, pay bills, salary statements, issue/dispatch transactions, accounting and financial management, account wise consumption, analysis report, sales report etc. There exist number of special purpose business system developed to meet the specific requirement of a company or business. Central to these software packages are modules to handle human resource, invoices, accounting etc. The requirement to bring all the activities of a business organization under single software has led to the development of ERP systems. The Enterprise Resource Planning (ERP) systems are bundle of the software which includes the standard business practices. These softwares are customized according to the need of an enterprise and provides the tailored solution to the enterprise. Information Technology is playing a significant role in standardization of different processes in banks. Banking has taken a major lead in past few years after deploying the Information Technology. Now it has become possible to transfer the balance, internet banking, Tele-services and using automatic tailor machines. Time, effort and money required to monitor the business processes in the banks has been reduced drastically in past few years. EDI (Electronic Data Interchange) has allowed the different automated/computerized organizations to transfer the documents electronically. EDI has reduced the cost of transportation, reduced paper work, minimum human interaction and faster exchange of the document within the organization. This is not all, Information Technology application to different areas such as hospitals, medicine, reservations, tele-shopping, manufacturing, communication etc., are very common. The process of updating the conventional practices through Information Technology in the different organization is still going on.

1.3 WHAT IS THE DIFFERENCE BETWEEN DATA AND INFORMATION ?

It is generally not easy to decide as to when a particular piece of text, numbers, tables, images, graphics serve as merely data and when they become information. In fact, there is no hardline to tell us that a piece of text or sample of numbers represent data or information.

Let us take an example. The government has launched a polio vaccination drive to eradicate polio from India. In this programme, officers or executives at different levels have been deployed. The top level of executives monitor the overall progress and might be interested about the success at the national level. Similarly, the next level of executives watches the progress at the state level, the next at the zonal, district, block and village levels. The top level has fixed a target that vaccination of a certain percentage of population at the national level be achieved. To monitor the overall progress at a particular time, the top level collects the data from each state and process that data to know the current status. Similarly, at State level, data are collected from Zones and processed subsequently. Data from lower levels are collected and processed to find the current status at the upper level. The result of processing of data at each level serve as **information** at the next higher level. For example, suppose there are 100 villages in a particular block. If executives at block level are provided with vaccination data of all one hundred villages, then it will probably not be of much importance. However, if after processing of all such hundred data, if the average percentage of vaccination at block level is obtained, then this figure will be of much importance to executives at the block level. The executives at block level then may take decisions based upon the figure obtained after processing the data. This processed figure thus serves as information at the block level.

The data are the basic facts and figures which may be used as a historical record about say, a company or an organization. These may be assembled together in the form of files, reports, graphs, payrolls etc. If raw data is processed as par certain rules or policy, the results obtained (if they are meaningful) are called information. The word meaningful here signifies that on which executives or the management may take decisions. It may be noted that information obtained at a certain level may serve as raw data for further information at another level. That is probably the reason that data and information words are used interchangeably. Strictly speaking, data consists of numbers, text etc. that a computer processes according to certain procedures to produce information. The computer can be used to organize the raw data in some order so that it becomes information. Preparing charts, tables, reports, work sheet etc. are examples of creating information from raw data.

We may therefore conclude that processing data is a cyclic process and at every hop we receive more meaningful data as evident from Figure 1.1.

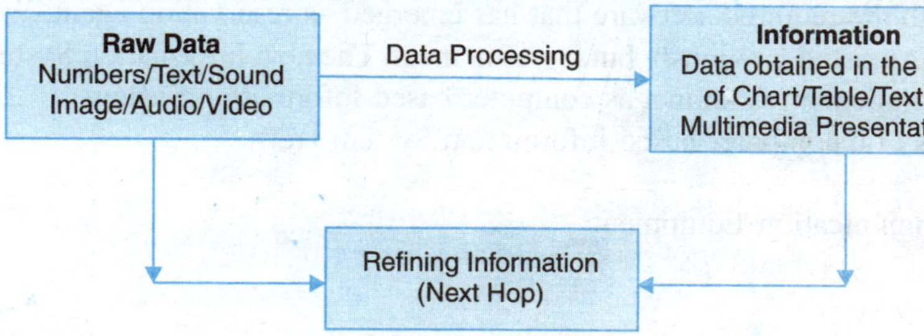

Figure 1.1

1.4 INFORMATION SYSTEM

The past decade has witnessed tremendous growth in the information innovation and application. Information Technology has become a vital component for the success of business because most of the organizations require fast dissemination of information, information processing, storage and retrieval of data. Today management of an organization involved in the business requires high speed processing of huge amount of data, fact and figures. High speed communication between organization, customers, clients etc. is also playing an important role to achieve high business goal. These requirements of modern business led to development of a business information system which provides appropriate information to appropriate person in desired format and at correct time. The timely processing of data also helps and enable management to take important decision at earliest possible time. **Information System** may be defined as organized collection of human, software, hardware and communication equipment and database, in which the person controls, process and communicate the information. The overall objective of the Information System is to gather the data, processing of data communicating the information to the user of the system. User group includes the person from all level i.e. top, middle and operational level. The information obtained from the information system allows the different persons to take decisions. To provide the appropriate information to user, it is necessary to collect the data, process and output of the data. Information System may include feedback mechanism under which processed data or output are fed back to the system to make changes in processing activities. **For example**, sales, inventory report generated may be fed back to appropriate managers to take appropriate decision in time. Therefore, the high end information systems are designed around feedback and control machanism, based on user-based criteria to produce and communicate the information for planning and control of business.

Information System may be broadly categorized into two categories (i) Manual (ii) Computer Based Information System (CBIS). As discussed before, the major objective of the information system is to collect, process and disseminate the data to appropriate user. Traditionally, the business analyst in the organization study the pattern of investment, expenditure, sales etc. to evaluate the performance and to take decision for future. These analyst used to collect the data and prepare the report in the form of chart, table, graph etc. to analyze the business. Now-a-days, the requirement of a business analyst may be programmed and a computer based system may be developed to study and analyze these reports. These Information System are called Computer based Information System. **For example,** in earlier days the rail reservation system was manual. Traveller used to fill application form and allotment of seat in different quota on different train. These reservation used to be on the basis of certain well defined rule. After the introduction of the computer, these rules and guidelines have been programmed in computer along with the required software that has emerged as reservation agent. We may say that the Information System existed previously but it was manual. The new Information System, which used computer as central component, is known as computer based Information System.

Basic components of a computer based Information System are:

1. Users
2. Hardware/Communication Equipment
3. Software
4. Database
5. Set of Methods

1. Users: are one of the most important components of the Information System. These users include the different group of persons who manages the system and those who retrieve the information from this system take decisions.

Another set of the users are those who not only retrieve the information but also provide the information to information system. **For example,** marketing and sales personnel provide the details of sale etc. to the Information System.

2. Hardware/Communication Equipment: In the modern business, it is not only necessary to gather and process information but the fast dissemination of the information is also essential. Lot of organizations maintain constant touch with a large customer base. It requires that the Information System at an organization must be computer network enabled and must be able to communicate the information through internet or other communication channel. All hardware, Network and communication equipment forms an important component for a computer based information system.

3. Software: A software is a collection of programs, which do a specific tasks. Different rules, methods and practices prevailing in a business organization are coded into the programs or software. The software once installed in computer system is considered as most important component of information system. These programs process the data and generate report such as sales report, invoice, bill etc. for customers and generate different reports for the managers.

4. Database: Database is a structured collection of data. The software or programs fetch the data from the database and process them as per the requirement. The database may contain the customer and employee record, data pertaining to sales, inventory, account etc. The raw data gathered from the field by sales or marketing persons, from customer etc. are stored in the database. To develop an efficient Information System, it is necessary to have a good design of database. The Information System are said to be built on top of database and performance of Information System depends on the underlying database.

5. Set of Methods: Set of methods is another important component of Information System. The set of methods refers to the tradition and practices prevailing in the business house where the Information System is used. Various traditions, practices, which govern the business, are laid down in the form of rules which are then coded into the programs. These rules or methods changes from time to time whenever any new business practice is adopted or any change in the business environment is observed. The Information System must be adaptable to these changes and must be flexible to incorporate the changes in the business environment.

1.4.1 Types of Information System

Following are the motivating factors for any business enterprise to use information system:

1. Information System's support for business processes and practices.
2. Information System's support for decision making.
3. Information System's support for the innovative planning.

Depending upon the specific requirement of users, various types of information systems may be developed. Based on the specific requirement of organization and need of user, information system may be categorized into the following categories:

1. Transaction Processing System
2. Management Information System
3. Work Flow System
4. Decision Support System
5. Expert System

1.4.2 Transaction Processing System (TPS)

A transaction processing system is a traditional system which is combination of people, software, hardware and database. The main focus in these systems is on completion of a business transaction. The objective of these systems are to reduce the cost, effort and automation of business activities in the organization. **For example,** business transcations in an organization includes activities like raising an invoice, acceptance of sales order, receipt and dispatch of item from store etc. A business transaction is considered as an atomic activity. It is therefore necessary to complete the business transaction otherwise the underlying database may enter into inconsistent state. Suppose, a sales order is received by an organization from a client, after the receipt of sales order a chain of activities needs to be invoked. These involves, informing manufacturing unit to raise requirement of items, sales department, accounts, shipping etc. If any of the related activity is not completed, required modification to the database may not occur. This situation may lead disaster because incomplete or inconsistent information may jeopardize the business activity. The nature of these transactions may vary from one organization to another. The information system processes these transactions as a basic activity which satisfies the organizations day to day need. There may exit a number of transactions in the organization which need to be completed for full assistance of persons working at operative level and top management. These systems ensure timely and correct completion of the job. A transaction processing system deals with the transaction in two different ways.

1. Batch Processed Information System
2. On Line Transaction Processing (OLTP)

In the **batch processing**, the different transactions are queued and they are executed one after another. These transactions keep modifying the data or database and preceding transaction operate on the data processed by previous transaction. Payroll system, electricity billing, telephone billing are examples of batch processed system. These activities are triggered at required time and result in fetching the data from the database and prepare the reports like marksheets, telephone bills etc. These transactions also modify the database when required. The **On Line Transaction Processing System** (OLTP), in contrast to batch processing, process the data instantaneously. The OLTP systems are becoming more popular now-a-days as they provide instant services to customer. The request raised by either customer or any other person are instantly (on line) processed by the computer. Good example of OLTP systems are railways reservation system banking system etc. However, OLTP, requests are processed instantaneously whenever they are submitted. The OLTP is the system in which operational level support to organization is provided by processing the data through business transactions. These requests retrieve and store the data in database on line. Any failure in these systems might become a costly affair, as recovery from the failure is time consuming and an intricate affair. There exist another type of transaction processing called Real Time Transaction Processing. In **Real Time Transaction Processing** System, not only transactions are processed on line but also the deadlines are maintained.

In the mission control operation, it is not only important to process the data but it is more of importance that the transactions are completed within deadline.

1.4.3 Management Information System (MIS)

On Line Transaction Processing Systems provide the operation level support to the organization by processing the data through business transactions. These business transactions are submitted to the system time to time. MIS is used in those organizations, where information in form of reports, presentations is required by the management to take decisions. The Transaction Processing Systems are based on merely processing a business transaction. In MIS, the requirement is much higher as different areas of an organization like accounts, inventory, sales, purchase, marketing etc. needs to be tightly integrated to provide collective information to the management. MIS provides reports or feedback to the management with appropriate data, which arises from transaction processing systems. For example, MIS may be used by finance controller of huge organization to view daily budgetary positions in the budget heads. A sales manger may seek the report from MIS to judge the performance and work of their sales representatives. MIS also helps getting scheduled report of income, weekly report of sales etc.

1.4.4 Workflow System

Workflow systems in an organization are used to manage and control the interrelated activities required to perform a business goal. These systems help users, employees and managers to evaluate and control the status of different interrelated tasks. These systems are based on certain rules that control the flow of the tasks. Primary objective of workflow systems is to provide tracking and routing of tasks or documents from one process to another. **For example,** in any typical university, a student falling short of attendance is required to take permission before appearing in the examination. Suppose the rules state that if a students attendance falls short up to ten percent then permission from head is required; if the attendance falls short up to twenty percent then permission from principal is required; if the attendance falls short of twenty-five percent or more then permission of dean is required. If all officers of university and students are connected via network, a student may download the application form and submit it electronically. The various steps i.e. routing of application from one desk to another will be monitored and permission from the concerned persons will be transmitted to student for the examination cell. There exist few workflow system tools out of which Lotus Notes, MS Exchange and Novell Group Ware are popular. Major advantages of workflow system include reducing time due to retyping, filling the option form and reports, and amount of work towards the reconciliation of several reports.

1.4.5 Decision Support System

As we have discussed that MIS is helpful in meeting the organization's requirement to automate the business process and produces required information to employee or manager. MIS helps the organization to do the different task correctly but lacks in decision-making capabilities. Decision Support System supports management solving business problems. It often may not be solved by management information system. **For example,** many time management needs to decide which product of company should be continued and which product be discontinued. Deciding the areas, location and condition where a particular product have better sales prospects. These decisions are based upon certain underlying fact and feedback obtained by a company and its representatives. Taking these decisions MIS which merely provides processing data and also provides the information, are not sufficient. It requires to prepare the information specific formats and certain organization specific methdos needs to be deployed to take appropriate decision. After introduction of MIS at a later stage, organization has started feeling that MIS are not able to meet the decision making requirement of the management, as management had to remain dependent on the MIS for getting appropriate information for decision making. **A Decision Support System** is a collection of software and hardware to support decision-making in specific environment or problem. The main objective of decision support system is to suggest the right options. Most of the cases, to solve complex problem where information to make effective decisions are difficult to obtain, the Decision Support System are used. Decision Support System are often designed as per the manager's requirement and plays a vital role in making managerial judgements. Decision Support System are designed around the business policies and methods for decision making and supporting database to provide information.

1.4.6 Expert Systems

Expert Systems are used to solve the problems of individual by providing expert decision making. These systems use Artificial Intelligence to solve the problem that requires significant human expertise. To the core, Expert Systems are computer based systems that emulate the decision making capability of human expert. Emulation means that computer system acts as an expert. The general purpose MIS are used to gather information from the database and decision support system helps us in decision making process, the expert system goes beyond the scope of MIS and DSS, Expert System provides the expert guidance to make use of a specialized knowledge required for decision making. These systems incorporate the knowledge which are not available to most of the people. The work Expert System and knowledge based system are often used interchangeably. One of the classical expert systems MYCIN was developed to provide the expert guidance to individual for medical diagnosis. In contrast to the expert system, several knowledge based system has also been developed for providing knowledge as an intelligent agent to human expert. Most of the expert systems are designed around knowledge base and inference engine. The user enters the information and expert system provides the response by invoking inference engine which draws the conclusion from the basis of information stored in knowledge base. One of the limitations posed by the expert system is that the knowledge and the techniques used by inference engines limit its performance. If the knowledge base does not have knowledge or information about any one of the facets, it may not provide the expert guidance.

1.5 IMPORTANT DATA TYPES

The most popular way of representing information is in the textual form. In this form, a combination of letters, numerals and some special characters are used. However, today there are several other ways in which data can be represented. These are Text, Image, Graphics and Animation, Audio and Video forms.

1.5.1 Text

Text is a collection of alphabets (both lower and upper case), numerals (0–9) and special characters (* , ? , : , #) etc. Data presented in textual form may be written and read. The information content in the text can be determined only after reading and interpreting it. Any collection of these characters does not constitute information; it is necessary to organize the characters according to some order or plan, then only it can have informative value.

1.5.2 Image

Images are another form of data type. Images refer to data in the form of pictures, photographs, hand drawings etc. Suppose we have to create a database for the employees of an organization to develop identity cards with photographs of the employees. To generate the identity card, it is required to store several attributes of employees. These are Employee Id, Employee name, Date of Birth, Address, Telephone Number etc. All this information may be stored in a textual form and may be printed on the identity card. A good and effective database of employees requires that the photograph of employees should also be stored. Collection of all attributes represented in textual form may not generate the photograph. While generating an identity card, the photograph of an employee will also be printed simultaneously with printing other textual attributes. A different software would be required to generate images like photographs.

Information may be represented in the form of images. These images may be processed and several software programs have been developed to process images. Editing of images includes changing the size of object in images, changing the background, modifying the colors, shading, zooming an object on image etc. All of these changes the image or photograph, thus changing or modifying the information contained in the image.

1.5.3 Graphics and Animation

Graphics and animations are another way of presenting information. For example, if you have to present the information about an organization systematically, it is possible to combine together the text, images and sound pertaining to that organization in order to prepare a good presentation. There are various progress for preparing this type of presentation, as for example, Microsoft Powerpoint tools. Powerpoint comes with music, sounds, and videos you can play during your slide shows. You can also insert music, sound, or video clips wherever you want it on the slide. It is also possible to add different animation effects to make the presentation more effective.

The following are popular graphics file extension used by Microsoft:

- Enhanced Metafile (.emf)
- Joint Photographic Experts Group (.jpg)
- Portable Network Graphics (.png)
- Windows Bitmap (.bmp, .rle, .dib)

1.5.4 Audio

Audio is the data in the form of sounds. Different type of sounds produce important information. For example, the sounds obtained through medical devices of the Heart, Speech or voice of any person provide important diagnostic information to the doctors. The meaning or value of information contained in audio can be interpreted by hearing. The audio may be stored in a database in the form of files. Audio data may be processed by the computer, as for example, mixing of sound, modifying the sound parameters like frequency, pitch, amplitude, bass etc.

1.5.5 Video

Video is another important data format to hold information. It basically combines sound and stack of images and these are displayed over a period of time. This format stores synchronized play of both sound and image, putting them as a sequence of images. These images are called frames. Different frames are juxtaposed and so produced that it seems as though the objects are moving as in real life. Storing a clip of video takes maximum storage space. Video can also be processed in a similar way as sound and images. 'avi' and '.dat' are popular extension of files holding video data.

1.6 VALUE OF INFORMATION

The need for information is a fundamental ingredient of any development process in society. The emergence of information triggers the development process. The modern society may be termed as Information Society, as it is characterized by increasing responsiveness towards the individual's need for information. This society motivates the individual human being to engage in productive businesses that are knowledge based and knowledge generating. The value of information has been seen as a dynamic resource.

The chronological development of society may be seen in three phases–Agricultural society, Industrial society and Knowledge based society. In earlier times, the society was mainly dependent on agriculture and agriculture based activities. Different societies during those times were quite isolated. During the past 400 years after the Industrial Revolution took place, industrial activities, business, trade and commerce grew rapidly. During this time it was realized that information about products technologies as well as customer needs plays a vital role in any business. This trend continued until last decade. In 1970's after the acceptance of digital computer by organizations for information storage, retrieval and processing, a new dimension to economic growth was added. The Industrial society is now rapidly moving towards knowledge based society. This society is centered around information, information processing tools and innovative ways for information communication. In the industrial society, the Capital resources were considered as the prime resource for individuals or organizations. In knowledge-based society, Information is considered as the prime resource for individuals or organizations. High speed telecommunication services also play an important role in information dissemination and communication. The rapid delivery of information has become a primary activity in this society.

The value of information plays an important role in decision making process. It is possible to quantify the amount of the information but it is difficult to compute the absolute value of the information. The value of the information is different to the different groups of persons. Value of information is related to the parameters like, who uses the information, under what circumstances the information is used and most importantly how it is used. The information for this purpose may be treated as a item or commodity to be used by different persons for different purposes. It may be understood from the example. The glass of water may have high value to a thirsty person in summer and may have different value to the person who just had a cup of water in the winters. Similarly, the information received from the meteorological department that it may have heavy showers in next week will have different impact or value to different persons. This information may have high value to the farmer looking for the rains but may not have greater value to those who are not farmers. Therefore, the value of information to different persons will have different effects and it greatly depends on the person, time and environment. There may be different types of value of information. These are given below:

1. Normative Value
2. Realistic Value
3. Subjective Value

Suppose the management of a electronic equipment manufacturing company gets the information that a bulk order for different equipment is going to be placed with them in coming days. Management of the company will estimate the cost of production and margins based on additional cost required to manufacture the required number of equipment. Based on these estimates, management will make a plan to quote the revised price of equipment to the purchaser. The computation may be carried out to estimate the profits by calculating the estimated cost of production with and without knowledge of information. The difference of estimated cost with prior knowledge of order and without the knowledge of order would be normative value of information. The normative values are obtained by theoretical procedures of decision making and assume that it will be an optimal decision.

The experienced managers will treat the information in different ways. The major drawback of normative value of information is that it is based on the theoretical and standard procedures and ignores the human factor, environment and other risk factors. The experienced manager will like to carry out some experiment to include the human and other environmental factors to study the impact of information. The gain in payoffs may be estimated after obtaining the information. When these payoffs are taken into the consideration to estimate the profit margin, it provides the realistic value of information. Therefore, the value of information obtained after taking the behavioural aspects into consideration is known as realistic value of information.

At number of times, it is not possible to calculate the normative or realistic value of information, most experienced persons make an intuitive guess for the expected profit margins. Based on these intuitive guess management will quote the price to purchaser. The value obtained by using the intuitive guess is known as subjective value of information. In real life, mostly we use the subjective value of information.

1.7 QUALITY OF INFORMATION

It may be noted that data in the form of audio, video, graphics or animation requires a high amount of memory in comparison to text and numbers for storage. Since many applications require storage, retrieval and processing of data in various formats and also that information be communicated from one place to another on communication channel. Band width requirement has become a prime area of concern and it is quite a costly affair.

It is always desirable that the information be presented in such a way that it enables one to take decisions. Quality of information refers to the extent to which it enables decision making.

The need for information in an enterprise arises because of the following reasons:

1. Opportunities before the organization and formalizing the short term or long term policy for the growth of the organization.
2. Resource allocation in an optimal way in order to attain the basic goals of an organization.
3. Adjusting with new and rapidly changing technological advancement and opening new vistas for overall progress of the organization.
4. To maintain the relationship with the management, suppliers, customers, government, banking institutions, etc.
5. Product survey, product marketing, sales of product etc. require the data to be gathered from the field and consequent processing to generate information.

1.8 DATA COMPRESSION

Images, audio, video take enormously high amount of storage ranging from kilobytes to gigabytes. It is always desirable to store the information in a compressed form. Data Compression may be divided into following two categories:

1. Lossless Data Compression
2. Lossy Data Compression

Lossless data compression refers to the compression where the exact input data value will be produced after decompression. In the case of **lossy compression,** data may loose some of content and the exact information will not be reproduced after decompression. There exist several techniques for lossless and lossy compressions. Images, Audio, Video are compressed using lossy data compression techniques as even after losses, the information retrieved after decompression will have certain value. Most of the lossy compression techniques may be adjusted to different quality levels. Lossy compression techniques are usually applied to images, audio, video as they result in certain loss of accuracy thus they are more suitable to formats (images, graphics etc.) other than text. In text cases, where it is not acceptable to miss or lose even a single digit, lossless compression techniques are applied. All the software, programs and important data are compressed using lossless data compression techniques. Suppose, a file containing bank account detail is compressed. After decompression each data or figure must appear without any loss to it. If any digit is lost or missed, the processing of that data may have catastrophic results. Therefore lossless compression techniques are normally applied to text files.

1.9 ENCODING vs COMPRESSION

There is a fine difference between encoding and compression. The objective of compression is to convert the input data into a format which requires less space for storage. The graphics, audio, video data usually take very high amount of storage ranging from several megabyte to gigabytes. Storage, retrieval, processing and communication of such huge data is a very costly affair. Basic principle behind compression is to code the input data using coding techniques in such a way that the coded data takes less amount of storage. For this purpose many coding techniques are used and this process is called **encoding**. Encoding is therefore a part of compression. The objective of compression is to minimize the storage requirement and produce the same input data at the decompression phase. The objective of encoding is to generate the code for input data which after decoding produces the same information.

Data compression is one of the applications of Information Theory. Information theory is actually a branch of mathematics which deal with information or data representation. Information storage, retrieval, processing and communication are also a part of Information Theory. Information theory mainly deals with computation and minimising the redundant information in a sample data. The audio, video, graphics and animation contain a lot of redundant information which can be easily notified without adversely affecting the value of information. Such modification is made in the values of some of the parameters. For example, if you take a original or new photograph and process it in such a way that some parameters like color, size of background objects etc. are slightly changed, then it will still have some information. The level of adjustment of such process must be controlled. If by doing some modification in the parameter pertaining to audio,video or text we save storage space, then this will always reduce the processing time, time for communication and enable fast storage and retrieval.

Data compression therefore consists of taking the stream of characters and converting them into codes. The resulting stream of code is smaller than the original stream. The compression is obtained by following a model of compression. The model of compression is collection of statistical data and rules of coding which determine which code to output.

1.10 ENTROPY OF INFORMATION

The prime difference between Loss Less and Lossy Data compression is that Loss Less Data compression algorithm compreses the data without any loss of the information. The original data compressed using Loss Less compression is obtained without any loss while Lossy data compression algorithm allows certain losses to occur. The information theory provides the basic frame-work for development of loss less algorithms. For data compression, it is essential to measure information contents in the data or degree of disorder/randomness in the data. Quantitative measure of information serves the basis for the data compression. Claude Shannon has done pioneering work in information theory and proposed the concept of self-information. Self-information is associated with outcome of every event.

Suppose, A and B are the possible outcome of an event. With every possible outcome there is self information associated.

Suppose P(A) = Probability of occurrence of 'A'

P(B) = Probability of occurrence of 'B'

Suppose Si (A) denotes Self Information associated with 'A' and Si (B) denotes Self Information associated with 'B'. According to Shannon Si (A) and Si (B) may be defined as,

$$Si\ (A) = -\mathbf{log}_m\ P(A)) = \mathbf{log}_m\ (1/P(A))$$

$$Si\ (B) = -\mathbf{log}_m\ (P(B)) - \mathbf{log}_m\ (1/P(B))$$

The base of the log function (m) defines the unit of information. For example, if the m=2, the unit is bits, if m=10 the unit is hartleys. Since we are always interested in knowing information in terms of bits, we generally set the value of m to '2'.

Let us analyze what is meant by self information. Since value of log (1)=0 and value of $\log_2$ (yx), where x is any number, increases as x decreases from one to zero. It is evident from the following table with assumption that base of the log is 2.

The following table shows that with decreasing values of P(A), self information associated with event 'A' increases. It clearly indicates that high probability event contains less self-information while low probability event associates much more self-information. Let us try to understand the meaning of it leaving the mathematics behind.

We know that sun rises in the east. Probability that sun will rise in the east tomorrow, is extremely high probable event. (The probability is very high and too close to 1). Since this event has high probability of occurrence therefore, it does not associate much information. Assume, one morning, the sun did not rise in the east (very low probability event.), it will have lot of self Information.

P(A)	**Self-Information Si (A)**
(Prob. of occurrence of event 'A')	**Si (A) = $\log_2$ (P(A))**
1.0	0.0
.60	0.74
.50	1.0
.25	2.0
.20	2.32
.15	2.74
.10	3.32
.05	4.32

Entropy of information may be defined as a measure of information contents in the input sample or message. The higher entropy of message indicates that more information contents are present in the message. Higher entropy of the message also implies higher potential for data compression.

Concepts of the self information may also be deployed to make inferences after associating two independent events. Suppose 'A' and 'B' are independent event. The self-information associated with two independent Si (AB) is the sum of self-information obtained from these events separately.

Since A and B are independent events therefore,

$$P\ (AB) = P\ (A) * P\ (A))$$

and self information of event 'A' and 'B' are

$$Si(A) = -\log_2 (P(A)$$
$$Si(A) = -\log_2 (P(B))$$

Self information associated with occurrence of event 'A' and 'B', Si (AB) may be defined as

$$Si(AB) = -\log_2 (P(AB))$$
$$= -(\log_2 (P(A) + \log_2 (P(B))$$
$$= Si(A) + Si(B)$$

1.10.1 Entropy Function

The term Entropy in the Information Theory has been borrowed from thermodynamics. Shannon used this term in Information Theory to determine degree of randomness or disorder in the data. The Shannon proposed following entropy function. Suppose there are 'n' possible of outcome of an event and Pi denotes the probability of i'th outcome, the Entropy may be computed as,

$$\text{Entropy} = -\sum_{I=1}^{I=N} Pi * \log_2 (Pi) \quad ...(1)$$

Let us understand the concept with following example.

Example

Suppose we have to examine the outcome of tossing a coin. There are two possible outcome Head and Tail. We will compute the self-information and entropy under following cases.

Case 1: The Coin is fair and probability of getting Head or Tail are equal.

Case 2: The Coin is biased and probability of getting Head or Tail are not equal.

Case 3: The Coin always falls on one side i.e. either Head or Tail.

Analysis for all cases are given below.

Case 1:

Assuming that coin is fair, probability of getting head or tail will be equal. It may be defined as

$$P(Head) = 1/2, P(Tail) = 1/2 \text{ and } P(Head) + P(Tail) = 1$$

The self-information of both outcome therefore may be computed as,

$$Si(Head) = -\log_2 (P(Head) = 1$$
$$Si(Tail) = -\log_2 (P(Tail)) = 1$$

The self-information associated with each outcome is therefore of 1 bit. We use the unit bit because the base of the logarithm is two.

Since the event tossing of a coin have only two possible out-come, if we compute following function:

$$E = -(P(Head) * \log_2 (P(Head) + P(Tail) * \log_2 (P(Tail))$$
$$= -(1/2 * \log_2 (1/2) + 1/2 * (\log_2 (1/2)) = 1$$

The term denoted by E is known as Entropy. In this example the value of entropy is 1.

Alternatively, the Entropy function may be written as,

$$E = (P(Head) * Si(Head) + P(Tail) * Si(Tail)) = 1/2*1 + 1/2*1 = 1.$$

Case 2:

Assuming that the coin is not fair and it is biased toward Head. The probability of getting a Head is .75 and probability of getting a Tail is .25.

$$P(Head) = .75, P(Tail) = .25$$

The self-information of both outcome therefore may be computed as,

$$Si\ (Head) = -\mathbf{log_2}\ (P(Tail) = -\ \mathbf{log_2}\ (.75) = .41$$

$$Si\ (Tail = -\ \mathbf{log_2}\ (P(Tail) = -\ \mathbf{log_2}\ (.25) = 2.0$$

If we compute the following Entropy function

$$E = -\ (P(Head) * \mathbf{log_2}\ (P(Head) + P\ (Tail) * \mathbf{log_2}\ (P(Tail))\ )$$

$$= -\ (.75 * \mathbf{log_2}\ (.75) + .25 * (\mathbf{log_2}\ (.25))\ ) = .807$$

For the Case 2, the Entropy value therefore is .807.

Alternatively, the entropy function may be written as,

$$E = (P(Head) * Si\ (Head) + P\ (Tail) * Si\ (Tail)) = .807$$

Similarly if the Probability of getting Head and Tail are .60 and .40 respectively, the Entropy function will yield the value .972.

Case 3:

If one of the outcome e.g. Head is guaranteed, the Probabilities of getting Head and Tail would be,

$$P\ (Head) = 1$$

$$P\ (Tail) = 0$$

Using the method given above the Entropy function will yield the value as under,

$$E = -\ (\ 1 * \mathbf{log_2}\ (1.0) + 0 * \mathbf{log_2}\ (0)\ ) = 0$$

Result obtained Case 1, Case 2 and Case 3 are presented in the following table.

Case	Probability	Entropy
Case 1 : Coin is Fair	P (Head) = P (Tail) = 1/2	1.0
Case 2 : Coin is biased Case 2 : Coin is biased	P (Head) = .60; P (Tail) = .40 P (Head) = .75; P (Tail) =.25	.97 .80
Case 3: Coin always falls on Head side	P (Head) = 1; P (Tail) = 0	0

Ealier we have observed that high probability event contains less self-information while low probability event associates much more self-information. It means when the high probability of event contains less self-information, therefore it requires less number of bits. From the table shown above, it is evident that entropy value decreases when the degree of disorder decreases. *Case 1* indicates that the coin is fair. Outcome of tossing a fair coin is completely uncertain as the probability of getting Head or Tail is 1/2. Hence both of the outcome are equally likely to occur. This also indicates that degree of disorder is maximum as any one of the outcome may occur with equal probability. In this case the entropy value is maximum. In the *Case 2*, when the coin is biased, two cases are considered when there is more probability that tossing a coin will result in getting a Head. The degree of disorder is reduced in the case when the probability of getting a Head is .60. In this case the entropy function yields the value .97 which is smaller than 1.0. When the degree of disorder is further reduced (high probability of getting Head) i.e. when Probability of Getting a Head is .75, the entropy value is further reduced (Entropy = .80). The extreme case is *Case 3*, when one of the outcome is certain as tossing of coin will always result in getting a Head (P (Head) = 1). This event is most certain and possesses no disorder. In Case 3, the entropy function yields the value equal to zero.

From the above discussion, it is therefore observed that under the certainty (degree of disorder is minimum) entropy reaches to minimum value and under most uncertain condition (Degree of Disorder is maximum) entropy reaches to maximum value. We may conclude that function of information is to reduce uncertainty by either reducing randomness or by decreasing number of choices. These observations made by the Shannon, were widely accepted by scientific community and it later found application in generating efficient code to be used in communication.

We may use the concept of self-information and entropy for generating efficient binary code for the different characters appearing in the text. Here efficient code means generating minimum size code. It means that when the codes of the different characters are communicated over communication channel, minimum number of bits are required to be sent over communication channel. This improves channel efficiency and reduces channel congestion.

Suppose the text or message contains N characters. Then entropy of whole message can be defined as average self-information of all (N) characters. The self-information of a character is also known as entropy of character.

$$\text{Entropy of Message} = 1/N * \sum_{1=1}^{1=N} \text{entropy of character} \quad ...(2)$$

Entropy of a character is related with the probability of occurrence of character. It is defined as follows:

Entropy (Self-Information) of Character = – $\mathbf{log_2}$ (Probability of character) ...(3)

The entropy of whole message is therefore the sum of entropy of individual characters. Entropy is also used to determine that how many bits of information are actually present in the message stream.

Example:

Compute the self-information and entropy of the following message stream:

"AABACDACDBABCAB".

Total number of Characters in Message (N) = 15

Total number of characters, their probability and self-information (entropy) is shown in the following table.

Character	Probability	Self-information (= $-\log_2$ (Probability of character))
"A"	6/15	1.32
"B"	4/15	1.90
"C"	3/15	2.32
"D"	2/15	2.90

Table shown below contains the character of the message and their associated self-information. Consider the equation (2). The entropy of message may be obtained as following:

A	A	B	A	C	D	A	C	D	B	A	B	C	A	B
1.32	1.32	1.90	1.32	2.32	2.90	1.32	2.32	2.90	1.90	1.32	1.90	2/32	1/32	1/90

$$\text{Entropy of Message} = 1/N * \sum_{1=1}^{1=N} \text{entropy of character}$$

$=1/15 * (1.32+1.32+1.90+1.32+2.32+1.32+2.32+2.90+1.90+1.32 +1.90+2.32+1.32+1.90) = 1.88$

The entropy of message indicates the average number of bit required to represent a character in the message.

We may also compute the entropy by the function given by equation 1.

$$\text{Entropy} = -\sum_{1=1}^{1=N} Pi * \log_2 (Pi)$$

$$= 6/15 * 1.32 + 4/15 * 1.90 + 3/15 * 2.32 + 2/15 * 2.90$$

$$= .528 + .506 + .464 + .386$$

$$= 1.88$$

1.10.2 Use of Entropy for Coding

As discussed before, the entropy function may be used for developing efficient code for purpose of communication or compression. Suppose we have to communicate the message stream containing several characters. We would like to assign a code to every distinct character and in place of a character a binary code may be communicated. Smaller the code, higher efficiency in communication will be achieved. While developing a code, entropy function reveals the scope of further refinement in coding scheme. The entropy of message is lower limit on average number of bits required to represent a character. Let us try to understand with following examples.

Example

Consider a message stream consisting of characters A, B, C and D. Suppose the probability of occurrence of every character is .60, .30, .08 and .02 respectively. Self-information associated with every character is shown below.

Character	Binary Code	Probability	Self-Information
A	00	.60	0.73
B	01	.30	1.73
C	10	.08	3.64
D	11	.02	5.64

If we generate shortest binary code for representation of every character without considering probability of occurrence, we will probably generate the code as shown in column 2 of above table. If we consider the probability of occurrence of every character, we may compute the self-information for every character. Entropy of message stream may be computed as follows:

$$\text{Entropy} = \sum_{1=1}^{1=N} Pi * \log_2 (Pi)$$

$$= .60*0.73 + .30*1.73 + .08*3.64 + .02*5.64$$

$$= 1.36$$

The entropy function suggests that minimum average size of the code for representing the character should be 1.36. However, if we generate the code through most simple method (column 2), the average size of code for representing each character is 2.0. This difference (between 1.36 and 2.0) suggest that there is still scope for improvement. We may use some other method or scheme for development of code for character where average size of code is more closer to 1.36 or less than 2.0. Generally, the entropy value serves as an estimate for average message length. We may define quantity of information as the average code size is necessary to represent a character.

Example

Suppose the probability of character '*' appearing in a particular text is 1/8. How many bits will be required to represent this character in compression? If a message string '*****' has to be compressed then determine number of bits saved in comparison to ASCII code.

Solution

The probability of character '*' = 1/8

Entropy of character = $-\log_2$ (Probability of character)

$= -\log_2 (1/8) = 3$ ...(1)

Thus the entropy of character '*' =3, this means that the character may be represented by a 3 bit code in compressed form.

Total number of characters in character string '*****'=5

Total number of bits required to represent a message string '*****' = 5*3=15 ... (2)

Characters or symbol requires 8 bit code to represent in ASCII code. Thus each character will require 8 bits for coding a character.

Total no of bits required to encode the text '*****' = 5*8 = 40 ... (3)

Total number of bits saved = 40 – 15 = 25 ... (4)

The difference in 15 bits of entropy and 40 bits to encode the message using standard ASCII code shows the potential for data compression.

1.10.3 Motivating Factors for Data Compression

Shannon's work in information theory has been widely accepted in communication and data compression. The concept of entropy and self-information are used to develop the efficient code. These codes require less amount of information bits to represent the data. Consider the following to understand.

Suppose a message consists of four character "A", "B", "C" & "D". The message consisting of these characters is to be sent over a communication channel. The receiver receives the message from the communication channel for further use. Suppose the probability of occurrence of each character is Pa, Pb, Pc & Pd respectively. Following condition holds on the probabilities:

$$Pa + Pb + Pc + Pd = 1 \quad \text{... (1)}$$

If equivalent binary code has to be generated then the total number of bit required to code each character distinctly may be obtained as follows:

$$\text{Total number of bits (M)} = \lceil \log_2(N) \rceil = \log_2 (4) = 2 \quad \text{... (2)}$$

If we assume that probability of occurrence of all characters in the message are equal then entropy function will yield the following:

$$\text{Entropy} = \sum_{1=1}^{1=N} Pi * \log_2 (Pi) \quad \text{... (3)}$$

$$= -(.25*\log_2 (.25) + .25*\log_2 (.25) + .25*\log_2 (.25) + .25*\log_2 (.25))$$

$$= 2$$

Therefore, size of code requires two bits to represent all four characters. Suppose the messages consist of 100 such characters then total number of bits to be transmitted will be 100*2=200 bits. According to this scheme, the possible code for the characters are shown below.

Character	Code
A	00
B	01
C	10
D	11

Computation above with equation 2 and 3, suggests that if the probability of occurrence of all characters is equal, entropy function yields the value equal to two. Total number of bits used for actual coding are also two. Therefore, the coding scheme which generates the two bit code as shown above in the table, is optimum because the entropy value is also equal to two. Using this code a message containing 100 characters will require 200 bit to code.

Consider another case, where the Pa, Pb, Pc and Pd are not same i.e. probability of occurrence of characters are not equal. Suppose Pa = .70, Pb = .15, Pc = .10 and Pd = .05. In this case, we will see that the equal size code as shown before in the table will not be efficient codes.

Let us compute the entropy for second case where the probabilities are not equal,

$$\text{Entropy} = -\sum_{1=1}^{1=N} \text{Pi} * \mathbf{log_2}\ (\text{Pi}) \qquad \cdots (4)$$

$$= -(.7*\log_2(.7) + .15*\log_2(.15) + .1*\log_2(.1) + .05*\log_2(.05))$$

$$= 1.31$$

The entropy value therefore is 1.31 for the case when the probabilities are unequal. This value suggests that average size of code for character with unequal probabilities should be closer to the value 1.31. The coding scheme shown above, which generates the code with size two proves to be inefficient code because there exist a scope for improvement in coding scheme. This is evident from the difference in average code size (=2) and new entropy value (=1.31). To generate better code than earlier code we must generate the code of different size according to the probability. High probability character must be assigned smaller size code. Let us examine the codes shown in following table without bothering how they have been generated.

Character	Code	Probability
A	1	.70
B	01	.15
C	000	.10
D	001	.05

If we use this coding scheme, the approximate number of bits to be transmitted over communication channel for a message containing 100 characters are:

No. of bits = 70*1 + 15*2 + 10*3 + 5*3

= 135

For 100 characters total 135 bits will be transmitted for the new coding scheme. It also implies that average number of bits transmitted per character is 1.35. This value is much closer to the entropy (1.31) for case of unequal probability of character. The difference in entropy value and actual number of bits transmitted can be used as factor for considering new and better strategy for generating code. Minimum difference will ensure minimum redundancy. This result is considered as a motivating factor to deploy better coding scheme for the communication and compression of messages.

Work on data compression started well before the introduction of Digital Computers. In the late 1940's, it was a major issue for mathematicians to code the information. Researchers started exploring the possibilities for efficient coding, redundancy and entropy in the text. Basically there are two ways of assiging a code to a character or symbol. These are **static** coding and **dynamic** coding. In the static coding scheme, fixed length codes are generated uniquely to identify each symbol. The whole message or text is converted into coded form by replacing each symbol with its code. This method has a disadvantage that it does not consider the frequency or probability of occurrence of a particular symbol in a message. In fact, statistical analysis of every text or message reveals that there are few symbols which have maximum frequency i.e. these symbols are repeated frequently in the text. If these symbols can be identified, then they can be addressed by smaller codes. We can then obtain a higher degree of compression. This type of coding is known as **dynamic** coding using a variable length code. The static and dynamic coding schemes are explained below:

1.10.4 Static Coding (Fixed Size Code)

In static coding, fixed sized codes are allocated to each symbol. Each symbol can be uniquely identified by its corresponding code. It is also possible to compute the minimum number of bits required to represent a symbol.

Suppose there are M symbols which are used to constitute a message or text:

Let N = minimum number of digits required to represent M distinct symbols.

Let I = base of number system.

$$N = \lceil \log_i (M) \rceil \quad \text{... (1)}$$

In digital computer system, we represent the data in binary form. Thus the minimum number of bits required to uniquely represent a symbol will be,

$$N = \lceil \log_2 (M) \rceil \quad \text{... (2)}$$

Example

Suppose a message is composed of five symbols 'a', 'b', 'c', 'd', 'e'. Compute the following:

1. Find the minimum number of bits required to represent/code each symbol uniquely.
2. Generate the code for all symbols.
3. Find the coded form of message string 'bddac'.

Solution

Total number of distinct symbol $M = 5$.

Total number of bits required (as par Eq. 2)

$$N = \lceil \log_2 (M) \rceil$$

$$= \lceil \log_2 (5) \rceil = 3$$

Thus 3 bit code will be required to represent each symbol or the minimum number of bits required to represent a symbol uniquely is 3.

The code may be generated in the following way. Using 3 digit, the following unique code may be generated.

Static Code	Symbol
000	'a'
001	'b'
010	'c'
011	'd'
100	'e'
101	–
110	–
111	–

Total number of unique code generated = $2^3 = 8$.

We may assign any five codes to these symbols as mentioned in the table above.

Using the scheme, coded string of 'bddac' is as follows.

'001 011 011 000 010'.

Thus string 'bddac' would require 5*3 = 15 digits to code.

Example

Consider the above example and show how many bits will be saved by using static coding over ASCII code for string 'bddac'.

Solution

Using static code, the total number of bits to represent string 'bddac' = 5*3 = 15

Using ASCII code, total number of bits to represent string 'bddac' = 5*8 = 40

So the total bit saving = 40 – 15 = 25.

Thus during compression, a text of size 40 bit may be compressed to 15 bit.

1.10.5 Dynamic Coding (Variable Size Codes)

We have seen that a fixed size code may be generated to uniquely represent each symbol of input text. If we code according to this, we may obtain a compressed form of input text. If the coded text is communicated over a channel, then the input text may be obtained at the receiving end by the decoding process. In this process, we reduce the size of input text which has to be communicated. The same process can be applied if we have to store the text and we will be able to save considerable amount of disk space.

Further compression may be obtained, if dynamic coding is done using variable size code. This method is based on the principle of identifying the symbols which appear frequently. Suppose a symbol 'a' appears in the text most frequently. This property may be exploited by assigning a minimum number of digits to represent 'a'. Since 'a' appears most frequently, then we may assign one bit code to save space. The symbols which appears in the text less frequently are assigned higher bit code. Any statistical model may be used to calculate the average frequency of occurrence of symbols. Consider the following example:

Example

Suppose a text or message may be composed of four symbols. These symbols are a, b, c and d. Frequency distribution of occurrence of each symbols is as under:

Symbol	Frequency
'a'	15
'b'	10
'c'	70
'd'	15

Suppose a text containing 1000 symbols has to be compressed. Compute the following:

1. Total number of bits required to represent the whole text using ASCII codes.
2. Total number of bits required to represent the whole text using fixed size code/static code. Generate the static code for all symbols.
3. Total number of bits required to represent the whole text using dynamic coding/variable length codes. Consider the frequency distribution. Generate the dynamic code for all symbols.

Solution

1. Number of bits used in ASCII code = 8.
   Total number of symbols in text = 1000
   Total number of bits to represent the whole text = 8000 bits.
2. Total number of distinct symbol $M = 4$.
   Total number of bits required to represent each symbol

$$N = \lceil \log_2 (M) \rceil$$
$$= \lceil \log_2 (4) \rceil = 2$$

Thus 2 bit code will be required to represent each symbol. The code may be allocated as below:

Symbol	Code
'a'	00
'b'	01
'c'	10
'd'	11

Total number of bits required to represent a text in
this scheme = 1000 * N = 1000 * 2 = 2000 bits.

3. In decreasing order of frequency, the symbols may be arranged as follows:

Symbol	Frequency	No. of Bits	Code
'c'	70	1	1
'a'	15	2	01
'b'	10	3	001
'd'	5	4	0001

Since 'c' is the most frequent symbol, it may be given one bit code. Thereafter symbols 'a', 'b' and 'd' may be allocated 2, 3, 4 bit code respectively as given in the above table. After using the above scheme, we may compute the total number of bit required.

Total bits required to represent text containing
1000 symbol = 1* Total occurrence of symbol 'c' + 2 *

Total occurrence of symbol 'a' + 3 *
Total occurrence of symbol 'b' + 4 *
Total occurrence of symbol 'd'

$$= 1 * 700 + 2 * 150 + 3 * 100 + 4 * 50$$
$$= 700 + 300 + 300 + 200 = 1500 \text{ bits.}$$

Thus using variable length code, the coded text would require 1500 bits.

It may be noted that this scheme of compression is suitable only if there is a large variation in the occurrence of symbols.

Example

Suppose a text is composed of four symbols. These symbols are 'a', 'b', 'c' and 'd'. Frequency distribution of occurrence of each symbol is as under:

Symbol	Frequency
'a'	15
'b'	10
'c'	70
'd'	5

Calculate the entropy and show the average number of bits required to represent a symbol.

Solution

Let P_i = probability of occurrence of ith symbol.

Entropy of symbol I, $E_i = \log_2 (1/P_i)$ ... (1)

Entropy of message, E_m $\text{E}_\text{m} = \sum_{1=1}^{1=N} P_i {}^* \log_2 (1/P_i)$ ... (2)

$$= .15 * \log (1/.15) + .1 * \log (1/.1) + .7 * \log (1/.7) + .05 * \log (1/.05)$$
$$= .41 + .33 + .36 + .21 = 1.31$$

1.11 NUMBER SYSTEM

We use the decimal number system in our day-to-day work. This system uses digits 0, 1, 2, 3, 4, 5, 6, 7, 8 and 9. This system is called decimal because it uses a total of ten digits and any number is represented as a string of these ten digits. However, a computer cannot use this number. Instead, the computer works on binary digits. A binary system has only two digits 0 and 1. This is because the computer uses integrated circuits with thousands of transistors which process the work submitted by the outside world in terms of electronic pulses.

1.11.1 Decimal Number System

The decimal number system uses ten digits (0, 1, 2, 3, 4, 5, 6, 7, 8, 9). It thus is said to have a base of ten. Using the various digits in different positions we can express any number. Since the base in decimal number system is 10, the number 4563 is written as $4563/_{10}$.

The digit used to represent a number carries a specific weight when it is used at a specific position. For example, the decimal number 4563 may be represented as

$$4563 = 4 * 10\text{^}3 + 5 * 10\text{^}2 + 6 * 10\text{^}1 + 3 * 10\ \text{^}0$$

1.11.2 Binary Number System

This system uses only two digits and thus it is known as the binary number system. These numbers are 0 and 1. Any number represented in the binary number system is a string of 0 and 1's. Hence this system has a base of 2. The abbreviation of binary digit is **bit**. A string of 8 bits is known as **byte**. A byte is the basic unit of the computer. In most computers, the data processed is in the string of 8 bits or some multiple of 8 bits. As in the decimal system, the binary number system is position weighted. For example, the binary number 1001 may be represented as

$$1001 = 1 * 2^3 + 0 * 2^2 + 0 * 2^1 + 1 * 2^0$$

1.11.3 Octal Number System

This system uses eight digits (0, 1, 2, 3, 4, 5, 6, 7). Since the octal number system uses a total of eight digits to compose a number, this system is said to have a base of eight. Using the different digits in different positions, we can express any number. Since the base in octal number system is 8, the number 4563 is written as $4563/_8$.

The digit used to represent a number carries a specific weight when it is used at a specific position. For example, the octal number 4563 may be represented as

$$4563 = 4 * 8^3 + 5 * 8^2 + 6 * 8^1 + 3 * 8^0$$

1.11.4 Hexadecimal Number System

This system uses sixteen digits (0, 1, 2, 3, 4, 5, 6, 7, 8, 9, A, B, C, D, E, F) to express a number. Thus it is said to have a base of sixteen. Using the different digits in different positions, we can express any number. Since the base in hexadecimal number system is 16, the number 4563 is written as $4563/_{16}$.

The digit used to represent a number carries a specific weight when it is used at a specific position. For example, the hexadecimal number 45AB may be represented as

$$45AB = 4 * 16^3 + 5 * 16^2 + 10 * 16^1 + 11 * 16^0$$

The following table presents four bit equivalent binary number of hexadecimal digits:

Hexadecimal Digit	Four Digit Binary Equivalent
0	0000
1	0001
2	0010
3	0011
4	0100
5	0101
6	0110
7	0111
8	1000
9	1001
A	1010
B	1011
C	1100
D	1101
E	1110
F	1111

1.11.5 Binary to Decimal Conversion

A binary number may be converted to a decimal number using the following process.

Example

Convert 11001 to decimal number system.

Since each position has a weight, first bit (Least Significant Bit) has a weight 2^0, if the position is n^{th} from the LSB, position has a weight 2^(n – 1).

Thus

$$\begin{aligned} 11001 &= 1 * 2^4 + 1 * 2^3 + 0 * 2^2 + 0 * 2^1 + 1 * 2^0 \\ &= 1 * 16 + 1 * 8 + 0 * 4 + 0 * 2 + 1 * 1 \\ &= 16 + 8 + 0 + 0 + 1 \\ &= 25 \end{aligned}$$

Hence equivalent decimal number is 25.

1.11.6 Decimal to Binary Conversion

To convert decimal to binary, a method of successive multiplication by 2 is used. After each multiplication, the integer part is noted and the fraction is again multiplied by 2 till the remainder become zero. Sometimes it is possible that the remainder doesn't become zero even after many stages. In such a case, approximation is made and the result is taken up to a certain number of bit after the binary point. A similar procedure is adopted for a number having both integer and fraction. Binary fraction is added and subtracted as the decimal numbers.

Thus this method involves successive division by 2 and recording the remainder (the remainder will always be 0 or 1). The division will be stopped when we get a quotient of 0 with remainder of 1. The remainders when read upward give the equivalent binary number.

Example

Convert decimal number 25 to binary number

		remainder
2	25	
2	12	1
2	6	0
2	3	0
2	1	1
		1

The procedure begins with the successive division by 2. Keep noting the remainder of division until '1' comes as the quotient. The string of remainder obtained from the successive division constitutes the equivalent binary number. Binary equivalent to decimal number 25 is 11001.

1.11.7 Hexadecimal to Binary Conversion

The hexadecimal number system is very convenient and extensively used because hexadecimal numbers are very short as compared to binary numbers.

Hexadecimal means 16. Thus the hexadecimal system has a base of 16. It uses 16 digits to represent all numbers. The digits are 0, 1, 2, 3, 4, 5, 6, 7, 8, 9, A, B, C, D, E and F.

Hexadecimal digits are converted to binary number by obtaining its 4-bit equivalent as per the conversion table.

Example

Convert 45A4 to binary equivalent.

Hexadecimal number	4	5	A	4
Each digits equivalent	0100	0101	1100	0100
Equivalent binary number	0100010111000100			

1.11.8 Binary to Hexadecimal Conversion

Convert each 4-bit binary into an equivalent hexadecimal.

Example

Convert 0001010001001101 to equivalent hexadecimal number.

Binary number :	0001	0100	0100	1101
	1	4	4	D
Equivalent hexanumber	144D			

1.11.9 Addition of Binary Number

The rules for addition of binary numbers are as follows:

0 + 0	1
0 + 1	1
1 + 0	1
1 + 1	10

It may be noted that 1 + 1 is represented as 10 i.e., the sum is 0 and carry is 1.

Example

Add two binary number 111010 and 1001.

Carry		1	1				
First number		1	1	1	0	1	0
Second number +				1	0	0	1
	1	0	0	0	0	1	1

1.11.10 Binary Subtraction

The rules for subtraction of Binary numbers are as follows:

0–0	0
1–0	1
1–1	0
10–1	1

In both the operations of addition and subtraction, we start with the least significant bit (LSB) i.e. start with the bit on the extreme right side and proceed to the left.

Example

Subtract 10001 from 110001.

First number	1	1	0	0	0	1
Second number –		1	0	0	0	1
	1	0	0	0	0	0

1.11.11 Multiplication of Binary Numbers

The four basic rules for multiplication of binary numbers are as follows:

- $0 \times 0 = 0$
- $0 \times 1 = 0$
- $1 \times 0 = 0$
- $1 \times 1 = 1$

The method of binary multiplication is similar to that in decimal multiplication. The method involves forming partial products, shifting successive partial products left one place and adding all the partial products.

Example

Multiply 10001 by 101

			1	0	0	0	1
×					1	0	1
			1	0	0	0	1
		0	0	0	0	0	
	1	0	0	0	1		
	1	0	1	0	1	0	1

1.11.12 Signed Binary Number

In binary number system the digit 0 is used for the +ve sign and the digit 1 for the –ve sign as the Most Significant Digit. The most significant bit is the sign bit followed by the magnitude bits. Numbers expressed in this form are known as signed binary number. The number may be written in 4 bits, 8 bits, 16 bits etc. In every case the most leading bit represents the sign bit and remaining bits represent magnitude.

1's Complement

The 1's complement of a binary number is obtained by complementing each bit.

Example

Obtain the 1's complement of 100001.

Number	1	0	0	0	0	1
	0	1	1	1	1	0

2's Complement

The signed binary number required too much electronic circuit for addition and subtraction. Therefore, positive decimal numbers are expressed in signed-magnitude form but negative decimal numbers are expressed in 2's complements.

2's complement of a number may be obtained by adding a binary digit '1' to the 1's complement of a number.

Example

Obtain the 2's complement of 100001.

Number	1	0	0	0	0	1
1's complement	0	1	1	1	1	0
+						1
2's complement	0	1	1	1	1	1

2's Complement Addition Subtraction

The use of 2's complement representation has simplified the computer hardware for arithmetic operation. When A and B are added, the bit are not inverted and so we get,

$$S = A + B$$

When B is to be subtracted from A, the computer hardware form's the two's complement and then adds it to A. Thus

$$S = A + B' = A + (-B) = A - B$$

Conversion of Hexadecimal to Decimal

One method to convert a hexadecimal into a decimal equivalent is to first convert hexadecimal to binary and then convert binary to decimal. A direct conversion of hexadecimal into decimal is also possible. Since the base of a hexadecimal is 16, the weight of different bits are 160,161,162, etc. starting with the bit on the extreme right. The decimal equivalent of a hexadecimal number equals the sum of all digits multiplied by their weights.

Decimal to Hexadecimal Conversion

One method is to convert the decimal to binary and then convert binary to hexadecimal.

The direct method is successive division by 16 and to write the hexadecimal equivalent of remainder.

1.11.13 Binary Coded Decimal (BCD)

In computer technology the numbers are represented in binary form while in our day-to-day functions, members are represented in the decimal form. The BCD codes are used to represent decimal number to binary. A weighted binary code is one in which number carries certain weight. A string of 4 bits is known as nibble. BCD means that each decimal digit is represented by a nibble (binary code of 4 digits). 8421 code is the most predominant BCD code. The designation 8421 indicates the weight of the 4 bits. When one refers to BCD code, it always means 8421 code. Though 16 number (24) can be represented by 4 bits, only 10 of them are used. The remaining 6 are invalid in 8421 BCD code. To represent any number in BCD code, each decimal number is replaced by the appropriate 4-bit code. BCD code is used in pocket calculator, electronic counter, digital voltameter, and digital clock. The early version of computers used BCD code. However BCD code was discarded later because it is slow and more complicated than the binary system.

BCD Addition

Addition is the most important arithmetic operation. Subtraction, multiplication and division can be done by using addition. The rules of BCD addition are:

1. Add the two numbers using binary addition. If the four-bit sum is equal or less than 9, it is a valid BCD number.
2. If the four-bit sum is more than 9 or carry is generated from the group of four bits, the result is invalid. In such a case, add carry to next four-bit group.

1.12 ALPHANUMERIC CODE

For proper communication, we need to represent numbers, letters and symbols. Alphanumeric code can represent all these three.

ASCII Code (American Standard Code for Information Interchange)

It is seven-bit code used extensively for printers and terminals of usually small computer systems. Many large computer systems also accommodate this code. The characters are assigned in the ascending order of binary numbers. Sometime an 8 bit is also added and this bit is either 0 or 1 or used as parity bit.

EBCDIC Code

This refers to Extended Binary Coded Decimal Interchange Code. EBCDIC is used in most of the large computers for communication. It is an eight bit code and uses BCD.

Error Detection Codes

Every digit of a digital system must be correct. An error in any digit can cause a problem because the computer may recognize it as something else. Many methods have been devised to detect such errors.

Parity

Parity refers to the number of 1's in the binary word. When the number of 1's in the binary word is odd, it is said to have odd parity. When the number of 1's in the word is even, it is said to have even parity. One method for error detection is to use 7 bits for data and 8th bit for parity. The parity can be 1 or 0. At the receiving end the parity is checked, and if an error has been committed, the data is required to be transmitted again.

In some computer systems even parity is used.

Check Sums

The parity check cannot detect two errors in the same word. One method to such cases is the check sum. As each word is transmitted, it is added to the previous words and the sum is retained at the sending end. Each successive word is added to the sum of the previous words. At the end of transmission, the sum is also sent and is checked at the receiving point. Check sum method is commonly used in Teleprocessing.

OBJECTIVE TYPE QUESTIONS

Multiple Choice

1. Data can be represented in a digital computer as
   (a) Text (b) Image (c) Both (a) & (b) (d) None of above

2. Which of the following are part of Information Technology?
   (a) Data Processing (b) Data Storage (c) Data Communication (d) All of above
3. Which of following is true for Information?
   i. Information is obtained by processing raw data.
   ii. Raw Data consist of numbers, text etc.
   iii. Information is meaningful.
   (a) Only (i) (b) Both (i) & (iii) (c) Only (iii) (d) All of above
4. Which of the following data file may be compressed?
   (a) Text (b) Image (c) Audio (d) All of above
5. Which of the following compression techniques loses some data contents?
   (a) Lossless (b) Lossy (c) None of above (d) All of above
6. Value of Information produced on the basis of intuitive guess is
   (a) Normative (b) Realistic (c) Subjective (d) None of Above
7. Which of the following are not graphics file extensions?
   (a) .JPG (b) .BMP (c) .DOC (d) .PNG
8. Entropy term is used to
   (a) Measure Information Contents (b) Represent value of information
   (c) Represent Information System (d) None of above
9. Lossless Data Compression technique is normally applied to
   (a) Image (b) Video (c) Text (d) Sound
10. Which of following may be compressed with Lossy data compression technique?
   (a) Image (b) Video (c) Sound (d) All of Above

Answers

1-c, 2-d, 3-d, 4-d, 5-b, 6-c, 7-c, 8-a, 9-c, 10-d

State True or False

1. Information plays a key role in decision-making. [True] [False]
2. Computer can process the data represented in the form of text only. [True] [False]
3. In Lossy compression, some data contents are lost. [True] [False]
4. Encoding of a text ensures compression in data. [True] [False]
5. Higher entropy of message implies high potential for data compression. [True] [False]
6. Dynamic code yields better compression result than static codes. [True] [False]
7. Normative value of information ignores the human errors and other risk factors. [True] [False]
8. Base of Hexadecimal number system is 16. [True] [False]
9. Graphics and animations also contains information. [True] [False]
10. Entropy of information is measure of information contents in message. [True] [False]

Answers

1-True, 2-False, 3-True, 4-False, 5-True, 6-True, 7-True, 8-True, 9-True, 10-True.

SELECTED EXERCISES

1. What do you mean by the term Information Technology? Express your views.
2. How digital computers are being used for storage, retrieval and processing of information?
3. List any five areas of IT application. Explain what do you mean by IT enabled services?
4. How a Video can hold information? Is it possible to process the video data? If yes, then explain what kind of operation may be performed on video data?
5. Explain the various data formats?
6. What do we mean by the term 'interactive multimedia'? Explain the reason why it is becoming popular in day-to-day life?

7. What do you mean by an image? How this format of storing data is different from animation and video ?
8. What are animations? How they are developed? Explain the role of computer in developing the animations.
9. What is the difference between data and information?
10. What do you mean by the term Information Representation? How is information represented in digital media or a digital computer?
11. Information is obtained by processing of raw data. Is it possible to process the data in an arbitrary manner and results be termed as Information?
12. Why is information required in an enterprise or an organization?
13. What do you mean by Quality of Information?
14. How is an image represented in the computer system? Is it possible to compress the image and obtain a copy of the original image after decompression? If yes, then how?
15. What do you understand by the term Graphics? Explain what kind of information may be contained in graphics? How are graphics represented in digital computer system?
16. Define Information System? Why an organization requires an Information System? How the employees of an organization are benefited with the Information System.
17. Define the steps, how would you develop an Information System for your college or university.
18. What are Computer Based Information Systems (CBIS)? How are they different from manual information systems?
19. What are the major components of an information system? Explain, why set of methods are considered as basis for Information System development.
20. How database are related to the information system? Explain why a good database design leads to development of efficient Information System.
21. How many types of information system exist today? List the name of any commercial information system.
22. Define Business Transaction? What are Transaction Processing Systems? List the limitations and advantages of transaction processing system.
23. What do you mean by On Line Transaction Processing? How it is different from Real Time Transaction processing?
24. What are Management Information Systems (MIS)? List the advantages of MIS.
25. What are decision support systems?
26. What are Workflow Systems? Under what circumstances, Workflow systems are required? Explain working of any workflow system you have seen in day-to-day life.
27. What are Expert Systems? Explain the role of inference engine and knowledge base in the design of expert system. How a knowledge base is different from database?
28. What do you mean by Normative Value of Information? How it is different from subjective and realistic value of information?
29. What do you mean by the self-information? Compute the self-information related to the event of tossing a coin.
30. Explain the relation of certainty with the self-information? Explain, why self-information is less for the most certain outcome of an event?
31. How the concept of self-information and entropy are used in data communication? Explain with example.
32. Write any four popular formats for storing the graphics.
33. What are the popular format for storing Video data?
34. What do you mean by the term Data Compression?
35. Explain what are Lossless Data Compression techniques? Detail the circumstances when data should be compressed using lossless data compression techniques.
36. What do you understand by Lossy Data Compression Techniques?
37. Explain why images are compressed by Lossy Data Compression Techniques?
38. What do you mean by the term Sound? Is it possible to store and process the sound using a digital computer? Can the audio data be compressed? List a few popular formats for storing audio data.

39. Write the essential differences between Encoding and Compression of Data.
40. Why is coding required in the process of data compression?
41. What to do understand by Entropy of information?
42. How do you measure the entropy of a message? What is the meaning of entropy of symbols and entropy of the whole message?
43. How many applications at home are found to be computer run or possibly they may be run through a computer by making some changes in them? Give your own account.
44. Convert the following decimal numbers to Binary, Octal and Hexadecimal Numbers:
    1000, 22, 556, 229
45. Write down the rules to add two binary numbers. Compute the addition of following binary numbers:
    (1001 + 10 + 11010), (1 + 1111), (10101 + 11100 + 10101)
46. Do the following operations on binary numbers:
    - Subract 1001 from 110001
    - Multiply 1001 by 110001
47. What are signed binary numbers? How is addition performed using signed numbers?
48. What are BCD codes? Explain.
49. What are Alphanumeric codes? How are they are used?

2

INFORMATION REPRESENTATION AND COMPRESSION

Contents

2 INFORMATION REPRESENTATION AND COMPRESSION

2.1 INTRODUCTION

The work on Information Science had started much before the introduction of digital computers. Development of new mechanism for information representation, redundancy and entropy had started in the late 1940's. Information science has been a major research area of mathematics. After the introduction of digital computers, the methodologies and techniques for information representation was used for handling and processing the data on digital computers. Thereafter we saw the emergence of a new area called **Information Technology**. Information Technology is a generic name given to a collection of techniques/methodologies for Information/Data Representation, Information/Data Storage, Information/Data Retrieval and Processing, Information/Data Communication on digital computers and communication networks. The computer is a tool to do the above-mentioned tasks effectively and efficiently.

Data compression is probably one of the most important areas of Information Theory. It has been a major concern to find efficient techniques to express the information contents in minimum storage. Information theory is actually a branch of mathematics, which deal with the information or data representation. Information Storage, Retrieval, Processing and Communication are also part of Information Theory. Data compression in information theory mainly deals with computation and minimization of the redundant information in a sample data. The audio, video, graphics and animation contain lot of redundant information which even after modification or alteration in the value of some of parameter will not adversely affect the value of information. For example, changing the color, size of object on the photograph up to certain limit may not adversely affect the phonograph or picture quality rather this process save lot of disk space when stored in the disk. Although there is a trade off on changing the parameter and quality of photograph. It means you may always identify your faded photograph, which was taken earlier. Level of adjustment of such process must be controlled. If by doing some modification the parameter pertaining to audio, video or text we save the space. It will always reduce the processing time, time for communication, and ensures fast storage and retrieval.

In the following sections we will deal mainly with Text Compression.

2.2 SHANNON-FANO ALGORITHM

Shannon-Fano algorithm was developed by Claude Shannon at Bell laboratories and RM Fano at MIT. The algorithm deals with text compression. It takes a stream of characters in the form of text or message and produces the code which when decompressed, produces the input text. The coded form of input text requires lesser number of bytes, and thus it will require less disk space to store. It would also enable faster processing and minimum time to communicate. Whenever the input text has to be reproduced, the coded input text may be decompressed to generate input text.

Motivations for Shannon-Fano algorithms are as follows:

1. Frequency of occurrence of all symbols in the text is not the same. There are few symbols which have a high probability or their frequency of occurrence is higher in the text.
2. The high frequency symbols may be identified by statistical analysis of sample data.
3. The high frequency symbols must be represented by a smaller code. Different codes will have different numbers of bits. Thus codes for symbols with high frequencies will have fewer number of bits and codes for low frequency symbols will have a higher amount of bits.
4. Although all of the codes are of different size i.e., each code may have different numbers of bits, but they will all be unique and will identify a symbol uniquely.
5. Shanon-Fano algorithm uses binary tree, called Shanon-Fano Tree, to generate the different codes.

The tree structure is helpful in allocating variable length binary code that are uniquely defined. The tree structure is easy to implement by using Tree data structures.

Let us try to understand the Shannon-Fano algorithm with an example.

Example

Suppose a message contains four symbols. The symbols and their frequency is given below:

Symbol	Frequency
'e'	60
'a'	20
'b'	15
'd'	5

Generate the code for each symbol using Shannon-Fano principles.

Solution

Step 1

Shannon-Fano algorithm requires to compute the frequency of occurrence and arrange them in the decreasing order of frequency. The table given in the problem contains symbols and their frequency.

Step 2

Divide the table horizontally in such a way that the sum of frequencies in the upper half and sum of the frequencies in the lower half are approximately the same. This may be done by taking one symbol from the top and putting it in the upper half. If the sum of all frequencies in the lower half is greater than the upper half, then move highest frequency from the lower half to the upper half. Keep repeating the process until the condition is satisfied.

The same process is applied to both upper half and lower half recursively until each symbol is left alone in its half. This process is shown below:

First Iteration

'e' 60 Sum of Upper Half = 60

____ First Division

'a' 20 Sum of Lower Half = 40

'b' 15

'd' 5

In this case the condition is satisfied in first hop or iteration. Now each subgroup/half is again divided. Since the upper half after the first division has only one symbol left, in this case no further subdivision has to be obtained. This process will be done for the lower half as now it contains three symbols.

Second Iteration

'e' 60 Sum of Upper Half = 60

____ First Division

'a' 20 Sum of Lower Half = 40

Sum = 20

** Second Division

'b' 15

'd' 5 Sum = 20

Third Iteration

After the second division, the upper half contains only one symbol but the lower has two symbols. Therefore we apply the same process for the lower half.

'e' 60 Sum of Upper Half = 60

____ First Division

'a' 20 Sum of Lower Half = 40

Sum = 20

** Second Division

'b' 15 Sum = 15

>>>>>>>>>>>>>>>>>>>>>>>>>> Third Division

'd' 5 Sum = 5 Sum = 20

Step 3

After dividing we start constructing the binary tree. At each level, the upper half will construct a left sub-tree and the lower half will construct a right sub-tree. This tree is called Shannon-Fano Tree.

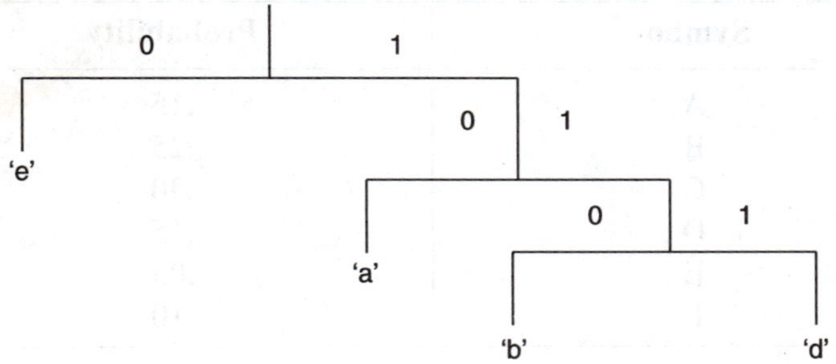

The tree constructed as above is Shannon-Fano Tree for the given set of symbols. Now we may generate the code for each symbol as shown below:

'e'	0
'a'	10
'b'	110
'd'	111

Evaluation of Performance

For the above example, the code for each symbol and the number of bits required to represent each symbol and its frequency is given below. We may observe that the highest frequency symbol is represented by one bit and the lowest frequency symbol by three bits. Thus the number of bits allocated correspond to the symbol frequency in an inverse ratio.

Symbol	Code	No. of Bits	Frequency
'e'	0	1	60
'a'	10	2	20
'b'	110	3	15
'd'	111	3	5

Total number of bits required to represent the text containing 100 symbols

= 60*1 + 20*2 + 15 *3 +5*3 = 160

Average number of bits per symbol using SF algorithm = 160/00 =1.6.

So using Shannon-Fano algorithm, the average number of bits required to represent one symbol is 1.6. This clearly is an improvement over the ASCII code which requires 8 bit code to represent each symbol.

Example

Suppose a message composed of six symbols need to be communicated over a communication channel. The symbols and their probability of occurrence is shown in the following table. Generate the Shannon-Fano code for each symbol. Compute the average number of bits required to communicate a symbol and estimate the amount of redundancy per symbol. Evaluate the performance over traditional ASCII codes.

Symbol	Probability
A	.15
B	.25
C	.30
D	.15
E	.05
F	.10

Solution

Step 1

Arrange the symbols into decreasing order of frequency. The following table shows the symbols placed in decreasing order of frequency/probability.

Symbol	Probability
C	.30
B	.25
A	.15
D	.15
F	.10
E	.05

Step 2

Divide the table horizontally in such a way that sum of probabilities in upper half and sum of probabilities in lower half is approximately same. The same process is applied to both upper half and lower half recursively until each symbol is left alone in its half. This process is shown below :

First Iteration:

C .30
B .25
Sum of Upper Half = .55

———————————————— First Division

A .15 Sum of Lower Half = .45
D .15
F .10
E .05

Second Iteration

C .30 Sum of Upper Half = .30

———————————————— Second Division

B .25 Sum of Lower Half = .25

———————————————— First Division

A .15
D .15
F .10
E .05

Third Iteration

C .30

Second Division

B .25

First Division

A .15
D .15 Sum of Upper Half = .30

Third Division

F .10 Sum of Upper Half = .15
E .05

Fourth Iteration

C .30

Second Division

B .25

First Division

A .15 Sum of Upper Half = 30

Fourth Division

D .15 Sum of Lower Half = 15

Third Division

F .10
E .05

Fifth Iteration

C .30

Second Division

B .25

First Division

A .15

Fourth Division

D .15

Third Division

F .10 Sum of Upper Half = .10

Fifth Division

E .05 Sum of Lower Half = .05

Step 3

At each level, upper half will construct a left sub-tree and lower half will construct a right sub-tree. After combining all the divisions, we obtain SF tree. The SF tree for this problem is shown below :

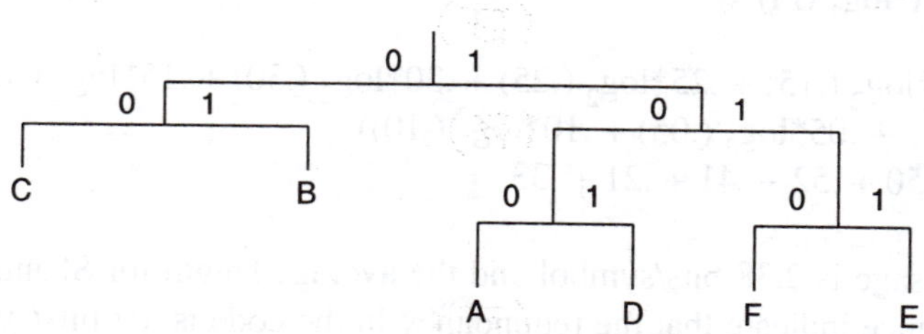

According to the SF tree shown above, we may generate the code for each symbol. The SF code for each symbol is shown below in the table:

Symbol	SF Code
A	100
B	01
C	00
D	101
E	111
F	110

Evaluation of Performance of SF Code

For the above example, code for each symbol and number of bit required to represent each symbol and frequency is given below. The third column indicates the number of bits required representing each symbol.

Symbol	Code	No. of Bits	Probability
A	100	3	.15
B	01	2	.25
C	00	2	.30
D	101	3	.15
E	111	3	.05
F	110	3	.10

Total number of bits required to represent the text containing 100 symbols

$$= 15*3 + 25*2 + 30*2 + 15*3 + 5*3 + 10*3$$
$$= 45 + 50 + 60 + 45 + 15 + 30$$
$$= 245$$

Av. No of bits per symbol using SF algorithm = 245/100 = 2.45

This clearly shows a improvement over ASCII code which required 8 bit per symbol.

Let us calculate the redundancy in the code. The redundancy in the code is defined as difference between entropy and average Number of bits required per symbol.

$$\text{Entropy} = -\sum_{1=1}^{1=N} \text{Pi}*\mathbf{log_2}\ (\text{Pi})$$

$$= -(.15*\log_2 (.15) + .25*\log_2 (.25) + .30*\log_2 (.30) + .15*\log_2 (.15) + .05*\log_2 (.05) + .10*\log_2 (.10))$$

$$= .41 + .50 + .52 + .41 + .21 + .33$$

$$= 2.38$$

Entropy of the message is 2.38 bits/symbol and the average length for Shannon-Fano code is 2.45 bits/symbol. The difference indicate that the redundancy in the code is .07 bits/symbol.

Example 3

Consider a transmitting string of characters. Suppose the characters are taken from the set (a1, a2, a3, a4, a5) with probabilities

P (a1) = .05
P(a2) = .15
P (a3) = .04
P (a4) = .50
P (a5) = .26

Compute the following.

(a) Calculate the entropy of the source.
(b) Obtain SF code for the characters.
(c) Find average length of characters.
(d) Compute the redundant bits/symbol in SF code.

Solution

(a) Entropy function is given by

$$\text{Entropy} = -\sum_{I=1}^{I=N} \text{Pi}*\log_2(\text{Pi})$$

$$= -((.05)*\log_2(.05) + .15*\log_2(.15) + .04*\log_2(.04) + .50*\log_2(.50) + .26*\log_2(.26))$$

$$= .21 + .41 + .18 + .50 + .51$$

$$= 1.81$$

(b) Table showing the character in decreasing order of probability is as follows:

Symbol	Probability
a4	.50
a5	.26
a2	.15
a1	05
a3	.04

The Shannon-gano tree for the given set of symbols may be obtained by following the steps of Shannon-Fano algorithm. The SF tree for the given problem is shown below.

The SF code may be obtained from the SF tree. The symbol, SF Code, Probability and size of SF code is shown below in the table.

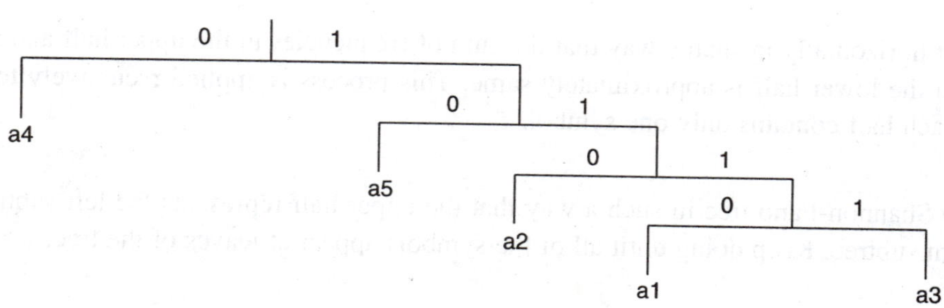

Symbol	Probability	SF Code	Size of SF Code
a1	.05	1110	4
a2	.15	110	3
a3	.04	1111	4
a4	.50	0	1
a5	.26	10	2

(c) Average length of character as per SF Code

= .05*4 + .15*3 + .04*4 + .50*1 + .26*2

= 1.83 bits

Therefore SF code will require 1.83 bits/character.

(d) Entropy define that best scheme we can found which will have no redundancy. The difference in entropy and average size of SF code will yield the redundancy in the SF code.

Redundancy = Entropy – Av. size of SF Code

= 1.83 – 1.81

= .02 bits/character.

2.3 SUMMARY OF STEPS OF SHANNON-FANO ALGORITHM

Compression for a text may be done by using Shannon-Fano algorithm through the following steps:

Step 1

Find the total number of distinct symbols which may appear in the text. Develop a list of frequency count for each symbol. To maintain the relative frequency of occurrence of symbols, the frequency should be calculated as under,

$$\text{Relative Frequency} = \frac{\text{Number of occurrence of symbol in text}}{\text{Total number of symbols in text}} \times 100$$

The computation of the frequency may be based on the statistical analysis of nature of text to be compressed. It is not mandatory to compute the frequency for every piece of the text being compressed.

Step 2

Arrange the symbols in the decreasing order of frequency.

Step 3

Divide the list horizontally in such a way that the sum of frequencies in the upper half and the sum of frequencies in the lower half is approximately same. This process is applied recursively to all of the halves until each half contains only one symbol.

Step 4

Construct the Shannon-Fano tree in such a way that the upper half represents the left subtree and the lower the right subtree. Keep doing until all of the symbols appear at leaves of the tree.

Step 5

Assign Shannon-Fano code to each symbol. It is done by representing the left branch of SF Binary Tree as '0' and the right branch of SF Binary sub-tree as '1'. Traversing from root to that symbol (leaf) will give the code for that symbol.

Example

For the given symbols and their respective frequency, compute the following:

1. The information content of each symbol and the total numbers of bits required to represent that symbol.
2. Improvement using Shannon-Fano Algorithm.

Symbol	Frequency
'e'	60
'a'	20
'b'	15
'd'	5

Solution

Refer to Example 1 for the following computations:

Symbol	Frequency	Code	No. of Bits
'e'	60	0	1
'a'	20	10	2
'b'	15	110	3
'd'	5	111	3

Information contents of a symbol (Entropy)

$$= -\log_2 (\text{Probability of symbol}) \quad \text{... (1)}$$

$$\text{Probability of symbol} = \frac{\text{Relative frequency of symbol}}{\text{Total sum of frequency}} \quad \text{... (2)}$$

Entropy of symbol 'e' = $-\log_2 (.6) = .74$

Entropy of symbol 'a' = $-\log_2 (.2) = 2.32$

Entropy of symbol 'b' = $-\log_2 (.15) = 2.73$

Entropy of symbol 'd' = $-\log_2 (.05) = 4.32$

Information bits for symbol 'e' = Entropy of symbol 'e' * Frequency = 44.4

Information bits for symbol 'a' = Entropy of symbol 'a' * Frequency = 46.4

Information bits for symbol 'b' = Entropy of symbol 'b' * Frequency = 40.95

Information bits for symbol 'd' = Entropy of symbol 'd' * Frequency = 21.6

Symbol	Frequency	Information Count	Information Bits	Code	Number of Bits	SF Size
'e'	60	.74	44.4	0	1	60
'a'	20	2.32	46.4	10	2	40
'b'	15	2.73	40.95	110	3	45
'd'	15	4.32	21.6	111	3	15
			Total = 153.35			Total = 160

Total Information count for the message = 153.35 bits

Total number of bit count for message using Shannon-Fano Code = 160 bits.

Total number of bit count for message using ASCII code = 800 bits

We may observe that the representation of the message containing 100 symbols will require 800 bits and the total information count or entropy of message is 153.35 bits. Shannon-Fano code will require 160 bits to represent text containing 100 symbols, which is very close to the entropy of message (153.35 bits).

2.4 HUFFMAN ALGORITHM

Huffman Algorithm for Text Compression is an improvement over Shannon-Fano algorithm. Although similar in approach, the Huffman algorithm differs from Shannon-Fano in the construction of the Binary Tree. The Huffman algorithm generates variable length code in such a way that high frequency symbols are represented with a minimum number of bits and low frequency symbols are represented by relatively higher number of bits. The decoding of the Huffman codes is done by using Huffman Decode Tree. Major difference in Shannon-Fano and Huffman algorithm, is that in SF algorithm, the tree is built on the Top-Down approach while Huffman Tree is built using the Bottom Up approach.

All the symbols in Huffman Tree are assigned leaf nodes similar to Shannon-Fano Tree. The steps of Huffman Algorithm are as follows:

Step 1

Compute or collect the total number of symbols and their relative frequencies.

Step 2

Arrange all the symbols in decreasing order of their frequencies.

Step 3

Construct Huffman Tree from the list of symbols.

Step 4

Assign the code.

2.4.1 Steps for Construction of Huffman Binary Tree

1. Pick up two symbols (a, b) from the list which has minimum frequency. These symbols will be the last two symbols in the sorted list of symbols.
2. Create two free nodes of the binary tree and assign A and B to these nodes.

3. Create a parent node for both nodes and assign it the frequency equal to the sum of frequencies of child nodes.
4. Delete these two nodes from the list.
5. Parent node is added to the list of free nodes.
6. Repeat steps 1 to 5 until the list of symbols becomes empty. This will generate the Huffman Tree.
7. Assign the bits similar to Shannon-Fano Tree i.e. left child is assigned '0' and right is assigned '1'. Traverse from the root node of Huffman Tree to the leaf containing a particular symbol. This traversal will generate a code for that symbol.

Let us understand Huffman Algorithm with an example.

Example

The symbols and their frequency are given below:

Symbol	Frequency
A	30
B	30
C	15
D	15
E	10

Construct Huffman Tree and generate code.

Solution

The Huffman Tree may be constructed in the following steps.

1. Find a sorted list of symbols in decreasing order of frequency. The list will be (A, B, C, D, E).
2. Pick up two symbols with minimum frequency. These symbols are 'D' and 'E'. Assign them two free nodes as shown below:

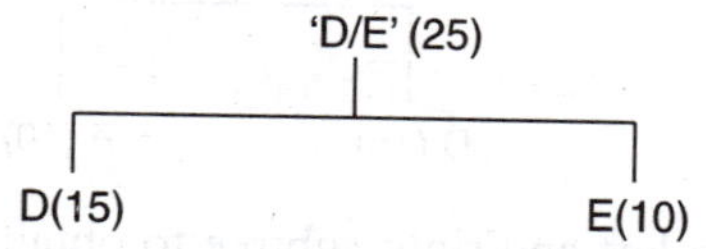

This subtree is called 'D/E'. Combined frequency of 'D/E' is 25.

3. Update sorted list as shown below:

   (A, B, (D/E), C)

   Pick up two symbols with the minimum frequency. These symbols are 'D/E' and 'C'. Assign them free node as under.

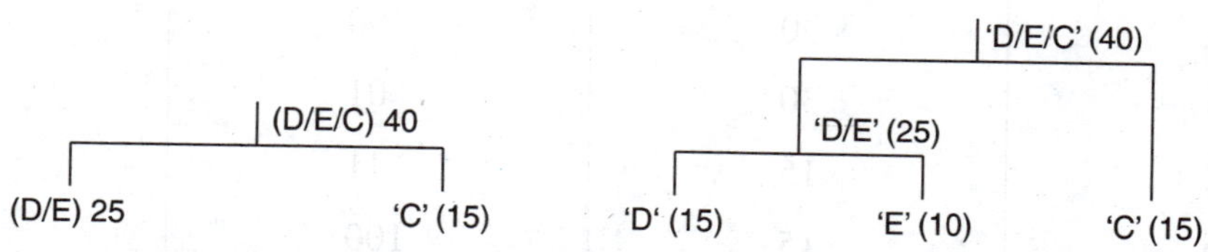

This subtree is called 'D/E/C'. Combined frequency of 'D/E/C' is 40.

4. Update sorted list as shown below.

('D/E/C', 'A', 'B')

Pick up two symbols with minimum frequency. These symbols are 'A' and 'B'. Assign them free node as given below:

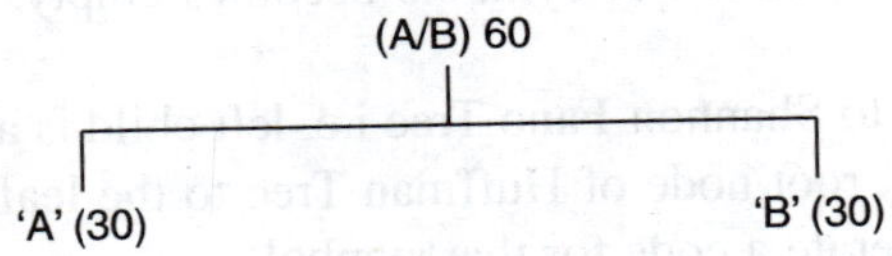

This subtree is called 'A/B' and combined frequency is 60.

5. Update sorted list as shown below.

(('A/B'), ('D/E/C'))

Pick up two symbols with minimum frequency. These are (A/B) and (D/E/C). Assign them free node as under:

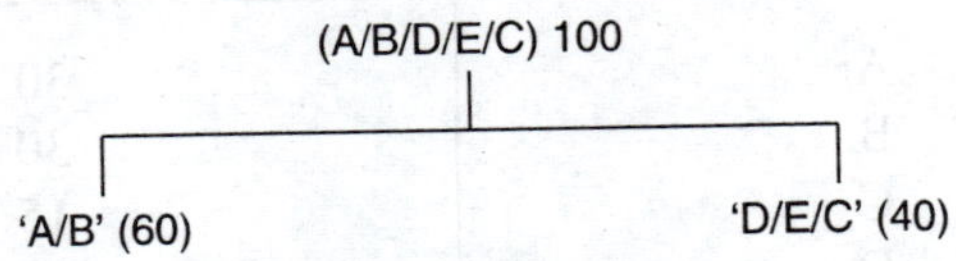

6. Update sorted list now it will contain only 'A/B/D/E/C' and no individual symbol is left. Therefore the process halts and final Huffman Tree is shown below:

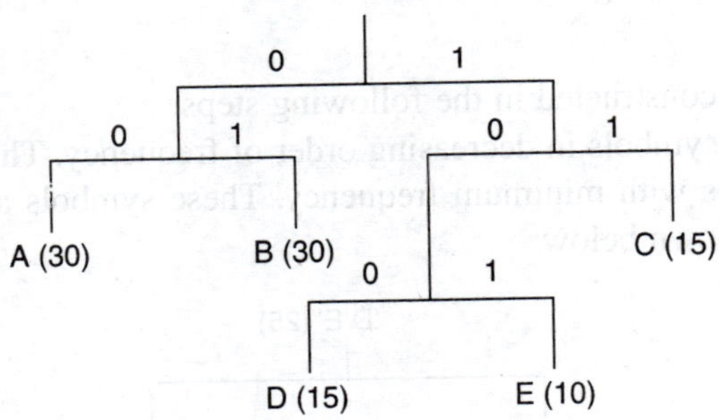

7. Assign the bit '0' and '1' to left and right subtree to obtain Huffman Code.

From above Huffman tree the code for all symbols are obtained. These codes are shown below in the following table.

Symbol	Frequency	Hoffman Code	Size of Huffman Code
A	30	00	2
B	30	01	2
C	15	11	2
D	15	100	3
E	10	101	3

Using Huffman code, the total number of bits required to represent a text of 100

$$= 30 * 2 + 30 * 2 + 15 * 2 + 15 * 3 + 10 * 3 = 225$$

Example

The symbols and their frequency is give below.

Symbol	Frequency
'e'	37
'h'	18
'a'	16
'b'	15
'd'	14

(a) Construct Huffman Tree and Generate Huffman codes.
(b) Compute the Entropy bits and calculate redundancy in the code.

Solution

(a) Steps for construction of Huffman Tree are shown below.

1. First find a sorted list of symbols in decreasing of frequency. The list will be ('e', 'h', 'a', 'b', 'd')
2. Pick up two symbols with minimum frequency. These symbols are 'b' and 'd'. Assign them to two free nodes as under.

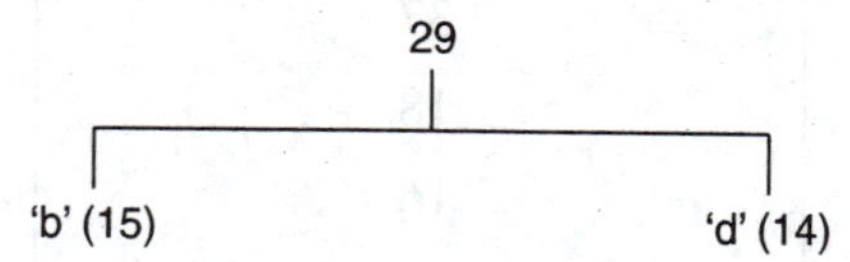

3. Remove the character ('b', 'd') from the list. From a new group (b, d). Now the sorted list is ('e', (b, d), 'h', 'a')
4. Pick up two symbols with minimum frequency. These symbols are 'h' and 'a'. Assign them to two free nodes as under. Remove character (h, a) from list and form a group (h, a). Now the list is ('e', (h, a), b, d).

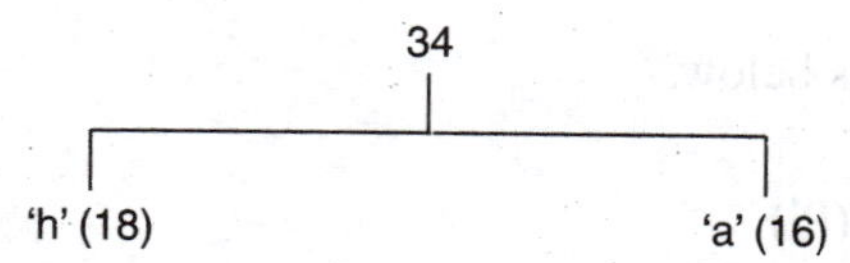

5. Ties the sub trees obtained at steps 4 and 2. Tree will appear as follows:

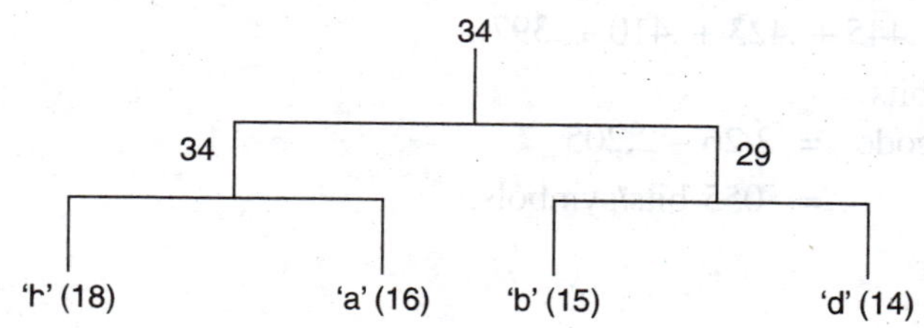

6. Remove the character ('b', 'd') from the list. Now the list is ('e'), i.e only one character. Create a free node for it. It will be as under

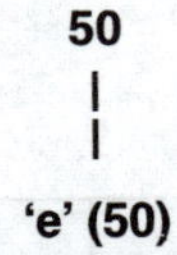

7. Tie up sub tree obtained n step 6 with sub tree of step 5. Since all the symbols have been incorporated, thus final Huffman Tree will be as under.

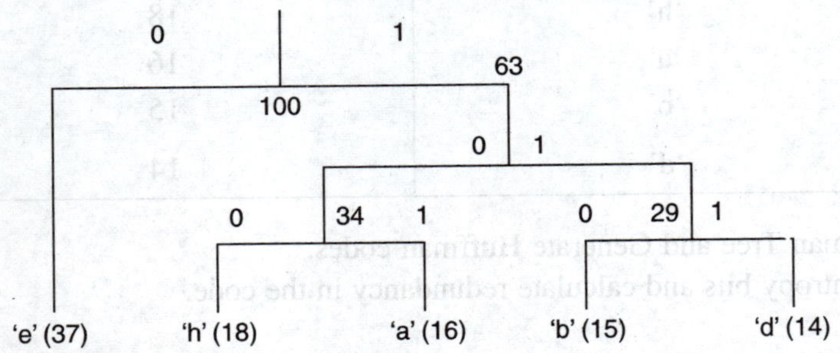

Thus from the above Huffman Tree codes for all symbols may be obtained. Following is the table containing Huffman Code, Frequency and respective symbols.

Symbol	Frequency	Huffman Code
'e'	37	0
'h'	18	100
'a'	16	101
'b'	15	110
'd'	14	111

Using Huffman scheme of code, Total number of bits required to represent a text of 100

= 37*1 + 18*3 + 16*3 +15*3 + 14*3

= 226

(b) Entropy may be calculated as below,

$$\text{Entropy} = -\sum_{1=1}^{1=N} Pi*\mathbf{log_2}\,(Pi)$$

$$= -(.37*\log_2(.37) + .18*\log_2(.18) + .16*\log_2(.16) + (.15)*\log_2(.15) + .14*\log_2(.14)$$

$$= .530 + .445 + .423 + .410 + .397$$

$$= 2.205 \text{ bits}$$

The redundancy in the code = 2.26 – 2.205

= .055 bits/symbols.

Example

Consider the following symbols and their relative frequencies.

Symbol	Frequency
A	20
B	18
C	16
D	15
E	15
F	10
G	4
H	2

For a text containing these symbols, develop Huffman Codes.

Solution

1. First find a sorted list of symbols in decreasing of frequency. The list will be (A, B, C, D, E, F, G, H)
2. Pick up two symbols with minimum frequency. These symbols are 'G' and 'H'. Assign them to two free nodes as under:

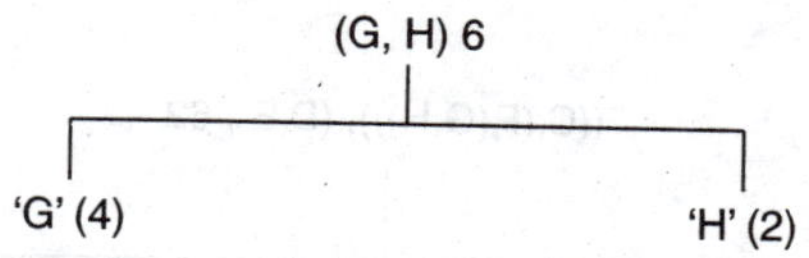

3. Remove the character ('G', 'H') from the list. Form a new group (G, H). Now the sorted list is (A, B, C, D, E, F, (G, H)
4. Pick up two symbols with minimum frequency. These symbols are 'F' and group (G, H). Assign them to two free nodes as under. Remove character 'F' and group (G, H) and form a new group (F, (G, H)). Now the sorted list is (A, B, C, (F, (G, H)), D, E).

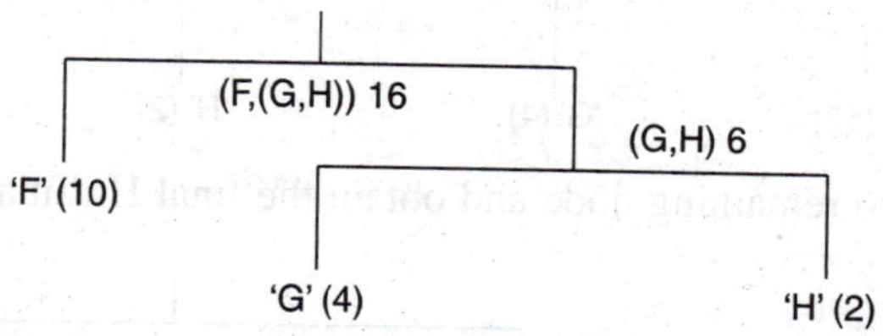

5. Select the two nodes from the list. Now these are ('D', 'E'). Delete the node 'D' from the list and generate the node for them and form a group of (D, E) and insert in to the list. Now the sorted list is (D, E), A, B, C, (F, (G, H)

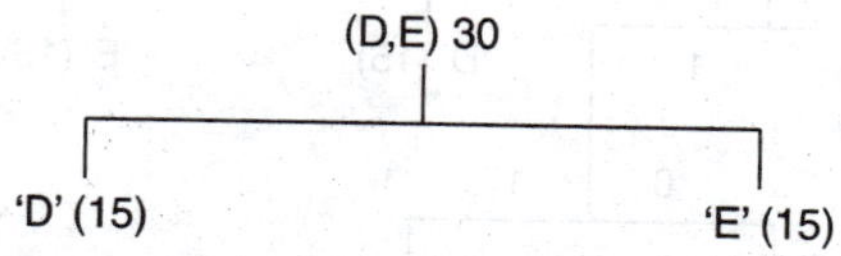

6. Select the two nodes from the list. Now these are 'C' and (F, (G, H). Delete these node the list and insert the node (C, (F, (G, H) into the list.

Now the sorted list is,

(C, (F, (G, H))), (D, E), A, B)

7. Select two nodes from list. These are (A, B). Delete these node from the list and add node (A, B) to the list. The sorted list, therefore is

(A, B), (C, (F, (G, H))), (D, E)

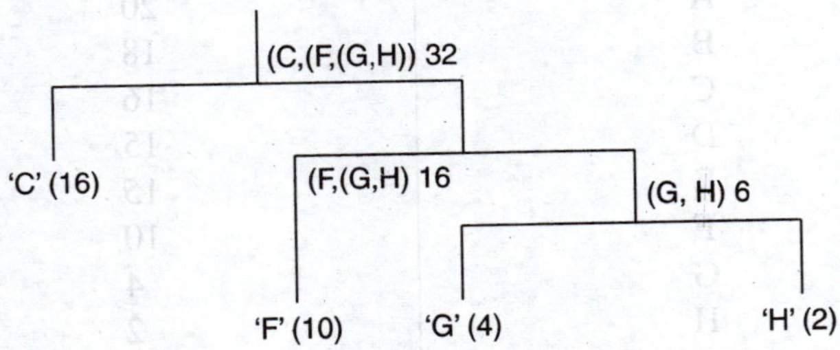

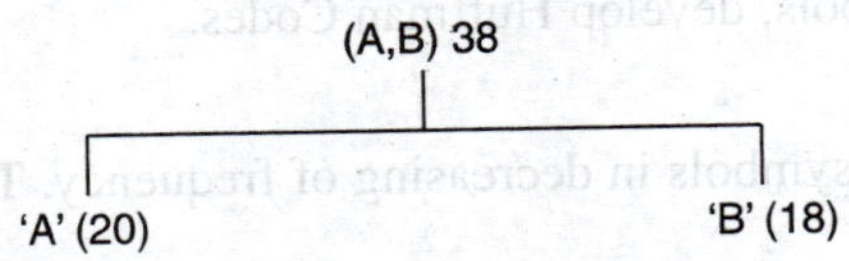

8. Select two nodes from list. These are (C, (F, (G, H) and (D, E). Delete these nodes from the list and add nodes ((C, (F, (G, H))), (D, E), to the list. The sorted list, therefore is as follows. (C, (F, (G, H))), (D, E)), (A, B)).

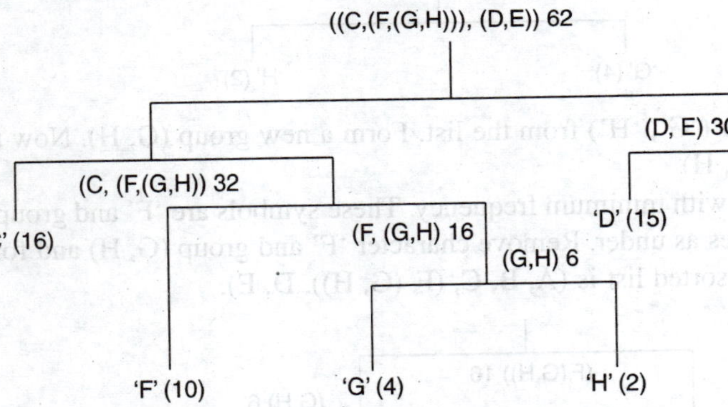

9. At last add up the two remaining node and obtain the final Huffman Tree.

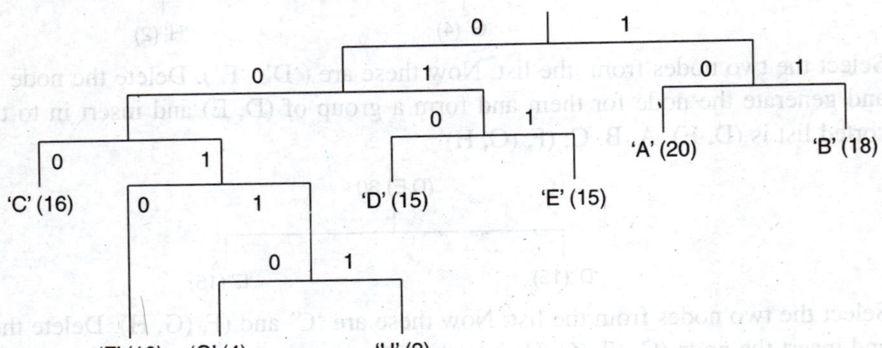

Assign the left branch with a code '0' and right branch with a code '1'. Now we may obtain the Huffman code for each symbol. These codes are given in the following table.

Symbol	Frequency	Huffman Code
A	20	10
B	18	11
C	16	000
D	15	010
E	15	011
F	10	0010
G	4	00110
H	2	00111

Using Huffman scheme of code, total number of bits required to represent a text of 100

= 20*2 + 18*2 +16*3 +15*3 + 15*3 + 10*4 + 4*5 + 2*5 = 284

2.4.2 Extended Huffman Code

In the previous sections, we have discussed Shannon-Fano and Huffman Codes. Both of the codes are so generated that each and every symbol is assigned a unique code. Whenever a symbol needs to be either compressed or communicated, the corresponding code replaces the symbol. The difference in entropy and average size of code length serves as a indicator for redundancy in the codes. Higher the difference, higher the redundancy. Our overall objective for designing Huffman code is that it gives minimum redundancy. Unfortunately, in all cases, we are not yielded with code which eliminates the redundant information up to considerable amount. Consider following example to understand.

Suppose a transmitter transmits three symbols. These symbols (A, B, C) have probabilitv P(A) = .85, P(B) = .10, P(B) = .05. Symbols, Huffman Codes, probability of these symbols are shown in the following table.

Symbol	Probability	Huffman Code
A	.85	0
B	.10	10
C	.05	11

Average size of Huffman code/symbol = 1.15 bits
We may compute the Entropy as

$$\text{Entropy} = -\sum_{i=1}^{i=N} Pi*\log_2 (Pi)$$

$$= .199 + .332 + .216$$

$$= .747 \text{ bit/symbol}$$

The difference in Entropy and average Huffman code size is considerably high. The redundancy for this code is .403 which is 54% of the entropy. Although we have generated variable length code but these codes does not yield good performance even after using Huffman Code, the redundant contents in the code are still 54%. In this example, we have considered the case where some of the symbols have exceptionally high probability of occurrence in comparison to other. We might observe that symbol 'A' occurs at high probability like .85 and other possesses significantly small probability of occurrence.

The Huffman Code generated for this problem requires 54% more bits than the minimum bits required. We might say that in this case the probabilities are skewed. The Huffman Code does not yield good performance when the probabilities are skewed.

The solution to this problem lies in using extended Huffman Codes. Extended Huffman Codes are obtained by grouping moe than one symbols in one group and Huffman code is obtained for whole group. Major advantage of using extended Huffman code is that it reduces the redundancy considerably. Limitations to these codes are that they work well for the case when the probability distribution over the different symbols are skewed.

Suppose N symbols are present in the message stream. Suppose we frame a group of M symbols where Huffman code for every group will be generated. In this way, total number of group formed would therefore be N^M. For this example, total number of symbols are three (A, B and C) and if we form the group of two symbols, total number of groups therefore are 3^2 = 9. We assume that transmitter will look for group of symbols to be sent and generate a code for the group. We may also calculate, the probability of occurrence of a group as under,

Suppose P(A) = Probability of occurrence of symbol (A)

P(B) = Probability of occurrence of symbol (B)

The probability of occurrence of group (AB) = P(A)*P(B).

The probability of occurrence of symbol A and B are .85 and .10 respectively. The probability for the groups 'AB' and 'BA' therefore are .85*.10 = .085.

The probabilities for the given symbols (A, B, C) in our example are .85, .10, .05 respectively. The following table shows the groups, where two symbols form a group, probability of occurrence of group.

Group	Probability
AA	.85 * .85 = .722
AB	.85 * .10 = .085
AC	.85 * .05 = .042
BA	.10 * .85 = .085
BB	.10 * .10 = .010
BC	.10 * .05 = .005
CA	.05 * .85 = .042
CB	.05 * .10 = .005
CC	.05 * .05 = .0025

A Huffman Tree for the group of symbols is shown below.

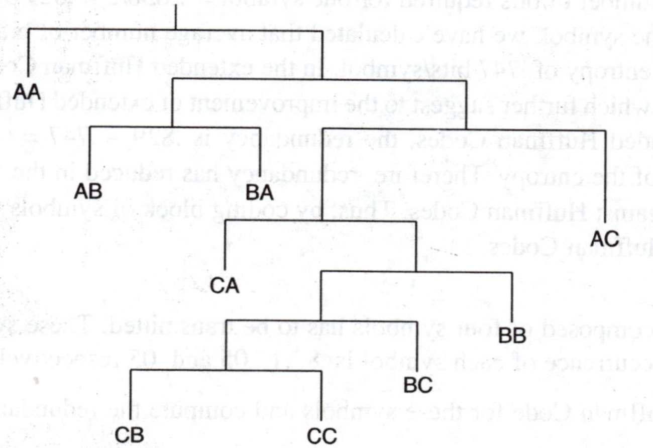

The Huffman codes for the groups of symbol are shown below in the table:

Group	Probability	Huffman Code
AA	.722	0
AB	.085	100
AC	.042	111
BA	.085	101
BB	.010	11011
BC	.005	110101
CA	.042	1110
CB	.005	1101000
CC	.0025	1101001

Let us evaluate the performance of the groups of the symbols i.e. extended Huffman Code. From the above table we may compute the average number of bits required to represent a group of two characters.

Average length of group of symbol = 1.658 bits/group

We may also calculate the revised entropy considering the group as a character as under,

$$\text{Entropy} = -\sum_{i=1}^{i=N} Pi*\log_2 (Pi)$$

$$= 1.490 \text{ bits/group}$$

In this scheme of generating the Huffman Code for a group

The redundancy = 1.658 – 1.490 = .168 bits/group

Therefore redundancy here is only 11.2% of the entropy value it proves that if we generate the extended binary code, we are left with only 11.2% redundancy.

In the extended Huffman Codes, average length of code for a group of two symbols is 1.658 bits. Therefore, average number of bits required for one symbol = 1.658/2 = .829 bits. While generating the Huffman Code for the symbol, we have calculated that average number of bits per symbol required is 1.15 bits against the entropy of .747 bits/symbol. In the extended Huffman Code, the average length of symbols is .829 bits, which further suggest to the improvement of extended Huffman code over Huffman Codes. In the Extended Huffman Codes, the redundancy is .829 – .747 = .– 082 bits/symbol. This redundancy is 11% of the entropy. Therefore, redundancy has reduced in the extended Huffman Code from 54% to 11% against Huffman Codes. Thus, by coding block of symbols together, we may reduce the redundancy of Huffman Codes.

Example

Suppose a message composed of four symbols has to be transmitted. These symbols are (A, B, C, D). The probability of occurrence of each symbol is .8, .1, .05 and .05 respectively.

(a) Generate the Huffman Code for these symbols and compute the redundancy.

(b) Generate the Extended Huffman Code. A Group of two characters should be formed for extended code.

(c) Compare the redundancy in extended Huffman Code (Obtained in (b)) with Huffman Code (obtained in (a)).

Solution

(a) Huffman Code for the Symbols A, B, C and D are shown in following table.

Symbol	Probability	Huffman Code
A	.80	0
B	.10	10
C	.05	110
D	.05	111

Average size of Huffman code/symbol = 1.30 bits

We may compute the Entropy as

$$\text{Entropy} = -\sum_{i=1}^{i=N} \text{Pi} * \log_2 (\text{Pi})$$

$$= .257 + .332 + .216 + .216$$

$$= 1.021 \text{ bit/symbol}$$

The difference in Entropy and average Huffman code size is .279 bits/symbol. The redundancy for this code is 27.3% of the entropy.

(b) The Huffman codes for the groups of symbol are shown below in the table:

Group	Probability	Huffman Code	Length of Code
AA	.64	0	1
AB	.08	1000	4
AC	.04	110	3
AD	.04	1011	4
BA	.08	1001	4
BB	.01	10100	5
BC	.005	10101000	8
BD	.005	10101001	8
CA	.04	1110	4
CB	.005	10101010	8
CC	.0025	10101100	8
CD	.0025	10101101	8
DA	.04	1111	4
DB	.005	10101011	8
DC	.0025	10101110	8
DD	.0025	10101111	8

Average number of bits required per group = 2.15 bits.

We may also calculate the revised entropy considering the group as a character as under,

$$\text{Entropy} = -\sum_{i=1}^{i=N} \text{Pi} * \mathbf{log_2}\,(\text{Pi})$$

$$= 2.036 \quad \text{bits/group}$$

The redundancy = 2.15 – 2.036 = .114 bits/group

Therefore redundancy in extended Huffman code is only 5.5% of the entropy value. It proves that if we generate the extended binary code, we are left with only 5.5% redundancy.

(c) Average length of code for a group of two symbols is 2.15 bits. Therefore, average number of bits required for one symbol = 2.15/2 = 1.075 bits. While generating the Huffman Code for the symbol, we have calculated that average number of bits per symbol required is 1.30 bits against the entropy of 1.021 bits/symbol. In the extended Huffman Code, the average length of code per symbol is 1.075 bits. It shows an improvement of extended Huffman code over Huffman Codes. In the Extended Huffman Codes, the redundancy is 1.075 – 1.021 = .054 bits/symbol. This redundancy is 5.2% of the entropy. Therefore, redundancy has reduced in the Extended Huffman Code from 27.3% to 5.2% against Huffman Codes.

2.5 COMPARISON OF SHANNON-FANO ALGORITHM AND HUFFMAN ALGORITHM

Huffman algorithm has been a matter of research to find algorithm which shows better performance. Huffman algorithm for construction of minimum redundancy code was proposed in early 1950's. Huffman algorithms performance is similar to that of Shannon-Fano, but Huffman algorithm has an edge over Shannon-Fano algorithm. Huffman codes, even in the worst case, will at least perform equal to Shannon-Fano codes.

We will now compare the performance of Shannon-Fano Codes and Huffman Codes which are generated for a given set of symbols and their relative frequencies.

Example

Consider the following symbols and their relative frequencies:

Symbol	Frequency
A	40
B	20
C	15
D	10
E	10
F	5

For a text containing these symbols, do the following:

1. Compute the information content of each symbol.
2. Compute information bits for each symbol.
3. Compute information content of text.
4. Compute Shannon-Fano code and the size of Shannon-Fano code for each symbol.
5. Compute the total number of bits required to represent each symbol. (Shannon-Fano bits)
6. Compute Huffman Code and the size of Huffman code for each symbol.
7. Compute the total number of bits required to represent each symbol. (Huffman bits).
8. Compare the performance of Shannon-Fano and Huffman Algorithm on the basis of Shannon-Fano bits and Huffman bits.

Solution

1. Information content of a symbol is entropy of a symbol. The information content of a symbol represents the minimum number of bits required to code the symbol.
   Information contents of a symbol (Entropy) = $-\log_2$ (Probability of symbol) ... (1)
2. Information bits of symbols is the total numbers of bits required to represent that symbol in the message based on the entropy of that symbol.

Information bits = frequency of symbol * Information Contents.

Information content and information bits are shown in the following table:

Symbol	Frequency	Information Contents	Information Bits
A	40	1.32	52.8
B	20	2.32	46.4
C	15	2.73	40.95
D	10	3.32	33.2
E	10	3.32	33.2
F	5	4.32	21.6
	100		228.15

3. Information contents of the message is the sum of all information bits of each symbols. Thus information contents in message = 228.15
4. Computation of Shannon-Fano Code requires the construction of Shannon-Fano Tree. The following is the Shannon-Fano Tree for the given set of symbols and their relative frequencies.

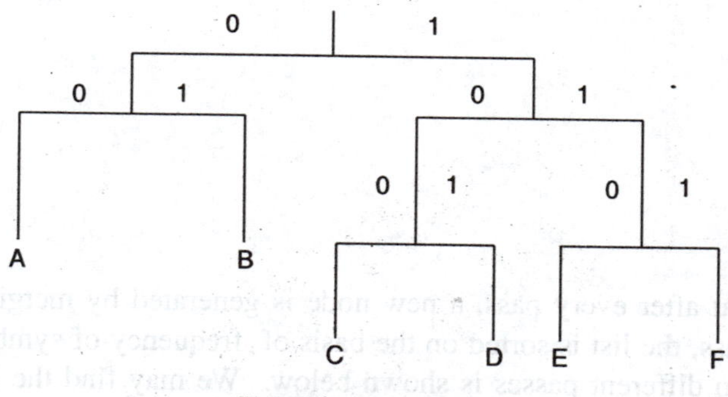

Shannon-Fano Tree

We may find the Shannon-Fano Code for each symbol from above tree. These Shannon-Fano codes, Size of Shannon-Fano Code, and the total number of bits required to represent symbol in Shannon-Fano code are shown in the table below:

Symbol	Frequency	Information Contents	Information Bits	SF Code	SF Code Size	Total SF Bits
A	40	1.32	52.8	00	2	80
B	20	2.32	46.4	01	2	40
C	15	2.73	40.95	100	3	45
D	10	3.32	33.2	101	3	30
E	10	3.32	33.2	110	3	30
F	5	4.32	21.6	111	3	15
	Total		228.15			240

5. Total numbers of bits required to represent message using Shannon-Fano code = 240
6. Computation of Huffman code requires the construction of Huffman Tree. Following is the Huffman Tree for the given set of symbols and their relative frequencies.

Various passes for the construction of Huffman Tree are shown below:

40	20	15	10	10	5
A	B	C	D	E	F

Pass 1

40	20	15	15	10
A	B	C	E/F	D

Pass 2

40	25	20	15
A	E/F/D	B	C

Pass 3

40	35	25
A	B/C	E/F/D

Pass 4

60	40
B/C/E/F/D	A

Pass 5

100
B/C/E/F/D/A

It may be noted that after every pass, a new node is generated by merging two least frequency symbols. After every pass, the list is sorted on the basis of frequency of symbols. The Huffman Tree constructed according to different passes is shown below. We may find the Huffman code for each symbol from this Huffman tree. These Huffman codes, size of Huffman Code, and the total number of bits required to represent symbols in Huffman code are shown in the table and are calculated as follows.

Size of Huffman code of symbol = Total number of bits in the Huffman code of that symbol.

Total Huffman bits = Total number of bits required to code the message using Huffman code.

$$= \sum_{i=1}^{i=N} = \text{(Relative Frequency * Size of Huffman Code)}$$

where N = number of symbols.

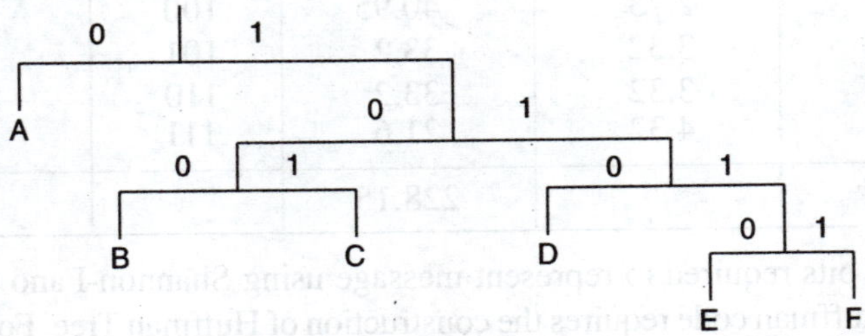

Huffman Tree

Sym.	Freq.	Info. Cont.	Info. Bits	SF Code	SF Code Size	Total SF Bits	Huffman Code	Huff. Code Size	Total Huff. Bits
A	40	1.32	52.8	00	2	80	0	1	40
B	20	2.32	46.4	01	2	40	100	3	60
C	15	2.73	40.95	100	3	45	101	3	45
D	10	3.32	33.2	101	3	30	110	3	30
E	10	3.32	33.2	110	3	30	1110	4	40
F	5	4.32	21.6	111	3	15	1111	4	20
		Total	228.15			240			235

7. Total number of bits required to represent a message using Huffman Code = 235.
8. We may see that the Shannon-Fano and Huffman codes are different for each symbol as well as they differ in the size. We have computed that the Information Content of the message are 228.15 bit. The same message requires 240 bits to encode using Shannon-Fano code and 235 bits using Huffman code. This proves a slight improvement using Huffman coding over Shannon-Fano coding.

The same message requires a total of 800 bits to code whereas the information content of the message is 228.15 bits. This reveals the scope for potential for improvement in coding. This potential may be exploited using Shannon-Fano or Huffman coding schemes.

Example

For the data shown in previous example, generate the code for the message string ACABDFAEA using Shannon-Fano coding and Huffman coding.

Solution

Message coded using Shannon-Fano code = "00 100 00 01 101 111 00 110 00"
Message coded using Huffman code = "0 101 0 100 110 1111 0 1110 0"

2.6 ADAPTIVE COMPRESSION TECHNIQUES

The Shannon-Fano and Huffman algorithm for data compression uses relative frequencies of occurrence of symbols. These relative frequencies may be computed once over a large sample of text data. Once the relative frequencies of all the symbols are known, then a static table containing the symbols and their respective frequencies is constructed. At the time of compression, a model of compression based on either Shannon-Fano or Huffman uses static data to encode the symbols. This is shown in the following figure.

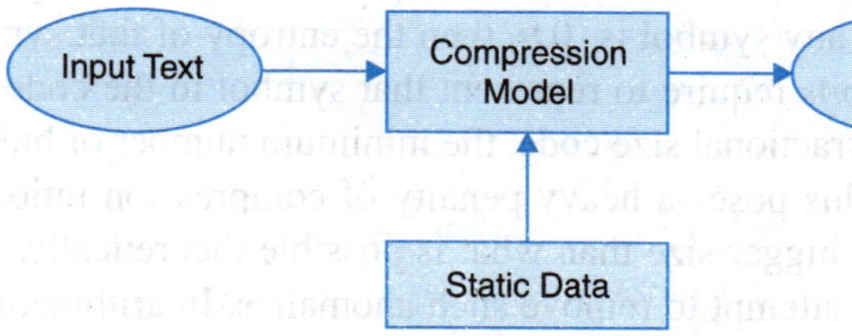

As shown in the Figure, this model uses static data and takes input text. It generates either Shannon-Fano or Huffman code based on the statistical data. Static data contains the code for each symbol computed previously and codes the current text. This model is called statistical model of compression. The major drawback of this model is that compression is done based on the previous statistical data. It is not always necessary that incoming text corresponds to static data. In such cases the compression ratio may be sacrificed.

The solution of this problem is to use the Adaptive Model. In *adaptive model*, data need not be scanned only once, instead static data is self-modified based on the frequency of symbols in the input text. The advantage of adaptive compression is that a better compression ratio is acquired. It also corresponds to the frequency of the symbols in the input text.

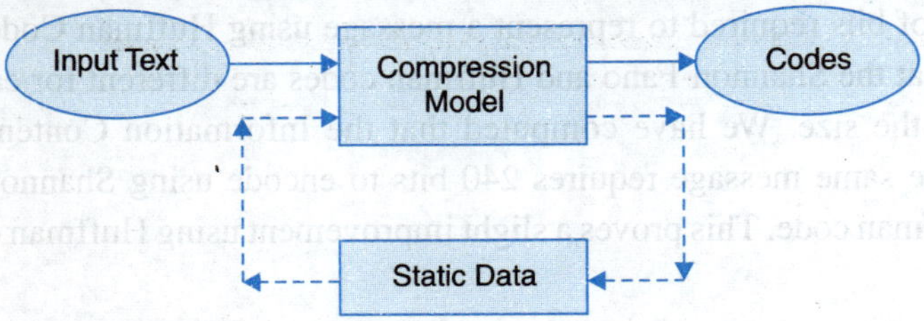

As shown in the figure, in adaptive data compression, the static data is updated according to input symbol and then it is coded as per the compression model. Therefore, adaptive compression techniques provide a better compression ratio. A similar process is implemented at the receiving end to decode the data. Huffman algorithm requires that a copy of the probability or frequency table be sent along with the compressed code. This compressed code will be decoded using the supporting information received along with the code. This is actually a major drawback of Huffman algorithm. This problem has been addressed in the adaptive Huffman Algorithm which is a significant improvement over the original Huffman algorithm.

2.7 ARITHMETIC CODING

The Huffman and Shannon-Fano algorithms produce the integral length code. For example, if the probability of occurrence of any symbol is 0.4, then the entropy of that symbol will be 1.3. The entropy of symbols represents the average number of bits required to represent those symbols. The number of bits allocated to the code representing a symbol would be an integral number, i.e., either one or two bits. If we opt to code the symbol with a two-bit number, then we will compromise with the redundancy and thereby with the compression ratio. If we choose to represent it with a one-bit code, then there will be penalty on another symbol for the number of bits. Thus, whichever option we choose, we will not be able to achieve an optimal compression ratio. The optimal criteria is important. For example, if the probability of occurrence of any symbol is 0.9, then the entropy of that symbol is .15. This indicates that the average number of bits require to represent that symbol in the code should be .15. But due to our inability to generate the fractional size code, the minimum number of bits required to represent that symbol would be one bit. This poses a heavy penalty of compression ratio. This mean that the compressed message will have a bigger size than what is possible theoretically.

Arithmetic Coding is an attempt to remove such anomalies. In arithmetic coding, it is not required to represent a symbol with a fixed integral length code. The arithmetic compressor takes the stream of symbols and produces a floating point number. This number is less than one and it represent the coded form of input text. The arithmetic coding technique also exploits the probability of occurrence of a symbol similar to Shannon-Fano and Huffman coding. The only problem with arithmetic coding is that it produces a large size floating point number and it is difficult to deal by digital computers.

Arithmetic Coding has proved to be efficient coding techniques for compression and communication of binary numbers. This method performs better than extended Huffman codes. As we have seen in the previous example, that for three symbols with the probabilities P(A) = .85, P(B) = .10, P(B) = .05 respectively. Following Huffman codes are generated:

Symbol	Probability	Huffman Code
A	.85	0
B	.10	10
C	.05	11

Average length of code in this scheme is 1.15 bits/symbol against the entropy of .747 bits/symbol. These codes may still have lot of redundancy. For this example the redundancy is .403 bits/symbol which is 54% of the entropy. Amount of redundancy left is highly dependent on the skews in the probability of symbols and higher skews among the probability will lead to high amount of redundancy in the code.

A significant improvement is achieved when we use extended Huffman Code. These codes are obtained by forming a group of symbols. When we obtain the extended code for group of two symbols together, average length of the group is 1.658 bits/group against the entropy of 1.490 bits/group. After forming a group of two symbols, the redundancy drops to .168 bits/group and it amounts to 11.2% of entropy value. In the same way, if we start forming the group of higher size (e.g. three symbols per group), the redundancy in the extended Huffman codes reduces. To get the acceptable, redundancy range, it is required to form group of eight symbols. With only group of eight symbols per group, it will be required to generate the three to power eight i.e. 6561 codes. Similarly, we form group of sixteen symbols, it would require 4304672 codes. These number may be exponentially large if the number of symbols are more than three. To generate such a large number of codes will be highly impractical. An alternative to these problems lies in arithmetic coding. In this technique, instead generating the code for all combinations, we generate the code for input stream only. Arithmetic coding not only eliminates the possibility of redundancy but also eliminate the requirement of generation of code for all the symbols. It rather emphasizes the replacement of input message with a single floating point number. More number of symbols in the input message will result in adding more number of digits in the output stream. Arithmetic coding produces a floating number between zero and one. Consider the following example to understand arithmetic coding.

Example

The following is the probability distribution of symbols:

Y	E	R	G	N	M	A	F	C
.1	.2	.1	.1	.1	.1	.1	.1	.1

Code the letter "GERMAN" using arithmetic coding.

Solution

Following are the steps to generate the code using arithmetic coding.

Step 1

Obtain the probability of occurrence of all the symbols. Check that the sum of probabilities of all symbols is equal to one. All symbols are given a range of probability from 0 to 1. Each symbol is then given an individual range which is equal to the probability of occurrence of that symbol. The given range for the symbols is as follows:

Table 1: Probability Table

Symbols	Probability	Range-From	Range-To
Y	.1	.00	.10
E	.2	.10	.30
R	.1	.30	.40
G	.1	.40	.50
N	.1	.50	.60
M	.1	.60	.70
A	.1	.70	.80
F	.1	.80	.90
C	.1	.90	1.00

As given in the table, for each symbol a range is created based on its probability of occurrence. For example, the first symbol 'Y' has probability ".10". Thus a range is allotted from 0.0 (Range-From) to .10 (Range-To). The next symbol 'E' has probability ".20". Its range starts from .10 (= Range-To of previous symbol) to .30 (Range-From of the Symbol + Probability of Symbol). This way the range of each symbol is allotted.

It is important to note that the range of a symbol includes Range-From but does not include Range-To. Therefore, the symbol 'A' falls in the range (>=.70 and < .80).

While coding the word "GERMANY", the first symbol "G" will be coded. "G" falls in the range (.40 – .50). Thus the final code, i.e., a floating number will be in the range (.40 – .50). The next symbol "E" would be taken into account and it will create a range (.10 – .30) within the range for "G". In this process, we will gradually keep restricting the floating number in a range.

Algorithm for Arithmetic Coding
Initialize

```
LOW _VALUE   = 0.0 ;
HIGH_VALUE   = 1.0 ;
Difference   = 1.0 ;
For Every Symbol in Input  REPEAT
{
LOW_VALUE = LOW_VALUE + Difference * RANGE-FROM (Symbol);
HIGH_VALUE =  LOW_VALUE  +  Difference *  RANGE-TO (Symbol);
Difference = HIGH_VALUE   –  LOW_VALUE ;
}
DISPLAY_OUPUT ( LOW_VALUE )
```

Now construct a table using the algorithm shown above. To code the word "GERMAN", all the symbols will be taken one by one. First symbol to be considered is "G". Calculate Low_Value, High_Value and the difference as per the algorithm. Consider the next symbol "E" and modify the Low_Value obtained in the previous pass. After considering the last symbol "N", the algorithm yields the coded fractional number as Low_Value. The following table shows the modification in Low_Value, High_Value on input of each symbol.

Table 2 : Coding Table

Action	LOW_VALUE	HIGH_VALUE	Difference
Initial →	.00	1.00	1.0
Input G	.00 +1.0*.40 = .40	.00 +1.0*.50=.50	.1
Input E	.40 + .1*.1 = .41	.40 + .1*.3 =.43	.02
Input R	.41 + .02*.3 =.416	.41 +.02*.4 =.418	.002
Input M	.416 + .002*.6 = .4172	.416 + .002*.7 =.4174	.0002
Input A	.4172 + .0002*.7 =.41734	.4172 + .0002*.8 =.41736	.00002
Input N	.41734 + .00002*.5 = .41735	.41734 + .00002*.6 = .417352	.000002

Output of this procedure is fractional number .41735. This number falls in the range ".4–.5" (see Table 1). Thus the first character of the code is "G". The decoding process follows as per the following decoding algorithm. This algorithm modifies the code on every pass and generates the (output) symbol of text.

Algorithm for Decoding

Do while (Code <> 0.0)

{

Find the Probability Range where code falls;

Output the Symbol corresponding to that range;

$$\text{Code} = \frac{\text{Code - Range\_From (Symbol)}}{\text{(Range\_To (Symbol) - Range\_From (Symbol))}};$$

}

Let us decode the fractional number ".41735" which is the coded form of the word "GERMAN". The various passes of this algorithm are shown in table. The Range_From, Range_To and symbols are shown in Table 1.

Table 3 : Decoding Table

Coded Fractional Number	Output	Range_From	Range_To	Difference
.41735	"G"	.4	.5	.1
(.41735 – .4) / .1 = .1735	"E"	.1	.3	.2
(.1735 – .1) / .2 = .3675	"R"	.3	.4	.1
(.3675 – .3) / .1 = .675	"M"	.6	.7	.1
(.675 – .6) / .1 = .75	"A"	.7	.8	.1
(.75 – .7) / .1 = .5	"N"	.5	.6	.1
(.5 – .5)/ .1 = .0				

This example shows how the text can be coded and decoded by using arithmetic coding schemes. The arithmetic coding has a little drawback as it does not know where should the decoding process end. This problem may be handled by introducing a special symbol. This symbol denotes the end of the string. When we reach at the end of coding, this special symbol is also coded but only once. At the time of decoding, the output of this symbol implies that there are no more symbols to output, and thus it thereby indicates the end of the decoding process.

Another drawback of this scheme is that it usually generates big or lengthy fractional numbers and most of modern day computers are capable of processing eighty digit long fractional numbers. If the computer is using 32-bit or 64-bit integer math, then these floating numbers are bundled and are represented as a combination. Thus, the single number formed by bundling may be as long as the number of bits of that computer.

Example

Use the Table 1 of previous example for symbols and their corresponding probability. Show the steps for coding the word "FRANCE" using arithmetic coding scheme. For the generated code, show the steps of decoding of code.

Solution

Using Table 1, we may generate the coding table to code the word "FRANCE" as follows.

Coding Table

Action	LOW_VALUE	HIGH_VALUE	Difference
Initial →	.00	1.00	1.0
Input F	.00 +1.0*.80 =.80	.00 +1.0*.90 =.90	.1
Input R	.80 + .1*.3 = .83	.80 + .1*.4 =.84	.01
Input A	.83 + .01*.7 =.837	.83 +.01* .8 =.838	.001
Input N	.837 + .001* .5 = .8375	.837 + .001* .6 =.8376	.0001
Input C	.8375 + .0001* .9 =.83759	.8375 + .0001* 1.0 =.8376	.00001
Input E	.83759 + .00001*.1 = .837591	.83759 + .00001*.3 = .837593	.000001

Thus the code generated for the word "FRANCE" is ".837591". This fractional number may be decoded to produce the word "FRANCE". The steps to decode the fractional number are shown below:

Decoding Table

Coded Fractional Number	Output	Range_From	Range_To	Difference
.837591	"F"	.8	.9	.1
(.837591 – .8) / .1 = 37591	"R"	.3	.4	.1
(.37591 – .3) / .1 = .7591	"A"	.7	.8	.1
(.7591 – .7) / .1 = .591	"N"	.5	.6	.1
(.591 – .5) / . = .91	"C"	.9	1.0	.1
(.91 – .9) / .1 = .1	"E"	.1	.3	.2
(.5 – .5) / .1 = .0				

Thus the above decoding procedure yields the word "FRANCE" by decoding the floating number ".837591".

Example

For the probability model shown below, use arithmetic coding to code the string "AACBC"

Symbol	Probability
A	.3
B	.2
C	.5

Solution

For the symbols with probabilities shown above, a detailed probability table may be obtained.

Symbol	Probability	Range-From	Range-To
A	.3	0.0	.30
B	.2	.30	.50
C	.5	.50	1.00

Probability Table

Obtain a Coding Table according to the algorithm for arithmetic coding. The coding table for the algorithm is shown below. This table is obtained by taking one symbol each repeatedly from the input text "AACBC".

Action	Low_Value	High_Value	Difference
Initial→	0.0	1.00	1.0
Input A	0.0+1.0*0.0 = 0.0	0.0+1.00*.30 = .30	.30
Input A	0.0+.3*0.0 = 0.0	0.0+.3*.3 = .09	.09
Input C	0.0+.09*.5 = .045	0.0+.09*1.0 = .09	.045
Input B	.045+.045*.3 = .0585	.045+.045*.5 = .0675	.009
Input C	.0585+.009*.5 = .063	.0585+.009*1.0 = .0675	.0055

Coding Table

Output of this procedure is .0630. This floating-point number represents the arithmetic code for the string "AACBC".

The output code .0630 may be decoded by using decoding algorithm. The Decoding table is shown below:

Coded Flaoting Number	Output	Range_From	Range_To	Difference
.063	A	0.0	0.3	.3
(.063–0.0)/.3 = .21	A	0.0	0.3	.3
(.21–0.0)/.3 = .7	C	0.5	1.0	.5
(.7–.5)/.5 = .4	B	0.3	0.5	.2
(.4–.3)/.2 = .5	C	0.5	1.0	.5
(.5–.5)/.5 = 0	–	–	–	–

Decoding Table

We may observe that after decoding of the number .063, the string "AACBC" is produced.

Example

For the frequency count shown in the table below:

Symbol	Frequency Count
A	20
B	10
C	30
D	10
E	30

(a) Find the arithmetic code for the sequence "DCBE" and "BACDAED"

(b) Decode the code obtained by you to verify the correctness of the code.

Solution

(a) Probability for the given symbols may be obtained from the frequency count. The Probability Table for the symbols is shown below:

Symbol	Probability
A	.20
B	.10
C	.30
D	.10
E	.30

Probability Table

(i) The Coding table may be constructed following the algorithmic step of arithmetic coding. Coding Table with steps for the string "DCBE" is shown below:

Action	Low_Value	High_Value	Difference
Initial→	0.0	1.0	1.0
Input D	0.0+1.0*.6 = .6	0.0+1.0*.7 = .7	.1
Input C	.6+1*.3 = .63	.6+1*.6 = .66	.03
Input B	.63+.03*.2 = .636	.63+.03*.3 = .639	.003
Input E	.636+.003*.7 = **.6381**	.636+.003*1.0 = 639	.0009

Coding Table

Therefore, the floating number equivalent to the string "DCBE" is .6381.

(ii) The coding table for the string "BACDAED" is shown below.

Action	Low–_Value	High_Value	Differecne
Initial→	0.0	1.00	1.0
Input B	0.0+1.0=.2	0.0+1.0*.3=.3	.1
Input A	.2+1*0.0=.2	.2+.1*.2=.22	.02
Input C	.2+.02*.3=.206	.2.02*.6=.212	.006
Input D	.206+.006*.6=.2096	.206+.006*.7=.2102	.0006
Input A	.2096+.0006*0.9=.2096	.2096+.0006*1.0=.209972	.00012
Input E	.2096+.00012*.07=.209684	.2096+.00012*1.0=.20972	.00036
Input D	.209684+.00036*.6=**.2097056**	.209684+.00036*.7=.2097092	.0000036

Coding Table

Therefore, the floating number equivalent to the string "BACDAED" is .2097056.

(b) In section (a) of solution, we have generated the code for the string "DCBE" and "BACDAED" which are 0.6381 and .2097056 respectively for the probabilities shown in the probability table. The correctness of these codes may be verified by decoding these codes. The decoding table of string "DCBE" is shown below.

Coded Floating Number	Output	Range_From	Range_To	Difference
.6381	D	.6	.7	.1
(.6381–.6)/.1 = .381	C	.3	.6	.3
(.381–.3)/.3 = .27	B	.2	.3	.1
(.27–.2)/.1 = .7	E	.7	1.0	.3
(.7–.7)/.3 = 0.0	–	–	–	–

Decoding Table

It may be seen that in the decoding process of number .6381, the symbols D, C, B and E are produced in order. Therefore .6381 is equivalent to the string "DCBE".

In the same way correctness of code of string "BACDAED" may be verified by decoding the number .2097056. The decoding table of string "DCBE" is shown below.

Coded Floating Number	Output	Range_From	Range_To	Difference
.2097056	B	.2	.3	.1
(.2097056–.2)/.1 = .097056	A	.0	.2	.2
(.097056–0.0)/.2 = .48528	C	.3	.6	.3
(.48528–.3)/.3 = .6176	D	.6	.7	.1
(.6176–.6)/.1 = .176	A	.0	.2	.2
(.176–0.0)/.2 = .88	E	.7	1.0	.3
(.88–.7)/.3 = 6	D	.6	.7	.1
(.6–.6)/.1 = 0.0	–	–	–	–

Decoding Table

2.8 COMPRESSION RATIO

Compression Ratio is defined as,

$$\text{Compression Ratio} = \frac{\text{Size of Original Data} - \text{Size of Compressed Data}}{\text{Size of Original Data}} \times 100$$

Example

A text containing 24 KB is compressed using Shannon-Fano coding. The size of compressed code is 15KB. Find the compression ratio.

Solution

Compression ratio = (24 – 15)/24 * 100%
= 37.5%

2.9 DICTIONARY BASED COMPRESSION METHODS

Compression methods like Shannon-Fano, Huffman and Arithmetic Coding take the symbols of input string and produce the code. In all these compression mechanisms, an equivalent code is produced after exploiting the probability of symbols. We emphasize that the compression is achieved when the size of the compressed code is less than the size of input text. One of the drawback of these algorithms is that the compression ratio depends on the program written to implement the compression model and obtaining the probabilities of the symbol. There exists a completely different mechanism which also compresses the input text.

Dictionary based coding depends on the concept of maintaining the indexes. Let us understand this concept. Suppose for a dictionary of all the words is existing which may appear in the incoming text for compression. We represent each word by the indices in which they appear in the dictionary. For example, a word may be represented by a combination of its page number in the dictionary and the index on that page. As this scheme becomes more effective, we can also generate the smaller codes for phrases and sentences. In all dictionary-based compression techniques, the word, phrases or sentences are represented by tokens. Suppose a text has to be transmitted over a communication channel, then an equivalent token of that is transmitted. These tokens are generated corresponding to the index where they have been stored in the dictionary. The dictionary may be generated according to the nature of the text to be compressed. Suppose, the data pertaining to the sales of a product of a company has to be transmitted frequently. A customized dictionary may be developed which contains only those words and phrases that appear frequently in the sales report etc. This customized dictionary will contain the minimum number of words/phrases and thus the index will also require fewer bits to represent these words and phrases.

The first algorithm proposed using dictionary-based compression was LZ77 developed by Ziv and Lampel. This algorithm with certain improvement was proposed by Ziv and Lampel in 1978 and it became known as LZ78 compression algorithm. The next variant of LZ78 was introduced in 1984, called LZW compression techniques. It was proposed by Teery Welch, who considered the implementation detail of LZ78 algorithm. One of the popular application of these algorithms is in the Compress program used in the UNIX operating system. The Compress was a program written in 'C' language for compression of the files on VAX machines. Another interesting application of LZ78 was the introduction of the ARC program. ARC was developed for MS DOS systems. Concept of compression using

ARC was similar to that of Compress program. It was possible to compress several files into one file in MS DOS environment just like the 'tar' files in UNIX. PKARC was also based on LZ78 compression algorithm. One of the most popular compression programs for MS DOS environment PKZIP was based on LZ77 compression technique. In the next sections, we will discuss LZ77, LZ78, LZW compression algorithms.

The dictionary based compression method exploits the semantic of the data to reduce the redundancy in the code. These methods shows significant improvement in compression over character based compression schemes. The dictionary based compression techniques generate the code not only for the single character but also for frequently appearing group of characters or phrases. It is possible to generate a reasonably small code for frequently appearing group of characters or phrases. It is also possible to generate a reasonably small code for frequently appearing statements which may be coded by a comparatively smaller codes. Dictionary based techniques may be both static and dynamic and they build and use the list of frequently occurring phrases. If one possesses the prior knowledge of source of information to be compressed, the use of static dictionary techniques are desirable. Suppose, we have to compress the text or data pertaining to employees of an organization. We might choose to use static dictionary techniques because some of the words and phrases will appear in the text most frequently. Suppose, employee list, salary bill and other similar report are to be compressed then name of employee, their employee codes, designations and certain other words specific to the organization will be repeated in that text. Under these circumstances, it would be fruitful to build and use a static dictionary which contains all the frequently appearing phrases and statements. These techniques work well for text when they are drawn from a specific domain. In the Dynamic Dictionary approach, the dictionary is built dynamically according to the patterns or phrases appearing in the text to be compressed. Most of the generalized dictionary based compression techniques build the dictionary dynamically.

Static Dictionary Compression

In the static dictionary compression, a dictionary of characters and all possible frequently appearing groups of the character is prepared. If we take all possible combinations of the characters appearing in the text, possibly this number will be very high to be accommodated in the dictionary. Since the dictionary is of fixed size therefore only those phrases or groups of characters are placed in the dictionary whose probability of occurrence in the text is relatively high. This technique also shows significant improvement on traditional Shannon or Huffman compression techniques. One such example of static dictionary based compression is **diagram coding**.

Suppose we wish to construct a dictionary of size 516 positions to accommodate all possible characters which appear in day-to-day life. Suppose total number of these characters are 100. Thus, in the dictionary first 100 positions will be occupied by 100 single characters and rest of the 416 positions will be occupied by the frequently appearing combinations of characters or phrases. Let us understand the concept with the following example.

Example

Suppose a text may be composed of total six characters A, B, C, D, E and F. If we decide to keep the size of dictionary to 16, a four bit code may be allotted to each character. We keep ten positions reserved for ten most frequently appearing phrases and first six locations are reserved for six characters. The characters, codes and ten most frequently appearing phrases in the text are shown in following dictionary structure. The phrases added to the library are those which appear in the text with relatively higher probability. These phrases may be identified by a statistical analysis of the texts.

Code	Character/Phrase	Code	Character/Phrase
0000	A	1000	BC
0001	B	1001	EF
0010	C	1010	DE
0011	D	1011	AAB
0100	E	1100	ABB
0101	F	1101	BAC
0110	AB	1110	BCDE
0111	AC	1111	AABB

Suppose a text "AFABDAABDEAABB" need to be coded then a code will be generated as the following.

A	F	AB	D	AAB	DE	AABB
0000	0101	0110	0011	1011	1010	1111

Therefore, the code for the text would be "0000 0101 0110 0011 1011 1010 1111". One of the limitations of this coding technique is that performance varies over the text to be coded and it is highly dependent on the actual occurrence of the phrases in the text. If the text does not confirm to the domain for which dictionary has been prepared then application of this technique does not work. The solution to these problems lies in adaptive or dynamic dictionary based compression. In the dynamic compression techniques, the dictionary is prepared on sequences of the characters appearing in the text being compressed. Using these techniques, we always get an optimum size codes. LZ family of algorithm e.g. LZ77, LZ78, LZW compression techniques builds the dictionary dynamically. In the following sections, we will discuss some of the dynamic dictionary based compression methods.

2.10 LZ77 COMPRESSION TECHNIQUE

First of dictionary based algorithm was presented by Ziv & Lampel in 1977, in their paper "A Universal Algorithm for Sequential Data Compression" in IEEE transaction on Information Theory. At a later stage, this algorithm was termed as LZ77 compression scheme. The LZ77 scheme implements the dictionary in a unique way. When a input text is taken for compression, it starts building the dictionary. Thus the symbols/words/phrases which have been scanned previously, appear again in the same text then a token corresponding to the entry of that phrase in the dictionary is generated. LZ77 scheme uses a text window, which is divided into two parts. One contains the previously scanned text and other contains the input text, which will be scanned next called look ahead buffer. The look ahead buffer is usually small and contains few phrases. If the symbol/string in look ahead buffer have been scanned before then an entry of it must exist in the dictionary. In that case only a token corresponding to that entry is generated.

1. The search buffer contains the part of input message being coded.
2. The look-ahead buffer contains forthcoming stream of characters.
3. Size of search buffer and look ahead buffer remains fixed. In this example, it is set to the values 4.

4. Look ahead buffer is moved over the input stream in forward direction. First character in the look ahead buffer is checked, if it is there in search buffer. A pointer is moved in search buffer to do it. The distance of match from the look ahead buffer is known as offset.
5. After the match occurred, the pointer is moved in forward direction to check if the next consecutive character has a match in next symbol in look ahead buffer. Total number of consecutive symbols matched is known as length of match. The compressor attempt to search the longest match in the look ahead buffer.
6. After match has been found, a token (offset to phrase, length of phrase, symbol) is generated. Symbol corresponds to the first symbol from where the match has been found.

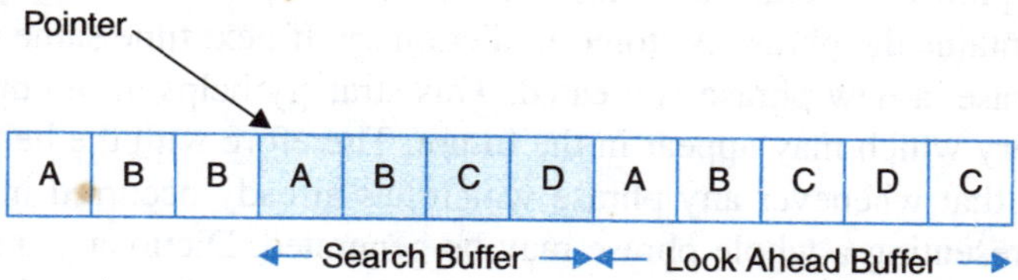

7. In the figure, match for the first symbol in the look ahead buffer "A" has been found as shown by pointer. String ABCD is matched as shown in look ahead buffer. Therefore a token (4, 4, 'A') will be issued for this match.

In this scheme the repeated occurrences of the phrases may be exploited and a token or code corresponding to the whole phrase is generated. This scheme has a drawback, that searching for phrases becomes complex and tedious affair if the size of the dictionary increases. If the compressed data has to be communicated over a communication channel then at receiving end, a copy of dictionary is also required. Sending a huge directory to recipient before sending a compressed text may be a costly affair. The solution to dictionary based compression techniques is to build the dictionary dynamically at receiving end. Bottleneck in the LZ77 compression scheme is to decide the size of text window. It is not possible to arbitrarily increase the size of text window. Performance of LZ77 depends on the size of text window, i.e., if it is higher then a better performance will be achieved. This is one of the major drawbacks of LZ77 compression. Since this algorithm uses a fixed size text window only a small size of data will fit in to text window in case of compressing a large text of data. This means once a text goes out of text window, corresponding entry in the dictionary will not be available even if the next match is found. Another drawback in LZ77 compression is that a limited size of phrase can be matched because of small size of look-ahead buffer. These drawback were taken care in an improved algorithm proposed by Ziv & Lampel in 1978. This algorithm is known as LZ78.

2.11 LZ78 COMPRESSION

LZ78 Compression algorithm was developed by Ziv & Lampel in 1978 which was an improvement of LZ77 compression algorithm. Details of LZ78 first appeared in IEEE transaction on Information theory in 1978. The LZ78 is similar to LZ77 in many respects that it takes input string and produces token. The major difference was that data structure fixed sized text window was replaced by a dictionary. This dictionary contains all the scanned phrases and any new phrase scanned is compared with the contents of dictionary. The LZ77 algorithm performs better whenever the string appearing in the look ahead buffer finds the matching string in the search buffer. Higher the size of look ahead buffer and search buffer provides high probability of successful match of the string. This also assumes that any phrase which appears at period longer than the size of window will not be available for successful match. This is considered as a major drawback, as the size of window cannot be increased arbitarily. In this case, if the same string occurs at a longer interval then a separate token will be issued for this phrase even though the string has already occurred in the past. This may cause serious drawback to LZ77 scheme as in the worst cases, instead of getting a compression we may end up with expansion. The worst case is when a phrase has a repeated occurrence but the size of phrase is longer than the window. In this case, repeated occurrence of longer phrase may not be captured. This gives a major advantage to LZ77, where the phrase could be matched with the contents of text window. Therefore in LZ78 compesssion begins with a new dictionary. It scans the input characters and an entry to the newly created directory is made. Whenever a new phrase is found which has a match with the phrase already stored in the directory, a new phrase which contains the phrase is stored in dictionary. If next time same phrase appears along with a new symbol/phrase, a new phrase is created. This strategy helps in building and entering new phrases into the directory which may appear in the future. Therefore with the help of dictionary LZ78 enjoys a major benefit that whenever any phrase which has already occurred in the past, will find a match and a token representing a whole phrase may be generated. Dictionary tree is also prepared to enter the new phrases of string to the dictionary. This dictionary tree also provides the fast fetch of the string at the time of decompression.

Consider the following example to understand the LZ78 compression.

Example

Consider the text string “WYS*WYGWYS*WYWWYSG”. Show all the steps of LZ78 compression including dictionary.

Solution

Scan the string from the Left character by character. Initially the dictionary is empty.

Step	Input Phrase	Output Phrase
1.	‘W’	<0, ‘W’>
2.	‘Y’	<0, ‘Y’>
3.	‘S’	<0, ‘S’>
4.	‘*’	<0, ‘*’>
5.	‘WY’	<1, ‘Y’>
6.	‘G’	<0, ‘G’>
7.	‘WYS’	<5, S>
8.	‘*W’	<4, W>
9.	‘YW’	<2, W>
10.	‘WYSG’	<7, ‘G’>

In LZ78 compression, with the progress in the encoding, the size of dictionary increases. After one stage, the dictionary builds up fairly large phrases. At the end of the input text to LZ88 compression, the dictionary looks like following:

1. ‘W’
2. ‘Y’
3. ‘S’
4. ‘*’
5. ‘WY’

6. 'G'
7. 'WYS'
8. '*W'
9. 'YW'
10. 'WYSG'

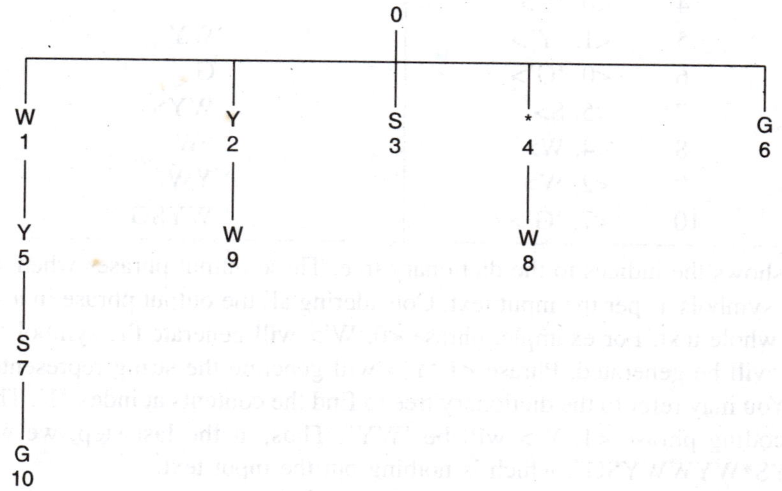

Dictionary Tree

The dictionary tree shown above is created after completely encoding the input text WYS*WYGWYS*WYWWYSG. The LZ78 compression algorithm's performance increases with the size of dictionary as after some time, it becomes possible to represent long phrases with a small code. But increased size of dictionary also poses problems in managing the dictionary tree. Although a large tree provides fast search of the phrases contained in the dictionary as well as storing a new phrase into the dictionary, yet it is always difficult to maintain a large tree. In coding of a binary file, the tree may require as many as 256 branches.

In the above example, the dictionary tree, grows on the occurrence of new symbols. The phrases stored in the dictionary are referenced by a set of pointers. This scheme of maintaining the dictionary is a better choice in the sense that it makes the best use of the available memory.

Decoding of the Text in LZ78

The LZ78 algorithm generates the output phrase. These phrases may be stored or communicated and they require lesser disk storage. For decoding, the output phrase is sent to the decoder which, with the help of the dictionary, decodes the phrase and produce the original text compressed. The generated series of output phrases are as follows:

Output Phrase	Text Generated
1 <0, 'W'>	W
2 <0, 'Y'>	Y
3 <0, S>	S
4 <0, '*'>	*
5 <1, 'Y'>	WY
6 <0, 'G'>	G
7 <5, S>	WYS
8 <4, W>	*W
9 <2, W>	YW
10 <7, 'G'>	WYSG

The number shows the indices to the dictionary tree. These output phrases when submitted to the decoder, generate symbols as per the input text. Considering all the output phrase in a sequential order will generate the whole text. For example, phrase <0,'W'> will generate the symbol 'W'. Then symbols 'Y', 'S', '*' will be generated. Phrase <1.'Y'> will generate the string represented by token '1' and symbol 'Y'. You may refer to the dictionary tree to find the contents at index '1'. Therefore the text generated by decoding phrase <1,'Y'> will be 'WY'. Thus, at the last step, we will get the text "WYS*WYGWYS*WYWWYSG", which is nothing but the input text.

Example

Compress the text "BABABBABUBABABAP" using LZ78 compression algorithm. Show the output phrase and the dictionary tree obtained after this compression.

Solution

All the symbols are scanned one by one. Following is the series of steps showing the input phrase and the corresponding output phrase generated.

Step	Input Phrase	Output Phrase
1.	"B"	<0, 'B'>
2.	'A'	<0, 'A'>
3.	'$'	<0, $>
4.	'BA'	<1, 'A'>
5.	'B$'	<1, '$'>
6.	'BAB'	<4, 'B'>
7.	'U'	<0, 'U'>
8.	'BABA'	<6, 'A'>
9.	'BAP'	<4, 'P'>

Dictionary Tree

Following is the dictionary tree for the input text shown in Example 10.

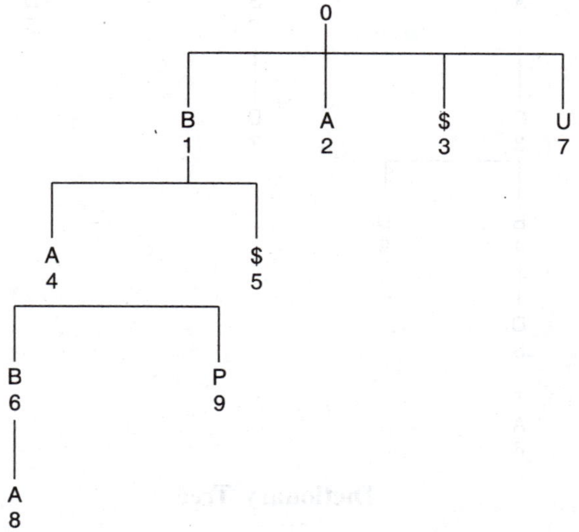

Decoding the compressed text takes place by placing the output text to the decoder in a sequential order. The following is the sequence of the output phrase generated.

(<0, 'B'>, <0, 'A'>, <0, '$'>, <1, 'A'>, <1, '$'>, <4, 'B'>, <0, 'U'>, <6, 'A'>, <4, 'P'>).

These phrases, when decoded with the help of the dictionary tree, produce the string 'BABABBABUBABABAP' which is similar to the input text.

Example

Encode the following string using LZ88 compression algorithm. Show the dictionary, dictionary tree and steps for decompression.

"ABACACBDACBDBDACBDAACD"

Solution

Scan the string from the left one by one character and generate the output. The input phrase and output phrase are shown in following coding table:

Step	Input Phrase	Output Phrase
1.	"A"	<0, 'A'>
2.	'B'	<0, 'B'>
3.	'AC'	<A, 'C'>
4.	'ACB'	<3, 'B'>
5.	'D'	<0, 'D'>
6.	'ACBD'	<4, 'D'>
7.	'BD'	<2, 'D'>
8.	'ACBDA'	<6, 'A'>
9.	'ACD'	<3, 'D'>

Coding Table

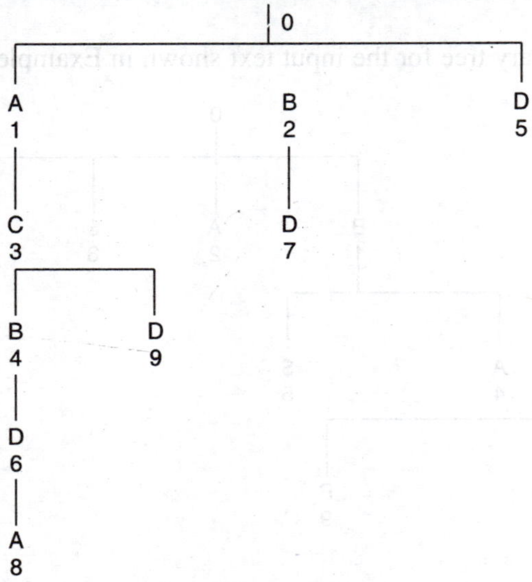

Dictionary Tree

Decoding the compressed text takes place by placing the output text to decoder in sequential order. The following table shows the token and output generated by the decoder:

Step	Token	Output
1.	<0, 'A'>	A
2.	<0, 'B'>	B
3.	<1, 'C'>	AC
4.	<3, 'B'>	ACB
5.	<0, 'D'>	D
6.	<4, 'D'>	ACBD
7.	<2, 'D'>	BD
8.	<6, 'A'>	ACBDA
9.	<3, 'D'>	ACD

Decoding Table

After combining the output, the string generated at decompressor is "ABACACBDACBDB-DACBDAACD" same as the string coded by the compressor.

The LZ78 compression algorithm has proved to be a landmark in the history of data compression because of its performance. The algorithm still contains a problem of handling the dictionary tree. However, the dictionary tree is quite efficient in finding the phrase matches. It is also not suitable for compressing a small amount of data, as in certain cases, the compressed code and the size of dictionary tree grows faster and the resultant code generated is larger than the input text. The Compress program used in UNIX is an extension of LZ78 algorithm. Compress manages the problem of the rising size of dictionary in such a way that, whenever the size of the compressed file becomes more than the size of the input text, it deletes the dictionary and the program is started from the beginning. The next version of LZ78 algorithm, LZW addresses to this issue.

2.12 LZW COMPRESSION ALGORITHM

Terry Welch proposed LZW compression algorithm in 1984. It is an improved version of LZ78 compression algorithm. It is different from LZ78 in such a way that LZW does not produce the character along with the output phrase. We have seen that, in LZ78, a combination of phrase and a character is produced when a string or phrase of input text is matched with the phrase in the dictionary and a combination such as < 4, 'W'> is produced. In LZW, only a code such as <201> is produced whose reference has been made to dictionary at the time of decompression. This minor improvement in LZW compression algorithm makes it more effective.

The following are the important points of difference between LZW and LZ78 compression algorithms:

1. The LZW algorithm uses an initialized dictionary. The dictionary is initialized with 255 characters stored in it. These are the characters which may be contained in the text e.g., all alphabets, numerals and special characters like '@', '&', '?' etc. All these characters occupy positions from 0–255 in the dictionary. Therefore any new entry to the dictionary will occupy the place at position 256. In this way, the dictionary keeps on growing and new phrases being added to dictionary are given a position number.
2. While scanning the characters of the text, at every character input, a phrase containing the character and the next character at input line, is entered to the dictionary. For example, at the entry of character 'c' of the string 'abcd', an entry corresponding to phrase 'cd' is made to the dictionary at the next available position in the dictionary. This is a unique feature which makes the dictionary more informative and efficient.

Let us understand the LZW compression algorithm with an example.

Example

Compress the text "WYS*WYGWYS*WYSWYSG" using LZW algorithm. Show the output code generated after compression with all the steps involved.

Solution

Suppose the entries for single character 'W', 'Y','S','*','G' occupies the positions at 63, 65, 59, 15, 47 respectively in the dictionary at the time of initialization. The following table shows the input symbol/phrase in their order of occurrence at input, output code and dictionary addition:

Input Symbol/Phrase	Output Code	Addition to Dictionary	
'W'	<63>	'WY'	256
'Y'	<65>	'YS'	257
'S'	<59>	'S*'	258
'*'	<15>	'*W'	259
'WY'	<256>	'WYG'	260
'G'	<47>	'GW'	261
'WY'	<256>	'WYS'	262
'S*'	<258>	'S*W'	263
'WYS'	<262>	'WYSW'	264
'WYS'	<262>	'WYSG'	265
'G'	<47>		
end of text			

Decompression of Coded String

A crucial advantage, which LZW coding offers is that it does not use the dictionary, created at the time of compression. Thus, after compression, the dictionary need not be passed to the decoder because the code itself creates the dictionary at the side of decompression. This saves lot of space and processing cost. The same dictionary which was created at the time of compression will be produced at the time of decompression using the information in the code. After the compression, the sequence of numbers (63, 65, 59, 15, 256, 47, 256, 47, 256, 258, 262, 262, 47) will be generated. This sequence of numbers is essentially the compressed form or code which represents the input text. At the time of decoding, the symbol/phrase will be generated according to the position index in the dictionary. The same code will produce ‘W’ for 63, ‘Y’ for 65 and so on. This way the final output will be ‘WYS*WYGWYS*WYSWYSG’ which is the input text compressed.

The steps for decompression in this example and for building the dictionary at the decompression phase are as follows:

Steps	Code	Generated Symbol/Phrase	Dictionary	
1.	<63>	‘W’		
2.	<65>	‘Y’	‘WY’	256
3.	<59>	‘S’	‘YS’	257
4.	<15>	‘*’	‘S*’	258
5.	<256>	‘WY’	‘*W’	259
6.	<47>	‘G’	‘WYG’	260
7.	<256>	‘WY’	‘GW’	261
8.	<258>	‘S*’	‘WYS’	262
9.	<262>	‘WYS’	‘S*W’	263
10.	<262>	‘WYS’	‘WYSW’	264
11.	<47>	‘G’	‘WYSG’	265

It is very important to note that at every step, a symbol or phrase will be added to the dictionary from the position starting with 256. For example at step 2, symbol equivalent to code 65 will be generated, i.e. ‘Y’. Here the content which will be added to the dictionary are the string produced at previous steps and the first character of the generated text or phrase at the current step. This content will be added to the next available position in the dictionary. Thus at step 2, string ‘WY’ will be added to the dictionary at position 256. It may also be noted that the dictionary will be initialized at the decompressor in the same way it was initialized at the compressor. At step 5, the string added to the dictionary is ‘*W’ at position 259. The ‘*W’ is formed by taking the previous output string and the first character of the current string generated.

Example

Encode the following string using LZW compression algorithm. Show the dictionary and steps for decompression.

“ABACACBDACBDBDACBDAACD”

Assume that characters A, B, C and D are placed at position 63, 64, 65 and 66 position in the initialized dictionary.

Solution

Following table input symbol/phrase in order of occurrence at input, Ouput Code and dictionary addition.

Input Symbol/Phrase	Output Code	Addition to Dictionary	
'A'	<63>	'AB'	256
'B'	<64>	'BA'	257
'A'	<63>	'AC*'	258
'C'	<65>	'CA'	259
'AC'	<258>	'ACB'	260
'B'	<64>	'BD'	261
'D'	<66>	'DA'	262
'ACB*'	<260>	'ACBD'	263
'D'	<66>	'DB'	264
'BD'	<261>	'BDA'	265
'ACB'	<260>	'ACBD'	266
'DA'	<262>	'DAA'	267
'AC'	<258>	'ACD'	268
'D'	<66>		
end of text			

After the compression the dictionary will contain the following symbols. Since dictionary is pre-initialized, it will contain all single characters up to 255 positions. Positions filled after 256 position onward in the dictionary are shown below.

Index	Phrase	Index	Phrase
256	AB	263	ACBD
257	BA	264	DB
258	AC	265	BDA
259	CA	266	ACBD
260	ACB	267	DAA
261	BD	268	ACD
262	DA		

The output of the coding of the string is a series of following tokens.
<63>, <64>, <63>, <65>, <258>, <64>, <66>, <260>, <66>, <261>, <260>, <262>, <258>, <66>.

The decoding of these series of token is done by decompressor. It generates the string stored in the dictionary at the place indicated by token. The steps for building the dictionary at the decompression phase are shown below:

Decoding

Steps	Code/Token	Generated Symbol/Phrase	Dictionary	
1.	<63>	'A'		
2.	<64>	'B'	'AB'	256
3.	<63>	'A'	'BA'	257
4.	<65>	'C'	'AC'	258
5.	<258>	'AC'	'CA'	259
6.	<64>	'B'	'ACB'	260
7.	<66>	'D'	'BD'	261
8.	<260>	'ACB'	'DA'	262
9.	<66>	'D'	'ACBD'	263
10.	<261>	'BD'	'DB'	264
11.	<260>	'ACB'	'BDA'	265
12.	<262>	'DA'	'ACBD'	266
13.	<258>	'AC'	'DAA'	267
14.	<66>	'D'	'ACD'	268

2.13 JPEG COMPRESSION

JPEG (Joint Photographic Experts Group) is a standardized image compression technique. International Standards Organization (ISO) had started a project on standardization of compression and decompression of still images and since 1992 it has been accepted as an ISO standard for image Compression and Decompression. JPEG is designed for compressing both full-color or gray-scale images. JPEG has laid down the guideline for compression of various real world images. It works well on photographs, naturalistic artwork, and similar material but it is not very effective for compressing text, animations or graphs. JPEG recommendations are used only for static images. JPEG is Lossy compression technique, therefore the image obtained by decompression will not be exactly similar to the original one.

2.13.1 Degree of Compression in JPEG

Color images are represented in their original form by a factor of 24 bits/pixel. Using the JPEG compression, the lossless compression may compress the image in the ratio of 2:1. This means that an image of size 10MB may be compressed to 5MB with lossless compression. JPEG may achieve 10:1 to 20:1 compression without visible loss, bringing the effective storage requirement down to 1 to 2 bits/pixel. 30:1 to 50:1 compression is possible with small to moderate defects, while for very-low-quality purposes such as pre-views or archive indexes, 100:1 compression is quite feasible. Another popular image format, GIF, would start out by sacrificing most of the color information to reduce the image to 8 bits/pixel. This provides 3:1 compression. GIF has additional "LZW" compression built in, but LZW doesn't work very well on typical photographic data; at most you may get 5:1 compression overall. If a file is made from full-color photographic data, using a quality setting just high enough to prevent visible loss, the JPEG file will typically be a factor of four or five smaller than the GIF file made from the same data.

2.13.2 Motivation for JPEG

JPEG is designed to exploit known limitations of the human eye. The human eyes work in such a way that small color changes are perceived less accurately than small changes in brightness. A image contained in a large file may be represented in a comparatively smaller file size without irritating our perception of it. Most of the parameters reduced or eliminated in a file are those which do not affect the quality of a picture upon viewing. JPEG is intended only for compressing images that will be looked at by humans. A very important feature of JPEG is that the degree of compression can be varied by adjusting compression parameters. Image makers can adjust the file size against the output image quality. It is possible to produce an extremely compressed file after sacrificing the quality of the picture.

Few important aspects of JPEG image compression are as follows:

1. JPEG compression is independent of source image. It implies that JPEG compresses the image irrespective of its size.
2. The decoders can trade off decoding speed against image quality by using fast but inaccurate approximations to the required calculations. It adds up high speedups in decoding the image.
3. JPEG works well without bothering about the type of image or color combinations.

2.13.3 Advantages of JPEG Compression

GIF does significantly better on images with only a few distinct colors, such as line drawings and simple cartoons. Not only is GIF lossless for such images, but it often compresses them more than JPEG can. For example, large areas of pixels that are all "exactly" the same color are compressed very efficiently indeed by GIF. JPEG can't squeeze as much data as GIF does without introducing visible defects. (One implication of this is that large single-color borders are quite cheap in GIF files, while they are best avoided in JPEG files). Generally speaking, JPEG is superior to GIF for storing full-color or gray-scale images of "realistic" scenes; that means scanned photographs, continuous-tone artwork, and similar material. Any smooth variation in color, such as highlighted or shaded areas, will be represented more faithfully and in less space by JPEG than by GIF.

2.14 MPEG COMPRESSION

MPEG (Moving Pictures Experts Group) is a group of people that meet under ISO (the International Standards Organization) to generate standards for digital video compression. A video is a sequence of still images or frames and audio. MPEG compression actually deals with the compression of still images and audio compression. MPEG standard were jointly developed by ISO (International Standard Organization) and IEC (International Electro Technical Commission). It has become a defacto standard for digital video compression recommended by ISO. MPEG groups meet roughly four times a year for roughly a week each time. MPEG does the data stream compression up to 1.2 MBPS which is equal to the CD ROM data transfer rate. Therefore, the motion pictures or movies may be stored in MPEG format and may be viewed without any synchronization faults. MPEG standards always make the use of JPEG compression because the digital video is represented as a sequence of still color images. MPEG may be used for following types of compression.

1. Asymmetric Compression
2. Symmetric Compression

In Asymmetric Compression, compression is done in a single shot but the decompression is done in multiple stages. Symmetric compression requires the same amount of effort for both compression and decompression.

2.15 MHEG

MHEG (Multimedia Hypermedia Expert Group) is a group of multimedia experts set up by International Standard Organization (ISO) for standardization of exchange format for Multimedia Presentation and Multimedia System. The main objective of this group was to create the standard method of storage, exchange and display of multimedia presentation. MHEG version 5 is the current work item for the group, and this was created in November 1994. It has been a DIS (Draft International Standard) since December 1995. Its basic goals are:

- To provide a simple but useful, easy-to-implement framework for multimedia applications using the minimum system resources.
- To define a digital final form for presentations, which may be used for exchange of the presentations between different machines no matter what make or platform.
- To provide extensibility i.e. the system should be expandable and customizable with additional application specific code, though this may make the presentation platform dependent.

2.15.1 Need for Multimedia Presentation Standard

The recommendations of JPEG and MPEG are of special importance for multimedia systems. In an interactive multimedia presentation, production of text, music or audio, video frames are of utmost importance. In order for products to have maximum commercial success, they must appeal to the largest number of consumers possible. There are various multimedia presentation packages available, but they are proprietary and do not work across different hardware platforms. One multimedia workstation uses its own standard for presentation and another uses a different standard for the presentation. In this way a Programmer or Content writer of the multimedia presentation who wants to publish an interactive multimedia presentation has to produce several versions that comply with different standards. This appears to be quite a cumbersome and undesirable job. The MHEG standard would do away with all this, allowing an author to produce Multimedia Presentation in one universally acceptable format. It also has advantages for the hardware and software suppliers. They are able to concentrate on producing the one standard MHEG engine rather than an engine for every presentation standard that is available.

2.15.2 Overview of MHEG Objects

The MHEG model is object oriented and a Multimedia Presentation contains several objects for defined classes. There are several classes, and these are used to describe the way video will be played, audio is presented and how the user can interact with the ongoing presentation. The relationship that is created between instances of these classes forms the structure of the presentation. In addition to just replaying existing multimedia data, MHEG also defines some types of its own.

There are primarily these classes in the MHEG Model, called Content Class, Behavior Class and User Interaction class.

Content Classes

Each piece of multimedia data e.g. video or audio clip has its own MHEG object. If the amount of data involved is small, then it may be contained in the MHEG object itself. If not, then the MHEG object will give a reference to the data e.g. a disk filename. Depending on the form of the data, extraction of smaller sections of the data may be possible e.g. one audio channel from an MPEG audio/video clip.

Behavior Classes

Classes under this heading control how and when data is presented to the user. They allow synchronizing of events and user interaction. It may further have two classes called Action Class and Link Class. The action class allows events to be triggered sequentially or in parallel, e.g., the replay of several clips of video one after the other. The link class establishes relationships between events and objects, i.e., what actions to take on what objects in response to a particular event.

User Interaction

The selection and modification classes allow the user to make selections, input information and trigger events. Several input methods are defined in MHEG: Push button, checkbox, radio button, slider, text entry field and text lists. These allow the user to control the information presented, and also to input information into the system.

There are many more classes defined by MHEG. Some are concerned with the structure of the presentation and grouping of objects, whilst others are involved in the interchange of information between machines. Several large companies including IBM are already developing software that conforms to the standard. This standard will allow the interchange and playback of multimedia information on any platform. The fact that a standard is now being agreed upon is creating new application areas for multimedia technology.

OBJECTIVE TYPE QUESTIONS

Multiple Choice

1. Which of following data compression techniques is lossy ?
   (a) Shannon Fano (b) JPEG (c) Arithmetic (d) Huffman
2. Shannon Fano coding yields
   (a) Variable length code (b) Static Codes
   (c) Both (d) None
3. Huffman Codes gives better results than Shannon Fano codes.
   (a) Always (b) Either Better or at least equal.
   (c) Never (d) None of these.
4. In Huffman coding, high frequency symbols are assigned
   (a) Minimum Number of Bits (b) Maximum Number of Bits
   (c) Average number of bits (d) None of these.
5. Arithmetic Coding produces.
   (a) Integer (b) Fractional Number
   (c) Variable length codes (d) None of these.
6. Which of the following is based on dictionary based compression ?
   (a) LZW (b) Huffman (c) Arithmetic (d) Shannon Fano
7. Which of the following uses a pre initialized dictionary ?
   (a) LZ 77 (b) LZ 78 (c) LZW (d) None of these.
8. Degree of Compression in JPEG may be
   (a) Varied (b) Can't be changed (c) always fixed (d) None of these.
9. Which of following are compressed with Lossy data compression technique.
   (a) Image (b) Video (c) Sound (d) All of these.
10. Which of the following is most developed method of dictionary based compression.
    (a) LZ 77 (b) LZ 78 (c) LZW (d) None of these.

Answers

1-b , 2-a , 3-b, 4-a, 5-b, 6-a, 7-c, 8-a, 9-d, 10-c

State True or False

1. Huffman Codes are based on relative frequency of occurrence of symbols. [True] [False]
2. Performance of Shannon Fano codes are better than Huffman Codes. [True] [False]
3. Arithmetic coding does not produce a distinct code for an input symbol. [True] [False]
4. Dictionary based coding is based on the concept of maintaining the index. [True] [False]
5. In LZ77 compression only a limited size of phrases can be matched. [True] [False]
6. LZW compression scheme uses a pre-initialized dictionary. [True] [False]
7. The degree of compression in JPEG can not be adjusted. [True] [False]
8. Main purpose of MHEG is to create standard for Multimedia System and Presentations. [True] [False]
9. JPEG compression is almost independent of source image. [True] [False]
10. In LZW, the dictionary tree created at compression need not be passed to decompressor. [True] [False]

Answers

1-True, 2-False, 3-True, 4-True, 5-True, 6-True, 7-False, 8-True, 9-True, 10-True.

SELECTED EXERCISES

1. What is meant by the term Information Representation? Describe various data format which can be used to hold information.
2. What is meant by Information Science? What are the areas of study in Information Science with respect to development in the area of IT.
3. What is the need for Information Compression ?
4. List the important features of Shannon-Fano algorithm for text compression. Discuss the performance of Shannon-Fano algorithm for different cases.
5. What is meant by frequency of character ? How is relative frequency calculated for symbols of different frequencies ?
6. Suppose a message is composed of twelve distinct characters. The various symbols and their frequency is shown below.

A	B	C	D	E	F	G	H	I	J	K	L
12	15	9	27	25	14	10	30	8	35	14	17

   (a) Complete the following:
      (i) Entropy of character.
      (ii) Entropy of a message containing 1000 symbols.
   (b) Generate the static code and compare the size of coded message with ASCII codes.
   (c) Develop a Shannon-Fano tree for this problem. Show all the steps involved.
   (d) Generate Shannon-Fano codes for each symbol and calculate the size of whole message. Compare its performance with static code and ASCII code.
   (e) Compression Ratio obtained in Shannon-Fano coding.
7. For Q 6, list a table showing all the symbols, frequency, relative frequency, information count, information bits, SF code and SF size.
8. What are the advantages of Huffman algorithm over Shannon-Fano algorithm ?

9. List all the steps required to construct the Huffman Tree. How is Huffman Tree more effective than Shannon-Fano tree ?
10. A text string contains total seven distinct symbols. The symbols and their frequency is given below.

Symbol	Frequency
A	35
M	25
E	15
P	10
D	5
L	5
Q	5

Construct the Huffman Tree and generate Huffman codes. Show the code for the input string "AEMPAALEQ". Show all the steps to decode the coded string.
11. For the data given in Q10, compute the following:
(a) the information contents of each symbol.
(b) the information bits for each symbol.
(c) the information contents of text.
(d) Shannon-Fano code and size of Shannon-Fano code for each symbol.
(e) the total number of bits required to represent each symbol. (Shannon-Fano bits)
(f) Huffman code and size of Huffman code for each symbol.
(g) The total number of bits required to represent each symbol. (Huffman bits).
(h) Compare the performance of Shannon-Fano and Huffman algorithm, on the basis of Shannon-Fano bits and Huffman bits.
12. For the string "DADDIADDVKAADRIDDRADD", deveiop the Shannon-Fano and Huffman codes. Compare the performance of Shannon-Fano codes with Huffman codes. Show the coded string equivalent to the input text with Huffman and Shannon-Fano codes. Show the steps at the decoding of coded strings.
Hint : To develop the table containing the symbols and frequency, count the occurrence of each symbol in input string.
13. What are the differences between Static length and Variable length coding schemes ? Why is Huffman compression called a Variable length coding scheme ?
14. What do you understand by Arithmetic Coding ? What are the features which make it different from Huffman and Shannon-Fano compression ?
15. What are adaptive compression schemes ? What is the basic difference between adaptive and statistical compression scheme ? Discuss with the model of adaptive compression.
16. Give reasons why Huffman and Shannon-Fano algorithms generate integral code length for symbols ? Is it a limiting factor for Huffman coding ?
17. What is adaptive Huffman coding ? How is it different from conventional Huffman coding ?
18. Following is the probability distribution of symbols appearing in on input text.

O	D	T	N	I	R	A	L	Y
.1	.1	.1	.1	.2	.1	.1	.1	.1

Code the following strings using arithmetic coding.
"INDIA", "ITALY", "IRAN", "INDIAN", "INDIANA", "LONDON"
19. Show how the arithmetic codes are generated. What is the algorithm for coding ?
20. How is the decoding of coded string done ? For the string given in Q 18. Show the steps for decoding.
21. What are the drawbacks of Arithmetic coding schemes ? How are they overcome ?
22. Discuss the relative advantages of arithmetic coding over Huffman coding ? In what way would you consider Huffman algorithm superior than arithmetic coding?

23. What are dictionary-based compression techniques ? How are they different from other conventional coding schemes. Discuss the relative merits and demerits of dictionary-based compression schemes. Discuss the genesis of dictionary-based compression schemes.
24. What is LZ77 compression scheme ? Discuss the main features of this algorithm. What are the drawbacks of this scheme.
25. What improvement Lampel and Ziv proposed in their LZ78 algorithm? Why LZ78 compression is considered superior than LZ77?
26. Show all the steps in building a dictionary in LZ78 compression. What is the role of dictionary tree in LZ78 compression ?
27. Consider the text string "DIDIDDIDI$DIDIA$DIDI". Show all the steps of LZ78 compression including dictionary formation. Explain the role of dictionary tree in compression. List the sequence of output tokens in LZ78 compression.
28. Show all the steps at decompression stage in Q 29.
29. What is LZW compression ? What are the advantages of LZW compression over LZ78 compression technique ?
30. What do you mean by dictionary initialization in LZW compression ? How a dictionary in LZW compression is initialized ?
31. For the text string "DIDIDDIDI$DIDIA$DIDI", show all the steps of LZW compression including dictionary formation. List the sequence of output tokens in LZW compression.
32. For Q 32, show all the step required for decompression of coded string.
33. Explain why LZW compression is considered a better choice, if a message has to be communicated over a communication channel. What are relative disadvantages in case of LZ78 compression for communication over channel.
34. Draw a comparative table to show relative advantages of LZ77, LZ78 and LZW compression scheme.
35. List popular compression program developed using dictionary based compression techniques.
36. What is meant by JPEG ? What are the recommendations of JPEG used for ? Explain the need for a image compression standard.
37. What is MPEG ? Explain the need for setting the standard for Motion Pictures ? Does MPEG use the recommendations of JPEG ? If yes, then explain why ?
38. What is meant by a Multimedia Presentation ? What are the problems in Multimedia Presentation ? How does the MHEG recommendation overcome these problems.
39. Explain in brief the meaning of Digital Video. How a digital video is represented in the Digital computers ?
40. What are extended Huffman Codes? Under what circumstances the extended Huffman codes are preferred over Huffman Codes?
41. Dynamic length codes are preferred over static length code? Explain the reasons.
42. What is redundancy? How the redundancy is measured? Explain with example. How the redundancy is measured in Huffman Coding.
43. Consider the following symbols and their probability of occurrences.

A	B	C	D	E
.80	.10	.04	.03	.03

Compute the following:

(a) Find Huffman Codes
(b) Find SF codes
(c) Calculate Entropy
(d) Calculate the redundancy in SF and Huffman Codes
(e) Generate the extended Huffman Codes and prove that these codes have minimum redundancy.

3

COMPUTER APPRECIATION AND PROGRAM DEVELOPMENT

Contents

3 COMPUTER APPRECIATION AND PROGRAM DEVELOPMENT

3.1 EVOLUTION OF COMPUTING MACHINES

The effort toward development of computing machines had started long back in the sixteenth century. An initial attempt in this direction was a mechanical computer developed by Blaise Pascal in 1640. This machine was based on wheels and it used to add and subtract numbers. Long before this, the first computing instrument known as ABACUS was developed in 400 B.C. Gradually, in course of time, Napier's bones (1600), Pascal's first computer (1642), Leibnitz's mechanical calculator (1771), Babbage's difference engine (1822) were developed. These devices eventually led to the development of present day computers. The development of the first computer, named MARK-1 marked the beginning of modern computer technology and generation of computers. In the field of software, the British mathematician Augusta Ada Byron became the first programmer in history to program Babbage's Analytical Engine (1836). BASIC was introduced by John Kemeny and Thomas Kurtz at Dartmouth College in 1965. IBM PC was introduced in 1981, the first Macintosh computer, the "MAC" with graphic interface, came in 1984. Windows 1.01 from Microsoft was introduced in 1985. Windows 3.1, which became very popular was introduced in 1992.

The computing machines developed initially were able to do restricted arithmetic computation, such as addition, subtraction, multiplication and division of numbers. Most of these were mechanical machines. In the mechanical computers, users had to compute the basic arithmetic operations and no programs were required to do it. Computation used to be carried step-by-step to get the desired results. The era of electronic computing started in 1940's after the invention of electronic valves. Now in the modern age, the computer is a general-purpose machine that processes data according to a set of instructions that are stored internally. The set of instructions according to which it performs operations are called programs. In other words, it is a programmable computing machine. Initially this machine was used for scientific and engineering computation but now it is used for a wide variety of jobs in practically all areas of human activity. There are three main types of processing functions, namely, calculating, comparing and copying, performed by the computer.

The digital computer manipulates the number represented in binary form. Any number in the decimal number system may be represented as an equivalent binary number. The basic technology for the generation of computers began with the electrical computers, which used electrical relay and switching circuits. Then came the electronic digital computers, whose generation is characterized by the type of switching circuit used in designing these computers. The output of a digital computer is also digital. The data and information used in the real world is in analog form. The analog data from the outside world is converted into binary form before it is processed. The output of the processing is also represented in digital form which has to be converted into the analog form so that it is intelligible.

The first general purpose digital computer was called ENIAC (Electronic Numerical Integrator and Calculator) developed at the University of Pennsylvania. It was a very huge machine and it did not become popular. Von Neuman was one of the chief architects of ENIAC computer. In ENIAC, the data and programs were stored in different memories. The computer's abilities to call in instructions and process them or follow them were known as the stored program concept. John Von Neuman introduced this concept which led to computers, with greater versatility in programming. The computer's ability of copying instructions into its memory from a disc, tape or other sources before any data is processed is referred to as the computer's copying ability. This copying ability also enables computers to directly start the processing of the first instruction in the program. By program we mean the set of instructions that are to be followed in a sequence, that is, one after the other. Because of its copying ability, the computer can hold the instructions in its memory from where, the first instruction is copied to the control unit circuit and match against the built-in set of instructions. Once the matching is found, correct processing is done, otherwise, the processing comes to an abnormal end. This ability enables the computer to execute the instructions of a program sequentially unit it finds GOTO instruction that tells it to go to different place(s) in the program. This feature gave facility to the computer to execute millions of instructions over and over again on the same set of data or on a new set of data. The latest trend in computer systems is overlapping of the operation of instructions. While one program is waiting for input from the user, the operating system directs the computer to simultaneously process another program from which data is available. Large computers are usually designed to allow input and output to occur simultaneously with the processing. This feature also allows the computer, while processing one user's data, to simultaneously, data from next user in queue can be retrieve the data from the next user in the queue. Based upon the technological advancement and areas of application, the evolution of the modern computer system may undergo several generations with truly amazing features.

3.2 COMPUTER GENERATIONS

The first generation of computers is said to have started in 1945. This generation may be marked with the appearance of UNIVAC-1 in 1950 where *vacuum tubes* were used, and their memory were made of thin tubes of liquid mercury and magnetic drums. Generally the period of the first generation is counted from 1945 to 1955. Most of the computer systems developed in this period used vacuum tubes. Most of the computer systems developed during this period were IBM 701, IBM 704, IBM 709. During this period, the stored program concept was introduced by Von Neuman. His idea was basically to store the instruction program in a separate memory. The high cost of memory, because of the high cost of vacuum tubes, had discouraged the manufacturers from using vacuum tubes for the memory. Instead, electrostatic memories were used to store the data in this generation of computers.

The second generation of computers lasted from 1955 to 1965. This period is considered to be a highly revolutionary one as a new technology called *transistor* was introduced in 1959. The new technology of transistors replaced the vacuum tube technology and it used ferrite core for memory. The size of computers was considerably reduced on account of using transistors. The transistors were made from germanium semiconductor material and they were also more reliable and faster than vacuum tubes. The second generation of computers marked a decisive breakthrough in the development of computer technology. Significant computer systems like IBM-1401, Honeywell-800, IBM 1620, PDP series were developed in this period. In the area of programming languages also, this period saw a significant advance. In this period higher level programming languages like COBOL, FORTRAN and ALGOL were developed. Greater reliability of electronic components and the higher speed of these devices also enabled the development of the operating system for these computers.

The third generation of computers started in 1965. The major development in this period was the introduction of the *integrated circuit* (IC). Integrated Circuit is one which contain a number of transistors. This generation computers used the Small Scale Integration (SSI) and Medium Scale Integration (MSI) technologies. In the case of SSI, it was possible to fabricate 10–100 transistors on a single wafer. MSI enabled to fabricate more than 100 transistors on a single wafer. Initially the computers used the memories made by ferrite core, but later in this generation computers started using semiconductor memories. Integrated circuits, the first Operating system and Data Base Management System (DBMS) were the significant advances in the third generation of computers. IBM-360 and CDC6400 computers are well known examples of this generation. In this generation, most processing was batch oriented using punch cards and magnetic tape. However on-line systems were also developed in this period. This generation lasted roughly from 1965–1975. Introduction of the operating system, database management system, use of semiconductor memories, use of magnetic tape and disk as secondary storage devices and introduction of cache memories were the major milestones of this generation.

The next generation of computers marked the introduction of the *microprocessor*. It became possible to fabricate the whole Central Processing Unit (CPU) on a single chip called the microprocessor. This happened because of the introduction of a new technology called LSI (Large Scale Integration). Later with VLSI (Very Large Scale Integration) it became possible to fabricate more than fifty thousand transistors on a chip. In this generation, the chip replaced the integrated circuit. Use of the microprocessor enabled manufacturers to introduce the Personal Computers which were very fast and compact as compared to earlier computers. Query languages, Report writers and Spread sheet, Graphics, Computer Aided Design were the major software developments in this period. This generation of computer started in 1975 and lasted until 1994 and it revolutionized life in the advanced countries. Data flow architecture was also introduced in this generation. Vector processor, array processor etc. were also used during this period.

The fifth generation started with major innovations in computer architecture like Parallel Processing, Intelligent programming, application of Artificial Intelligence and Knowledge based systems. The ULSI (Ultra Large Scale Integration) has triggered a new era as it has become possible to have the fastest microprocessor with a clock speed ranging from 100 MHz to 1 Ghz. This generation is considered to be in the developmental stages. Voice recognition, natural language processing, language translation, speech processing, other multimedia application, video databases, optical discs and artificial intelligence capabilities characterise the fifth generation computer. This generation of computer started in 1994. This period saw the wide use and popularity of personal computers. Personal Computer have made a revolutionary change in our culture and have become most common in public services and offices. They have replaced the typewriters used earlier. Paper technology is in threat; paper currency is also on the verge of being replaced by electronic currency. Personal Computers have entered from offices to our homes and are now a part of our daily life.

3.3 ERA OF PERSONAL COMPUTING

The introduction of fast and reliable microprocessor led to the era of personal computing. Personal computers have become very popular because of their compact size and fast processing. CDs, floppy disk, zip drive, high capacity hard disk drives can all be used with personal computers. The era of personal computer started in 1980 with the introduction of IBM Personal Computer. Microsoft also fuelled the usage of personal computers after development of Disk Operating System (DOS). Later Microsoft introduced the Graphical User Interface (GUI) based operating system WINDOWS which changed radically the whole scenario in personal computing since users of this OS were saved from writing the textual commands of DOS. Continuous development and upgradation in computer technology has led to the Pentium, a high speed computer, which can be used individually or in a group at a truly cost effective price. The first PC was designed by IBM with the name IBM Personal Computer and was introduced in 1981. In general, any machine compatible with IBM PC, which used a microprocessor and understood the same programs and languages as the PC, qualified as IBM PC compatible. IBM design was accepted by the industry and became the industry standard (1981–1987). After 1987 the term IBM compatible was abandoned. In course of time, however, no PC really fulfilled the standards as laid down by ANSI (American National Standards Institute), IEEE (Institute of Electrical and Electronics) or ISO (International Standards Organizations). Nor did any government make these standards mandatory. Two major organizations Multimedia PC (MPC) marketing council and Microsoft Corporation have also promoted PC certified standards. In fact Multimedia PC marketing council developed the first certification of PC standards for assuring that it can run multimedia software. As a result, the concept of multimedia PC was floated. Such a PC was supposed to be equipped with all peripherals necessary for producing sound and images. Such specificiations became general industry standards. Similarly when Windows-95 was developed, Microsoft specified certain minimum requirements on PCs that could run it. This set of requirement were later known as PC 95.

3.4 DIGITAL COMPUTERS

A digital computer is a programmable machine which reads the binary instruction and processes the data which are presented in binary form. Digital computers are different from analog computers in the

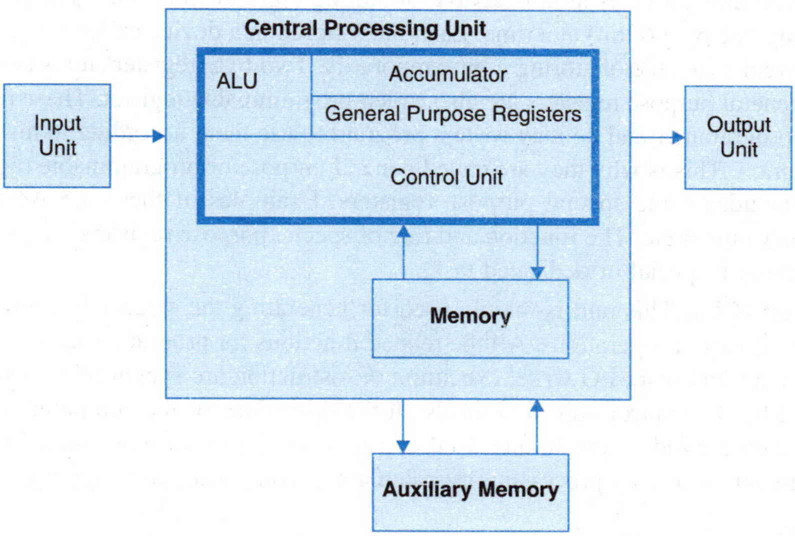

Fig. 3.1: Functional Units of a Digital Computer

sense that analog computers process the analog data. Here the term *analog* represents continuous data or real world data. Analog computer may process the real world data like current, voltage, speed, etc. in the real time frame. The digital computer takes the binary data at input, processes according to the set of instructions called program and produces the digital output. The computers we commonly use today are digital. A digital computer may be represented by the following schematic diagram:

As shown in Figure 3.1, the following are the main functional units of a digital computer.

1. Central Processing Unit (CPU)
2. Memory
3. Input/Output
4. Auxiliary Memory

3.4.1 Central Processing Unit (CPU)

The Central Processing Unit (CPU) is the brain of a computer where all kinds of processing is done. This unit takes the input data from the input devices and processes it according to the set of instructions called program. The outputs of processing of the data are directed to the output devices for use in the outside world. The major function of the CPU is to store the data temporarily in the registers and perform arithmetic and logical computations. This unit also controls the operation of all other functional units of the computer such as memory, input and output devices. CPU has four major parts called ALU and Control Unit.

Arithmetic and Logical Unit (ALU): This is responsible for carrying out (i) arithmetical operations on data by adding, subtracting, multiplying and dividing one set with another, and (ii) logical operations often known by comparing by using AND, OR, NOT and exclusive OR operation which is done by analyzing and evaluating data by matching it with a set of known data that are included in the program or called from the memory. This unit further performs increment, decrement, and shift and clearance operations as well.

Central processing unit also contains a set of registers as well as a special register called Accumulator. The set of registers is classified into two categories, general purpose registers and dedicated registers. A *register* may be thought of as a unit capable of storing eight or more bits. The one byte register is capable of storing one byte (8 bit) at a time. Each bit is stored in a device called *flip flop*. Flip Flops are the electronic circuits capable of storing a bit temporarily. Two byte register stores two bytes or 16 bits at a time. The general purpose registers are also called programmable register. These registers are at the disposal of the programmer and he may write a program to use them according to his needs in order to execute his program. This is why they are called general purpose or programmable registers. The set of registers also includes some special purpose registers. Examples of these are Accumulator, Stack register Program Counter etc. The function and role of special purpose registers are predefined and they are used to carryout a special or dedicated task.

Control Unit (CU): This unit is mainly used for generating the electronic control signals for the synchronization of various operations. All the related functions for program execution such as memory read, memory write, I/O read, I/O write, execution of instruction are synchronized through the control signal generated by the control unit. It controls all the operations of the computer. The computer can copy or move data around to create any kind of report or listing of any order. Thus the computer accomplishes all forms of data processing by calculating, comparing and copying.

3.4.2 Memory

The memory in a computer is analogous to a notebook where we may note down various things for future reference. Memory is also known by the term *storage* and its function is to store coded form of information from the human operator through the input device or from other computers connected to it. The information stored may be used immediately or it can be kept for later reference for processing by CPU. The memory can be classified into the following categories:

1. Main or Primary Memory
2. Auxiliary or Secondary Memory

Primary or Main Memory is the fastest memory in a digital computer system. This memory is primarily used to store the data and program temporarily during the execution of a program. It stores program along with data to be processed. It also stores necessary software programs which themselves are required for processing of user's program. CPU directly accesses this memory. Primary or Main memory is further classified into two categories called Random Access Memory (RAM) or Read/Write Memory (R/WM) and Read Only Memory (ROM). This classification is done on the basis of temporary or permanent storage of data.

Random Access Memory (RAM) is also called *volatile memory*. The term volatile is used for RAM because it holds the data temporarily and when the power is switched off, all data stored in this memory is washed. RAM is also referred to as Read Write Memory because it is used by the CPU to temporarily load the program instruction and intermediate results. The program instructions and data keep on changing by the process of reading and writing to it therefore it is also called read/write memory. The accessing of data from this memory takes place randomly and thus it is referred to as Random Access Memory (RAM). Its access time is in nano second (ns). *Secondary memory* or *auxiliary memory* is used to store the Operating System, Compiler, assembler, application programs, data files etc. Those are not read by CPU directly. If any information is needed to be processed from the secondary memory, it must be first transferred to the primary memory. The secondary memory is used for mass storage. Hard disks are used for this purpose. Accessing of information from the Hard disk (or similar media) is much slower (in mili-seconds). Random Access Memory may be classified into two categories as shown below:

1. Static RAM
2. Dynamic RAM

Static RAM is made-up of Flip Flops, an electronic device, which stores a bit as a voltage. Static RAMs are fast but the disadvantage is packing of flip flops. A comparatively lesser on number of flip flops are packed on a memory chip and therefore the memory density of static RAM is low.

Dynamic RAM is based on a technology called MOS transistor gates. The advantage of MOS transistor gates is that a comparative higher number of MOS gates may be packed on the memory chip, and therefore the memory density of dynamic RAMs is high. The drawback of dynamic memory is that its flip-flop, based on MOS transistor gates, uses charge as a bit. This charge is stored across the capacitor. The property of capacitor is that the charges leak with time. Therefore, a special circuit, called *refreshing* circuit, is placed with the dynamic RAM to refresh the memory.

Read Only Memory (ROM) is also a part of primary memory and it is called non-volatile memory. As the name indicates, the ROM can be used only for reading or fetching of data from it. The data or program are written into ROM only once and once it has been written, it cannot be modified or altered. ROM is used to store the programs or data which are critical and used frequently. The term non-volatile mean that even if the power is switched off, the data or program stored in ROM is not destroyed. Whenever the power comes, the same data appears once again. This so happens because of the permanent hardware pattern used to store the data in ROM. One of the important usage of ROM is to store the Basic Input Output Software (BIOS). This program is very important as it is used by the operating system at the time of starting up or booting the system. Since this program is used every time the computer is turned on, it must be stored in the ROM.

Why is ROM Non-volatile?

The data stored in the ROM are of permanent nature. When the power to ROM is switched off, the data is not deleted. When the power is switched on ROM retains the data stored in the memory ROM is based on the fact that there is a mesh of diodes or fuses placed in a matrix form. The selected fuses are burnt as per the data to be stored in the ROM. Similarly the presence or absence of the diode or fuse denotes whether bit 1 or 0 is stored. Since the pattern of placing diode or fuses is decided by the manufacturer of ROM, it becomes a permanent pattern. There are four types of ROM, namely Masked ROM, Programmable ROM, Erasable Programmable ROM and Electrically Erasable Programmable ROM.

Masked ROM is manufactured by the masking and metalization process. The pattern or matrix once created is permanent and no change or alteration is permissible afterwards.

Programmable ROM (PROM) may be programmed by the programmer. PROM is manufactured by placing a fuse at all the positions. A special devise called PROM programmer is used to store the desired pattern by selectively burning the fuses. Those fuses are burnt wherever a bit 0 has to be stored. The presence of a fuse represents the presence of bit 1. The pattern stored through this process is permanent in nature.

Erasable PROM are programmable ROM which may be programmed again and again. This so happen because the pattern stored on EPROM is semi permanent.

Electrically Erasable PROM (EEPROM) are the same as EPROM, the only difference being that electrical signals are used to program ROM.

3.4.3 Input Unit

Input Unit in the functional diagram of a digital computer (Fig. 3.1) represents the various input devices which are used to input the real world data into the computer. The function of the input unit is to accept coded information from the human operator or from an electromechanical device or from other computers connected to it through the Internet or by any other media. Input devices convert the human data into the form which is acceptable by the digital computer. Keyboard, mouse, scannner are examples of input devices.

3.4.4 Output Unit

The Output unit is used to represent the information processed by the digital computer. The function of the output unit is to store the processed information and display it as and when needed by the user. Cathode Ray Tube (CRT) terminal and printers are example of output devices. In fact, input and output equipment, is usually combined under the term input-output unit. The simplest example is the cathode-ray tube (CRT) terminal, consisting of a keyboard for input and a CRT display for output. However one must note that input and output functions are separated within the terminal. Thus, the computer sees it as distinct from each other but humans see it as being one of the same unit.

3.5 MICRO COMPUTERS

Using the Very Large Scale Integration (VLSI) technology, it has become possible to place all the circuits related with the CPU on one chip. When a CPU with its related control circuit is available on a single chip, it is called the *microprocessor*. All the essential ingredients of the CPU like Arithmetic and Logical Unit (ALU), set of registers, control circuit constitute the microprocessor. A digital computer, which uses the microprocessor as the Central Processing Unit, is called *microcomputer*. The difference between a microprocessor and a microcomputer is that the microprocessor is one part of the microcomputer. A microcomputer contains the microprocessor, Input and Output devices, memory and other components. All these make the microcomputer a complete digital data processing machine. The general schematic diagram of a microcomputer is shown below (Fig. 3.2).

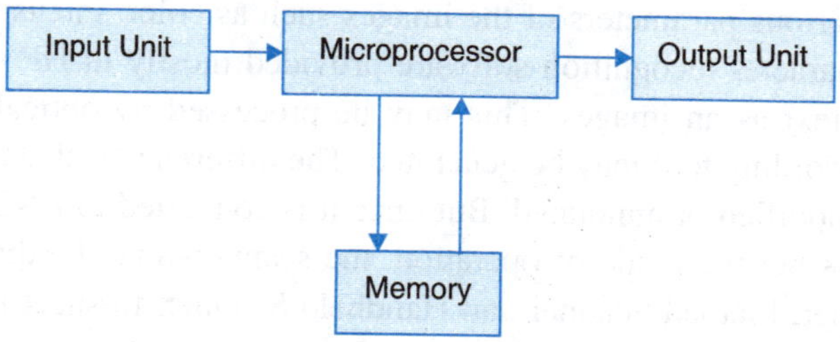

Fig. 3.2: Micro Computer

Comparing Figures 3.1 and 3.2, we observe that figure 3.2 contains the microprocessor in place of the CPU. In a digital computer, the microprocessor indicates that most of the control functions are centralized in a single unit. The microprocessor is capable of doing all the tasks of the Central Processing Unit like execution of instructions of programs, sequencing and selection of statements. The microprocessor therefore contains the Arithmetic and Logical Units, set of general purpose and dedicated registers, memory and related control circuitry. The currently most popular microprocessor is Intel Pentium-IV. The other microprocessors are Intel 8085, 8088, 80286, 80386, Motorola 6809, Zilog Z 80.

3.6 INPUT/OUTPUT DEVICES

The microprocessor takes the data from the real world, processes as it according to a program and sends the results to the output devices so that the results can be presented in the real world. In the following section, we will discuss the commonly used I/O devices. The communication between the microprocessor and the outside world (User) is established through I/O devices only. These devices are also known as *peripheral* devices.

3.6.1 Input Devices

Input devices are used to enter the command, program, images as well as the devices which are used to control various operations related to games and graphics etc.

Keyboard

This is the most popular and common input device for entering textual commands data and programs to the digital computer. The keyboard contains three types of key; one each for each alphabet and numerals; secondly, for various special characters; and the third set of keys are the special purpose keys known as Function keys. Whenever a key is pressed, it generates a string of electronic pulses which is decoded by the microprocessor. Identifying the purpose or the task related with a key, the microprocessor takes appropriate decision. There are many types of keyboards, namely, QWERTY, Ergonomic, Cordless and Dvork keyboards. The number of the keys on a keyboard is not fixed and the manufacturer decides the number of keys as per the need of the user. The enhanced keyboard now has one hundred and one keys.

Scanners

These are input devices used for inputting images in the graphics format. The colored images may be scanned by the scanner and may be stored and processed in the graphical format. There are some scanners which can also read the text as images that may be converted into text files. The most popular form of storing images is the bit map format. In the *bit map* format, an image is divided into various small segments and the various parameters of the images such as color, intensity etc. are recorded by a scanner. The Optical character recognition software provided mostly in HP scanners allows you to input pieces of paper or text as an images. This may be processed by optical character recognition software and a text file according to it may be generated. The difference is that a text represented as an image cannot be edited, modified or annotated. But once it is converted to ASCII text, it may be used by various text editors. As per the mode of operation, the scanners may be divided into three forms, namely, Sheet Feed Scanner, Flatbed Scanner and Handheld Scanner. In sheet feed scanners mechanical rollers are used to scan the paper with the help of the scanner head. The limitation is that only single regular size sheets can be scanned. The image is captured very accurately. Flatbed Scanner moves the scan head past the stationary paper. It uses a series of mirrors to keep the image focused on the lens. The lens give feedback to a number of sensors. As the name indicates Handheld Scanners are holded by the hand and are moved over the paper which needs to be scanned. Normally the output of handheld scanners is not as good as Sheet Feed Scanners.

Mouse

This is one of the most widely used input devices after the keyboard. The mouse is used as point and click device with the operating system or programs which have the Graphical User Interface. In the traditional textual interfaces like DOS, the user had to write the lengthy commands and instruction using the keyboard. It was quite troublesome for the users to write the commands again and again. In the Graphical User Interfaces (GUI) e.g. Windows 95/98 operating system, it is not necessary for the user to write the commands and instructions. Instead the user is supposed to select a graphical object, then point and position the mouse cursor and click it. The clicking on a particular object has the same effect as of writing a command. The mouse may be of two or three buttons and a ball. With every movement of the mouse, the ball is moved and accordingly the mouse cursor moves on the CRT screen. Touch Pad Mouse are also very common and are used with the laptop computers. In the touch pad mouse, the finger is moved on the pad and accordingly, the mouse pointer moves on the CRT display. A soft press on the mouse pad is treated equivalent to the pressing of a button of the mouse.

Digitizer

This input device is used for drawing free hand images and graphics. This is a pad with a grid of sensor's wire. A pen is moved on to the grid and every movement of the pen on the pad is captured. This pen is also known as stylus.

Apart from these input devices, there are many other popular input devices like Digital Camera for recording the motion and images; Joystick for use by children while playing computer games; Bar Code readers for reading the bar code or magnetic code; Mike for recording the voice etc.

3.6.2 Output Devices

The output devices are used for producing and presenting the data processed by digital computer to the real world. The examples of output devices are Printers, Plotters, Video Display Unit etc.

Video Display Unit

This is another form of the Cathode Ray Tube (CRT), which is used for displaying the images, text video etc. The VDU is the most widely used output device. All the commands, data and programs typed through the keyboard are visible on the CRT monitors of the digital computer. VDU also shows the output of processing of the data. A CRT display contains an electronic gun which sends electronic beams. A varying electromagnetic beam controls the direction of the electronic beam. When this electronic beam meets the screen, it displays the image. The coordinates of the screen are determined by the CPU. Regular refreshing of the screen is required because whenever the electronic beam hits the screen, it displays an image or text. To display another image or character, the screen has to be refreshed. The refreshing of the screen is a burden on the CPU. Therefore a video memory is provided which is used to refresh the screen. The smallest area which may be affected by the electronic beam is called *pixel.* It is the smallest display element of any picture. In the CRT display, the trio of Red, Green and Blue (RGB) phosphor dots represents the pixel. An electron gun shoots out a stream of electrons, one for each of the three primary colors. The holes (or dots) are arranged on a metal plate, called the shadow mask. Dot pitch is the shortest distance between two dots of the same color. It determines the precision and sharpness of a picture. Thus, the smaller the dot pitch, the better is the picture. Normally, display units support dot pitches form 0.39 to 0.22 mm. Smaller dot pitches are possible, but would result in more expensive display devices. The screen refresh rate of the monitor is vital in eliminating screen flicker. A high refresh rate demands a correspondingly high performance requirement on the display adapter and its memory. Today's monitors have a refresh rate of 75 Hz. This means that the monitor will be refreshed seventy five times per second. For the higher screen size, a higher refreshing rate is required. There are several options in which monitors are available today. There are energy compliance, standby and sleep monitors. Energy compliance monitors save power. In the standby mode, the electron beam and gun in the monitor shuts down, and there is about a 74 per cent reduction in power consumption. In the sleep mode, the monitor components shut down to cool the gun and the components, resulting to nearly zero watt consumption. The latter takes several seconds to return the working mode, compared to a few seconds of the former.

Printers

These are also commonly used output devices. While the monitors enables us to see or view the output the printers enable to make a hard copy of it. The processed data in the form of tables, spread-sheets, diagrams, pie chart, schedules, reports, image and graphics etc. may be printed on a piece of paper using the printer. The printer may be classified broadly into two types namely, Impact printer and Non-impact printers.

The *Impact printers* print the document character by character. Every character is pressed in a sequential order over a ribbon onto the paper. The drawback of impact printers is that since these printers print character by character, they are slow. Dot matrix printer is an example of an impact printer. The *Non-Impact* printer prints the document on to the piece of paper in a block. For example, the Line printers print the document line by line. These printer are usually costly and are used for high speed printing. The Line Printer is an example of non-impact printer. The Impact or Character printers are of two types, Dot Matrix and Daisy Wheel printers. All the character printers contain a moving head and a drum over which the paper is rolled.

Dot Matrix Printers: These are the most widely used printers. The maintenance cost of most of the dot matrix printers is very low. In dot matrix printers, a moving pin strikes on the ribbon that is coated with ink. When the pin is stroked to the ribbon, a dot is printed on to the paper because of the ribbon. These printers are called dot matrix because their printer head is composed of several pins. A 24 pin head contains total twenty four pins. A character is formed because of striking of selected pins on to the ribbon. The paper on which the document has to be printed is kept rolling over the drum and repeated strikes of the pins on the head prints the characters on the paper. All the characters printed by dot matrix printer are made up of various vertical dot patterns. Normally these printers are slow and noisy. But now several dot matrix printers are available which are quiet and fast.

Daisy Wheel Printers: These printers use a special plastic head, whose different edges are embossed with different characters. This head look like a wheel and whenever any character has to be printed, then the edge of the head which contains the embossed form of that character is stroked. Daisy wheel printers are used for high quality printing.

Laser Printers: They are popular now-a-days and are generally used in making official presentations and Desk Top Publishing (DTP). Their print quality is very good. The operation of laser printers is very similar to that of photocoping machines. The laser beams are used to create the image of the document on a drum coated with photoelectric material. When a paper comes in contact with the drum, a permanent image is printed on to the paper with the help of a toner or ink. Laser printers are also available with color options. Speed of the laser printer is measured as dots per inch. Higher DPI (dots per inch) indicate higher print quality of the document.

Ink Jet Printers: These are generally used for color printing. These printers are non-impact printers. The running cost of these printers is quite high but the purchase cost of ink jet printers is quite moderate. The size of these printers is quite small and the noise level is also very low. These printers use cartridges which contain ink. In the color cartridge, three color ink is available. Printing is done by the process of squirting the ink through the tiny nozzles of the cartridges. The working is similar to the dot matrix printer. The Ink-jet printer also has a printer head that moves over the page, printing an entire line with each pass. The only difference is that the head spews out the ink onto the paper. The print head contains four ink cartridges (one each for cyan, magenta, yellow and black). Many ink-jet color printers also come with two cartridges, one cartridge for black and the other for the rest of the colors. The size of the dots printed by the Ink-jet is smaller than the ones printed by the Dot matrix printer. This results in greater clarity of the output. They are also available with Black & White printing as well as color printing options.

Plotters: These are also output devices. Plotters are used for printing high quality graphs with multi colored pens. The plotters come in different sizes. They have a flat board on which paper is kept. They also contain several ink pens. Stepper motor is used to operate the pen. While printing a document, the required color pen is picked up and moved over the paper. The movement of different pens prints the document over the paper.

3.7 AUXILIARY STORAGE DEVICES

These are also known as the secondary storage devices. They are used to take the back-up (copy) of important files and data. The data and the programs are loaded into the main memory prior to the execution of the program. The processed data and the results are kept in the secondary storage device for future reference. The speed of the main memory is comparable to the CPU and the capacity of the main memory is also very small. Auxiliary storage devices are slower than the main memory and are almost inexpensive in comparison to the main memory. The main purpose of using the secondary or auxiliary storage devices is to provide a large storage at lower cost. Magnetic tapes, magnetic drum, disks are popular examples of auxiliary storage devices. The hard disk of the computer is also a auxiliary storage device. Based on the access method, these devices may be classified into two categories; Sequential access devices and Direct or Random access devices. The *sequential access* devices are those where the required data is to be fetched sequentially. The recording of the data on to the sequential access devices is done in a sequential order, but in the case of *direct access* device, the recording or access to required data may be done in a random order. The direct access device maintains the index or directory of all the data which contains the name of the file and address of the data. Whenever a required data is to be fetched, the head is directly placed to the place where the data exists on the device. Floppy disk and hard disk are examples of direct access devices.

3.7.1 Magnetic Tape

The magnetic tape (Fig. 3.3) is similar to the tape of music cassette. It is a long tape having a length between 2000–3000 feet. The tape contains the magnetic material capable of storing digital data. The data and programs are written to the magnetic tape using a device called head. The tape is rolled over the spool through the tape head. The tape reader or head is the fundamental part of the tape unit and when any part of tape passes through the head, the head reads or write the data. The storage capacity of magnetic tapes is measured in bytes per inch. This indicates the data density on the tape. A 10 feet long tape having the density 200 bytes per inch will be able to save 24000 bytes. The data may be written and erased any number of times in the magnetic tape. The magnetic tapes are sequential access device.

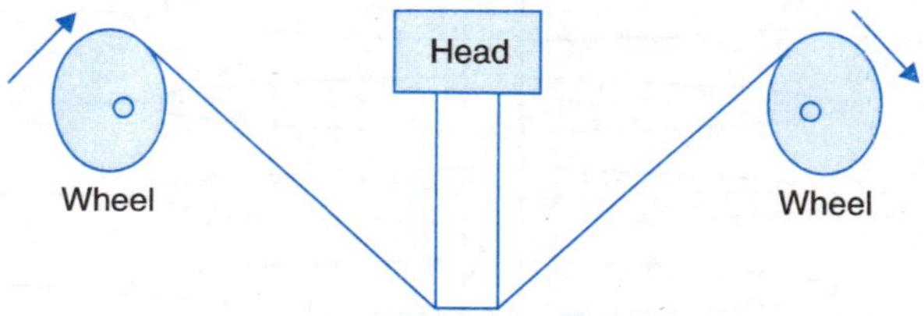

Fig. 3.3 : Magnetic Tape

3.7.2 Floppy Disk

The floppy disk is a small sized auxiliary storage device commonly used for storing the data and program. Microcomputers are available with either one or two floppy disk drives. The floppy disk are inserted into the disk drive before writing or reading the data from the disk. The floppy disk are the best choice for low cost and high capacity data storage device. The floppy disks are available in two sizes 3.5″ and 5.25″. The 5.25″ floppy disks are now not being used. Sony was the first to introduce the 3.5″ floppy disk. Floppy disks are made of magnetic oxide-coated tape material. Floppy disk may logically be thought of a magnetic disk. It is logically divided into several circles called tracks. Floppy disks are highly portable which is the main reason for their popularity. Disk drives for floppy disks are called floppy drives. They are slower to access than hard disks and have less storage capacity, but are less expensive and portable.

The floppy disks are covered by a rigid envelope. For reading and writing on the disk, the head has to be in contact with the disk surface. The head inside the disk drive is used to store or read the data stored in the floppy disk. The capacity of the floppy disk is measured as the maximum storage size. The floppy available today may store as much as 1.44 MB data.

3.7.3 Hard Disk

Hard disks are similar to the floppy disk but they contain number of platters. The Hard disk provides the storage for a large amount of data. The data storage and retrieval on the hard disk is faster in comparison to the floppy disk. The hard disk may logically be thought of as a collection of several magnetic disks. These magnetic disks are placed in such a way that they form a stack. One stack may contain as many as 5 to 10 magnetic disks. The storage capacity of the hard disk is much higher than the floppy disk. Now-a-days, hard disks are available with a storage capacity of 10 GB to 40 GB. The data is written to the hard disk using the hard disk head. As shown in Figure 3.4, the head is placed over the track to read or write the data. The magnetic disk is divided into several tracks and each track is divided into several sectors. Whenever the data is to be written on to the disk, the track and sectors are selected and are positioned according to the position of head. The head which remains in a fixed position writes or reads the data on the tracks. Two heads, one on each side of the disk, read or write the data as the disk spins. A hard disk/drive unit comes with a set rotation speed varying from 5400 to 7200 rpm. Disk access time is measured in milliseconds. Hard disks provide the required performance to support on-line data access. A typical server that supports hundreds of users at a time will require high-performance disk interfaces and drives.

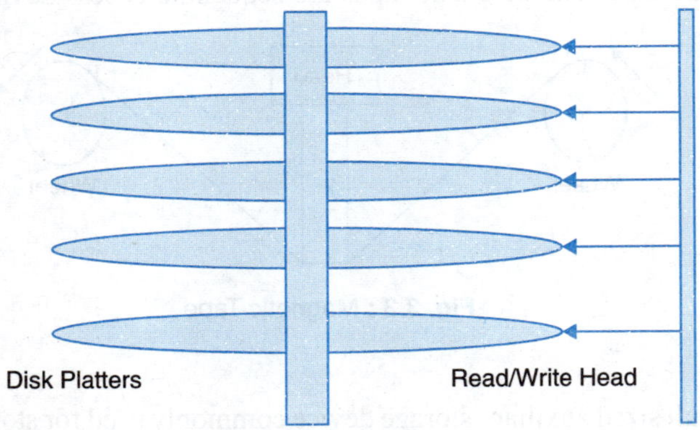

Fig. 3.4: Stack of Magnetic Disk

3.7.4 Optical Storage Devices

The Optical Storage devices use a different technology for storing the data or programs. CDROM (Compact Disk-Read Only Memory) is an example of these devices. They differ from conventional storage device in as much as the conventional devices use the magnetic material to store information. The data on the optical storage devices are written by using optical rays. In the CDROM, the data is stored by using a laser beam. Information is written on to the CDROM by creating pits on the disk. These optical disks consists of a metal disk coated with the material tillerium. Pits on the disk are created by directing laser beams on the disk. The presence of a pit denotes the digit 1 and its absence denotes the digit 0. By the process of stamping the data of one disk is copied on to another. The stamping process produces CDROMs in bulk quantity. A laser head moves radically in and out to the specified position. As the disk rotates, the laser beam and the sensing head translate the pits and lands to 0's and 1's by its electronic interface. There are two types of CDROM available according to their writing function. Write Once, Read Many (WORM) CDROMs are recorded only once. After recording, the data cannot be altered. In re-writeable CDROMs, it is possible to modify the contents by using a device called CD writer. The WORM disks can be only written to once and not overwritten. WORM technology is also called CD-R (Compact Disk-Recordable). With re-writeable disks, data can be stored and also erased. CD-E (Compact Disk-Erasable) or CD-RW (Compact Disk-Read Writeable) format is in the making. These three technologies are not compatible with one another. Each requires a different type of disk drive and disk. The CDROMs are far more compact than the traditional storage devices. The storage capacity of CDROM ranges from 500 MB to a few GB. These devices have become very popular because of their portability and compact size.

Important characteristics of CDROMs are given below:

1. CDROMs are very useful in distributing large amount of information to different users.
2. Mass replication of the data by stamping CDROMs is inexpensive and fast.
3. Since the CDROMs are removable and portable, therefore they are good choice for constructing archival storage.
4. The CDROMs have a disadvantage that once the data is written, it cannot be changed.
5. Access time of CDROMs is higher than magnetic devices.

3.7.5 Digital Versatile Disk

Digital Versatile Disks (DVD) are high density disks that can hold upto 20 GB of data. DVDs and CD ROMs look similar to each other since they have the same shape and size. The advantage of DVD is that with the same size, it can store nearly twenty times more data than the CDROM. DVD are different from the conventional storage devices in as much as the conventional storage devices use a head which comes in contact with the device to read or write while in the case of DVDs, the head does not come in contact with any such device and therefore, the DVDs last for a longer time.

3.7.6 Zip and Jaz Drive

Zip disks were developed by Iomega Corporation for storing large amount of data. These high-capacity disks are available in 100 MB, 250 MB and 750 MB size. The Zip discs are used in Zip drives. A Zip drive is a small, portable disk drive used primarily for backing up and archiving personal computer files. Zip disks are slightly larger than conventional floppy disks, and are about twice as thick. Zip drive is not backward compatible with older 3.5-inch 1.44 MB diskettes. The Zip drive comes with a software utility that lets you copy the entire contents of your hard drive to one or more Zip disks. Data transfer rate supported by Zip drive is much higher than any traditional floppy drive. Since they are relatively inexpensive and durable, Zip disc are popular and convenient mechanism for backing up hard disks and for transporting large files. These disks are useful for storing unusually large files, graphics, images and transporting high volumes of data from one to another computer system. Jaz is computer disk drive made by Iomega that enables users to save about 1000 megabytes or 1 Gigabyte of information on their special disks. Iomega has now discontinued the manufacturing of JAZ drive due to introduction of much faster media, however some of the computer system still uses Jaz drive. Jaz drives are similar to Zip drives but can store larger volumes of data and more expensive. The removable cartridges hold up to 1 GB on each disk. They are faster than most hard drives. The Jaz drive has a 12 millisecond seek time and a transfer rate of 5.5 Mbps. Like Zip drives, they are portable and make transporting information easier. The fast data rates and large storage capacity make it a viable alternative for backup storage as well as for everyday use.

3.8 PROGRAMMING LANGUAGE

A computer program is basically *a set of instructions* which when executed by the computer, do a specific task. The Microprocessor or CPU processes the data as per the instruction given to it. These instructions are written using various syntax and rules. Programming language provides the set of rules/ syntax/instruction format in which the various instruction are written. A sequential collection of instructions is called *program*. The program may be written in many languages. Programming languages may be divided into three broad categories:

1. Machine Language
2. Assembly Language
3. High Level Language

3.8.1 Machine Language

Each processor or CPU has its own set of instructions. As discussed earlier, these are binary instructions and they are written in a sequence of 0's and 1's. Any program written using these binary instructions is said to have been written in machine language. The machine language for every processor is different. A machine level instruction may be divided into two parts. The first part is called the *Operation Code* or Op Code while the second part presents the binary data or list of *operands*. Consider the following machine language instructions of the microprocessor 8085. This program adds two hexadecimal numbers 20H and 30H stored in registers A and B. The result is stored in register C.

Sl No.	Hexadecimal Code	Binary Code	
1.	3E	00111110	: Instruction 3E moves the data 20 to register A
2.	20	00100000	
3.	06	00000110	: Instruction 06 moves the data 30 to register B
4.	30	00110000	
5.	80	10000000	: Instruction Code 80 adds the contents of registers A and B
6.	4F	01001111	: Instruction Code 4F moves the result to register C from the Accumulator

As shown in this example, this machine code corresponds to the following set of operation:

Load Data byte 20 H in register A	:	3E 20
Load Data byte 30 H in register B	:	06 30
Add register A to B	:	80
Move result to register C	:	4F

We can see that the first two instructions have two parts; '3E', '06' are operation codes and '20', '30' are operands for the first two instructions, respectively. The next instruction '80' has only the operation code and the operands are implicitly known.

Computer programs are written in machine language as it is the language which a processor understands and it executes only those programs written in this language. However, writing a program in machine language is very cumbersome and difficult as for every task the machine codes are to be searched or remembered. The fact that different processors follow different machine languages further prevents the programmer from using the code written for one machine and executing it on another machine. The advantage of the machine language code is that a processor can execute it without any translation.

3.8.2 Assembly Language

Consider a program written in machine language for addition of two numbers. The programming would become easier and it would be similar to understand the code if it is written using letters and digits and carries some meaningful identifier. These issues are addressed in assembly language which uses mnemonic, that is meaningful names which makes assembly language programming easier than machine language. Consider the following:

Sl No.	Assembly Code	Hexadecimal Code	Binary Code	
1.	MVI A, 20h	3E	00111110	: Instruction 3E moves the data 20 to register A
2.		20	00100000	
3.	MVI B, 30h	06	00000110	: Instruction 06 moves the data 30 to register B
4.		30	00110000	
5.	ADD B	80	10000000	: Instruction Code 80 adds the contents of registers A and B
6.	MVI C, A	4F	01001111	: Instruction Code 4F moves the result to register C from the Accumulator

In the above program, the assembly code is written which is a substitute for the machine code. Instruction code MVI A, 20h transfers the data '20' to register A.

It should be noted at this point that the processor cannot understand the code written in assembly language. Therefore, it would not be able to execute assembly language instructions. The processor understands the machine language and, therefore, assembly language programs have to be converted into machine language. This task is done by the assembler.

Assembler

The assembly codes are easier to write but the processor still executes the machine code. Therefore a translator is required to translate the assembly language program into a machine language program. The assembler is a program which converts an assembly language program into the machine code (Object Code) which may be executed by the processor. This is shown in Figure 3.5.

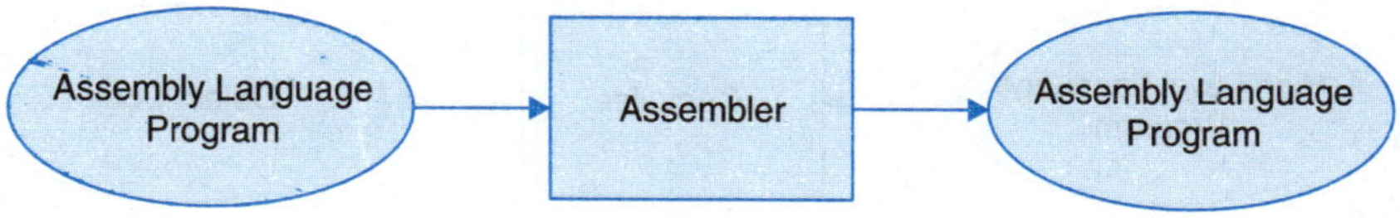

Fig. 3.5: Assembler

Assembly language and machine language are also known as lower level languages. These languages are dependent on the processor or are processor specific. The advantage of assembly language over machine language is that it is more convenient for the programmer to write programs in assembly language. The disadvantage of assembly language is that this language is machine or processor specific. Therefore, it is not possible for a particular processor to execute the assembly language programs written for another processor if the architecture of the two processors is different. This means that another programming language is required so that the program code written for one processor is executed on another processor without needing to know the architectural details of the processors. Such languages are called High Level Languages.

3.8.3 High Level Language (HLL)

High Level Languages are machine independent. It is not necessary for the programmer to know the rigorous details of the architecture of a processor to write programs in these languages. COBOL, BASIC, PASCAL, ADA, C are all high level languages. Each language provides its own construct/syntax and set of statements. The programs written in any of these languages can be executed on any machine. Writing programs in High Level Languages is more convenient as they provide the construct and set of statements which are easy to use and meaningful. Consider the following program written in high level language BASIC, which adds two numbers:

```
10  LET A = 20
20  LET B = 30
30  C = A + B
40  PRINT C
50  END
```

Each statement is coded with the meaningful construct. The first statement initializes the variable A with 20, the second initializes variable B with 30, the third adds the number A and B stores the sum in C and the next statement prints the value of C. Writing a program for a problem in a high level language is easier than machine and assembly language. Therefore, the program development time in high level languages is considerably low.

Translation of High Level Language Program

The program written in a high-level language needs to be translated into the language which a machine understands. The processor or machine understands the code written in assembly language or machine language. Therefore all programs developed in high level languages have to be translated into lower level languages before they are executed. This translation of program from high level language to low level language is done by the software called Compiler and Interpreters. This process is shown in Figure 3.6. In the figure, the program written in high level language is translated into its object code by the compiler. The processor or machine executes the object code.

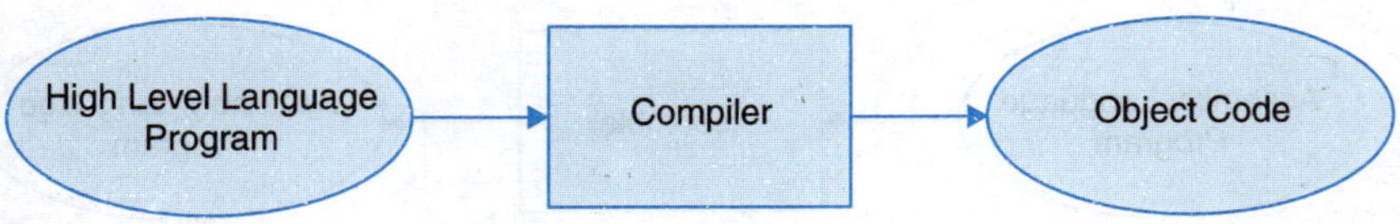

Fig. 3.6: Compiler

3.8.4 Compiler vs. Interpreter

The compiler and interpreter are software which translate the code written in High Level Language. The difference between the two is in the methodology of translation. The compiler takes the whole program and generates the object code while the interpreter executes the program line by line. In the compilation process the whole program is scanned for syntax errors and the compiler lists all the errors at one time.

In the interpretation process, the translation is done line by line and the interpreter check only one line at a time for the syntax error. The execution time of the compiled code or object code generated by the compiler is faster than the code generated by the interpreter. The debugging of a program is difficult in the compilation process because all the errors are listed at every compilation attempt. However, the interpreter is best suited for the debugging process because the errors are reported line by line.

3.8.5 Comparison of High, Assembly, Machine Level Languages

The comparative analysis of various languages are shown in the following table:

High Level Language	Assembly Language	Machine Language
Program developed in High Level Languages are most understandable.	Program are less understandable than High Level Language but more than Machine Language.	Programs are less understandable.
Program are portable.	Not portable; portable to processor of the same architectures only.	Not portable; portable to machine of the same architecture only.
Debugging is easier.	Debugging is more complex than in high level languages.	Debugging is most difficult.
Most suited for software development.	Not good for large programs.	Difficult to write large programs.
Programs are not machine dependent	Programs are machine dependent	Programs are machine dependent
Provides flexible construct for program development	Does not provide flexible construct for development	Not good
Programs are translated using Compiler and interpreter to generate object code.	Uses assembler to generate object code.	No translation is required.

3.9 FOURTH GENERATION LANGUAGES (4GL)

High level languages are considered to be third generation languages. Examples of third generation languages are BASIC, COBOL, PASCAL, FORTRAN etc. All these languages are procedural languages. Programmers writing programs to solve any real world problem must specify the procedure in the program. This procedure is reflected in the program in which the executions of the statements are done in a sequential order. These languages are based on the *textual* interface and programs are executed after writing a textual command on the operating system prompt.The machine and assembly languages are considered to be first and second generation languages respectively. It is very easy to write programs in high level languages in comparison to assembly and machine language. With gradual development in the field of information technology, the need for *graphical* interfaces was realized where the user has to type the minimum number of textual commands. Several operating systems and other software were developed which requires only the minimum entry of textual command.

Consider a case of preparation of the result of a large competitive examination. Suppose one Lac students appear in this examination. The organization, which conducts this examination would require several operations to be done on the data bank of students, starting from the data entry, preparation of roll list, allotment to the different centers, merit list preparation, preparation of mark sheet, admit card etc. All these activities are required to be done in order to achieve a successful conclusion of the examination. Writing programs for all of these activities and managing such a huge data bank is a challenging job. One cannot think of writing these programs in the assembly or machine languages. Writing programs for a huge database in any high level language also requires lot of efforts and it will not be an easy task. Typing all the textual command required in a program is quite cumbersome and time consuming.

Structured Query Language (SQL) and Query by Example (QBE) considered fourth generation languages. These languages are used to gather the data from a database with visual interface like Visual Basic (VB). Developer for Oracle, Application Program Tools (APT) for Sybase works well and requires a minimum amount of effort to query the database. Most of the fourth generation languages are used for developing large and complex software systems. These languages use automated report generator, menus etc. Most of the time, various visual objects are to be placed on the canvas and a routine has to be written to specify the task. In Figure 3.7 a record of a student is shown. The format in which various attributes like Name, Father's name, etc. are shown appears to be more user friendly. Simple queries to search the record for a particular student, etc. may be served by pressing a button with mouse.

Following is the query written in SQL to print the Roll Number, name and father's name of the student whose name is "Pawan Kumar Tripathi" (Fig. 3.8). The data of all students are stored in file 'Student'.

***Select** Rno, Name, Fname*

***From** student*

***Where** Name = "Pawan Kumar Tripathi"*

Pressing the "Find" button on the layout may do the same process. Once the "Find" button is pressed, a new window appears where one may enter the name of a student and click "Find First" or the relevant button.

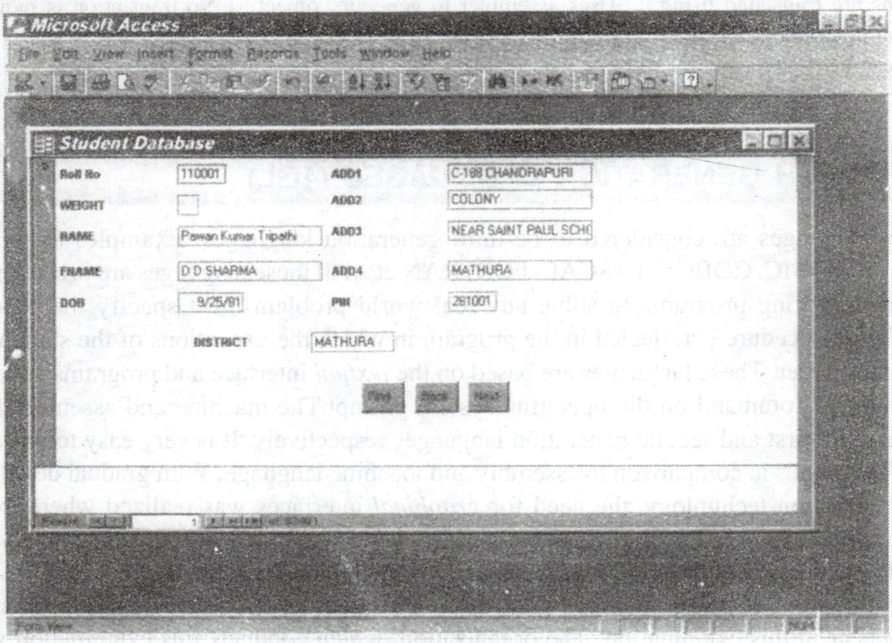

Fig. 3.7

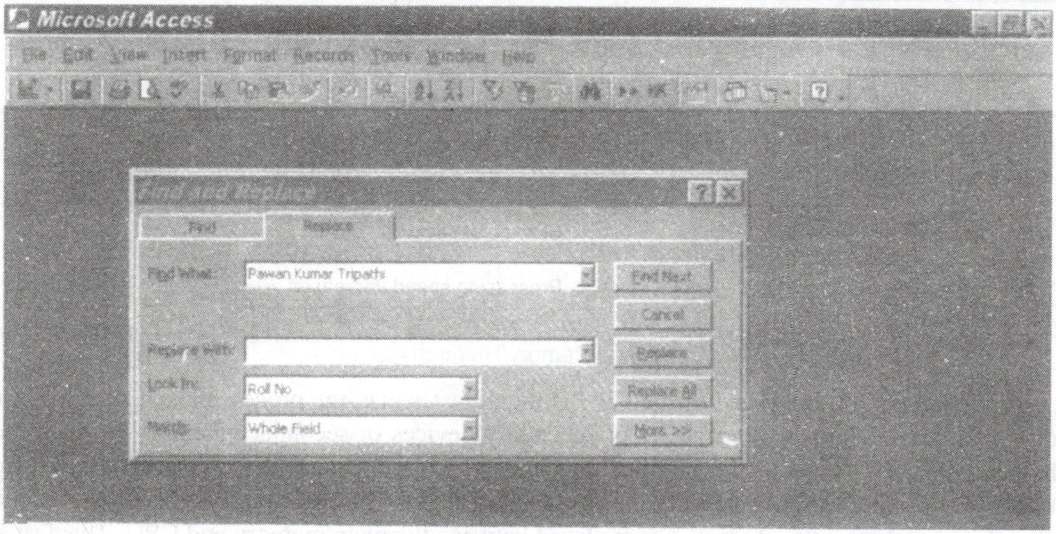

Fig. 3.8

These languages are tightly integrated with GUI screens which are used to generate complex reports and provides user defined graphical user interface. All these languages finds a wide application in software development for business and commercial activities. However for scientific and technical work, the third generation languages continue to be regularly used.

3.10 APPLICATION PROGRAM vs SYSTEM PROGRAM

Software is a collection of programs, which are used to do any specific task. Software may be divided into two categories; Application program and System program.

The *application* programs are written by the programmer to solve any real world problem. For example, writing a program for report generation, queries, preparation of report are all application programs. These programs are written in either Higher Level Languages or using 4GLs. The application program may be altered, modified as per the change in the reqirement by the programmer. The *System* programs are generally used to create the environment for the development and execution of application programs. These programs are required to make the computer system operational; the computer cannot function without these programs. Therefore, they are known as system programs. Most of these programs are written and developed by the manufacturers. Operating systems, compilers are examples of system programs or system software. The compiler is used to convert the application program written in a high level language to the machine language program. Operating System (OS) is a collection of several system programs and the OS facilitates the user to interact with the hardware.

3.11 MEMORY HIERARCHY

There are several storage devices which may be categorized on the basis of storage and retrieval time, capacity and technology. Another way of classifying these memory devices is on the basis of hierarchy. By hierarchy we mean that the memory will be used first by the central processing unit. This classification is done on the basis of speed of the processing of the memory device.

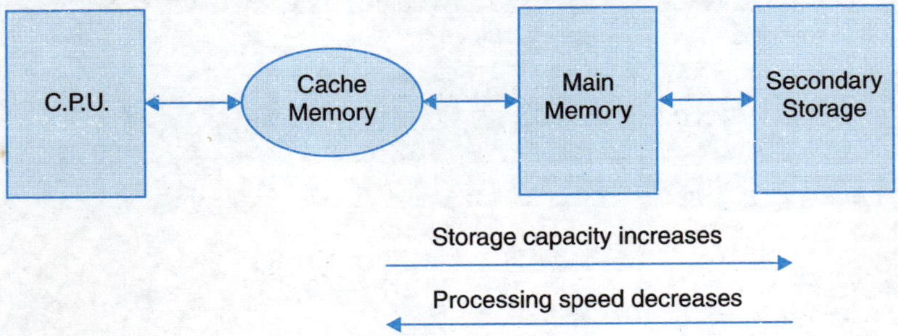

Fig. 3.9: Memory Hierarchy

As mentioned before, the speed of the CPU is much faster than the processing speed of main and secondary memories. The storage capacity of secondary devices or secondary memory is much more than the main memory. To get the best output, the data and programs must be stored and retrieved from the memory at the rate, which matches with the speed of CPU. The main memory is slower than the CPU, therefore a fast memory of small size is placed between the main memory and CPU. This fast and compact memory is called *cache memory*. The data and the program instructions which are to be fetched frequently by the CPU are placed in the cache memory. The diagram (Fig. 3.9) shows the memory hierarchy. It may be observed that the secondary memories are the slowest, main memory is faster than secondary memory and cache is the fastest. The storage capacity of secondary devices are the maximum and these storage devices are used for archival storage. The main memory capacity is more than cache memory. The size of cache is kept small because of its higher cost.

3.11.1 Cache Memory

This is the fastest and the most costly form of storage. The size of cache memory is very small and use of the cache is managed by the operating system. Since the CPU works much faster than main memory, the most frequently accessed data are kept in cache memory, so that they can be made available to the CPU on demand without time delays.

3.11.2 Main Memory

Main memory is the storage media used for data that is available to be operated on. The general-purpose machine instructions operate on the main memory. Although it may contain several megabytes of data, the main memory is generally too small to store the entire database. Main memory is sometime referred to as core memory, a reference to technology used in 1960s and early 1970s to implement the main memory. The content of main memory is usually lost if power failure in system crash occurs.

3.11.3 Secondary Storage

Secondary or Disk Storage is the primary medium for the long-term storage of data. Typically the entire database is stored on disk. Data must be moved from the disk to the main memory in order for the data to be operated on. After operations are performed, the data must be returned to the disk. It is also referred to as direct access storage because it is possible to read the data in a disk in any order (unlike sequential access storage). Disk storage devices themselves may fail and destroy data but such failure are significantly less frequent than system crashes. Tape storage is used primarily for back up and archival data. Although a tape is much cheaper than a disk, access to data in it is much slower. Tape storage is referred to as sequential access storage and is used primarily for recovery from disk failure. The head is a device, which stays close to the surface of the platter and reads or writes information encoded magnetically on the platter. The platter is organized concentric tracks of data. The arm can be positioned over any one of the tracks. To read or write information, the arm is positioned over the relevant track. Since the platter rotates at a high speed, it does not take very long for the content of an entire track to pass under the head. This amount of time is referred to as the disk *latency* time. Relative to the latency time, it takes a long time to reposition the arm. The time for repositioning the arm, the *seek* time, increases as the distance that the arm must move increases. Multi-platter disks are called disk packs when we wish to distinguish them from a single platter disk. Whenever we use the term disk, we shall be referring to multiple platter disks. All the disk arms are used as the unit actuator. Each arm has two heads: one to read and another to write. Data is transferred between disk and the main memory in units called *blocks*. A block is a continuous sequence of bytes from a single track of one platter. Block size ranges from 512 bytes to several thousands bytes. The simplest way to optimize block access time is to organize the block on disk in a way that corresponds closely to the manner in which we expect the data to be accessed.

3.12 FILE ORGANIZATION

A file is organized logically as a sequence of records. These records are mapped on to the disk block of the physical storage device. As we have seen while discussions memory hierarchy, the data and programs are kept in the secondary storage devices for archival purpose. Whenever these data and programs are required by the CPU, they are transferred to the main memory and used by the CPU via cache memory. The data and program are contained and stored logically in files. Files are provided as a basic construct in operating systems.

A *file* is a collection of records, many records may reside on one page. Therefore a file may also be logically seen as a collection of pages. Each record is identified by a unique address called record number or record ID.

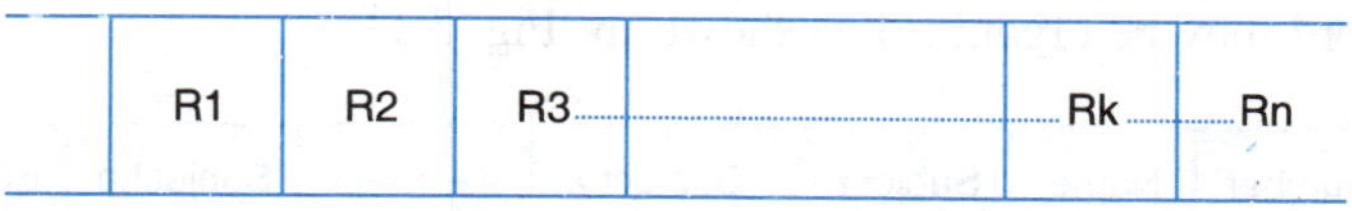

Fig. 3.10: A Logical View of File.

3.12.1 Types of Record

Data are contained in files in the form of records. A record may be a variable length record or fixed length record.

Fixed Length Record

Consider a case where data pertaining to a student are to be stored in a file. Following is the format for record:

Record Student {
Roll_Number Integer;
Name String (30);
}

These records are called fixed length record. Every attribute of these records will require a predefined space. Managing fixed length record is simpler. The drawback of this scheme is that every record will require a predefined space. Consider a case where the subjects being studied by the student are also to be stored. This will require to have a record inside the record, i.e. Student record will contain the record of the subjects—which he has studied. Problem with the fixed length record scheme is that the total number of subjects studied cannot be bounded as one student may have taken only one subject and an other may have taken many. If a number bound the number of subjects then it will create problems when the number of subjects taken by students is large. Otherwise the space will be wasted. The following should be the scheme of this record as fixed length record.

Record Student {
Roll_Number Integer;
Name String (30);
Subject Record;
}

Record Subject {
Sub_Name String;
Teacher String;
Marks Integer;
}

This scheme of using fixed length is not efficient as it cannot be determined how many subjects will be taken by a student. Therefore another scheme of holding a record, called Variable Length Record, is used in order to reduce space anomalies.

Variable Length Record

In this scheme, it is possible to have records which allow variable size for one or more attributes and permits the duplication of attributes. There are many scheme/representation which may be used to implement variable length records. One such scheme is byte string representation. In this scheme, the end of a record is specified by a special notation called 'end of record'. For the example shown above, the variable length record may be organized as shown in Fig. 3.11.

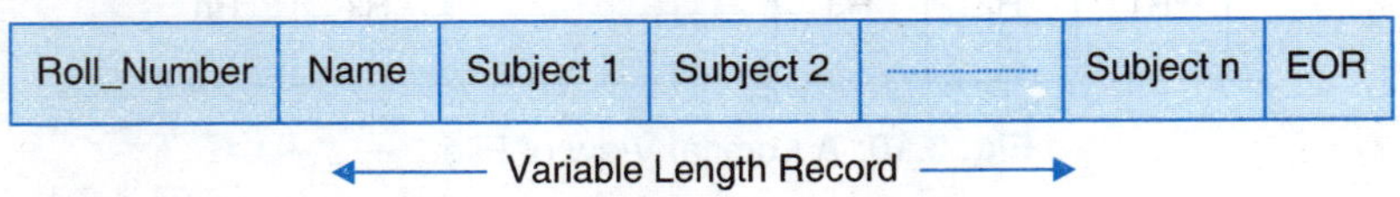

Fig. 3.11: Variable Length Record

As shown in the figure, a student record may contain one or more record of the subject and the end of a student record is marked by a special symbol called EOR (end of record). The next record of another student follows it.

3.13 FILE TYPES

A file may be viewed as a collection of records. A file organization is way of arranging the various records on the disk. Accessing a record on the file is of utmost importance. Records in the file may be organized in several ways and this yields different access mechanisms. Since data is transferred between disk storage and main memory, and the basic unit of transfer is page or collection of records, it is worthwhile to arrange the records in a file in such a way that the search for a desired record takes minimum time and effort. If the records are placed randomly in the file, then a page containing other unordered records would be accessed. To locate the next record according to a certain order will require another page to be transferred to the main memory, which may once again contain other undesired records. If several records on the basis of certain criterion have to be accessed and the records appear in the file in random order, we may have to make several disk accesses which takes a lot of time and becomes a bottleneck. If the records are arranged according to certain criteria, we may be able to save multiple disk accesses and the collection of records in the form of a page will be transferred to the memory. Therefore access mechanism of records is one of the performance criterion. On the basis of access mechanism and organization of records, files may be considered to be of the following types:

1. Heap Files
2. Sequential Files
3. Indexed Files

3.13.1 Heap Files

Here the records are placed in random order. The records are placed one after another in the file and are totally unordered. This creates lot of problems in basic file operations such as insertion of a record, deletion of a record, modifying the contents of record and searching a desired record. A heap file may be logically viewed as shown in Fig. 3.12.

To search a desired record requires the sequential scan of all the records from the beginning until the desired record is found. Therefore, search of the desired record takes a long time.

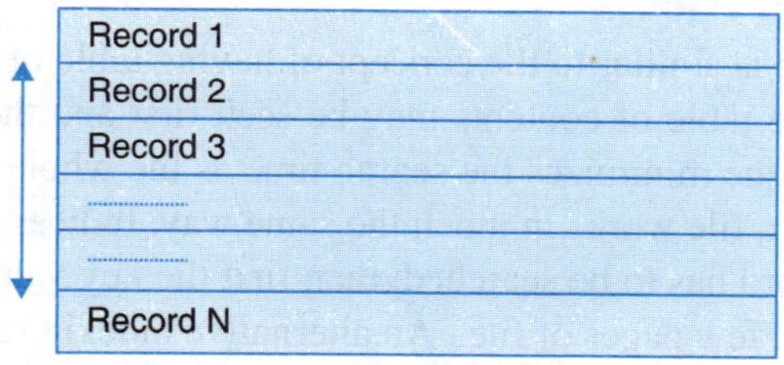

Fig. 3.12: A Heap File

3.13.2 Sequential File

The disadvantage of heap files is that the various records are kept unorganized. A large heap file requires more time for search because the search is started from beginning until the record is found. In this process every record is checked which leads to loss of productive time. A sequential file is designed for efficient processing of records. The search for a record in sequential files is based on a key. Every record contains a key by which it can be uniquely identified. These keys are called *search keys*. For the fast retrieval of a record, the search key is used and a pointers chain is developed among the record. The key is so selected that it may uniquely identify a record. For example, storing the records of students of a college, the roll number may be treated as the search key. The roll numbers are supposed to be unique and searching a roll number will locate the correct record. Sequential files are also called *sorted files*. The pointers are so placed between the record that they start from the first record and point to next record in the order of key. This chain allows fast retrievals of records in search-key order. The sequential files are either sorted or nearly sorted. This means that the records are placed physically in the file in order of the key. Consider the record of student (Roll Number, Name, Father Name, Marks) as shown in Fig. 3.13.

Roll Number	Name	Father Name	Marks
101	Pawan Tripathi	S K Tripathi	55
102	Ram Sagar	B R Sagar	42
103	Anil Kumar	H M Chauhan	80
104	Dheeraj Singh	M S Bose	45
105	S P Tripathi	P K Tripathi	60

Fig. 3.13: Logical View of Sequential File

All the records in the sequential file are placed in the order of the search key, which is the roll number (Fig. 3.13). While storing the records on the disk, they are physically placed in the order of the roll number. Organizing the records in the order of keys eases the fundamental operations like insertion, deletion and updation of records. This process also reduces the search time as all the records are stored on a criterion based on keys.

3.13.3 Indexed Sequential File

The concept of index for a file is similar to the concept of having table of contents in a book. To search an item or topic in a book, the table of contents may be seen first and then the item is searched at the appropriate place. This technique minimizes the search time as the whole book need not be searched in sequential order. An index for a file works in much the same way. Indices for a file are created to search a record in the file. If any record has to be searched, then first the key value is matched in the index and the search is confined to only a few pages of file. An alternative indexing technique is called *hashing*. In Hashing, a hash function is used which maps the key value to the physical address. Both of these techniques have their advantages and disadvantages. Following are the performance criteria for indexing.

Seek Time

The Seek Time is defined as the total time to locate a desired record. Access time is minimum using indexed file.

Insertion Time

Insertion Time is defined as the time to insert a new record to an appropriate position. Insertion time includes the time required to find the appropriate location where the new record will be inserted as well as the time required to rebuild the index.

Deletion Time

This is the time required to delete a record, Deletion Time include the time required to find the record (access time) and the time taken to rebuild the index after deletion of a record.

In the indexing process, an index structure is used to locate the record in a file. In order to store the index structure, additional storage is required. It seems to be advisable to have a fast access to the records at the cost of additional space. Faster access to the records in a file also improves the performance of the system. When we use a sequential file and generate an index structure, the file is known as indexed sequential file. It is not mandatory to use one attribute in the index. Two or more than two attributes or keys may be used to generate the index structure. For example, index structure for the student file may be generated on the basis of attribute roll number and name. One of them is called the primary index. The attribute or set of attributes used to look up the records in a file is called the search key. It is also possible to have more than one index structure for the same sequential file. This index structure will be based on the different set of attributes. Each indexed structure is associated with a particular search key. If the file is sequentially ordered, and if several indices are used, the index on which the search key is based, is called *primary index* for the file. The other indices are called the *secondary indices*. The search key of a primary index is usually the primary key.

A logical view of an index sequential file is shown in Fig. 3.14. A sequential file containing eight students' records have the pointer from the index structure. The index structure uses 'roll number' as the primary index and it has three records with value of roll number as '101', '105' and '108'. It also has a pointer field which contains the addresses of students required whose roll numbers are '101', '105' and '108', respectively. In other words, every entry in the index structure points to a corresponding record in the sequential file. The advantage of doing this, is that whenever any record with a given roll number has to be searched, it is first matched in the index structure; after that, appropriate pointer is used to select the record. This minimizes the access time. For example, searching a record with roll number 107, the pointer from '106' in index structure will be used to find the desired record. This will eliminate the sequential search from roll number 101. This technique is very useful for large files.

Based on the number of pointers from the index structure, two types of indices are used. These are called Sparse index and Dense index. In the *dense* index scheme, an index record in the index structure appears for all key values in the file. In this case, for every distinct value of the roll numbers from 101 to 108, there will be a record and corresponding pointer in the index structure. The disadvantage of this indexing scheme is that a comparatively larger index structure has to be created and deletion of records become difficult. In the *sparse* index scheme, index records in the index structure are created for a few key values. To search a record, the search value is compared with the values in the index structure and the pointer is used to identify the block where the desired record lies. The index structure shown in the Figure 3.14 is an example of sparse index.

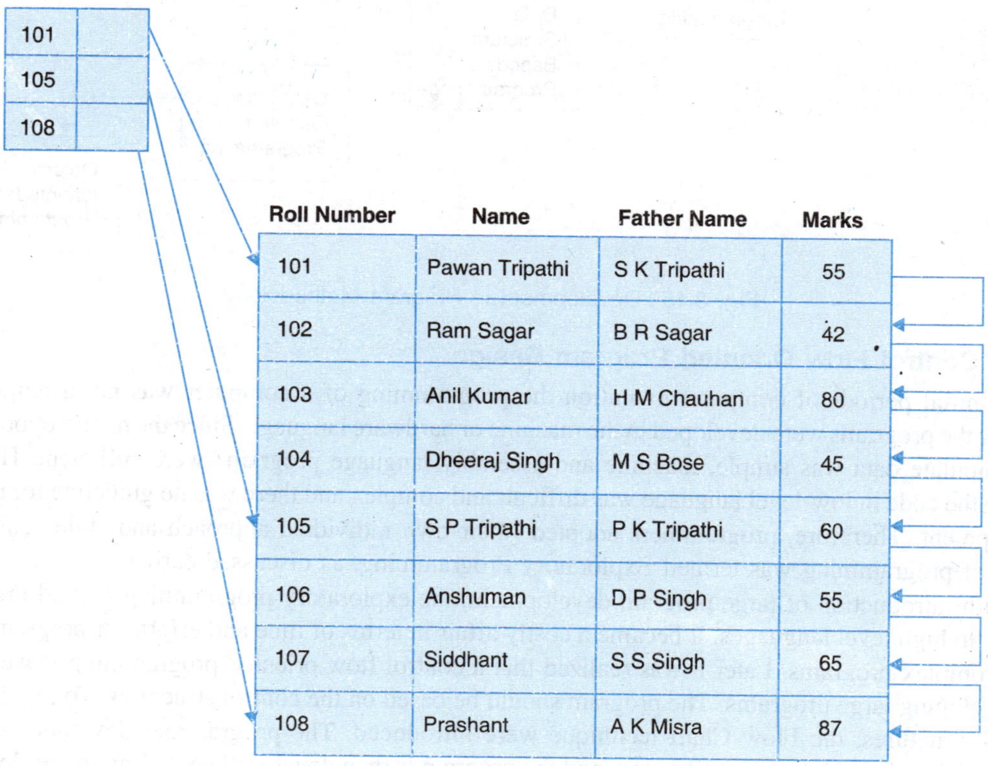

Fig. 3.14: Indexed Sequential File

3.14 OVERVIEW OF PROGRAM DEVELOPMENT METHODOLOGIES

During early programming days, every programmer had his own programming approach and the codes were written in adhoc style. This type of programming is known as Exploratory Style of Programming. When the size and complexity of progress increased with time, this approach was proved to be inefficient and control structure based programming was introduced. To develop the programs with control structure required the use of flow charting techniques. It was realized that a good control flow through flow charting is necessary to deal efficiently with the increasing size and complexity of code. Jackson then proposed his Jackson Structured Programming (JSP) methodology with three constructs—sequence, selection and iteration which were considered sufficient to express a large problem. Gradually, Data Structure based programming technique and Data flow oriented techniques were evolved to solve large and complex problems. For development of large software products data flow oriented design approach was most preferred. This approach requires the use of data flow diagrams (DFD). With further advancement in the field, the data flow oriented techniques evolved into Object Oriented Design techniques. The Object Oriented Design is relatively a new paradigm for software design. This concept is entirely different from the traditional function oriented approach. Figure 3.15 shows the developments in program methodologies.

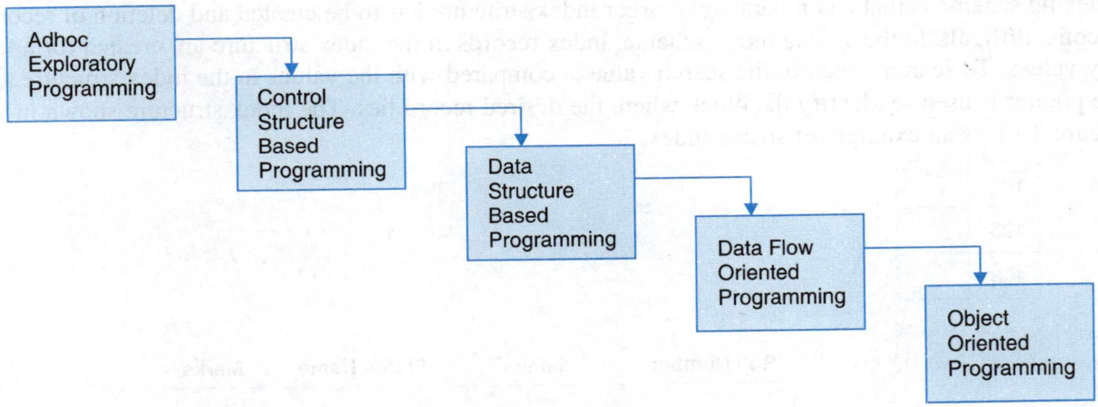

Fig. 3.15 : Development in Program Methodology

3.14.1 Control Flow Oriented Program Design

In the initial periods of computer evolution the programming of a computer was not a major issue. Initially the programs were developed in the machine or hardware language. Since the nature of operations to manipulate data was simple, machine and assembly language programs were sufficient. However, writing the code in low-level language was difficult and complex and there was no guideline for program development. Therefore, programmers adopted their own individual approach and style. This adhoc nature of programming was termed Exploratory Programming, as discussed earlier.

With introduction of large program development, the exploratory programming proved ineffective even with high level languages. It became a costly affair in terms of time and effort, for programmers to write complex programs. Later it was realized that a control flow oriented programming is well suited for developing large programs. The program should be based on the control structures. To provide good control structures, the Flow Chart technique were introduced. The programmer developed the flow chart which indicated the execution flow and the program is then developed according to the flow chart.

A flow chart to find the average of M numbers is shown in Figure 3.16. For a moderate size problem, it is necessary to plot the flow of control before the actual program is written. The motivation for doing so is twofold. First, the flow chart depicts a clear picture of the logic and the code written is maintainable. If the number of lines of code for a particular problem exceeds 1000, then another programmer would find it difficult to modify the code. However, he can refer to the flow chart which would help him to understand the code logic. Therefore, the flow chart considerably help in maintaining the source code. Another advantage of developing the flow chart prior to program development is that the programmer can then accurately define the various steps for controlling the flow of execution.

Control Flow Design is well suited for moderate sized programs. Many suggestions were made by different researchers for a robust design of programs. Dijkistra, a famous computer scientist, proposed that unconditional GOTO or JUMP-like statements must be restricted in the program design. Later it was proved that the three construct "Sequence", "Selection" and "Iteration" may represent any program logic. A program is said to be structured when the program logic is based only on "Sequence", "Selection" and "Iteration". At a later stage it was detected from experience that programmers are more prone to errors while using the control structures statement like if-then-else, for statements, do while statement etc. normally fail or produce logical errors at boundary conditions. With the pressing need to solve more complex and larger problems, another programming methodology was proposed which was called Data Structure Oriented Design.

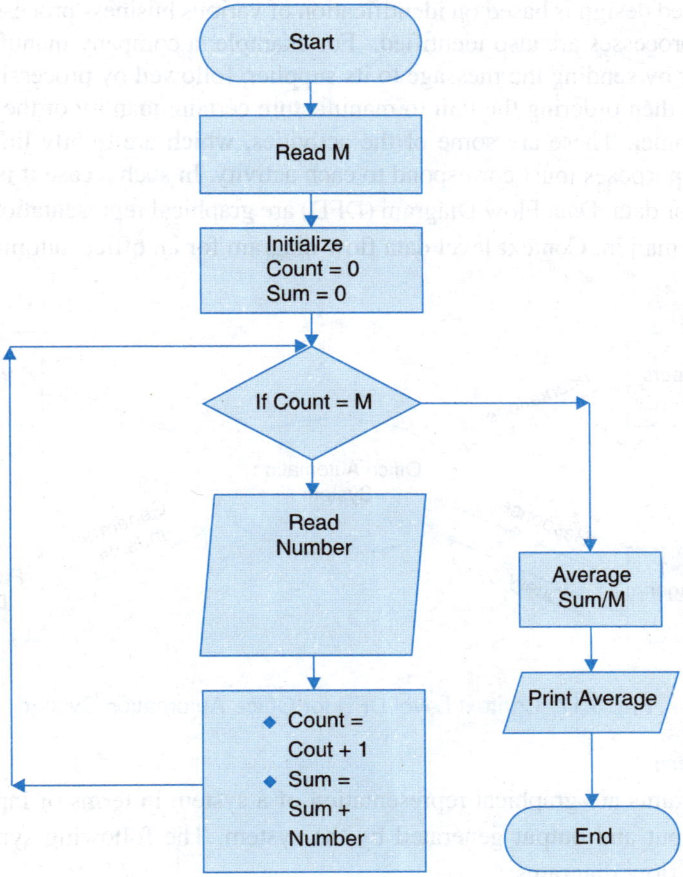

Fig. 3.16: Control Flow Oriented Design

3.14.2 Data Structured Oriented Design

With continuous growth in the problem and data size, the control flow oriented program design proved to be ineffective. Software engineers and programmers felt that a robust data structure is more suitable to represent the data instead of control flow. Data structures like Linked List, Stacks, Queues, Tree and Graph etc. provide a logical way of arranging the data. The program is then developed around the data structure. It was also proposed that the program structure must correspond to the data structure.

3.14.3 Data Flow Oriented Program Design

This approach is very good for solving moderate sized problems. Rapid development in processor speed and cheaper cost memory has motivated software engineers to develop the software which can cater to the needs of the whole organization rather than specific sections. Data flow oriented program design is suited for development of large software products. The difference between a software product and a program is that the software product caters to the need of many users in an organization and is developed by a team of software engineers. However, the program is written by an individual programmer or by a small team. Let us consider a large organization striving to automate its business activities. The organization has multiple divisions, sections, sub-sections and so on. To develop a software which is used by multiple users from different divisions and which automates the various processes would require the writing of several programs. The Data Structure oriented design will not work well for the development of such a huge software product.

Data flow oriented design is based on identification of various business processes. The dependencies among the various processes are also identified. For example, a company manufacturing an item, will process a sales order by sending the message to its supplier, followed by processing of the order by the account section, and then ordering the unit to manufacture certain quantity of the item and shipment of the item to the customer. These are some of the activities, which are tightly linked, and the program written for different purposes must correspond to each activity. In such a case it is necessary to find the flow of information or data. Data Flow Diagram (DFD) are graphical representation of various processes and the flow of information. Context level data flow diagram for an office automation system is shown in Figure 3.17.

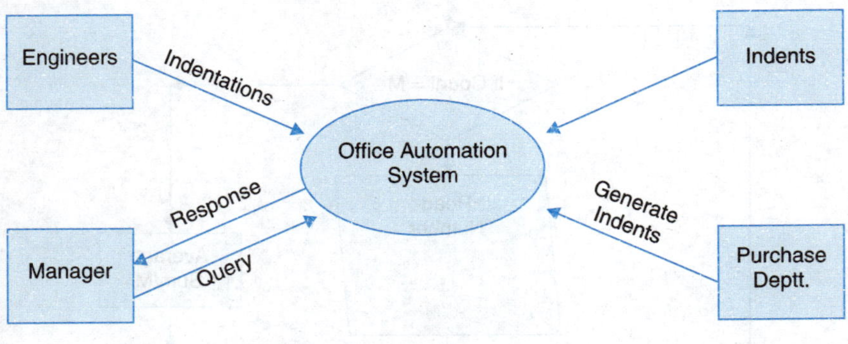

Fig. 3.17: Context Level DFD for Office Automation System

Data Flow Diagram

Data Flow Diagrams are graphical representation of a system in terms of input to the system, and processing of the input and output generated by the system. The following symbols are used in the construction of data flow diagrams:

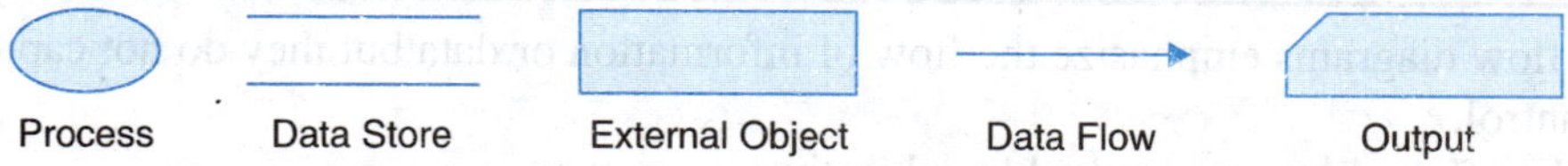

As shown in the context diagram for Office Automation System, in an office there are some engineers who request the OAS for the indent of an item. The indent generated is shown as output of the system. Similarly, the external object, the Manager puts his queries to the Office Automation System and in turn the manager receives the response from the system. Context level means the first level of the system. In context level, the system is viewed as one or single process. At the next level, the process activities are bifurcated and all the subprocesses and data flow is shown appropriately.

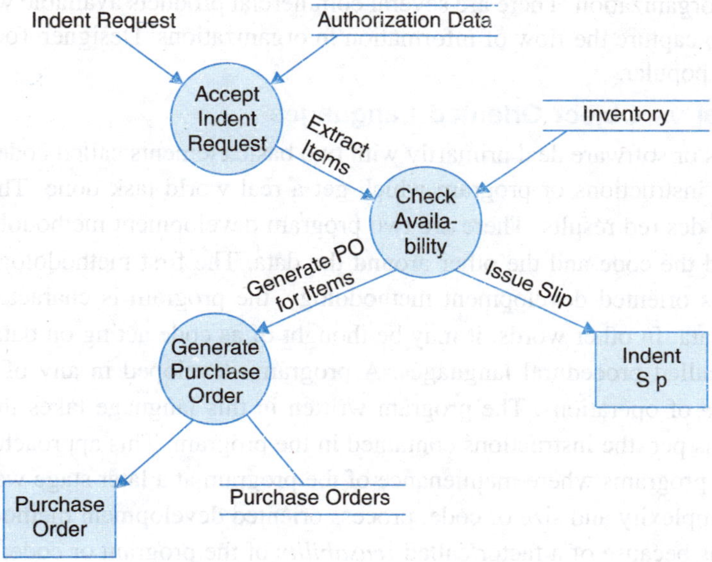

Fig. 3.18: Level 1 Data Flow Diagram

In the context diagram or level 0 data flow diagram, various external entities like engineers and manager are shown and it shows also how they interact with the Office Automation System (OAS). Level 1 data flow diagram shows (Figure 3.18) the various bifurcated steps as to how the indent requests are processed. "Accept Indent request" is a process which checks for the authorization. It takes the input from the data store called Authorization data. The items to be issued are extracted and their availability is checked using the inventory data. If the items are available in the store, then an issue slip is generated by the system, else the purchase order for the items is generated. The purchase order is an output of the system and it is kept in the data store called purchase orders. These three processes (Level 1) may further be decomposed to highlight the data flow in their processing. This will provide the next level data flow diagram. The data flow diagrams are very helpful in defining the organizational needs and the flow of information within the organization. However the data flow diagrams have some shortcomings.

Shortcomings of Data Flow Diagram

1. While data flow diagrams are helpful in capturing the data flow inside an organization, however, at every stage or level, they leave sufficient scope for further enhancement. Therefore, they are not exhaustive.

2. Data flow diagrams emphasize the flow of information or data but they do not capture the flow of control.
3. The data flow diagrams are highly subjective.
4. The data flow diagrams do not specify the dependencies among the process. For example, if any report is prepared late, or any other activity is delayed, then how will the process work ? Under such cases, DFDs do not provide any useful information and some alternative must be there.
5. The data flow diagrams do not provide any guideline as to how the process should be decomposed to get next level data flow diagram.

Inspite of these shortcomings, data flow diagrams remained a major tool to understand the software requirements of an organization. There are several commercial products available which are used in the software industry to capture the flow of information in organizations. Designer Tools, Power Designer of Sybase are very popular.

3.14.4 Procedural vs Object Oriented Languages

Computer programs or software deal primarily with two basic elements called code and data. The code refers to the set of instructions or program which get a real world task done. The program uses the data to produce the desired results. There are two program development methodologies; one develops the program around the code and the other around the data. The first methodology is called *process-oriented.* In process oriented development methodology, the program is characterized as a series of operations on the data. In other words, it may be thought of as code acting on data. BASIC, COBOL, Pascal and C are called procedural languages. A program, developed in any of these languages, is nothing but a series of operations. The program written in this language takes the data as input and processes the data as per the instructions contained in the program. This approach was well suited for writing small sized programs where maintenance of the program at a later stage was not a major issue. With increasing complexity and size of code, process oriented development methodology proved to be inefficient. This was because of a factor called *reusability* of the program or code. The other approach where the program is developed around the data is called *object-oriented* programming. To solve large and complex problems, object-oriented programming was developed. Object-oriented programming develops the program around the data. It also provides a well-defined interface to the data. An object-oriented program can be characterized as data controlling access to code. Large and complex programs are more prone to errors. The reason is that large and complex software is developed not by a single programmer but a team of software engineers working together. The coding part becomes an expensive affair because of repeated debugging and modification in the code. Object-oriented programming offers a new and powerful way to cope with this complexity. It seeks to develop clear, more reliable, more easy and more maintainable programs. Object oriented programming involves the concepts of data hiding, encapsulation and polymorphism. These concepts are the basis for object oriented programming. These concepts are new to programmers working with the conventional high level languages like BASIC, COBOL, PASCAL, etc. Examples of object oriented programming languages are C++ and Java. Although programs statements in C++ and Java are similar to statements in procedural language like C, yet they are based on a different paradigm of program development.

3.14.5 Drawbacks of Conventional Programming Approach

As programs grow ever larger and more complex, the procedural programming languages with structured programming approach prove to be ineffective. It is evident from the experiences of the software industry that, as the project's complexity grows, the schedule slips, more programmers are added, complexity increases, costs escalate, the schedule slips further and many more problems occur. In prodcedural languages, the emphasis is on function oriented approach. This approach cracks the problems into sub-problems with sub-problem into their sub-sub-problem. The subdivision of a program into functions continues this emphasis. The data in the organization which has to be used by the program remains a secondary issue and more emphasis is placed over the complexities and functionalities of the programs. It is quite often that a programmer creates a function that accidentally corrupts the data when he is not fully aware of the complexities of the program. This can easily happen because every function has complete access to the data. Any public data can be corrupted by a function that has no business to change it. Many programs may be required to be written for several purposes which use the same set of data. This is another issue and the organization of data cannot be changed without modifying all the functions that access it. On adding new data to the databank or modifying the data, all the functions which use the data would also need to be modified. It is a difficult job to find all such functions, add even harder to modify all of them correctly. Object oriented programming gets rid of all such problems. In the procedural programming languages like PASCAL, C, BASIC, thrust is on the construct which are suited for sequence, selection and iteration. In this programming environment, the code or program is written first which act on the set of data i.e., each statement in the language tells the computer to do some operation on data such as input data, arithmetic and logical operation on data and finally, print the processed data. When programs become larger, a single list of instructions becomes unwidely. Few programmers can comprehend a program of more than a few hundred statements unless it is broken down into small units. The idea of breaking a program into functions can be further extended by grouping a number of functions together into a larger entity called a module, but the principle is similar: a grouping of components that carry out specific tasks. Programming by dividing a program into function and modules is called *structured* programming.

3.15 OBJECT ORIENTED PROGRAMMING

The obejct-oriented approach is relatively a new paradigm for software design. The fundamental idea object-oriented language is to combine into a single unit both the data and the functions that operate on that data. Such a unit is called an *object*.

3.15.1 What are Object and Member Functions?

Objects are real world entities which may be distinguished from each other. Object is considered as collection of data which identify the object, and a set of procedures that operate on that data. For every specific operation on the data, the object function called *member* function is invoked. The member function is the only way to access the data. Reading, modifying, adding the data items in the object have to invoke the corresponding member function which does a specific task. Data cannot be accessed directly. The data is hidden, so it is safe from accidental alteration. Data and its function are said to be a single entity.

Consider the case where an operation is to be done on the set of students of an Institute. The student is considered as an object and may be modelled as shown in Figure 3.19.

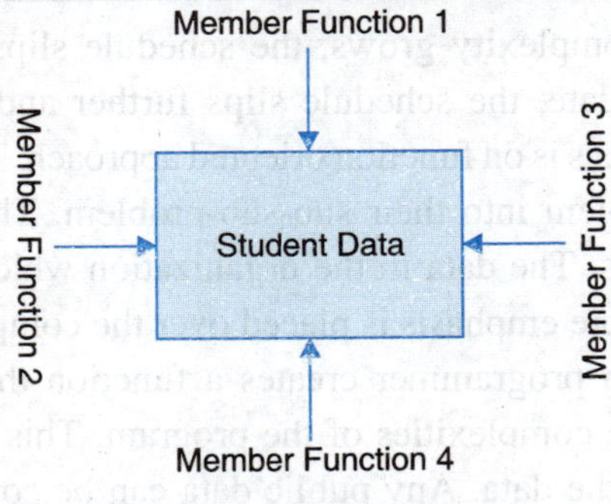

Fig. 3.19: Representation of Object

A student may have the following attributes:

Roll Number	:	*Roll Number of Student*
Name	:	*Name of the Student*
Father Name	:	*Father Name of the Student*
Marks	:	*Marks in Qualifying Examination*
Hostel	:	*Name of the Hostel Allotted*
Degree	:	*Name of Degree Program*
Tel No.	:	*Telephone Number of Student*
Address	:	*Address of Student*

There may be several operations which are required to be done on the students. Some of these may be;

1. Finding the address and telephone number of students.
2. Preparation of merit list on the basis of Marks.
3. Prepare a list of hostel wise allotment.

Here it may be noted that each object contains an information or data pertaining to it. The data internal to the object are called *attributes* of an object. The Roll Number, Telephone Number etc. are attributes of students on the basis of which a particular student is identified. The members function like "finding the address and telephone number of a student" are supported by the object and are allowed to operate. There is no other mechanism by which the data corresponding to the student may be fetched.

Class is defined as a collection of objects, which depict the same behaviour. The set of students may be considered as class and a particular student is treated as object. Each object is defined as an instance of a class. Motorcycle is an object belonging to the class of Two Wheelers.

All object oriented programming languages provide mechanisms that help you implement the object-oriented model. They are encapsulation, inheritance and polymorphism.

3.15.2 Encapsulation

Data encapsulation and data hidings are key terms in the description of object oriented languages. Modifying and accessing the data of an object is possible only through member functions which interact with it. No other functions can access the data. This simplifies writing, debugging and maintaining the program. It may be emphasized that object-oriented programming is not primarily concerned with the details of a program.

The property of an object which interfaces with the outside world in terms of messages is referred to as *encapsulation*. It is the mechanism which binds the code and the data. This keeps both code and data safe from interference. Encapsulation may be considered as a protective wrapper that prevents the code and data from being arbitrarily accessed by other code defined outside. Access to the code and their data inside the wrapper is tightly controlled through a well-defined interface. In Java, the basis of encapsulation is the class. A class defines the structure and behaviour (data and code) that will be shared by a set of objects. Each object of a given class contains the structure and behaviour defined by the class. For this reason, objects are sometimes referred to as instances of the class. Thus a class is a logical construct an object is a physical reality. Since the purpose of the class is to hide complexity of the implementation within it, each method or variable may be declared private or public.

3.15.3 Inheritance

Inheritance enables the creation of a new class by deriving or extending the existing class properties. It is a process by which one object acquires the properties of another object. Inheritance supports the concepts of hierarchical classification. It is the inheritance mechanism that makes it possible for one object to be a specific instance of a more general case. Inheritance interacts with encapsulation as well. If a class encapsulates some attributes, then any subclass will have the same attributes plus any that it adds as part of its specialization. Most people naturally view the world as made up of objects that are related to each other in a hierarchical way. This is a key concept, which enables object-oriented programs to grow in complexity linearly rather than geometrically. A new subclass inherits all the attributes of all its ancestors.

Consider Figure 3.20 to understand concept of inheritance.

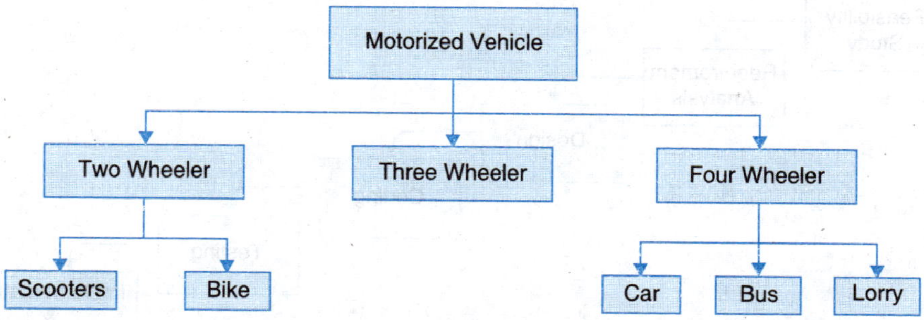

Fig. 3.20: Inheritance

As shown in the figure, the class 'Motorized Vehicles' is called the base class. The 'Two Wheeler' is a derived class which inherits some of the properties of the base class 'Motorized Vehicle'. The base class contains the properties, which are common to all of its derived class.

3.15.4 Polymorphism

The word polymorphism may be dissected as Poly (multiple) and Morphism (Forms), i.e. *polymorphism* means multiple forms. Polymorphism is a feature that allows one interface to be used for a general class of actions. One message may initiate several actions when received by different objects. Any specific action is determined by the exact nature of the situation. Polymorphism is often expressed by the phrase "one interface, multiple methods". This indicates that it is possible to determine a generic interface to a group of related activities. This helps reduce complexity by allowing the same interface to be used to specify a general class of action.

3.16 SOFTWARE DEVELOPMENT LIFE CYCLE

As discussed before, the term software is now considered as a product which may be used by a variety of users and serves several purposes. In an organization, the complete enterprise software solution will require a software product which has the capacity to handle various activities of an enterprise in a systematic way. These activities are account and financial activities, administration, inventory and stock control, customer support, marketing, product design, human resources and so on. The software development life cycle is used to facilitate the development of a large software product in a systematic, well-defined and cost effective way. The life cycle divides the various activities into several phases. The following are popular of software development life cycle:

1. Waterfall Model
2. Prototyping Model
3. Spiral Model
4. Evolutionary Model

3.17 WATERFALL MODEL

Here the software development is carried out in six phases. This classical model suggests well-defined activities to be carried out in every phase of development. This method is called waterfall model because it is similar to a waterfall and all the activities are done sequentially. Figure 3.21 shows the various phases of the classical waterfall model.

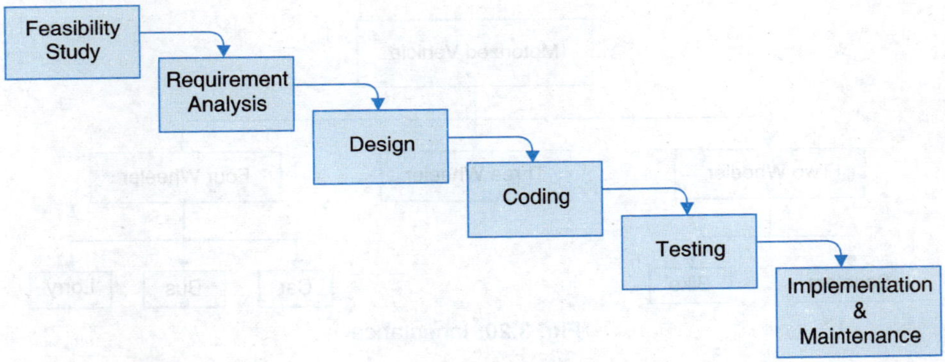

Fig. 3.21: Waterfall Model

3.17.1 Feasibility Study

The first phase is known as feasibility study. This is done to assess whether the software project is technically and economically viable. This involves the following steps:

1. Problem is defined.
2. Determination of technical and economic viability.
3. Study of alternative solution to attempt the problem. A cost/benefit analysis is done.
4. A layout of the plan is prepared to get the project executed. Scope of all the activities/phases are determined. It is also subject to the risk analysis in order to determine threats due to technological advances and economic changes.

At the end of this phase, a report called feasibility study is prepared by a group of software engineers. The client or the customer is also consulted through a questionnaire. This report determines whether the project is feasible or not. After being successful in the feasibility study, the requirement analysis is carried out.

3.17.2 Requirement Analysis

The customer who may be company or an individual, requires the software solution. The ultimate objective of the customer for software solution is to boost its business and minimize the procedural delays. Once the project is found to be feasible, the requirements of the customer are studied in detail. Major steps in the requirement analysis phase are as follows:

1. Information about the customer's organization is gathered. The detailed study of the various processes in the organization and information flow between the processes is determined. Special chat sessions or interviews are the popular ways by which the system analyst gathers information about the organization. The customer may also be given an questionnaire to determine his requirement.
2. Information gathered in the first phase is analyzed to find any ambiguities. If an ambiguity is found, then a special interview or questionnaire is prepared. This part is very important in the sense that if any ambiguity remains unsolved, it may lead to serious errors at later stages. Ambiguities and contradiction are to be totally removed at this stage.
3. Once the information is available about the organization, a document called Software Requirement Specification (SRS) is prepared. The SRS document is most important and it may be understood as a contract between the customer and software team. All the software development activities are done according to the SRS document. An SRS document must contain following:
   - Detailed statement of problem.
   - Possible alternative solution to problem.
   - Functional requirement of the software system.
   - Constraints on the software system.

The SRS document must be precise, consistent and complete. There is no scope for any ambiguity or contradiction in the SRS document. A SRS document may be organized as problem statement, introduction to problem, functional requirement of the system, non-functional requirement of the system, behavioural description and validation criteria.

Software Project Mangement Plan Document

After preparing the SRS document, the Software Project Management Plan document is prepared by the Project manager with the help of the system analyst. The objective of the software project management plan is to enable the group of software engineers to work towards a common goal and completion of the project. The software development team works under the supervision of the Project Manager. The Project Manager is responsible for completion of the project. The Software Project Management Plan contains the following:

1. Introduction
   — Overview of Major Functionality's
   — Objectives and constraints
2. Estimation
   — Software Size Estimation
   — Software development cost/effort estimation
   — Project development plan
3. Scheduling
   — Scheduling of various activities
   — Use of PERT and GANTT chart to schedule the project.
4. Staffing
   — Allocation of staff to various phases.

5. Risk Management
   — Analysis of future risk, their identification and abatement plan.
6. Project Monitoring and Control Plan

3.17.3 Design Phase

The design phase is a vitally important phase. It starts only after the SRS document and software project management plan documents have been prepared. In the design phase, attempts are made to transform the software requirements into such a form that the program may be written easily. Design may be carried out in any of the traditional methodology or object oriented design methodology. The traditional design procedures include the following steps:

Traditional Software Design

1. Carry out structured analysis. This analysis yields the different functions or processes and a data flow among the processes are obtained. A pictorial representation (DFD) is used to represent the structured analysis.
2. Obtain high level design. The data flow diagram is used to obtain high level design. This design contains the information about the various functions and how a particular function invokes the other functions.
3. Obtain detailed design. This design is obtained using high level design. This fine design uses the algorithm and data structure. The objective of the detailed design is to transform the requirements into well defined steps, which may be coded without any further clarification.

Object Oriented Design

This is a new paradigm. Various objects in the system are identified. After the identification of objects, the relationships among them are also explored. Details of objects, their internal data and methods are listed.

3.17.4 Coding

The outcome of the design phase is the detailed design. The various modules and functions identified in the detailed design are coded. Several software companies have formed their own rules for coding. Determining the coding standards is necessary to provide a uniform appearance by a group of programmers. It makes the code understandable and increases the potential for reusability of the code. Some of the important rules and guidelines for determining the coding standard are:

1. There must be rules for restricting the use of global variables.
2. Give meaningful names to the variables, functions etc.
3. Header contents like name, date, author and modification history of code.
4. Exception handling conventions.
5. Restrict the use of an identifier for multiple purposes. It makes the program difficult for others to understand.
6. Restrict the use of clever programming.

   Clever Programming:
   ```
   DO 10 I = 1, N
   DO 10 J = 1, N
   A (I,J) = (I/J)* (J/I)
   ```
   These lines are written by the programmer to make the diagonal element of a N*N matrix to set to 1. It will be difficult for other programmers to understand the intentions behind writing this 3-line code.
7. Avoid the use of unconditional GOTO and Jump statement.

8. Length of a function in terms of total number of lines must not increase 10–15 lines.
9. Guidelines for internal and external documentation.

Internal and External Documentation

The documentation of the code written is a must. Large software development companies employ multiple programmers. One programmer may understand well the code written by another if it is properly documented. There are two types of documentation—Internal and External. *Internal* documentation is done along with the code. Writing the comments line with the code serves as documentation and is helpful to other programmers to understand the code. Most of the software firms adhere to 3:1 documentation. This means that for every three lines of source code, one comment line must be there. The *external* documentation is done outside the code. The procedures, functions and rules which describe the code are kept in the form of manuals or directories.

Debugging Techniques

It is very common for a programmer to make syntactical and logical errors while writing the code. Debugging is process of fixing the bug. When a code contains bugs, it generally does not yield the desired result. Following are popular techniques for debugging:

Brute Force Debugging: The programmer appends the print or write statement which, when executed, display the value of a variable. The programmer may trace the value printed and locate the statement containing the error. Earlier when the time for execution was quite high, programmers had to use the core dumps. The core dumps are referred to as the static image of the memory and this may be scanned to identify the bug.

Back Tracking: In this technique, the programmer back tracks from the place or statement which gives the error symptom for the first time. From this place, all the statement are checked for possible cause of error. There are several other debugging techniques used. These are Program Slicing, Fault Tree Analysis, Cause Elimination etc.

3.17.5 Testing of Software

Once the code for a module or function has been written, it is tested under several conditions. Testing of the code is done to observe whether it behaves as per the expectation. For testing a module or function, several test cases are generated and the behaviour of the program is observed. If the output at any test case is different than expected, then its code would have to be corrected or it may have to be rewritten. The exhaustive testing of a program is very difficult and might take a lot of time. The test cases are so developed that they cover almost possible conditions. The testing of a software may be categorized as follows:

1. Unit Testing
2. Integration Testing
3. System Testing

Unit Testing

The module or function code is first unit tested upon completion of code writing. In unit testing, a module is tested in isolation. Therefore unit testing is also called *isolation testing*. The module is tested against several test conditions. There are two ways of code check called Code Walkthrough and Code Inspection. *Code walkthrough* is an informal technique for analyzing the quality of code. Here a team checks whether the programmer has followed the various rules and guideline of the software company in writing the code. *Code inspection* is a formal process where the code for a module is checked in terms of the commonly made errors. Following are the commonly made errors by a programmer:

1. Use of unbounded loop.

2. Improper storage allocation.
3. Use of Jumps and GOTO statement.
4. Use of goto statement inside a loop.
5. Using a variable without initialization.
6. Arithmetic operation on a mix of integers and floating numbers.

Consider Figure 3.22. In certain cases it is not possible to test the module in totality at the point where it calls a function or another function calls itself. As shown in Figure 3.22, module M1 calls module M2 and M3 and Module M3 calls module M4, M5 and M6. Suppose the module M3 is under unit testing. The M3 cannot be tested without module M1, M4, M5 and M6. M1 passes certain values to M3 and M3 passes the values to M4, M5, M6 modules. If other interacting modules are not ready, then a simulation is carried out. In simulation a dummy function is created which either accepts the value or passes the value as the case may be. This will create an environment for testing and a proper unit testing of module may be carried out. The unit testing is carried out in two ways called Black Box Testing and White Box Testing.

Black Box Testing: of a module is done without bothering about the internal architecture of the module. The test cases are developed in the line of SRS document and the behaviour of the module is observed.

White Box Testing: mainly focuses on the internal architecture of the module. The test cases are developed to find the bugs and errors in the code written for the module.

Integration Testing

After the unit testing of modules, the module developed undergoes integration testing. Various modules developed are integrated according to a certain plan and the test cases are executed to check whether the various modules work as a single entity. It is not necessary to put all the modules together to perform integration testing. For example, as shown in Figure 3.22, the modules may be integrated and test cases are executed to check that they are properly integrated.

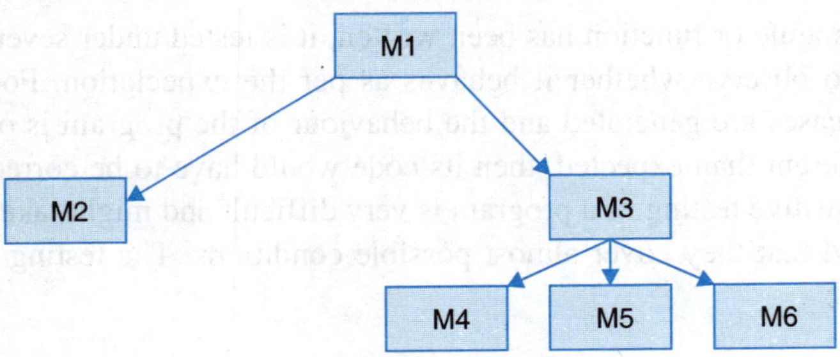

Fig. 3.22

System Testing

The final test is performed after developing all the modules according to the requirement. The objective of system testing is to determine whether the software system performs as per the requirements mentioned in SRS document. This testing is known as system testing. A fully developed software product is system tested. The system testing is done in three phases called Alpha, Beta and Acceptance Testing.

- **Alpha Testing** is conducted by the software development team at the developers site. The software product containing all the modules are intermarried and test cases are executed. If the product is successful, then the next phase called Beta Testing is performed.

- **Beta Testing** is performed by a group of friendly customers in the presence of the software development team. The problems noted and the suggestion made by the customer are considered. There are several cases where the customer is not one party, instead the software is developed for the masses. For example, Operating Systems like MS WINDOWS, DOS, UNIX, database management systems like Oracle, Sybase, Ingress, Web browsers like Internet explorer, Netscape navigators and other products which are developed for masses are beta tested in a different way. The evaluation copy of such software is freely distributed among the target audience and feedback from the users are noted. The development team collects various views and suggestion of the selected users and modifies the code if necessary. Once the product is successful in Beta testing, it undergoes Acceptance Testing.
- **Acceptance Testing** is performed by the customers themselves. If the software is successful in acceptance testing, the product is installed at the customer's site.

3.17.6 Implementation and Maintenance

When the software product is successful in the testing process and finally passes the acceptance testing, it is installed at customer's site. The most critical phase of its life cycle then starts. This phase is known as *maintenance* of the software product. The maintenance of the product is done usually at customer's site. After installation, when the customers start using the product for their routine work, several problems are reported by the customers or their employees. The product is then modified, sometimes a patch-up is sufficient, and sometimes a new module is written.

3.18 PROTOTYPING MODEL

The prototyping model is similar to the waterfall model with some differences. It has been noticed by several system analysts that most of the time, the customer is not sure about the functionality he requires in the software product. He may not clearly express his requirements in terms of the software product he wants. In such cases, it is not considered a good practice to develop a product as only perceived by the software development team. Before preparing the SRS documents, the customers must also understand the functionality of the product.

Under such circumstances, the prototyping model for software development is used. In this approach a quick design of the product is prepared and shown to the customer. Prototype is the toy representation of the software product. As per the suggestion of the customer, the prototype is rebuilt and modified. Once the design is accepted by the customer, the design phase according to the waterfall model starts. The schematic of the prototyping model is presented in Figure 3.23.

The development in the prototyping model starts after collecting the basic data about the customers requirements. Based on the initial requirement a rapid design of the product is created by simulation. The customer evaluates it and his suggestions are noted. Once the suggestion are incorporated, the modified design is shown to the customer. This process is carried out until the customer is satisfied. Then the SRS documents are prepared. After this point, the software development process follows the phases of the traditional waterfall model. The design, coding, testing, implementation and maintenance are carried out in similar ways.

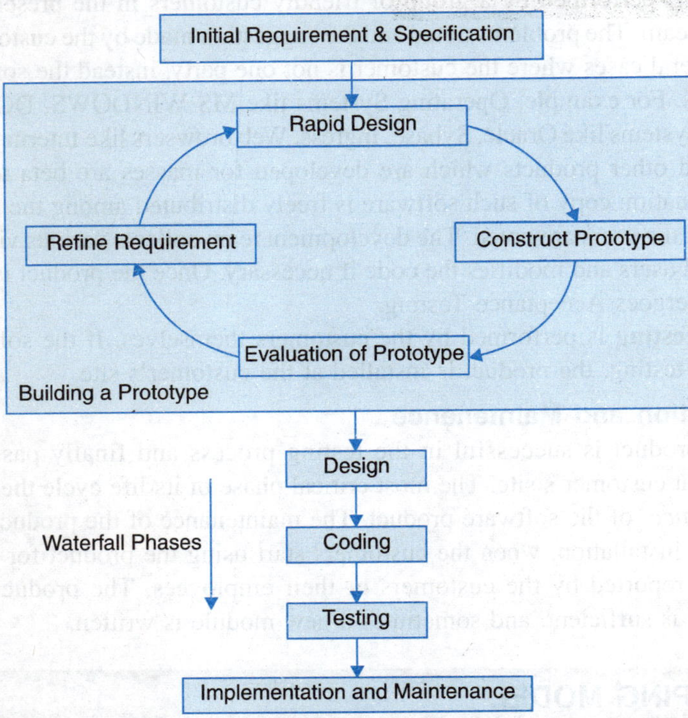

Fig. 3.23: Prototyping Model

3.19 SOFTWARE QUALITY ASSURANCE

The motivation behind software quality assurance is to enable the software industry to develop high quality software products and adhere to the standard software development practices. We will discuss the salient feature of ISO certification and SEI Capability Maturity Model (CMM) in this context.

3.19.1 ISO 9000

The International Organization for Standardization (ISO) is a worldwide federation of national standards bodies from some 100 countries. ISO is a non-governmental organization established in 1947. The mission of ISO is to promote the development of standardization and related activities with a view to facilitating the international exchange of goods and services, and to developing cooperation in the spheres of intellectual, scientific, technological and economic activity. ISO published its ISO 9000 standard in 1988. ISO 9000 consists of three standards for external quality assurance. These are ISO 9001, ISO 9002 and ISO 9003. ISO certification is used as a reference model for a contract between the external independent parties. It must be remembered that ISO certification does not guarantee a high quality product. It focuses mainly on the processes. ISO is now being used as the standard and basis of evaluation for international bidding. ISO 9000 specifies a set of guidelines for repeatable organizations. A repeatable organization is one where the production process is person independent.

ISO 9001 standard is applicable to the organization engaged in design, development, production and services of goods. ISO 9001 applies to software industry.

ISO 9002 standard is applicable to only those organizations which are involved in the manufacturing of a product. These organization do not design a product.

ISO 9003 standard applies to service industry. The organizations who are involved in only installation of product, services and testing of product are eligible for ISO 9003 certification.

3.19.2 How Does ISO 9001 Apply to Software Industry ?

These days, software customers are clearly going global and are demanding high quality software products. Given the stakes involved, it is important for software organizations to understand all the rules for self-improvement and for doing business in the international marketplace. The ISO 9001 standard has become a basic feature of these rules. ISO 9001 is an international "quality management system" standard used to assess an organization's management approach regarding quality product development. ISO 9001's focus is directed internally at an organization's processes and methods and externally at managing the quality of products and services delivered to the customer. Software products are very different from other products. As they are intangible and difficult to control. The only raw material in the software product is data. ISO has released ISO 9000 part-3 in 1991 for the software industry. Since software development life cycle includes requirement, specification, design, coding, testing, maintenance and installation, most of the software industry takes on turnkey software projects. ISO 9001 is the most suited certification required by the software industry.

3.19.3 Why ISO Certification is Required by Software Industry?

There are several reason why a software industry must get an ISO certification. Some of the important reasons are listed below:

1. It is a sign of customer confidence. This certification has become a standard for international bidding.
2. It motivates the organization to follow a well-defined process towards product development.
3. It makes the processes more focussed, efficient and cost effective.
4. It leads to high quality repeatable software products.
5. It focusses on the weak points of an organization process and suggests corrective measures.
6. It facilitates the development of optimal processes and total quality management.
7. It considers proper documentation as an important activity. In fact, proper documentation is vital in the software industry.

There are several shortcoming in the ISO standard; most important one being that it is not a full proof system and does not guarantee that the product developed will be of high quality.

3.19.4 Capability Maturity Model (CMM): a Standard for Software Industry

The Capability Maturity Model for Software (SEI-CMM) is a model for judging the maturity of the software processes of an organization and for identifying the key practices that are required to increase the maturity of these processes. The Software Engineering Institute (SEI) of Carnegie Mellon University developed this model. The SEI-CMM has become a *de facto* standard for assessing and improving software processes. Through the SW-CMM, the SEI and the software community have put in place an effective means for modelling, defining, and measuring the maturity of the processes used by software professionals. The software industry, based on their software development processes, may be categorized into one of the five levels proposed by SEI-CMM. These levels are shown in the Figure 3.24.

Level 1: The software company where the software development activities are adhoc and processes are not defined and not documented. The success of a project in this organization depends on individual efforts. These organization are categorized as Level-1 or initial.

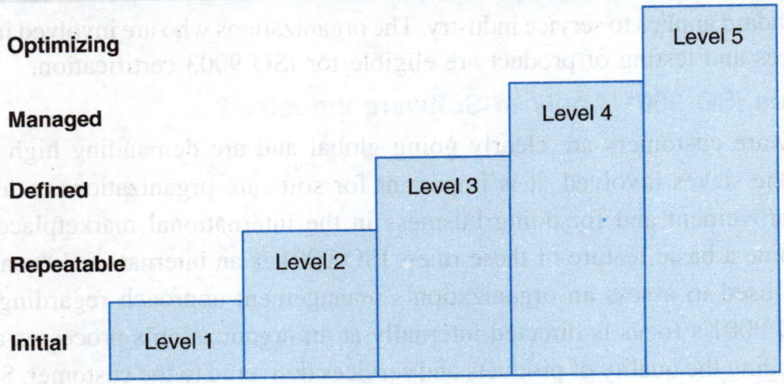

Fig. 3.24: CMM Levels

Level 2: Software companies where the basic management practices are defined but the procedure is followed normally on adhoc basis. These companies are categorized as Level-2 or Repeatable. In these companies, the previous efforts done towards success of software project may be repeated.

Level 3: Software companies where the management practices are defined, processes are well defined and documented. In these companies, the processes and practices are defined but are not quantitatively analyzed. These software companies are categorized in Level-3 or Defined.

Level 4: Software companies where the management practices and development processes are not only but also measured, are categorized in Level 4 or Managed. In these companies, the software processes are not only defined but are also controllable. These companies use modern cost estimation, effort estimation techniques.

Level 5: The Level-5 or optimizing software companies, perform error analysis and process monitoring for continuous process improvement. These companies analyze the innovation and new technologies and intend to optimize the current processes in the Industry.

Both SEI-CMM level certification and ISO certification have become a must for a software organization in this global era. There are several Indian software companies which have been awarded SEI-Level 5 and Level-4. WIPRO, TCS, Infosys, Infotech are a few of these companies.

OBJECTIVE TYPE QUESTIONS

Multiple Choice

1. Which of following is not hardware.
   (a) Printer (b) Operating system (c) Keyboard (d) Mouse
2. Which of the following is not a operating system
   (a) UNIX (b) LINUX (c) DOS (d) BASIC
3. Which of the following is not a system software.
   (a) Operating System (b) Compiler (c) Payroll System (d) None of above.
4. BIOS is
   (a) Software (b) Hardware (c) Both (d) None of above
5. Program written in Higher Level language is translated in to machine code by.
   (a) Operating system (b) Machine language (c) Assembler (d) Compiler
6. Access time of RAM is in the order of .
   (a) Seconds (b) Millisecond (c) Nanoseconds (d) Microseconds
7. Refreshing circuit is required in
   (a) Static RAM (b) Dynamic RAM (c) Both (d) None of above

8. Which memory is non-volatile
   (a) RAM (b) ROM (c) Both (d) None of above
9. CDROM is example of
   (a) Magnetic Storage Device (b) Optical Storage Device
   (c) Both (d) None of above
10. Which type of keyboard is suitable for a person who suffers from stress and pain while typing.
   (a) DVORK (b) ERGONOMIC (c) QWERTY (d) None of above
11. Operating system is a software interface between
   (a) User and Hardware (b) Software & Hardware
   (c) Compiler and Interpreter (d) CPU and Memory
12. Objective of Information system is to assist in
   (a) Decision Making (b) to define business processes
   (c) Innovative Planning (d) All of above
13. OLTP system processes the data .
   (a) On Line (b) Off Line (c) Both of above (d) None of above.
14. Which of the following language is machine dependent.
   (a) 4GL (b) Machine Language
   (c) Assembly language (d) High Level Language
15. Which memory is considered to be fastest?
   (a) Main Memory (b) Cache Memory (c) Auxiliary Memory (d) Secondary Memory
16. Which of the following is not true for Data Flow Diagrams.
   (a) DFD is highly subjective
   (b) DFD help in capturing dataflow inside organization
   (c) DFD helps identifying
   (d) DFD does not exhibit rule to time dependencies decompose processes
17. Which of the following is based on OOP Concepts
   (a) C (b) COBOL (c) FORTRAN (d) C++
18. Basic building block of an infromation system are
   (a) Set of methods (b) Software/Hardware
   (c) Database (d) All of above
19. Data Processing is required
   (a) To produce information (b) To assist in managerial decision making
   (c) Both (d) None of above
20. Major design issue in real time operating system is
   (a) To make the processor (b) Meeting job deadlines fast
   (c) To enhance throughput (d) Memory management

Answers

1-b, 2-d, 3-c, 4-c, 5-d, 6-c, 7-b, 8-b, 9-b, 10-b, 11-a, 12-d, 13-a, 14-b, 15-b, 16-c, 17-d, 18-d, 19-c, 20-b

State True or False

1. A program is collection of instructions. [True] [False]
2. System software is written to solve day to day problems. [True] [False]
3. Information plays a key role in decision making. [True] [False]
4. Data Processing refers to administration of data stored in files. [True] [False]
5. Data stored in RAM can not be removed. [True] [False]
6. Compiler translates the program written in HLL to machine code. [True] [False]
7. Microprocessor is a CPU fabricated on a chip. [True] [False]
8. Cache memory is faster than secondary memory. [True] [False]
9. Masked Rom are manufactured by Masking and Metallization process. [True] [False]
10. Optical storage devices uses magnetic material to store data. [True] [False]
11. Beta Testing of software is carried by section of customers. [True] [False]
12. Waterfall model is example of software development life cycle. [True] [False]

13. SEI-CMM model is a model to judge the maturity of software processes of an organization. [True] [False]
14. White Box Testing mainly focuses on internal architecture of the module. [True] [False]
15. Customers at customer site conduct alpha testing. [True] [False]
16. PERT and GANTT chart are prepared for job scheduling. [True] [False]
17. JAVA is a programming language based on concept of object-oriented programming. [True] [False]
18. For development of large software product, it is not necessary to adhere to SDLC. [True] [False]
19. ISO 9003 is applicable to service industry. [True] [False]
20. CMM level-5 organization does error analysis and process monitoring for continuous improvement. [True] [False]

Answers

1- True, 2-False, 3-True, 4-True, 5-False, 6-True, 7-True, 8-True, 9-True, 10-False, 11-True, 12-True, 13-True, 14-True, 15-False, 16-True, 17-True, 18-False, 19-True, 20-True

SELECTED EXERCISES

Digital Computer and Devices

1. What is meant by a digital computer? Draw a schematic to show various functional units of a digital computer.
2. Explain how the digital computer captures the real world data. How the result produced by the digital computer is analyzed in the real world?
3. What are Peripheral Devices? Explain the working of any two peripheral device in brief.
4. Differentiate between computer hardware and software. Explain how firmware is different from software and hardware. Support your answer with a suitable example.
5. What do you mean by Computer Generations? List the major advances in each generation in the development of computer technology.
6. What is meant by Personal Computing? Comment on the era of personal computing.
7. What are I/O devices? List some of the important I/O devices.
8. What is a Microprocessor? What are the differences between a microprocessor and a microcomputer?
9. Explain the differences between a microprocessor and the CPU?
10. What are motherboards? How are the microprocessor associated with Motherboards?
11. What do mean by Memory Devices? Explain the differences between the Primary and Secondary memory.
12. Distinguish between RAM and ROM and auxiliary memory.
13. What is BIOS? Is BIOS hardware or software? Justify your answer.
14. What is the function of the Control Unit?
15. What are Static RAMs? How are they different from Dynamic RAMs? Explain the function of Refreshing Circuit used in dynamic RAM.
16. Distinguish between Online/near line and offline data storage.
17. What are Auxiliary Storage Devices? Can a Hard Disk be categorized as an auxiliary storage device? What are the performance parameters of HDD.
18. What is a floppy disk? How many sizes and capacity floppy disk are available these days?
19. What is ROM? Why is the data stored in the ROM not erased even after the power is switched off? Justify your answer with an example.
20. How many types of ROMs are available? What are Masked ROM? How Programmable ROM (PROM) are different from EPROMs?
21. What are CDROMs? What technology is used to store the data onto CDROM? Explain with a suitable examples as to when the use of a CDROM is desirable.

22. What are recordable CDROMs? Explain how the recording is done in CDROM.
23. What are Scanners? How they are used?
24. Why a digitizer is called an I/O devices? Explain with a example as to how digitizers are used?
25. What is the Video Display Unit (VDU) considered as one of the most important output device? Explain the working of a VDU in brief.
26. What kind of device is a keyboard? How many types of keyboards are available for use in computers?
27. List the different types of printers available. What technology does the Laser Printer use to print a document?
28. Explain how an Ink-jet Printer works.
29. What is the main function of UPS? How many types of UPS's are available.
30. If you intend to buy a computer, how would you decide which computer should be purchased and what peripherals it should have?
31. What are Magnetic Tapes? Explain how the data is recorded onto the tape. What are magnetic disks? How is the recording done on a magnetic disk?
32. What are the advantages of using Ergonomic Keyboard ?
33. What is a Monitor? Explain how the color graphics is displayed on the monitor.
34. What are Optical Storage Devices? How is the data recording done on an optical storage device? Explain the differences between the CDROM and Digital Versatile Disk? How are the DVDs being used in day-to-day life?

Programming & Languages

35. What are programming languages? Explain the difference between Machine, Assembly and a High Level languages? Give some examples of High Level language.
36. Explain the drawbacks and difficulties in writing programs in low level languages. Why is a large software product not written in a low level language?
37. Explain with an example as to which language is more suitable to write a program; an assembly or a machine language? Justify your answer.
38. Why programs written in a High level Language or Assembly language are translated before execution?
39. What are Compilers? How are they different from Interpreters? Compare the features of Compilers and Interpreter.
40. What are assemblers?
41. Give a comparative analysis of High Level Language, Assembly Language, and Machine language.
42. What are Fourth generation languages (4GL)? Explain where these languages are used and how they are different from third generation languages?
43. What are Application programs? What are differences between an application program and system program? Cite any two examples of each.
44. What is meant by memory hierarchy? What is cache memory and why is it used ?

File Organization

45. What is file organization?
46. What do you mean by a file? How is the information stored in a file?
47. What is the difference between a variable length record and a Fixed length record? Explain how these records are logically represented. What are the advantages of using variable length record?
48. What are Heap Files? How heap files are represented? Explain how the insertion, deletion and updation operations on a record takes place in a heap file?
49. What are sequential files? How are they different from Heap files? Explain with a suitable example as to how records are inserted, deleted and updated in the sequential file.
50. What is Key? How is key used to search a desired record?
51. What is meant by Indexing? How is a file indexed? Explain the difference between Indexed sequential file and a sequential file?
52. Discuss the performance parameters on which an indexed sequential file may be evaluated.
53. Explain what are Seek Time, Insertion Time and Deletion Time? How is the time for seeking a record improved in index sequential files?

54. Show the structure of a sequential file containing the record of ten employees of an organization. The key to the file is Employee No. Show the index structure of the file and explain how a record is inserted, deleted and updated.
55. Create an index structure of the students of your class. Which index, a sparse index or dense index, will be used by you to create the index structure? Discuss with an example.

Program Development Methodologies

56. Why is program development considered as an important activity? Justify your answer with a suitable example.
57. What is the difference between a program and a software product?
58. What is exploratory style of programming? Why is exploratory programming considered inadequate for developing a software product?
59. Give a systematic description of evolution of program development methodologies.
60. What is control structure? Why a control structure based programming is considered a better option than exploratory programming?
61. What are the reasons for adopting control flow oriented programming? Under what circumstances is the control flow oriented programming recommended?
62. What are software development life cycle models? What is it important to adhere to software development life cycle model for developing a large software product? List the various phases of the waterfall model.
63. What is meant by data flow oriented programming methodology? List the shortcomings of control flow oriented programming methodology and show how these can be tackled well in data flow oriented design.
64. What are Data Flow Diagrams? What are their shortcomings?
65. What is Object Oriented Programming? Why is object oriented design considered a good option for design?
66. What is the prototyping model? Under what circumstances is this model used?
67. Explain the salient features of Waterfall Model for software development. List the shortcoming of waterfall model if it is employed for all types of software product development?
68. What do you mean by Jackson Structured Programming? How are the three constructs Sequence, Selection and Iteration sufficient to express any programming logic?
69. Why is the use of GOTO and JUMP statements in programming considered harmful? Explain with an example.
70. What is Data Structure oriented design? Explain its salient features.
71. What do you mean by structured programming? Is it possible to write a structured program using languages like C and Pascal? What are the advantages of writing structured programs?

Software Development

72. Explain the salient features of the classical Waterfall model for software development. Explain the activities in which are required in each phase.
73. What is meant by software project planning? What is software project management plan? Explain the issues covered in software project management plan.
74. Why is a feasibility study of a project carried out as the first activity in software development?
75. How is the requirement analysis done? What is SRS document? Why is the SRS document considered as a contract between the software development team and customers.
76. What is meant by coding? Why is it necessary to set down the guidelines for coding? Why is clever programming not preferred?
77. What is meant by testing of a software product? What are the differences between Unit testing, Integration testing and System testing.
78. What is documentation? Why is documentation considered as an important activity in large software development? What are the differences between Internal and External documentation.
79. What is System Testing? How is system testing carried out? What are the dfferences between the Alpha, Beta and acceptance testing?

80. What is meant by Black Box testing? How is it different from white box testing? What are the conditions against which the black box testing is done? List the objectives of white box testing.

Software Quality Assurance

81. What do you mean by software quality assurance?
82. What is ISO? Why should the software industry get ISO certification? Explain why it is important for the IT industry to get ISO 9001 certification.
83. What is meant by SEI capability maturity model? List the various levels of SEI-CMM model.
84. Explain the requirement for every level of SEI-CMM certification.
85. Explain with examples, the types of software organization to which ISO 9001, ISO 9002 and ISO 9003 is applicable.
86. Discuss the requirement to be satisfied by an IT firm to qualify for the Optimizing level of SEI-CMM.

4

OPERATING SYSTEM

Contents

- **Introduction**
- **Operating System Evolution**
- **Operating System Functions**
- **Resource Management**
- **Operating System Classification**
- **Case Studies**
- **Future Trends**

4 OPERATING SYSTEM

4.1 INTRODUCTION

Operating System may be defined as an interface between computer hardware and human. It allows the user to effectively utilize the hardware without much worrying about complex hardware details. The Operating System may be considered as collection of software and program which allows user to interact with the hardware. Computer System consists of several hardware devices like processor, memory, peripheral devices. The Operating System provides several routine which control the hardware and provide an environment for a user to execute their application program without worrying for the details of hardware. Working with computers, without an Operating System (OS), would be a difficult task because the task like loading an application program from disk to primary memory, allocation of memory scheduling etc. would require hours of work. Application programs themselves would be longer, more complicated and more expensive than they are now. This will result in writing complicated application program which not only deals with the logical details of program logic but also include other function which allows the application program to use hardware. Luckily, the availability of standard Operating System has prevented all of this and more. It may be emphasised that Operating System therefore, is a collection of program which act as an interface between user and hardware and provides an environment for executing application programs. An abstract view of computer system along with Hardware, Operating System, Application Software and Users are shown in the Figure 4.1.

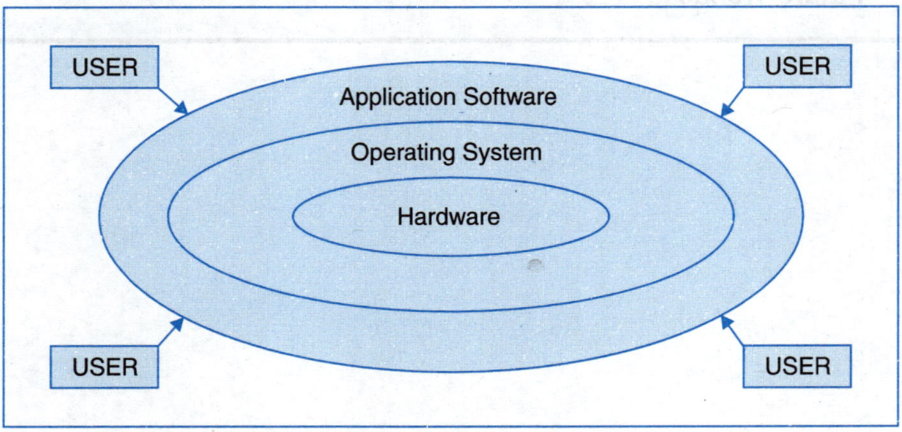

Fig. 4.1: View of Computer System

4.2 OS EVOLUTION

In the early stage of computing the operating systems were developed for specific computer system. VMS and CMS operating systems were developed for IBM 360 and IBM 370 computers. CP/M was developed for the microprocessor system Z80 of Zilog Corporation. Microsoft developed MS-DOS for the Intel 8086 range of processors. This approach of developing operating system proved to be ineffective when the two or more than two computers used to be integrated. Since each computer system running its own operating system, it was difficult to transfer files, use of the resource available at different computer was difficult to achieve due to compatibility problems. Sometime, it is also not possible to run same application program or software on different computer system. In all such cases, significant amount of work used to be redone. Extreme cases were those where the entire application program used to be rewritten. Many of the operating system used support only a subset of programming languages, and many programming language were supported by only few of them. Therefore, in the early days due to problem of compatibility of file formats and other simple job, the strategy of developing different operating system for different processor did not last long and people have started developing operating systems which are not machine dependent. Due to the problem of compatibility raised by early days operating, operating systems were being developed that could be easily transferred across different computer systems. This has become possible by development and design of operating system which were not dependent of architecture of the underlying computer system. This is probably the reason when attempts were made to write operating system in high level language or at least a language which supports the high-level language constructs.

The 'C' programming language was considered as a suitable language which is a high-level language closer to machine-level language. First of popular implementation of this strategy was design of UNIX operating system which was written in the C programming language. Due to the portability of this operating system, it has become very popular and allowed the users and programmers to work on the computer system without worrying for the architectural details of underlying computer system. A programmer can now use same programming tools, skill and environment to write programs to run without modifications on one system to another. A user can learn one set of procedures and commands, and use it across all systems, supporting his chosen OS. The first effort towards writing whole set of program required for operating system was the development of CP/M. The Control Program for Microprocessor (CP/M) was developed by Gary Kildall in 1973. He first of all developed the programming language called PL/M, (Programming Language for Microcomputers) and then wrote the operating system CP/M in the programming language PL/M. CP/M later was adopted by personal computer based on Z80 based computer system and supported floppies and hard-disk drives. After the introduction of CP/M, the small computer built around microprocessor became very popular because not only they were available at affordable prices but also this Operating System allowed the user to use hardware more effectively.

Microsoft introduced Disk Operating System (DOS) in eighties. This led IBM Personal Computer to revolutionise the personal computer market. IBM PC loaded with MS DOS has become a choice for the independent programmer and programmers found them very useful. At the same time, when MS DOS emerged as a choice for personal computer, UNIX has established itself as a platform for larger mainframe computers. The major problem with the Disk Operating System (DOS) and UNIX was that they had textual interface. This problem was more acute with the users of personal computer running with MS DOS. Since the low cost PCs were targeted at general audience, remembering the commands and syntax of DOS were not easy to remember. Microsoft has realised it and they came up with their solution called Windows in 90s, which was introduced as a replacement of DOS. Earlier version of Windows used to run on top of DOS. Later with introduction of Windows 95/98 with fully functional graphical user interface, it has become very easy for general users work with PCs and get their task done at few clicks of mouse. Windows NT was introduced for the network of computer and it is very easy for frequent tasks like sharing of file/folders, transfer of data with single click of mouse. Main advantage of Graphical User Interface (GUI) based Operating System like Windows was that users can get rid of typing and remembering the command of DOS.

4.3 OS FUNCTIONS

An Operating System is perhaps the most important program which creates a user-friendly environment for a user to interact with the machine and is the essential part of any computer. It co-ordinates and controls the operation of computer hardware and software resources. These resources are mainly processors, main memory, secondary memory, input-output devices and files. The operating system functions can broadly be categorised into two categories called Resource Management and providing friendly interaction of user with hardware by allowing him to write command to do specific tasks. The major function of operating system is, therefore, to bridge the gap between the hardware and the user. The operating system not only manages the hardware but also provides services to application programs by allocating the hardware resource which are essential for execution of the program. These services and resources include file systems, memory management, process management, process communication, and networking. Whenever an application program is written and executed by a user, it accesses several software and hardware resources. These resources are processors, main memory, secondary memory, input-output devices and files. Operating Systems' major role is to allocate these resources to application program efficiently and effectively. The Operating System lies between the application programs and the computer hardware. Operating System also resolves conflicts, attempts to optimise performances and simplify the effective use of the system.

Modern Operating System makes the life of a user easy by providing him easy access to hardware. Early days Operating System used to provide a textual interface. This means that a user may access the functionalities of Operating System by writing textual command. The Operating System interprets these commands and translates them into sequences of further instructions to the hardware. For example, if you have to create a file, the user may submit a command for creation of file and Operating System does rest of the task. It will find the free space on the disk which is responsible for saving your work as long as the user want to keep his file on the disk. These files may be copied, edited, deleted at the wish of the user. The only thing required by the user is to type it in an appropriate command using keyboard. Therefore, Operating System performs tasks, such as recognising input from the keyboard, sending output to the display screen, keeping track of files and directories on the disk, and controlling peripheral devices, such as disk drives and printers. User interacts with the OS through a set of commands. The user-commands are submitted by user through keyboard. The Command Interpreter, which is subset of operating system software routine, reads the command entered by the user and converts it into a stream of electronic pulses. These commands are executed by the Operating System on the hardware and the required task is done without forcing user to learn rigorous details of hardware. For example, a copy command submitted to the Operating System may copy the file from hard disk to floppy, or vice versa without letting the user to know the details or working principle of either floppy-disk drive or hard-disk drive.

The textual interface to the Operating System at the later stage found to be little more cumbersome and started proving difficult to operate. The main reason to this was that users used to remember the lengthy command, their syntax etc. This has paved the way to design and develop the Operating System where the user need not remember large and complex commands. The Microsoft was the first who came with such Operating System called Windows. The Windows have proved to be an alternative to textual interfaces to Operating System. Windows has provided Graphical User Interface (GUI) which allows user to enter commands by pointing and clicking at objects and icon displayed on the monitor by mouse. Windows hides the internal details of hardware components and presents a simple, usable working environment. Example of textual interfaces are Disk Operating System (DOS), UNIX etc. Windows 95/98/NT are graphical-user-interface based Operating Systems. The Operating System is therefore system software, which is loaded in the memory of the computer at the time of booting process. It remains there all the time and provides a platform on top of which application programs may run. The Operating System apart from allowing the users to run their commands and application program also helps the user for housekeeping activities in the computer system. This includes maintenance of files, allocation of resources, etc. Every general-purpose computer must have an OS to run other programs, and provide the base upon which application programs can be written.

4.4 RESOURCE MANAGEMENT

Most of the operating systems work in two modes, single-user mode and multi-user mode. In single-user mode, it is assumed that only one user will have access to all the resources of computer system. These resources are mainly memory, processor, I/O and files. In the multi-user mode, the Operating System is designed to allow several users at a time. Most of the large computer systems work in multi-user mode. Microsoft Disk Operating System (DOS) is considered as single user Operating System and all of the resources available are at the disposal of the user. In this environment, a user may submit only one task at a time. If he wishes to run another application, in that case he need to terminate the previous one. This feature excludes the DOS being multi-tasking or multi-processing Operating System. The UNIX is considered as multi-user Operating System which allows more than one user to work at a time. In the conventional UNIX-based system, the multiple user sitting at their terminal may send request to the CPU and these requests are served by the CPU one by one. The requirement and methodologies of management of resources (memory, processor, I/O devices and files) varies in single- and multi-user Operating System. Based on the resources, chiefly Operating System performs four management functions namely Memory Management, Processor Management, Device Management and File Management.

Memory Management

The memory-management function finds all available free space in memory and allocates it to the processes. The process is program/task under execution stage. The Operating System manages whole memory by dividing it into several blocks and partitions. Every job under execution stage requires memory. If there exist two or more than two processes, then Operating System allocates the memory segments as per requirement of the job. In case any job execution has to be suspended or it has been terminated, the Operating System combines the memory freed by the process and allocates the memory to other process. The Operating System therefore decides which process gets memory, when and how much and allocates the memory when that process requests it. It finally frees the allocated memory space as and when the process is executed completely. Memory Management is the important function carried out by Operation System. It is also the responsibility of the Operating System that memory be allocated in such a way that the utilisation is maximum.

Processor Management

The Processor Management function of operation is related with allocation of process or job to processor. The speed of processor or CPU is much faster than peripheral devices. Every process is completed only after its processor and I/O requires. Since the speed of CPU is much faster than I/O devices, the scheduling is done in such a way that CPU remains idle for minimum amount of time. When a process waits for I/O to be completed, during that wait time, the CPU may be allocated to other process waiting for processor. There exists several scheduling techniques which maximizes CPU utilisation.

Device Management

This function of Operating System deals with allocation of devices to process. Operating System schedule the I/O devices, I/O channel to process whenever it requires. For managing the different requests arising from different processes for grant of devices, scheduling of I/O devices are done according to some strategies. In I/O scheduling, after finding the status of device, channels, a schedule is prepared to which state, which process, which device is allocated to the process.

File Management

The File Management of Operating System is related with management of files stored on to secondary storage. The file is considered as collection of logically related data item which are organised in records. These files may contain set of commands, executable codes or reports. Purpose of file management is to hide the complex details of device specific aspects from the user. Users wish to rely on a uniform set of file manipulation services which are independent of details of devices from users perspective. File Management of Operating System keeps track of all information on files. It finds and records the following for all files: location, size, usage (attribute), status etc. It also finds as to which process which file is required, checks through the protection routine, opens the file if allowed, and allocates it to the process. It essentially does the task of mapping the request of file from process to physical disk, swapping the file contents between primary and secondary memory, keeping track of allocation and de-allocation of space and support for protection and sharing of files.

4.5 OS CLASSIFICATION

The Operating System provides software layers between user and hardware which creates an environment for user to run his application and control hardware without knowing the rigorous details of hardware. Users submit their jobs to the Operating System and Operating System schedule their jobs. The job may be handled by the Operating System serially or concurrently. The serial-processing means that the resources of the computer system are allocated to single job and remain allocated until job is finished. In concurrent processing, the resources may be dynamically allocated to the jobs as and when required. Current application requires the distributed Operating System, which co-ordinates the allocation of resources located at different sites or computer system. For the job requiring the resources located at different computer system, all of the computer system has to follow a common set of protocols. These types of requirements are being served by distributed Operating System. Based on the nature of application and functionality of Operating System, the Operating System may be classified into several categories. We will discuss some of the modes of Operating System and different types of Operating Systems in this section.

Batch Operating System

One of the major design issues for the Operating System is to increase the resource utilisation. It also includes the reduction in CPU idle time by removing the manual or programmers intervention during the execution of program. Batch Operating Systems are based on the concepts that if several programs are batched together on input they can be executed one after another without programmer intervention. This reduces the overhead for each program, as the program need not require slower human intervention. The batch processing is suitable in programs with large computation time with no need of user interaction or involvement. For pay roll, forecasting, statistical analysis and large scientific number crunching programs, user need not wait while the job is being processed. The instructions are provided by embedding the commands in a batch stream. These commands are written in a language called Job Control Language (JCL). JCL commands are required to mark the beginning and end of the job, to announce their resource need and memory requirements. Batch Monitor, a part of batch operating system, reads and interprets the commands written in JCL. The total time from submission of job into the queue till it get completed is called *turn around time*. The major disadvantage of batch operating system is non-interactive environment. It also imposes several drawbacks from programmer's point of view, e.g., the programmer is bound to do off-line debugging. The time taken between job submission and job completion is generally very high, although the time lapsed in actual execution of program may be quite less. Since the programmer does not have any control over intermediate results of a program, batch operating systems are considered quite inflexible in software development. Off-line debugging also does not permit the programmer to correct the bugs whenever they occur, but has to correct them at later stage.

Multiprogramming Operating System

In Batch Operating System, the jobs are submitted in the batch and all of the resources are reserved to one job at a time. This practice improves the turn around time but shorter length jobs are suffered adversely because they have to wait for a longer time for their turn. Another disadvantage of batch operating system is that it does not maximise the resources utilisation. This drawback of batch operating system is reduced in multiprogramming operating systems. The multiprogramming allows the interleaved execution of two or more than two programs. Multiprogramming operating systems are fairly sophisticated compared to batch operating systems. Multiprogramming improves both system throughput and resource utilisation. The job submitted to the Operating System requires CPU for computation and I/O for their I/O needs. During the serial execution of program when CPU completes the computation, it remains idle for the time when I/O operations of the job are under progress. This idle time of CPU poses heavy penalty on the jobs waiting for CPU intervention. Multiprogramming operating system allows concurrent execution of two or more than two jobs and schedules them in such a way that whenever computation work of one job is completed and it goes for I/O, this idle time of CPU may be utilised by allocating another job to the CPU who wants_the services of CPU. This improves throughput of Operating System. The number of jobs active in the system is known as degree of multiprogramming. Higher degree of multiprogramming ensures higher resource utilisation. Concept of multiprogramming is illustrated in the following schematic.

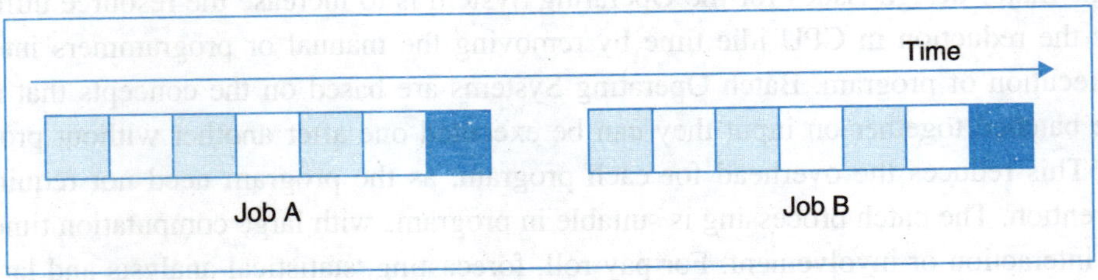

Fig. 4.2 (a): Sequential Execution of Job A and B

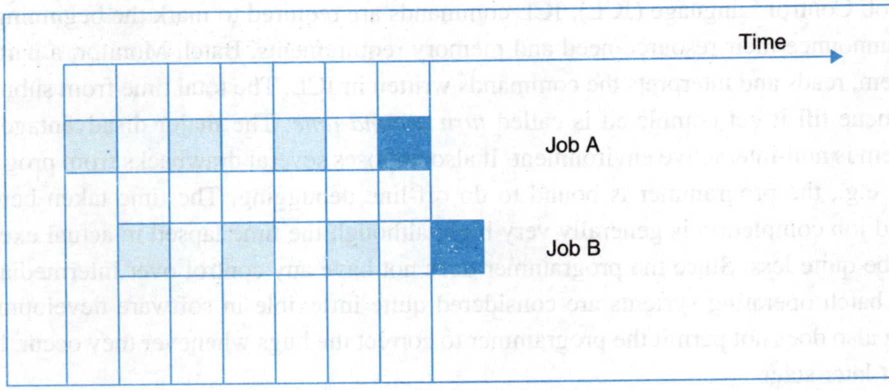

Fig 4.2 (b): Concurrent Execution of Job A and Job B

Figure 4.2 (a) shows the sequential execution of two jobs A and B. Their time requirement for CPU is shown as shaded box. The Fig. 4.2 (b), shows the interleaved or concurrent execution of both the jobs in such a way that when Job A does its I/O bound work, the CPU is utilised for computation work of Job B.

Multitasking Operating System

A Multitasking Operating System allows two or more than two active processes. The instance of a program execution is known as *process*. Multitasking is implemented by maintaining code and data of several processes simultaneously in the memory. Multitasking is often coupled with hardware and software support. During execution of more than two processes, it is the responsibility of the Operating System to protect the memory space reserved for one process from other process. Most of the multitasking systems out of multiple processes, only process and accept the input from keyboard, mouse or other input devices. This process is known as *foreground process*. Rest of the processes are said to be running in background. These processes are therefore called *background processes*. Those who have been extensively in the Windows 95/98 environment might have observed the concept of foreground and background process. Background processes can not accept interactive input from a user, but they can access data stored on a disk and write the data to the video display. One may open several applications in several windows. If you have opened a word file and have given print command the computer will keep printing the document in background and Windows allows you to work at the same time in another application, e.g., Access, Word editing etc. Out of the several Windows, you have opened only one which remain active and at a time you may interact with only one application. This means that only one process will work as foreground process. This concept is called SPOOLing. (Simultaneous Peripheral Operation On Line). In addition, many communication programs are designed to run in the background. Background processes generally have a lower priority than foreground processes so that they do not interfere with interactive applications.

There exist two types of multitasking called pre-emptive multi-tasking and cooperative multitasking. In pre-emptive multitasking, CPU time is shared among the different processes. In this case, fixed time slice are allocated to each process in rotation. Time slice is amount of the time allocated to each process for CPU utilisation. In cooperative multitasking, each process may hold the CPU for the duration it wants. A process not utilising the CPU may allow others to process program to use it temporarily. Windows 95, Windows NT, and UNIX Operating System are the examples of pre-emptive multitasking operating system. Windows 95/98 are considered as multitasking operating system but DOS does not qualify as multitasking operating system. Although DOS allows some of the tasks to be done in back ground like printing in the background. MS Windows 95/98, Mac OS, UNIX are the examples of Operating System which are full multitasking operating systems.

Multiprocessing Operating System

A Multiprocessing or Multiprocessor Operating System manages operations of computer system which has two or more than two (multiprocessor) processors. The multiprocessor operating systems are also multitasking operating systems because they allow multiple processes to be executed at a time on different processors. It may be noted that multitasking may not be allowed on different processors. The multiprocessor operating system provides all features of operating system along with the management of multiple processor. Multiprocessing can be done in two ways called symmetric and asymmetric multiprocessing. In asymmetric multiprocessing different jobs may be allocated to different processors. The disadvantage of asymmetric multiprocessing is that some processors may be overloaded while other processors remain idle. In the symmetric multiprocessing, the same job may be executed simultaneously at different processors.

Multi-user Operating System

A Multi-user OS allows two or more users to work simultaneously. It is achieved by allowing two or more users to connect to the computer system from different terminals. Multi-user Operating System does not guarantee that multi-programming or multitasking will be done. The general purpose time sharing system incorporates features of both multi-user and multiprocessing operating system.

Multithreading

Threads are used to increase the performance of operating system by reducing the context switching time.Threads are a good mechanism for achieving high degree of concurrency. Each thread represents a process and they are also called *light-weight processes*. Each thread corresponds to exactly one process and represents a flow of control and have its own state. Concept of threads has been implemented in operating system Mach OS and OS/2. Threads are individual processes that execute simultaneously in multitasking operating systems. The programmer must carefully design the program in such a way that all the threads can run at the same time without interfering with each other. Programmers writing programs for multitasking operating systems can design processes that can be split up into threads. These threads may be executed simultaneously. It is always beneficial to do multitasking with threads on multiprocessor system. Even in case of single processor system, each thread is executed in turn, one after the other. A single thread does not dominate the processor, but instead is given a small amount of time to complete some or all of its tasks.

Time Sharing System

Time Sharing is extension of multi-programming where multiple jobs are executed simultaneously by the CPU. The switching between the processes occurs so frequently that its users may interact with each job in execution state. It is like a form of multi-programmed OS that operates in an interactive mode with a quick response time. The user types a request to the computer through a keyboard. The computer processes it and a response if any, is displayed on the user's terminal. A time-sharing system allows many users to simultaneously share the computer resources. Since each action or command takes a very small fraction of time, only a little CPU time is needed for each user. The CPU switches so rapidly from one user to another, that each user is given impression that he has his own computer, while actually it is one computer being shared among many users.

Real-time Systems

Real-time Systems are used in the environment where most of the input or events are accepted from the environment external to computer systems. These jobs must be processed meeting their deadlines. In real-time system meeting the deadline of job is a must. Thus, real time systems are defined as those systems in which the correctness of the systems depend not only on the logical result of computation but also on the time in which the results are produced. Real-time Operating System intends to complete the submitted job within the time limit. The job is said to have served successfully only if the job has met the deadline. Real-time systems are deployed in mission critical application, flight control, simulation, military operation where meeting the deadline is as important as job completion. Primary objective of real-time systems are, therefore, to meet the deadline. Examples of real-time operating system are Maruti II, VRTX (Virtual Real Time Executive) and HART OS (Hexagonal Architecture for Real Time Operating System). The deadlines in the real-time operating system are met by maintaining the calendar management. A resource-allocation chart for a job is prepared first before the execution of job. All the resources are made available to the job so that it completes the execution, meeting the deadline. General overview of a real-time system is presented in the following schematic:

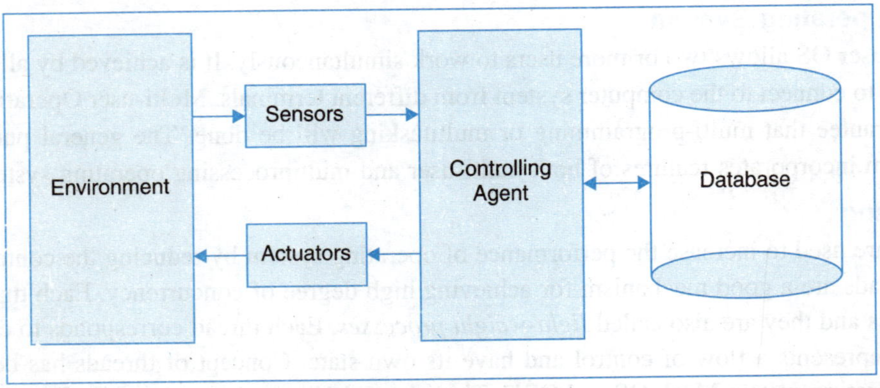

Fig. 4.3: Real-Time System

As shown in Figure 4.3, typically a real-time system consists of a controlling system and controlled system. The controlled system can also be viewed as the environment with which the computer interacts. The controlling system interacts with its environment based on the information available about the environment from various sensors. The state of the environment, as perceived by the controlling system, be consistent with the actual state of the environment. Otherwise the effects of the controlling system activities may be disastrous. Hence periodic monitoring of the environment as well as timely processing of the censored information is necessary. Timely processing of the information in real-time system is necessary because of the physical impact of the controlling system's activities upon its environments. For example, if the computer controlling a robot does not command it to stop or to run on time, the robot might collide with another object on the factory floor possibly causing serious damage.

There can be two types of the task which may be submitted to Real-Time Systems. These are called periodic and aperiodic.

- *Periodic task:* A periodic task is one that is activated at regular time intervals (T). The deadline for each activated instance may be less than, equal to, or greater than the period T. For example, a radar that tracks the flights produces data at a fixed rate.
- *Aperiodic task:* An aperiodic task is activated at unpredictable times, e.g., an object falling in front of a moving robot.

Database Operating System

Database Management System provides the set of programs for creating and processing database. Conventional database management system, e.g., Oracle, Sybase etc runs on top of the Operating System. With growing demands of heavy data processing, it has been found that some of the operating systems do not yield good performance for database management system because of incompatibility in the configurations. The database management systems performance remains under-utilised as Operating System does not provide sufficient functionality to the database implementation. Database Operating Systems are those, which are designed for supporting the function needed by database management system. Development of such operating systems from the scratch is a costly affair, therefore, the existing Operating System may be modified whenever interface to the underlying database management system is changed. Conventional operating system handles the job submitted to them by following process creation, synchronisation of process, memory handling for process and file management. The database systems are based on the concept of transaction. The transaction is a unit of atomicity. The atomicity of transaction means that either the transaction be executed fully and affects of its execution must not be reflected in database if the transaction has been aborted. It is required in the database system that they handle volume of data efficiently, provide concurrency control, to store the data temporarily in the storage when fetched from the secondary storage. All this has to be done without sacrificing the integrity of data. The Operating System designed by emphasising the database systems need is called database Operating System.

Network Operating System (NOS)

Computer Network refers to the collection of several computing machines, peripheral devices, storage units. The computer systems may communicate over computer network and shares the resources. These networks enable the computer to communicate a remote computer where the remote computer may be located at a distance of few meters to several thousand kilometres. The users of a computer system on network are able to share the software resources such as programs, databases, and program utilities. These computers may communicate the data to each other, participate in solving a problem collectively, share the resources available. A computer network installed in a very small area, e.g., a room or building is known as Local Area Network (LAN). Network operating systems provide features for controlling LAN. Network Operating System is designed and developed towards the need of computer user on network e.g. the users may transfer or copy files from one machine to another machine, and can log in to remote machines on network. A network OS may provide a shared file system and a set of security features and controls to control user access to network resources. Some typical characteristics of network operating system are as follows.

- Every computer system has its own operating system which provides an environment for a user to use that computer system as stand alone system.
- Instead of providing a whole network wide operating system which controls all the machines on the network, Network Operating System provides an environment where certain application user of one computer may interact with other computer for sharing resources. Most of the time, user works on his system and whenever he wants to use the resources available at other system, NOS allows him to do it by means of transfer of files, remote log-in etc.
- Network Operating System allows all users aware of the locations of the different files and resources on the network. Users are also allowed to transfer file from one computer to another by means of file transfer protocols.

In NOS, many operating systems provide point-to-point resource sharing, e.g., file/printer sharing similar to the services offered by full-featured network operating systems. These environments usually lack the security and access controls. Most of these systems are not fault tolerant.

Salient features of the Network Operating System (NOS) are summarised below:

- NOS allows the multiple users to share the resources available on the network.
- It also provides location transparency. It means user at one system may access the resources available. NOS provides authorisation and authentication features.
- NOS also controls and restrict access of the resources by adopting the security features like password etc. at other system without worrying for the locations of resource.
- NOS also provides some fault tolerance using clustering and back-up services.
  It includes the common services like documentation of activities on network, software and hardware inventory, replication of data and file etc.

Novell NetWare and Windows NT are popular network operating systems being used for the management of local area networks. They support one or other features of network operating system. All the network operating systems available today have their own set of functions and provide features, which may or may not exist in other NOS. Now-a-days, the NOS are using some of the standard protocol to implement the common services, e.g., TCP/IP protocol for Internet working.

Distributed Operating System

A Distributed System is defined as a collection of cooperating computer system that do not share either memory or clock. These computer systems may be geographically located. Each computer in a distributed system has its local memory and its own Operating System. Whenever the users on different computer system works, they generally realise the need of sharing the resources like data file etc and other costly resources. The distributed system allows the users to share the resources over a communication network. Distributed operating system appears to its users like a centralised operating system but it runs on multiple-independent processors. The user views the system as virtually single processor but not as a collection of distinct machines. This is known as transparency. The resource located at different computer systems are so managed that users are not even aware of where their programs are being actually run or where their files are residing. These all activities are handled by distributed operating system. The major limitation of distributed systems are:

- Absence of global clock.
- Absence of shared memory.

Major issue in the design of distributed operating system is the lack of global knowledge. These problems occur because the different computers not only have their own operating systems but also they do not share the memory and clock. In scheduling the job in distributed system, it requires to know the up-to-date status of the system resources. Other important issues in design of distributed operating system are related with the scalability, naming conventions, processes synchronisation, mutual exclusion and deadlock detection. Distributed operating systems allow the job to be executed on different processors at the same time. They also require deploying complex scheduling algorithms as compared to centralised operating system. The different computer system cooperate towards execution of a job which requires the resources available at different sites. The only method of obtaining the knowledge of other site or computer system is by exchange of messages. These messages are often time stamped and delivered at destination after arbitrary time delays. This also imposes serious restriction over the distributed operating system. Fault tolerance is another area in which distributed operating systems are different from centralised operating system. Fault tolerance on distributed system is quite stronger in the sense that most of the time, the system has the ability to recover from the failure of job, data link or malfunctioning of hardware.

We may, therefore, define distributed system as a pool of different computer systems located geographically and they do not share memory or clock. Interprocess communication among the processes running on different computer systems is established by the exchange of messages over communication channel. Advantages of distributed operating system may be summarised as below:

- ***Price/Performance Advantage***

  It has been noticed that if few less powerful computer systems are interconnected and are used as collective resources, then their computing power is enormous. Therefore, for high-end application, instead of going for costly and powerful processor like main frame computer, it is always a better option to interconnect low cost less powerful computer system. Collective computing power of these cheaper, less powerful computer system is enormous. Therefore, distributed systems clearly have a price/performance advantage over more traditional systems.

- ***Resource Sharing***

  In distributed system, a computer may request for a service or resource located at another computer system. These requests are sent in the form of messages over the communication network. This allows the different computer systems to use the hardware and software resources and the power of over all distributed system is multiple times increased.

- ***Reliability***

  The distributed operating system provides high reliability as few components of the system may fail without affecting the rest of the system. The services, files and data are still accessible even if a computer system fails. This is achieved by replication of data and services.

4.6 CASE STUDIES

4.6.1 Microsoft Products

Microsoft has a family of OS products, designed to fully utilise the range of PC hardware available in the market today, while providing a consistent user interface for end users and a programming environment for developers. Windows 3.x and Windows for Workgroups 3.x on MS-DOS are designed for mainstream portable and desktop PC platforms. Windows 95 and 98 are successors of the aforementioned products running atop the same or improved hardware configuration. Windows NT 3.x and 4.0 and Windows NT 2000 (Windows NT5) are designed for the high-end business and technical workstation platforms and Windows NT Advanced Server is designed as a server platform.

MS-DOS (Microsoft Disk Operating System)

Tim Patterson originally developed MS-DOS in 1980. From the very beginning, it was designed to be a full-fledged OS for 16-bit personal computers built around the 8086 microprocessor. Patterson originally christened it 'QDOS' for 'Quick and Dirty Operating System'. The initial versions of DOS were very simple and resembled CP/M. Work began on MS-DOS because, digital research was very slow to release a CP/M based OS to go with the new 8086 chip. Eventually they did, but by then MS-DOS was well established. In 1981, IBM (International Business Machines) released its Personal Computer (PC). At the same time, it announced that MS-DOS (renamed PC-DOS) was the OS of the choice for the new machine. Practically overnight, MS-DOS became the standard OS for virtually all 16-bit microcomputers, not just the PC. Although CP/M and MS-DOS differ significantly in detail, IBM persuaded Microsoft to create some similarities, making easier for people familiar with CP/M to move to MS-DOS. Since IBM's selection of MS-DOS, many programs originally written for CP/M have been rewritten in 16-bit versions to run under MS-DOS or PC-DOS. A great deal of new software has been written under it as well. Subsequent versions have become increasingly sophisticated as they incorporated features of minicomputer operating systems. However, DOS is still a 16-bit Operating System and does not support multiple users or multitasking.

Windows 95

It was a major release of the Microsoft Windows OS in 1995, and the successor to Windows 3.x and Windows for Workgroups 3.11. Windows 95 represented a significant advancement over its precursors, Windows 3.1 and Windows for Workgroups 3.11. It is a pre-emptive, multithread, multitasking, networking 32-bit OS with advanced file systems, running on Intel-based machines. For customers, Windows 95 presented a major step forward in functionality on mainstream desktop platforms by providing a system that is easy to use, offering responsive multitasking performance, and providing a great platform for communications. Ease of use is delivered through the Plug and Play architecture and an improved, intuitive user interface. Windows 95 is a complete, integrated protect-mode OS that does not require or use a separate version of MS-DOS. In addition to wearing a new user interface, Windows 95 also included a number of important internal improvements, implementing the Win32 API (Application Programming Interface), providing pre-emptive multitasking and multiple threads of execution for 32-bit applications, which meant that applications written specifically for this OS would run much faster.

It has essentially removed DOS as the underlying platform. It included MS-DOS 7.0, but took over from DOS completely after starting. This means, removal of many of the old DOS limitations, such as 640 KB of main memory and 8-character filenames. The communications capabilities of Windows are enhanced with integrated, high-performance networking, built-in messaging, and features such as Remote Network Access and File Synchronisation, designed for mobile and remote computer users. Windows 95 implements new working set management technologies that optimise the use of memory on low-configuration systems. Windows 95 runs most of the current applications for Windows and MS-DOS. Windows 95's new shell provides a complete set of services that is tightly integrated with the OS components. It allows full access to hardware, hence it is useful for older games. Home users prefer it, as games run unobstructed.

The Windows 95 user interface offers dramatic gains in ease of learning and ease of use for the broad range of people using PCs today. Instead of mastering different kinds of tools to work with different resources on their computers, users will be able to browse for and access all resources in a consistent fashion with a single tool. This is much easier than learning separate applications such as Program Manager, File Manager, Print Manager, Control Panel, etc. as users of Windows must do. Windows 95's smart set-up technology uses the current system settings to present an initial configuration that is familiar for the current Windows-based user. And for corporate customers and individuals who may not want to make any user interface changes initially, Windows 95 enables them to continue running their current Program Manager and File Manager configurations. A system toolbar that is always accessible makes it much easier to start and switch between full-screen tasks. The direct manipulation of data through drag-and-drop in the user interface makes working with documents easier and more intuitive. The set-up program enables customers to uninstall Windows 95, assuring customers a way to remove it if they are in any way unhappy with it, and have provided tools for system administrators to customise the configuration of Windows 95.

Windows NT

It is a robust, pre-emptive, multitasking, 32-bit OS with symmetric multiprocessor support. It is intended for use in network servers, workstations and software development machines. Windows NT Workstation 4.0 version has come a long way since its coming out in 1996, so that the mainstream desktop PCs and laptops now come with Windows NT Workstation preinstalled, and has now become a great solution for all business users, not only power users but also engineers, and developers. Windows NT 4.0 comes in two versions, as Windows NT Server, designed to act as a server in networks and Windows NT Workstation for stand-alone or client workstations. Corporations prefer this version and a lot of businesses are standardising their desktops and laptops on Windows NT workstation because it is cheaper, fast, reliable, efficient, and powerful. The Windows NT's user interface is very similar to that of Windows 3.1 and Windows 95, internally it is totally different from either of them. Windows NT ensured fully protected applications, wherein all programs are protected from each other, with virtualised hardware access. Windows NT does not allow access to hardware like UNIX. The Windows NT file system, NTFS (New Technology File System) provides lot of security and reliability.

Windows 98

The successor to Windows 95 was released in 1998. Originally it was called Memphis, and then Windows 97, but Microsoft changed the name when it realised that it was going to miss its target 1997-release date. Windows 98 offers support for a number of new technologies, including AGP (Accelerated Graphics Port), MMX (Multimedia Extensions), USB (Universal Serial Bus), DVD (Digital Video Disk) etc. Its most visible feature is the Active Desktop, which integrates the Web browser Internet Explorer, with the OS. The Microsoft Windows 98 Second Edition is downloadable from the Internet. It consists of two parts: Microsoft Internet Explorer and revised core components of the OS, called Windows 98 Service Pack 1. The only new feature that is not available for download is Internet Connection Sharing (ICS), which lets networked Windows 98 systems share a single user connection. To get ICS, one needs to buy a new CD-ROM containing the complete Second Edition. Users, who already have Internet Explorer 5 installed over an existing Windows 98 setup will see no obvious differences. The Desktop, Start Menu, and Explorer windows look the same. Windows' built-in applications look and act exactly as before. The Windows 98-Second Edition, is more stable than the original, reflecting many bug fixes in the core Windows files, but performance seems identical. The most obvious change is Internet-Connection Sharing, which adds a feature previously available in Windows 98 only through third-party networking software. When ICS is installed on a home or small-office network, all networked client computers can access the Internet through a single-host computer. The host can use any existing Internet connection. The Second Edition does smarter networking.

Windows 2000

Microsoft is continually enhancing its Windows OS product line. There is a great deal of interest in speculation about the Windows 2000 project, the technology development effort which will deliver the next major release of Windows for the mainstream desktop and portable PC. Windows 2000 is advertised as the state of the art OS that uses the latest hardware. It is supposed to be a major upgrade aimed at the OS market, which is largely dominated by the different features variants of UNIX. Windows 2000 uses a new security protocol with an encryption facility to authenticate users logging in to the network. It maintains encrypted passwords in the active directory and ensures that user connections are secure. The interface of Windows 2000 is similar to that of Windows 98, with a lot of hidden features waiting to be discovered. All Explorer windows have customisable toolbars. In the previous versions (both of Windows NT and Windows 98), you could view or hide various toolbars. In this, you have control over which buttons to view in the toolbar. For example, you can open My Computer, and add the Map network drive button in the toolbar, or add buttons necessary for Internet activity (like home page, refresh, stop, etc.). The display properties have also been changed in the new addition. You can view all the display modes and refresh rates for your display adapter. There is also a colour management option built in.

4.6.2 UNIX and Linux

UNIX is a powerful, flexible and manageable OS with good utilities, communication abilities and GUIs. The UNIX project was justified to the management, as a vehicle for document preparation—the first users of UNIX were in the Bell patent department, which used the system's document preparation software. Dennis Ritchie wrote a C compiler under UNIX, and in 1973, Thompson and Ritchie rewrote the UNIX kernel in C.

Linux is a free, powerful, UNIX-like OS. It is a 32-bit OS that runs on a variety of platforms, including Intel, SPARC, PowerPC, and DEC Alpha processors as well as multiprocessing systems. A young computer science student, Linus Torvalds, at the University of Helsinki in Finland initially created it as a hobby. He developed the original OS as a college project. When he realised that the lack of UNIX programming facilities was hampering its work, he decided to rectify it, by writing his own UNIX-like micro-kernel on a 386 machine. Linus had an interest in Minix, a small UNIX system, and decided to develop a system that exceeded the Minix standards. He began his work in 1991 when he released version 0.02, including all the source code of the software. Source code is the exact specifications by which a computer makes an executable program. With the help of literally thousands of volunteers, Linux grew dramatically. Linux is a 'user-developed' product, meaning that users around the world who ran the OS for their own use have developed many of its components and drivers. Linus worked steadily with the assistance of developers around the world, and in 1994, version 1.0 of the Linux Kernel was released. Torvalds remained the co-ordinator of the project, and determined which of several competing designs for feature implementations would make the next distribution, often combining the best of several implementations to make a tool far better than any of the original designer's intentions. The current full-featured version is 2.2, released on 25th January 1999, and the development continues. Linux is now well-supported and gaining ground as a respectable OS despite its home-grown roots. Linux also has an official mascot, the Linux Penguin, which was selected by Linus Torvalds to represent the image he associates with the Operating System he created.

The Linux OS is available at free of cost. Its source code is freely available to everyone. This however, does not mean that Linux and its various distributions are free; companies and developers may charge money as long as the source code remains available. Thereby, a number of companies have developed their own 'distribution' of Linux, so there are many different Linux distributions, or versions available in the market. A 'distribution' is the compiled Linux source code, usually combined with extra features and software, and some are equipped towards specific types of computer systems. You can download Linux from the Web. Some distributions are available for download at no charge while others are available at affordable prices on CD-ROM from Linux retailers world-wide, the top commercial Linux vendors today being Caldera and Red Hat. Other options include purchasing Linux pre-installed on a computer, or purchasing a book or magazine containing a complimentary CD-ROM. You can purchase a book that includes a CD-ROM with the entire OS. In India, PC-Quest magazine has recently issued several versions of Linux Red Hat distributions in its CD-ROMs. Each distribution has its own purpose, and a number of factors should go into deciding which distribution is best for each user. Some distributions are better suited to home users, others are excellent for commercial settings. Some are better suited for Intel or Macintosh PCs, other are excellent for use on high-performance computers. The only problem with this approach is that drivers and fixes are only available if some user decides to develop them. Support is another issue since you cannot call any particular vendor. Anyone that plans to use this OS for production use should first make sure that applications run on the OS and that appropriate drivers are available to support hardware and software.

4.7 FUTURE TRENDS

A number of clear trends are emerging which will point the way the future Operating Systems will be designed. These are:

- Multiprocessing feature will be much more common because of development of VLSI (Very Large Scale Integration) chips and the decline in the cost of hardware.
- Micro-code will support all the functions of Operating System integrated into it, currently performed by software, therefore, the execution will be faster.
- The trend is towards distributed control among the localised processors in place of centralised system. Therefore, the use of distributed Operating System will increase.
- The concurrency is becoming an important feature of programming language. Hardware and Operating Systems are being designed to execute concurrent programs more efficiently.
- Developments in software engineering will result in Operating Systems that will be easily maintainable, more reliable and simpler.
- Lots of developments are taking place in computer networking. The data transmission rate is also increasing. Therefore, the use of networking operating systems will also increase.
- Practically, all Operating Systems (especially desktop operating systems) will be supporting multimedia (video and graphics) applications in the near future.

OBJECTIVE TYPE QUESTIONS

Multiple Choice

1. Operating System serves as interface between
   (a) Hardware and software (b) Software and human
   (c) Hardware and human (d) Human and human
2. Which of the following is not a function of Operating System
   (a) Loading an application program (b) Memory allocation
   (c) Scheduling of job (d) Writing a program
3. Which of the following is not an Operating System?
   (a) UNIX (b) PROLOG (c) Windows 98 (d) Linux
4. Which of the following OS is fully supported by Graphical User Interface?
   (a) UNIX (b) PROLOG (c) Windows 98 (d) Linux
5. Which of the following is an advantage of Distributed Operating System?
   (a) Price/Performance (b) Reliability (c) Availability (d) All of above

6. Which of the following Operating System is not a member of Microsoft family?
   (a) DOS (b) Windows (c) UNIX (d) None of above
7. Major limitation of Distributed Systems are
   (a) Absence of global clock (b) Absence of shared memory
   (b) None (d) Both
8. Which of the following is not a Real-Time Operating System?
   (a) Windows (b) HARTOS (c) MARUTI (d) VRTX
9. In Real-Time Operating System, a job must
   (a) Meet deadlines (b) Not complete
   (c) Not interact with other jobs (d) All of above
10. Multiple process execution of several processes at a time is characteristic of
   (a) Multi-programming OS (b) NOS
   (c) DOS (d) Real time OS

Answers

1-c, 2-d, 3-b, 4-c, 5-d, 6-c, 7-d, 8-a, 9-a, 10-a.

State True or False

1. Operating System allows users to run application programs. [True] [False]
2. Principal concern of designing real-time Operating System is meeting the job deadlines. [True] [False]
3. Concurrent execution of two or more programs is not supported by operating systems. [True] [False]
4. Distributed Operating System supports management of resources located at different sites. [True] [False]
5. Linux OS is first known OS which is available for free of cost. [True] [False]
6. Microsoft Disk Operating System was based on Graphical User Interface. [True] [False]
7. In Batch operating system all resources are made available to a job under execution. [True] [False]
8. Threads are also known as light-weight processes. [True] [False]
9. Principle concern behind development of Database Operating System is concept of transactions. [True] [False]
10. Time sharing system allows various processes to share the CPU on rotation basis. [True] [False]

Answers

1-True, 2-True, 3-False, 4-True, 5-True, 6-False, 7-True, 8-True, 9-True, 10-True.

SELECTED EXERCISES

1. What do you mean by Operating System?
2. What are the functions of an Operating System? How it provides easy access of hardware to user?
3. Explain the hierarchy of application programs and operating system? What do you mean by the statement that all application programs run on top of the Operating System?
4. Explain the functions of Operating System in brief.
5. What do you mean by the Command Interpreter? How it executes the command entered by the user?
6. What do you mean by the management of resources in Operating System? Explain the different type of resources managed by the operating system.
7. What do you mean by the memory management in Operating System? Explain the issues in memory management.

8. What is file management? Explain how the data from the secondary memory are brought to the processor for execution?
9. Explain the salient features of Batch Operating System?
10. What is Time-Sharing System?
11. What do you mean by multiprogramming? Explain the term degree of multiprogramming? Explain how multiprogramming affects throughput?
12. Explain in brief, how turn-around time is affected in Batch Operating System?
13. What is the difference between Multiprogramming Operating System and Multitasking Operating System? What are the similarities in multiprogramming and multitasking Operating System?
14. What are threads? Explain the advantages of Multithreading Operating Systems?
15. Explain Real Time System?
16. What are the two main functions of Operating Systems? Describe them in detail?
17. Give type of Operating Systems came into existence. Describe the most popular Operating Systems that are in wide use.
18. What are multiprocessing operating system? Explain weather multi-programming may be done on uni/ single processor system? If yes, then justify your answer.
19. What do you mean by Multiuser Operating System? List any two Multiuser Operating System.
20. Describe the components of any Operating System along with their functions?
21. Enlist the functions of an Operating System?
22. Give brief details on how Operating System manages various component of a computer?
23. Give a classification of Operating Systems and indicate their merit and demerits, if they are used?
24. What are the difference between Network Operating System and Distributed Operating System?
25. Discuss the role of Command Interpreter in brief.
26. Write a short note on the Process Management in Operating System.
27. Discuss the salient features of Controlled Program for Microcomputers (CP/M).
28. What do you mean by time sharing operating system? Explain how the time sharing improves the performance of Operating System.
29. What are the main advantages of Distributed System? Explain in brief, why Distributed System offer better price/performance ratio?
30. Draw a comparative chart to explain the gradual improvement in the Windows product of Microsoft.
31. What are real-time systems? Under what circumstances it is necessary to meet the deadline of job?
32. What do you mean by periodic and aperiodic jobs?
33. Write a short note on Operating System of Microsoft family.
34. How Window NT is different from Windows 98?
35. List the important features of MAC OS.
36. How LINUX is different from UNIX?
37. Discuss the Operating System product of Sun Microsystems.

5

DIGITAL FUNDAMENTALS

Contents

5 DIGITAL FUNDAMENTALS

The basic building block of any digital computer is logic gates. All digital devices are logical in their operation. Digital logic is the fundamental principle used by digital computers to represent the information and processing inside the computer. Digital logic uses two values 0 and 1 and these values may be represented in the digital electronic system as Low Voltage High Voltage. We have discussed the number system in previous chapters and in this chapter we will discuss the basic digital devices like Gate, Flip Flops, Registers, Counters and Boolean algebra.

5.1 BOOLEAN ALGEBRA

Named after the famous mathematician George Boole (1850), Boolean Algebra found its application in digital computers during the 1930s. A digital computer consists of digital components and devices which work logically. In a digital system, the information is represented by a combination of two digits 0 and 1 and Boolean Algebra also deals with two values 0 and 1.

The Boolean functions are represented as a combination of three basic operation called NOT, AND and OR operation. It may be understood as a combination of relays as shown below:

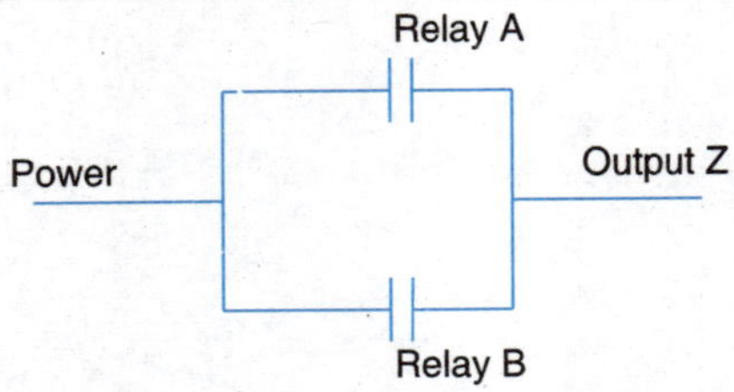

Fig. 5.1 A: OR Operation

Fig. 5.1 B: AND Operation

The relay operates by an input signal A and B as shown in Figure 5.1. Figure 5.1A shows the logical OR operation. The output Z is high only if either relay A or relay B operates, (either A = 1 or B = 1). If both A and B are non operated (A = 0 and B = 0), the output would be low (no power). Similarly, to get a high output as shown in Figure 5.1B, both relays must operate. These basic operations are captured and well defined by Boolean Algebra.

5.1.1 Boolean Postulates

A mathematical system consisting of a set of variables (Boolean variables) together with binary operations (AND, OR) is called Boolean Algebra if and only if the following postulates hold. The variables are called Boolean when they can assume one of the values from set (0,1).

1. Operation AND (.) and (OR) (+) are commutative
   a. $A + B = B + A$
   b. $A.B = B.A$
2. Each operation is distributive over the other
   a. $A.(B + C) = (A.B) + (A.C)$
   b. $A + (B.C) = (A + B) . (A + C)$
3. Operation of a Boolean variable A with values 0 and 1 is defined as
   $A + 0 = A$
   $A.1 = A$
4. For every Boolean variable A, there exists complementary element $\overline{A}$ such that
   a. $A.\overline{A} = 0$
   b. $A + \overline{A} = 1$
   c. $\overline{A} = A$

The A and B are Boolean variables and the values assigned to them are either 0 or 1. Based on the Boolean postulates, the following operations are valid:

$1 = 0$	$0 + 0 = 0$	$0.0 = 0$
$0 = 1$	$0 + 1 = 1$	$0.1 = 0$
	$1 + 0 = 1$	$1.0 = 0$
	$1 + 1 = 1$	$1.1 = 1$
	$0 + 0 = 0$	$0.0 = 0$

$A + 0 = A$	$A + 1 = 1$	$A + \overline{A} = 1$	$A + B = B + A$
$A.0 = A$	$A.1 = A$	$A + A = A$	$A.B = B.A$

5.1.2 Demorgans Theorem

Following are two theorem proved by Demorgan

$$\overline{A + B} = \overline{A}.\overline{B} \quad ...(1)$$

$$\overline{A.B} = \overline{A} + \overline{B} \quad ...(2)$$

5.1.3 Boolean Function

The prepositions NOT, AND, OR may be combined with the Boolean variable to form Boolean Expression. A Boolean Function f (A, B, C) is combination of Boolean variables A, B and C combined by preposition operations. Some of the examples of Boolean Function are as follows.

$$F(A,B) = A + \overline{B} \quad ...(1)$$

$$F(A, B, C) = \overline{A} + B.C + A.\overline{B} \quad ...(2)$$

5.1.4 Truth Table

The truth table of a Boolean function shows the output for all possible combinations of input. This table is also known as the *characteristic table*. The table contains all possible combinations of input which may be assigned to Boolean variables and the corresponding output or value of the function.

Example 1

Draw the truth table for the following Boolean function:

$$F(A, B, C) = \overline{A} + B.C + A.\overline{B}$$

The truth table for the expression shown above is presented in Table 5.1. The table contains a total of eight rows (Total eight distinct input). For all possible combinations of the input, the output of the function is shown in the table.

Table 5.1

A	B	C	A´	B.C	A.B´	F(A, B, C)
0	0	0	1	0	0	1
0	0	1	1	0	0	1
0	1	0	1	0	0	1
0	1	1	1	1	0	1
1	0	0	0	0	1	1
1	0	1	0	0	1	1
1	1	0	0	0	0	0
1	1	1	0	1	0	1

Example 2

Draw the truth table for the following Boolean Expression:

$$F(A, B, C) = A + \overline{B}.C$$

The truth table for the given expression is shown below (Table 5.2).

Table 5.2

A	B	C	F(A, B, C)
0	0	0	0
0	0	1	1
0	1	0	0
0	1	1	0
1	0	0	1
1	0	1	1
1	1	0	1
1	1	1	1

5.2 LOGIC GATES

The fundamental units for performing digital operations are called logic gates. These gates allow the input signal to be processed in logical ways. There are three basic gates called NOT, AND and OR. Other gates are NAND, NOR, EX-OR (Exclusive OR), EX NOR (Exclusive NOR). Their characteristic table or truth table defines the characteristic of the gates.

5.2.1 NOT Gate

The NOT gate is also known as Inverter. It has one input and one output line. Status of the signal at input (High or Low) is inverted by the NOT gate. Figure 5.2 shows the representation of the NOT gate.

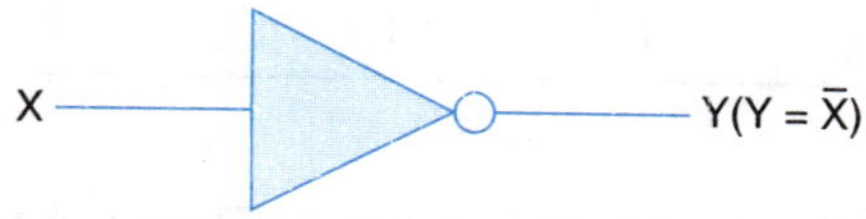

Fig. 5.2

The characteristic table of NOT gate is shown below (Table 5.3).

Table 5.3

X	Y
0	1
1	0

5.2.2 OR Gate

There may be two or more than two input signals at the OR gate. An n-input OR gate takes n input signals and produces one output according to the following Boolean expression:

$$Y \text{ (output)} = X1 + X2 + X3 \text{ .... } + Xn$$

Here X1, X2, X3, ..., Xn are the input signals. If any of the input signals is high, the output of n-input OR gate will be high. The symbolic diagrams of 2-input OR gate is shown in Figure 5.3.

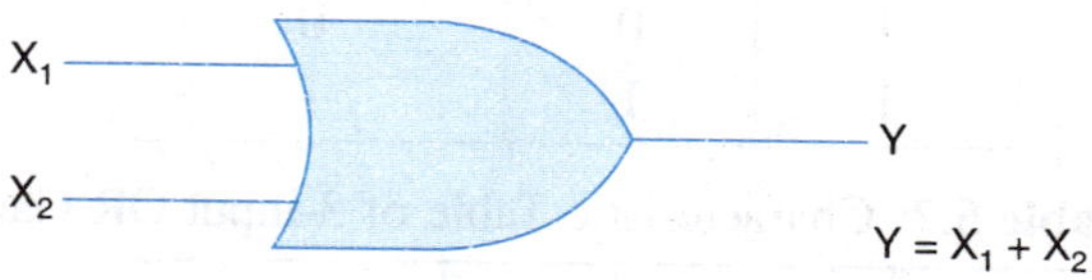

Fig. 5.3

The characteristic table of 2-input OR gate and 3-input OR gate are shown in Table 5.4 and Table 5.5.

Table 5.4: Characteristic Table of 2-input OR Gate

A	B	A OR B
0	0	0
0	0	1
0	1	0
0	1	0

Table 5.5: Characteristic Table of 3-input OR Gate

A	B	C	Z = A + B + C
0	0	0	0
0	0	1	1
0	1	0	1
0	1	1	1
1	0	0	1
1	0	1	1
1	1	0	1
1	1	1	1

5.2.3 AND Gate

There may be two or more than two input signals at the AND gate. An n-input AND gate takes n-input signals and produces one output according to the following Boolean expression.

Y(Output) = X1.X2.X3. ....Xn

Here X1, X2, X3, ..., Xn are the input signals. If any of the input signals is low, the output of n-input AND gate will be low. The symbolic diagram of 2-input AND gate is shown in Figure 5.4.

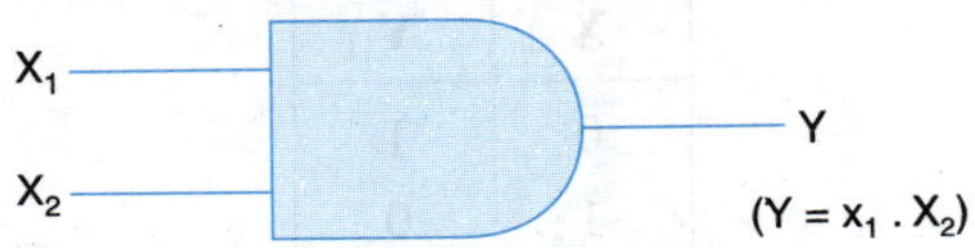

Fig. 5.4

The characteristic table of 2-input AND gate and 3-input AND gate are shown below:

Table 5.6: Characteristic Table of 2-input OR Gate

A	B	A AND B
0	0	0
0	1	0
1	0	0
1	1	1

Table 5.7: Characteristic Table of 3-input OR Gate

A	B	C	Z = A.B.C
0	0	0	0
0	0	1	0
0	1	0	0
0	1	1	0
1	0	0	0
1	0	1	0
1	1	0	0
1	1	1	1

5.2.4 NAND Gate

A NAND gate is functionally equivalent to combinations of AND and NOT gate in series. It may be represented as shown below:

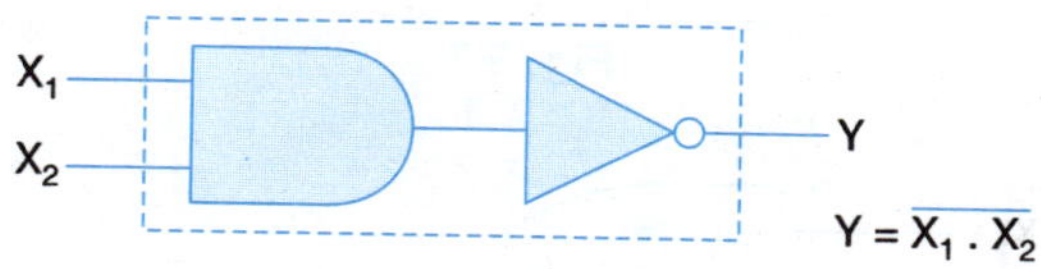

Fig. 5.5

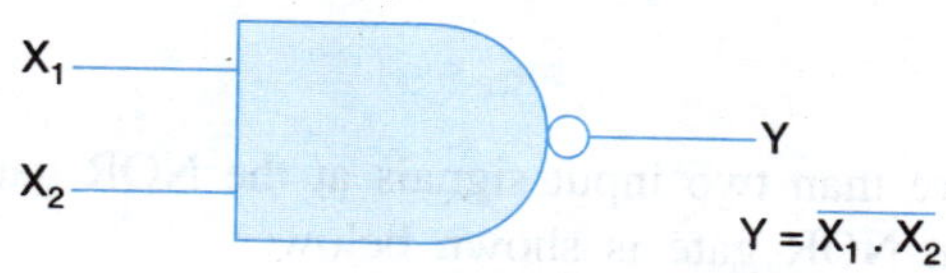

Fig. 5.6

There may be two or more than two input signals at the NAND gate. The characteristic table of 2-input NAND gate and 3-input NAND gate is shown below:

Table 5.8: Characteristic Table of 2-input NAND Gate

A	B	$Z = \overline{A.B}$
0	0	1
0	1	1
1	0	1
1	1	0

Table 5.9: Characteristic Table of 3-input NAND Gate

A	B	C	$Z = \overline{(A.B.C)}$
0	0	0	1
0	0	1	1
0	1	0	1
0	1	1	1
1	0	0	1
1	0	1	1
1	1	0	1
1	1	1	0

5.2.5 NOR Gate

A NOR gate is functionally equivalent to combinations of OR and NOR gate in series. It may be represented as shown in Figure 5.7.

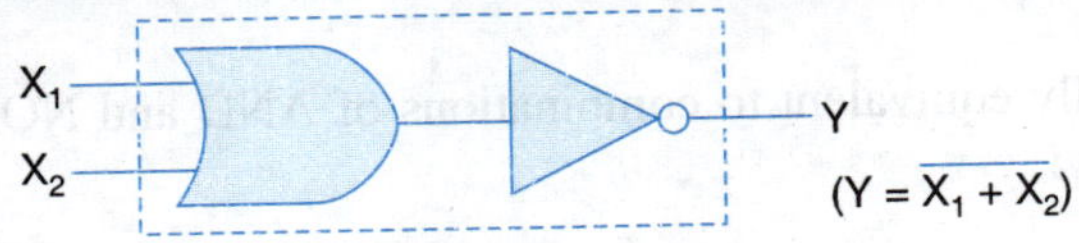

Fig. 5.7

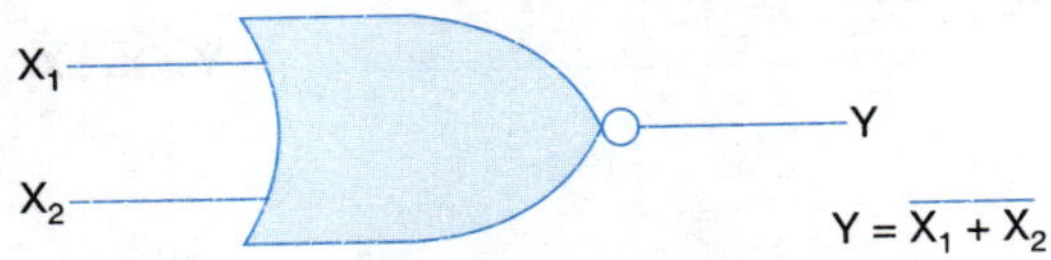

Fig. 5.8

There may be two or more than two input signals at the NOR gate. The characteristic table of 2-input NOR gate and 3-input NOR gate is shown below:

Table 5.10: Characteristic Table of 2-input NOR Gate

A	B	$Z = \overline{A + B}$
0	0	1
0	1	0
1	0	0
1	1	0

Table 5.11: Characteristic Table of 3-input NOR Gate

A	B	C	$Z = \overline{(A + B + C)}$
0	0	0	1
0	0	1	0
0	1	0	0
0	1	1	0
1	0	0	0
1	0	1	0
1	1	0	0
1	1	1	0

5.2.6 EX-OR (Exclusive OR) Gate

The EX-OR gate is functionally represented shown in Figure 5.9.

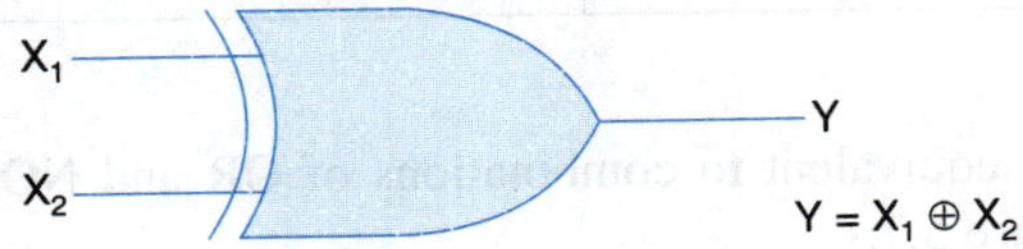

Fig. 5.9

As shown in the figure, the output of the EX-OR gate is high if the input lines are at different levels. If the input lines are at the same level, the output of EX-OR gate is low. The characteristic table of EX-OR gate is shown below (Table 5.12).

Table 5.12

A	B	Z (Output of EX-OR Gate)
0	0	0
0	1	1
1	0	1
1	1	0

The EX-OR operation may be represented as

$$Z = A \oplus B = \overline{A}.B + A.\overline{B}$$

5.2.7 Ex-NOR (Exclusive NOR) Gate

The EX-NOR gate is functionally represented as in Figure 5.10.

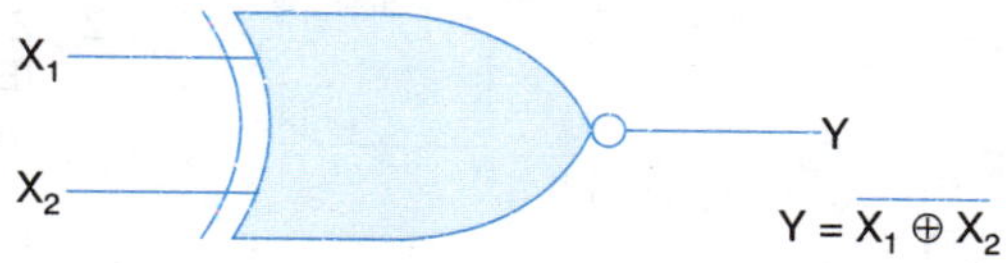

Fig. 5.10

As shown in the figure, the output of the EX-NOR gate is low if the input lines are at different levels. If the input lines are at the same level, the output of EX-NOR gate is high. The characteristic table of EX-NOR gate is shown in Table 5.13.

Table 5.13

A	B	Z (Output of EX NOR Gate)
0	0	1
0	1	0
1	0	0
1	1	1

The EX-OR operation may be represented as

$$Z = \overline{A \oplus B} = A.B.+\overline{A}.\overline{B}$$

5.2.8 Universal Gates

The NAND and NOR gate are considered as universal gates because all of the gates may be realized using these two gates. They are used for fabrication of Integrated Chips and require less power consumption. The realization of various gates using the NAND gates is shown in Figure 5.11.

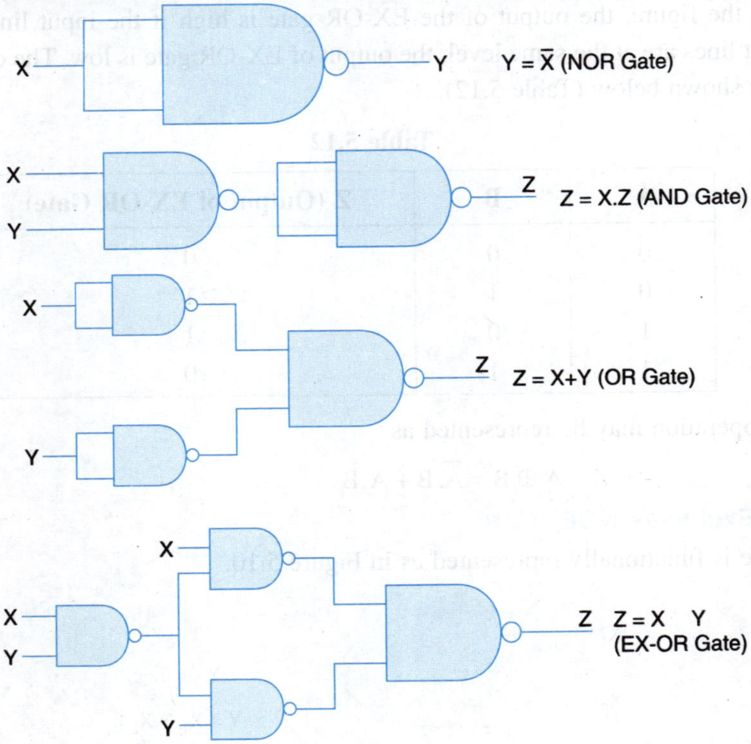

Fig. 5.11

5.3 REPRESENTATION OF BOOLEAN EXPRESSION AS DIGITAL CIRCUIT

As mentioned in the previous sections, the Boolean operations Complement, AND (.), OR (+) may be represented by the NOR, AND and OR gate, respectively. Any Boolean expression may be converted to equivalent Digital Circuit consisting of gates. Characteristic table of the digital circuit will be the same as that of characteristic table for Boolean expression. Consider the following example:

Example

Obtain digital circuit for the following expression:

$$Z = A + B.\overline{C}$$

The digital circuit for the expression is shown in Figure 5.12.

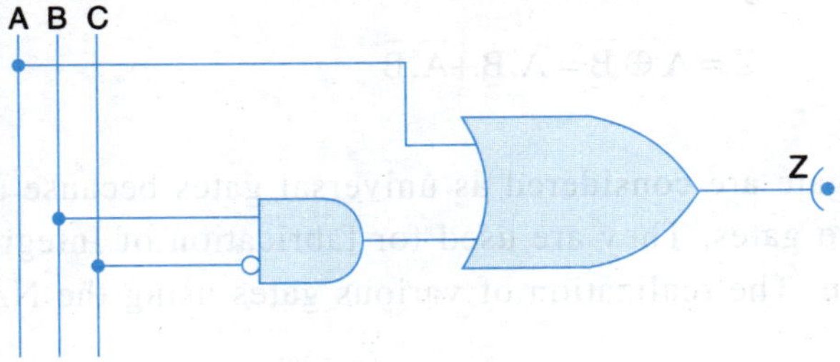

Fig. 5.12

Example

Obtain the digital circuit for the following expression:

$$Z = A.B + B.\overline{(A + C)}$$

The digital circuit for the expression is shown below (Figure 5.13).

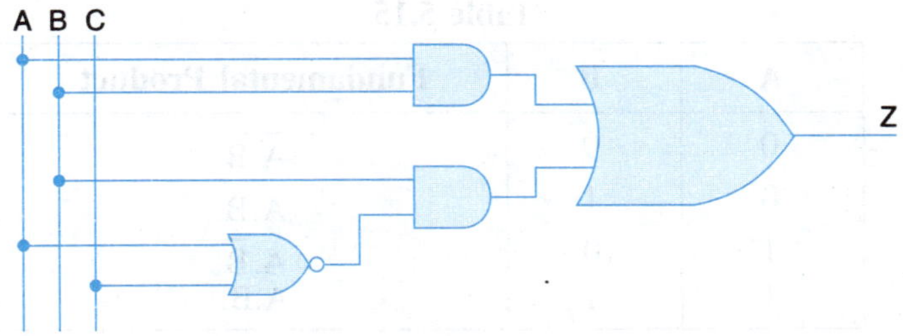

Fig. 5.13

5.4 SUM OF PRODUCTS

The digital design starts with the construction of the characteristic table for an expression. The characteristic table contains the output values (0 or 1) corresponding to all possible combinations of input. The characteristic table may be converted to the equivalent digital circuit. The sum of product (SOP) is used to represent the expression and is obtained from the characteristic table.

Example

Covert the following expression into sum of product form:

$$Z = A.B + B.\overline{(A + C)}$$
$$= A.B(C + \overline{C}) + B.(\overline{A}.\overline{C})$$
$$= A.B.C + A.B.\overline{C} + \overline{A}.B.\overline{C}$$

The expression has been represented in Fundamental products. It may be verified by constructing the characteristic table for the expression of the example (Table 5.14).

Table 5.14

A	B	C	$Z = A.B + B.\overline{(A + C)}$
0	0	0	0
0	0	1	0
0	1	0	1
0	1	1	0
1	0	0	0
1	0	1	0
1	1	0	1
1	1	1	1

As shown in Table 5.9, the functions output is high (1) at three input values for A, B, C. These are (0, 1, 0), (1, 1, 0) and (1, 1, 1). Any entry in the characteristic table represents the fundamental product. The input set (0, 1, 0) produces high (1) at output, therefore, the first term to be included will be

$\overline{A'}.B.\overline{C'}$. Similarly other terms will be $A.B.\overline{C'}$ and A.B.C. Therefore, if the expression needs to be converted into the sum of fundamental products, collect the fundamental products for those input where the output is high. The fundamental product for the Two Variables and Three variables are shown below in tables 5.15 and 5.16 respectively.

Table 5.15

A	B	Fundamental Product
0	0	$\overline{A}.\overline{B}$
0	1	$\overline{A}.B$
1	0	$A.\overline{B}$
1	1	A.B.

Table 5.16

A	B	C	Fundamental Product
0	0	0	$\overline{A}.\overline{B}.\overline{C}$
0	0	1	$\overline{A}.\overline{B}.C$
0	1	0	$\overline{A}.B.\overline{C}$
0	1	1	$\overline{A}.B.C$
1	0	0	$A.\overline{B}.\overline{C}$
1	0	1	$A.\overline{B}.C$
1	1	0	$A.B.\overline{C}$
1	1	1	A.B.C

Minterm

An expression may also be written in terms of Minterms. Consider the following expression written as minterm:

F(A, B, C) = {m2, m6, m7} or {2, 6, 7}

Both of the representation for the minterms are used. Here minterm m2 represents the input combination where the value of function is high, similarly m6 and m7 also represent the input combinations where the value of function is high (1). Minterms and function value for the expression F(ABC) = {2, 6, 7} are shown in Table 5.17.

Table 5.17

A	B	C	Minterms	Z = {2, 6, 7}
0	0	0	m0	0
0	0	1	m1	0
0	1	0	m2	1
0	1	1	m3	0
1	0	0	m4	0
1	0	1	m5	0
1	1	0	m6	1
1	1	1	m7	1

Table 5.17 shows the respective minterms for three variable expression. A set of minterms represents the function in such a way that wherever input conditions correspond to minterms, the output of the function is high (1).

5.5 FLIP FLOPS

These are basic memory elements capable of storing a bit. A Flip Flop is a bistable device which remains in one of two states. The state of the flip flop is changed by the appropriate excitation at the input. The states of a flip flop are called SET and RESET. Since the flip flop remains in one of the states until an approrpiate excitation is applied at input, this behaviour of the flip flops is captured in such a way that one state represents storage of bit 1 and another state the storage of bit 0. The behaviour of a flip flop is represented by two types of tables called Characteristic and Excitation Table. The characteristic table shows the possible input signal and cross pending output. The excitation table of a flip flop shows what excitations are required at the input to get the desired changes. The examples of flip flops are D, RS, JK and T flip flop. We will present the behaviour and functional circuit for these flip flops. All of the flip flop are built around the basic storage element called Latches or RS Latches. There are two types of latches possible called NOR latch and NAND latch. The NOR latch is built around the NOR gates and NAND latch uses NAND gates.

5.5.1 NOR Latch

The NOR latch is shown in Figure 5.14.

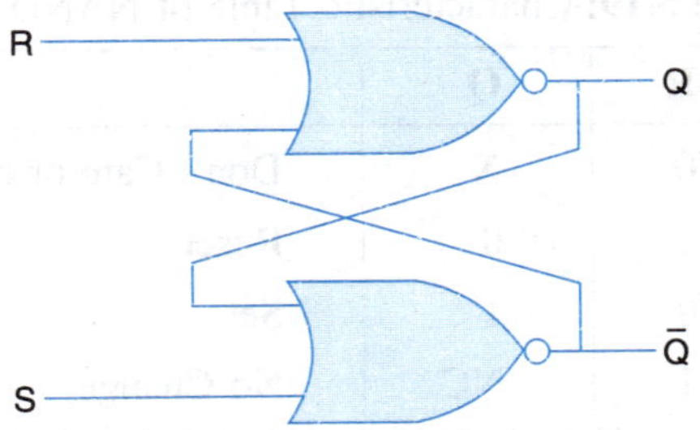

Fig. 5.14

As shown in the figure, the NOR latch has two input lines called R and S. The output has two lines called Q and $\overline{Q}$. When the output line Q is at high level, it is said to have stored a bit '1' and this state is called the SET state. The RESET state is one where the status of output line Q is low (0). The characteristic of this latch is shown in Table 5.18.

Table 5.18: Characteristic Table of NOR Latch

S	R	Q	
0	0	NC	No Change in the state
0	1	0	Reset
1	0	1	Set
1	1	X	Don't Care or Not Allowed

As shown in the table, at the first line when S = 0, R = 0 is applied, there appears no change in the state of the latch. If the Q is high, it will remain high and if it is low, then it will remain low.

The second row, when S = 0, R = 1 is applied at input, the latch is Reseted. This means the status of Q shall be 0. When S = 1, R = 0 is applied, the flip flop enters into SET state and stores the bit '1' at output line Q. The S = 1, R = 1 condition is called Don't Care or Not Allowed state. When both the excitations R and S are placed at high level, the state becomes unstable. This situation is also called Race condition. The flip flop are so designed that this situation is never allowed to occur.

5.5.2 NAND Latch

The NAND latch is shown in Figure 5.15.

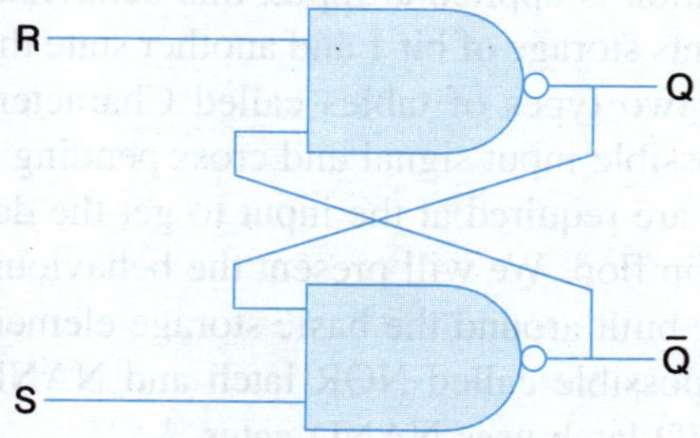

Fig. 5.15: Nand Latch

The characteristic table of NAND latch is shown in Table 5.19

Table 5.19: Characteristic Table of NAND Latch

S	R	Q	
0	0	X	Don't Care or Not Allowed
0	1	0	Reset
1	0	1	Set
1	1	NC	No Change

In the NAND latch, the only difference is that S = 0, R = 0 excitation is not allowed. This excitation forces the latch to enter in an unstable condition. The input S = 1, R = 1 causes no change at the output line Q. If it is at level high, it continues to remain at level high.

5.5.3 SR Flip Flop

The schematic of a Clocked SR flip flop is shown in Figure 5.16.

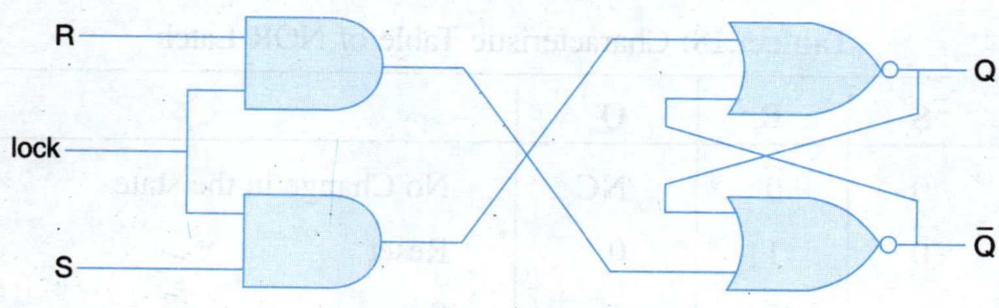

Fig. 5.16: Clocked SR FF

The latches are edge-triggered devices. The state of the latches reflect changes at the rising or falling edge of the signal. The disadvantage of this is that a short spike may change the state of the latch. This is the main reason for using an input conditioning circuit before the latch. As shown in Figure 5.16, SR input are conditioned and are loaded with the clock. The changes at SR lines are allowed to pass when the clock is high.

The following is the characteristic table of SR flip flop:

Table 5.20: Characteristic Table of SR Flip Flop

S	R	Q	
0	0	NC	No Change in the state
0	1	0	Reset
1	0	1	Set
1	1	X	Don't Care or Not Allowed

The changes are not effective when the clock is low. The SR flip flop will respond as per the characteristic table shown above only when the clock is high. All of the operations in the microprocessor are synchronized with the system clock, therefore the system clock is used to load the changes to the flip flop.

The general schematic of the SR flip flop is shown below in Figure 5.17.

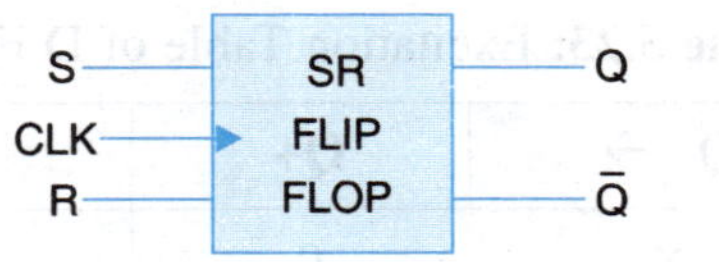

Fig. 5.17: Schematic of SR Flip Flop.

The excitation table of the SR flip flop is shown in Table 5.21.

Table 5.21: Excitation Table

Q →	Q +	S	R
0	0	0	X
0	1	1	X
1	0	0	1
1	1	X	0

5.5.4 D Flip Flop

The schematic of Clock D flip flop is shown below (Figure 5.18).

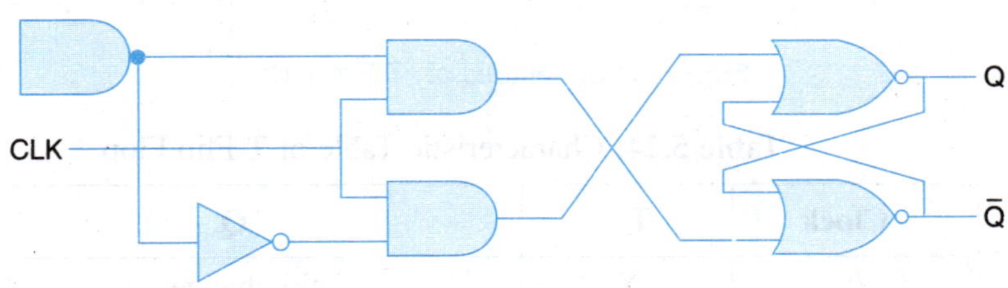

(a)

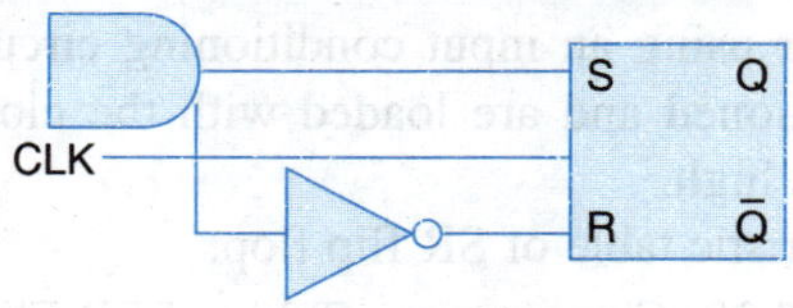

(b)

Fig. 5.18: Schematic of Clocked D Flip Flop

The characteristic table of D flip flop is given in Table 5.22.

Table 5.22: Characteristic Table of D Flip Flop

Clock	D	Q
0	×	No Change
1	1	1
1	0	0

It may be noted that the clocked D flip-flop stores the bit which appears on input line 'D'. Change in the input is allowed only when the clock is high. The excitation table of D flip flop is shown below:

Table 5.23: Excitation Table of D Flip Flop

Q →	Q+	D
X	0	0
X	1	1

As shown in Table 5.23, the input required to change the state from X to 0 is low at D and input required to change the state from X to 1 is high at D.

5.5.5 T-Flip Flop

T-Flip Flop, also known as Toggle Flip Flop, toggles the state as the input signal with clock. The schematic of T flip flop is shown in Figure 5.19.

Fig. 5.19: Schematic of T Flip Flop

Table 5.24: Characteristic Table of T Flip Flop

Clock	T	Q
0	X	No change
1	0	No change
1	1	State changes 1→0, 0→1

Table 5.25: Excitation Table of T Flip Flop

Q →	Q+	T
0	0	0
0	1	1
1	0	1
1	1	1

The T flip flop toggles the state when input 'high' is applied at T input line and the clock is high. If 'Q' is at level low, it changes to high and if it is at the high state, then it changes to the low state.

5.5.6 JK Flip Flop

This removes the drawback of SR flip flop. Whenever excitation S = 1, R = 1 is applied to SR flip flop, it enters into the race condition and this input is considered as undesirable. The JK flip flop works similarly as SR flip flop but when J = 1, K = 1 excitation is applied, the JK flip flop changes the state or the next state is the complement of the previous one. If the level of Q line before applying J = 1, K = 1 input is low, it is converted to high and if it is high, then it is converted to low. The JK flip flop may be constructed over SR flip flop. The schematic diagram, Characteristic table and Excitation table for JK flip flop are shown below:

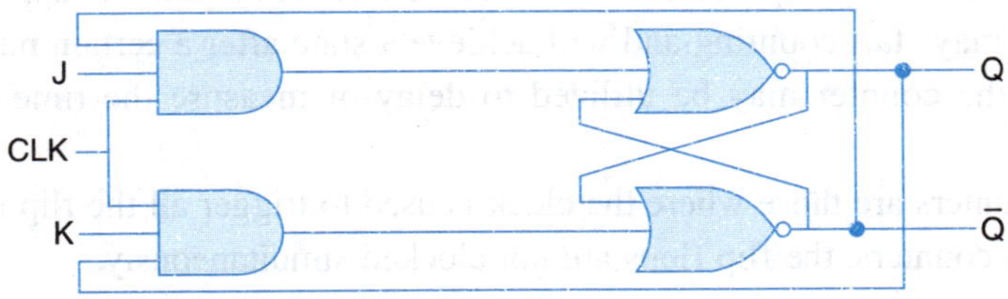

Fig. 5.20: Schematic of JK Flip Flop

Table 5.26: Characteristic Table of JK Flip Flop

Clock	J	K	Q
0	X	X	No Change
1	0	0	No Change
1	0	1	0
1	1	0	1
1	1	1	Toggle

Table 5.27: Excitation Table of JK Flip Flop

Q →	Q+	J	K
0	0	0	X
0	1	1	X
1	0	X	1
1	1	X	0

5.6 SEQUENTIAL CIRCUIT vs COMBINATIONAL CIRCUIT

Sequential circuits are digital circuits containing the memory elements such as flip flops. The Combinational circuit does not contain the memory element. The Sequential circuits may be defined as follows:

$$Z\text{ (Output)} = f\text{ (Input, Current State)} \quad \text{...(1)}$$

In the Combinational Circuit, the

$$Z\text{ (Output)} = f\text{ (Input)} \quad \text{...(2)}$$

Output of the sequential circuits depends on the external excitation to the circuit as well as on the present state of the system. In the Combinational circuits, the output of the cirucuit is dependent on the input to the system. Registers, counters are examples of sequential Circuits.

5.7 COUNTERS

Counters are sequential circuits, consisting of flip flops. The major functions of counters are to count the number of pulses at the input line. Counters are also used to measure the time and synchronize several activities inside the microprocessor. If a specific frequency pulse is applied to the input of a counter, the counter may start counting and will achieve a state after a certain number of counts. The time delay used in the counter may be utilized to delay or measure the time interval for another activity.

Synchronous counters are those where the clock is used to trigger all the flip flops simultaneously, but in Asynchronous counters, the flip flops are not clocked simultaneously.

5.7.1 Ripple Counters

Ripple counters change the state sequentially from one state to another at each clock pulse. The state diagram for 3-bit ripple counter is shown below:

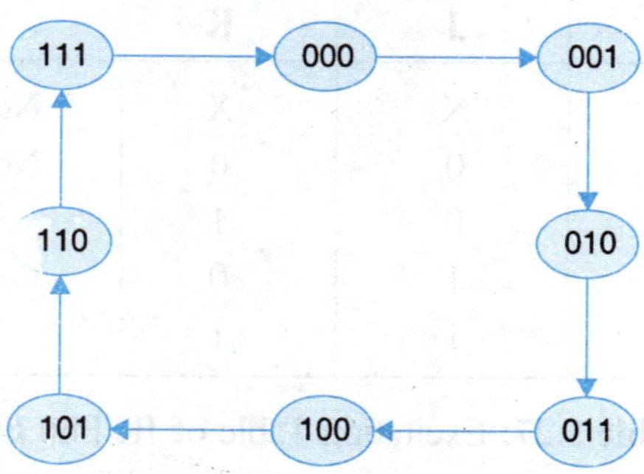

Fig. 5.21: State Diagram

5.7.2 Mod-10 Counter/Decade Counter

The mod-on counter contains total n states which are changed to the next one on every clock pulse. A Mod-10 counter has total 10 states, therefore Mod-10 counter is also called decade counter. State diagram and state table of decade counter is shown below:

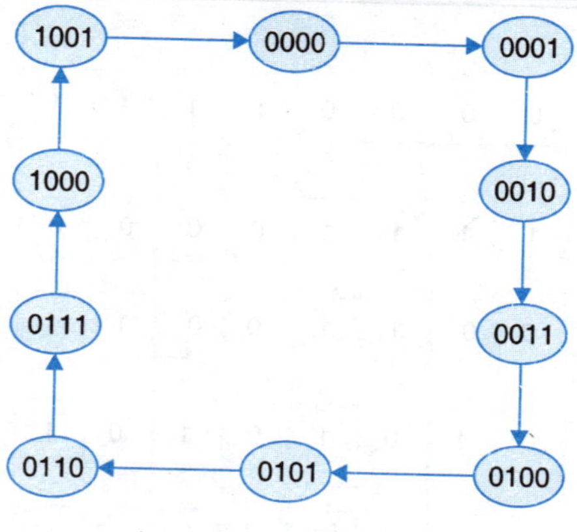

Fig. 5.22

Characteristic Table of Decade Counters

Table 5.28

Q_3	Q_2	Q_1	Q_0	Q_{3+}	Q_{2+}	Q_+	Q_{0+}
0	0	0	0	0	0	0	1
0	0	0	1	0	0	1	0
0	0	1	0	0	0	1	1
0	0	1	1	0	1	0	0
0	1	0	0	0	1	0	1
0	1	0	1	0	1	1	0
0	1	1	0	0	1	1	1
0	1	1	1	1	0	0	0
1	0	0	0	1	0	0	1
1	0	0	1	0	0	0	0

Digital circuit for four stage ripple counter (mod-16) is shown below:

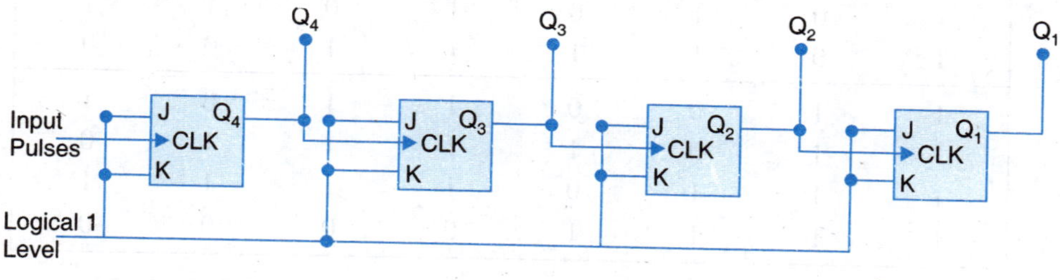

Fig. 5.23

As shown in the figure, the circuit is composed of four JK flip flop which change their state (Q4, Q3, Q2, Q1) at every input pulse applied to the clock input of the first JK flip flop. The changes state as per the following timing diagram:

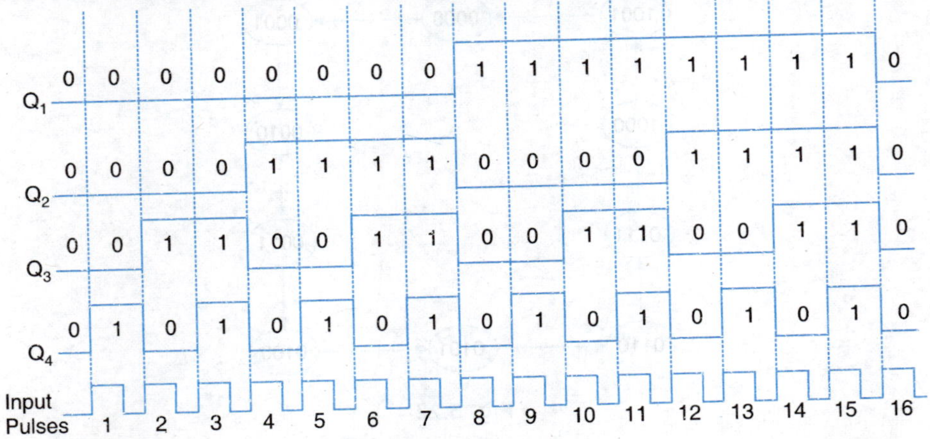

Fig. 5.24

Characteristic Table for Mod-16 ripple counter is shown below:

Table 5.29: Characteristic Table for Mod-16 Ripple Counter

Q_1	Q_2	Q_3	Q_4	Q_{1+}	Q_{2+}	Q_{3+}	Q_{4+}
0	0	0	0	0	0	0	1
0	0	0	1	0	0	1	0
0	0	1	0	0	0	1	1
0	0	1	1	0	1	0	0
0	1	0	0	0	1	0	1
0	1	0	1	0	1	1	0
0	1	1	0	0	1	1	1
0	1	1	1	1	0	0	0
1	0	0	0	1	0	0	1
1	0	0	1	0	0	1	0
1	0	1	0	1	0	1	1
1	0	1	1	1	1	0	0
1	1	0	0	1	1	0	1
1	1	0	1	1	1	1	0
1	1	1	0	1	1	1	1
1	1	1	1	0	0	0	0

5.8 REGISTERS

A flip flop is a basic storage or memory element which is capable of storing one bit. The Register is made of flip flop and it is capable of storing more than one bit. A 4-bit register is capable of holding a nibble a 4-bit number.

Shift Register is a special type of register. It consists of a number of flip flops connected in such a way that whenever a control pulse is applied, it shifts the data from one flip flop to another. Basic Operations in 4 bit shift register are shown below:

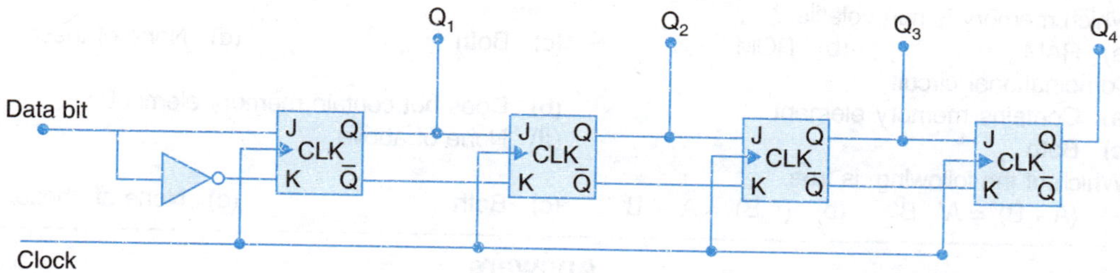

Fig. 5.25 : 4-bit Shift Register

As shown in the figure, the bit to be stored is applied at 'Data bit' line. Suppose a nibble 0 1 1 1 has to be stored in the 4 bit shift register and initially all flip flops are reset. The bits are applied to data bit line one by one and register stores the bit in the first flip flop. At every Clock input, the bits are sequentially shifted to another register. The movement of bits are shown in the following table:

Table 5.30: Contents of Register

Date bit input	Q_1	Q_2	Q_3	Q_4	
	0	0	0	0	(Initial state)
1	1	0	0	0	
1	1	1	0	0	
1	1	1	1	0	
0	0	1	1	1	

Parallel Register

In shift register the bit are shifted at each clock input. Therefore to store an 8 bit number, 8 clock pulses will be required to enter 8 bits. The parallel register loads all the 8 bits in a single clock pulse.

OBJECTIVE TYPE QUESTIONS

Multiple Choice

1. Which of following is a memory element
   (a) NAND Gate (b) SR Flip Flop (c) NOT gate (d) Universal Gate
2. Flip Flop is a basic memory element capable of storing
   (a) One Bit (b) One Byte (c) One Nibble (d) Two Byte
3. Which of the following is a universal gate.
   (a) NOT (b) NAND (c) OR (d) AND
4. in Sequential circuit , Output depends on
   (a) Input Only (b) Present State only
   (c) Both Input and Present (d) None of above State
5. Function of Register is to
   (a) Store Data Bytes (b) Count the numbers
   (c) Compile the Program (d) None of above.

6. Which of the following is not a Flip Flop?
   (a) JK (b) D (c) T (d) NOT
7. Refreshing circuit is required in
   (a) Static RAM (b) Dynamic RAM (c) Both (d) None of these
8. Which memory is non volatile ?
   (a) RAM (b) ROM (c) Both (d) None of these
9. Combinational circuit
   (a) Contains memory element (b) Does not contain memory element
   (c) Both (d) None of above
10. Which of the following is true.
   (a) $(A + B)' = A' . B'$ (b) $(A.B)' = A' + B'$ (c) Both (d) None of these

Answers

1-b, 2-a, 3-b, 4-c, 5-a, 6-d, 7-b, 8-b, 9-b, 10-c

State True or False

1. Basic building block of any digital computer is logic gates. [True] [False]
2. Characteristic table of Boolean function shows output for all possible input. [True] [False]
3. AND gate is also known as Inverter gate. [True] [False]
4. OR gate is a Universal gate. [True] [False]
5. A flip-flop is a bi stable device, which remains in one of two states. [True] [False]
6. JK flip-flop removes the problem of Race Conditions. [True] [False]
7. All counters are sequential circuits. [True] [False]
8. All registers are combinational circuit. [True] [False]
9. NOT gate is used to invert the input signal. [True] [False]
10. EX-OR operation may be represented as $A'.B + A.B'$. [True] [False]

Answers

1-True, 2-True, 3-False, 4-False, 5-True, 6-True, 7-True, 8-False, 9-True, 10-True.

SELECTED EXERCISES

1. What are fundamental products for each of the following input words:
   ABCD = 0100 ABCD = 1100 ABCD = 1111
2. Draw the logic circuit for the following expressions:
   a. $ABC + A\overline{C}$
   b. A.B (C+D) + B.C
   c. $A.\overline{B}.C.D.+A.B.C.D + \overline{A.B.C.D}$
3. For the following truth table, draw the AND-OR digital circuit:

A	B	C	Z
0	0	0	1
0	0	1	1
0	1	0	1
0	1	1	0
1	0	0	0
1	0	1	0
1	1	0	1
1	1	1	1

4. Write the expression for the truth table shown in problem 3.
5. Draw the truth table for the following Boolean expression:

$$F_1(ABC) = A.B+\overline{C}$$

$$F_2(ABC) = \overline{(A.B.C)}$$

Draw the truth table for the expression

F_1, $F_1.F_2$, $F_1 + F_2$

6. Explain the NOT, AND, OR operation with suitable examples. Draw the truth table for these operations.
7. What are flip flops? Explain the working principles of a clocked flip flop. What are excitation tables?
8. What is the difference between a sequential circuit and a combinational circuit? What do you mean by the state of a circuit? Explain with a suitable example.
9. What do you mean by the complement operation? Obtain the complement of functions F_1 and F_2 of problem 4. Draw the truth table of the complement of the function and compare the entries with the truth table of the function.
10. What are NAND gates? Why is a NAND gate called a universal gate. Draw a digital circuit to obtain a EX-OR and EX-NOR gate using NAND gate.
11. What is meant by basic memory cell? How is a NOR cell different from NAND cell? Give the characteristic table of both the cells and compare them.
12. What are the problems in SR flip flop? Explain by using the characteristic table of SR flip flop.
13. What is a counter? Why is a counter characterized into the category of a Sequential Logic Circuit? What do you mean by Mod-n counter? Draw the state diagram of a MOD-10 counter.
14. What are Ripple counters? Draw the logical circuit of a MOD-16 counter. What is the difference between a Synchronous and Asynchronous counter?
15. What are registers? What are used for? Draw a schematic diagram of 4-bit register.

6

DATA COMMUNICATION AND COMPUTER NETWORKS

Contents

6 DATA COMMUNICATION AND COMPUTER NETWORKS

Communication has been a basic requirement for the sharing and exchange of information over decades. The telephone network is one of the earliest modern communication medium for the exchange of information. The current information technology trends requires high capacity communication methods and medium to transfer large volumes of data at a higher speed. Communication refers to the data communication of information represented in several formats like Audio, Video, Text, Animation etc. All these Multimedia applications require high data transfer rate on the communication channel. Now-a-days, communication is not restricted to the use of telephone lines; several other modes of communication have evolved like Optical communication and wireless communication, e.g. Satellite and Radar communication. The primary objective of data communication is to provide reliable and high speed communication between the digital computers. The underlying infrastructural requirement for Computer Networks is the establishment of high speed communication channel. The local networks of computers which are confined to a room or a building, can use telecommunication cable for communication of data, but the geographically dispersed computers require that communication be established in the wireless mode. In this chapter, we will study the basic requirement for data communication and issues in computer networks.

6.1 MODEL OF DATA COMMUNICATION

A general model for data communication containing real world data is shown in Figure 6.1.

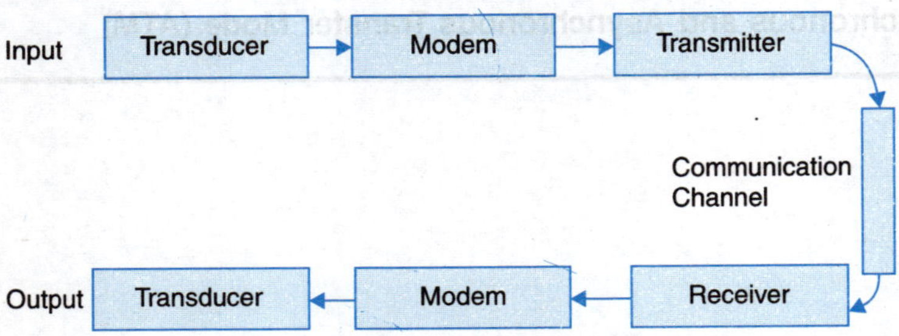

Fig. 6.1: General Model of Communication

As shown in the figure, the real world input is submitted to the transducers. The transducers are devices which convert the real world data into the electrical signals. These electrical signals are converted into the form which may be communicated over a channel by a device called Modem (Modulator Demodulator). The process of conversion at the sender's end is called modulation. Transmitters are the devices which load the modulated data on to the communication channel. The data, upon being received by the reciever at the receiving end, is passed on to the modem and the transducer in order to produce the real world output. The communication channel is the physical medium which is used to carry the signals from the source to destination.

6.2 ANALOG AND DIGITAL SIGNALS

The data to be transmitted may be in either of two forms—Analog or Digital. The analog signals are continuous electromagnetic waves. These waveforms may be periodic or aperiodic. The amplitude which represents the value of the signal at a particular instant of time, changes continuously with the time in analog signal. There are basically three characteristics which defines the analog data. These are Amplitude, Frequency and Phase. The analog signal is shown in Figure 6.2.

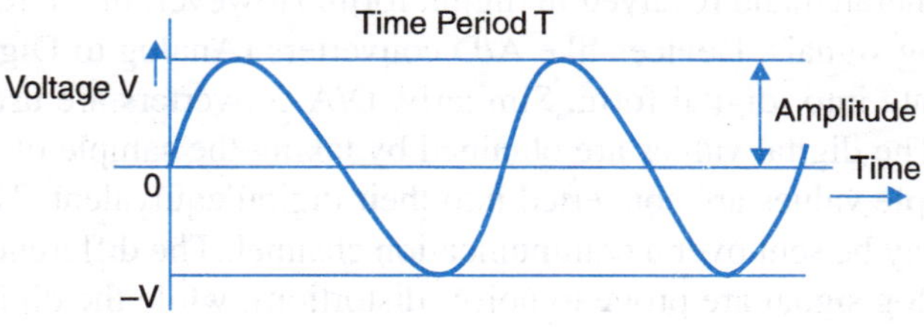

Fig. 6.2: Analog Signal

6.2.1 Amplitude

The amplitude is defined as the value of analog signal at a particular instant of time. It may be noticed that the plot represents the varying voltage over time, or in other words, we may say that the amplitude of the signal is changing with time. Amplitude of the signal may be represented in Voltage, Current, speed etc.

6.2.2 Frequency

The frequency of the signal is measured as the amount of time required by the signal to complete one cycle. In Figure 6.2, the time period for one cycle is T. Therefore, the frequency of the signal is 1/T. The frequency of a signal is not of great importance in the case of aperiodic signals.

6.2.3 Phase

The term phase is a relative notion. The phase difference in two signals is the difference of phases when the two waveforms are compared. It is measured in degrees.

These three signal characteristics may be exploited to transform the signal for communication over a communication channel. Characteristics like amplitude of the voice, voltage current etc, frequency of a radio signals are all used to communicate the analog signals. At the transmission end, these signals are superimposed on to the carrier signal and sent over the channel. At the receiving end, the signals are detached from the carrier signals and produced in their original form. For example, in Radio signals, the voice of the singer or news reader is transmitted by capturing the amplitude and superimposing it on the high frequency carrier signal from the studio. At the radio instrument, the waveforms are detached from the carrier signal and the original voice is produced.

6.2.4 Digital Signal

The digital signals are the strings of electronic pulses. A digital signal contains only two discrete values called high or low. The following figure shows digital signal.

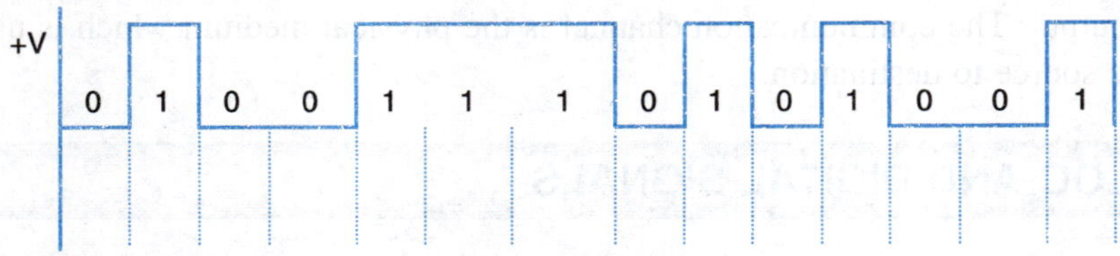

Fig. 6.3: Digital Signal

As shown in the Figure 6.3, the digital signal logically represents the digital data "01001110101001". The dotted line shows the period of the signal. Value of the signal at a particular instant of a time is either high or low. The data in analog form has to be converted into the digital data. In the computer systems, the data are generated and received in digital form. However, in the real world, the data needs to be presented in analog signals. Devices like A/D converters (Analog to Digital Converter) are used to convert the analog data into digital form. Similarly, D/A converters are used to convert the digital data into analog form. The digital values are obtained by taking the sample of analog values at regular time intervals. The sample values are converted into their digital equivalent. These digital values form a digital signal which may be sent over a communication channel. The difference in Analog and Digital transmission is that analog signal are prone to noise (distortion), while the digital signals are generally not affected by the outside interference. Therefore the quality of digital transmission is higher than analog signaling.

6.3 ISSUES IN ANALOG TO DIGITAL DATA CONVERSION

In the discrete time system, the values of a signal are specified at only discrete time intervals. In these systems, the signal changes at discrete time intervals only. As the analog signal varies in continuous time, the conversion of the analog signal into the digital signals requires two processes called Sampling and Quantization. Depending upon the requirements, the signal may be quantified in time and amplitude. In *sampling*, the samples of analog signals are taken at fixed time intervals. The sample values contain amplitude and these values are quantified by the process called *amplitude quantization*. For quantization, the A/D converter are used. Figure 6.4 shows this process.

Figure 6.4 shows a model of digital transmission. The continuous waveform or analog signal is applied to the sampler circuit. As discussed earlier, the sampler circuit takes the sample values of the signal at different time intervals. The values are then quantified by the process of amplitude quantization. The circuit called A/D converter does the job of generating digital equivalent of analog samples. The digital values are then sent over the communication channel and received by the receiver. At the receiving end, these digital values are converted into analog values by D/A converter. These analog values represent the sample output at discrete times. These samples are further subject to hold circuit which generates a waveform in continuous domain.

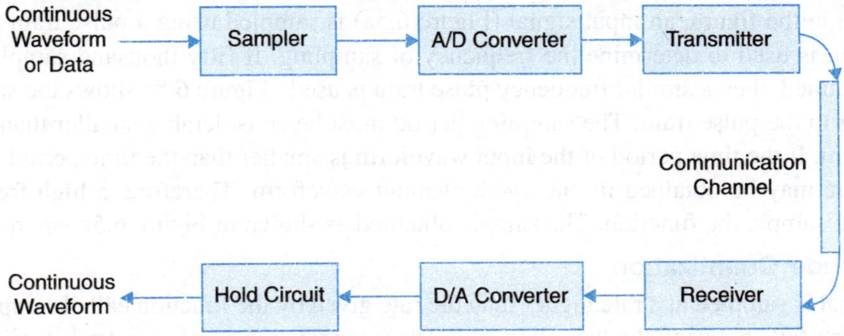

Fig. 6.4: Digital Transmission

6.3.1 Sampling Process

The sampling process is a basic operation in digital systems. The sampling process generates a train of pulses. Sampling may be non-uniform or uniform. In non-uniform sampling, the samples are taken at non-uniform time intervals but in the case of uniform sampling, the samples are taken at uniform intervals. In general, for all practical purposes, uniform sampling is preferred. In uniform sampling, the clock signal is used for synchronization. The sampling process is shown in Figure 6.5.

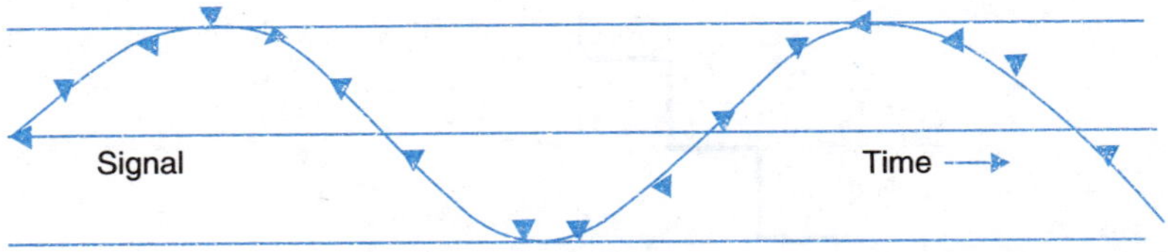

Fig. 6.5 (a)

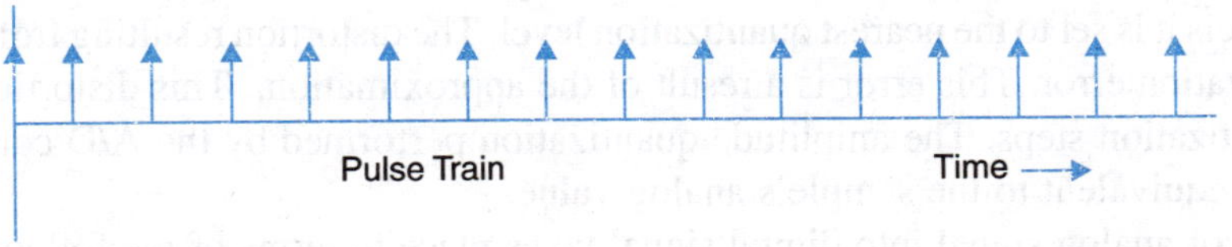

Fig. 6.5 (b)

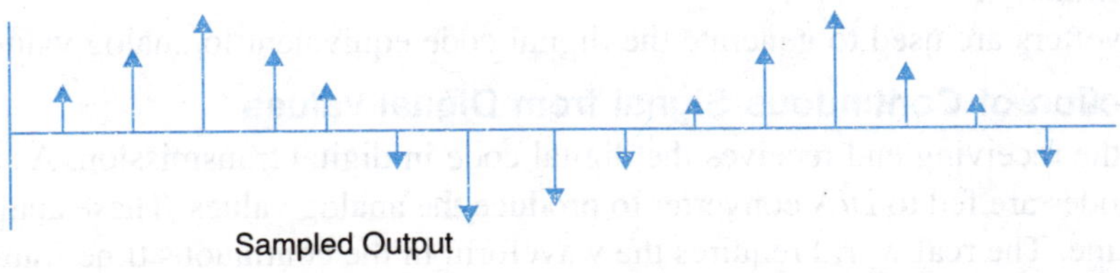

Fig. 6.5 (c)

Fig. 6.5: Sampling of Signal

As shown in the figure, an input signal (Figure 6.5a) is sampled using a pulse train (Figure 6.5b). The pulse train is used to determine the frequency of sampling. If fifty thousand samples per second have to be obtained, then a similar frequency pulse train is used. Figure 6.5c shows the sampled values corresponding to the pulse train. The sampling period must be considerably smaller than the period of input waveform. If the time period of the input waveform is smaller than the time period of pulse train, then no sample may be obtained in one cycle of input waveform. Therefore, a high frequency pulse train is used to sample the function. The sample obtained as shown in Figure 6.5c are quantified next.

6.3.2 Amplitude Quantization

The input signal is sampled at a rate higher than the rate given by the function called sampling function. A sample which falls between the two allowed levels (quantization level) is rounded off to the nearest quantization level. This process of approximation of a signal by discrete values is known as amplitude quantization. The process of amplitude quantization is performed by the A/D converters. Figure 6.6 shows the uniform quantization characteristics.

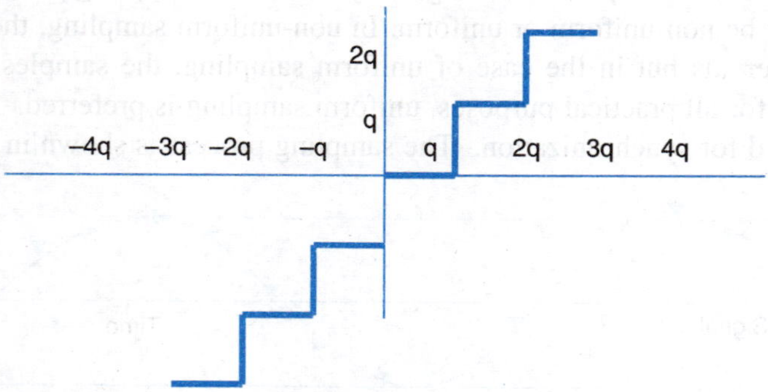

Fig. 6.6: Quantization Levels

The various levels of quantization are shown in Figure 6.6. If the signal value is between the two quantization levels it is set to the nearest quantization level. The distortion resulting from the quantization is called quantization error. This error is a result of the approximation. This distortion depends on the size of the quantization steps. The amplitude quantization performed by the A/D converters generates the digital code equivalent to the sample's analog value.

Conversion of analog signal into digital signal takes place in terms of the following steps:

1. The samples of analog signal are taken in accordance with the sampling function (train of pulses).
2. The sample values are subject to the quantization level and produce the nearest possible value by approximation.
3. A/D converters are used to generate the digital code equivalent to analog values.

6.3.3 Construction of Continuous Signal from Digital Values

The receiver at the receiving end receives the digital code in digital transmission. As shown in Figure 6.4, the digital codes are fed to D/A converter to produce the analog values. These analog values are on discrete time frame. The real world requires the waveform in the continuous time frame. A continuous waveform is generated using Hold circuits. The process of constructing of continuous signals from digital values is shown in Figure 6.7.

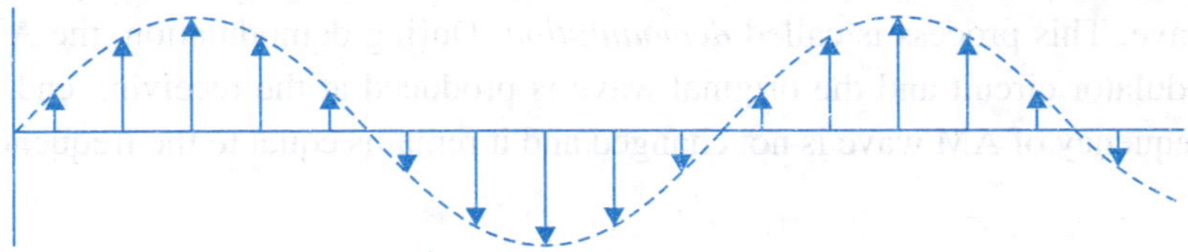

Fig. 6.7: Data Hold Operation

The train of pulses is converted into continuous analog output by the Data Hold circuits. This process is similar to the extrapolation of the values of signals between the sampling instants.

6.4 MODULATION

The process of modulation is of utmost importance in communication. This process uses a high frequency carrier wave to transmit the waveform. The various characteristics of the carrier wave are changed in accordance with the variation in the selected parameters of the waveform to be transmitted. This process is also called the *superimposition of waveform the over the carrier* wave. The characteristics of waveform to be exploited for superimposition are amplitude, frequency or phase. In order for the waveform to be transmitted, it is necessary to be converted into the high frequency signal. This process is called *modulation.* In analog modulation, analog signal is used as carrier and in pulse modulation, the digital carrier is used. If the amplitude of the carrier wave is changed according to the varying amplitude of waveform, the process is called *amplitude modulation.* Basically there are three types of modulations for analog signals:

1. Amplitude Modulation
2. Frequency Modulation
3. Phase Modulation

All modulations use high frequency analog signal as a carrier. The modulation method, which uses digital pulses as carrier, is known as *pulse modulation.* Pulse modulations are basically of four types:

1. Pulse Amplitude Modulation
2. Pulse Duration Modulation
3. Pulse Position Modulation
4. Pulse Code Modulation

In the following section we will discuss the basic concepts of these modulation principles.

6.4.1 Amplitude Modulation

Here, the amplitude of high frequency carrier wave is changed as per the variation in the amplitude of input waveform. This process is called superimposition of waveform over carrier wave. The resultant waveform is called modulated waveform. This process is explained graphically in Figure 6.8.

As shown in the figure, the input waveform (Figure 6.8a) is superimposed on a high frequency carrier (Figure 6.8b) and a resultant wave (Figure 6.8c) is generated. This resultant wave is called Amplitude Modulated Wave. In amplitude modulation, amplitude of the high frequency carrier wave is modified in accordance with the amplitude of the input waveform. The AM wave is transmitted over the transmitting end, and at the receiving end, the reverse procedure is adopted to detach the input wave from the AM wave. This process is called *demodulation*. During demodulation, the AM waveform is fed to the demodulator circuit and the original wave is produced at the receiving end. It may also be noted that the frequency of AM wave is not changed and it remains equal to the frequency of the carrier wave.

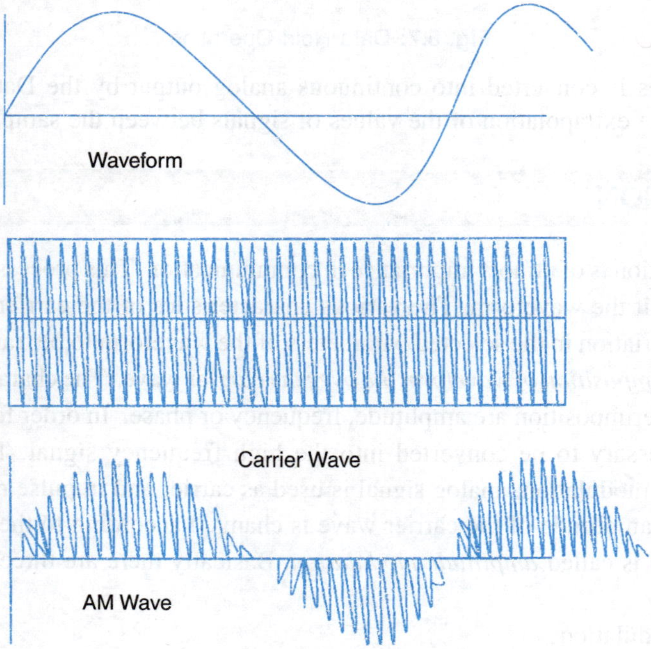

Fig. 6.8: Amplitude Modulation

6.4.2 Frequency Modulation

Here, the frequency of the carrier wave is modified in proportion to the modulating signal. The frequency of the carrier wave is increased according to the increase in the amplitude of the input waveform. The frequency of the carrier wave decreases upon the decrement in the input waveform. The process of frequency modulation is shown in Figure 6.9.

Figure 6.9 shows the process of frequency modulation. The input waveform (Figure 6.9a) is superimposed on the high frequency carrier wave (Figure 6.9b). The resultant wave after the superimposition is called Frequency Modulated Wave (FM Wave). The FM wave is shown in Figure 6.9c. It may be noted that the amplitude of the carrier wave remains unaffected but the frequency of the carrier wave is changed in accordance with the changes in the amplitude of the input waveform. The amplitude of FM wave remains unaffected. The FM wave is transmitted over the communication channel and the original waveform is produced at the receiving end by a reverse process called demodulation. The demodulation process is carried out at the receiving end. There are several advantages of communication through frequency modulation over amplitude modulation. The noise level in frequency modulation is minimum. An audio signal transmitted by amplitude modulation suffers from low quality or noisy reception.

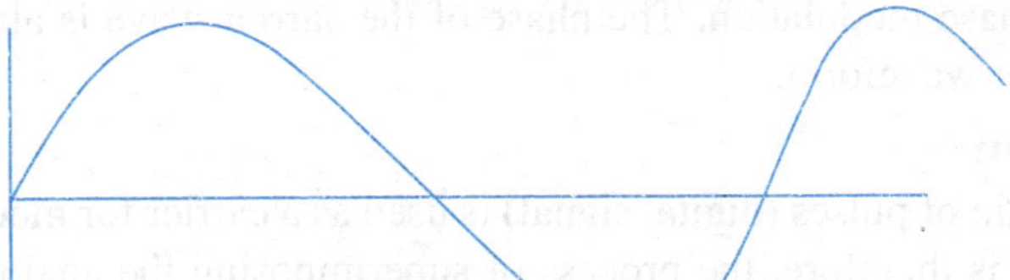

a. Waveform

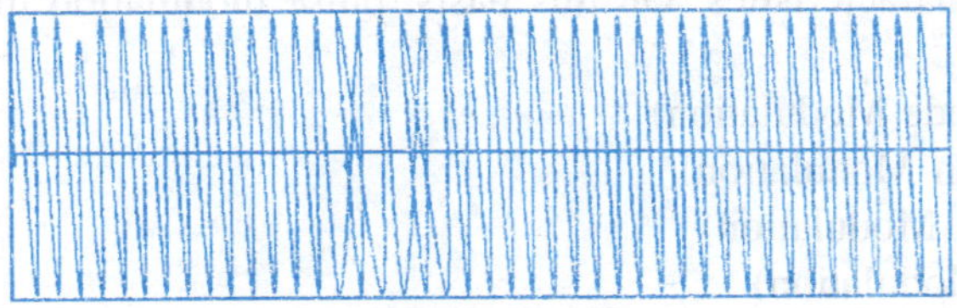

b. Carrier Wave

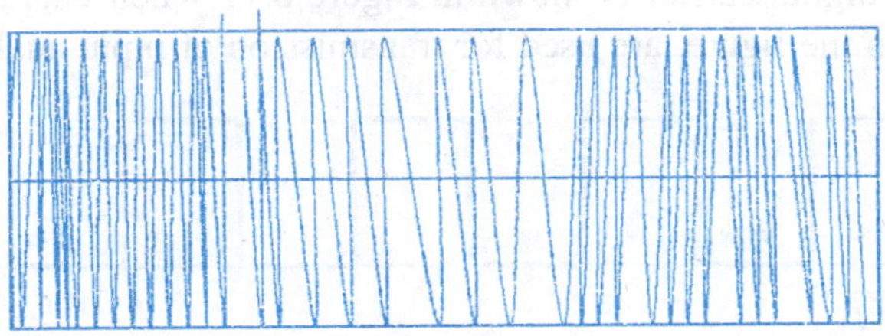

c. FM Wave

Fig. 6.9: Frequency Modulation

6.4.3 Phase Modulation

Under phase modulation, the phase of the carrier wave is varied in accordance with the variations in the input waveform. The phase angle of the carrier wave is changed in terms of the corresponding changes in the amplitude of the input waveform. The phase shift increases when the amplitude of the input waveform increases and phase shift decreases when the amplitude of the input waveform decreases. Normally, the change in the phase angle also affects the frequency of the signal. Therefore, the phase modulation is very similar to the frequency modulation. The pictorial representation of the phase modulation is given in Figure 6.10.

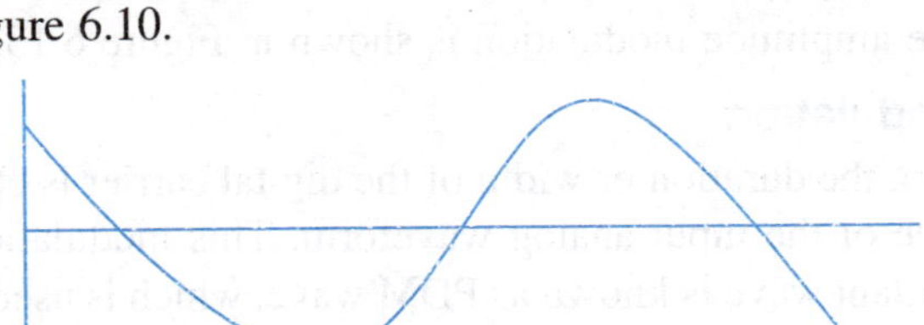

a. Input Waveform

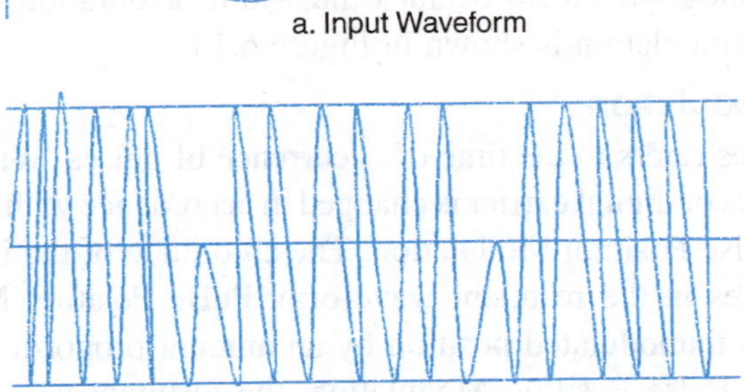

b. PM carrier

Fig. 6.10: Phase Modulation

Figure 6.10 shows the phase modulation. The phase of the carrier wave is altered in accordance with the amplitude of the input waveform.

6.4.4 Pulse Modulation

In pulse modulation, a train of pulses (digital signal) is used as a carrier for modulating the input analog signal. Pulse modulation is therefore, the process of superimposing the analog signal onto the digital train of pulses. Various characteristics of the train of pulses may be varied or changed in accordance with the input waveform characteristics. On this basis, pulse modulation may be divided into four categories:

1. PAM (Pulse Amplitude Modulation)
2. PDM (Pulse Duration Modulation)
3. PPM (Pulse Position Modulation)
4. PCM (Pulse Code Modulation)

The train of pulses or digital carrier is shown in Figure 6.11. Their characteristics like amplitude, duration position, shown in the figure, are used for transmission of input analog waveform.

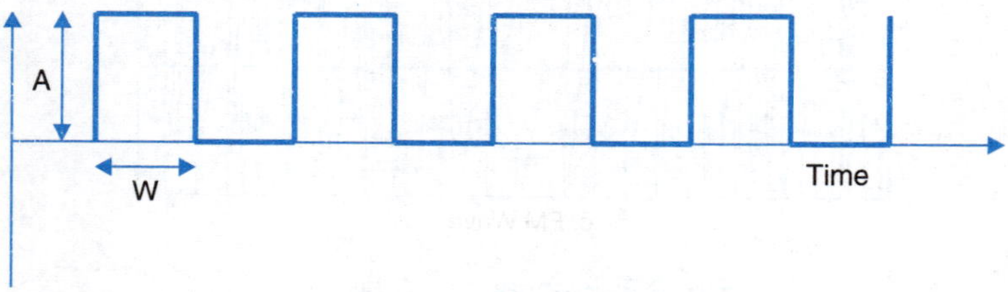

Fig. 6.11: Train of Pulses (Digital Carrier)

In Figure 6.11 the amplitude of the pulse is shown by 'A' and width of the pulse by 'W'.

6.4.5 Pulse Amplitude Modulation

In pulse modulation, the train of pulses is used as a carrier wave. When the amplitude of the train of pulses is changed in accordance with the input analog waveform, the process is called Pulse Amplitude Modulation (PAM). The process is also known as superimposition of analog waveform over train of pulses (digital carrier). The resultant waveform is known as Pulse amplitude modulation wave (PAM Wave). The process of pulse amplitude modulation is shown in Figure 6.13.

6.4.6 Pulse Duration Modulation

In pulse duration modulation, the duration or width of the digital carrier is changed in accordance with the changes in the amplitude of the input analog waveform. This modulation is also known as Pulse Width Modulation. The resultant wave is known as PDM wave, which is used for transmission purpose. Amplitude of the input analog waveform decides the width or duration of the train of pulses. The process of Pulse Duration Modulation is shown in Figure 6.13.

6.4.7 Pulse Position Modulation

The position of digital pulses refers to the time of occurrence of pulses. When the time of occurrences of pulses in the train of pulses or digital carrier is changed in accordance with the input analog waveform, the modulation is called Pulse Position Modulation. The amplitude of the input waveform decides the time of occurrence of pulses in the resultant waveform. Pulse Position Modulation is achieved by shifting each pulse from its unmodulated position by an amount proportional to the amplitude of the input analog waveform. In Pulse Position Modulation, the resultant waveforms are known as PPM wave. The concept of Pulse Position Modulation is shown in Figure 6.12.

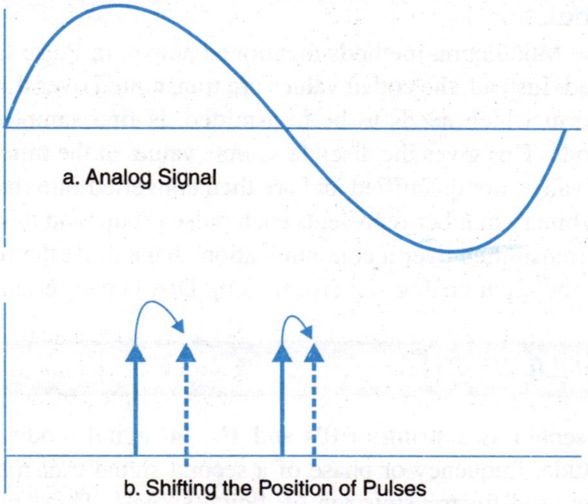

Fig. 6.12: Pulse Position Modulation

As shown in the figure, the dark arrows represents the original position of pulses in the digital carrier. In the PPM wave, the position of the pulses are shifted by an order proportional to the amplitude of the analog signal. The dotted arrow shows the actual pulse position generated in the PPM wave.

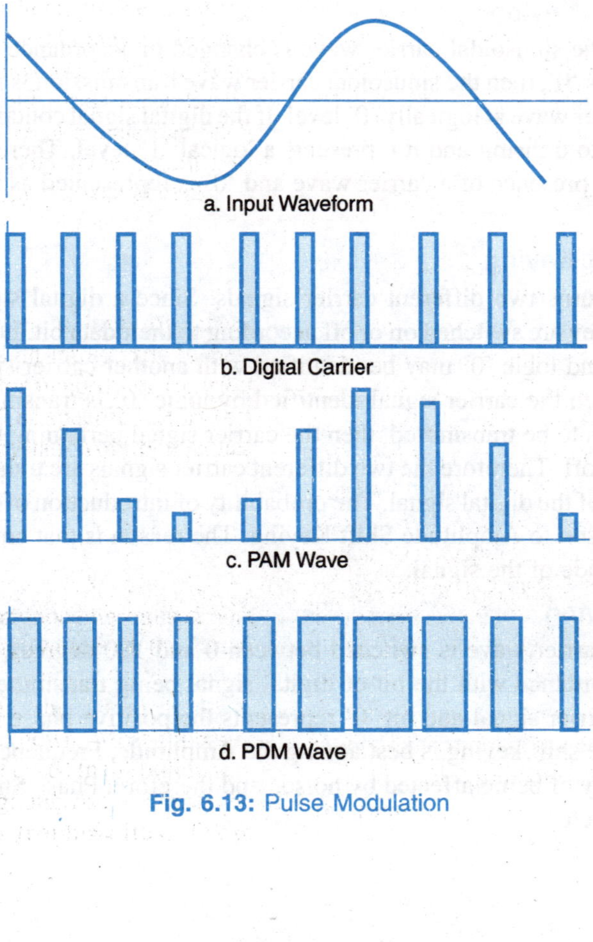

Fig. 6.13: Pulse Modulation

6.4.8 Pulse Code Modulation

As distinct from the Pulse Modulation methods mentioned above, in Pulse Code Modulation the train of pulses is not transmitted. Instead, the coded values are transmitted over the communication channel. The input analog waveform which needs to be transmitted, is first sampled using Pulse Amplitude Modulation (PAM) methods. This gives the discrete sample values at the time interval corresponding to the digital carrier. These values are quantified and are then converted into the digital values using A/D converter. Under PCM, a binary number represents each pulse group, and this pulses group represented by the binary number, is transmitted over a communication channel. At the receiving end, the signal is decoded and it generates the input analog waveform using D/A converter and a filter.

6.5 DIGITAL MODULATION

Digital signals are represented as a string of 0's and 1's. In digital modulation techniques, varying properties such as amplitude, frequency or phase of a second signal transmits the digital signals. The sinusoidal carrier wave is used for transmission of digital signals. Three properties of carrier waves such as amplitude, frequency and phase are used to alter the characteristics of the carrier wave in accordance with the digital signal. Commonly used digital modulation techniques are:

1. Amplitude Shift Keying
2. Frequency Shift Keying
3. Phase Shift Keying

6.5.1 Amplitude Shift Keying

Here, the amplitude of the sinusoidal carrier wave is changed in accordance with the digital signal. If the digital signal contains '0', then the sinusoidal carrier wave transmission is switched off. It represents the amplitude of the carrier wave at logically '0' level. If the digital signal contains '1', then the sinusoidal carrier wave is allowed to transmit and it represents a logical '1' level. Therefore in the digital signal, '1' is represented by the presence of a carrier wave and '0' is represented as the absence of the carrier signal.

6.5.2 Frequency Shift Keying

Frequency shift keying uses two different carrier signals. Since a digital signal is represented as a string of '0's and '1's , they are switched on or off according to their data bit. Logic '1' may be identified with one carrier signal and logic '0' may be identified with another carrier signal. Whenever a bit '0' has to be transmitted, then the carrier signal identified by logic '0' is transmitted and the other one is kept off. If the bit '1' has to be transmitted, then the carrier signal pertaining to logic '1' is transmitted and the other one is kept off. Therefore the two different carrier signals are transmitted one after another, according to the data bit of the digital signal. The probability of introduction of noise is less in Frequency Shift Keying in comparison to Amplitude Shift Keying. The reason is that environmental disturbances affect mostly the amplitude of the signal.

6.5.3 Phase Shift Keying

Here, the phase of the carrier wave is switched between 0 and 180 degrees. The phase of the carrier wave is changed in accordance with the bit of digital signal being transmitted. The bit '1' represents negative phase of the carrier signal and bit '0' represents the positive phase of the carrier signal. The performance of the phase shift keying is best among the Amplitude, Frequency and phase shift keying. It has the least probability of being affected by noise, and therefore, Phase Shift Keying is preferred in satellite communication etc.

In all these schemes of modulation the modulation is carried out at senders end and demodulation is done at the receiver's end. These operations are performed by a device called Modulator/Demodulator, popularly known as the Modem.

6.6 MULTIPLEXING OF SIGNALS

The increase in the bandwidth of a channel has always been a prime issue in the design of networks. Full utilization of the bandwidth available is of utmost importance when the computers associated with the network are slower and do not usually transmit a lot of data. To optimise the utilization of the channel bandwidth, multiplexing of signals is done. Multiplexing of signals enables the transmission of more than one signal at a common communication channel. The transmission of two or more signals that use different carrier frequencies for communication over a common communication channel at a time is known as *multiplexing of signals*. Common examples of multiplexing are television or radio signals. Each station is allotted a channel frequency that broadcasts the programs. The signals at the corresponding station are modulated with the designated carrier and are broadcasted simultaneously. In this way, multiple channels may broadcast their programs. Multiplexing is of two types:

- Frequency Division Multiplexing
- Time Division Multiplexing

6.6.1 Frequency Division Multiplexing (FDM)

This is a technique to send more than one signal over a communication channel. The FDM technology is used with transmission of analog signals and it employs multiple carrier frequencies to transmit the signals. The multiplexer at the sender's end receives all the signal from the computers. These signals are combined together and modulated with the designated carrier frequencies. The resultant complex waveform is transmitted over a communication channel, transmitting multiple signals at a time. The process is shown in Figure 6.14(a). As shown in the figure, the signals generated by the different computers

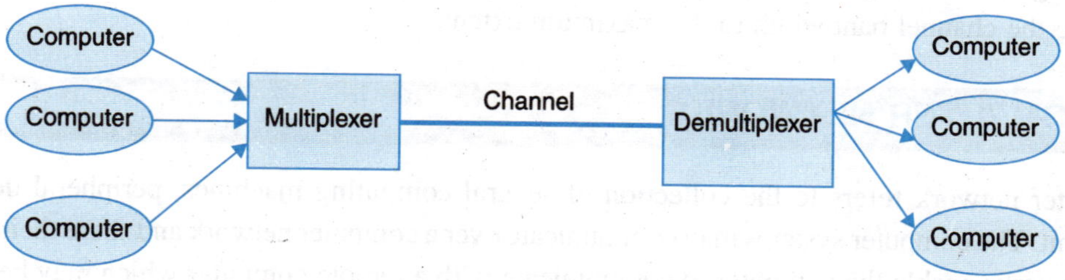

Fig. 6.14 (a): Frequency Division Multiplexing

are modulated with the different carrier frequencies and are communicated over a single channel at a time. A multiplexer combines the various signals and transmits them over the channel. This technology allows multiple senders to communicate with multiple receivers. FDM is carried out in several steps. The available bandwidth is first divided into several ranges. Each range corresponds to the transmission of one signal.

6.6.2 Time Division Multiplexing

Here, a communication channel is shared among the different senders. In this scheme, different signals are combined together like Frequency Division Multiplexing. These signals are sampled and communicated over the channel in distinct time frames. The scheme is shown in Figure 6.14(b).

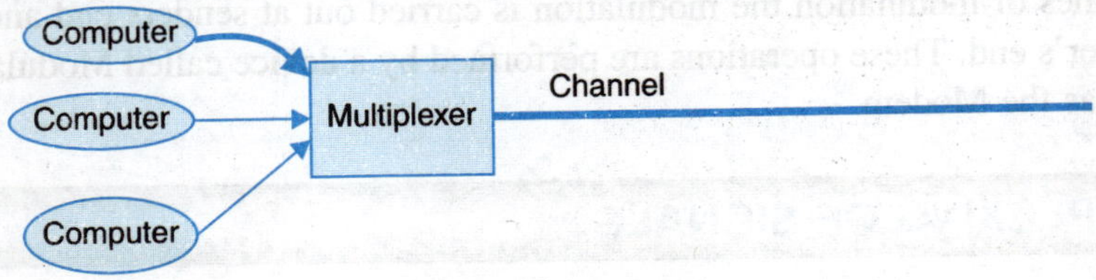

Fig. 6.14 (b): Time Division Multiplexing

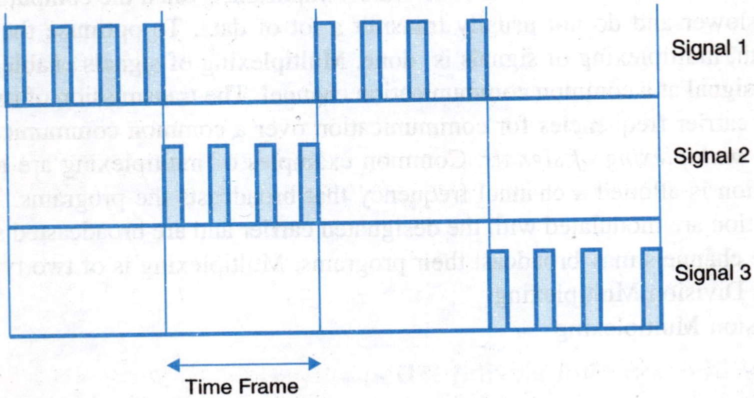

Fig. 6.15: Digital Time Division Multiplexing

As shown in the figure, three senders send the data over a communication channel in different time slots. First, computer 1 sends the data, then computer 2 and all of the computers get their turn in round-robin order. Figure 6.15 shows, the different time slots. In the first slot, signal 1 is communicated, then signal 2, signal 1 and signal 3 are communicated next. Therefore, a multiple number of slow devices can utilize the channel bandwidth to the maximum extent.

6.7 COMPUTER NETWORKS

A computer network refers to the collection of several computing machines, peripheral devices and storage unit. The computer systems may communicate over a computer network and share their resources. These networks enable the computer to communicate with a remote computer which may be located at a distance of a few meters to several thousand kilometers. The users of a computer system on the network are able to share the software resources such as programs, databases, and program utilities. The computer network has become a basic necessity and has triggered the development of several applications. The conventional concept of installing a high performance and large computer system has now been replaced with computer networks where several low cost and low performance computer systems collectively exhibit high performance at lower cost. The computer network connects several peripheral devices, databases and computer systems as shown in Figure 6.16.

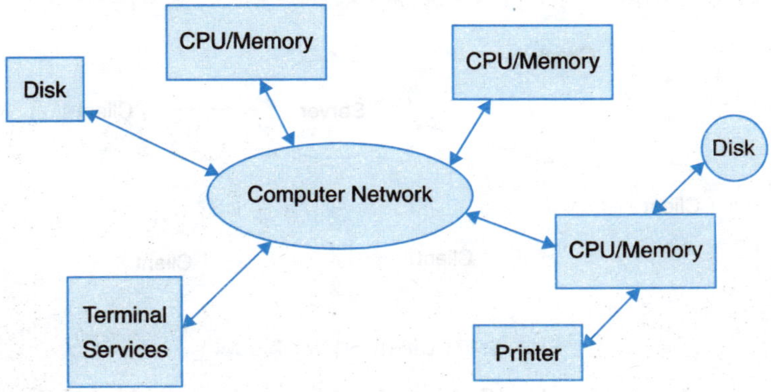

Fig. 6.16: Computer Network

The main benefits of Computer Networks are:

- Resource Sharing
- Enhanced Performance
- Improved Reliability and Availability
- Modular Expandability

Resource sharing implies the sharing of software/programs/data of remote computer systems. This eliminates the replication of resources. The overall performance is increased as data migration and distributed scheduling of programs or jobs may be done by using the computer network. The availability of the components increase as whenever any system or component is down, the other similar resource from another system on the network may be used. These factors have motivated most organizations to establish their own network.

6.7.1 Distributed System

The distributed system consists of several computers that do not share a memory or clock. All computers in the distributed system run their own operating systems and communicate to each other by exchange of message over the network. A set of users working together would like to share the database, communicate with each other and share other resources. It has been proved that providing a pool of relatively less powerful processors increases the total computing power exponentially. The main advantage of a distributed system is a better cost/performance ratio.

6.7.2 Client Server Model

A process in the operating system may be characterized as a program in the execution state. In the client server model, the processes may be characterized as clients and a server. Processes that need some service are called clients and processes that provides the service are called servers. Examples of a client could be a program requesting for some data available at a remote computer. The client sends the request to the server and server replies back to the clients and sends the result after performing the required processing. The client-server model is presented in Figure 6.17.

As shown in the figure, the client process located at different computer systems may send the request to the server process located at a remote computer system. The server, after serving the processing request, passes the result to the client process.

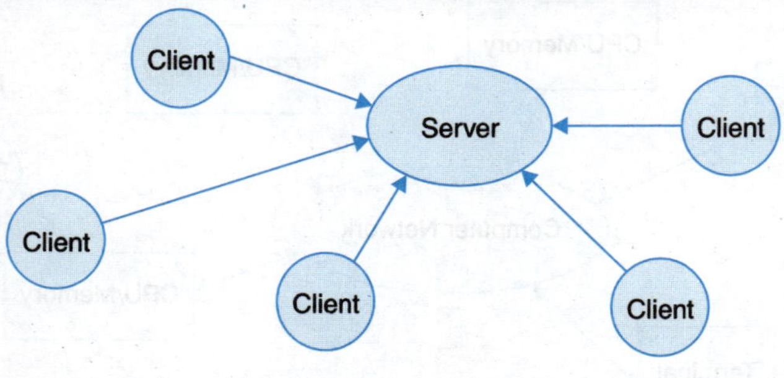

Fig. 6.17: Client Server Model

The computer networks may be classified into three categories called LAN (Local Area Network), MAN (Metropolitan Area Network) and WAN (Wide Area Network).

6.7.3 LAN/MAN/WAN

Local Area Networks connect the computers and other resources located in a small locations such as a room, building, office or institute etc. LANs are privately owned and cater to the need of resource sharing for a particular organization. The LANs are located in small geographical boundaries ranging from 100 meters to 2 km.

Metropolitan Area Networks (MAN) connects the computer system, other resources and some times local area networks to a range from 5 to 50 km. It uses high speed data transfer medium like Fiber Optics.

The Wide Area Networks are used to connect the computer system and devices spread over a larger geographical area. The wide area networks are also known as Long Haul Networks. WANs use the switches and are based on store and forward mechanism. The data are communicated in the form of small pieces and sent over the network. The packets follows different routes to their destination and computers or switches in the path store the packets and forward to the next computer or switch in the path.

6.7.4 Circuit vs Packet Switching

The main use of a computer network is to share resources. These resources includes the software/ program utilities or data. A frequent communication of data and programs is the common usage of the computer network. The data being communicated over a communication network may be sent in one of the following two modes:

- Circuit Switching
- Packet Switching

In circuit switching, a dedicated path between a sender and receiver is established for data communication. This path remains intact until the whole set of the data is transmitted. An example of circuit switching is the conventional telephone network. In the traditional network when a subscriber dials a number, a dedicated path between the caller and called party is established and it is terminated when either party wishes to do it.

In packet switching, the message or the data is sliced into small packets and these packets are transmitted over the communication network. All the packets contain the information about the source and destination address including the data byte. These packets are communicated on the 'store and forward' principle. Every node in the path forwards the packet to the node on the route. It is important to note that not all packets follow the same path. In packet switching, the communication path is not reserved for data communication. The same node may receive the packets from different sources and forward them to different destinations.

6.7.5 Simplex vs Duplex Communication

While transmitting the data between the sender and receiver, three types of data communication may be established over a communication channel based on the utilization of the channel. These are:

- Simplex Communication
- Half Duplex Communication
- Duplex Communication

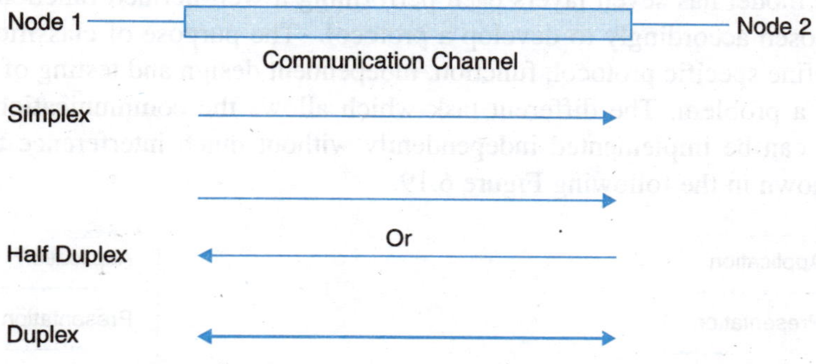

Fig. 6.18: Communication Modes

As shown in Figure 6.18, Node 1 and Node 2 may use a communication channel for the data communication between them. In *simplex communication*, the data travels only in one direction over the communication channel. In some systems, the data may travel in both directions simultaneously. This mode is called *duplex communication* mode. In the duplex communication mode, both the nodes may communicate to each other simultaneously. In the *half-duplex mode*, the communication channel may be used to communicate the data in both directions but with the restriction that at a time, the data may travel in only one direction.

6.7.6 Baseband vs Broadband Technology

The Frequency Division Multiplexing is widely used technology to design the computer network. FDM allows multiple data stream to be sent simultaneously over a communication channel. Use of Twisted Pair, Coaxial cable & optical fiber are most popular transmission medium for design of small to large distance network. One of the major advantages of deployment of Frequency Division Multiplexing is to obtain high throughput. The Broadband technology allows the bandwidth to be divided into multiple ranges of frequency spectrum and each allows the transmission of a data stream over network. If we have used Coaxial cable for data transmission, the multiple data stream are communicated over the coaxial cable. The Cable TV is one of the examples of multiple signal transmission. The bandwidth available in broadband may be utilized for transmission of variety of signal. This technology resulted in offering Cable TV, Internet and other services over same communication channel simultaneously. The baseband technology utilizes a small part of the frequency spectrum and transmits only one data stream at a time. In the local area networks, only one data stream is transmitted at a time. The main difference in broadband and baseband technology is that broadband adopts the technology to communicate multiple data stream over a communication channel simultaneously while baseband technology focuses on communication of single data stream over communication channel.

6.8 AN OVERVIEW OF ISO OSI LAYERS

In current days, computer network employs heterogeneous environment including different types of computers, printers, database, modem, switches, router and other networking equipment's. International Standards Organization (ISO) has proposed Open System Interconnection (OSI) reference model which provides a framework for data communication protocols. An open system is referred to as set of protocols, which allows the communication to take place between two independent computer systems. OSI model addresses the problem of interconnection of different computer and associated devices. The OSI reference model has seven layers each performing a well-defined function. The function of layer should be chosen accordingly to develop a protocol. The purpose of classification of layers in OSI model is to define specific protocol, function, independent design and testing of components for a particular class of a problem. The different task which allows the communication to take place in computer network can be implemented independently without much interference from other. These seven layers are shown in the following Figure 6.19.

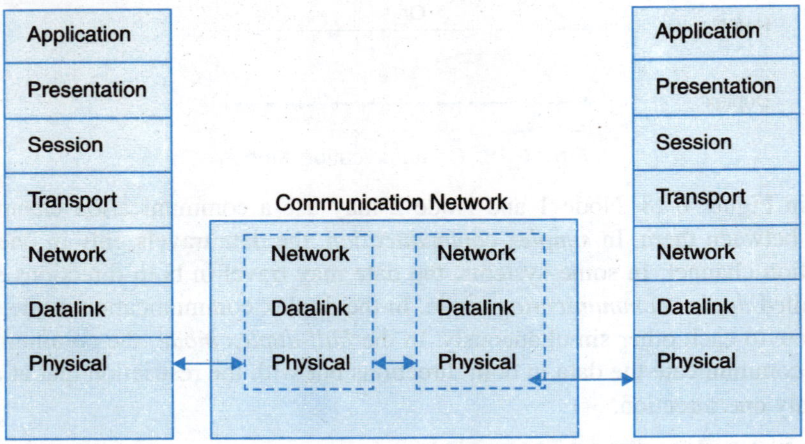

Fig. 6.19: OSI Reference Model

When an application at the host computer sends a message to the application at a remote computer, several activities takes place. The OSI layers bound these activities. The application or program runs in the application layers. OSI reference model is only a recommendation, therefore it does not specify the exact services or protocol to be used in that layer. The function of each layer is presented below:

Physical Layer

The main function of this layer is to send the data bit stream over a communication network. The design issues in this layer confirm that the bit sent by the sender is received in original. For example, bit '1' sent must be received as bit '1'. This layer is not concerned with the transmission errors.

Datalink Layer

The function of this layer is to recover from the transmission errors. Data link layer takes care of the speed mismatch between senders and receivers. Any disparity in the speed of sending a data and receiving it is taken care by data link layer.

Network Layer

The network layer is mainly concerned with routing and congestion control. In packet switching, the message is divided into the pieces called packets and these packets are sent over the communication network. This layer decides which outbound communication channel must be used to reduce the congestion. It also decides the optimal path for routing of a packet.

Transport Layer

Role of transport layer is to receive the data from the session layer and divide it into pieces in order to pass it to the network layer. A major function of this layer is to hide the details of communication network and provide a network independent device-to-device communication.

Session Layer

This layer establishes a session for communication between the two hosts. Establishing a connection involves authentication of the hosts, who want to communicate as well as authentication of transportation service.

Presentation Layer

This layer serves as an interface between the application and the communication network. Typical function of this layer is to code the data into mutually agreed formats. The presentation layer performs the compression of data and forms a sequence of symbols according to the standard format.

Application Layer

The major role of application layer is to provide the facility to use the other layers. It contains several protocols that are generally needed to perform a job. The contents of the application layer are determined by the user themselves.

6.9 NETWORK TOPOLOGY

The computer network contains several computers which communicate with each other. The principle of locality of reference states that a computer which is physically near to another one is likely to communicate more as well as a particular computer will have repeated communication with a particular class of computers. Network topology refers to the connection of different computers and deals with problem of how best various computers can be interconnected. Based on the interconnection scheme, the computer network uses three types of network topologies, as follows:

- Bus Topology
- Ring Topology
- Star Topology

6.9.1 Star Topology

In the Star Topology, the various computers are attached to a single point. The center of the star network is called Hub. The function of the Hub is to facilitate the communication between the two computers. It receives the request from the computer sending the data and delivers the data to the destination computer. The Star Topology is shown in the Figure 6.20.

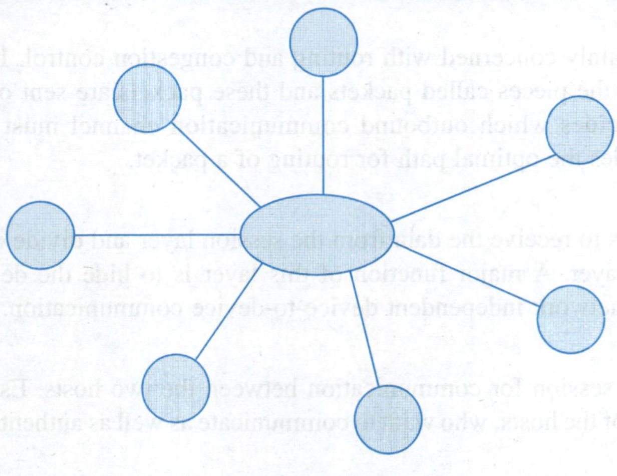

Fig. 6.20: Star Network

6.9.2 Bus/Tree Topology

In Bus/Tree topology, the bus is used as a carrier for data packets. The computer communicates by sending various packets and each packet contains the address of destination. Packets are traversed along the bus and all the computers on the network have access to the bus. The common bus is used by all computers as a medium for communication. Tree network is a collection of several bus topology networks with a common bus. Figure 6.21 shows the Tree Network. In the figure, several local area networks based on the bus topology are connected to a common bus (shown as thick line). The data to be communicated by a sender is placed on the bus in the form of packets. All computers on the network have an access to the medium (bus). The packets are then delivered to the destination.

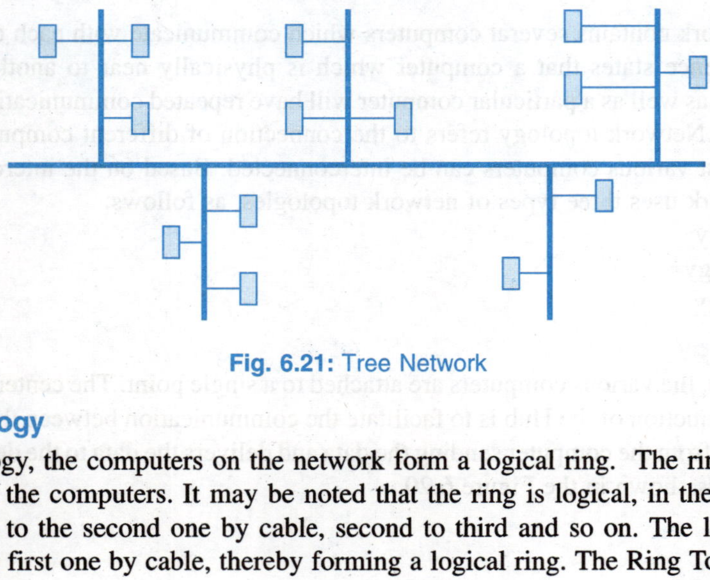

Fig. 6.21: Tree Network

6.9.3 Ring Topology

In the Ring Topology, the computers on the network form a logical ring. The ring represent a cable which connects all the computers. It may be noted that the ring is logical, in the sense that the first computer connects to the second one by cable, second to third and so on. The last computer in the network connect to first one by cable, thereby forming a logical ring. The Ring Topology is shown in Figure 6.22.

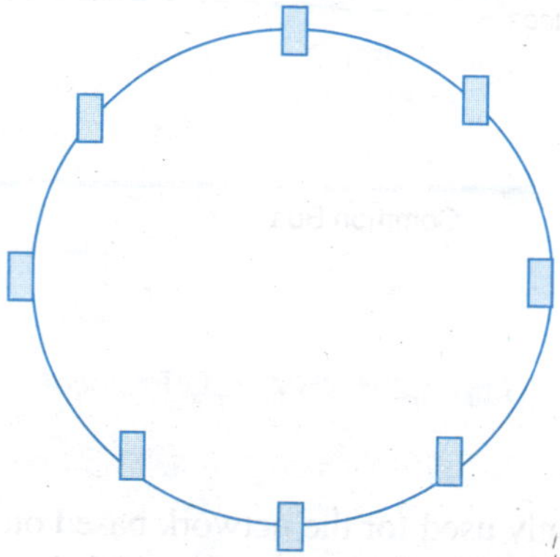

Fig. 6.22: Ring Network

6.10 PROTOCOL FOR NETWORK ACCESS

Various protocols have been developed for communication of data arising from one node of computer to another node of computer for different network topologies. Ethernet is one of the popular network technology which uses Bus Topology. Ethernet standards are now governed by IEEE. A Ethernet LAN employs a coaxial cable called ether to connect to different computers on the network. CSMA/CD (Carrier Sense Multiple Access with Collision Detection) Protocol is one of the popular protocols used for bus topology. Token bus protocol is also used for networks. Token ring protocol is employed by ring network. These protocols are known as access control protocol for networks. In the following sections, the salient features of these protocols are presented:

6.10.1 CSMA/CD Protocol

The Carrier Sense Multiple Access with Collision Detection (CSMA/CD) protocol is most widely used for access control on bus topology. The access of common medium (bus) is available to all the nodes on the network. The node which wants to communicate to another node senses the medium, and if there is no data in transit, it places the data on the bus and the destination node receives the data. The protocol is presented in the following steps.

1. A device or node wishing to transmit the data listens to the medium (bus) to determine whether any other transmission is in progress.
2. If other communication is under progress, then the device waits for a random amount of time and again listens to the medium if the transmission has completed.
3. If the device wishes to send the data and no other communication is under progress, then it starts transmitting the data and listens to the medium until the transmission is over.
4. If at the time of transmission, any other device starts transmitting his own data, then collision is said to have occurred. In case of collision, a short jamming signal is transmitted over the bus.
5. In case of collision, the device waits for some time and again starts transmitting.
6. The receiver node receives the data on the bus and the receiver also continues to listen to the medium.

The advantage of this protocol is its simplicity while the major disadvantage of this protocol is that under heavy load, the performance degrades drastically. If many devices are attempting to communicate the data, the frequency of collision increases, which affects the performance adversely.

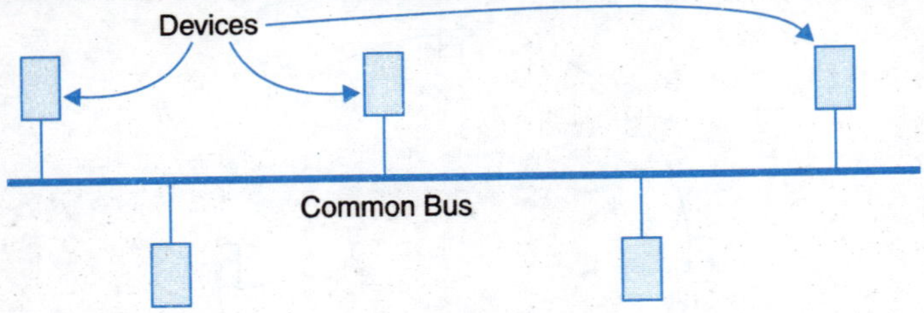

Fig. 6.23: CSMA/CD Protocol

6.10.2 Token Bus Protocol

Token bus protocol is also commonly used for the network based on the bus topology. In this case, the devices connected to the bus form a logical ring. This protocol uses a control packet called *token*. The token is circulated in the logical ring and passes from one node to another. The device holding the token becomes the owner of the bus for the period it continues to hold the token. The holder of the token may transmit the data. Holder of the token may poll another device and may send the requests. The main features of this protocol are as follows:

1. Only holders of token may communicate the data.
2. Devices not holding the token are not allowed to transmit the data. However, they may respond to the request of the holder of the token.
3. A device may hold the token for a specified amount of time. After the expiry of the time, it passes the token to its neighbour device in the logical ring.

6.10.3 Token Ring Protocol

This protocol is widely used in the ring network for access control. The protocol employs a token which is circulated in the logical ring as shown in Figure 6.24.

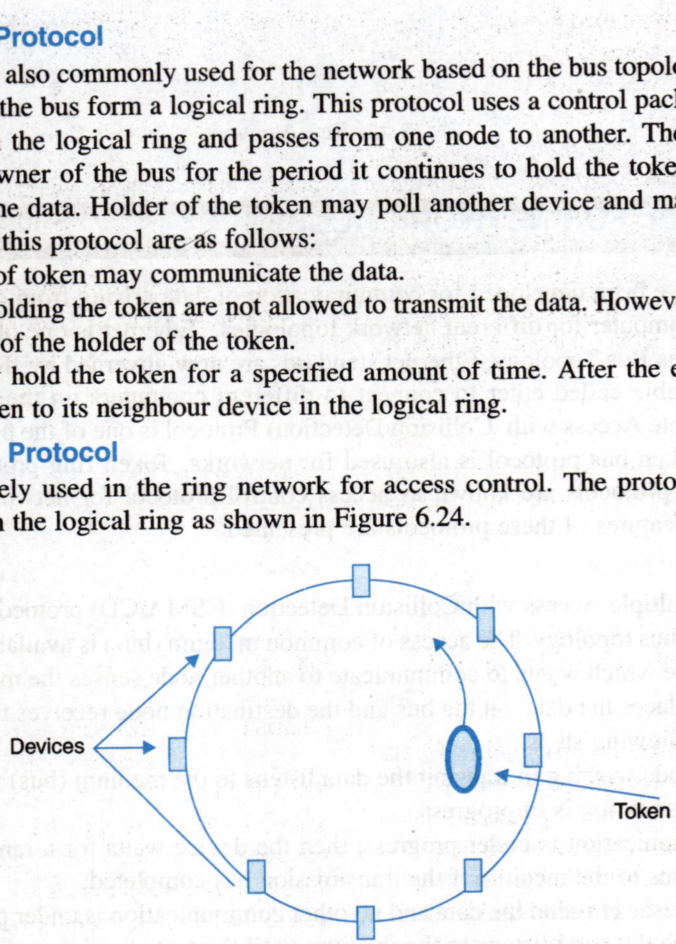

Fig. 6.24: Token Ring Protocol

The salient features of this protocol are as follows:

1. The token is used as a primary object to access control in Token Ring Protocol.
2. Token is marked either free or busy. The mark 'busy' indicates that some device is transmitting the data. The free token indicates that no device is transmitting the data.
3. Whenever a device wishing to transmit the data receives the token marked free, it changes the status to busy and pass the token to its neighbour.

4. The device immediately marking the token busy, starts transmitting the data.
5. Another device wishing to transmit the data waits for the token to come and may start transmission only if it is marked free.
6. The device, after completion of transmission, marks the token free and passes it to its neighbour.

The advantage of this protocol is that it utilizes the bandwidth of the medium to full benefit. The disadvantage of this protocol is its complexity.

6.10.4 Slotted Ring Protocol

Slotted ring protocol is used in ring networks. Unlike token ring protocol, there are several fixed length slots continuously travelling in the logical ring as shown in Figure 6.25.

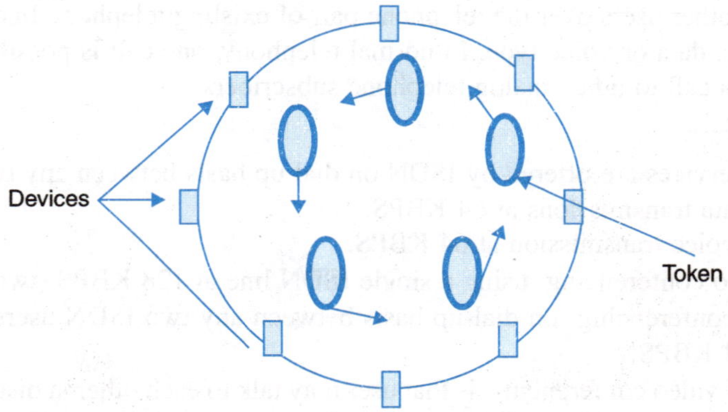

Fig. 6.25: Token Ring Protocol

The salient feature of this protocol are as follows:

1. The fixed length slots (tokens) circulate in the logical ring. These slots are marked free or busy.
2. If any device wants to communicate and receives the free token, it marks the token busy and loads the data on to it. The destination address is also inserted into the token.
3. When this token reaches the destination, the receiver device unloads the data.
4. When the busy token returns to the sender device, it marks it free , if it has completed the transmission of data.
5. A device which is transmitting the data, is not allowed to retransmit until the busy token returns to it. Some of the special bits (flags) are also stored in the token which carry the status of the transmission. The acceptance, rejection or acknowledgement by the device is also marked on the token by setting or resetting the special bits.

6.11 INTEGRATED SERVICES DIGITAL NETWORK (ISDN)

Integrated Service Digital Network is the most powerful tool for various services such as voice, images, and video and multimedia data communication over the telephone network. ISDN may be viewed as a logical extension to the digitalization of telephone network and has became very common in the western countries. In India too, the various mail network service provides as well as DOT, VSNL and MTNL are providing this service to users. In ISDN, the voice, image, video and multimedia data is transmitted over the telephone line in digital form. The ISDN works in the following modes:

1. BRI (Basic Rate Interface)
2. PRI (Primary Rate Interface)

Users can opt for a BRI connection from the local ISP or users can opt for PRI connection in BRI, also called, 2B+D, two 64 kbps channels are available to the user. The other, PRI is used for ISDN compatible EPABX etc., with the induction of state-of-the-art digital technology. In the telecom network in India, these services are being offered by the new Technology Exchange laid down by DOT or MTNL. The ISDN connection is provided at the user's premises located within permissible distance for digital exchange.

6.11.1 ISDN Line vs Analog Telephone Line

In the normal telephone line, the user can make a voice call and the voice data is transmitted in analog form, which is normally vulnerable to distortions. In ISDN, the multimedia data i.e. voice data or image graphics is transmitted over the telephone lines in digital form. In ISDN the user may establish two independent calls to other users over the telephone pair of existing telephone line. These simultaneous calls can be of image, data or voice type. In normal telephony, one call is possible at one time. ISDN user may also make a call to other analog telephone subscribers.

6.11.2 ISDN Services

The following four services are offered by ISDN on dial up basis between any two ISDN subscribers:

1. High speed data transmissions at 64 KBPS.
2. High quality voice transmission at 64 KBPS.
3. Desk top video conferencing using a single ISDN line at 128 KBPS (two B channel).
4. High quality conferencing on dial-up basis between any two ISDN users by three ISDN lines (3*128) = 384 KBPS.

The advantage of video conferencing is that user may talk to each other at distant places thus saving time and money. This is done by transmission of voice and video images of both users as well as by transmitting images, drawing, text or still produces of document at a high speed. Data files on the PC may also be transmitted at a very high speed of 64 KBPS.

6.11.3 ISDN Terminals

Normally when a user wants ISDN connection at it's own premises, DOT or MTNL provide a NT (Networking Terminal) equipment. The user may also procure the terminal from the open market. The telephone line from electronic exchange is terminated at NT box. Up to 8 ISDN terminal equipment may be terminated to NT box. This ISDN terminal may be a ISDN telephone set, videophone, fax, personal computer (PC), video conferencing equipment. These equipment must be compatible with ISDN and it is a mandatory requirement to procure a DOT/MTNL certified equipment. Details of the equipment are as follows:

Normal ISDN Phone

It is the ISDN Phone in its most simple form and contains the hand set phone unit. It converts the user's voice into a digital signal, which may be carried over the ISDN line to its destination.

Advance ISDN Phone

Advance ISDN phone, in addition to normal ISDN phone is required. The additional keys and functions are as follows:

Display: The ISDN phone contains a liquid crystal display. The user may dial the number, which is displayed on LCD. The calling takes place when the button (digit) is pressed. In this calling, a recipient of the call may see the number of calling user.

Logging: Logging facilities provide automatic storing of numbers dialed when the call could not be answered. The calling number may be recalled from the log.

Terminal Adapter: Devices such as 44 fax, answering machine, push button telephone, cordless phone may be connected to ISDN line through a terminal adapter. Any PC with RS232C port (serial port) can be connected to ISDN line. In such cases data communication may take place in 9600 KBPS. In this communication, the PC does not require modem.

6.11.4 Video Conferencing

Video conferencing is the process of simultaneous participation of various users where video and audio from one user to another is sent. The participant on video chat may see and talk to each other. The video conferencing equipment requires a computer, color monitor, digital camera and other control units. This equipment is connected to the telephone network using three ISDN lines. A similar equipment is also required at the other end. The conferencing is established by dial up through the network. Moving images are communicated from one point to another during the conversation. It is also possible to send graphs, report diagrams and still picture through video conferencing equipment. Other control equipment and software help the user to focus and zoom on the participants conferencing. The equipment from Picture Tel is one of the popular options for video conferencing.

6.11.5 Video Phone

This is an subset of video conferencing equipment. In video telephony, a user may dial up another user who has the same equipment.The equipment consists of compact screen and camera. This requires only one ISDN line and the moving images are sent at 128 KBPS (2B) channel. Videophone could be made available as an add-on facility to the Personal Computer.

6.12 SYNCHRONOUS AND ASYNCHRONOUS TRANSFER MODES (ATM)

There are many technologies which have evolved over the time for data communication for a Wide Area Network (WAN). Some of the technologies/ protocols are ARPANET, X.25, Frame Relay, SMDS (Switched Multi Megabit Data Service and ATMs). The ATM (Asynchronous Transfer Mode) is a widely used technology. To understand the difference between asynchronous and synchronous transfer, one must understand Synchronous Time Division multiplexing and Asynchronous Time Division multiplexing. We have already referred to Time Division Multiplexing in section 6.6.

In the Synchronous Time Division Multiplexing, the time slots are allocated to all the devices one by one. Therefore all the devices get an equal share of channel bandwidth. The disadvantage in the synchronous time division multiplexing is that the bandwidth allocated to the device that is not transmitting the data is wasted. In the Asynchronous Time Division Multiplexing, the device which has data ready for transmission gets the available bandwidth. Therefore, in the later scheme, the optimum utilization of bandwidth is obtained.

6.12.1 Asynchronous Transfer Mode (ATM)

ATM scheme is widely used for data communication in telecommunication network. ATM network uses an ATM switch which receives the request for data transfer from different computers. The ATM switch facilitates the data transfer in asynchronous mode. Various computers are connected to the ATM switch. The ATM switch connects the sender's and receiver's computers and transfers the packets to destination at a high speed. ATM network is similar to the Star network as is evident from Figure 6.26, where several computers are interconnected via the ATM switch.

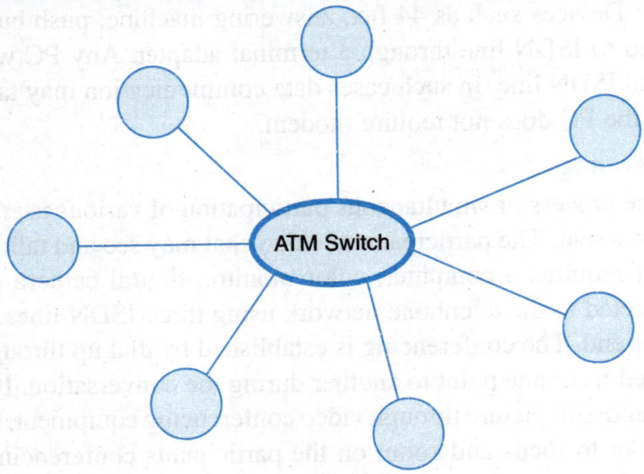

Fig. 6.26: ATM Switch

ATM is an ANSI (American National Standardization Institute) standard for cell switching and it may be used to connect the LANs with the WANs. Switching speed of ATM is from 1.544 MBPS to 10 GBPS. In ATM networks, one to one connection is established by virtual channel which may transfer the data without interference.

ATM switch is most suitable for multimedia data transfer which contains the text, audio and video data. The speed of communication between the computers and ATM switch is 156 MPBS.

ATM Cell

To provide fast data transfer, the ATM switch divides the data received from the sender into small sized packets called ATM Cell. ATM cell size is of 53 octets (one octet = 8 bits). The five octets are reserved for the header information and the rest 48 octets contain the data bytes. Since ATM is an attempt to provide the multimedia services across the network, the multimedia data is divided into several octets containing text, audio and video data. The chopping of the data is so done that it synchronizes the receipts of text, audio and video packets. ATM switch allows the users to specify the quality of service requirement of communication.

OBJECTIVE TYPE QUESTIONS

Multiple Choice

1. Which of following parameter determines the characteristic of Analog Signal?
   (a) Amplitude (b) Frequency (c) Phase (d) All of these
2. Which property of carrier wave is modified in FM?
   (a) Amplitude (b) Frequency (c) Phase (d) All of these
3. Which of the following modulation technique uses train of pulse as carrier.
   (a) Amplitude Modulation (b) Frequency Modulation
   (c) Pulse Code Modulation (d) All of these
4. Which of following technique is used for transmitting digital signal?
   (a) Amplitude Modulation (b) Frequency Modulation
   (c) Pulse Code Modulation (d) Amplitude shift keying
5. Which of the following is an advantage of computer network?
   (a) Resource Sharing (b) Improved reliability and availability
   (c) Enhanced Performance (d) All of these

6. A network spreading in different geographical location is known as
   (a) LAN (b) WAN (c) Both (d) None of these
7. A communication which allows data transmission in both directions simultaneously is called
   (a) Simplex (b) Full Duplex (c) Half Duplex (d) None of these
8. Which of the following is a token based protocol.
   (a) CSMA/CD (b) Slotted Ring (c) Both (d) None of these
9. BRI mode of ISDN uses two data channel each of
   (a) 64 KBPS (b) 256 KBPS (c) 1 MBPS (d) 64 MBPS
10. Number of layers in ISO-OSI reference model are . 0
   (a) 5 (b) 7 (c) 9 (d) 6

Answers

1-d, 2-b, 3-c, 4-d, 5-d, 6-b, 7-b, 8-b, 9-a, 10-b

State True or False

1. Digital signals are trains of pulses. [True] [False]
2. Continuous signal may be constructed from digital values by data hold operation. [True] [False]
3. Amplitude Shift Keying is example of Analog Modulation. [True] [False]
4. FDM allows sending more than one signals over communication channel. [True] [False]
5. Point to Point dedicated path is established in Packet Switching. [True] [False]
6. Single direction communication is known as Simplex. [True] [False]
7. CSMA/CD protocol is used for network access. [True] [False]
8. ISDN may be used for video conferencing. [True] [False]
9. Bandwidth denotes the amount of data communication over channel. [True] [False]
10. Optimum bandwidth utilization is achieved in Asynchronous Transmission. [True] [False]

Answers

1-True, 2-True, 3-False, 4-True, 5-False, 6-True, 7-True, 8-True, 9-True, 10-True.

SELECTED EXERCISES

1. What is meant by Data Communication? Why is a communication networks required for Information Transfer?
2. Explain the general model of data communication. What is the role of the modem (modulator and demodulator) at the sender's and receiver's ends?
3. What are analog signals? Explain briefly the parameters defining analog signal. How are analog signals different from digital signal?
4. What are transducers ? Explain the role of the transducer in communication.
5. Explain the general model of digital transmission of data. Why is the analog data sampled? Explain how the sampled data is quantified.
6. What do you mean by amplitude quantization? How are the samples quantified?
7. What is meant by communication channel? Explain different types of communication channels.
8. What is the importance of sampling process? How are the samples of analog waveform taken? Explain the role of train of pulses.
9. Explain how the input waveform is reproduced at the receiving end in digital communication.
10. What do you understand by modulation? What are essential differences between amplitude, frequency and phase modulation?
11. What is meant by pulse modulation? How is it different from analog modulation?
12. Explain the salient features of amplitude modulation? What are the disadvantages of amplitude modulation?

13. Explain the salient features of frequency modulation. What are the advantages and disadvantages of frequency modulation?
14. Explain the salient features of phase modulation.
15. Explain the different pulse modulation techniques. What are the relative advantages/disadvantages of these techniques?
16. What is pulse code modulation? Explain the steps of pulse code modulation? Why PCM is less susceptible to errors?
17. What do you mean by digital modulation? Explain the various digital modulation techniques.
18. What is amplitude shift keying? How is it different from frequency keying? Compare the performance of both the techniques.
19. What do you mean by phase shift keying?
20. What do you mean by multiplexing of the signals? Why is multiplexing of the signals required in communication? Explain different techniques of multiplexing of signals.
21. What is meant by time division multiplexing? How is digital time division multiplexing done?
22. What is frequency division multiplexing? Explain the issues in frequency division multiplexing?
23. What are computer networks? Explain the motivation behind the computer network.
24. How is the availability of a computer system increased on a computer network?
25. What are Distributed Systems? Explain the problems of distributed systems? How is a distributed system different from network operating system?
26. What do you mean by Client Server model?
27. What are the differences between the Local Area Network and Wide Area Network? How are they different from Metropolitan Area Networks?
28. What are the differences between the circuit and packet switching? For what are these techniques used?
29. What do you mean by Simplex transmission mode? How it is different from Duplex transmission mode? Explain what are Half duplex transmission mode.
30. What are ISO OSI reference model? Explain the role of all the layers of OSI reference model.
31. What do you mean by the network topology? Explain the following in brief.
    - Star Topology
    - Tree/Bus Topology
    - Ring Topology
32. What do you understand by communication protocols?
33. Explain the salient features of CSMA/CD protocol. In which type of topology, is this protocol used?
34. Explain the steps of Token Bus protocols? Compare the performance of token bus protocol with CSMA/CD protocol.
35. What is meant by Token Ring protocol? What is the role of token in the protocol?
36. Explain the salient features of slotted ring protocol? What are advantages and disadvantages of slotted ring protocol? Compare the performance of slotted ring protocol with token ring protocol.
37. What is Asynchronous Transfer Mode? What is ATM switch? Under what circumstances is the ATM switching used?
38. What do you understand by ISDN? Explain the salient features of ISDN. Under what circumstances are the ISDN lines required.

7

MS WINDOWS & MS OFFICE

Contents

7 MS WINDOWS & MS OFFICE

7.1 INTRODUCTION

Windows, a product of Microsoft is an operating system that manages scheduling of work and hardware accessories. The entire task performed in an operating system can be accomplished in Windows 95 environment. Unlike previous operating system DOS (disk operating system), it is a Graphical User Interface (GUI) based operating system. You may enter the command by clicking desired objects using mouse. Windows 98, a successor of DOS removed the major limitation of Disk Operating System. Though, there exists several versions of MS Windows, we choose to restrict our discussion to MS Windows 98. Main features of Windows 98 are as follows:

- Windows is Graphical User Interface (GUI) based system, while DOS was based on the textual interfaces.
- While working with Windows, it is not necessary to remember the lengthy DOS command and with syntax.
- Windows allows the user to get rid of typing commands and all major operations are performed by a few clicks of mouse.
- Basic operating system services, file and folders are shown in the graphical form as Icon and using the mouse pointer to those Icons and clicking on top of them invoke the services.
- Management of file and folder like Copy, Delete, Create operation may be performed by mouse and it also allows drag and drop operation.
- Windows allows the multitasking while DOS is not a multitasking system. It is possible to open several applications in windows at the same time.
- Windows exhibit a better mechanism to show and remove the error occurred in different operation.

Windows allows the user to control the hardware in the most simple way. It allows the user to add new hardware, configure the system and enable them to work together. It allows users to run different program or application in windows. Microsoft Office package which includes MS Word, MS Access, MS Excel etc. are compatible with the Windows. It also allows the ease of the organizing users information in form of files and folders. It provides the user all the tools and services to copy, delete, sort, move the files and folders.

When a computer running on Windows 98 operating system is turned on, after few seconds it displays a screen as shown in the Figure 7.1. This area is called desktop, which contains various objects such as task bar, mouse pointer and several icons.

Fig. 7.1: Desktop

7.2 KNOWING OBJECTS OF WINDOWS

7.2.1 The Desktop

Total visible area on the screen, which you get immediately after turning on your computer, is called Desktop area. You may keep your important folders on desktop or you may create shortcut to the program that you use very frequently. You may customize the desktop according to your requirements and ease by adding the shortcut to program, folders or documents. You may also change the setting such as desktop colour, screen saver, size, background, appearance and other effects. For this you have to right click the mouse button on the desktop, and select the properties. The desktop may contain many items like My Computer, Network neighbourhood, My Documents, Recycle Bin along with the items which a user creates. The Desktop is shown in the Figure 7.1.

7.2.2 Task Bar

At the bottom of the screen a horizontal strip is seen which is called taskbar. It contain the Start button on the extreme left side, which is used to start an application or program. On the right hand side you may view the various icon which represent various process running by the system. To know about the programs or process under active condition, you may move mouse pointer to them and see their name. At the extreme right side you can see the clock running.

Fig. 7.2: Task Bar

7.2.3 Start Button

You may click on the start button to start various programs or applications. When you click on the start button the screen as shown in the Figure 7.1 appears. By navigating the mouse pointer you may select & click on the appropriate icon. This will start your application. For example, going through program-accessories-entertainment-CD player, you may start CD player application. You have to use this button if you want to change in the setting or to find a file or folder on your disk.

7.2.4 My Computer

You can use My Computer to see everything stored on your computer. All you need to do is to double click on My Computer icon on the desktop to browse through files and folder stored onto your disk. It will show you all the accessories attached to the computer. As shown in Figure 7.3, My Computer lists Floppy Drive A, Disk Drive C & D, CD Drive, Control Panel etc. On clicking to the drive icon like A, C, D or CD Drive, you may explore the contents of either floppy, disk or CD.

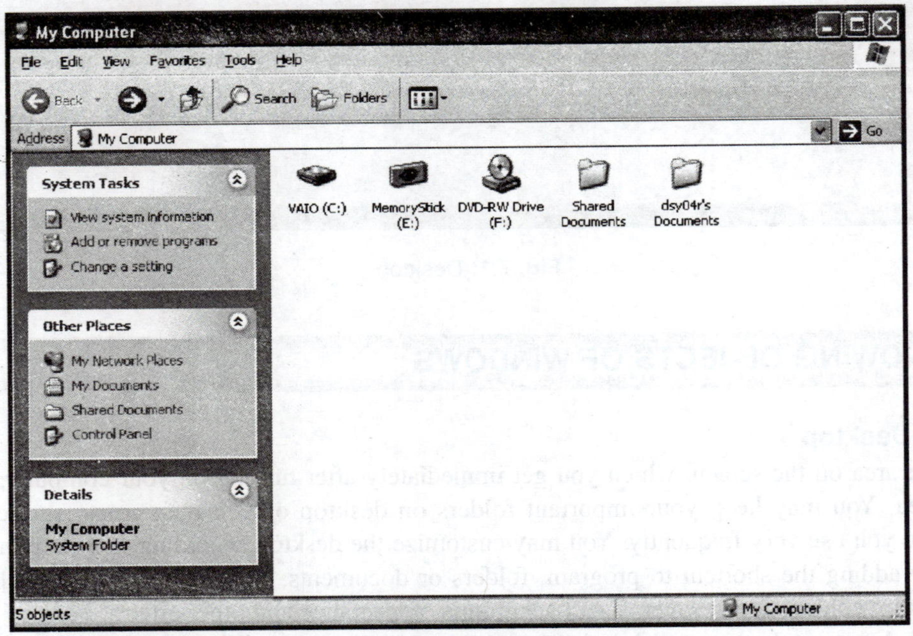

Fig. 7.3: My Computer

If you want to the find out the current amount of space available/used on hard disk, floppy disk, CD etc., then point to the corresponding disk icon and right click the mouse select properties. This will show you the total disk space available and used in graphical form as shown in the Figure 7.4.

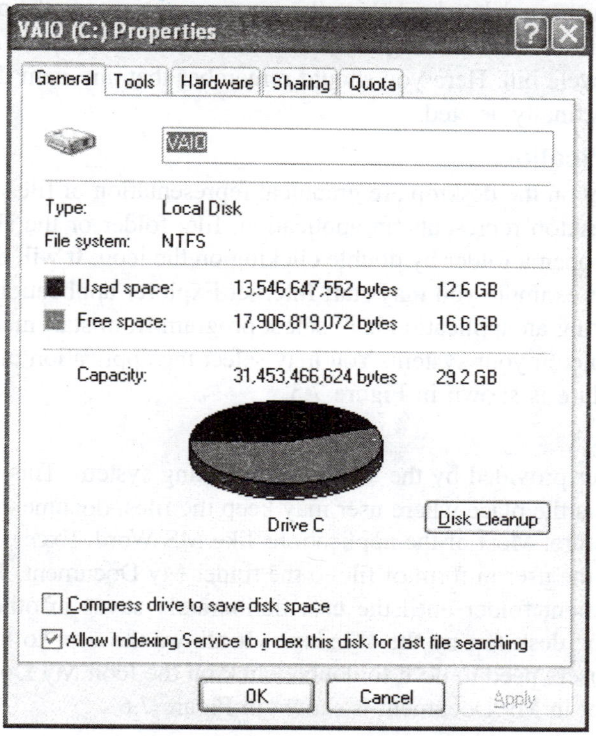

Fig. 7.4: Display of Disk Space

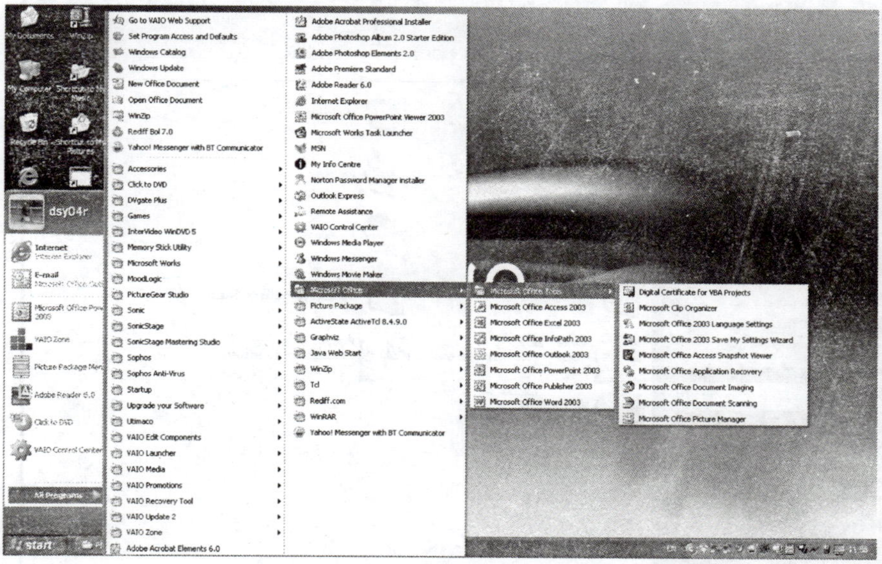

Fig. 7.5: Starting an Application

7.2.5 Recycle Bin

You may delete any file or folder or program or shortcut etc. After deleting any object, it is not actually deleted but it is sent to the recycle bin. This avoids the possibility of accidental deletes. If any point of time, you feel that a file has been deleted accidentally, you may restore it to the original location by right clicking the mouse on that object in the recycle bin. If you run short of space on the disk, you should first delete the item in recycle bin. Here you should remember that any item deleted from recycle bin cannot be restored i.e. it is finally deleted.

7.2.6 Starting an Application

Various other icons present on the desktop are graphical representation of files or programs or applications. Any icon on the desktop represents an application, file, folder or the shortcut. You can start a program or application or open a folder by double clicking on the icon. It will then start the application or open the file/folder. For example you may start Internet Explorer application by double clicking the icon. Another way of starting an application is to select program from start menu. It will present you a list of applications available on your system. You may select the application of your choice which you want to start. This procedure is shown in Figure 7.5.

7.2.7 My Document

My Document is the folder provided by the Windows operating system. This folder is the utility provided by the Windows. It is the place where user may keep the files, documents etc. which needs to be accessed by the user in future. Most of the applications like MS Word, Excel, PowerPoint etc. attempt to save the work done by the user in form of file to the folder My Document. These files are automatically saved in My Document folder until the user deliberately saves in other folder. The Icon My Document is placed on the desk top by the Windows. It allows the user to have quick access to the previous work done. All users need to do it to double click on the Icon My Document on the desk top. The view of file and folder in My Document is shown in Figure 7.6.

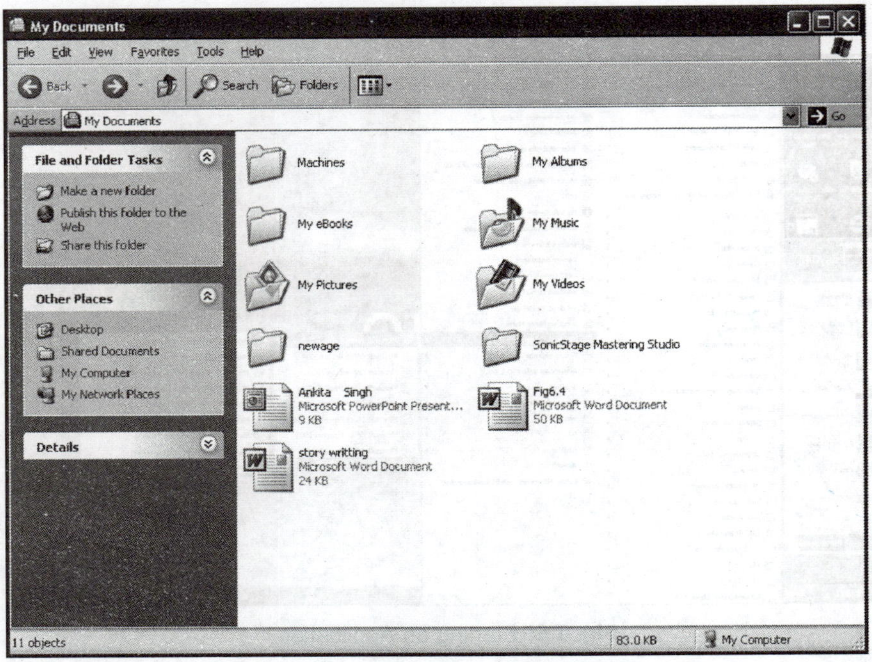

Fig. 7.6: My Document

The documents, files and folders contained in My Document may be customized according to users requirements like size of icon, arranging the file/folders in order of their size, alphabetically etc.

7.2.8 My Briefcase

My Briefcase is another utility provided by windows. The Icon for My Briefcase folder is placed by the windows on the desktop. This utility is very useful to those persons who travel very frequently with the electronic documents. Frequent travellers carry the documents electronically in the form of files and folders. These files and folders may be kept in floppy disk or laptop while travelling. Major advantages of this folder is that the user may get rid of subsequent changes in the documents. For example, if the user have saved one document in the My Briefcase for the purpose of transportation. If any change has occurred in the document, you may select the utility of 'Update All' of My Briefcase contained in briefcase menu for subsequent changes in the file.

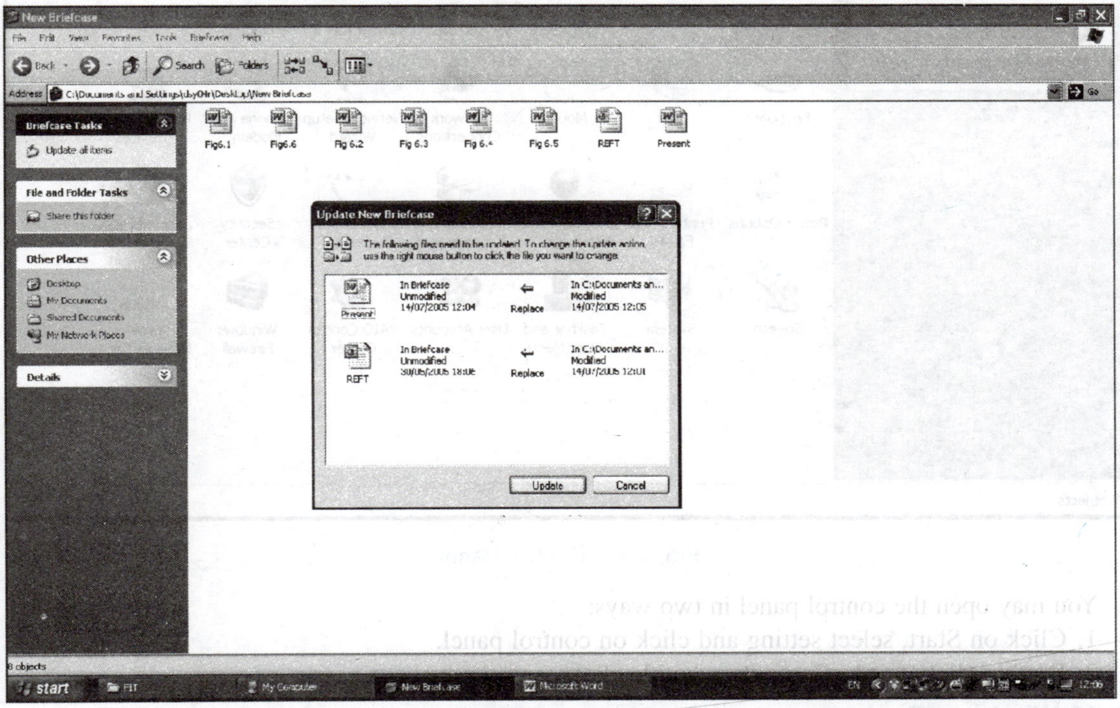

Fig. 7.7: My Briefcase

As shown in Figure 7.7, you may open My Briefcase by double clicking on the icon My Briefcase placed on desktop. It will display the files contained in the My Briefcase folder. By selecting briefcase option from the top of My Briefcase and clicking on update all, Windows will open a new screen (Update My Briefcase) which will display the file which have been deleted from My Briefcase and the files which have been modified outside my briefcase. You may choose the action accordingly to modify the contents of My Briefcase.

7.2.9 Control Panel

Control Panel is one of the most important utility provided by MS Windows 95/98. It allows you to change the parameters and setting. In fact, Control Panel contains a number of small utilities. You may change the setting of the desk top, printer, mouse, screen savers, keyboard and other hardware devices. A view of contents of the control panel are shown in Figure 7.8. All the facilities are provided at one point from which user may customize the setting or windows environment according to his choice.

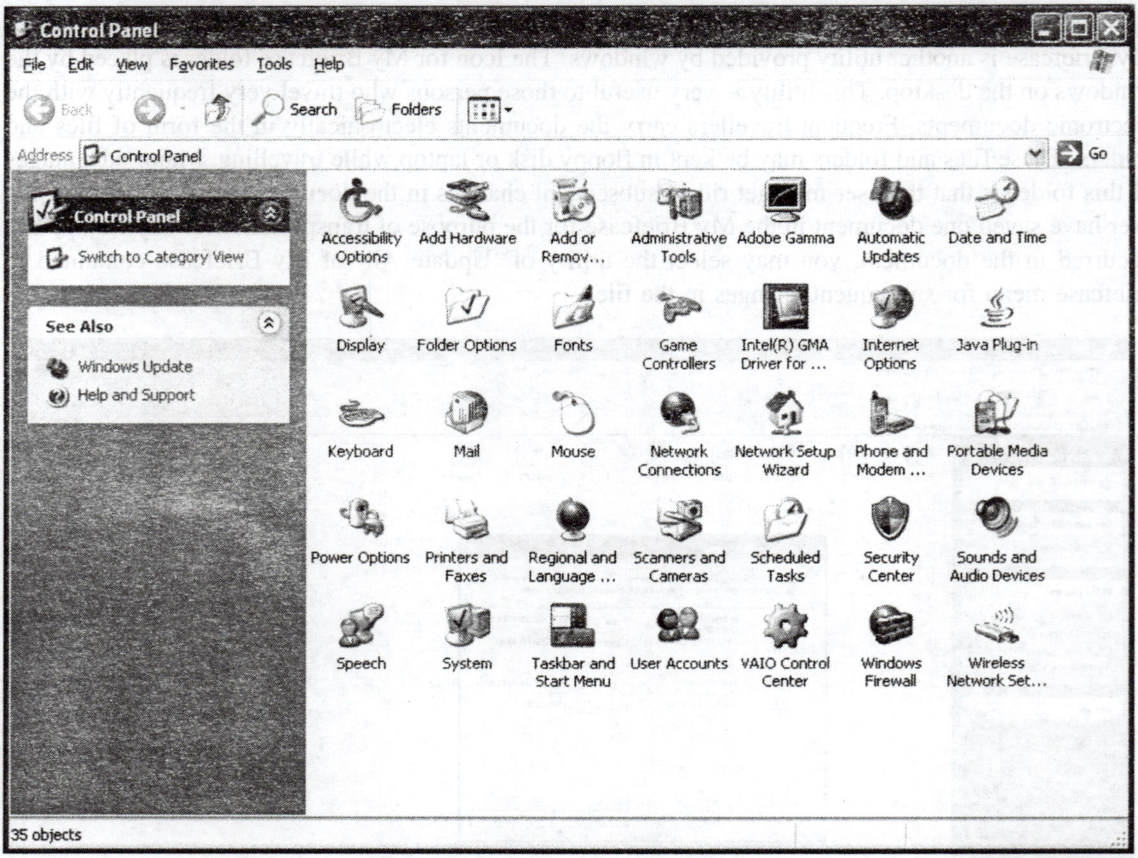

Fig. 7.8: Control Panel

You may open the control panel in two ways:

1. Click on Start, select setting and click on control panel.
2. Double click on My Computer, double click control panel.

7.2.10 Windows Explorer

Windows Explorer is one of the most important utilities provided in the windows which allows you to view various files and folders placed on floppy disk, hard disk and CD. It can also be used to locate the file and folder on your computer system. Windows explorer is two pane window, when any element in left pane is clicked, right pane displays the contents of that folder. Windows explorer can be started from start menu, program and windows explorer. Typical snap shot of windows explorer is shown in Figure 7.9.

As shown in Figure 7.9, windows explorer displays the contents of all hard drives, CD and floppy disk. In the left pane, if you click on to any item e.g. Floppy, the contents of floppy disk will be displayed in right pane. You may use drag and drop operation to copy the files and folders from one place to another in windows explorer.

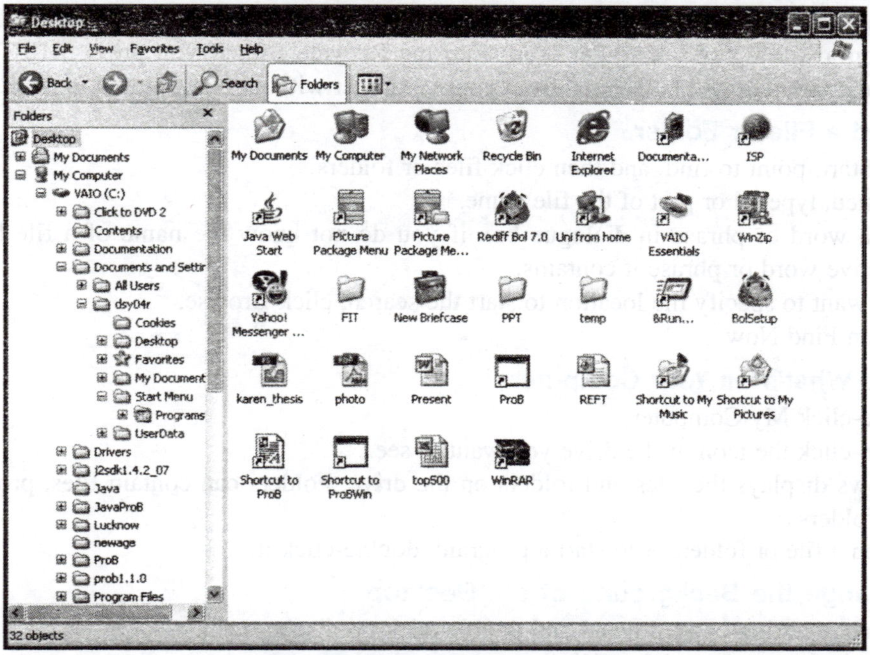

Fig. 7.9: Windows Explorer

7.3 IMPORTANT FUNCTIONS

In this section, the tips for doing some important functions in the windows are given.

7.3.1 To Open a File or Folder

1. Double-click My Computer on the desktop.
2. Double-click the drive that contains the file.
3. Double-click the file or folder you want to open.

It will then open the file for you.

7.3.2 To Open a File You've Used Recently

1. Click Start, and then point to Documents.
2. Click the document you want to open.

7.3.3 To Copy a File or Folder from One Disk/Folder to Another

1. In My Computer or Windows Explorer, click the file or folder you want to copy.
2. On the Edit menu, click Copy.
3. Open the folder or disk where you want to put the copy.
4. On the Edit menu, click Paste.

7.3.4 To Change the Name of a File or Folder

1. In My Computer or Windows Explorer, click the file or folder you want to rename.
2. On the File menu, click Rename.
3. Type the new name, and then press ENTER.

7.3.5 To Delete a File or Folder

1. In My Computer or Windows Explorer, click the file or folder you want to delete.

2. On the File menu, click Delete.
3. You can also drag file or folder icons into the Recycle Bin. If you press SHIFT key while dragging, the item will be deleted from your computer without being stored in the Recycle Bin.

7.3.6 To Find a File or Folder

1. Click Start, point to find, and then click files or folders.
2. In Named, type all or part of the file name.
   Enter a word or phrase in dialogue box if you do not know the name of a file but know a distinctive word or phrase it contains.
   If you want to specify the location to start the search, click Browse.
3. Click on Find Now.

7.3.7 To See What's on Your Computer

1. Double-click My Computer.
2. Double-click the icon of the drive you want to see.
   Windows displays the files and folders on the drive. Folders can contain files, programs, and other folders.
3. To open a file or folder, or to start a program, double-click it.

7.3.8 To Change the Background of the Desktop

1. Go to start-setting-control panel and double click on display icon.
2. Alternatively you may right click the mouse and select properties.
3. In Wallpaper, click the background you want to use or click Pattern to choose or modify the background.
4. Click Apply to see the changes before you close the dialog box, or click OK to accept the changes and close the dialog box.

7.3.9 To Set up a Screen Saver

1. Go to start-setting-control panel and double click on display icon.
2. Alternatively you may right click the moue and select properties
3. To open the Display Properties dialog box at the Screen Saver tab.
4. In Screen Saver, click the screen saver you want to use.
5. To customize the screen saver, click Settings.

Display properties are shown in Figure 7.10.

7.3.10 To Adjust the Rate at which the Cursor Blinks

1. Go to start-setting-control panel and double click on keyboard icon
2. On the Speed tab, drag the Cursor blink rate slider.

The test cursor to the left of the slider area blinks at the new rate.

7.3.11 To Send a File or Folder to a Disk

1. If you are copying a file or folder to a floppy disk, insert the disk in the disk drive.
2. In My Computer or Windows Explorer, click the file or folder you want to copy.
3. On the File menu, point to Send To, and then click the drive you want to copy the file or folder to.
4. After selecting a file or folder to copy, right click the mouse and select Send To Floppy Disk.

7.3.12 To Move a File or Folder

1. In My Computer or Windows Explorer, click the file or folder you want to move.
2. On the Edit menu, click Cut or Copy.

3. Open the folder where you want to put the file or folder.
4. On the Edit menu, click Paste.

7.3.13 Creating a Shortcut

A shortcut is a quick way to start a program or open a file or folder without going to its permanent location in Windows Explorer. Shortcuts are especially useful for programs, files, and folders you use frequently. There are three ways you can create a shortcut.

7.3.14 To Put a Shortcut on the Desktop

1. In My Computer or Windows Explorer, click the item, such as a file, program, folder, printer, or computer, for which you want to create a shortcut.
2. On the File menu, click Create Shortcut.
3. Drag the shortcut icon onto the desktop.

7.3.15 To Create a Folder

1. Click the drive in Windows Explorer where you want to create the new folder.
2. On the File menu, point to New, and then click Folder.
   The new folder appears with a temporary name.
3. Type a name for the new folder, and then press ENTER.

7.3.16 To Add a Program to the Start or Programs Menu

1. Click Start, point to Settings, and then click Taskbar & Start Menu.

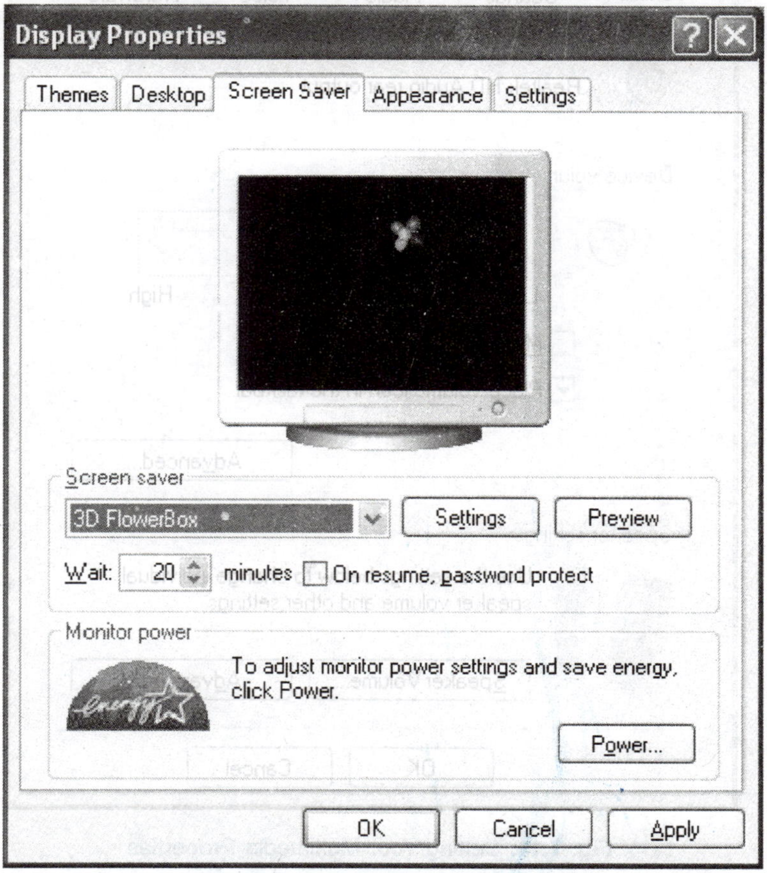

Fig. 7.10: Setting Your Screen Saver

2. Click the Start Menu Programs tab.
3. Click Add, and then click Browse.
4. Locate the program you want to add, and then click it.
5. Click Next, and then double-click the menu on which you want the program to appear.
6. Type the name that you want to see on the menu, and then click Finish.
7. If Windows prompts you to choose an icon, click one, and then click Finish.

7.3.17 To Add a New Font to Your Computer

1. Click Start, point to Settings, click Control Panel, and then double-click Fonts.
2. On the File menu, click Install New Font.
3. Click the drive, and then click the folder that contains the fonts you want to add.
4. Click the font you want to add.

7.3.18 To Adjust the Playback Volume

1. Open the Multimedia Properties dialog box at the Audio tab.
2. In Playback, click the Volume icon to display Volume Control. Adjust the volume for the appropriate device.

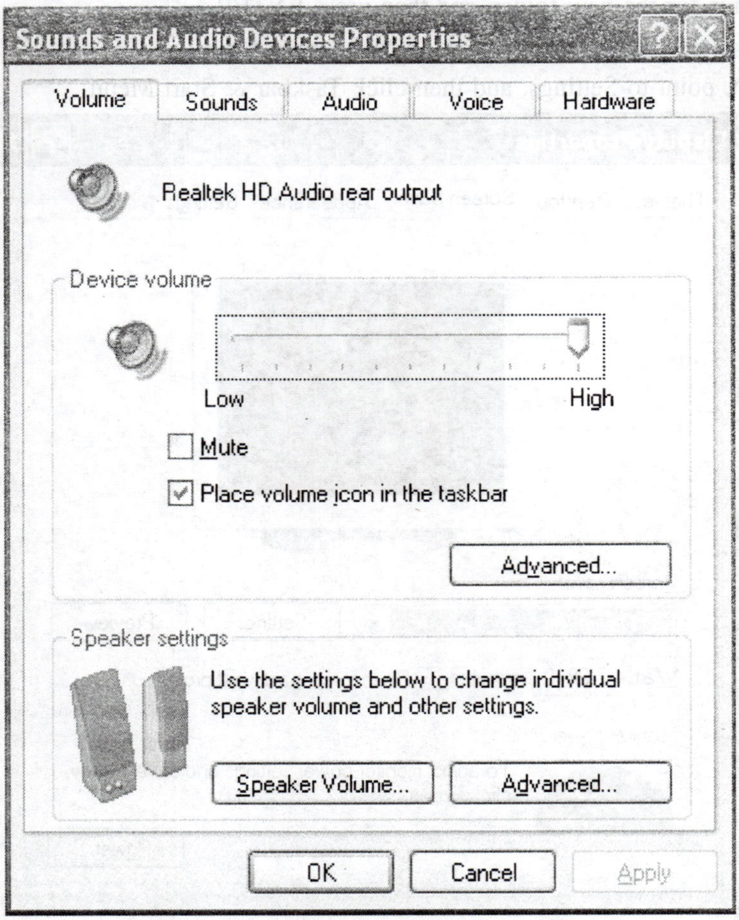

Fig. 7.11: Setting Your Multimedia Properties

7.4 STARTING AN APPLICATION (PROGRAM)

Starting an application means, starting a program with which you want to wok. For example, you may like to open internet explorer, MS Word, MS Access, MS Excel or any other similar program. There are several ways to start an application. Most simple way to start an application is by navigating through Start button. All you have to do is to click on the start button, which is at the left corner of the task bar. When you click on it Task Menu is displayed which contain many pads. Select Program menu which contain all applications including Accessories, Windows Explorer, MS Word, MS Access, MS Excel, MS-DOS prompt and many other applications of windows. You may find several applications on entertainment, system tool, communication, calculator etc. in the accessories of program menu. For starting any application, you should first select the application and click on the application by mouse.

There is another faster way to start an application. You may create a short cut of that application and place the short cut on your desktop. This is very helpful for the application, which you run very frequently. All you have to do is to create a short cut, is to move mouse pointer to that application using My Computer or Start button, press right button of mouse, select create short cut. Then you may drag it to the desktop. Many accessories such as Games, Multimedia, Calculator, Paint, Wordpad are provided in Windows 95. The folder Games contains many games based on windows. Multimedia has a CD player, Media player and Volume control to operate multimedia programs. In System Tool, Scan disk is a very important utility which enable hard disk to operate smoothly and prevent it from problem. Paint is used for painting with colour, Calculator to calculate some mathematical operation and word pad to write a letter or to print a report.

7.5 KNOWING YOUR WINDOWS

Windows 98, if you start an application, it will always run in windows. You may run more than one application at a time in Windows 98. This feature of Windows 98 is called multitasking. All the windows you open has the following component. For example when you start Windows explorer application, it will run into a new window which is shown in the Figure 7.12

7.5.1 Title Bar

The application executed will run in a window. It displays the title of window on the top. The dark colour bar is called title bar. On the right hand side you may see the three boxes which are used to minimize, restore or close the application. Title bar is also used to move a windows. Double clicking on title bar either restores or maximizes the windows. The left corner icon on the title bar is called control box, which when clicked invokes a Control Menu, used to control the window. If the windows is already maximized then the restore button is used to restore the windows.

7.5.2 Menu Bar

The next bar below the title bar is Menu bar. This is divided into many menu items such as File, Edit, View, Go, Favourite, Tools and Help. Clicking on any menu item displays a menu list. This list contains several menu Item, clicking on it will issue a command of appropriate nature.

7.5.3 Tool Bar

The bar next to the menu bar is seen with many small buttons. The common commands, which are given through menu bar, can be issued by tool bar. Clicking on any button is sufficient to give a command by tool Bar. In some application such as Microsoft Word. Two-tool bars are seen.

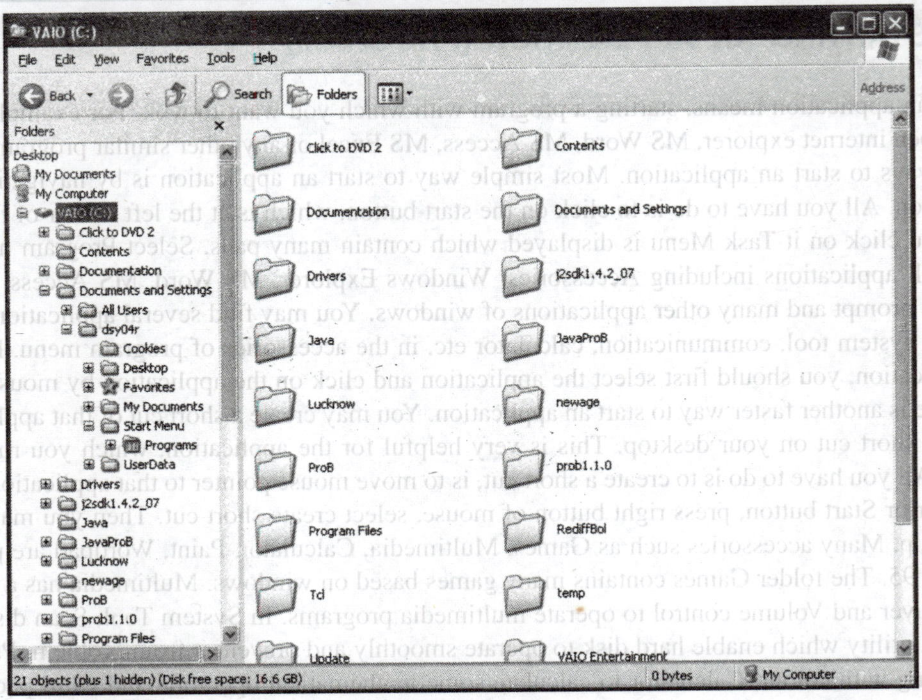

Fig. 7.12: Windows

7.5.4 Status Bar

The bar at the bottom of any window is called the status bar. It shows the status of the application.

7.5.5 Scroll Bar

There are two scroll bar called horizontal and vertical which are seen if the content of the window are larger than the window. Small button of the scroll bar is used to navigate in a window.

7.5.6 Control Menu Box

Control Menu appears when the icon of the left side in the title bar is clicked. This Menu is used to control the whole application window to move a window on the desktop, Move is selected. To change the size of application window, Size is clicked. Maximize and Minimize are used to maximize or minimize the application window. The last option is to close which is used to close the application. To activate the control, menu by keyboard press Alt+Space bar keys simultaneously. Use arrow keys to select an option.

7.5.7 How to Close an Application

You may quit the application or close the application in one of the following ways:

1. Click the button on the title bar, which is seen as X on the right corner.
2. Choose the file on menu bar and select exit command from menu bar.
3. Press the Alt + F4 keys simultaneously.
4. Activate the Control Menu of the application window by Clicking on the Control menu icon at left corner in title bar and select Close.

7.5.8 Clip Boards

Clipboard is a utility provided by the Windows 98 to add the process of copying information between the application. It is temporary storage area on which we can clip a small amount of information. This information stays on the clip board unless it is replaced or exit windows. Using clip board portion of the text, graphic or sound can be marked in one application and dropped into other.

7.6 HOW TO SWITCH BETWEEN THE VARIOUS APPLICATIONS

By virtue of being a multitasking operating system, windows 98 allows you to run more than one application simultaneously. You may see the status of various applications which are displayed on the status bar. You may click on to the appropriate item on the status bar to switch to that application. Alternatively you may also use alt and tab keys of your keyboard to switch between the applications.

7.7 MANAGING YOUR FILES THROUGH WINDOWS EXPLORER

Windows explorer is a powerful tool of Windows 98, which allows you to manage your files and folders on the disk. You can start windows explorer by navigating through start button then select windows explorer in program files. All the information on your disk is saved in the form of files. This information may be a document, letter, image, video, sound or any other format supported by a specific application. All files in a computer are stored in directory, which is called Folder. A Folder contains many files and folders. Double clicking any folder opens it and lists the contents of it. Windows Explorer is used to copy, move and delete files/folders. Properties of the file can also be seen in the explorer. We can also find the location of a file in the explorer. To move file or folder click on the files/folder and drag it to desired location. To copy/folder to other location click it and drag it to desired location by holding the Control key down. To Create a new file/folder go to file menu on menu bar and select new option. A screen shot of Windows Explorer is shown in the figure.

7.8 STARTING DOS APPLICATION

Although Windows 98 is an operating system yet you may work on Microsoft Disk operating system in the Windows 98. All you have to do to start a DOS application is to click on start button and navigate through program and select MS DOS prompt. By clicking on this item you may start DOS application. The DOS has almost no use in Windows but it is provided only to assist the old users who are familiar with DOS. You will see the DOS prompt on the DOS window and you may issue any DOS command.

7.9 HOW TO SHUT DOWN YOUR COMPUTER

Never switch off your computer when your applications are running. This may corrupt your window file system. It has been recommended to shut down your computer by navigating through shut down on start button. On clicking this item following window will appear. You may select to shut down, restart or restart in MS DOS mode your computer. If you select shut down, then click in the box provided and press OK button. You must wait until the message "It is now safe to turn off your computer" comes on to your screen.

Fig. 7.13: Shut Down Menu

7.10 INTRODUCTION TO MS OFFICE

Microsoft office package consists of several softwares which are frequently used by MS Windows users. The MS Windows provides the platform for office tools. These are given the name Office tools because they are very useful in disposing various day-to-day office work. The office tool is a bunch of several other tools like Word, Access, Excel, PowerPoint etc. The office tools are tightly integrated with the MS Windows and gives best performance with MS Windows platform. The documents created in one of the office tools may be used in another office tool. For example, the MS Excel may use the MS Word files. These tools use graphical user interface and are quite easy to learn. Most of the tasks in these tools may be accomplished by few clicks of the mouse. These packages may also be utilized at other places also for specialized work. This package is a bunch of following important softwares or tools:

1. MS Word : used for word processing
2. MS Excel : used for calculation and analysis of data
3. MS PowerPoint : used for business and technical presentations
4. MS Access : used for database applications

In the following sections of this chapter, we will discuss the basic tips to use these softwares.

7.11 MS WORD

The MS Word package is one of most important and widely used tools for word processing applications. This package allows you to type the text, format the text and helps generating documents. The documents, once entered, may be saved for longer time and whenever the documents need to be reproduced with modification, it can be done with little effort. MS Word allows you to do the following:

1. Create, open, save and print the documents.
2. Typing, editing, copy, paste and justifying the text.
3. Search for spelling and grammatical errors.
4. Formatting the paragraphs.

5. Create and manipulate the tables.
6. Page setup, paper size, margin, header, footer, page numbering.

The MS Word may be started in MS Windows by the following steps:

1. Go to start
2. Select Programs
3. Click MS Word.

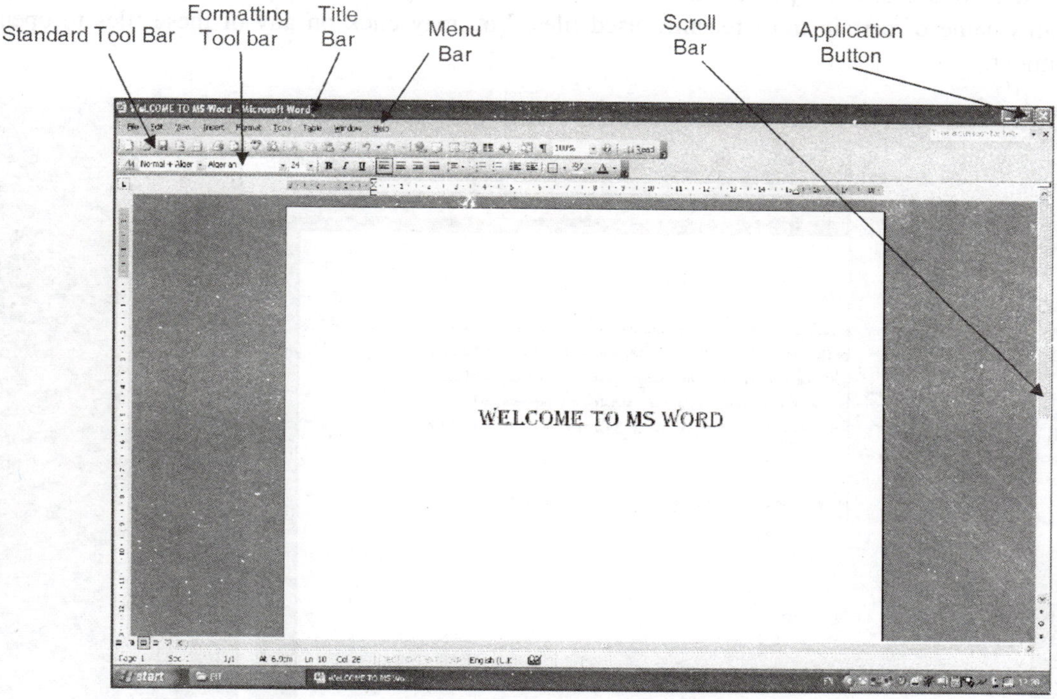

Fig. 7.14

7.11.1 Create, Open, Save and Print the Documents

Following operations may create a new document:

1. Go to File on menu bar.
2. Select New.

Alternatively by clicking on a new button on the standard tool bar, a new document may be created. The MS Word allocates the default name to the document like Document1, Document2 etc. to the newly created document. Name of the document currently being used is displayed in title bar.

To open an existing document, go to the menu item File on Menu bar and select 'Open'. Immediately after clicking on 'Open', the MS Windows will open a directory listing. You may choose to select appropriate file. To save a document, you may again select, Save option from File Menu item of the Menu bar. The existing or newly created document may be printed by the same procedure by selecting Print option from File Menu Item at Menu Bar. The Create, Open, Save and Print option contained in menu item File are shown below in Figure 7.15.

As shown in Figure 7.15, options available in menu item 'File' are divided into several groups. First keeps the option New, Open, Close. These options are used to create a new file, open an existing file and close the current file. Second group contains the item save, save as, Save as HTML. With these options, the document may be saved on the disk in different formats. Last option allows you to save the document as a HTML file. Third group contains the items Page Setup, Print Preview and Print option. With these options, you may change the page set up, view the document before printing and may print the document by clicking print. The fourth group contains the 'Send To' and 'Properties' items. With the 'send to' option, you may send or move the document to the desired place like desktop or My Document folder. The 'Properties' item will list the various profiles of the document. The last group contains name of certain most recently used files. You may click on any of these files to open the document.

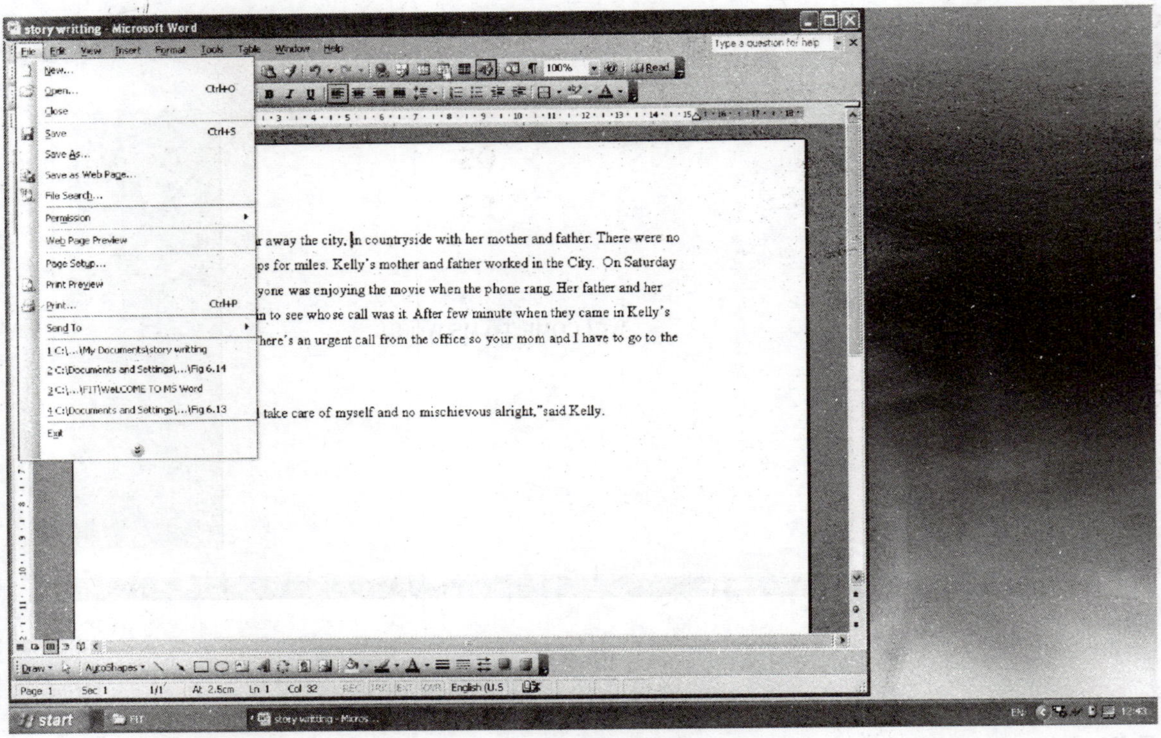

Fig. 7.15

7.11.2 Typing, Editing, Copy, Paste and Justifying the Text Selecting Fonts

After creating a new document or opening an existing document you may start typing the text. After the typing of the text, the various characters or phrases may be edited and annotated. You may do following operations on the phrase or text:

1. To change the font size.
2. To change colour of text.
3. To change the font itself.
4. To make the text in Bold, Italics or Underline.

To do these operations, use the Font window. It may be opened by positioning the mouse pointer on 'Format' menu item on menu bar and clicking the 'Font' option. The window is shown below in the Figure 7.16. Alternatively, these jobs may be done by selecting the text and using an appropriate icon on formatting tool bar.

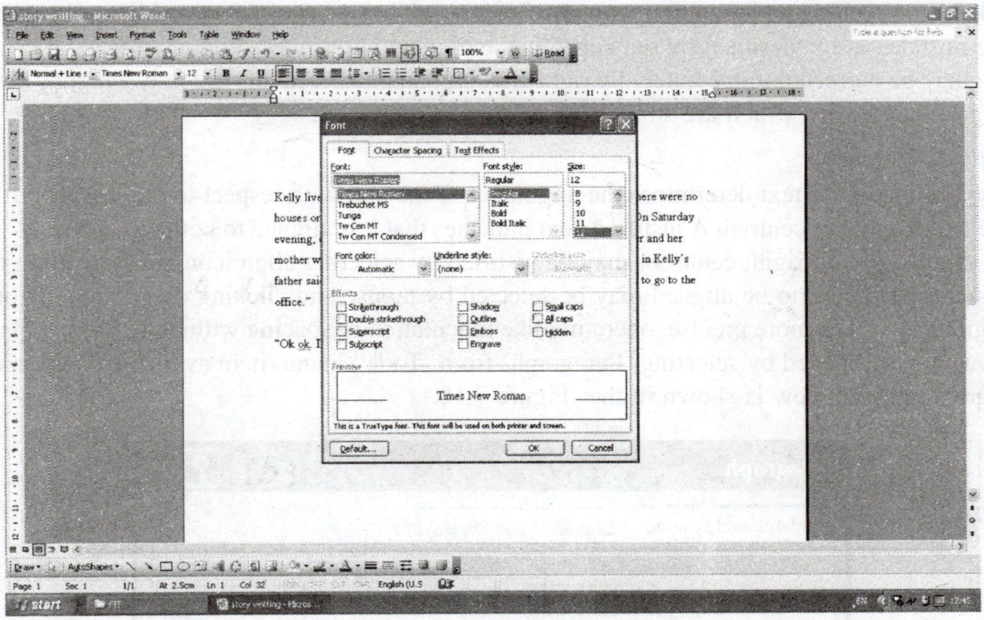

Fig. 7.16

Editing the Text and Using Spell-checker

The most important operation used for editing the text is "Copy Paste" and "Cut Paste" option. Mouse may select any portion of the written text. The selected text may be 'Cut' or 'Copy' by selecting an option on 'Edit' menu item on menu bar. After positioning the cursor on the destination, where the text needs to be pasted, the text may be pasted by selecting 'Paste' option available at 'Edit' menu item on menu bar. The difference between "Copy Paste" and "Cut Paste" option is that, in the later option the text vanishes from the original place or the place from where it was selected.

The text once entered may be checked for the spelling or grammatical errors. To accomplish this option a spell checker is built in the package may be invoked by clicking on menu item 'Tools' and selecting 'spelling and grammar' from it. The window showing the spelling and grammar error is shown in the Figure 7.17.

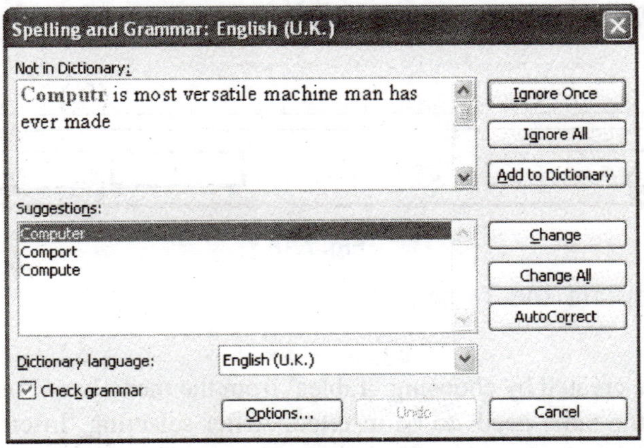

Fig. 7.17

A check for the spelling and grammar may also be done while typing of the text. All words, which have spelling mistake, are underlined by red curly line and green curly lines show grammatical errors. The spelling may be corrected immediately by right clicking the mouse. In this process, you may also select the suggestion of word which are similar to what you have typed.

Justifying the Text

Justification of the text determines the alignment of the text with respect to the margins. It may be aligned to left, right or centred. A justified text indicates that it is aligned to both left and right. The text may be aligned to left, right, center or may be justified by selecting align icon on formatting tool bar. For this, the text needs to be aligned may be selected by mouse and clicking on one out of four icons will align the text. For more precise, operating like indentation or spacing within the lines, a 'paragraph ' window may be opened by selecting 'Paragraph' from 'Tools' menu item available on the menu bar. The 'Paragraph' window is shown in the Figure 7.18.

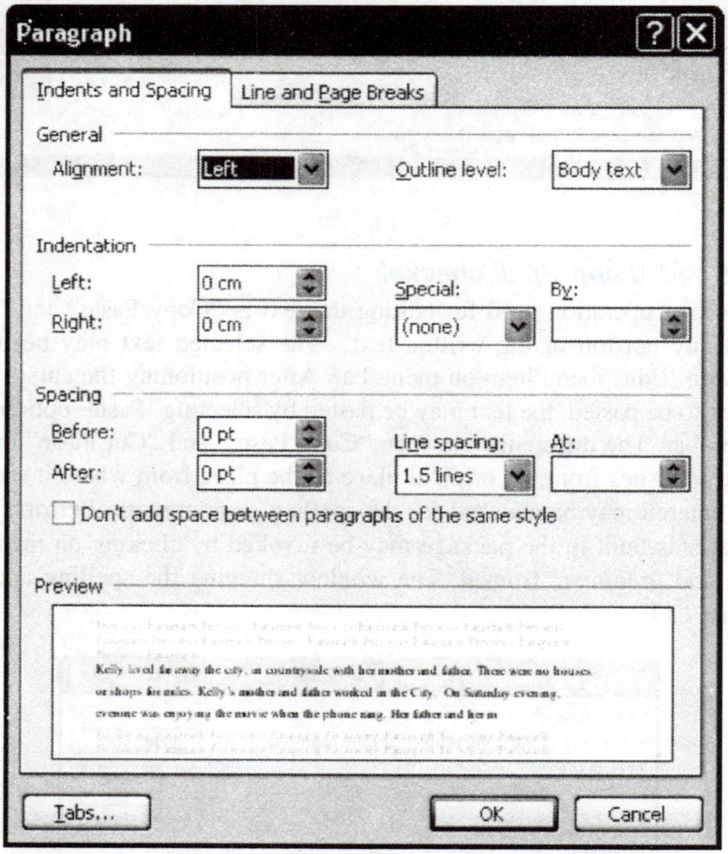

Fig. 7.18

7.11.3 Create, Manipulate the Tables

Creating a Table

A new Table may be created by choosing 'Tables' from the menu bar. You may position the cursor on the text area where the table needs to be inserted. Affter selecting 'Insert a Table', it asks for the number of rows and column in the table. The window 'Insert Table' is shown in the Figure 7.19.

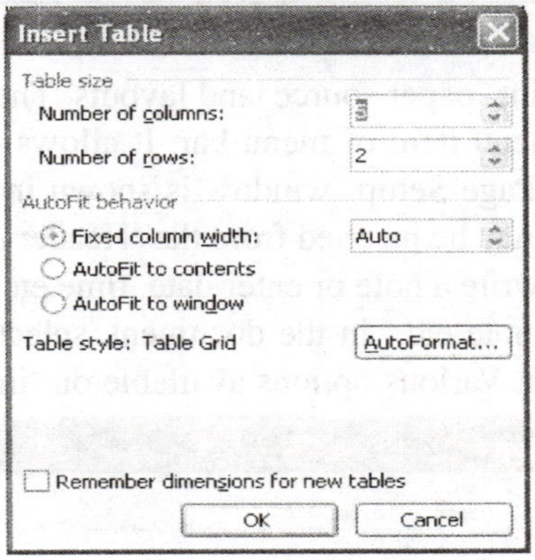

Fig. 7.19

Inserting Rows and Column

The new rows and columns may be inserted, even after a table has been created. The table is divided into the cells. You may enter the text or numbers in the cells. The table may be formatted with the different option available with MS Word. To change the orientation of table, you may choose the 'Table Autoformat' option from the 'Table' at menu bar. 'Table autoformat' window is shown in the Figure 7.20.

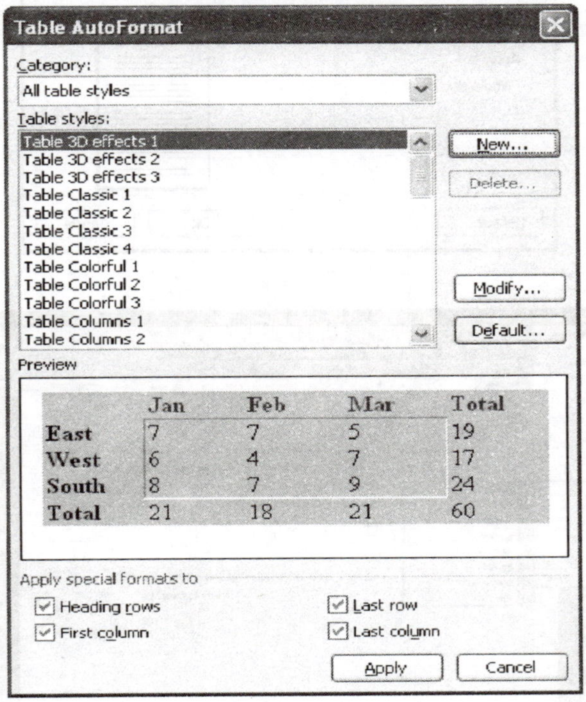

Fig. 7.20

Various rows and cells may be inserted and deleted. It is also possible to sort the contents of the table and using simple formulas for calculating the values.

7.11.4 Page Setup and Header Footer Notes

The page setup indicates the margins, paper source and layouts. The page setup utility may be invoked from the 'Page Setup' of 'File' menu item of menu bar. It allows you to set the paper margins from top, bottom, left, right etc. The 'Page Setup' window is shown in the Figure 7.21.

The Header and Footer notes may be inserted from the 'Header & Footer' item available on 'View' menu item of menu bar. You may write a note or enter date, time etc. at header or footer. To insert page numbers, symbol, comment, foot note etc. in the document, select the appropriate item available on the 'Insert' menu item of menu bar. Various options available on 'insert' are shown in the Figure 7.22.

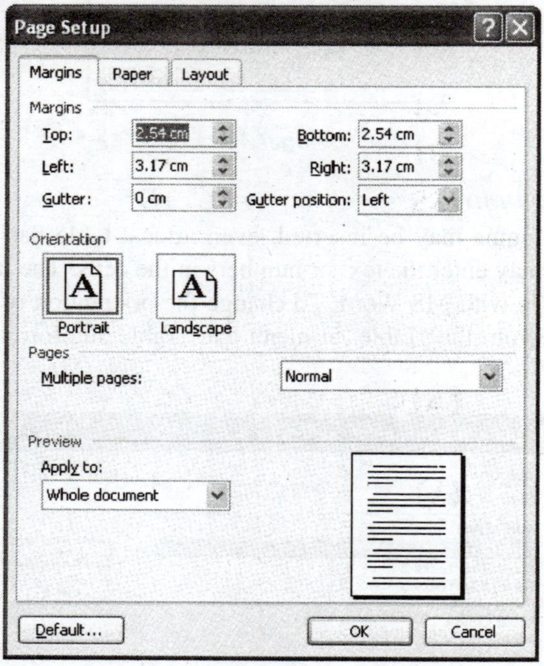

Fig. 7.21

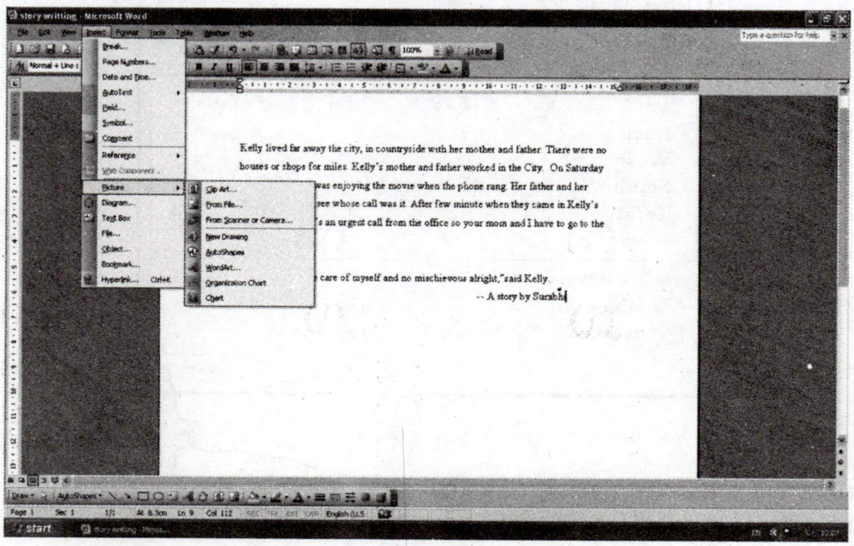

Fig. 7.22

7.12 MS EXCEL

MS Excel is another widely used software which is a part of MS Office package. It is used mainly for simple calculation and tabular management of data. Various analysis of data may also be performed by MS Excel. MS Excel is considered to be a good tool for organising numerical data. It not only helps to organise and manage the data but queries may also be performed on the data. MS Excel application may be started by clicking MS Excel on 'Program' option of 'Start' button. The different parts of the excel windows are shown in the Figure 7.23.

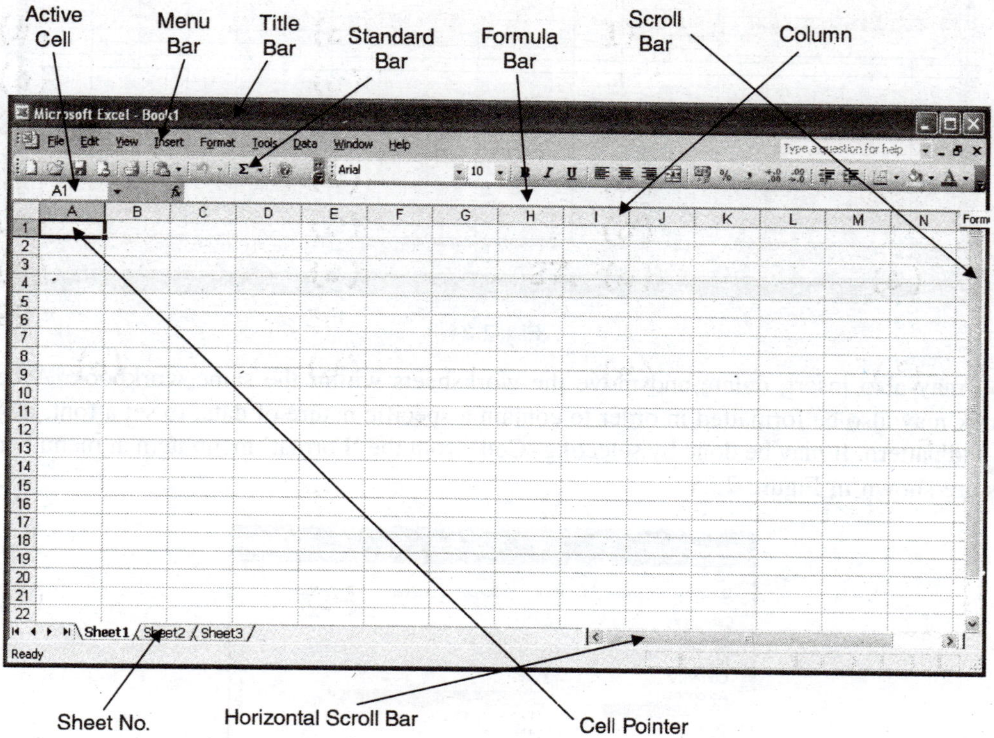

Fig. 7.23

The major operations done by MS Excel are given below:

1. Create, Open, save, edit work book.
2. Page Setup, Menu Commands, Alignment.
3. Calculation in the worksheet, Entering & Editing a formula.
4. Working with Charts.

7.12.1 Create, Open, Save and Edit Workbook

A new workbook is opened by following the steps given below:

1. go to 'File' menu item on menu bar.
2. Select 'New' .

You may also open an existing work book by selecting a 'Open' option of 'File' menu item. Similarly, a workbook may be saved by 'Save' option. Various options available on 'File' menu item are shown in the Figure 7.24.

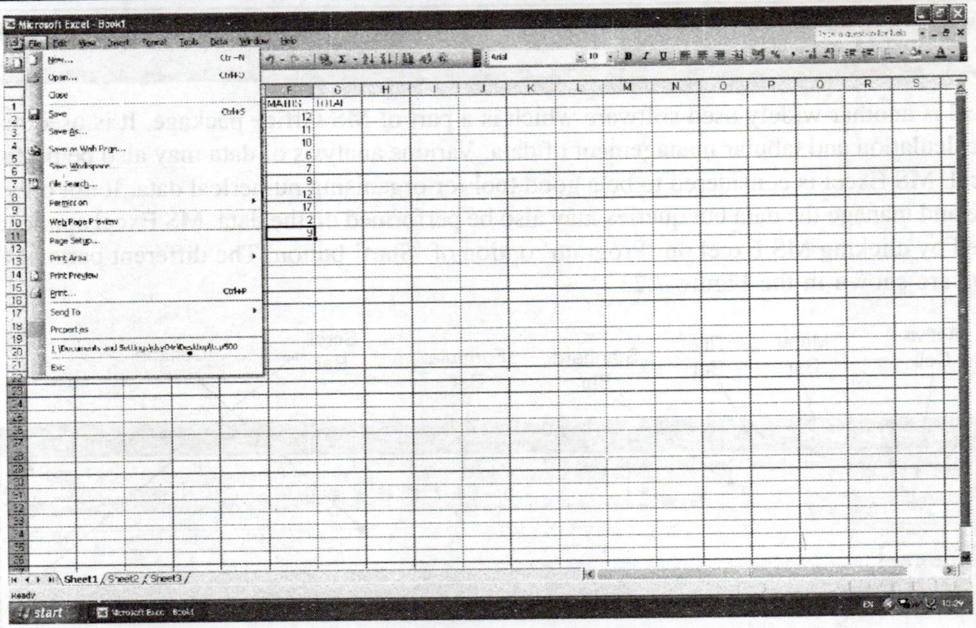

Fig. 7.24

You may also insert, delete and move the worksheets within the same workbook. A cell on a workbook may also be formatted in order to contain a specific nature of data, to set a font, alignment, border and pattern. It may be done by selecting 'Cell' from the 'Format' menu item at menu bar. These options are shown in Figure 7.25.

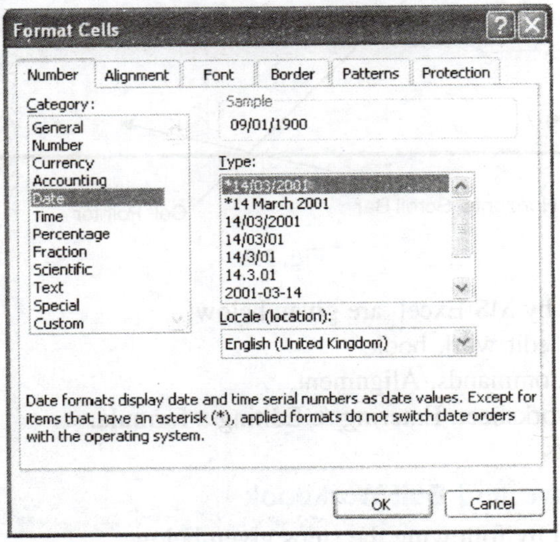

Fig. 7.25

Entering the Data

You may enter the data in the different cell by simply selecting the cell and typing the text. Various cells are also referred by row and column number. Cell in first row and first column is referred as A1.

7.12.2 Page Setup, Menu Commands, Alignment

The page setup allows you to set the page options like orientation of print, paper size etc. You may also set the margins and write header/footer notes. These notes will be displayed on the top or bottom of every page according to the case. To do these settings, you should select 'Page setup' from the 'File' menu item of menu bar. The 'Page Setup' window is shown in the Figure 7.26.

7.12.3 Calculation in the Worksheet, Entering & Editing a Formula

MS Excel allows to not only store the data but also to manipulate the data. The data manipulation is done by writing simple formulas. These formulas use mathematical functions like addition, subtraction, multiplication, division apart from special functions like average, maximum etc. When a formula is set to a cell, MS Excel automatically changes the value in a cell if the changes in the values occur in the dependent cell. A formula essentially contains the Cell Number, operator and begins with '=' sign.

As shown in the Figure 7.26, the values entered in the column B (from row 2 to 11) may be added by writing the formula for the cell B12 in formula bar. It is written as " =SUM(B2:B11) ". This means that cell B12 will always contains the value which is sum of values entered in the cell from B2 to B11. If any values in these cells are changed then the value for B12 will be changed automatically according to the formula.

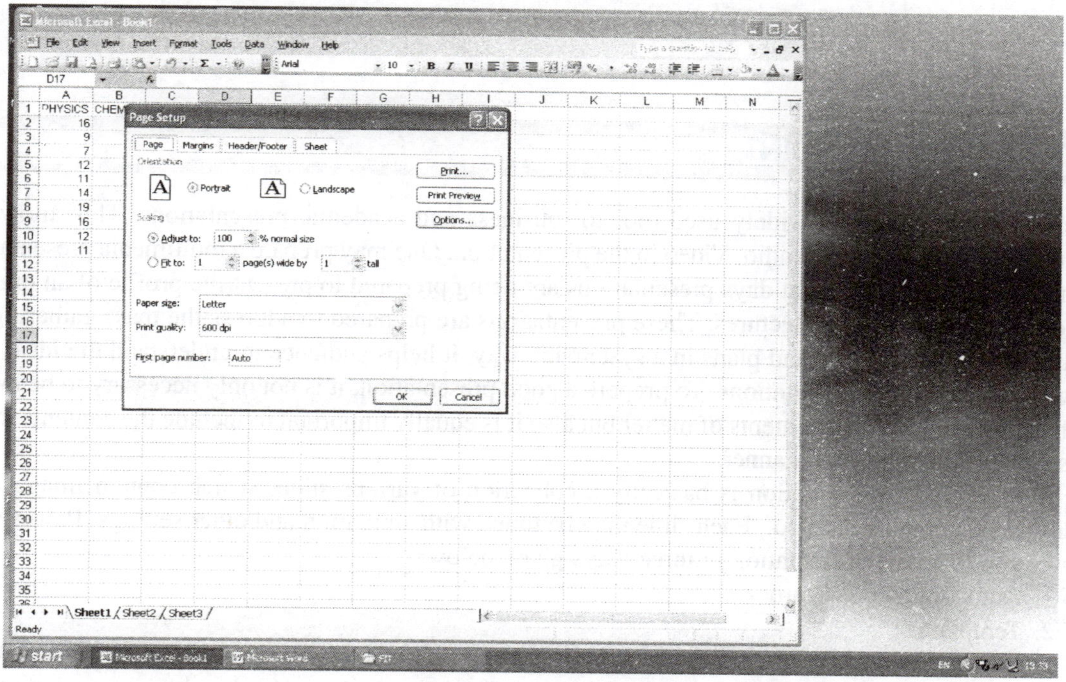

Fig. 7.26

7.12.4 Working with Charts

MS Excel allows you to view the data graphically in different form of charts. Number of chart types like Pie Chart, Bar Chart, Line Chart etc. may be drawn from the data entered in the worksheet. To do this, select 'Chart' from the menu item 'Insert' menu item from menu bar. Here, you have to specify the data range for which the chart to be drawn. Bar chart for the physics marks is shown in Figure 7.27 for the first student (A2 to A11) to 10th student.

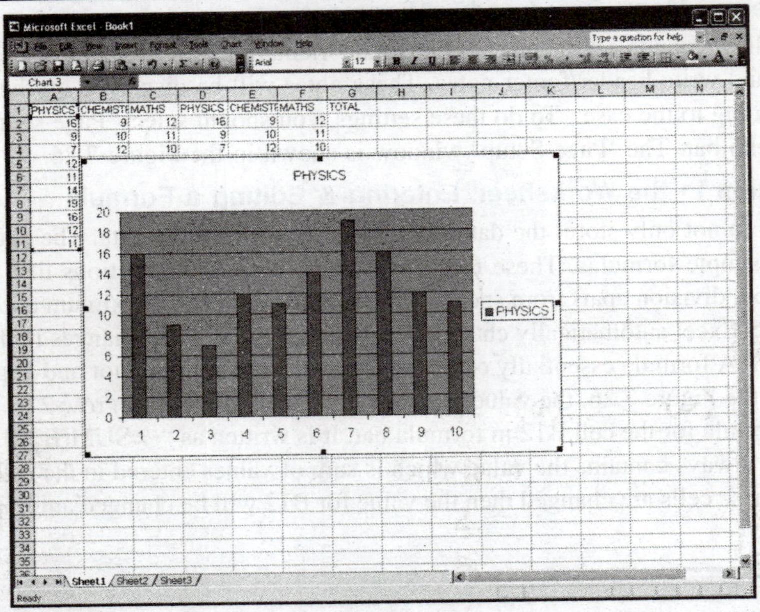

Fig. 7.27

7.13 MS POWERPOINT

The MS PowerPoint is a widely used tool for business and academic presentations. This allows to include images, Graphics, Audio, Video in the presentation. One may prepare a multimedia presentation using this tool. In the current days presentations are being prepared to present the profile of an organization, strategies, policies, lectures. These presentations are prepared to address the mass gathering by putting the different ideas and plans in a systematic way. It helps audience to understand the ideas and views narrated in the presentations. To prepare a good presentation, it is not only necessary to be aware of the audience level and contents of matter but also it is equally important to include the contents in the presentation in simplified manner.

A PowerPoint presentation is basically a collection of various slides which contain Images and audio visual components also. Each slide may be tuned with animation and other settings. PowerPoint allows you to create presentation in three ways given below:

1. Auto Contents Wizard
2. Templates
3. Blank Presentation

You can start by working with the AutoContent wizard, in which you begin with a presentation that contains suggested content and design or with design templates which determines design of the presentation but doesn't includes content or by using blank presentation which does not suggest either.

Creating Presentation through Auto Contents Wizard

MS PowerPoint allows you to select one of the above mentioned methods for creating your presentation as shown in the Figure 7.28.

AutoContent wizard helps you create a presentation on suggested contents and designs. The AutoContent wizard contains sample presentations for a variety of topics. To start AutoContent Wizard you may follow the following steps:

1. Go to File menu, click New, and then click the Presentation tab.
2. Double-click AutoContent Wizard.

After doing so, a window as shown in the Figure 7.29 will appear.

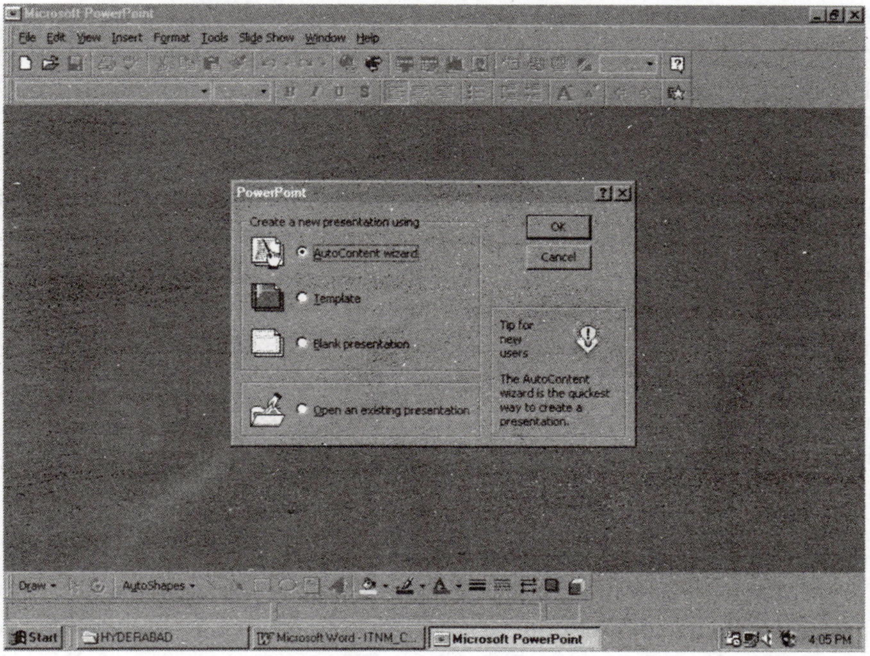

Fig. 7.28

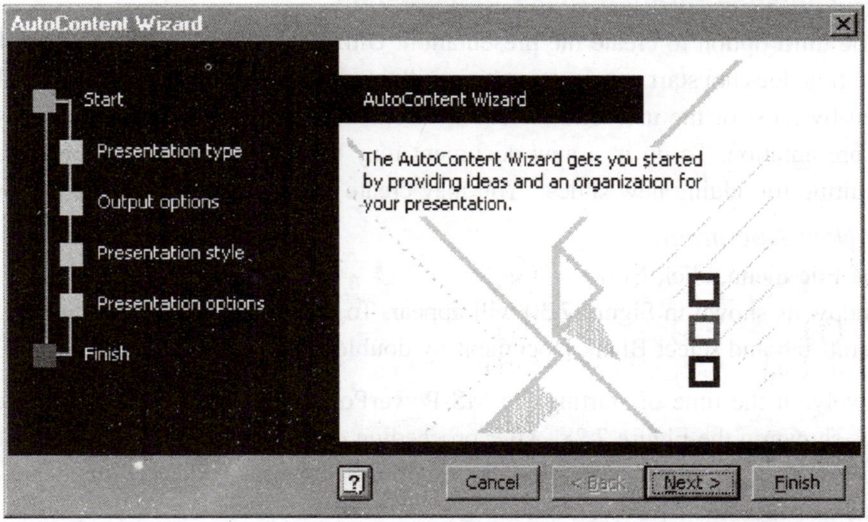

Fig. 7.29

PowerPoint creates sample presentations by following the instructions. You may double-click the slide 1 to switch to slide view, and then type the title of your presentation. You may further continue to type in the text at the place of sample text. After typing the text, you may save your presentation by selecting Save option from the 'File' menu. You can add your own words and pictures to it and it displays it in outline view.

Creating Presentation through Templates

Another way to prepare the presentation is to use the Template. You may begin by selecting a design template that determines the design of presentation but doesn't include content. You can also begin with an outline you import from another application, such as Word, or with a blank presentation that has neither suggested content nor design.

PowerPoint uses two types of the templates called design templates & content templates. Design templates contain some standard formats and colour schemes. These colour schemes and formats may be applied to the presentation made by you. Content templates not only contain formats and color schemes but also suggest the contents for specific subjects. Various template options are displayed in the window and any one of them may be used as basis for the presentation being made by you. If you decide to create a new template based on an existing presentation, all the text, graphics, and slides in that presentation appear in the new template.

The various template options may be chosen by the following steps given below:

- Go to the 'File' Menu on Menu Bar
- Select New
- Click on Presentation Designs on window shown in Figure 7.30.

Various design templates are listed in the window, you may select any one based on the design layout as displayed next to it. After selecting a layout for your presentation, type in the text as per your requirement to the slide. Keep doing it until you prepare the required number of slides. After creating different slides, you may save all slides in your presentation by 'Save' option on 'File' menu.

Creating Presentation through Blank Presentation

This is the third option to create the presentation. Unlike AutoContent Wizard and Template, the blank presentation does not start your presentation with predetermined scheme or formats. It is a general option chosen by most of the user of PowerPoint users and allows great amonut of flexibility while creating the presentation. To do it, a new document may be created or existing presentation may be opened for editing for adding new slides. You may create a new document by the following steps:

Creating a New Document

1. On the File menu, click New.
2. A window as shown in Figure 7.30 will appear. To create a new blank document, click on the 'General' tab and select Blank Document by double-click.

Alternatively, at the time of starting the MS PowerPoint application, you may select the 'Blank Document' as shown in the Figure 7.28. After proceeding either way, PowerPoint presents a screen as shown in the Figure 7.31 for creating a new presentation. For every slide, you may choose any of the layout scheme as suggested by PowerPoint.

You may enter the text in the selected layout as shown in Figure 7.31 and add number of slides as per the need. A view of total six slides of a presentation is shown in the Figure 7.32. The more frequent operations, which may be done on the presentation, are given below:

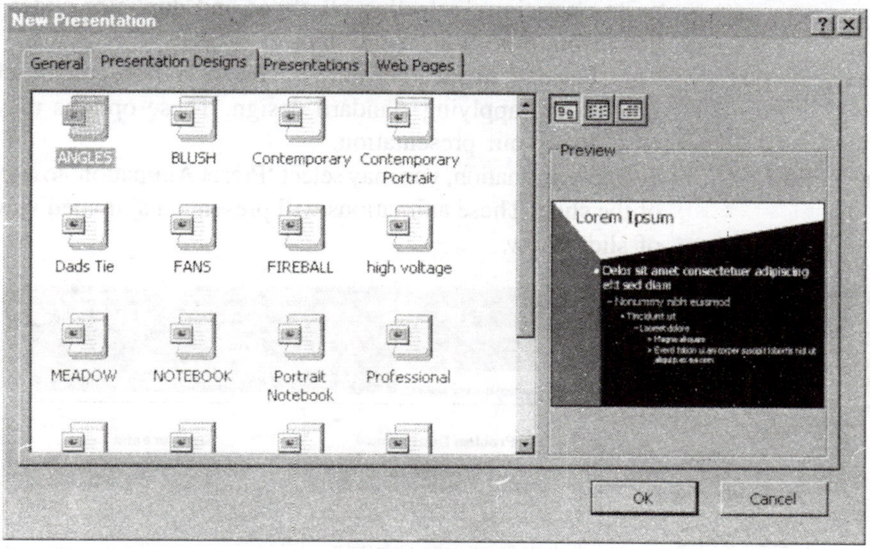

Fig. 7.30

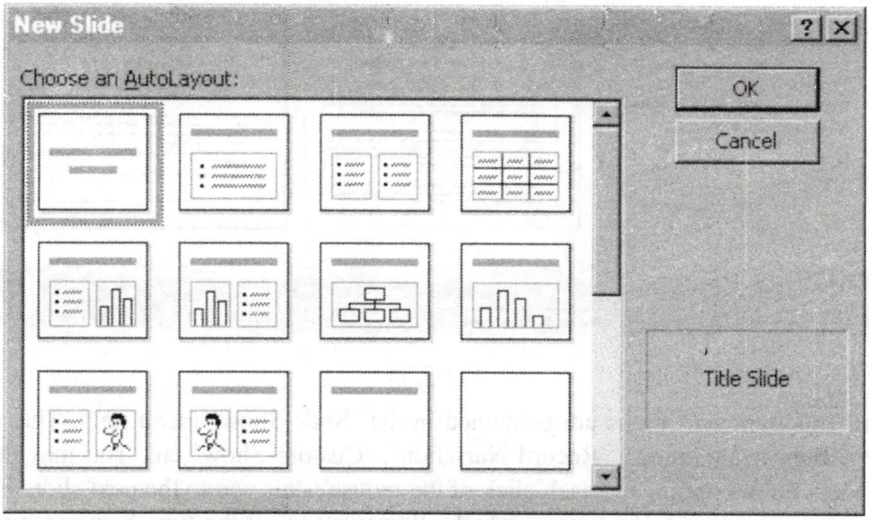

Fig. 7.31

To Save the Presentation : Select 'Print' from 'File' Menu.

To Add New Slide : New slides may be inserted from 'Insert' Menu item. The creation of duplicate slide, insertion of slides from different file, insertion of sound may also be done from 'Insert' Menu Item.

To View the Presentation : from 'View' menu item, you may view the slides in different form.

To Start Slide Show : Select 'Slide Show' from the 'View' menu item. This option will take you to the presentation of slides or slides show.

To Delete a Slide : A slide may be deleted from 'Delete Slide' of 'Edit' menu item. Various editing operations like copying of slides from one presentation to another, paste operations, selecting all slides and duplicate slides etc. may be done from this 'Edit' menu item.

To Change the Formatting : The 'Format' menu item allows you to layout, colour scheme, background and applying standard design. These options may be used to customize your presentation.

To Apply Animation : To apply animation, you may select 'Preset Animation' to different objects of the slide. These animations will present an animated view at the time of slide show.

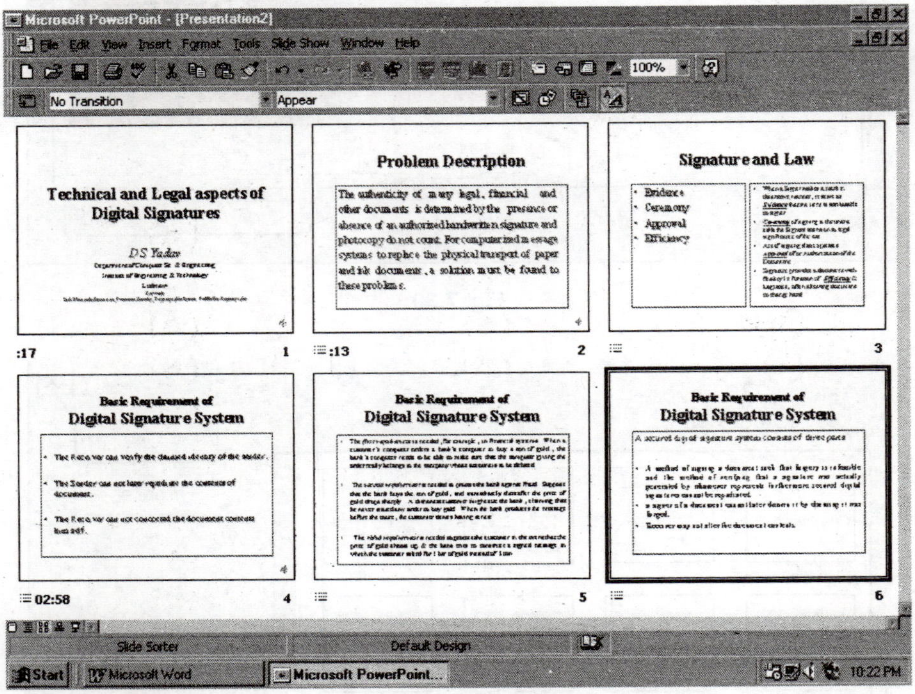

Fig. 7.32

The other important operations are contained in the 'Slide Show' menu item. These options are 'View Show', 'Rehearse Timing', 'Record Narration', 'Custom Show' etc. You may start the slide show using 'View Show' option and each click of the mouse takes you to the next slide. For automatic presentation, you may rehearse the timing, which allows you to set the time between different events contained in the presentation. The full show may be customized using 'Custom Show' option.

7.14 MS ACCESS

MS Access is perhaps the most sophisticated tool widely used for database application. Using Microsoft Access, you can manage all your information from a single database file. A database is a collection of information related to a particular area or domain. The MS Access uses Relation Database concepts and data are stored in the table. Various tables may exist in the database and contents of these tables may be modified or inserted or deleted. The MS Access allows you to create the forms by which you may view, add, and update table data. All you require is to have little knowledge of databases.

Creating a Database

Clicking on 'MS Access' may start the MS Access application. Very first activity that needs to be done is to create a database for your application. 'File' menu item contains the option to open an existing database to create a new database. Microsoft Access provides two methods to create a database. First method is to create a blank database and then add the tables, forms, reports, and other objects. Another method is to use the Database wizard. It is perhaps the easiest way to start building the database. Database Wizard creates in one operation the required tables, forms, and reports. Either way, you can modify and extend your database at any time after it has been created. To create a database, go to the following steps:

1. Click 'File'.
2. Select 'New Database'.

Once you have created the Database, then you have to create basic objects like Tables to contain the data and other objects like Query, Form, Report etc. may be created according to the need. The screen view after creating the database is given in Figure 7.33.

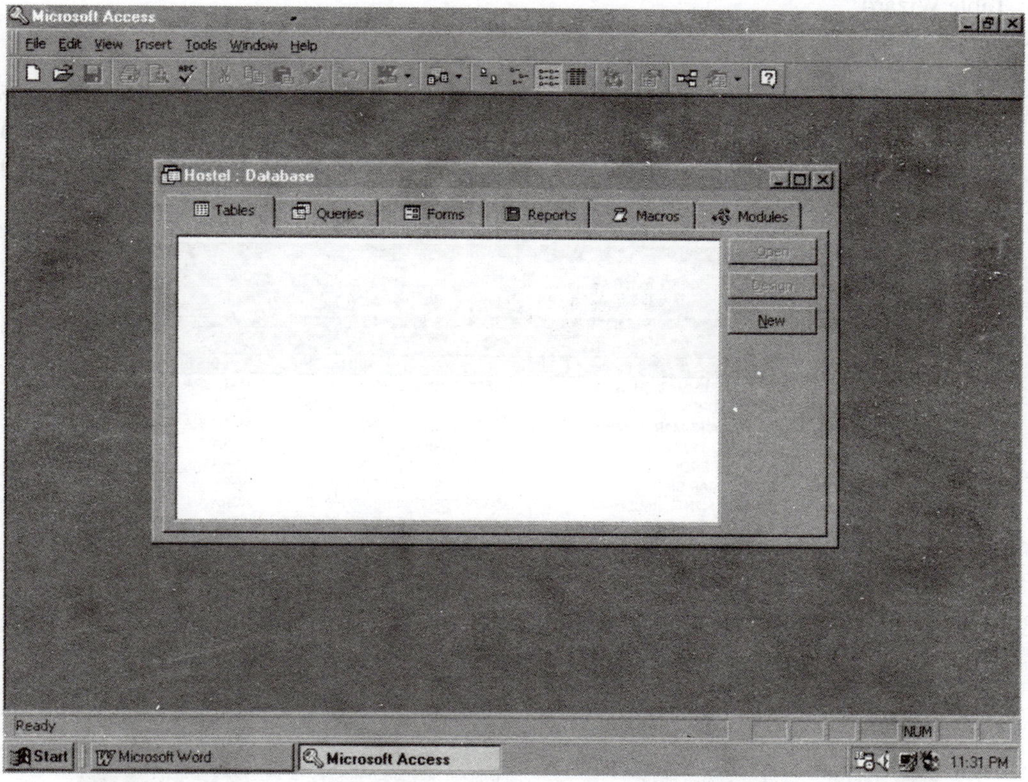

Fig. 7.33

Creating a Table

A Table is the most important object used in the databases. The various data are stored in the table. A logical view of the table is given below. Each column of the table is known as field and each row is called a record. Following table contains four fields: Roll Number, Name, Father Name and Marks.

Roll Number	Name	Father Name	Marks
102	Ram Sagar	B R Sagar	42
103	Anil Kumar	H M Chauhan	80
104	Dheeraj Singh	M S Bose	45
105	S P Tripathi	P K Tripathi	60

Logical View of Table

A table may be created in multiple ways in the MS Access. Creation of a table includes the definitions of the fields and entering the data into the table. You may create a new table in the database by selecting 'Table' tab and clicking on 'New' as shown in the Figure 7.33. These options are:

1. Datasheet View
2. Design View
3. Table Wizard
4. Import Table
5. Link Table.

The naïve users may use the table wizard to create a new table. This wizard helps you to create a new table with field definitions. After creating the table, wizard will help you to enter the data into the table. A view of the table opened in the MS Access is shown in the Figure 7.34. You may use the scroll bar or record number to locate a record in the table.

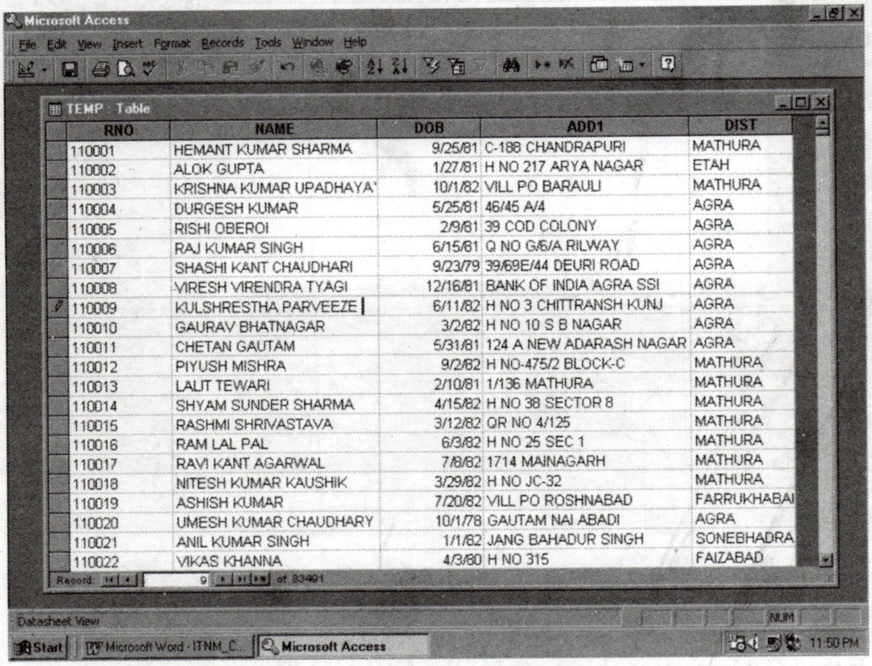

RNO	NAME	DOB	ADD1	DIST
110001	HEMANT KUMAR SHARMA	9/25/81	C-188 CHANDRAPURI	MATHURA
110002	ALOK GUPTA	1/27/81	H NO 217 ARYA NAGAR	ETAH
110003	KRISHNA KUMAR UPADHAYA'	10/1/82	VILL PO BARAULI	MATHURA
110004	DURGESH KUMAR	5/25/81	46/45 A/4	AGRA
110005	RISHI OBEROI	2/9/81	39 COD COLONY	AGRA
110006	RAJ KUMAR SINGH	6/15/81	Q NO G/6/A RILWAY	AGRA
110007	SHASHI KANT CHAUDHARI	9/23/79	39/69E/44 DEURI ROAD	AGRA
110008	VIRESH VIRENDRA TYAGI	12/16/81	BANK OF INDIA AGRA SSI	AGRA
110009	KULSHRESTHA PARVEEZE	6/11/82	H NO 3 CHITTRANSH KUNJ	AGRA
110010	GAURAV BHATNAGAR	3/2/82	H NO 10 S B NAGAR	AGRA
110011	CHETAN GAUTAM	5/31/81	124 A NEW ADARASH NAGAR	AGRA
110012	PIYUSH MISHRA	9/2/82	H NO-475/2 BLOCK-C	MATHURA
110013	LALIT TEWARI	2/10/81	1/136 MATHURA	MATHURA
110014	SHYAM SUNDER SHARMA	4/15/82	H NO 38 SECTOR 8	MATHURA
110015	RASHMI SHRIVASTAVA	3/12/82	QR NO 4/125	MATHURA
110016	RAM LAL PAL	6/3/82	H NO 25 SEC 1	MATHURA
110017	RAVI KANT AGARWAL	7/8/82	1714 MAINAGARH	MATHURA
110018	NITESH KUMAR KAUSHIK	3/29/82	H NO JC-32	MATHURA
110019	ASHISH KUMAR	7/20/82	VILL PO ROSHNABAD	FARRUKHABAI
110020	UMESH KUMAR CHAUDHARY	10/1/78	GAUTAM NAI ABADI	AGRA
110021	ANIL KUMAR SINGH	1/1/82	JANG BAHADUR SINGH	SONEBHADRA
110022	VIKAS KHANNA	4/3/80	H NO 315	FAIZABAD

Fig. 7.34

Creating a Form

Forms in the MS Access are used for building a GUI based interaction to database. It helps you to enter the view, edit, enter the data into the table. These are also used to create the dialog boxes to accept the input from the user and perform the related tasks. It also works as a tool to open other forms or printing the reports. A form contains different icons either to accept the data from the user or display the data to user. A form may be linked to one or more table to display or enter the data. You may also put different buttons on the forms which when pressed does a specific task. A sample form, which manages the data entered in the table, is shown in the Figure 7.35.

Creating Queries & Reports

Queries are used to view, change, and analyze data in different ways. Queries may also be used as the source of records for forms and reports. For example, you may write the queries for performing the calculations, displaying the selected records, calculating minimum, maximum, total etc. from the data stored in the table. A table on which the query has to be served must accompany every query. The most common type of query is a select query. A select query retrieves data from one or more tables using criteria specified by you and it displays in desired way as mentioned by the user. A wizard may create the queries. Selecting the 'Query' tab and then pressing 'Design' button as shown in the Figure 7.33 may activate this wizard.

The data entered in the tables or database may be retrieved to be printed in desired format. Example of the reports include, the telephone bill generated by telephone department, electricity bills, mark-sheets etc. Therefore, a report is an effective way to present the data in a desired printed format. Since the size, appearance and the format in a report may be adjusted, you can display the information in report in desired format. Most of the information in a report comes from an underlying table, query, or SQL statement, which is the source of the report's data. Other information in the report is stored in the report's design. You can create a report using a Report Wizard. It is easy to use report wizard as wizard will take you to design a report in desired format. While using a Report Wizard, it prompts you for information and creates a report based on your answers.

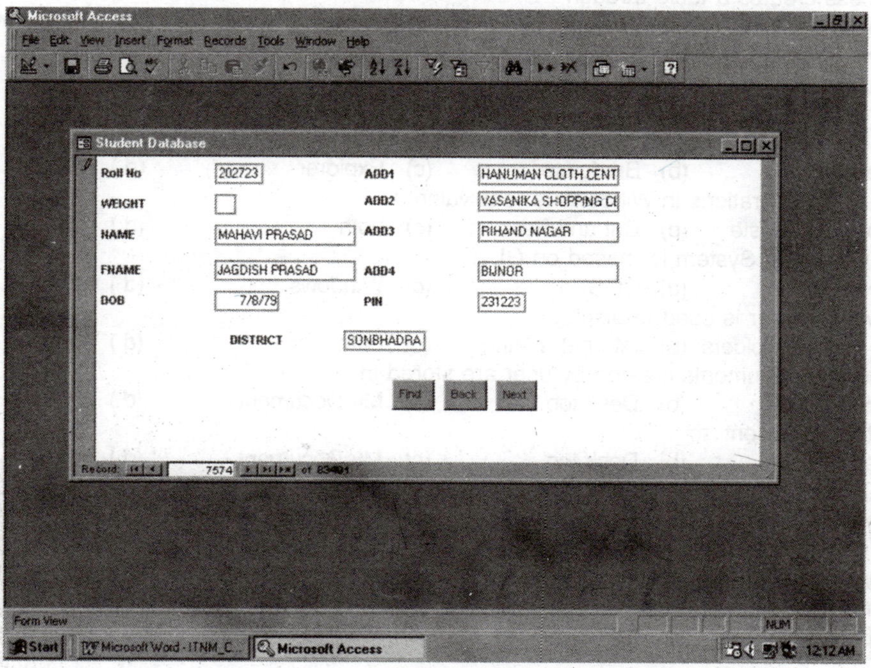

Fig. 7.35

OBJECTIVE TYPE QUESTIONS

Multiple Choice

1. Which of the following is used for word processing?
   (a) MS Word (b) MS Excel (c) MS PowerPoint (d) MS Access
2. MS Access is used for
   (a) Database Applications (b) Word Processing
   (c) Spreadsheet Application (d) None of above
3. Which of the following is used for managing E-Mails in Windows?
   (a) MS Outlook Express (b) MS Excel
   (c) MS PowerPoint (d) MS Access
4. Which operation may be done by MS Excel?
   (a) Data Analysis (b) Drawing the Charts
   (c) both (d) None
5. You may create presentation in MS PowerPoint using
   (a) AutoContent Wizard (b) Templates
   (c) Blank Presentation (d) All of above
6. What you can do with MS Word?
   (a) Create Document (b) Check Spelling Mistake
   (c) Check Grammatical Error (d) all of above
7. Which of the following may be included in PowerPoint Presentation?
   (a) Graphics (b) Audio (c) Video (d) all of above.
8. PowerPoint presentation file has extension
   (a) .ppt (b) .ppi (c) .ptp (d) .ppp
9. Which of following objects may be created in MS Access?
   (a) Forms (b) Report (c) Queries (d) all of above
10. MS Access creates a table through
    (a) Datasheet View (b) Design View (c) Wizard (d) all of above
11. Windows is based on
    (a) Multitasking (b) Parallel Processing
    (c) Time Sharing (d) Batch processing
12. Visible area on the screen after turning on the computer system is called
    (a) Desktop (b) Briefcase (c) Explorer (d) Folder
13. Drag & Drop operations in Windows is equivalent to
    (a) Copy and Paste (b) Cut and Paste (c) both (d) none
14. Which Operating System is based on GUI?
    (a) UNIX (b) DOS (c) Windows (d) none
15. Windows Explorer is used to display
    (a) all files and folders (b) Internet surfing (c) both (d) none
16. All important documents created by user are stored in
    (a) Recycle bin (b) Desk top (c) My Document (d) none.
17. A deleted file is sent to
    (a) Recycle bin (b) Desk top (c) My Document (d) none.
18. Which of the following are system folders provided by Windows?
    (a) Recycle bin (b) Desk top (c) My Document (d) all
19. Which of the following is used for managing the files and folders?
    (a) My Briefcase (b) Control panel (c) My Documents (d) Window Explorer
20. Which of the following is a word processor?
    (a) MS Access (b) MS Excel (c) MS Word (d) MS PowerPoint

Answers

1-a, 2-a, 3-b, 4-c, 5-a, 6-c, 7-a, 8-d, 9-d, 10-c
11-a, 12-a, 13-b, 14-c, 15-a, 16-c, 17-a, 18-d, 19-d, 20-c

State True or False

1. MS Excel is used for spreadsheets. [True] [False]
2. A MS Word document is saved in a file with extension.doc by default. [True] [False]
3. MS Word cannot open Rich Text Format (RTF). [True] [False]
4. A word document may be saved as HTML file. [True] [False]
5. MS PowerPoint is meant for managing the E Mails. [True] [False]
6. MS Office suite provides GUI interface to user. [True] [False]
7. Database in MS Access contains Forms, Table, Queries and Reports. [True] [False]
8. One Form may be linked to only one table in MS Access. [True] [False]
9. PowerPoint Presentation is contained in series of slides. [True] [False]
10. MS Office suite has been integrated with MS Window. [True] [False]
11. Windows Explorer may be used to move the files from one folder to another. [True] [False]
12. Control Panel is used to customize the Windows setting as per user requirement. [True] [False]
13. Windows is based on the textual interface to user. [True] [False]
14. Recycle Bin helps user to prevent from accidental deletes. [True] [False]
15. A file may also be placed on the desk top. [True] [False]
16. Windows allows the user to add new hardware to system. [True] [False]
17. Windows is a Multitasking Operating System. [True] [False]
18. Multitasking operating system does not allow more than two active processes. [True] [False]
19. You may install new fonts to your system through control panel. [True] [False]
20. Windows allows you to start multiple applications. [True] [False]

Answers

1-True, 2-True, 3-False, 4-True, 5-True, 6-True, 7-True, 8-False, 9-True, 10-True,
11-True, 12-True, 13-False, 14-True, 15-True, 16-True, 17-True, 18-False, 19-True, 20-True

REVIEW QUESTIONS

1. What is MS Office? Why MS Office suite is popular?
2. What do you mean by Word Processing? List important features, which makes MS Word suitable for word processing applications.
3. What do you mean by Page Margins? Write the steps to set the margins in MS Word.
4. How the charts are prepared in MS Excel? List the types of charts which may be prepared by MS Excel.
5. What are Sheets in the MS Excel? How would you do the following in MS Excel.
   a. Create & Save Workbook.
   b. Calculations in worksheet.
   c. Editing formula.
6. How would you carry out the following in MS Word.
   a. Create, Open and Save a document.
   b. Inserting a table
   c. Writing footnote.
   d. Page setup/margins.

7. How the following may be done in MS Access?
   a. Create a table..
   b. Generating a form through Wizard.
   c. Manipulating the table data through forms.
8. Write complete steps to generate workbook, which keeps the record of the marks obtained by different students of your section.
9. Develop a complete application, which contains the form for editing and entering the marks to student database. Print the mark-sheets of all students through report.
10. What are Macros in the MS Word? What does they do?
11. Why Windows is called GUI based system?
12. What is Desktop? What are the major icons present on your desktop area?
13. What is the role of Recycle Bin? How it helps to prevent accidental deletes?
14. What are the contents of My Document Folder?
15. What is the role of Start Bar? What are the contents of menu item Program & Accessories?
16. How will you open a folder using Windows Explorer?
17. Explain the purpose & role of Windows Explorer?
18. Explain the steps to change the background of your screen.
19. How will you install a screen saver of your choice to your system?
20. How will you find a file or folder of your interest using Windows Explorer? Explain the process of searching a file/folder.
21. Give complete history of WINDOWS 1.0 to WINDOWS 98. Distinguish the development with supporting features that advanced version possessed?
22. Enlist the important functions that WINDOWS 98 has in it?
23. Give possible reasons that might crash WINDOWS 98 in your computer?
24. Explain the process of adding your favourite program to Start or Program Menu.
25. What are the reasons for calling "Windows 98" operating system as Windows?
26. Explain the process of Shut Down? What happens if you do not shut down the machine properly?
27. Suppose you have started many applications in Windows. If you want to close some of them, what steps you will take?
28. Explain the process of switching between the several applications running on Windows.
29. Give complete history of WINDOWS 1.0 to WINDOWS 98. Distinguish the development with supporting features that advanced version possessed.
30. Enlist the important functions that WINDOWS 98 has in it.
31. Give possible reasons that might crash WINDOWS 98 in your computer.
32. Explain in how many different ways an application may be started in Windows 98.
33. Explain briefly the important menu item present in start bar.
34. Explain how will you do the following functions in the Windows.
    a) Copying the file from one to another directories.
    b) Changing the attribute of the file.
    c) Create the short cut of an application.
    d) Adjust the rate of cursor blink.
35. What is Control Panel? How the control panel is used?
36. How will you close an application?

8

INTERNET AND WORLD WIDE WEB

Contents

8 INTERNET AND WORLD WIDE WEB

8.1 INTRODUCTION

Nearly twenty years back, the Defence Department of USA had started a project for information communication among its various computers. The main objective of this project was to prevent its computers from failure, that is, this project was to ensure that even if one computer system failed, another was ready to take up the job and no information or data content was lost. This event was probably the first step in the construction of a large network of computer systems. Earlier, these networks were being primarily used for scientific and research activities. In course of time, computer networks kept growing larger and larger and they now fulfill a wide variety of requirements including information, education and even entertainment. Today approximately 20 million computers are connected together forming a massive computer network called the Internet. Communication between these computers is established using telephone lines, fiber optic cables and satellite transmission. Earlier this network was being used for communication between various scientists and researchers; a major break-through was achieved with the launch of the web browser. After the launch of the web browser, it became possible for even the common man to use the Internet. Web browser is a tool to view the large information contents stored on different computers worldwide. Its use has enabled the gathering of information about any topic of interest on the Internet. Now one can find out a product of one's choice, place an order, search for new audio, video, news groups, send mail to friends on the Internet. The Internet is not governed by any person or company. However there are certain voluntary organizations such Internet Architecture Board (IAB), Inter NIC, and Internet Society (ISOC), which are meant to regulate it. Nobody pays for Internet usage but one thing must be remembered that nothing comes free of cost. There has been a misconception that use of the Internet is free. Users pay to Internet Service providers for getting an access to the Internet and they also pay for using the telephone line. These are called direct costs. However, users also pay for the hidden cost like advertisements and commercial message they get every day on their mail account. Thus users of Internet pay directly for the usage of Internet in the form of telephone tariff and fee to Internet Service Providers and indirectly for the advertisement and cost of information hiring to web site.

8.2 INTERNET: A GLOBAL NETWORK

Whenever we speak of a network in the context of the Internet, essentially we speak about computer networks. In the early a 1990's various organizations, corporate offices and government offices had started setting up their own computer network within their premises. This was required for faster transfer of data from one desk to the computer at another desk. Slowly it became possible to access the network of one organization from the network of another organization. This eventually gave birth to the Internet, where any computer located anywhere may be accessed from any distant computer through the communication channel. In 1983–84, there were only around 500–600 computers on the internet, but it grew very fast reacting 1.2 million in 1993, 15 million in 1996, and now there are more than 20 million computers on the Internet. Internet is based upon the need to share information between two or more computers. This is done by interconnecting or networking the computers. The computers may be connected through various media such as fibre optic cables, telephone lines and satellites. The Internet may be thought of as a huge network comprising various small networks, on which a user can store information and share it. The network of computers installed within a room or a building is called Local Area Network (LAN). Campus Area Network comprises the computers located in the campus containing one or more building. All these computers constitute the network and they are able to communicate with each other. When the connectivity of computers crosses the boundaries of a building and the user gets access to the computers located in different areas of the city, that network is called Metropolitan Area Network (MAN). When the connectivity of these computers crosses the limits of city/town/state, then this type of networking falls under the category of Wide Area Network (WAN). It is also possible to have a network comprising computers which are located very far from each other. For example, they may be in different countries or even continents. This type of network is called Long Haul Network. It should be remembered that the purpose of all kinds of networks is to share the information available in different computers on the network. The Internet is therefore a global collection of numerous computers worldwide with the objective of sharing resources.

There are a few large networks owned by some major companies like America OnLine, CompuServe etc. One may get an access to the computers available on these private networks with the permission of their owners, However, there is no person or organization which governs the internet.

The Internet is a decentralized global network of millions of computers and computer networks. These networks are used to communicate messages or information to each other and they all follow a common set of protocols called TCP/IP. These protocols make the Internet an effective and efficient tool for communications between different people and organizations. The Internet growth is exponential and the addition of more computer networks and computers is happening at a rapid speed. Since more people gaining access to the Internet, it is becoming more and more useful by providing additional information and resources.

In summary, may say that the Internet is a very large network of computers which are interconnected for the purpose of sharing information. Internet offers a variety of services such as Electronic Mail, Telnet, File Transfer etc. and with the help of software, it provides access to remote data stored in other computers.

8.3 TRANSMISSION CONTROL PROTOCOL / INTERNET PROTOCOL (TCP/IP)

TCP/IP is a very popular term used in conjunction with the Internet. To establish a link between two computers on the Internet, it is required to frame certain rules and regulations so that the data communication between the computers may take place. A protocol means a set of rules which is accepted globally. TCP/IP is the protocol which defines the rules and algorithm for data communication between different computers.

To establish a link between two or more computers, it is required to define the address of the computer. This address must be unique. Rules and regulations for secure transmission of data over the communication channel are also required. TCP/IP is divided into two set of protocols one is called TCP or Transmission Control Protocol and other is called IP or Internet Protocol.

Transmission Control Protocol

This deals with packets over networks. The packets are small pieces of data meant for effective and safe communication over the network. To send a block of data over a communication channel, the data is divided into various pieces and these pieces of data are communicated as packets. These packets have to follow a long path, traversing from one computer or node to another computer. This process is called routing. The size of packets is decided on the basis of network capability. The TCP also ensures the safe delivery at the destination and the assembling of all the packets to get the complete lot of data at the destination computers.

Internet Protocol

This mainly deals with the addresses of computers. The Internet Protocol decides the address of computer to be labelled on the packet. This allows various computers or intermediate nodes to read the address of the destination computer and route the packet to the destination node.

8.4 COMMON PROTOCOLS USED IN INTERNET

Transmission Control Protocol and Internet Protocol (TCP/IP) are most commonly used protocol in the Internet. They mainly deal with slicing the data into small sized packets and routing them along the communication channel. These packets are routed to their destination and passed through from node to node and are assembled in order to form the data at the destination computer.

8.4.1 Simple Mail Transfer Protocol (SMTP)

This protocol is used for the delivery of E Mail. When an E mail is to be sent, then the Mail Transfer Program contacts the remote machine and forms a TCP connection over which the mail is transferred. Once the connection is established, then Simple Mail Transfer Protocol (SMTP) identifies the sender itself, specifies the recipient of mail and then transfers the E mail message. Other features included in the SMTP are that it allows the sender to ask whether the mailbox to whom the mail is directed, does exist on the remote computer or not. It also enables the sender to keep a copy of the mail until it is actually delivered. This enhances the reliability of message delivery.

8.4.2 Point to Point Protocol (PPP)

This is used when the Internet is accessed using a telephone line. Normally, in India, the server of the Internet Service Provider (ISP) is accessed from the home or office through the telephone line. PPP is the set of rules which specify how the data will be communicated over telephone line from your computer when the connection with your ISP has been established. This protocol is used in conjunction with Serial Line Internet Protocol (SLIP). This protocol is used when the communication is done over a serial transmission line like the telephone line. The protocol allows the user to use GUI based web browsers like Netscape and MS Internet Explorer. Internet Service providers use the PPP and SLIP account to enable users to view graphics on the Internet. These accounts assign an IP address to your computer when a connection is established.

8.5 WORLD WIDE WEB

World Wide Web (WWW) is one of the most popular services on the Internet. It can be thought of as a network of millions of servers, hosts and users. It is based on on-line documents containing text, image, video and sound. The document which contain these items are arranged systematically. The contents stored on World Wide Web are accessed through an interactive software called web browser. Some examples of web browsers are Netscape and MS Internet Explorer. The information contents are displayed on the browser and it requires only a few clicks of the mouse to interact with the browser. The GUI based web browsers are easy to handle as they have point and click interface. Information displayed on the browser may have text, image, graphics etc. Some of the text or image items may contain a pool of information. The information pertaining to these text or keywords may be obtained by simply pointing the mouse on that object and clicking on it. These items or objects are called selectable items. These documents are written in a language called HTML (Hypertext markup language). HTML is a scripting language in which various information on the web is published.

Hypertext is similar to the normal text but it is linked to another text or page or information content. Hypermedia is an advanced version of the hypertext document as it contains sound, image or video apart from the text. The entire documents on World Wide Web are accessed through a standard or protocol. This protocol, known as Hypertext transfer protocol (HTTP), is used for transferring Hypertext documents from the host to the client computer. Hypertext contains the items which are selectable and they provide a link to the various web pages. Usually, the link from the selected object of one document to another document is so provided that the next document contains the detailed information about the object selected earlier. We may emphasize that the World Wide Web is a distributed hypermedia system. A distributed hypermedia system is one where all the information resides on multiple web sites or servers. Therefore, on the Internet, it is common to see the links from one document to another, from one site to another.

In summary, we may say that the World Wide Web is a collection of millions of documents written in Hypertext Markup Language (HTML). Various software programs known as Web Browsers are used to seek these documents and display them on the user's local computer. These documents may reside on different computers located in widely distant geographical locations. HTML documents or web pages may contain many different forms of information such as text, pictures, video and sound. These documents are available in various web pages and web sites and they are accessed through links provided by hypertext documents. The ability of users to jump from one site to another site for sake of searching a relevant document or information is called surfing the Net. The World Wide Web is by far the most heavily used application on the Internet.

Web Page is a collection of text, image, graphics arranged in systematic way and provides the information about a subject. The very first page or root page which is encountered first while visiting the web site is called the Home Page. All the links are provided from the main or home page to other pages. Normally, the home page is so designed that it portrays all the information stored at that site and presents a representative picture of that site.

8.6 HYPER TEXT MARKUP LANGUAGE

The HTML document is based upon a script and it follows a standard syntax. Usually various HTML documents provide links to several other HTML documents. HTML is used for creating web pages. Browsers such as Netscape and MS Internet Explorer understand this language and display these pages on the computer screen. World Wide Web is a collection of millions of on-line documents/pages written in HTML and they provide a link from one document/page to another page. These pages are called web pages. Hypertext, as the name indicates is something more than a simple text. In fact, hypertext itself is a source of a related pool of information. HTML allows the formatting of documents on the web. The documents are prepared in such a way that they are linked to each other. By simply clicking on the text/objects on the screen, it navigates you to the desired information pool.

For example, if you are collecting information about tourist places of India on the net, you may be provided with various destinations on one screen. If you would like to know about the Taj Mahal or Agra in detail you should click on the text Taj Mahal or Agra to seek more information Figure 8.1(a). Figure 8.1(b) shows the home page of the web site of Indian Institute of Technology, Kharagpur. The information pertaining to various departments, sections, alumni, research and academics is arranged in a defined format. Upon downloading the page, you may click the appropriate block or icon to get more detailed information. For example, you may click to see the latest on Academics or News to get the latest news from IIT Kharagpur.

HTML is based on a set of predefined tags. These tags are used to prepare the documents in a presentable form. Using these tags, you may underline a piece of text, or use bold, blinking, italics, a desired font type and size for the text in your web page. If all the formatting is done in a systematic way, the document would be converted into a presentable form and would look pleasing to the eyes. A web page may be created using HTML and HTML tags are used to structure the information contents on the web page. HTML, therefore provides the tools to define the various forms of text, insertion of graphics and placement of hyperlinks. Hyperlink on the web page are the points from where you may traverse to a new web page or a new block of information. HTML is different from conventional languages like C, C++, etc. Writing a program in 'C' for Graphical User Interface would be a complex job and would require much effort. With the help of a web language like HTML and other web tools, programming becomes very easy, HTML is perhaps the most popular language for creating web documents. Another advantage of HTML is that it is a portable language. It can be interpreted with web browsers like Netscape and MS Internet Explorer. A document written in HTML can be viewed on any platform or OS like UNIX or MS Windows, which has a web browser.

8.7 WEB BROWSER

The web pages can be viewed by using web browsers. Web browsers are programs which are used in viewing documents or pages written or coded to HTML. Most popular web browsers are MS Explorer and Netscape Navigator. MS Internet explorer is provided with the windows 95/98 operating systems. Web browsers may be of two types, and GUI based or text based. GUI based web browsers permit the user to move the mouse and click on the desired item, selecting a hypertext of choice and the appropriate tool bar button. When you use web browser for net surfing, it acts as a client and connects you to the desired server after specifying the URL address (Universal Resource Locator). It then takes you to the home page of the server. The home page is usually the first page by which you may navigate to the other related pages. The home page provides the link to the other relevant pages available at the server.

8.8 INTERNET ADDRESSES

8.8.1 Domain Names

Since many organization 'universities, educational institutes, private and public units and commercial firms develop and maintain their web sites, it belongs necessary to properly categorise these various web sites. Domain name identifies the general class in which particular web sites are grouped. Any two web sites may not have the same domain name. It also indicates the address and type of server. The domain name is separated by dots. There may be one or more dots in a particular domain name. Most commonly used domain names are as follows:

.com	Commercial	.in	India
.edu	Educational	.my	Malaysia
.gov	Government	.uk	U.K.
.org	Organisation	.de	Germany
.mil	US military	.sg	Singapore
.net	Network	.fr	France
.ac	Academic	.au	Australia

The domain name of an organization represents the type of organization and the country it belongs to.

8.8.2 Uniform Resource Locator (URL)

Each web page on the Internet is accessed by providing an address. This unique address is called Uniform Resource Locator or URL in short. In a number of cases, each web page may contain several URLs, as clicking on hypertext you may navigate from one page to another. All these pages are addressed by specifying their address. While using any web browser, you have to specify the URL in the space provided for it.

Here are some examples of URL:

http://www.iitkgp.ernet.in
http://www.unisa.edu.au
gopher://gopher.kent.edu
http://www.wmich.edu/admi/gradapp.htm

Let us analyze the URL *http://www.wmich.edu/admi/gradapp.htm*. This address contains three parts. The first part *http* specifies the protocol. In this case, the Hyper Text Transfer Protocol will be used to transfer the contents of this web site. The second part *www.wmich.edu* specifies the address of the site. Here *edu* specifies the domain name, i.e. this is an educational site. WWW, which stands for World Wide Web, specifies that this site is on world wide web. *wmich* is the name of the organization which has hosted this web site. Here, the name of organization is University of west Michigan. The third part */admi/gradapp.htm* specifies the path of the file gradapp.htm which is stored in the directory /admi/.

8.8.3 IP Address

The IP address is an actual address of a node or computer or server on the Internet. This IP address is also sometimes called IP number or Internet address. These addresses are of following type.

144.16.202.19

An IP address is divided into four blocks or numbers each separated by a dot. These numbers uniquely identify the network or location or the machine itself. These numbers are provided in consultation with the Internet Service Provider and InterNIC. InterNIC is an international body for allotment of domain names and addresses. These addresses are given in such a way that no two computers or servers get the same IP address. The Internet is not governed or controlled by anybody but there are some bodies which set the rules for Internet usage. The popular bodies are InterNIC, Internet Society, an international body for membership, IAB (Internet Architecture Board). IAB frames the rules for allocation of addresses on the Internet.

8.9 ELECTRONIC MAIL

Electronic Mail, popularly known as E-mail has become an important means of communication in this decade. E-mail is now one of the popular medium of communication. This medium is being widely used to send and receive letters/notes or draft, let it be personal or official. One of the main advantages of this medium is that these mails are delivered almost instantly. Technically, E-mail refers to the sending of documents in electronic form from one computer to another computer. Every recipient of the E-mail must have an E-mail address. This mail address is used to send the mail. Earlier E-mail was considered good for sending and receiving only short messages but because of a rapid growth in the bandwidth of the channel, it is now possible to send large messages with attachment which may have images, graphics or animation, voices etc.

E-mail is probably one of the most important service available on the Internet. It may be used to transfer letters, text, images etc. over the network. E-mail are normally delivered almost instantly to the recipient. Because of this, it has in a very short time gained an edge over the conventional methods of communication. The conventional methods of communication, which include ordinary mail, takes several days or weeks to get the mail delivered. Further, letters can be misplaced, lost or damaged in conventional mail delivery. E-mail is a much more reliable and cost effective mail service. To send or receive messages using E-mail service, every recipient must has a unique E-mail address. The letters or message are sent electronically to the recipient over communication channels like telephone links, radio links, satellite etc. The E-mail is delivered to the inbox of the mail recipient. E-mail addresses appear to be little complex, but they have a simple meaning. E-mail address is usually divided into two parts comprising the name of the user and the name of the server on which the user has his address. Following are few examples of email address:

dsy_iet@cse.ietlko.com
girish@cse.iitk.ac.in

Here the first portion, e.g., dsy_iet or girish is called Mail Id. The second half is the address of the server where this Mail Id is registered.

The general Syntax for the mail is Username @ address of Server 'where dsy_iet is the name of the user who has a mail account at server cse.ietlko.com server. The letter after the dot (.) denotes the type of server and its location.

One can easily see that the mail address *rkag@unisa.edu.au* has the user name rkag and is present at University of South Australia (unisa), an educational institution located in Australia.

8.10 HOW ARE E-MAILS SENT ?

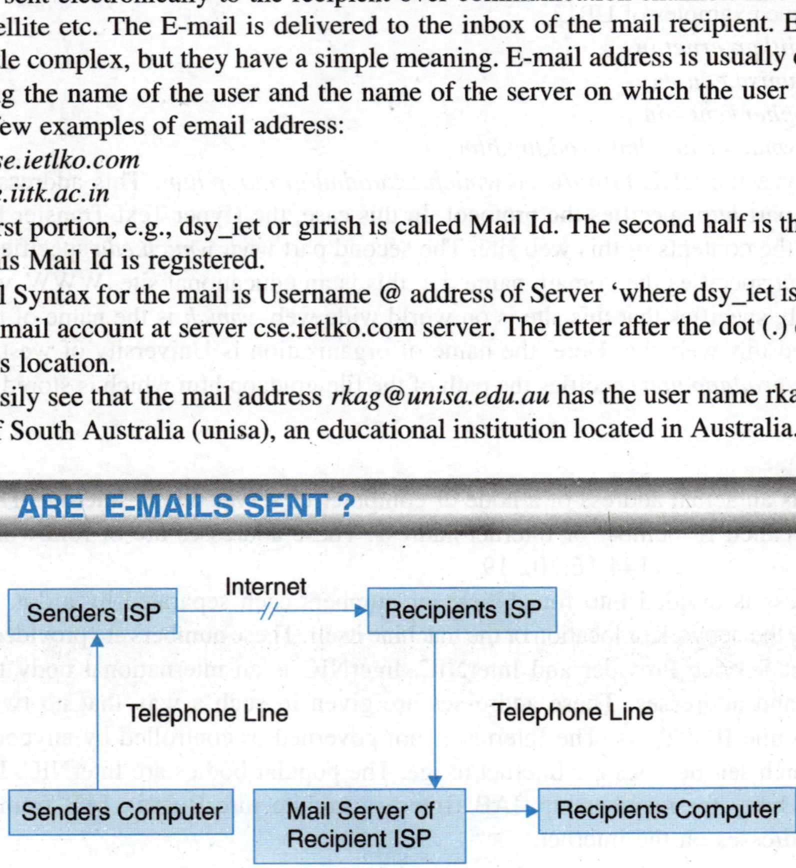

Fig. 8.6: Delivery of E-mail

Sending and receiving an E-mail is very simple and it requires only a few clicks of mouse. Any person who wishes to use this medium for communication need not know the rigorous details of the computer system.

Figure 8.6 shows the process of sending and receiving E-mail. The sender has to specify the mail address of the recipient of mail. Before sending a mail, the sender must connect to the local ISP (Internet Service Provider) server (e.g. Satyamonline, Avadhonline, DOT, MTNL, etc.). When a sender sends the mail, it first get converted into an analog message by the modem and is delivered to the local ISP server. It then goes to the recipient ISP and is stored in the mail server of the recipient's (recipient mail box) ISP. The recipient may receive the mail to its own computer when it connects to its ISP. It is essential to write the correct mail id of the recipient otherwise it will not be delivered to the recipient. Whenever a sender enters an incorrect mail address of the recipient or if the mail is not delivered to recipient's mail box because of other reasons, the sender receives the message about non delivery of the mail. In most of the cases, however after sending a mail, the user is informed that his mail has been sent.

Sending a Mail

You may open your mail account with your local internet service provider. You can also open a mail account with free email service providers like Hotmail, rocketmail, yahoo, 123india, lycos, rediffmail etc. The advantage of keeping account on global free email service providers like hotmail or yahoo is that these accounts may be accessed by browsing from any place in the world. In the case of accounts with the local ISP, it might be a little cumbersome or costly to connect to the local internet service provider and access the account from far off places.

8.11 HOW TO GET E-MAIL ADDRESS AT HOTMAIL ?

Hotmail is one of the largest free e-mail service providers. It has to be accessed on World Wide Web and it maintains all mail accounts at its site *http://www.hotmail.com.* An Indian professional in USA initially started Hotmail. It became very popular in couple of years. At present Microsoft owns it. It is considered as one of the biggest free e-mail service providers. Hotmail provides its services in several languages. In order to open an account at Hotmail, you have to visit their web site. For this, just type in *www.hotmail.com* at the address box of your browser. Your monitor will then display the screen as shown in Figure 8.3. You may sign up by clicking the mouse at sign up if you are a new user. After this procedure, you will get an email address and a password which would provide you an access to your mail box.

8.12 HOW TO MANAGE MAILS AT HOTMAIL

You may compose your messages, receive and reply to incoming mail, make folders, and keep track of various addresses on Hotmail. Before sending a new mail, you should compose the mail by clicking on *compose*. After composing the mail, you can send the mail after clicking on *send.* You may also specify the addresses of all recipients to whom you want to send a copy of this message. Similarly, you may check the spelling, save the draft of outgoing mail or you may use the dictionary. To send any file attachment to the mail, you have to click on *attachment* to attach the file you want to send along with the mail. On doing this your monitor will display the screen as shown in Figure 8.4. Now you may select the file of your choice from the hard disk or floppy by specifying the drive and file name. It may take a few minutes to upload the file and attach it to your mail. If you have received an attachment with the mail, you may click on attachment to download the file. This process may take from a few minutes to an hour depending upon the size of the file and the bandwidth you are using.

8.13 OTHER SERVICES PROVIDED BY INTERNET

Internet provides several types of services. Some of popular services are explained below.

8.13.1 Telnet

Telnet is a protocol or set of tools, which allows you to log on to any computer on the Internet. Telnet is a service on the internet which enables an Internet host to become the terminal of remote computer. It is therefore a very strong and powerful facility where one host may get the full command of another machine. After logging in you may use the software and other programs stored on the remote computer you logged in. By telnet you can therefore, use the computer you had logged in, as if you have full control of that computer. But one should not suppose that through Telnet one can connect to and use any computer on the Internet. To use Telnet you should have access permission usually in the form of an account and password. Telnet facility is normally used to search an information archive such as a public library or a public database. Telnet is very useful in accessing various services, which are not available on the host computer. For example, if you want to use the GUI developed by any other user, then you may log on to his remote computer using telnet. You can run the desired program there and see the results on your computer. Whenever any person develops any utility or service on his host computer, Telnet users can access those services or programs from their computers. You can also use Internet facility to log on to your machine if you are out of city to read or send your mails. Telnet is very similar to the utility called login (Remote Login). It also called emulation protocol as once the connection between the host computer and the remote computer is established, the host computer's commands are executed on the remote computers and the results are displayed on the host computer. The following command at prompt may open Telnet session.

➢ Telnet 144.16.202.14

Here 144.16.202.14 is the IP address of the remote machine. It will then ask you to enter your id and password in order to log onto the remote machine.

8.13.2 FTP (File Transfer Protocol)

File transfer from one computer to another is a major function enabling users to share the resources on the internet. FTP is an utility for transfer of files from one computer to another. FTP stands for file transfer protocol which means the method of transferring files from a remote host computer to your computer. The Internet contains several archives of files comprising the source code for any software programs, audio, pictures, images, graphics etc. These files can be transferred from the remote computer to your computer permanently. On Internet there are thousands of FTP sites from which you may transfer the files to your computer. FTP tools are used to transfer any type of file from one computer to another. However, access authority is required. After the FTP program establishes a connection between your computer and the remote computer, you can browse through the directories and view the files contained in the directories. Several sites allow you to enter even if you do not have an account on the remote host. They allow you to enter their anonymous accounts. Therefore by using anonymous FTP, you may have an access to public archives. The word file includes all kinds of digital documents such as images, text drawing, audio music, video files or any software. Anything which can be stored on the computer may be copied to another destination or vice-versa with FTP. Many computers on the Internet have FTP archives containing public access files.

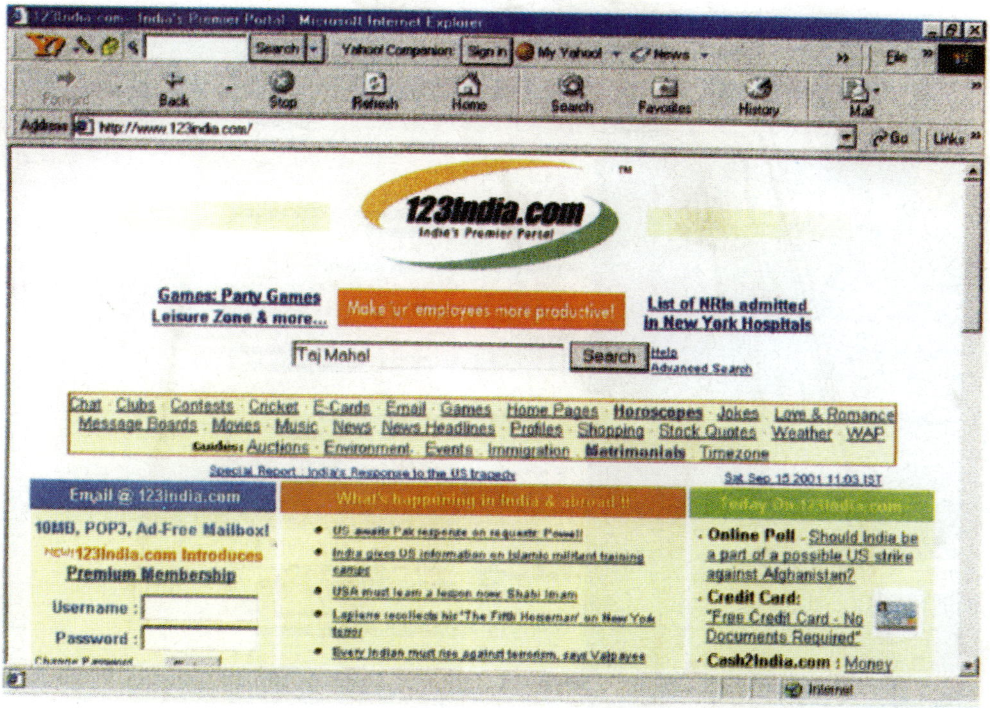

Fig. 8.1 (a): Home Pages of Websites

Fig. 8.1 (b)

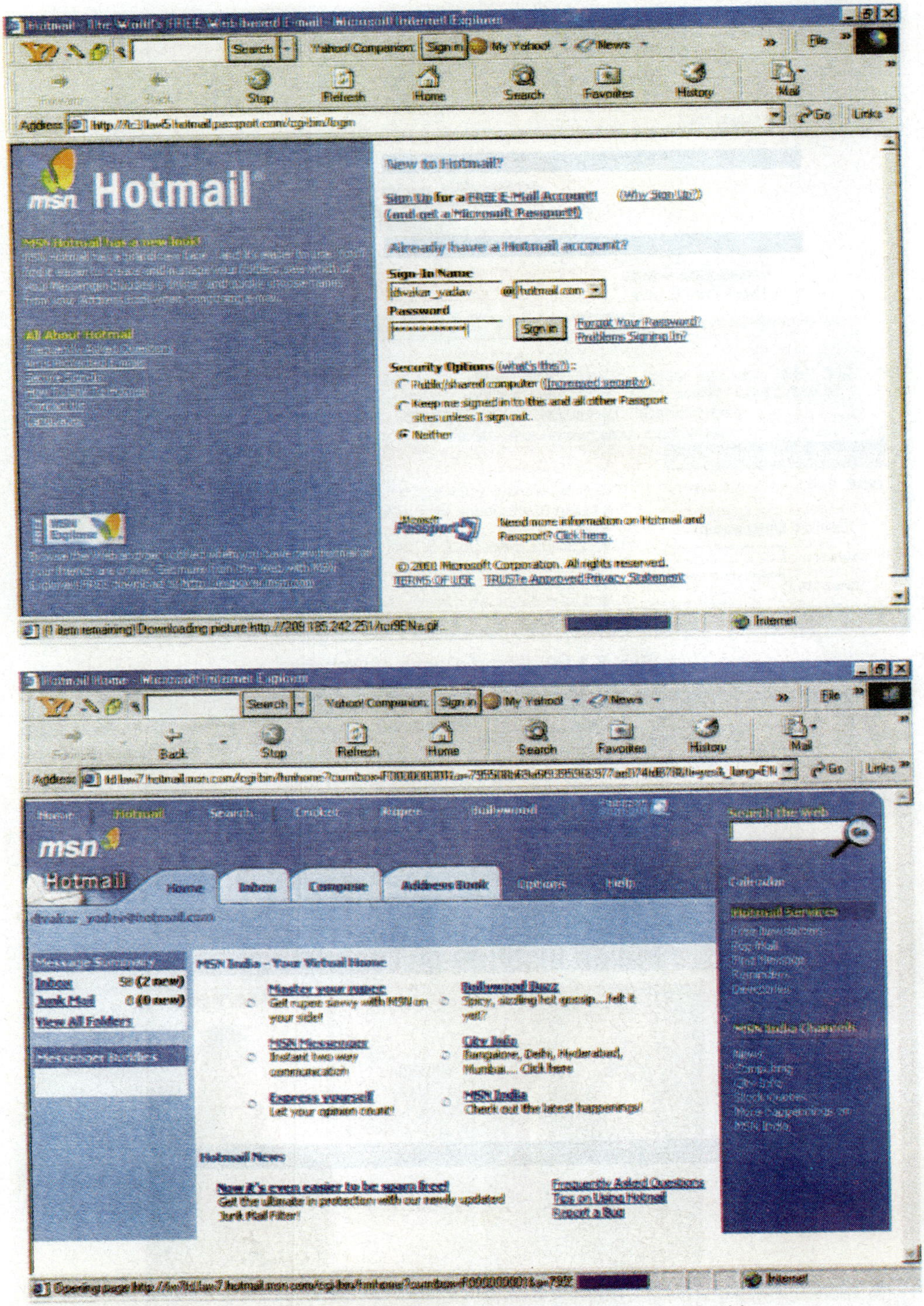

Fig. 8.3: Snap Shot of Hotmail, a Free E-mail Service Provider

Fig. 8.4: Replaying and Attaching a File to Mail

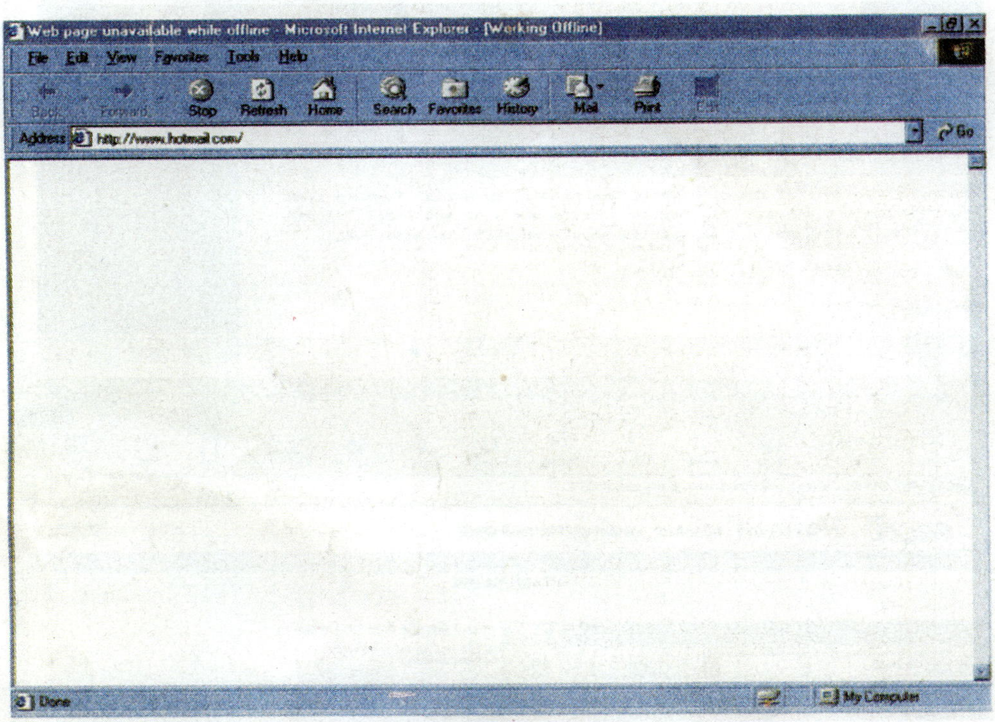

Fig. 8.5: Know Your Internet Explorer

You may establish an FTP session by the following command:

>ftp 144.16.202.14

Here the 144.16.202.14 is P address of the site. After user verification, you may enter the following command and specify the file name to be transferred. These are as under:

>Get Filename

>Put Filename

You may copy the whole directory containing several files. A better approach is to do it by compressing all the files using a suitable compression program.

8.13.3 Usenet

Usenet stands for Users network. Usenet allows the users from different geographical locations to share their views on any topic of interest. It was first started in 1979 and today it has more than 10 millions users. Usenet is the international meeting place where people gather to meet and discuss various subjects ranging from business, academic, sport, music, tourism, games etc. It is very similar to the Bulletin Board System (BBS) that serves the local users using a direct dial up to Internet Service Providers. The Usenet is related to news groups. The News Groups have actually nothing to do with news but they work as bulletin boards. The person may put a notice highlighting his views etc. on some topic. This notice may be seen by all the users of news groups. Each message from a user appearing on the Usenet is called an article. Each article contains a header just like an e-mail. To read and post the articles, the Usenet news servers are required. The local Internet Service Provider makes available this server. There are millions of people world wide talking in thousands of Usenet news groups. The Usenet is a global bulletin board service that uses the Internet as an access point.

8.13.4 Gopher

Gopher is a service on the Internet, which allows users to access resources such as files or text. Gopher is a protocol used for searching and retrieving information from remote sites on internet. It is an alternate way of accessing information which is little different from visiting web sites using hypertext transfer protocol. Gopher is based on client server architecture just like web browsers. It is the same as the World Wide Web with the difference that information in it is stored in a hierarchical order. Mostly educational institutions and universities create Gopher resources like, for examples, university directories. The information contained in the Gopher space is usually reliable and stable. A Gopher menu may always call another Gopher menu. Gopher service is faster in the sense that it contains the listing only in an indexed manner.

The difference between web browsing and visiting a Gopher space is that in the former, you see the graphical pictures/text etc. while Gopher presents you with a menu. The web pages are full of hyper text, and clicking on them you may navigate from one pool of resources to another. In Gopher service, the menus are presented before you. These menus are clickable items and clicking on them, you may go to another menu or get the information in the form of text. To use the Gopher service, you have to use Gopher Protocol. The Gopher service may be accessed by specifying its URL as stated below,

gopher :// gopher.kent.edu

The URL of the site has to be accessed using Gopher protocol just like you use Hypertext transfer protocol (http) to access normal web pages.

8.13.5 Archie

Archie is a simple service on the Internet that searches for FTP Archie on the Internet. It is a sort of search program that looks through different anonymous FTP sites. Files and other information may be downloaded through FTP tools. Archie is a search tool that searches FTP servers. Archie is now becoming obsolete as there are many other ways to search FTP sites and tools for file transfers. Archie indexes file names that are available on public FTP servers. If you search for a particular file, then you will be presented a list of FTP sites which contains that file. Since many other user friendly software are available today which makes a quick search for the file, Archie is not used often now.

8.13.6 Veronica

Veronica is also a search tool like Gopher. Veronica enables the user to perform a keyword search of Gopher space. The result of the search is presented on the user's screen as a menu with items leading to more specific information. Veronica is accessed through a Gopher server just like gopher itself. Veronica searches for a string or text in the Gopher space only. Once the item is found or searched, then a menu is presented before the user to select the item. Here it is important to note that the World Wide Web has a number of search engines with which you may search for an item or site on World Wide Web but the Gopher space offers only one search engine. The Veronica servers may be found at different sites but in fact they execute only one software for search, thus there is no reason to search again on a different server. If the search is unsuccessful at one server, it will again be unsuccessful at another server. Since the number of Veronica servers are few, it is possible that your request for the search at one server is denied. Veronica, after the search is completed over Gopher space, returns the menu item which has a pointer to that Gopher.

8.14 EXTERNAL AND INTERNAL MODEM

Modem (modulator/demodulator) is a device by which you may connect your computer to the ISP over the telephone line. Since our telephone line uses analog communication, thus computer or digital data from your computer cannot be transferred over the telephone line. Modem is a device which converts analog data to digital data and vice versa.

A modem translates the digital data from your computer into analog data and transmits it over the telephone line. Modems are available in various ratings in the range of 14.4 kbps to 33.6 kbps and 56 kbps. The rating kbps stands for kilobytes per second. Thus a 33.6 kbps modem is capable of transferring 33600 bytes per second.

External modems are small devices which can be connected/installed to your PC easily. GVC and Motorola manufactured modem are considered to be good and are available in range of Rs. 2000 to Rs. 5000. Internet modem comes along with your motherboard and lies under the cabinet of your computer. The internal modems are cheaper than external modems. Installation of the internal modem may be a little more complex than the external modem. If you wish to install your modem on different computers, then external modem is the right choice.

8.15 WHAT CAN THE INTERNET DO FOR YOU?

Now-a-days the Internet is being used for multiple purposes. The following are popular services being offered by the Internet.

E-mail is probably the most common and important service offered by the Internet. Various documents, letters, greetings etc. can be delivered almost instantly to people located in widely distant geographical areas through the E-mail.

Job hunting and job finding on the web is also a very important usage of the internet. The popular web sites www.dice.com, www.Jobserve.com, www.employment.com.au etc. are dedicated to job hunting. These are the site popular for IT jobs at USA, Europe and Australia respectively. You may find out a list of jobs upon entering a suitable keyword in the search box. You may also post your resume for appraisal by different organizations.

Marketing/Shopping on Internet is also becoming popular. The concept of e-markets has become a reality. Many of the sites allow you to see the product details on the web and place the order. Through these sites, you may choose or search for a product of your choice and order for purchase may be placed online.

Banks and stock exchanges are also offering their services over the internet. It is now possible to make payments electronically on the web. Stock Exchanges are offering their services by announcing the current rate of scripts. It is also possible to sell and purchase a script through your banker or merchant on the web.

Latest News and features are also available in the Internet. Almost all news paper, magazines and TV channels, offers their services on their web sites. You may also subscribe to the electronic version of many magazines and newspapers. These newspapers and magazines send their publications to the customers by E-mail.

Accessing Libraries located world wide is also a major use of the internet. Almost all major libraries are on the web. It is possible to search through the Internet for an article, author, book or journal available in various libraries.

Universities and colleges provide their information on the web. One can access the information about admission to the various courses, fee structure, scholarship details or any other relevant information about a University or Institute from its web site. It is necessary for the university or institute to have its own web site for the display of all the relevant information.

Games and Puzzles are offered by many of the entertainment sites. You may search for news on any Sport, Game, Puzzles or Tourism on the web. There are various web sites which provide specialized services in these areas.

Movie Clips, Music, Chat and information about other entertainment activities may be found on the web. It is possible to search, download the latest, movie clips, music etc. Chat on the net is also a very common.

These are some of the commonly used facilities on the Internet. A multitude of organizations relating to finance, business, entertainment, tourism and much more have their web sites on the Internet. You can access any information relevant to your needs by browsial through their web sites.

8.16 SELECTING AN INTERNET SERVICE PROVIDER

Internet Service Provider (ISP) is the agency which enables users to access Internet services. The ISP is equipped with all tools and technology to provide you the Internet services. The computers at home or at offices have to be connected to the ISP first for accessing the Internet. The connection to ISP can be made over a telephone line, leased line or wireless/radio link connections. Following are some of the important issues relating to ISPs.

Cost

Cost of accessing the Internet is one of the prime factors which should be looked at while selecting an ISP. Generally, different ISPs offer different schemes and they charge Rs. 500 to Rs. 10000 for providing an Internet access for hours ranging from 10 hours to 500 hours. This period indicates the maximum number of hours you may use various Internet services through your service provider. Several ISPs provides unlimited Internet access to you for a fixed duration ranging from one to twelve month for a fixed charge. It would be advisable to estimate your Internet access hours and decide among the various options by ISPs.

Connectivity

To get a good and sustainable connectivity of your computer to the ISP, over the telephone line is also a prime factor. It is very common that you get disconnected from your ISP. This could be because of two reasons; a problem with your telephone or disturbances over your telephone from your ISP. Before you finalize your ISP, you should also enquire about the connectivity from your friends who may be regularly using the internet service.

Dial up region

If you are frequent traveller across the country/regions with your own laptop, then you should check whether your ISP provides the facility for getting an internal access of your account from other cities of the country without charging any additional amount. If the ISP allows you to have an access to your account while you are on a tour, then you may think of choosing this ISP for your internal service.

Technical service offered by for ISP

Many ISPs provides a help desk for the benefit of users. In case of any technical trouble, you may dial a specific number provided by your ISP. In most of cases these systems are IVRS (inter radio voice response system) where you will be asked by the computer to press the required key on your telephone set. Or you may ask the ISP to send a person for your specific query. Before choosing an ISP, you should also enquire about the technical support service of the ISPs available in your city.

Personal disk space

Your ISP also provides a disk space to your PC for the purpose of keeping your mails. The total size of your mail should not exceed the space reserved for you in the range of 1MB to 10MB depending on the internet service provider. You should also estimate the size of your mail to be kept in the mail account.

8.17 NATURE OF INTERNET ACCOUNTS

VSNL, a government organization in India, is considered to be largest Internet Service Provider. It provides the internet access in India through GIAS (Gateway internet access service). Similarly, DOT (Department of Telecom) provides this service through DOT internet access service. VSNL and DOT primarily provide Shell account or TCP/IP account to users for Internet access. Earlier the Shell Accounts were quite popular but now the use of Shell account has been abandoned.

These two services are offered on normal dial up telephone lines available at your work place or home. To get an access to either account, your computer will dial a number through your modem and within 30 sec. - 1 minute, you will get a message on your screen about the connection status.

8.17.1 Shell account

Using a dial up access, the user may be connected to the ISP server with a Shell account. It is a UNIX based account on an ISP's server. In this account, the user is able to get almost all the services available on the Internet but limitation of this account is that the user cannot get graphics etc. on the screen. Web browsers like Nestcable, Navigators or MS Internet Explorer cannot be used for this account. Since you can receive only text with the Shell account, thus it imposes a severe restriction on the services which can be availed on the Internet. This account is also known as text account. Earlier this account was available especially to the student for the sole purpose of sending and receiving text based mails. This uses PINE for maintaining the mails. PINE is a popular program in UNIX to access and keep records of mails.

8.17.2 TCP/IP Account

TCP/IP account is a more comprehensive option for Internet access through dial up. Users can use transmission control protocol (TCP) and internet protocol (IP) to connect to the host system and access it. In this mode, a user will be able to use graphical web browsers like MS Internet Explorer and Netscape Navigator. You can also view moving picture; graphics animated design and can listen to music or sound. Shell account also imposes restrictions on sending and running mail through the account, whose size is limited. But in TCP/IP account, after using web browsers like MS Internet Explorer/Netscape Navigator, you may view and attach graphic/animated design. While working on TCP/IP account, you can use easily the free email service at yahoo, hotmail, rediffmail to send and receive the mail to/from your computer. Since a large percentage of web sites on the Internet have graphics, video and animation, it is essential to use a GUI based browser to access the Internet and view these sites. TCP/IP accounts enable the use of graphics based browsers like MS Intenet Explorer and Netscape Navigator.

8.18 KNOWING YOUR MS INTERNET EXPLORER

Title bar. Displays the title of the web page you are viewing currently (Figure 8.5). At the right side are the minimize, maximize, and close buttons.

Menu bar. Contains menu items file, edit, view, go, favorites and help. These are pulldown menus.

Tool bar contains various graphical buttons, which are widely used in navigation.The bar is as follows:

Address bar contains the address, provided by you, of the web site you wish to view. It is a pull down text area containing the history of the web site accessed by you. You may also pull down and select the website address if you have already visited the site in part.

Document area. This is the target area and contains the text, graphic, animator etc. for the site you are visiting.

Status bar. Shows the process of downloading a page. It graphically shows how much of the quantity of web pages which have been loaded.

8.19 SEARCH ENGINES

Since there are literally thousands of web sites on the Internet, it is usually a great problem for the user to find the appropriate site or sites of his interest. The solution to this problem is to use a search engine. Search engines are actually web sites and they contain links to millions of web pages. All you have to do is to type in the URL of the search engine and type in the keyword of the document you are searching. The method of inputting the keyword varies slightly according to the search engine. After typing the keyword in the dialog base for search, press the button "search" and you will get a list of hyper text documents which contain the keyword you have entered. The next step is to select an appropriate document and click on it to enter its site. You can then view its pages and browse through its content.

Some popular search engines are as follows:

- *www.google.com*
- *www.lycos.com*

- *www.altavista.com*
- *www.hotbot.com*
- *www.yahoo.com*
- *www.webcrawler.com*
- *www.excite.com*

The screen for the first page of search engine yahoo is shown in Figure 8.7. You may enter the search string in the text box and start search by pressing the search button with the mouse.

8.20 REQUIREMENT FOR INTERNET ACCESS

To get an access to the Internet, following are the mandatory and basic requirements:

- A legal account with your local ISP.
- A computer (486 or above) with the required software to access Internet.
- Intel 486 or higher processor, Windows 95/98, 16 MB RAM, 70 MB of disk space (minimum)
- CD ROM drive, color monitor (preferred), sound card and speaker (preferred)
- A modem (14.4 kbps or above)
- A telephone connection

A higher speed access to the internet may be obtained if you get an ISDN connection or may be a leased line.

8.21 MANAGING E-MAILS IN MS WINDOWS 9X/NT

Outlook Express is a program which helps you to send and receive e-mails. It organises the mail items into various folders, namely, Inbox, Outbox, Sent items, Deleted Items and Drafts. It is a user friendly tool for managing mails. The Figure 8.7 shows the Outlook Express screen.

8.21.1 Composing a Mail

To compose a mail, click on, *new mail* icon at the standard tool bar. You will get a new screen as shown in Figure 8.8. You may then type recipient's e-mail address, subject of the e-mail and finally type the message in the space as shown in the same figure. You should enter the e-mail address of all the recipients, to whom you want to send a copy of the mail. After putting in the mail text, you may click on the *send* button to send the mail.

8.21.2 Attachment to Mail

You may send the file of your choice as an attachment along with your mail. All you have to do is to click *attach* icon on the tool bar. By this process you may attach a file of your interest and send it with the mail as shown in Figure 8.9.

8.21.3 Opening the Attachments

You may also receive the attachments sent to you by your friends along with the mail. The attachment can be opened before saving it to your disk or you may choose to directly save it to your disk. For viewing the attached files, go to your Inbox and select the mail. Every mail that contains the attached file displays an icon at the lower half of the screen. The arrow sign shows this icon in Figure 8.9.

You should click on this icon to view the attachment. This will open a dialogue box and will ask you to enter one of the following choices.

1. Open it.
2. Save it to disk.

After clicking the appropriate choice in the dialogue box, you may choose to open th attached file or opt to save it to the disk. If you opt to open the file, Windows will attempt to open th file using the program most suitable for it. If you opt for saving it to your disk, then it will ask you to specify the location/path on the disk.

8.21.4 Forwarding a Mail

If you want to pass the mail you have received to someone else, this process is called forwarding the mail. This can be done in following two ways:

1. Select the mail to view it. Click *forward message* icon on the Outlook Express tool bar.
2. Go to *compose* and then select forward.

Now you may enter the recipient's address in the address box and send the mail. It is also possible to insert your comments at the same time with the contents of the mail forwarded by you.

8.21.5 Deleting a Mail

You can delete a message with the following steps:

1. Select the message from the Inbox.
2. Press the right button of mouse. Press delete.
3. It will delete the current selected mail and send it to the deleted item folder.
4. You may further delete the mail from the deleted items folder, but you must remember that the item deleted from this folder is never retrieved.

8.21.6 Address Book

Outlook Express allows you to enter the details of your contacts including the e-mail addresses of your friend and relatives. In fact, the address book is like a diary where you may store various attributes of contact addresses of your friends. You may open the address book by choosing the address book option from the tools icon on the menu bar of Outlook Express.

The screen as shown in Figure 8.10 will appear. If you wish to add a new contact to the address book, press the icon New on the tool bar. This opens a screen as shown in Figure 8.10 where you may enter the various attributes including his default e-mail address.

You may also opt for entering other attributes, e.g. Home, Business, Personal, Others, NetMeeting, Digital Ids, by moving on the respective tab page. If you choose to send a mail to a friend whose address is listed in the address book, his name will appear in the address field of the compose screen. You may also delete or modify the current contact stored in your address book. Selecting address book from the tools menu on Outlook Express can do this job. You may click to the field which you wish to modify, then select properties. It will allow you to modify the contents.

8.21.7 Creating Signature

You may create your own signature in Outlook Express. Here signature means your address which will be added automatically to every mail sent. To create the signature, go to Outlook Express menu bar and select stationary. Fill up your address (signature) in the dialogue box. You may also choose to add this signature to all outgoing mails.

8.22 MANAGING MAIL IN UNIX : PINE

PINE is an easy-to-use full-featured menu-driven mail program for sending, receiving, and filing Internet messages and Netnews messages. PINE is a mail program developed at the University of Washington. PINE has easy-to-remember single characters command structure and a menu interface, which displays the options available at each point. It uses folders to store incoming mail and addresses. It also lets you send attachments, which have non-text files, such as graphics files or spreadsheets.

PINE is a mail program developed at the University of Washington, Office of Computing and Communications. It is made available to the world-wide Internet community as a public service. To start PINE, type **pine** at the shell prompt. You see the 'Main menu'. At the bottom of the screen is a list of PINE commands you can use. PINE uses the bottom of the screen to show you what keys you can press to issue commands. Looking over these commands is very important if you don't know what to do next.

PINE Command Structure

Command	*Description of Command*
?	Shows the help screen.
C	Composes and sends a message.
I	Displays messages in the current folder.
L	Selects a folder to view.
A	Creates or modifies address books.
S	Accesses setup options.
Q	Quits PINE.
O	Shows all other available commands.
P	Selects the next item displayed on the menu.
N	Selects the next item displayed on the menu.
R	Displays release notes, which contain information for using PINE.
K	Locks the keyboard, preventing others from accessing it when you are not at your computer.
G	Goes to a specified folder.

In some of the PINE's screens, the list of commands may show a caret (^) in front of a letter. This refers to the control key (Ctrl) plus the desired command. This means to press and hold the Ctrl key while typing the letter. For example, **^C** exits the editor when you are composing a message.

Here are some tips on how to use PINE:

- Choosing Option 1 (E-mail) from the VSNL menu will start the PINE e-mail system.
- Press the **q** key to quit PINE (this will not disconnect you from VSNL).
- Always look at the menu at the bottom of the screen if you don't know what to do next.
- Check your e-mail frequently—people expect immediate reply.
- Delete old e-mail messages or move them to folders rather than keeping them in the inbox.

8.22.1 Entering PINE Command

The bottom two lines of the screen are always used to show the commands you can use. You press the key that is highlighted to give the command. On some screens, there is a command labelled Other Cmds. Selecting this will change the bottom two lines to show you the other commands available. Note that a command does not have to be on the screen for you to use it. This is a useful feature once you memorise the common commands.

On some screens you will see a ^ character next to a highlighted letter. This indicates you must hold down the key while you tap the highlighted letter once. Release the key after you tap the letter. You can use the arrow keys to move up or down a line. Be sure the Num Lock is off to enable the arrow keys on the numeric keypad; otherwise numbers will appear.

The + and – keys are used for moving to the next or previous page. Note that you can also use **V** and **Y** to page up and down. These keys are often used in the message composer.

You can use L to redraw the screen. Sometimes things just look weird; that's when you use this command.

8.22.2 Composing the Mail

You may compose a mail using the *Compose Message*. It will invoke the e PINE message composer and allow you to create and send a new message. You will see four lines at the top of your new message: **To, CC, Attachment**, and **Subject**. Enter an e-mail address or an address book name on the To line. If you want anyone else to get a copy, enter their e-mail addresses (or address book names) on the CC line; otherwise leave this line blank. If you want to send a file with your message, you enter its location here (see view attachments described in the Folder Index section of this Chapter for more details); otherwise leave this line blank. Enter a general one-line overview of your message as the subject.

At this point, the cursor has moved into the message area. Essentially, just start typing. As you add text, it automatically wraps as you type past the end of the line, you don't have to hit at the end of each line. To send the message, press **X**.

How to abandon the mail

You will be asked if you are sure that you want to abandon your message. If you reply Y, the message is discarded; it is neither sent nor saved: if you reply **N**, you are returned to your unsent message.

How to send the mail

When you press **X**, you will be asked to confirm that you want the message to be sent. If you answer **N**, you are returned to your unsent message; if you answer **Y**, the message is sent and copied to your sent-mail folder.

Justifying the text

Justify **(J)** command reformats the text of that paragraph which the cursor is in. Paragraphs are separated by one blank line. This is useful when you have been editing the paragraph and want to make it look neat again.

Copying the text from other files to your mail

Read File **(R)** command allows you to copy the text from an existing file into your message. You will be prompted for the name of the file to be inserted into the message. The filename is relative to your home directory or must be a full path name. The contents of the entire file are inserted at the cursor location. Note that you can read files only on the UNIX machine. If your file is on a PC or Mac, you must transfer it to the UNIX machine before using the PINE Read File command.

How to search a string

The **(W)** command will search the message for a word or phrase. The search does not include the header. The search starts from the cursor and moves down; if found, the cursor is moved to it. The entire document is searched; when the end of the message is reached, the search wraps to the top and continues. To find the next occurrence, press W and it will use the previous word again.

How to run spell checker

You may call the UNIX spell checker to check your mail for spelling mistakes. Spell Check **(T)** tool of PINE invokes the spell checker of UNIX. This will check the whole mail text but it does not suggest alternative spellings. Because of the sorting, your cursor will move up/down/sideways as it highlights the unknown word in the message text; don't be concerned with this — it is just showing you the context of the unknown word.

8.22.3 Managing the Folders in PINE

PINE allows you to store your messages in folders. Folders are simply files where messages are kept. Every message has to be in a folder. New messages are automatically kept in your 'Inbox'. Whenever you are reading a message, you can also shift and put them in another folder. You can move messages between folders by highlighting a message and using the Save command. When you choose 'Save' **(S)**, you will be prompted for the name of the folder. You can type the name of a new or existing folder. If the folder does not exist, it will be created for you. You can also press **Ctrl T** to go to a list of your folders. Using folders is an effective way to organise your messages. All the commands for reading, replying to, deleting, and printing messages work in folders. Folders make it easy to organise your messages; for example, you might have a folder for your study group, another for mail from professors, and another for your social correspondence with friends.

Pressing **I** takes you to a screen that displays captions for each message in the currently open folder. This is useful if you want to quickly find a particular message. The current message is always highlighted, and its message number is shown in the status line. To highlight a different message, use the arrow keys. When you press Enter, the highlighted message is brought into the Message Text screen.

8.22.4 Replying or Forwarding a Mail

Replying and forwarding are your two alternatives for following up on the message you are reading. You would use reply if you want to get the e-mail back to the author of the message (and/or other people who have already seen it). You use forward if you want someone new to see the message.

How to view the Attachment Files

You may receive an attachment along with your mail. After viewing the mail text, you will like to view the attached files. Attachments are files sent with the message, but not actually shown in the message text. View Attachment **(V)** command allows you to see the attachment to the mail. Attachments are useful in sending large files and especially binary files (programs). If the file is in the text, you will be able to read it by selecting it and pressing. If the file is not text, you can save it to your home directory.

Managing mail folders

If you wish to see the names of all the message folders or wish to delete, rename or add folders, use Folder List (**L**) tool. This will help and allow you to view, rename, delete and add folders. You can open a different folder by highlighting it (using the arrow keys to move around), and pressing; this will take you to the Folder Index screen.

Managing the Address Book

Address Book is the place where you keep the mail addresses and other attributes of your contacts. It will also help you to block the mail. Address Book toll **(A)** helps you do these jobs in PINE. Blocking the e-mail means that you will not receive any mail from person whose address has been blocked. While putting the mail addresses in the address book, you may specify the short name of the person whose address it is. After this, whenever you wish to send a mail to that person, you need not enter the complete e-mail address of the person.You may specify the short name of that person in the first column instead of typing in the long e-mail address in the third column. You can add the address from a current message into your address book while reading the message by pressing **Ctrl T** together with pressing **A.** This will take you to the Address Book management screen. From here, your personal address book(s) may be updated. You can also use it as a short cut for addressing a new message; if you highlight an address and select **C** to compose a new message, the address is automatically inserted as the addressee.

Besides your own address book(s), there may be some global address books maintained by the system administrator. The global address books are shared, and everyone can see them. You can use them like you would use your own address books (except that you cannot make changes in the global address books).

8.22.5 Details of Attributes of Address Book

1. Nickname

Nickname is a short, easy-to-remember label to identify an entry. You can type this in as the address in the Compose Message screen, and it will automatically use the real address associated with the nickname.

2. Full name

This is longer field where you can put the full name of the person. Usually in the full names, the last name appears first so they can sort nicely. Note that all address books are sorted by the full name. Whatever you put here will appear on the message when it is finally delivered.

3. Address

This is the actual e-mail address itself. It must be a valid Internet address.

Editing the entries in the Address Book

You may edit or correct or modify the current contents in the address book. Edit **(E)** command will help you in modifying. To modify an existing entry, you use this command. You can only edit one field of the highlighted entry at a time. You will be asked which field to modify.

8.22.6 Block Sending of Mail

There are several occasions when you would like to send the mail to a large number of persons. For example, you may like to send festival greetings, invitations etc. to your all friends. This you can do by Create List **(S)** command in the PINE. This command allows you to create a distribution list, which is a collection of e-mail addresses. These addresses are related in some way, such as all the person working in your organization, your relatives or all your friends. While sending a message to a distribution list, the message automatically gets sent to each address listed in the distribution list.

8.22.7 Creating Your Signature

Normally you enter your name and address at the end of each message that you send. Doing this job again and again may be little boring. The best solution to this problem is defining your signature. Your signature will contain all of the possible attributes of your address, e.g., your name, mailing address, e-mail address, URL to your home page, telephone number etc. This job can be done in PINE using signature **(S)** command. You can make use of the signature option provided. You can store the information that you want to attach at the end of the messages as your signature. Now you can configure your system in such a way that all the out-going messages will automatically have your signature at the end of the message.

The signature can be anything from your name and address, to your URL or contact information.

8.22.8 Quitting PINE

You may quit PINE by entering quit (**Q**) command. On entering this command, you will be asked if you are sure you want to quit, if your option is **Y,** you will exit PINE and return to the UNIX prompt.

8.23 E-MAIL ETHICS/NETIQUETTE

Sending an E-mail is exactly similar to writing a letter. When you write a letter to someone, whether personal or business letter, you follow some unwritten rules. Writing a letter is an art and it not only communicates the matter but also communicates the mood and sentiments of the sender. The recipient may like or dislike the way of presenting the matter. These unwritten rules are called ethics. Since e-mails are also letters, the same rules also apply. The ethics on the internet is called Netiquttee (Internet Etiquette). While you interacting with some known or unknown person or the Interact, you must follow certain rules. A few netiquettes are listed below:

1. The mail should not be written using lot of Bold letters. Conventionally the bold letter indicates emphasizing the word or statement. Too much use of bold letters is similar to shouting.
2. Do not leave the subject field blank. If you leave it blank, it appears that you have nothing concrete to say.
3. While communicating to elders or in official mails, do avoid acronyms.
4. Do not forget to check your draft of the message for spelling mistakes. It is better you make it a point to use spell checker before you actually sending the mail.
5. While writing the mail, you must remain cool and use humor while writing the mail.
6. While sending a copy of the mail to someone, please make sure that it is really necessary to send a copy to him. Otherwise it is very confusing embarrassing for the receiver on deciding what to do with the mail.
7. Do not send junk mails. Junk mail is considered as the mail which was neither expected nor requested by the receiver.
8. Please remember that no recipient likes a document with long, boring and broken statements. Your message must be sharp and clear.
9. If you have to present a certain point, it is always better to break it into small pieces of numbered statements.
10. Try to write your mail off-line and read the mail again before sending it.
11. You must see your mail regularly. It is a belief on the net that if an answer or confirmation is expected, it would come immediately.

Before sending a mail make sure that it conveys exactly what you want to communicate. You should remember that it is like a bullet which when fired, cannot be taken back.

OBJECTIVE TYPE QUESTIONS

Multiple Choice

1. Which of the following protocol may be used for accessing World Wide Web?
   (a) HTTP (b) SMTP (c) SLIP (d) None of these.

2. Web pages are created in a language called
   (a) SLIP (b) HTML (c) HTTP (d) WWW
3. Which of the following protocol may be used for transfer of files?
   (a) SLIP (b) HTML (c) FTP (d) WWW
4. Which of the following are Web Browsers?
   (a) MS Internet Explorer (b) Netscape Navigator
   (c) Both (d) None
5. Which of the following is a valid domain name?
   (a) .com (b) .gov (c) .net (d) All of these
6. URL stands for
   (a) Unique Resource Locator (b) Universal Resource Locator
   (c) Uniform Resource Locator (d) United Resource Locator
7. Search Engines are used
   (a) to search document on web (b) search the file on host computer
   (c) to search data in a file (d) None of above.
8. Which of the following is used as mail program?
   (a) PINE (b) ELM (c) MS Outlook Express (d) all of these
9. Which of following is a search engine?
   (a) Google (b) Yahoo (c) Altavista (d) all of these
10. Which of the following are free e-mail service provider?
   (a) Hotmail (b) Rediffmail (c) Yahoo (d) all of these

Answers

1-a, 2-b, 3-c, 4-c, 5-d, 6-c, 7-a, 8-d, 9-d, 10-D

State True or False

1. Address Book is used to keep E Mail addresses. [True] [False]
2. IP address is an actual address of a server on Internet. [True] [False]
3. IP (Internet Protocol) is mainly responsible for routing of packets. [True] [False]
4. HTML is a general purpose programming Language. [True] [False]
5. Images can not be sent through E-Mail. [True] [False]
6. IP Address of two different servers must be different. [True] [False]
7. No body owns the Internet. [True] [False]
8. ISP provides basic internet facilities in the region. [True] [False]
9. Web Documents are created in HTML. [True] [False]
10. Veronica enables user to search a keyword in Gopher space.. [True] [False]

Answers

1-True, 2-True, 3-True, 4-False, 5-False, 6-True, 7-True, 8-True, 9-True, 10- True

REVIEW QUESTIONS

1. What is Internet? List the important usage of Internet.
2. Explain with the reasons why the number of computer/computer network added to Internet at a exponential rate.
3. Explain how E-mail are important and how they are sent?
4. Who governs Internet? List various societies who are responsible for laying the guideline for Internet users.
5. Why an E-Mail is considered as most important service offered by Internet? Comment on whether an E-Mail is secured?

6. What do you mean by Local Area Network? How it is different from Metropolitan Area Network? Explain with a suitable example.
7. Give detail on how same message through E-mail can be sent to more than one person at a time?
8. Justify the statement "Internet is a decentralized network of million of computers".
9. What are attachment files? Explain the conditions when attachment files are sent . How the attachments are down loaded at recipient end?
10. Explain the process of E-Mail delivery system. How the mails are delivered to the recipients?
11. What do you mean by TCP/IP? Why TCP/IP is so important for Internet uses?
12. What are Transmission Control Protocols? What is the difference in Transmission Control Protocol and Internet Protocol?
13. What do you mean by Simple Mail Transfer Protocol (SMTP)? Explain the objectives of this protocol.
14. What do you mean by Point to Point Protocol? Explain the objectives of this protocol.
15. What is World Wide Web? How world wide web is related with the term Web Site?
16. Why the documents to be placed on world wide web are written in HTML? Is it the only language for writing the text for web documents?
17. What do you mean by URL? Explain the component of URL with a suitable example.
18. What are Internet Address? Explain the process of allocation of Internet Addressees.
19. Why are domain name? Name the society which govern the usage and allocation of domain names?
20. What are IP address? How are they different from URL? Does there exist one to one correspondence among them?
21. What are Free E-Mail Service Providers on Web? What are the possible reason for providing the free servive to the users?
22. What is address book? How the address book are used ?
23. How the mails are composed? How will you reply to a mail, you have received?
24. What are signatures? How will you send the signature with the E-mail.
25. List few popular free E-Mail provider on the Web.
26. Explain the process of opening a E-Mail account on a Web based E-Mail service?
27. What are the possible advantages of opening a mail account on Web based E Mail service provider?
28. What do you mean by Telnet? How a Telnet session is started? Under what circumstances the Telnet is used?
29. What are Netiquette? List any five important netiquette which you consider important.
30. Explain the various services that are available on internet.
31. Give configuration of a computer that is essential for accessing an Internet?
32. What are Modems. Distinguish between internal and external modem?
33. Give complete detail about VSNL and also enlists what are services provided by VSNL.
34. What are search engines? What for the search engines are used? List any two popular search engines.
35. What to do you mean by File Transfer Protocol (FTP)? What are FTP sites? Under what circumstances the FTP is desirable to be used?
36. Explain with suitable example, how a FTP session is established? Explain the basic command for downloading and uploading a file?
37. What are Usenet's? Under
38. What is meant by Browsing the WEB or NET surfing, and how it is performed?
39. Give details about the search engine and how they are accessed?
40. What are E-mails? and How they are sent?
41. What are Network? what are the difference between LAN , MAN and WAN?
42. What do you mean by Internet? Give a brief account of growth of Internet .
43. Give the Syntax of E-mail address?
44. What is World Wide Web?
45. What do mean by FTP service? Under what circumstances you would like to use FTP?
46. Explain the Telnet service in the brief? What are the major advantage of this service?
47. What are USENET? Explain in brief how it is similar to the Bulletin Board System?
48. What do you mean by Gopher? How Gopher service may be utilized to search an item or information on the net?

49. What is Archie? How an Archie service is used to search an FTP site?
50. What do you mean by Veronica? What are the similarities of Veronica with the Gopher?
51. List various application of Internet and explain how Internet may be used for Day to Day problems?
52. What are the advantages of ISDN over normal telephone line?
53. How would you get ISDN connection to your office or home? Give detail of expected expenditure.
54. What is PRI? How it is different than BRI? What advantage you would get if you opt for PRI while applying for ISDN?
55. What do you mean by the term Video Conferencing? Is there any difference between video Telephony and Video Conferencing?
56. What is the role of Internet Service Provider? List any five popular ISP in your city.
57. Explain the grounds on which you would like to select a Internet Service provider.
58. What are differences between a Shell and TCP/IP account?
59. What do you mean by Dial Up region?
60. What are the difference between the TCP/IP and shell account offered by DOT?
61. Explain the various components of your Web Browser?
62. What are Search Engines? How will you search for a good university in US for admission to PG course?
63. What do you mean by URL? How will you visit a specific site?

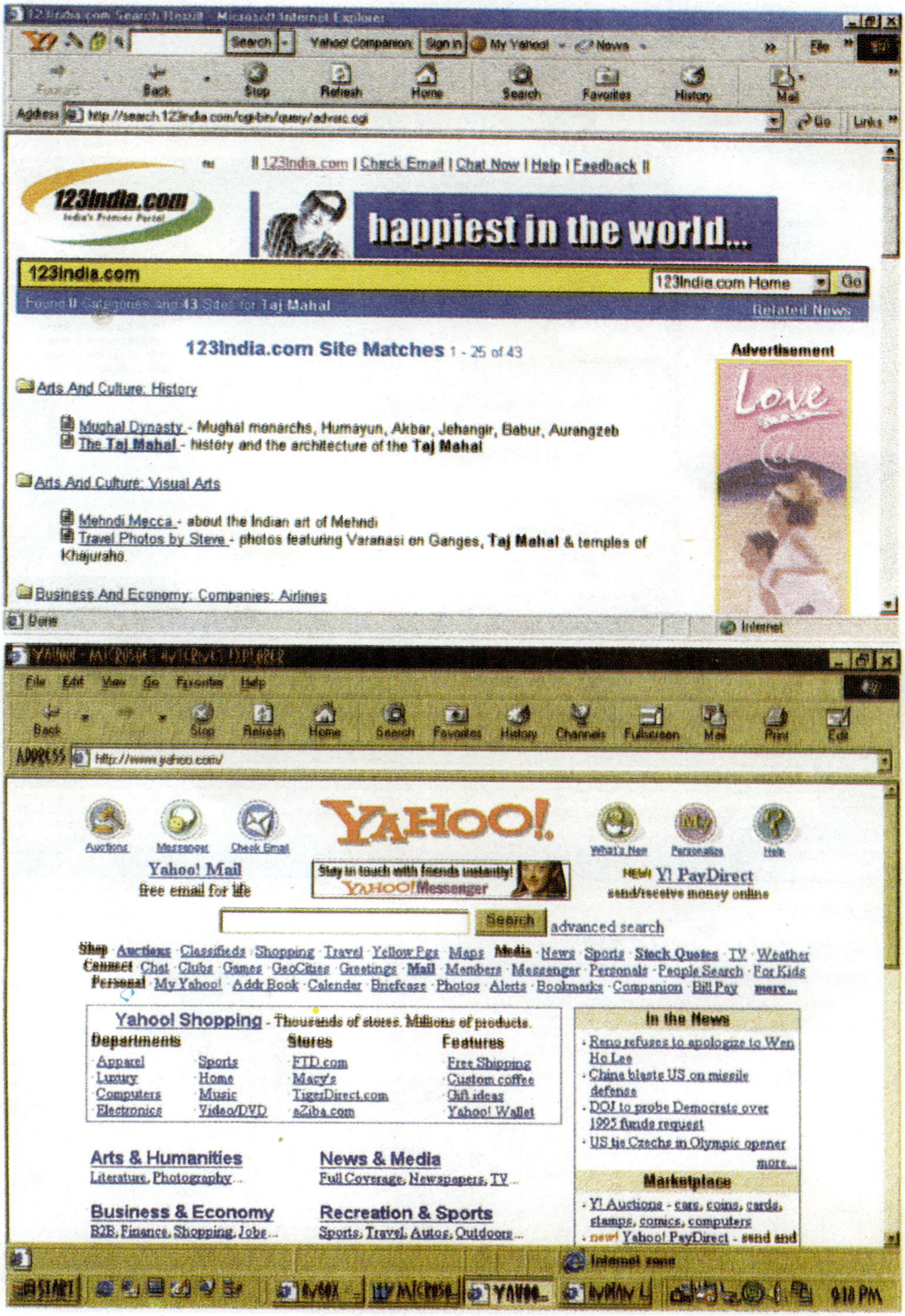

Fig. 8.6: Search Engines

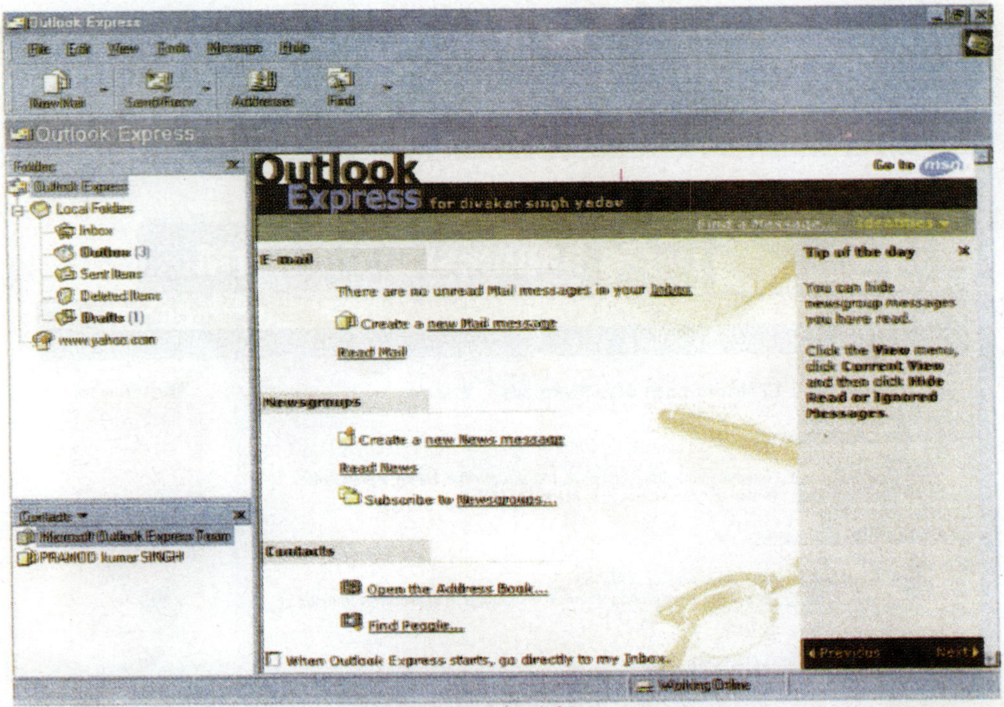

Fig. 8.7

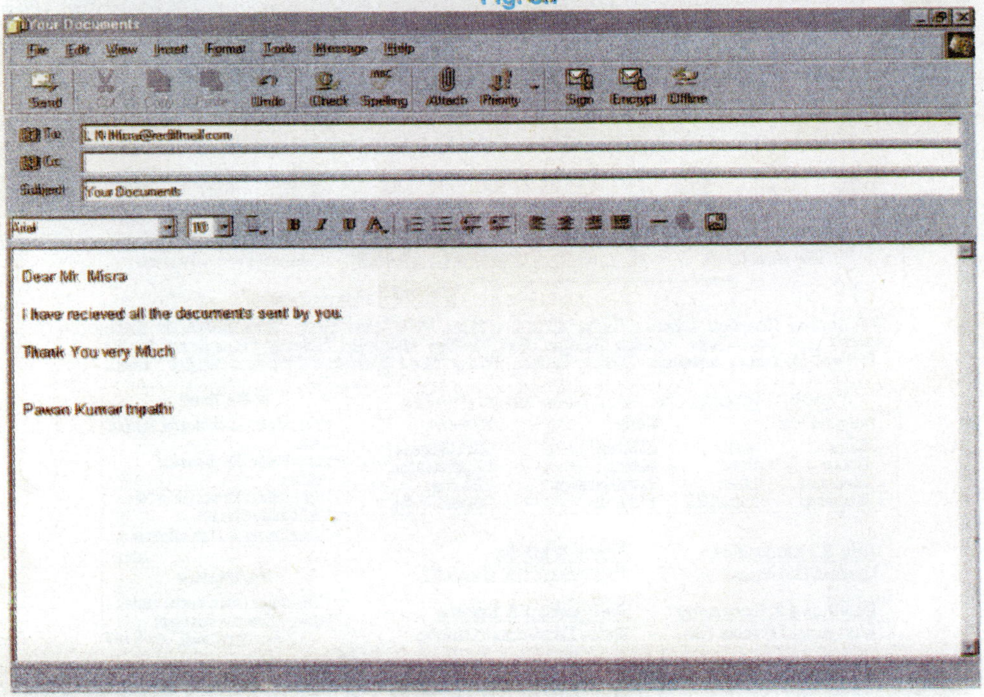

Fig. 8.8: Composing a Mail

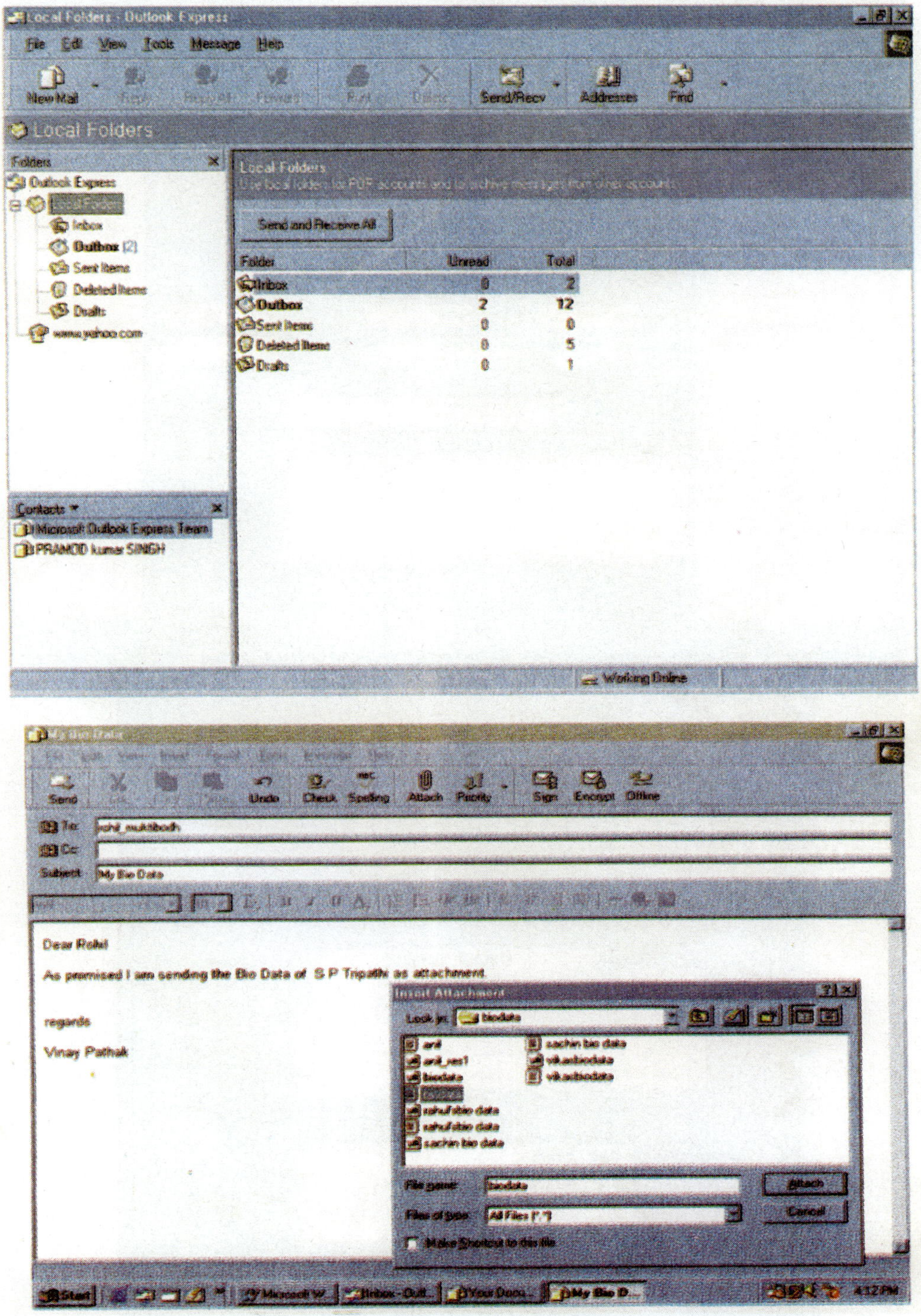

Fig. 8.9: Attaching a File

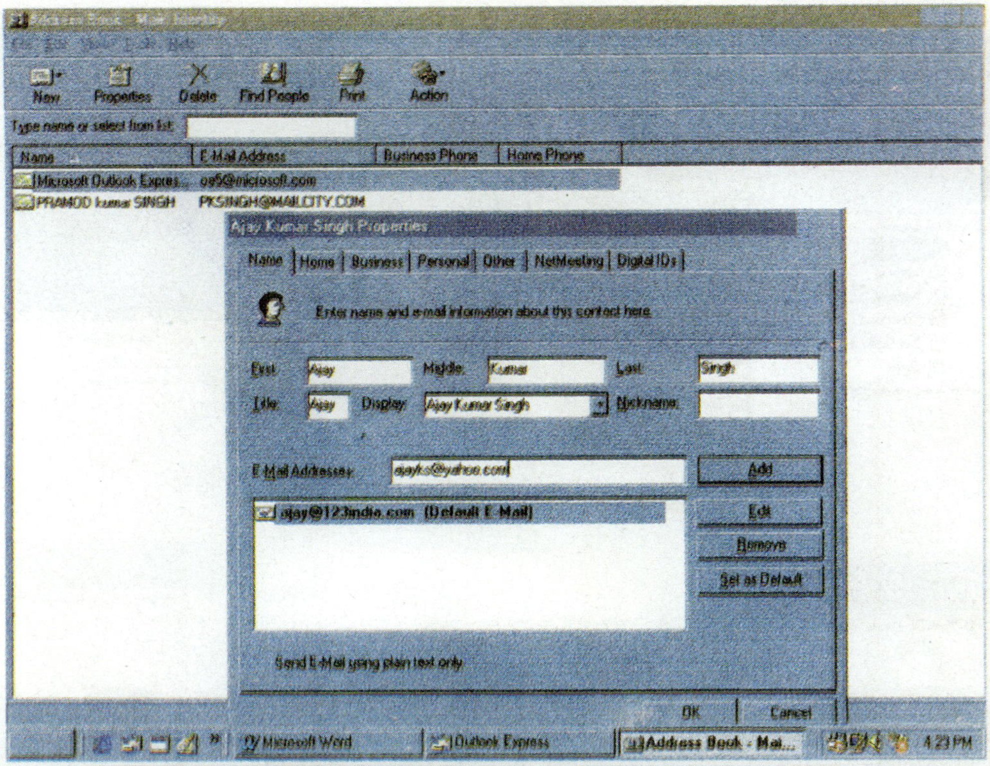

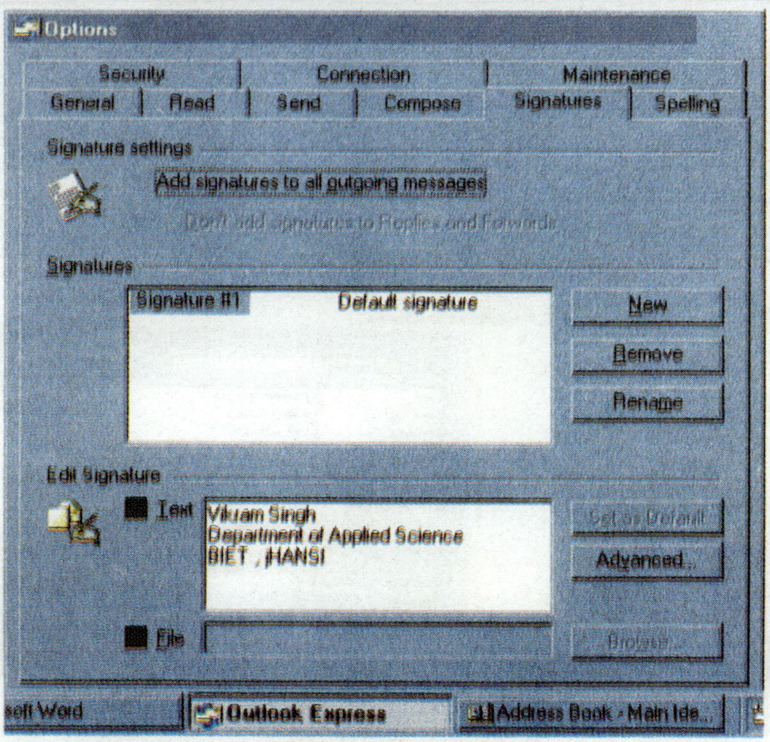

Fig. 8.10: Adding Signatures

9

ELEMENTS OF ELECTRONIC COMMERCE

Contents

9 ELEMENTS OF ELECTRONIC COMMERCE

9.1 INTRODUCTION

The exponential growth of the internet led to the search of new techniques for conducting effective business and commercial activities on the Internet. Commerce is now undergoing a revolutionary phase where the medium of communication between the customer and the merchant is electronic. The cutting edge for business today is Electronic Commerce (E-commerce). There are many other current buzzwords similar to E-commerce, like, Electronic Trading, Electronic Business, Electronic markets. In fact, E trading, E business, E markets are all parts of computer based commerce. Shopping on the Web is only a small part of E-commerce.

We define E-commerce as a business activity which is done using electronic medium. E-commerce is not a very new concept, as it started in 1995/1996. Actually, in a broader sense, E-commerce had started much earlier when telephones and fax machines were used to place an order for buying a product. This type of shopping also falls in the category of E-commerce. In early days of telecommunication in Europe, the electronic exchanges used to provide multiple facilities to subscribers on a telephone call. In India also, you may open the STD/ISD facility after dialing a number, for example, using a telephone, you can find your railway reservation status as soon as you dial a ticket number; you can come to know about a pending bill after dialing a number. There are several applications which are done by using a telephone connection even without the intervention of a telephone operator.

Another of the good example of using an electronic medium (telephone line) is Interactive Voice Response System (IVRS). You must have noticed that many organizations make available certain information using IVRS. IVRS is a system which plays an appropriate recorded voice on the telephone line when a customer presses some predefined digits on the telephone. For instance, you may enquire about your examination center after dialing your role number, get to know your result, merit positions etc. by pressing your role number in the telephone. In such cases, the telephone at the recipient end is connected to a computer data base. It searches your roll number in the database and then plays the recorded voice which corresponds to your examination center or result or merit position.

E-commerce refers to buying products without ever going to a shop. E-commerce covers activities like delivery of information, product and services and payments through electronic medium. There are some products which may be purchased online in electronic form. You may buy many items on the net whose delivery will be almost instantaneous. These are music, books, software, video, games, puzzles etc. These are products which can be represented in electronic form. However, a majority of the products may not be delivered instantly. Examples are television, computers, printers, hardware, household items etc. These products are delivered at a later state by courier or manually. There exists another form of E-commerce where large organizations place an order directly to another organization using business-to-business connection that makes purchasing easier for that organization. While there is no one standard definition of E-commerce, it is generally described as a method of buying and selling products and services electronically. The main vehicles of E-commerce remain the Internet and the World Wide Web. However, E-commerce is also done through e-mail, faxes and telephone.

9.2 E-COMMERCE

It may be defined as a modern business activity that includes the delivery of information, product and services and payments using electronic medium such as the Internet. This medium of business reduces the cost of services, and improves the quality of items and service. There are several activities which actually are not related with the buying or selling of a product, i.e., these activities are simply business related and no commerce is involved in them. These activities may include the inquiry about a product, selling price, delivery time or any other information pertaining to the business. These types of information exchanges may occur using an electronic medium like telephone, fax or e-mail. This will in fact not be a part of E-commerce activities but a part of E-business. Therefore the term E-business is broader than E-commerce and all E-commerce activities are subsumed in E-business.

E-commerce is mainly concerned with the business processes prevalent in an organization. It requires an information base of customers, creation of various information resources and an effective interaction between sellers, buyers, consumers etc. Thus the major requirements to establish E-commerce activity are the creation of information base, processing capability of information and an effective mechanism for information communication within and outside the organization. The impact of e-commerce may be seen in almost all areas of business, whether it be customer service, rapid product design, customized design of product, identifying the potential customers and transmitting electronically relevant information to customers about new products. It also helps the customers through online advertising and marketing, online-order taking and on-line customer service etc.

9.3 E-COMMERCE ADVANTAGES

E-commerce helps reduce the effective selling price of a product or service by eliminating various components of the distribution chain. We may take the example of a distribution chain, where the producer of an item sends the product to wholesellers, who in turn sell the item to retailers and they sell it to customers. Imaging the cost incurred in transportation from the producer to the wholeseller and from wholeseller to the retailers. Wholesellers and retailers would have their profit margins plus other costs. All this would be added to the cost of the product and its selling price would increase appreciably. The cost may be minimized if the customer orders the product directly from the producer and upon receipt of the order, the producer sends immediately the product to the customer. This will reduce lot of time as well as cost. For this exchange to take place, there has to be an interface between producers and customers which enables both parties to communicate directly with each other. E-commerce provides this interface. E-commerce is most suitable for items which may be produced in electronic form such as music, videos, interactive games, electronic books, and information-on demand and information based services. These items are easily handled in E-commerce as they can be delivered online to the customer and the payment can also made at the same time in an electronic form. Electronic commerce therefore offers a lot of lucrative advantages to both producers and consumers. It opens new vistas in contacting new consumers located around different geographical areas, and it also helps the producers to develop a good rapport with the existing customer base. The Customer Relationship Management (CRM) is another area which can be effectively managed through E-commerce technology. The information about customers, customers purchasing habits, customers profile and needs may be stored in databases and processed electronically. Based on this customized solutions or specific products for the customer can be instantly designed. All this helps in establishing a better customer relationship. This is probably one of the major activities to boost business through E-commerce. It helps the organization to minimize the paper work as the processing of various orders is done electronically, and therefore, it saves time, energy and cost for both producers and consumers.

Major advantages of E-commerce are listed below:

1. Cost reduction due to competitiveness in the procurement of products. Many suppliers of the product compete for customer patronage in open electronic markets. This competition brings down the product price.
2. Cost reduction due to reducing the paper work. The cost effective electronic document transfer ensures that both the customers and supplier's documents will be delivered almost instantly and safely. This enables both parties to take quick decisions.
3. Information dissemination at a wider level is possible. Information about the product, cost, size, specification etc. may be made available to the customer located at widely distant geographical boundaries.
4. Improved customer relationship may be achieved by fast dissipation of the information to the potential consumers.
5. Because all orders and inquiries are processed online, the product is directly supplied to the customer. This eliminates the need for whole sellers and retailers and brings down the product price.
6. Total time reduction in the order processing, as E-commerce minimizes the time taken from order to delivery.
7. Provides better, fast and effective linkage with the clients. Since all information has to be processed in the electronic medium, that is online, it is possible to identify the customers requirements which leads to quick product design.
8. Opens new vistas for the organization and generates better business avenues because of easy and cheap reach to the potential customer base.
9. Enhances the organizations product and market analysis as the organization gets faster feedback from the customer. These feedback may be processed online.

Thus we may see that E-commerce provides lots of benefits to both producers and customers.

9.4 VIRTUAL ORGANIZATIONS

It happens a number of times that the manufacturer of a product buys the raw material from different suppliers. Here the manufacturer is himself the customer of organisations supplying the raw materials. Dealing with the different types of organisations is cumbersome and manufacturer would look for a customized solution or product. Virtual organizations perform this rcle by networking with various suppliers who may be located in different cities. Virtual organisations announce themselves and advertise their services through their websites. They are like a common platform where the goods services from various suppliers are offered by the central agency. The customer may feel that all of the services are being offered from one organization. Virtual organizations therefore are industrial organizations in networked form. Virtual organizations may be encountered on the web in form of networks and they are different from the conventional set up. Virtual organizations are not based on the characteristic of traditional organizations such as inflexible hierarchical structure etc.

Intermediary are those people or organizations who are engaged in business on the interact and they provide a single point of contact between the customers and a group of suppliers. Customers normally have complex needs to be fulfilled. For example, a person engaged in the construction of a house may have to look after different suppliers for different items like cement, bricks, furnishers, wood, coal, electricity, telephone connection, cable TV, labor for construction, interior decoration, plumbing etc. These are all separate activities undertaken by different suppliers. In such cases, the customer requires a full solution instead of having to interface with different agencies or suppliers on different aspects. Intermediary is one who provides a single point of contact between the customer and different service providers or suppliers. Intermediaries are usually non-competing suppliers with a common customer using E-commerce to enable the customer to do single step/point purchasing with a guarantee that a one time contact will ensure the right materials to the right location at the right time.

Advantages of an intermediary are that it reduces the time of processing of customers requests, provides business avenues to suppliers and can offer the products or services of different organizations in new ways.

9.5 ROLE OF METAMEDIARY ON THE WEB

Metamediary is similar to the intermediary in the sense that it offers a point of a contact between the consumers having different requirements of products and services and different suppliers and organization offering a wide range of products and services. It will appear to the customers that he is getting a full solution to his requirements at one point.

A customer looking forward to purchasing a two-wheeler may be looking for different items and services offered while purchasing the two-wheeler. The relevant information on the subject may include the consumer reports on satisfaction from different brands, reports of the brand in news papers, information from insurance companies, the different schemes for different brands, manufacturer's advertisement for different specifications, spare shops, service centers. Multimediary provides all this information from different companies related with the purchase at a single point to customer. The customer is, thus, enabled to make a better choice according to this needs.

9.6 E-COMMERCE APPLICATIONS

E-commerce offers a number of applications to different people, organizations etc. Anything, which suppliers and consumers do in the market place can also be done on the web. There are a number of application possible; we list a few important ones.

Education and Training

It is a very important area of E-commerce application. Many institutes and universities offer interactive classroom teaching through video conferencing and virtual classrooms. Even the presence of a virtual universites on the web may be seen now-a-days.

Entertainment

Entertainment is a major application of E-commerce. You may select and buy audio and video disks in electronic form. Video on demad, multi user games and online discussions are other major activities related to entertainment which are all possible using E-commerce. There are a number of organizations which offer a variety of entertainment products on the web.

Banking and Financial Transactions

Banking and Financial transactions also may be realized using E-commerce. Home banking through credit cards, e-currency, Stock market information, bidding for tenders, financial news, bank to bank transfer, money transfer, debit and credit of accounts and other related activities may be performed well on the web. All these activities are a part of electronic or Web commerce.

Essential Services

Essential services required in day-to-day life like medical, health and, telephone, electricity, Housing, transportation etc. are the areas where E-commerce is quite useful. All the relevant information and services may be obtained online, thus, making day-to-day life more convenient.

9.7 A BUSINESS TRANSACTION IN E-COMMERCE

A customer oriented business transaction involves all the activities starting from identification of product, to order, processing of order by the manufacturer, delivery of the product and realization of payments. The following are the broad activities involved in settlement of a business transaction, through E-commerce:

- *Search of the product:* This step involves the selection of a product from various choices and a comparative study of value of the product. Time and money are required to obtain the information about a product.
- *Price negotiation:* Is that part of a business transaction where negotiation on the product design, cost, delivery time etc. is done.
- *Settlement:* This involves the order processing by the supplier. A business transaction settlement includes the delivery of goods or services to the customer and the realization of payments by the supplier.

E-commerce pertains to commercial activities, which may involve the following types of products. These are Tangible items, Digital goods and services.

Tangible Items: These are the physical products, which may be seen, touched and felt. Commercial activities involve purchase and exchange of tangible goods. The product identification, order processing, payments may be made in the electronic form but the goods delivery to the customer is done using the traditional meant. Therefore, E-commerce helps partially in the trading of tangible goods.

Digital Goods: These goods have an electronic rather than a physical form. They include the digital form of books, documents, information, audio, video software, news, pictures, animation, games etc. These items may be traded in electronic medium since they can be transmitted online. A business transaction involving the buying or selling of digital goods is settled instantly.

Services: Services is an extremely important area of E-commerce which probably is the most sought after the users. Stock market information, railways booking, airline information, insurance activities, payment of electricity, water, telephone bills and medical and health services are important examples of services. Different government organizations and industrial houses offer up to date information about their services on their websites. Customers at remotes places can log on to their servers and access these services and also obtain relevant information about the status of any requests/ orders which they might have placed.

9.8 SAFETY OF BUSINESS TRANSACTION ON WEB

A business transaction on the web involves mainly three activities; search of product, price negotiation and delivery of product and payments. There are several ways of making payments on the Internet using credit and debit cards, this is, electronic currency. Since the data pertaining to the payment has to travel on the network from one computer to another over a communication channel, no e-commerce system can be considered as 100 percent safe. But you are more safe in these electronic payment system in comparison to the conventional shopping where you're more likely to get your pocket picked! There have been cases reported about Internet security breaches. Inspite of these cases most customers, banks and researchers are of the view that E-commerce transactions are far safer than those in the physical world. With the newer versions of web browsers like Netscape Navigator and MS Internet Explorer, transactions can be encrypted using Secure Sockets Layer, a protocol that creates a secure connection to the server and protects the information as it travels over the Internet. Secure Socket Layer uses a public key encryption, considered to be the strongest encryption method. The document may be signed by the customers which involves the payment details. These documents are coded in such a way that it is almost impossible for an intruder to decode it. All Credit Card companies are promoting an additional security standard called Secure Electronic Transactions. This standard encodes the credit card numbers in such a way that it can be decoded only by their bankers and credit card companies. The security of electronic fund transfer or electronic payment transaction is intimately related to the model of encryption used in encrypting it. Algorithms have been developed where the possibility of decoding an encrypted message is one out of million attempts. Therefore, we may say that electronic transactions are far safer than what is generally imagined.

9.9 BASIC INFRASTRUCTURE REQUIREMENT FOR E-COMMERCE

Although E-commerce is still in its infancy, it has already made a huge impact on the traditional methods of doing business. The main motivating force behind E-commerce is an access to large data stores using the Internet. To do business on the net, the basic infrastructural requirement is *bandwidth*. All E-commerce applications require the transmission of multimedia data which consists of text, graphics, audio and video. If the bandwidth available is not sufficient, then bottleneck would be created in accessing the interact. Business across the globe in electronic medium requires Information Superhighways, fueling multimedia contents to interact with customers.

Information Superhighways

Effective and efficient linkage between the customer and the supplier is a precondition for E-commerce. Including more and more multimedia content can be considered as a fuel for E-commerce applications. Multimedia information includes combination of text, audio, video and graphics. Its purpose is to combine the interactivity of a user-friendly interface with multiple forms of content. E-commerce applications require a variety of multimedia content and packaging. Large databases and high speed networking are therefore required to store and distribute large amounts of information with multimedia content to customers.

Traditional business activities require basic infrastructural support like electricity, water, communication, transportation and even law and order. The delivery and distribution of goods in traditional business requires good transportation infrastructure. This includes high quality interstate highways, expressways and fine local roads with an excellent connection from one city to another. In the same way, to give a boost to E-business, customers and suppliers require better and improved ways of information communication. The problem becomes more intricate when multimedia data has to traverse on the information path ways. Sustained E-business requires better bandwidth to communicate the information presented in the form of multimedia data. Multimedia information itself requires a high bandwidth for communication.

The concept of *Information superhighway* or *Information corridors* is used in E-commerce just as physical highways and roads are used in traditional business activities. This concept is not limited to any particular geographical region. It has taken the shape of a global phenomena. The Information Superhighways would be a key element in business transformation through E-commerce. Information Superhighway is not a single high-speed data link between two points. It is a *nested collection of high speed data links* designed according to long-standing, well-defined rules and regulations. The Information Superhighway might not be based on one type of data communication link; it would require telephone wires, wireless link, radio link, satellite, cable TV wire etc.

The other requirement for E-commerce applications is the forming of the standards for E-commerce. These standards include public policy and technical requirements. These two requirements serve as a basis for infrastructural support for E-commerce.

Standardization of Public Policy

Standardization of public policy means the framing of rules and regulations to prevent frauds and forgeries. The noticeable difference in doing business on the Web and traditional business is that traditional business is done in a limited domain, thus all aspects related with the business may be controlled or predicted as one deals with them personally. In E-commerce there is no personal meeting or physical interface between the supplier and the customer. The business is conducted over the Internet without the two parties even coming in physical contact with each other. In such a situation, there is always a possibility of fraud or cheating. Therefore, public policy pertaining to E-commerce needs to be framed and standardised to ensure proper functioning of E-Commerce. Further issues like universal access and information pricing also need to be standardized. In most countries, E-business has been given a legal status, however, in some countries it is yet to be given legal status standardised to become E-commerce is truly international in its nature and scope. Several other issues like maintaining the privacy, payment realization require great amount of attention.

Technical Standards

Technical standards refers to the issues of information publishing and user interfaces. The way of presentation of information about the product using graphical user interfaces and embedding multimedia applications requires a technical standard to be followed by different organization.

These two standards are as stated above, should be addressed in order to bring about uniformity in business on the Web.

9.10 E-COMMERCE CATEGORIES

E-commerce business is expected to grow up to 300 billion dollars in 2002 as per the Forester research. This includes trading of goods and services involving individual consumers and large organizations. Based on the nature of business, E-commerce may be categorized into the following three categories:

- Business to Business (B to B) E-commerce

- Business to Consumer (B to C) E-commerce
- Business to Government (B to G) E-commerce

9.10.1 Business to Business (B to B) E-commerce

The most popular form of doing E-business is by establishing the web sites of business houses and letting the different customers interact with those web sites. These web sites generally present multimedia contents to provide a better image of their products and services. B to B E-commerce requires the establishment of B to B extranets which is a secure network of various houses which cooperate with each other. This may be understood as the business alliance between different companies for their mutual benefit. These cooperating companies can include various suppliers, customer companies and trading partners. Internet can connect all businesses to each other, located in different geographical boundaries. Internet also helps to do business transactions between companies regardless of their position in the supply chain.

Thus B to B E-commerce is settlement of business transactions among large organizations. This type of electronic business alliance poses a threat to traditional intermediaries like wholesellers and brokers. Internet connections facilitate the ability to bargain directly with a range of suppliers, thereby eliminating the need for such intermediaries. The methods of doing business in B to B E-commerce differ from traditional commerce in a number of ways as electronic commerce combines information technology, telecommunications technology, and business processes to make it practical to do business in ways that could not otherwise be done.

Let us take the example of a large computer manufacturer. The manufacturer may have to handle a large number of queries from customers which include the normal inquiries about product availability, product specification and prices. The manufacturer accumulates the orders for sales and buys the components or other hardware from different companies. This includes buying mother boards, processor chip, HDD, FDD, jumpers and connecting wires, modem etc. from different companies. A business alliance with these companies on the web will facilitate the manufacturer to reduce labor intensive interaction and cost and ensure higher profit margins. The B to B extranet will help different organizations to understand their common needs and goals. Therefore, the objective of B to B E-commerce is to enable trading partners, organizations, suppliers and customers to form a tight business relationship over a secured network.

B to B E-commerce's main focus is on Supply Chain Management. A supply chain is the network of suppliers, manufactures and vendors within which the business works. Supply Chain Management has become a vital issue as it is difficult for different companies and manufacturers to do their business in isolation. Non-competing organizations are forming business alliances so that the goals of all the companies are profitably achieved. It should be noted here that wholly non-concepting companies or companies which are not competing with each other form business alliances. For instance, a company manufacturing mother boards would not form an alliance with another company manufacturing mother boards; instead it would form an alliance with a company distributing mother boards or a company producing the raw materials for the manufacturer of mother boards. As we have discussed earlier, a computer manufacturer forms a larger network of suppliers of floppy disk, mother boards, CD's etc. It can also form a network of customers comprising retailers and end consumers.

9.10.2 Business-to-Consumer (B to C) E-commerce

In B to C E-commerce the focus is on the consumers. Obtaining the feedback, from consumers and responding to their inquiries about product and design, services and price are the main functions in B to C, E-commerce. This type of E-commerce binds the relationship between the consumers and the company. Common activities involved in B to C, E-commerce include retail selling of products, marketing relationships, consumers survey forms, customizing the product and services according to the consumers needs, and providing opportunities for consumer satisfaction.

Shopping on the Web is probably one of the most common activities on the internet, where a customer looks for different products and services offered by various companies and on the basis of comparison, he places a purchase order to the selected company on the Web. All these activities involve the organization's web sites which contain the details of products and services. Secure web transactions enable companies to allow consumers to purchase products directly over the Web. The Internet has enabled, Electronic Markets where products are electronically bought and sold. Relationship marketing is also a major activity in B to C, E-commerce. It allows companies to track the actions of consumers on the Web and thereby, gauge their preferences. Companies are experimenting with this methodology as a tool for market research and relationship marketing. This relationship gets strengthened when companies obtain filled consumer survey and feedback forms from their consumers. These forms provide vital data about the nature of buying habits of persons belonging to different sects, professions, locations, age groups etc. This feedback helps the companies to customize their products and services according to the customer needs and profiles.

Determining technological feasibility of a B to C E-commerce application is very important. It has been noticed in the past that many of E-commerce companies and web sites failed because of lack of technological and behavioral feasibility. Upon determination of business goals, it is necessary to establish the technological feasibility of various E-commerce plans that could meet the goals. The starting point should be a clear sense of what functions each E-commerce technology can perform in order to improve business activity and achieve the objectives. It must be remembered that the success of any E-commerce web site or organization, particularly metamediaries, depends on customer satisfaction, after taking into consideration the behavioral and technological feasibility aspects.

We may conclude that B to C, E-commerce is consumer oriented and B to C web sites normally offer retailing, personal investment and personal finance, home banking along with a vast amount of information on various products and services. There are two technologies which are used to build any B to C E-commerce application. These are Generation, Reading and understanding of Bar Codes printed on the product and implementation of Electronic Shopping Cart.

Shopping Basket/Cart

An electronic shopping basket or shopping cart is similar to the normal shopping cart which a customer uses in real life shopping. Shopping on the internet begins by visiting the web site of a company. If you are visiting a general store on the net, you may like to purchase a number of items available on the shop. As you browse through an online store, you can keep the selected items in your virtual shopping cart, which keeps a track of the items you have purchased. It also simultaneously shows the item quantity, price etc. Once you finish shopping, you will have to click on the *quit shopping* or other related link that shows you what you've placed in your virtual shopping cart. You may remove items that you're no longer interested in purchasing and then enter your shipping and payment information to process your order. This concept of a shopping basket is implemented in almost every E-commerce web site. The program or software is so developed as it gives the feeling of shopping in real life.

Bar Codes

Bar codes are rectangular pattern of lines of varying widths and spaces. Specific characters are also assigned to these unique patterns. These codes are used for automatic product identification by the computer. A special *bar code reader* reads the bar codes. Almost all the packaged items contain the bar codes. They include all the cosmetic items, books etc. These items are scanned through by the bar code reader to scan the price printed. These prices are input to the computer and it adds up the prices of all the items purchased. As the product is identified, the price is entered in the cash register, while the internal systems such as inventory and accounting are automatically updated. This technology carries tremendous potential to improve any business requiring tight control over material flow.

9.10.3 Business to Government (B to G) E-commerce

A new trend in E-commerce applications is the B to G E-commerce. Many government departments are setting up their web sites to directly reach the common citizens. They announce various government policies, rules and regulations on their web sites. A common citizen may interact with these web sites to know the various details. The concept of Smart City has also been introduced. One such project launched by few state governments is to bring various government departments under a single point of reach for the citizens. This is shown in Figure 9.1.

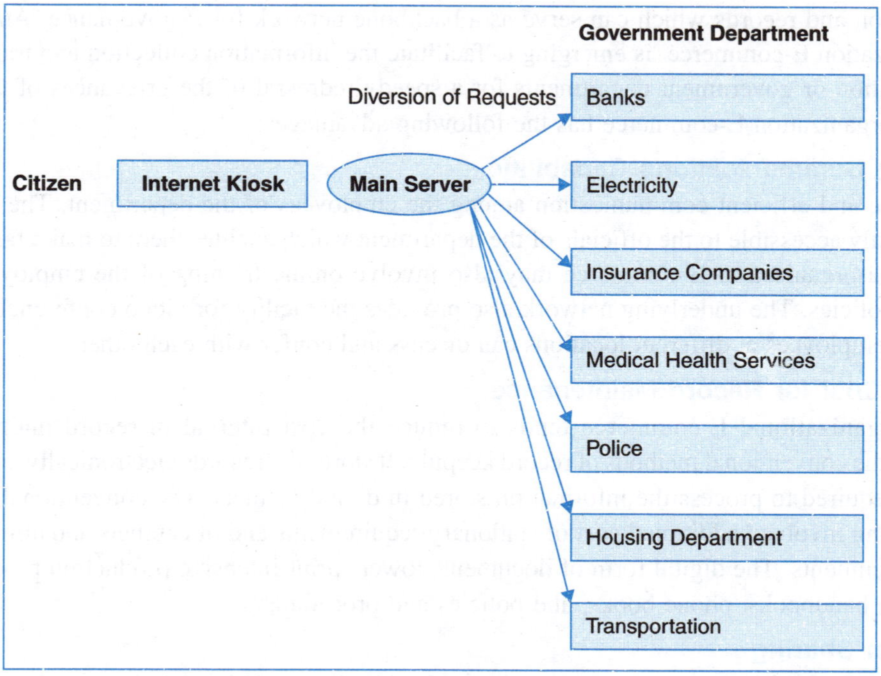

Fig. 9.1: A Model of a Smart City

The diagram shows the concept of a Smart City. All the services and information for which a common citizen has to struggle from one office to another in day-to-day life, can now be accessed from one place. A person while sitting on a computer at Internet Kiosk, may log on to main server of the government. From this place he will find the links to various other departments servers. These servers may be kept and maintained in the individual offices of Transportation, Housing, Banks, Electricity etc. The requests submitted to the main server will then be directed to the departmental server and, in return, a person will get the desired information. This concept can provide a lot of convenience to the common man and it is very important for E-governance.

9.11 E-GOVERNANCE

The former chairman of Nasscom, Dewang Mehta once said the when common citizen will be able to do various jobs on the net like lodge a FIR in a police station on the net, submit telephone and electricity bills on the web, booking railway tickets, reminders of insurance premium and deposit premium, obtain land records and housing development information, and perform common banking operations then, E-governance is said to have been achieved.

Truly, E-governance is the process of bringing the government departments close to common citizens by using Information Technology. Beneficiaries of E-governance are the common citizens and government officials and machinery. There is no doubt that a lot of time and effort is wasted in collection of information from various fields taking decisions and forming new rules and policies. All this happens as the records are kept and maintained manually. Therefore the processing of any information takes lot of time and the cost of transmitting information is also very high. All this creates inefficiency within the government departments. To facilitate better efficiency, it is necessary to first establish a common pool of information and records which can serve as a backbone network for E-governance. An area called Intra-organization E-commerce is emerging to facilitate the information collection and transfer within the organization or government departments for a speedy redressal of the grievances of the common man. Intra-organization E-commerce has the following advantages:

Enhancing Communications Capability

Effective and efficient communication among the employees of the department. The information becomes easily accessible to the officials of the department which enables them to make fast decisions. Further, intra-organisation E-commerce may also involve online training of the employees on new issues and policies. The underlying network also provides the facility for video conferencing whereby the various employees at different locations can discuss and confer with each other.

Reducing Cost for Record Maintenance

Intra organizational E-commerce tends to reduce the cost internal in record maintenance by eliminating the conventional methods of record keeping. It stores the records electronically and minimum efforts are required to process the information stored in digital formats. The conventional methods of record keeping involved additional cost of stationary requirements and of cabinets and almirahs for the safety of documents. The digital form of documents lowers print-intensive production processes such as employee handbooks, phone books, and policies and procedures.

Information Sharing

In most government departments, collection and reconcilement of information is a prime concern. Lot of effort and energy is wasted in the collection of relevant records and information. By storing records in Digital formats, intra organization E-commerce provides an effective way of not only sharing information but also a platform for sharing expertise and ideas. Further it is easier, creating and updating content when it is stored in a digital format.

Increased Customer Satisfaction

When information is electronically stored and processed, the customers get the required information at a click of the mouse, and they do not even have to visit the office premises. This enables the government/organizations to have a better communication with the customers and citizens.

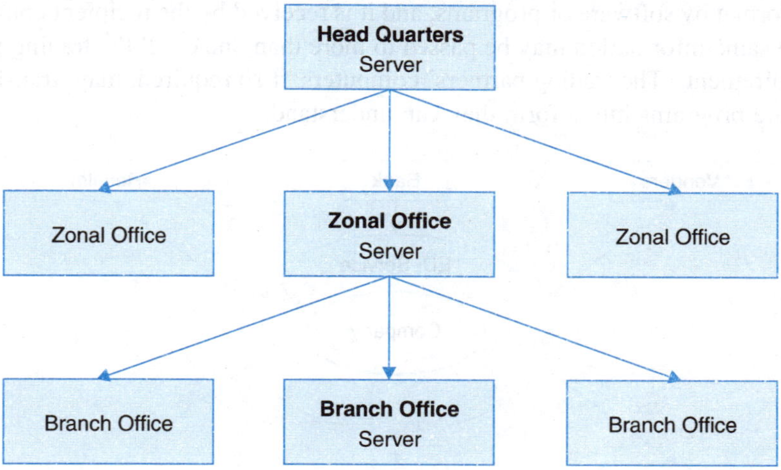

Fig. 9.2

Figure 9.2 shows the structure of an Intra organization network. A server may be placed at Head Quarter, Zonal office and Branch office and so on. The required information at appropriate levels is kept in the dedicated servers. If any information is to be passed on to other level of office, one may connect to that server to get the information or data. The Network enables the government department and organization to keep a track of all the information record and provide appropriate information to its employees and then to customers.

9.12 ELECTRONIC DATA INTERCHANGE (EDI)

The growth of multidimensional business activities and innovations in Information Technology are pressing business organisations to become automated. Many organizations are using computers not only to store and, process the data but also to get information and pass it in various formats to other organizations as well as to their customers. Suppose a computer manufacturer, upon getting a big order for the supply of computers, places orders to his business partners like the suppliers of FDD, hard disk, mother board etc. This requires the manufacturer to send different types of letters and invoices to the partner organizations. These documents are formatted in the manufacturer's computer, printed out and mailed to the partners. On being received at the partner's organisation, the documents are entered again into the computer by the partners. Therefore in the supply chain, the various forms, invoices etc. are to be entered into the computer again and again. The entire process of creating reports by one company, printing them with printers, posting to the destined company, receipt of reports or documents at destination and computer entry of relevant data at the destination computer requires a lot of time. Thereby delays occur and a prompt response to the customer's inquiries and orders is not made. Further, mistakes can also occur in the data entry of orders etc. the receiving end. The solution to this problem, mostly arising because of adhoc usage of computing facilities, is Electronic Data Interchange.

Electronic Data Interchange refers to the computer-to-computer exchange of structured business information in a standard electronic format. Using Electronic Data Interchange, the various trading partners can establish links between their computers to exchange the information electronically. EDI may also be defined as the transfer of structured data between the computers on mutually agreed formats known as EDI formats. The information stored in the source computer in an organization is converted into EDI format by software or programs, and it is received by the recipient computer system for direct usage. The same information may be passed to more than one or all the trading partners depending upon the requirement. The trading partners' computers, if so required, may translate the information using software programs into a form they can understand.

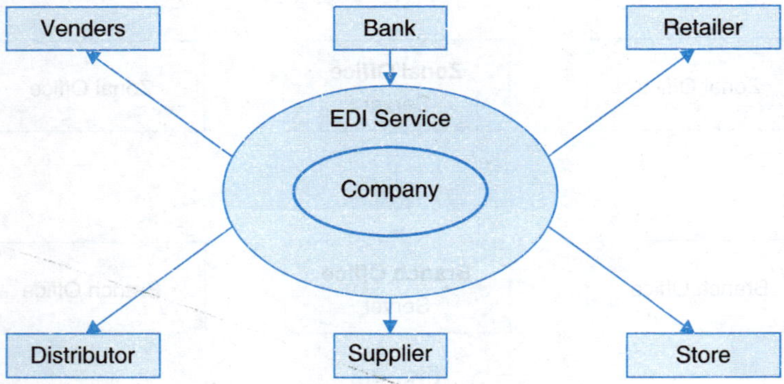

Fig. 9.3

Figure 9.3 shows, a company and its various partner companies like as vendors, banks, retailers, distributors, suppliers and warehouses. The company sends various reports, documents, queries etc. to different partner companies from time to time. In conventional business practices these documents are printed and posted to the partner companies. Upon receipt, these documents are re-entered into computers. EDI interface is essentially a software, which converts or prepares the document into mutually agreed format which is accepted by the computer in partner companies in its original form or without requiring any further processing. Thus EDI interface converts various documents into mutually agreed formats which are automatically accepted by different computers.

9.13 BENEFITS OF ELECTRONIC DATA INTERCHANGE

The main difference between the Electronic Data Interchange and other conventional methods of electronic communication using Fax, E-mail and other business formats is that the data sent by the sender's organization wing EDI is understood by the receiver company's computer without any manual intervention by the operators. This happens because of translation or conversion of the document into mutually agreed digital formats. The main advantages of EDI, therefore are the following:

- The information or the data sent by one company's computer may be directly used by the recipient's computer without any manual intervention. The mutually agreed format of documents enables both companies to reduce paper work.
- Since standard formats are used for information or data exchanges between the computer systems of both organizations, it eliminates the data entry errors to a considerable extent.
- It improves the business cycles of both organizations by providing a link for electronic communication between them. A considerable reduction in time is observed in the completion of a business cycle.
- Electronic data Interchange may be used for communication between more than two companies. In such cases the various cooperating companies agree to common digital formats for communicating the electronic data and information.

- Electronic Data Interchange may also be used to communicate between the various components of the organization itself. Various departments, or sections of an organization may transfer the document in structured formats.
- Instant delivery of information or data on the prescribed digital formats enables quick execution of orders, lower stock levels, and therefore, more productivity and profitability.
- The EDI format can also be applied to the feedback forms/inquiry forms from the customers. This promotes a better organisation-customer relationship and also reduces the response time of the organisation.

A common example of EDI is that of various organizations providing electronic forms to this customers. These forms may correspond to market survey form, feedback form, purchase order form etc. Here the customers provide the relevant information in a specified format. When these form are submitted electronically to the company, they are stored in the company's computer database. Since the customer fills the appropriate contents at the specified location on the form, customers data may be directly transferred and stored in the database. These databases are generally organised in the form of tables and customer's data is automatically transferred to the appropriate tables.

9.14 ELECTRONIC DATA INTERCHANGE vs DATA EXCHANGES BY E-MAIL

Sometimes EDI is confused with E-mail. However, the two are totally different applications. This may be understood by an example. A customer may place the purchase order for an item by writing an E-mail. This E-mail contains the text which has been written by the customer in his own way. The Mail may be delivered to the recipient computer instantly. But the processing of that E-mail requires manual intervention as it has be read by a person, understood and is then processed by entering the relevant data from the mail into the company's computer. The mail is then acknowledged by the company. Thus, considerable intervention is required at the receiver's end. If the customer places the purchase order electronically on the format prescribed by the company, all of the information which the customers wanted to write in the mail, would be entered in the digital form at the appropriate pre-specified locations on the form. After entering the complete information on the form, on the click of a mouse, the information is transferred to the company's computer database without any manual intervention. The receipt of the information may be generated by an auto-mail generator at the company's computer which reads the information supplied by the customer and posts it in the company's specified format. This saves a lot of time and the customer gets an acknowledgement immediately upon sending the digital information form.

We may summarize the essential differences between EDI system and E-mail as follows:

1. In EDI systems, there is no human intervention as the documents are transferred through a software in a mutually agreed format. E-mail requires human intervention for reading the mail, processing the information and storing the data.
2. The EDI documents are composed by one software and processed by another set of software. These software are compatible in the sense that they produce the document in the format which can be taken as input by another software for processing. E-mail messages are composed and. interpreted by human beings and the reply documents are also composed and drafted by human beings.

9.15 NETWORK INFRASTRUCTURE REQUIREMENT FOR EDI

EDI is mainly concerned with the electronic exchange of documents between various companies, in such a way that the documents are received and processed without any human intervention. The EDI standard for large business companies was developed during 1970s and they are under the control of American National Standardization Institute (ANSI). The communication of documents requires an underlying secured network. Conventionally, this requires a leased line between organizations or an entry to the Value Added Network (VAN).

Value Added Network (VAN) was established basically for the communication of information. This network, apart from communicating the data or information, provides many other services to add value to the network. Following are the some of the main services provided by VAN:

1. Time Stamping of the document
2. Acknowledgement of the document
3. Routing of the document
4. Reliability of document delivery
5. Integrity of network
6. Safety of business transaction

A value added network time stamps the document, i.e. time at which the document was sent and the time it was received are tracked. The acknowledgement of delivery is managed by VAN. It also ensures integrity, privacy, safety of business transaction and routing of the document.

Transportation of EDI documents is far more complex than simple mailing of the documents or sharing of the files. The EDI documents are highly structured and processed by the software at the sending and receiving ends. EDI service software executes the procedure and functions for safe and secure delivery of the documents, tracks the routing of the documents on the network and ensures delivery of the documents. It is the responsibility of VAN service provider or network service provider to communicate the message. VAN works on the concept of store and forward mechanism, where the documents are sent by the sender without knowing whether the receiver is ready to receive them. The documents are kept preserved and delivered whenever the recipient becomes ready to accept the document.

There are a number of ways in which company may adopt Electronic Data Interchange. One such way is to connect the company computer, which is pre-installed with EDI software, to computer, VAN. The EDI software converts the document into EDI format and once the documents reach the destination computer, the EDI software converts them into the format acceptable to the recipient computer. The types of software which are required to be installed for EDI are:

1. Application Software
2. Translation Software
3. EDI service Software
4. Network Access Control Software.

Figure 9.4 shows the various software installed on the sender's and receiver's computers. Application software has the same role as conventionally defined. The application software produces and processes the information or documents. After generation of the document, it is passed to Translation Software, which translates the document into EDI format, a commonly agreed format of the document. EDI service software processes the EDI document in such a way that it becomes compatible to VAN. EDI Service software also keeps track of the document on the network and executes the functions to ensure the safe delivery of the document at destination. There are specially written software which allows the company's computer to access the network. These software allow the document to enter into the network and execute the services provided by the Value Added Network.

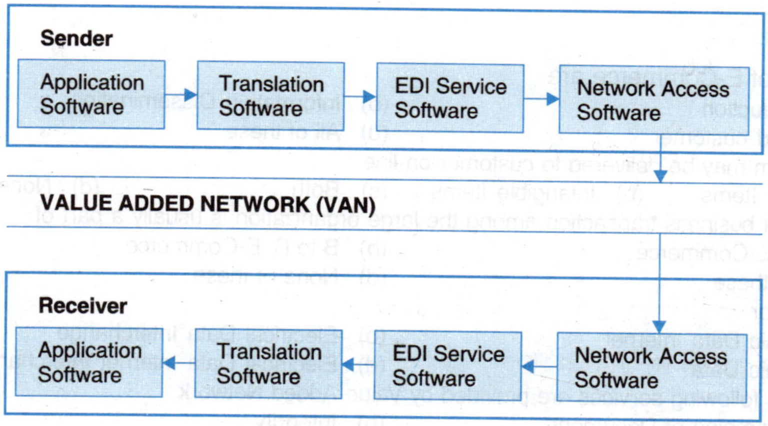

Fig. 9.4

9.16 ELECTRONIC FUNDS TRANSFER ON EDI NETWORKS

EDI allows the document transfers among the partner companies without any manual intervention. It is thus, a suitable technology for banks and financial Institutions which are concerned with payments and final transfers. Suppose a customer orders his bank to transfer money from his e-account to another account in a different bank. Documents corresponding to fund transfer are to be sent over EDI network to the recipient bank. These types of documents must have minimum data interchange between the banks since security is the most important issue related with this type of data transfer. Fund transfer documents not only require encryption but also requires a secured network. At present there are several secured networks which are providing secured transmission of these types of documents. A major one is FedWire, which is the oldest EDI network for bank transactions.

ISO 7898 model defines the standards required to be fulfilled for safe and secure delivery of electronic fund transfer over a network. Some of the important features defined in the model are authentication of various entities in the network, restricting the access to network by only authorized entities, preventing modification of information on network, detection of unauthorized alteration of information etc.

We may conclude this chapter by observing that E-commerce is a novel way of processing business transaction on the Internet. It allows the customer to search for a product, purchase and pay for it on the internet. The underlying infrastructure required for E-commerce is computer and telecommunications networks. As more and more computers are being added to the Internet, increase in the bandwidth of communication channel is fuelling the potential of E-commerce. Traditional systems like, EDI are now being converted into full E-commerce applications. E-commerce application uses the most popular service on the Internet called World Wide Web. This is also encouraging the business companies to expand their business by opening their web sites on the internet which provides new directions for growth. As awareness of the Internet throughout the commercial world and the general public increases, competitiveness will force lower entry barriers, continued rapid innovation and further expansion of markets.

OBJECTIVE TYPE QUESTIONS

Multiple Choice

1. Advantage of E-Commerce are
   (a) Cost reduction (b) Information Dissemination
   (c) Improved customer (d) All of these
2. Following item may be delivered to customer on line
   (a) Tangible Items (b) Intangible Items (c) Both (d) None of these
3. Settlement of business transaction among the large organization is usually a part of
   (a) B to C, E-Commerce (b) B to B, E-Commerce
   (c) Both of these (d) None of these
4. EDI stands for
   (a) Electronic Data Internet (b) Electrical Data Interchange
   (c) Electronic Data (d) Electrical Data Internet Interchange
5. Which of the following services are provided by Value Added Network
   (a) Time Stamping of Document (b) Integrity
   (c) Safety of Business (d) All of these
6. EDI software convert the document in to EDI format with
   (a) Human Intervention (b) Without Human Intervention
   (c) Little coding work (d) None of above
7. Which of the following may be downloaded online?
   (a) Music (b) Video (c) Software products (d) All of these
8. Which of the following are typical part of a business transaction
   (a) Search of a Product (b) Price Negotiation
   (c) Price settlement (d) All of these
9. Which of the following are web browsers?
   (a) MS Internet Explorer (b) Netscape Navigator
   (c) Both (d) None of these
10. IVRS stands for
    (a) Interactive Voice Response System (b) Iterative Voice Response System
    (c) Interactive Value Response System (d) Iterative Value Response System

Answers

1-d, 2-b, 3-b, 4-c, 5-d, 6-b, 7-d, 8-d, 9-c, 10-a

State True or False

1. E-Commerce includes the business activities done in electronic medium. [True] [False]
2. Virtual Organizations have presence on the web. [True] [False]
3. B to B, E commerce focuses on retailing, personal interaction. [True] [False]
4. Standardization of public policy is a must to enable E Governance. [True] [False]
5. A high bandwidth data internet enables the E Business. [True] [False]
6. EDI may be used for communication in two or more organizations. [True] [False]
7. E Mail and EDI are similar concept. [True] [False]
8. EDI can be used for electronic fund transfers. [True] [False]
9. Bandwidth denotes the amount of data communication over channel. [True] [False]
10. E-Commerce enables customer relationship. [True] [False]

Answers

1-True, 2-True, 3-False, 4-True, 5- True, 6-True, 7-False, 8-True, 9-True, 10-True.

SELECTED EXERCISES

1. What is meant by Electronic Commerce? How is E-commerce related with Electronic Business?
2. Explain the benefits a consumer gets in E-commerce.
3. What are potential benefits of E-commerce for the business firms?
4. What is meant by supply chain management? How E-commerce affects the supply chain management?
5. What are virtual organizations?
6. What are the differences between E-commerce and Electronic Data Interchange (EDI)?
7. What are the difference between goods and services? What kind of services may be offered in E-commerce? Explain with suitable examples.
8. What are tangible goods? How can one buy a tangible good using E-commerce? Show with a diagram. How will the product be delivered to the consumers?
9. Explain how the services costs may be reduced in E-commerce?
10. How can E-commerce help a company to reach its customers and maintains a healthy relationship with the customers. Explain with suitable examples.
11. How does a greater access to the Internet affect the prospects of E-commerce?
12. What are the essential differences between the E-commerce and Print and Broadcast mediums?
13. Explain the roles and function of Intermediary on the web. How does the intermediaries work on the web? Explain with suitable examples.
14. How can E-commerce improve the customer satisfaction?
15. How E-commerce helps to reduce the cost of a product for the consumer? Explain with an example.
16. Show with the help of an example as to how E-commerce helps to get better customer satisfaction? Show how business strategies has to be mixed with innovation in E-commerce activities?
17. What is the importance of Electronic Data Interchange in E-commerce? The EDI application is a part of E-commerce. Justify the statement.
18. What are partially integrated EDI systems ? Can partially integrated EDI system take up financial transactions?
19. What is the role of Metamediary on the Web? How does the function of Metamediary differs from the Intermediary?
20. Comment on the failure of E-commerce sites? What are the reasons behind the failure of E-commerce site ? Under what circumstances can E-commerce be successful ? Explain with proper examples.
21. What is meant by Value Added Network? Must EDI use a underlying VAN in order to get financial transactions executed.
22. List any five advantages of EDI over conventional E-Mail system of information exchange.
23. What do you mean by a business transaction? Show the various states of execution of a business transaction? How a simple business transaction is different from a financial transaction?
24. Describe the types of E-commerce? Compare the requirement goals of B to B, B to C and B to G commerce.
25. Define the network infrastructure requirement of E-commerce application. What precaution must be taken in order to get safe and secure execution of business transactions on the web.
26. Define the network infrastructure requirement for EDI applications. What is the role of the following software on the clients computer?
    - Application Software
    - Translation Software
    - EDI service Software
    - Network Access Control Software.
27. What is meant by the concept of E-governance ? What are the requirement goals of E-governance ? How E-governance is related with the set up of a smart city?
28. What are Bar Codes? How are they scanned and what information are coded into Bar Codes? How are bar codes used in E-commerce applications.
29. What is meant by E-markets or E-malls? How is shopping done on the web? Explain the role and usage of e-basket or e-shopping cart.
30. Main focus of B to C, E-commerce is on consumers. Justify the statement.

10

INTERNET SECURITY AND SAFE ELECTRONIC COMMERCE

Contents

10 INTERNET SECURITY AND SAFE ELECTRONIC COMMERCE

10.1 INTRODUCTION

Various business organizations have been exploring different ways to increase their profits and innovative methods to reach their consumers. With the increase in the popularity of the Internet, these business organizations have seen the World Wide Web as a potential tool for multiplying their profits and directly reaching their consumer base. Information Technology application to all commercial and business activities is called E-commerce, which is an integration of communication, data management and security capabilities to allow the various business organizations to do commercial activities on the Internet. A business transaction on the web requires safe and secure completion. A secured system requires protection from unauthorized access to hardware and software. All E-commerce activities use the computer systems and underlying networks for communication of information. The safe and secure delivery of information to its destination is the most critical part of a business transaction. An electronic payment, legal document, services contracts, pay roll, future planning and strategic goals are all not only most important but also totally private types of information. No business organization can afford misuse of this type of information. Any alteration, leakage or damage of the information content may prove to be catastrophic to the organization. For example, where data pertaining to a payment has to travel over the communication network from one computer to another, any damage or alteration or leakage of credit card details may be fatal to customer, bank and business organization. No electronic commerce system is hundred percent safe even though most customers, banks and researchers are of the view that E-commerce transactions are far safer in cyberspace than in the physical world. All this is possible because of the application of many safe approaches to electronic commerce.

With the growing usage of the Internet by a variety of users, security and protection of computer systems and networks has become a matter of prime concern. A safe electronic commerce should not only protect from misuse of information but destruction of such information should also be checked. Many different safe electronic payment systems and methods for safe delivery of information are emerging. Experts are of the view that security aspect must be addressed first, in order to make any company start E-commerce activities.

Security in E-commerce addresses the following issues:

1. Safe and secured delivery of information.
2. Safe and secure execution of business transaction on the web.
3. Secure network.

Safe and secure delivery of information from the source to the destination computer protects against tapping of information contents, alteration of contents or destruction of the contents. For a successful completion cycle of a business transaction on the web, it is necessary that safe delivery of all the information from various sources to various destinations has been made. The above two requirements may be fulfilled only if the protection mechanism prevents intruders from getting an access to the network. No unauthorized person is allowed to access the network.

10.2 SECURITY THREATS TO E-COMMERCE

Privacy, integrity, authentication and availability of the documents are the basic objectives of a secured computer system. Privacy of document means the isolation of the information contents. This is achieved by providing passwords and appropriate access control systems. *Integrity* of the document or information means that data and application should not be changed or modified without the consent of the owner. *Authentication* means that the people using computer are authorized users of the computer system or information. *Availability* of the document implies that the document will be available for users whenever the owner of the document needs it.

Potential security threats on the Internet for the successful completion of business transactions are information release or destruction, information modification and denial of service.

10.2.1 Information Release and Destruction

Any information released to an unauthorized person means the access to information on the network or on the computer system. This information may be misused to provide an undue advantage to a person or conversely damage to a person. This category of security threat also includes any destruction of the information. The partial or full destruction of information would also prove to be catastrophic to customers and banks. The potential ways of release of the information are unauthorized entry to the network and unauthorized use of the program or software on remote computer system.

10.2.2 Information Alteration

This is another security threat to E-commerce. This occurs when an intruder enters into the computer system or network and changes the information contents. Examples include changing the account balance in a bank, alteration to product price, invoices, purchase order, specification of the product etc.

10.2.3 Denial of Service

Sometimes an intruder may prevent the authorized user from using the resources. The authorized user of a program or software or computer system may be denied because of any alteration in the authorization details of the user, like change in password etc. The various services to an authorized user may also denied because other reasons like overloading or change in the scheduling algorithms.

10.3 ELECTRONIC PAYMENT SYSTEMS

Electronic payments are the central part of E-commerce activities as it deals with the strategies for the payment of goods and services by online customers. Electronic payments also refers to the activity of account settlement where the prompt settlement of payments is crucial. If the debit and credit to the bank account, customer and the company are not settled immediately or suffers due to conventional processing delays, then the entire business chain may be interrupted. Payment and settlement of the business account are the bottleneck in all E-commerce activities. Conventional instruments for payments such as demand draft, credit notes, cheques are not suited to E-commerce. The electronic versions of these instrument also may not work well, particularly when small payments are to be made. The supplier as well as the customer would like to settle the payment online when the amount to be paid is small. Conventional instruments are too slow to be processed and the overheads in processing such instruments may be high.

Various instruments which may be used to make payments on the Internet are Credit/Debit cards. Smart Cards, Electronic Cash, Electronic Wallet etc. Important issues related to the Electronic payment systems include the methods, form and characteristic of payment instrument such as e-cash, credit/debit cards, how to minimize the financial risk such as leakage of information, mistakes and frauds and finally devising methods for the completion of electronic payment cycle.

Several protocols have been devised and deployed to provide the necessary security to payment transactions. The Netscape Navigator and MS Internet Explorer have promoted their payment protocols for safe payment transaction and these have been implemented in their web browsers. Some of the commonly used protocols for secured transactions are as follows:

1. Secure Electronic Payment Protocol (SEPP)
2. Secure Electronic Transaction Protocol (SET)

SEPP has been developed by MasterCard and Netscape. It has been implemented in the Netscape web browsers. Secure Electronic Transaction protocol is a new E-commerce industry standard. Many companies are implementing SET protocol and it has many features in common with SEPP. SET is also one of the popular protocols for safe electronic transaction. It was developed by Microsoft and VISA. SET uses the cryptographic standard and digital signatures to secure the document and information. The card holder's authentication and verification is done using digital signatures.

10.4 ELECTRONIC PAYMENTS THROUGH SEPP PROTOCOL

This protocol was developed jointly by MasterCard, CyberCash, Netscape and IBM. SEPP is open vendor free and license free specification for online payment transactions. SEPP works on the simple conventional process of signing and submission. This protocol involves three way communication involving to customer, company and the bank. The whole process is illustrated in Figure 10.1.

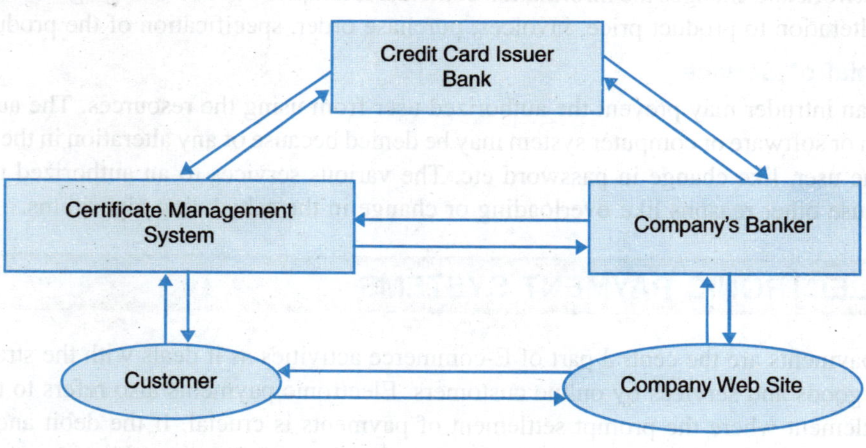

Fig. 10.1

As shown in the figure, the customer is a person who buys the product or services from a company. He does it by visiting the web site of the company. The customer is also a holder of a credit card and intends to pay for the purchased product and services through his credit card.

The company's web site displays and sells the items such as goods and services. It also accepts the payment from the customer against the purchased items and services.

Company's Banker is essentially a bank that services the company's account and processes credit card based transactions for the company.

Certificate management system represents the agent or broker who creates and distributes the digital certificate to customers and other financial institutions. The agent works on behalf of the credit card issuer bank. The whole process of purchase is done in the following steps:

1. The customer sends an initial message to the company web site.
2. Company response by sending the Invoice message, enabling the customer to validate goods and services of the company.
3. The customer then prepares the Purchase Order and credit cards details. The credit card details are so encrypted that can only be decrypted by the Bank.
4. The company receives the purchase order. The company then sends the encrypted credit card details to its banker.
5. The banker decrypts the credit card details and may verify from the credit issuer bank.
6. When the company's banker verifies the authenticity of the credit card, it sends an authorization response to the company. The authorization response essentially contains the verification results of credit card.
7. The company then sends to the customer a purchase order response.
8. Next step is the delivery of the product to the customer. The non-tangible items are delivered to the customer immediately and if the purchase order contains the delivery of a tangible item, the same are shipped by conventional means.

10.5 SECURE ELECTRONIC TRANSACTION (SET) PROTOCOL

This is a new industry standard which is now being adopted by many organization for their E-commerce applications. SET provides the full of confidentiality of the data containing the payment details with full integrity. Like the SEPP protocol, it also provides the authentication details of customer's credit card to the company through the credit card company. SET offers more security to the customers and provides the credit card details to the company in an encrypted form. SET encodes the credit card details in such a way that it can be decoded only by the bank. Therefore, the credit card details are available only to the customer and the bank. The card holders, comapny and the financial institution like the bank, all hold a digital certificate which ensures everybody that they are authorized entities. The digital certificate may also be issued by the authorized agents of the credit card company. Some of these popular agents are VeriSign and GTE Inc. There is one drawback in the SET protocol; SET only encrypts the credit card number and rest of the purchase details are sent as plain text. Some of the features of SET are as follows:

1. Confidentiality and privacy of the information is obtained by encryption.
2. Digital signatures are used to authenticate the documents.
3. Authentication of the company is also done by the use of digital signatures.

Following is the credit card purchase model proposed in SET (Figure 10.2).

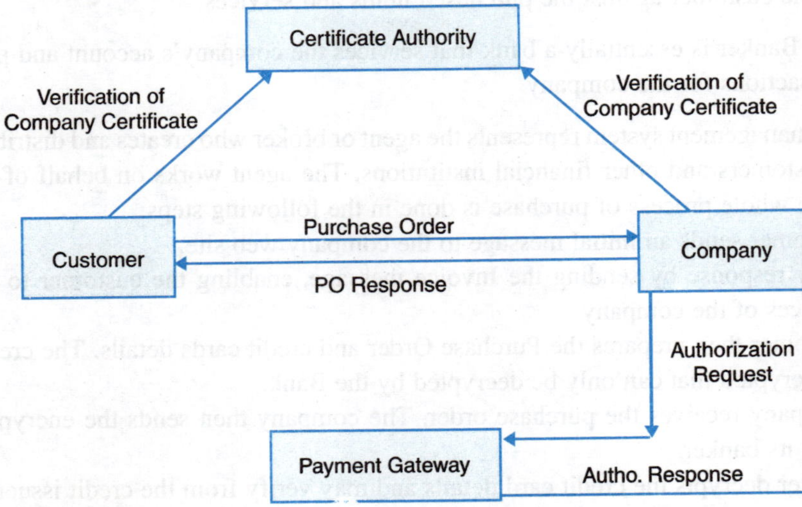

Fig. 10.2

The various steps in the payment processing in SET are as follows:

1. Customer places Purchase Order with company.
2. Company contacts payment gateways for authorization.
3. Company receives the authorization response.
4. Customer is notified by PO Response about the authorization result.
5. Company requests the issue of token from the payment gateway any places it before the bank for the transfer of money to its account.
6. Items, if they are tangible, are delivered by conventional courier service or they may be downloaded by the customer, if they are intangible.

10.6 ELECTRONIC TOKEN BASED PAYMENT SYSTEM

We have seen that in Secure Electronic Transaction Protocol, an electronic token is issued to the company by the payment gateway which may be deemed to the bank for the account transfer. The Electronic Tokens are also being used as payment instruments like E Cash or E Cheques. Electronic token is similar to the various other payment instruments used by many financial instituions, Electronic token guarantees that a certain amount will be credited to the account. Electronic tokens may be used in the following ways:

1. Online Settlement of Electronic Tokens

Payment transactions are settled immediately on online. This type of electronic token is called electronic cash. Using electronic cash, the money is exchanged instantly.

2. Prepaid Electronic Token

In prepaid electronic token system, the customer pays in advance to get the required item or services. The product or services are delivered to him later on. Smart Cards which store the money values and Electronic Purses are good examples of prepaid electronic tokens.

3. Post Paid Eletronic Token

In this mechanism, the purchase may be made and the accounts are settled afterwards. The company authenticates the customers by verifying that they have adequate money for the settlement of the purchase values. This is done online. After the verification, the purchase is allowed. Examples of post paid electronic token are Credit and Debit cards.

10.7 PAYMENTS INSTRUMENTS USED IN E-COMMERCE

The payments instruments are the method of making the payment for the product and money exchanges. There are multiple ways in which money can be exchanged for the product or service. The popular payment instruments being used in E-commerce are as follows:

10.7.1 Electronic Cash (E-cash)

Many customers are used to buying products by using cash. Various statistical analysis reveal that people like to pay in cash for the items they have purchased as long as the amount is not very large. The same is the trend on Internet shopping. The payment instrument known as Digital cash or E-cash, allows person to pay for goods or services by transmitting a number from his computer subsystem to the merchant's computer system. These numbers, just like those on a dollar bill, are issued by a bank and they represent specified sums of real money. One of the key features of digital cash is that it's anonymous and reusable, just like real cash. E-cash must have monetary value, interoperability, preservability and security. Here monetary value means that it must carry surety of a particular amount. When E-cash is issued by the currency server or bank, it must be accepted by the bank and reconciliation must be done without any problem. *Interoperability* of E-cash can be converted into paper cash or currency or any other type of payment instrument. E-cash must be preservable in the sense that it should be possible to store E-cash and use it whenever a customer wishes. Security of E-cash is related with prevention from theft. Here the theft indicates the copying, tampering of the E-cash information.

10.7.2 Credit Cards

Credit Cards are another payment instrument which have now become very common. Credit cards are issued by a financial institution which allows you to make purchases upto a certain limit on credit. Most of the credit card companies recognize the organization or shop etc. from where you may purchase the item. Payment of these item is made by the credit card company on your behalf. The credit card companies regularly send the bill to the customers for the shopping they have done. In E-commerce, use of credit card is very common. If consumers want to purchase a product or service, they simply send their credit card details to the service provider involved and the credit card organization will handle this payment like any other transaction.

Figure 10.3 shows the various steps when items are purchased on the Internet through Credit Cards.

The figure shows the processing of the credit card when an item is purchased from a company on the web. When the customer wishes to purchase items from a web site, he places the purhcase order electronically and sends encrypted credit card number. This information will be sent to the customer bank through the credit card processor. After checking the authenticity of the credit card, the bank allows the company to go ahead with the purchase. The bank will issue an electronic token to the company. The customer bank will realize the payment through monthly or fortnightly bill sent to the customer.

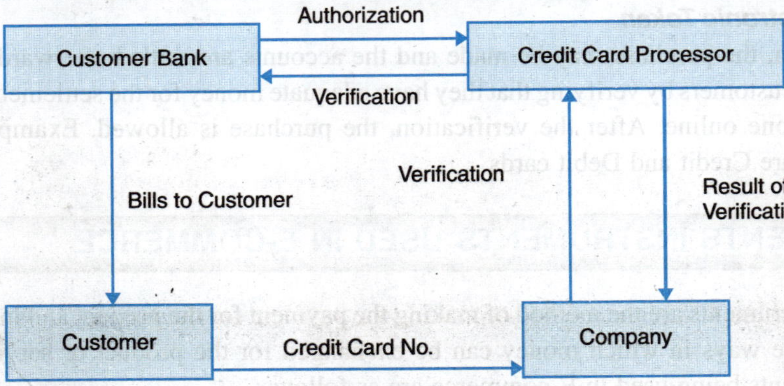

Fig. 10.3

10.7.3 Smart Card

These are similar to the credit and debit cards containing a microprocessors chip with memory capable of holding more information than the traditional magnetic stripe. The chip can store significantly greater amounts of data, estimated to be 80 times more than a magnetic stripe. This card contains an encrypted key that is compared to the secret key stored on the customer's computer. Whenever a customer pays for an item from his smart card, the value is deducted from the card. Relationship based smart credit cards contain more features than a normal smart card. These cards contain the services that a financial institution delivers to its customers via a chip-based card. These new services may include access to multiple financial accounts or other information which card holders may want to store on their card.

10.7.4 Electronic Purses

Electronic purses are another form of Smart Cards. These are wallet-sized smart cards embedded with programmable microchips that store the money value. Every time a customer pay for an item from his card, the value is deducted from the electronic purse. Customers use this card instead of cash for buying anything from food to paying for railway or train fares. The Cash Card is an another form of electronic purse.

10.7.5 Electronic Cheques

Electronic cheques are another form of payment instruments popular on the Web. These cheques work on the same principle as the real world cheques. This instrument is helpful to those customers who like to pay later for the product or service they have bought. The customer in the real world must have an account in a Bank to avail the cheque facility. When a customer issues a check, it indicates that the money printed on the cheque will be delivered to the holder of the cheque from his bank account. In a similar way, a customer, to avail the E-Cheque facility, must be registered with a bank or financial institution. The customer upon buying an item, may issue E-Cheque to the company, which will be deposited or transferred to the company's bank for the realization of money from the account of the customer. The E-Cheque are good instruments for paying small amounts on the web. The "NetCheque" is an example of electronic cheque. It was developed by the Information Science Institute and contains all the software for issuance of the Cheque, identification of signature and depositing into the account. Many organizations are using "NetCheque" for internal applications.

10.8 INTRODUCTION TO CRYPTOGRAPHY

The word *cryptography* has Greek origin and is combination of two Greek words, Krupto and grafh, which mean secret and writing. Cryptography is the science of converting a stream of text into coded form in such a way that only the originator and receiver of the coded text can decode the text. Cryptography plays a very important role in Internet based commercial activities as many secret documents which include payment details, money transfer, contract document, business plans and other confidential information are to be transferred from one computer to another. Cryptography become important during the First World War when military messages used to be encrypted and then sent to the recipients. In encryption, a very basic approach is *shifting by three methods.* For example, the word "message" may be encrypted as "phvvdjh" by using shift by three method. In this method, every letter is advanced by three letters. Of course, today's cryptographic systems are much more advanced and far more complex to decode. In this example, the key to decode the message is "Shift By Three". If the key or method of encryption is known to any person, he may decode the text using the key. We may define cryptography as follows:

Cryptography is a technique that allows a piece of Information to be converted into cryptic form before being stored in the computer database or transmitted over an insecure channel.

As we have discussed earlier in this chapter, security and protection of messages related with electronic payment system are of prime importance. The security and protection mechanisms help to prevent any unauthorized user to access the resources and communication network. However, it may be possible that an unauthorized person may tap the information under communication after bypassing the security and protection mechanism. Encryption of message is done to provide extra protection in order to maintain the confidentiality of the document. For example, if an unauthorized person succeeds in tapping the channel, then the information he has copied may not be of his use, if it is encrypted. Cryptography is primarily used to protect the confidentiality of information from an intruder. The information may be of following types:

1. Stored information.
2. Tapping the information from the channel.

10.9 MODEL OF CRYPTOGRAPHY

The terms used commonly in a cryptographic system are as follows:

- **Intruder** : Intruder is a person who is not authorized to access the information or the network.
- **Plain Text** : Intelligible message that is to be converted into unintelligible message (encrypted message).
- **Cipher Text** : Message in an encrypted form.
- **Encryption** : Process of converting plain text to cipher text.
- **Decryption** : Process of converting cipher text to plain text.
- **Key** : Parameter (process) required for conversion of the message.

Figure 10.4 shows the basic mode of a cryptographic system. As shown, the sender converts the plain text into the coded version by encryption for transmission over a communication channel. Sender uses a key (encryption algorithm) to convert the plain text into a cipher text. The recipient of the cipher text will require the key (decryption algorithm) to decrypt the message. After decryption, the receiver will get the cipher text converted into plain text.

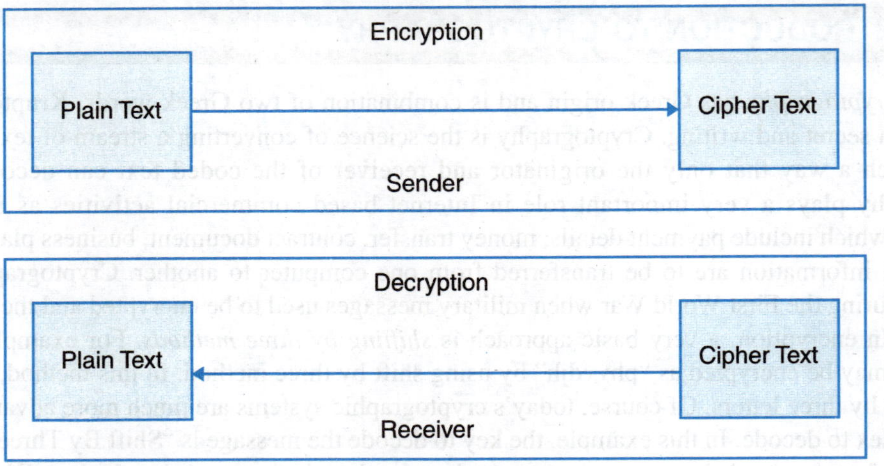

Fig. 10.4

The key required for encryption and decryption may be the same or different. If the key for encryption and decryption is the same, then it is called *symmetric key.* If the key for both encryption and decryption are different, then the key is called *asymmetric key.*

Figure 10.5 presents a general model of a cryptographic system.

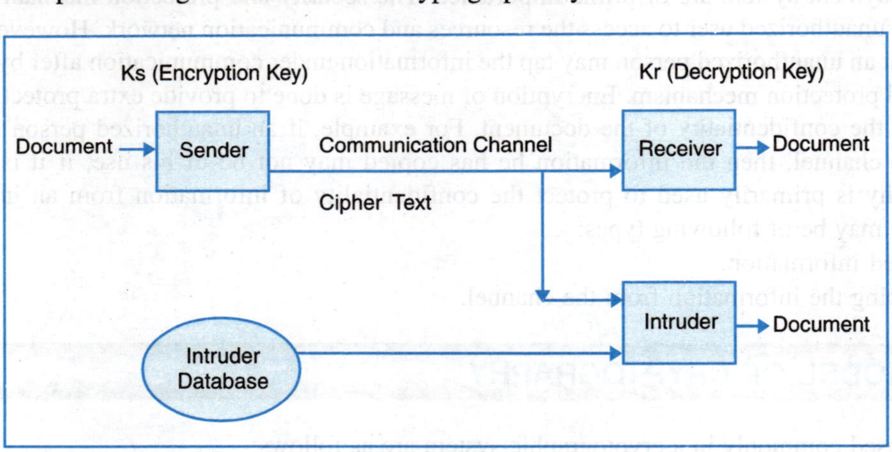

Fig. 10.5

This schematic illustrates the process of encryption and decryption of the document which is being sent over an insecure communication channel. The sender of the document encrypts it with a key Ks (encryption key). Therefore, the cipher text may be represented as :

Cipher Text = E Ks (Document)

The above equation means that a document is encrypted using the Ks key. Here Ks may correspond to any algorithm or method of encryption.

After the cipher text has been received, the receiver will use a decryption key Kr to decrypt the cipher text. This process of decryption will convert text into the original document.

Document = D Kr (Cipher Text)

This indicates that the document is obtained by decryption (of cipher text) using Kr as decryption key.

If the communication channel is insecure, then an intruder may tap the information on this channel. The intruder will not be able to decrypt the information or document if he does not have knowledge of the decryption key (Kr). The model shows that the intruder may still decode the document without knowing the decryption key Kr based on the information he has gathered in the past. The intruder's information is shown in the figure as Intruder database. Intruder database may contain the information about the origin, frequency of documents or size of document or other statistics about the cipher text. However, the intruder will not be able to decrypt the entire cipher text without knowledge of the decryption key Kr. This shows the strength of an encryption system. If the algorithm for the decryption key is strong, intruder will find it more difficult to decrypt the cipher text. Therefore, the performance of the encryption system is dependent on the encryption and decryption keys and these keys must be implemented after detailed analysis.

10.10 THREATS IN CRYPTOGRAPHIC SYSTEM

There are three possible ways in which an intruder may capture the message. An intruder may capture the cipher text from the channel. If the message is being transmitted over an insecure communication channel, the cipher text may be captured by the intruder but it will have very little utility for him because in the absence of the decryption key, he will not be able to decide it. He may try to, however, decrypt the document using the information he has. This type of attack is called *cipher text attack*. When an intruder has insufficient knowledge about the plain text, but on the basis of the little information available to him about the plain text, he may attempt to decrypt the document. This type of attack is called *known plain text attack*. The systems are more vulnerable to failure is known plain text attacks rather than cipher text attacks. The threat to the system is more when the intruder captures the plain text corresponding to the cipher text and goes to the extent of making the system generate the cipher text as par the choice of intruder. These types of attacks are known as *chosen plain text attacks*.

- Intruder may have attack cipher text.
- Intruder may have attack both cipher text and plain text.
- Intruder may attack the key.

10.11 ISSUES IN DOCUMENTS SECURITY

There are several issues related with the security of the documents on the network. Following are the important issues related with the documents for payment transaction:

1. Integrity of the documents.
2. Authentication of the documents.
3. Maintaining the confidentiality of the documents.
4. Non-repudiation of the documents.
5. Authorization issues.

10.11.1 Integrity of the Documents

In the E-commerce a lot of documents such as purchase orders, invoices, bank statement, service contracts etc. are sent over the network. The customers as well as the suppliers or the senders and receivers would like to ensure that the correct document has been transmitted. The receiver will like to verify that the document sent by the sender has not been changed and the sender too will like to ensure that the document received by the receiver is the one which was sent by him. If any alteration or change in the document is made after sending it the documents are said to have lost their *integrity*. A safe and secure system must ensure the delivery of documents in their original form, i.e., without alteration.

10.11.2 Authentication of Documents

When a customer places the purchase order to an E-commerce company, the company would like to identify the customer before delivery of the items. This requires that the document (purchase order) must be authenticated. An authentication of the documents ensures that the document was sent by a genuine customer. There are several processes or mechanisms in digital systems to authenticate the documents. Digital Signatures is one of them.

10.11.3 Maintaining the Confidentiality of the Document

This is one of the major issues relating to the security of the system. There are several examples where both the sender of the document and receiver would like to maintain confidentiality. For example, two parties contract for a strategic alliance. The contract signed between the two parties may be of utmost importance and neither party would like to reveal the information pertaining to the contract to any third party. Confidentiality in digital systems is maintained by using cryptographic techniques. This is done be encryption of the document by the sender and decryption of the document by the receiver.

10.11.4 Non-repudiation of the Document

Repudiation means a refusal by either the sender or receiver that neither one has ever sent a document or that one has not received a document. This may be understood with an example. Suppose a customer places the purchase order to a company for buying a share. If the price of share goes down on the same day, the sender may create a dispute that he has never placed such a purchase order. Similarly, if the price of the share goes up during the same day, the company may raise a dispute that it has never received such a purchase order. This problem is called repudiation. An effective way to prevent repudiation is that both parties digitally sign the document. These problems are usually addressed in the digital signature system.

10.11.5 Authorization Issues

Authorization issues are very important in E-commerce and attention has to be paid to ensure that any privilege is enjoyed only by an authorized person who is authorized. For example, only authorized persons should be able to access the software resource or the documents. These issues are handled by providing the privileges and rights to various entities in the E-commerce system.

10.12 TYPES OF CRYPTOGRAPHIC SYSTEM

The cryptographic systems may be categorized into the following two categories:

1. Conventional Cryptographic Systems.
2. Modern Cryptographic Systems.

Conventional cryptographic systems are based on the encryption of messages or text written in plain language. These systems primarily use the substitution method. In this method, various characters are replaced from the text by another character or symbol. There has to be a one-to-one correspondence between the symbols to be replaced and the replacement symbols. Example of the substitution method is the Ceasar Cipher. This was named after the Julius Ceasar, the ancient ruler of Rome. Julius Ceasar was the first person to send a cryptographic message to his colleagues, as he did not trust his messengers. He used to use the "Shift by Three" substitution method. Thus a symbol in the text was replaced by the third symbol in the alphabetic order. This system suffers from two defects; one, that since the transformations or encryption are linear, searching the key is simple, and secondly, that the number of keys are significantly limited.

Modern cryptographic systems are more advanced and are based on exhaustive search mechanism. The information storage, retrieval, communication and processing is done in digital media. Therefore, these systems use binary information. The plain text and cipher text are to be represented in binary codes. The encryption and decryption algorithms and procedures are publicly known but the keys for encryption and decryption are kept secret. In these systems, a cipher text may be decrypted only by using a decryption key and may be encrypted only by using an encryption key. For both encryption and decryption, both the keys must correspond to each other.

10.13 SYSTEM OF KEYS FOR ENCRYPTION/DECRYPTION

10.13.1 Secret Key Cryptography

In Secret Key cryptography, both the sender and receiver of a message possess the same "secret password" (key). The sender uses the key to encrypt the message, rendering it unintelligible. The message cannot be deciphered without the key. The receiver will also use the same key to decrypt the message. These types of cryptographic systems are also known as Symmetric Cryptographic Systems. The secret key cryptographic systems are shown in the diagram below (Figure 10.6). .

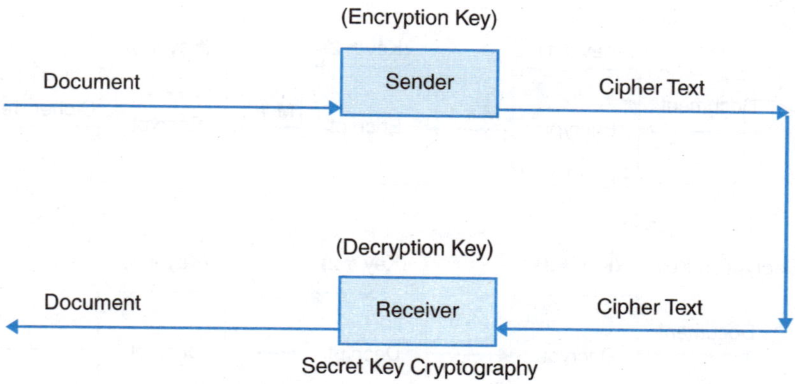

Fig. 10.6: Secret Key Cryptography

As shown in Figure 10.6, the sender takes the document or a piece of text and encrypts it using a secret key. The cipher text is communicated to the receiver who upon receiving it, decrypts it using the secret key. If both sender and receiver of the cipher text use the same secret key to encrypt and decrypt the message, the system is called a *secret cryptographic system*. The system is well suited for communication between parties who agreed to share the secret key. The secret key may also be used to store the data on an insecure medium. A user may store the information by encrypting it using the secret key and may decrypt it using his own secret key whenever he wants to use the information.

This works well as the key is shared among only two persons. But suppose another sender wants to send documents to the same receiver, if the second sender uses the same key, and the first sender eavesdrops on the conversation, he can decode the message! The receiver could generate a separate key for every potential sender, but that would be a massive exercise and impractical for any organization which has to communicate with a large number of customers. In such cases, the organisation may have to generate a large number of keys, one for each customer. This problem is called the scalability problem.

10.13.2 Data Encryption Standard

Data Encryption Method is an example of secret key cryptography. Data Encryption Standard (DES) was developed by IBM for US Government Departments. DES is a block cipher based scheme which encrypts the 64 bit data block using 56 bit key. Encryption of the whole text is not done at one instance. The block cipher scheme takes a block of 64 bit data and produces a 64 bit cipher text. It proceeds in the following steps:

1. Plain text block undergoes an initial permutation, in which the 64 bit of the text are scrambled.
2. The permuted block is transformed in such a way that it involves 16 iterations. This is done using a secret key.
3. This block undergoes a final scrambling, which is the inverse of the first scrambling.

The output produced as a result of these steps is the cipher text. This cipher text can be decrypted using the reverse of all of the three steps using the same secret key.

10.13.3 Multiple Encryption Schemes Using Secret Keys

To make the secret key encryption more powerful, it is also possible to encrypt the text multiple number of times. The DES encryption strength is increased by multiple encryption. In this scheme, a secret key is used to encrypt a message, and the cipher text generated is further encrypted by another secret key. The decryption of the final cipher text is done by using the same keys, which were used at the time of encryption, but in reverse order. The following schematic (Figure 10.7) shows the triple encryption using secret keys.

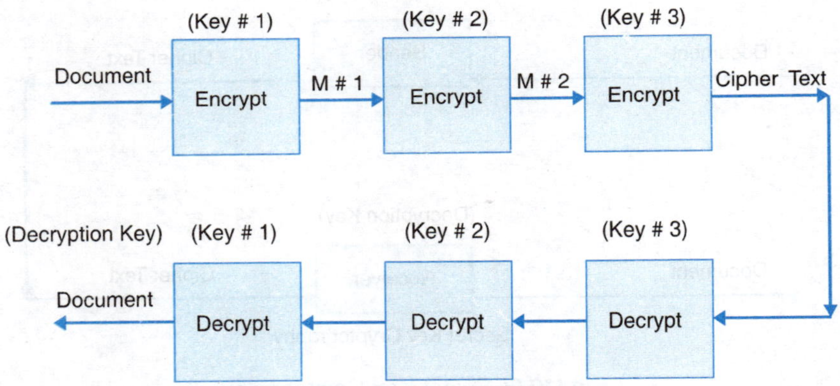

Fig. 10.7: Multiple Secret Key Cryptography

The figure shows the multiple secret key cryptography, which includes triple encryption. The document is encrypted by secret key (#1) to produce message M#1. The M#1 is further encrypted by secret key (#2) to produce message M#2. The message M#2 is again encrypted by secret key (#3) to produce the cipher text. The cipher text is then transmitted over the communication channel. The recipient of the cipher text decrypts the message thrice using the secret key (#3, #2, #1) sequentially to produce the plain text. This scheme was applied to DES standard to provide additional strength to it.

10.14 PUBLIC KEY CRYPTOGRAPHY

Public key cryptography is quite similar to the secret key cryptography. Public key cryptography is a solution to the problem raised in the secret key cryptography. Secret key cryptography requires the distribution of the secret key to all the recipients or the generation of a secret key for every recipient.

This becomes a problem for the company sending confidential documents over the communication channel. Public key cryptography addresses this problem.

In Public key cryptography, the sender and receiver use two different keys called public key and private key. Following are the main features for encryption and decryption of cipher text in public key cryptography :

1. The sender uses one key (sender key) to encode the message, and the receiver uses another key (receiver key) to decode the message.
2. The receiver publishes the sender-key, so that everyone who wants to send him a secret message can do so, but he keeps the receiver-key secret. This enables the receiver to ensure that only he can decode any of the messages.
3. Since sender-key is known to all the senders it is called a public key, and the receiver-key is called the private key.

The concept of public key cryptography may be understood as follows. Suppose a sender (A) wants to send the message (M) over a communication channel to receiver (B). In the process the following actions are taken :

1. Sender (A) will encrypt the message (M) using the encryption key (Ek_b) to produce the cipher text. The key Ek_b is called the public key of receiver (B).
2. Receiver (B) upon receiving the cipher text will decrypt it using its decryption key (DK_b) to get the message (M). The key (DK_b) is known as the private key of receiver (B).

The process in the schematic form is shown below in Figure 8.8. The public key of the receiver (B) is published on the web and it is available with all the potential senders. Since the decryption key or private key is kept with receiver (B), only the receiver (B) can decrypt the message (M). Therefore, in the public key cryptographic system, anyone who knows the public key of the receiver (B) can send the message but only receiver (B) will be able to decrypt it with its private key. This system of cryptography is very useful for companies who wish to communicate confidentially with a large group of customers.

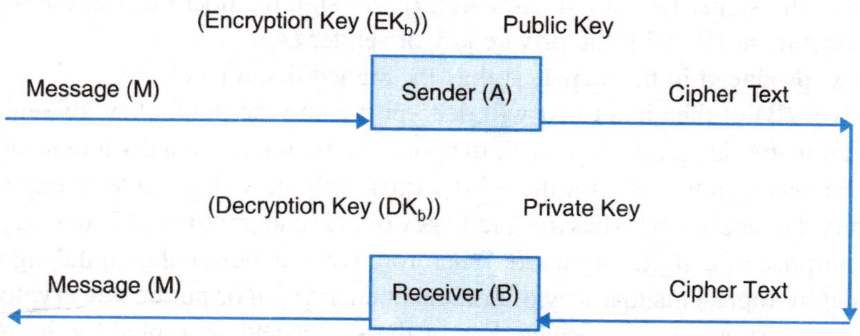

Fig. 10.8: Public Key Cryptography.

10.15 DIGITAL SIGNATURES AND PUBLIC KEY CRYPTOGRAPHY

Signatures on documents in the real world are the specialized or unique mark or impression made by the person with the help of ink. It is assumed that no two persons would have the same signature. The signature of a person on the document implies that the document is attributed to him. Signature are made by the person to authenticate the documents. The authenticity of many legal, financial and other documents is determined by the presence or absence of an authorized handwritten signature. For computerized message systems to replace the physical medium of paper and ink documents, a solution must be found to the problem of authenticating the messages. The solution to this problem in digital media is called Digital Signature.

10.15.1 Relating Digital Signatures with Public Key Cryptography

As we have seen in the public cryptographic system, a sender encrypts the message using the receiver's public key. The encrypted message is then decrypted by the receivers's private key. Digital Signatures are based on the same concept but the difference is that the sender encrypts the message with its private key and the receiver decodes it with the sender's public key. Thus the mechanism of public key crytography is reversed in the implementation of digital signature system. The signer or sender encodes the document with his own private key. This allows anyone with his public key to decode the document. Since the documents can be decoded with his public key, and he's the only one who has access to the corresponding private key, everyone knows that he really did encode (sign) it. This proves the authenticity and the integrity of the document. A model of a general Digital Signature is shown in the schematic below. (Figure 10.9).

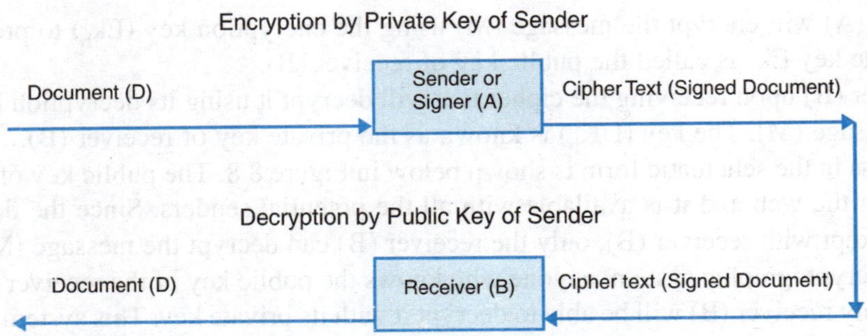

Fig. 10.9: Digital Signature Model

The sender or the signer (A) of a document (D) will sign the document in the following way:

1. Encrypt document (D) with the private key of sender (A).
2. Cipher text produced in the step 1, is thus the signed document.
3. The receiver (B) of the cipher text will decrypt it using the public key of sender (A).

The sender publishes his public key to all the potential recipients of a document signed by him. The private key of the sender remains with the sender thus, only he will be able to encrypt the document with this key. Only the receiver who has the public key of the sender will be able to decrypt the document. This serves the purpose of a digital signature. Therefore we may define the digital signature as follows:

Digital Signature represents that way of document encryption or public key cryptography, in which the documents are encrypted by the private key of the signer and decrypted by the receiver using the public key of the signer.

10.16 REQUIREMENTS OF A DIGITAL SIGNATURE SYSTEM

The digital signature system is another form of public key cryptographic system. Basically, the digital signature system requires a system where one party can send a "signed" message to another party in such a way that

1. The receiver can verify the claimed identity of the sender.
2. The sender cannot later repudiate the contents of the message.
3. The receiver cannot possibly have connected the message himself.

The first requirement is needed where the receiver of the signed document wants to verify the identity of the sender. For example, in E-commerce systems, a customer places a purchase order to a broker to buy the shares of a company. The broker will like to ensure that the computer giving the order really belongs to the customer whose account is to be debited. The first requirement in the system is guaranteed because no one else knows the private key of the customer other than himself, i.e., no one can create the digital signature on the purchase order other than the customer himself.

The second requirement is needed to protect the broker against frauds. Suppose the broker buys the required shares for the customer and immediately thereafter the share price drops. A dishonest customer might create a controversy claiming that he has never issued such an order. When the broker produces the message before the court, the customer denies having sent it. The digital signature also serves the second requirement making sure that no one else could encrypt the message this way because only the sender knows the private key.

The third requirement is needed to protect the customer against frauds. For example, the share price shoots up on the same day and the broker says that he has never received any such order from the customer or tries to construct a signed message in which the customer asked for a lower number of shares.

To serve this requirement public digital signature systems are required where both the sender of the document and the receiver use different public keys to sign and decrypt the documents. This problem is addressed in the Public Digital Signature System.

10.17 PUBLIC DIGITAL SIGNATURE SYSTEM

The fundamental requirement in the public digital signature system is the deployment of an encryption/decryption algorithm where the following two conditions are satisfied:

$$E(D(P)) = P$$
$$D(E(P)) = P$$

Here E, D and P denote the encryption, decryption and plain text respectively. These indicate that decryption of a plain text using a key other than encryption key will produce the same plain text P. Similarly, that encryption of plain text using a key other than the decryption key will produce the same plain text P.

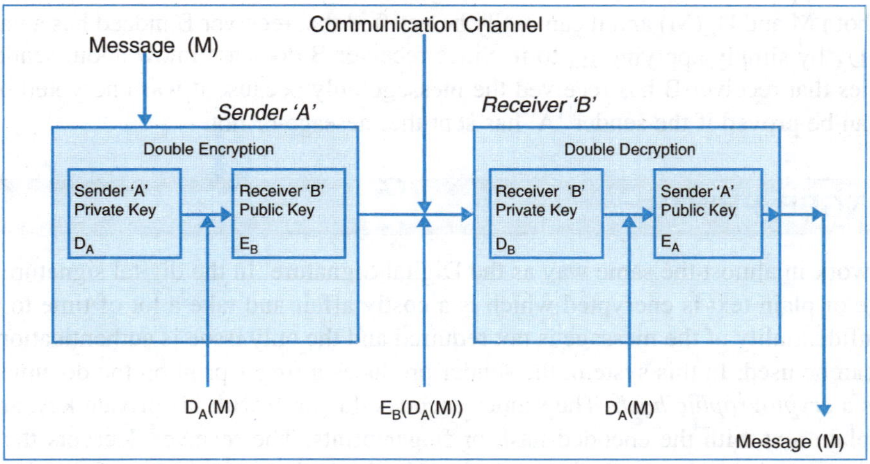

Fig. 10.10: Public Digital Signature System

Consider the case when sender 'A' sends a document to receiver 'B'. The process is shown in the schematic below. (Figure 10.10).

In this scheme, both sender (A) and receiver (B) have two keys, private and public keys. Either one knows the public key of the other, that is, the senders knows the public key of the receiver and the receiver knows the public key of the sender. But the private key is kept secret and lies with the owner only. Here

D_A = Private Key of Sender A
D_B = Private Key of Receiver B
E_A = Public Key of Sender A
E_B = Public Key of Receiver B

The Sender 'A' encrypts the message M in the following two stages:

1. Encrypts the message M with its private key. The message is threfore $D_A(M)$.
2. Further, encrypts the message $D_A(M)$ using the public key of Receiver B. This step will produce the message $E_B(D_A(M))$.

The cipher text $E_B(D_A(M))$ is then communicated over the communication channel. Remember the cipher text has been produced after double encryption of the message M. Therefore at the receiving end, the cipher text has to be decrypted twice in order to receive the message M. The steps taken at Receiver end for decryption are as follows, or Receiver B decrypts the cipher text in the following steps:

1. First decrypt the cipher text $E_B(D_A(M))$ using private key of receiver B. This will generate the text $D_A(M)$.
2. The second decryption is done using the public key of sender 'A'. This step will produce the message M.

The scheme of Public Digital Signature satisfies the three basic requirements of digital signatures. The first requirement in the system is guaranteed because no one else knows the private key of the customer other than himself, i.e., no one can create the digital signature on the purchase order other than the customer himself. The encryption at the sender's end is done twice using his private key and the receiver public key. The private key is known to only the sender or customer. Therefore, the receiver can verify the claimed identity of the sender.

The second requirement of digital signature system is that sender cannot later rapudiate the contents of the message. Suppose that sender A denies having sent the message M to receiver B. The receiver B may produce both M and $D_A(M)$ and it can easily be verified that receiver B indeed has a valid message encrypted by D_A by simply applying E_A to it. Since receiver B does not know about sender A private key, this implies that receiver B has received the message only because it was encrypted by sender A. Therefore it can be proved if the sender 'A' has sent the message or not.

10.18 FINGER PRINTS

Finger prints work in almost the same way as the Digital Signature. In the digital signature system, the entire message or plain text is encrypted which is a costly affair and take a lot of time to encrypt and decrypt. If confidentiality of the message is not required and the only issue is authentication, the digital finger prints can be used. In this system, the sender produces a finger print on the document, which is also known as a *cryptographic hash*. The sender encodes this hash with his private key, and sends the document in plain text with the encoded hash or finger prints. The receiver decrypts the hashes and decodes the signature with the sender's public key to check the authenticity of the document. The

Finger Print does not ensure the integrity of the document because the document is sent in the original form. The digital signature system, however, ensures the integrity of the document whereby the messages cannot be altered or changed. This is achieved because the entire document is encrypted and only the receiver can decrypt it.

10.19 PROBLEMS IN DIGITAL SIGNATURE STANDARD

RSA (Rivest-Shamir-Adelman) algorithm is one of the standards for digital signatures. It is the most widely used authentication algorithm. The crux of RSA algorithm is that it basically takes a large piece of binary plain text and it is divided into blocks which are numbered between 0 to n–1. These algorithms have the following shortcomings:

1. It lacks key exchange capability. The cryptographic methods used are too recent and have been subjected to too little scrutiny for users to be confident of their value.
2. Verification of signature with DSS is too slow.
3. DSS was originally proposed with a fixed 512 bytes key size but after much criticism that this is not secure enough, NIST revised DSS to allow key size up to 1024 bits. This makes RSA algorithms very slow.

10.20 FIREWALLS

The term Firewall have been taken from the construction industry where a protection mechanism has been deployed in buildings against fire hazards. In the computer world, the term *firewall* is used to protect the network from the outside world against any unauthorized access to network, computer hardware and software. Firewalls is conceived by different persons in different ways. An organization, which has its local area network for sharing the various resources, will also have a gateway to the outside world or global network. The mechanism is required to protect the network of the organization from the users in the outside world, in such a way that only authorized users from outside may access the software and hardware resources of the organization. The firewalls are typically the hardware or software that are placed on the gateway. The most common way of doing this is by placing a dedicated computer at the gateway, which verifies the authenticity of various users. The firewalls are also known as *secure internet gateway.* Thus we may define firewalls as a system which is a collection of devices, computer software, routers, host or collection of hosts. The firewall operates by screening the message packets that are passed through the gateway for the purpose of accessing the internal network. The following schematic (Figure 10.11) explains the function of firewalls :

As shown in the diagram, all the inbound and outbound traffic is screened by firewalls. The purpose of installing a firewall to the network is that it collectively safeguards from unauthorized attacks from the outside world. In the absence of the firewall, all the nodes in the network must emphasize their own security mechanism. Firewall may be configured as per the following policies:

1. Restrict the access from outside users in such a way that some specific users from the outside world are denied access. Otherwise, the network becomes open to all. This provides a weaker restriction on the users from the outside world.
2. Restrict the access from the outside user in such a way that only the permitted users are given an entry into the network. This provides a stronger restriction on the users from the outside world.

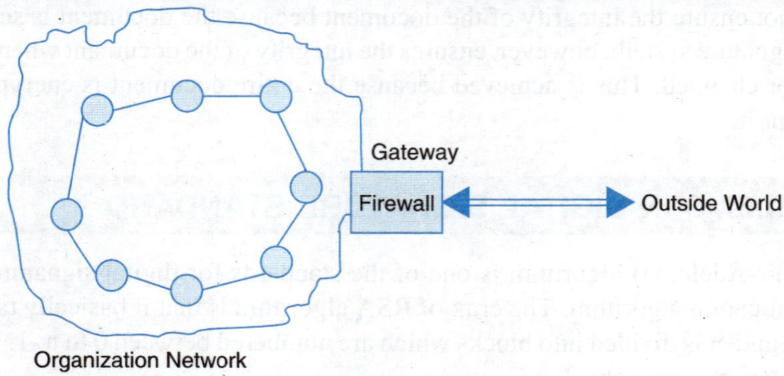

Fig. 10.11

Generally, an outside user is allowed to log on to any computer system inside the network provided the user is a valid user and enters the correct password. The firewall provides security to the network but it is not a full proof system. It provides a robust set of protocols and routines but yet it is possible for an intruder to break the security mechanism.

10.20.1 Types of Firewall

Depending on their functions firewalls may be considered as:

1. Static Firewall.
2. Dynamic Firewall.

The *static* firewall are generally pre-configured and they allow or deny the access from the outside world by default. *Default* allow policy allows the inbound traffic by default and blocks only specified traffic. In such a mechanism, only the specified user will be denied access to the network or resources of the enterprise. In the *default deny* policy, only the specific users who exhibit their authentication are permitted to access the network. The default deny policy is more restrictive as compared to default allow policy of static firewalls.

The *Dynamic* firewall uses an allow and denial of the services policy at the network on the time basis. Some services on the network may be allowed and others may be denied for a specific time interval. The configuration of such firewall is slightly more cumbersome and complex.

Firewall works in such a way that it scrutinizes the packets entering into the network through the gateway. The message or application is divided into small sized packets which contain the address of the host and the address to which it has to be sent. The Choke, a component at Gate, screens the packets and decides whether it should be passed to the internal network on the basis of firewall policies. The Gate is the final point of entry where access will be decided on the basis of default policy.

10.20.2 Firewall as Proxy Server

A proxy entity is one which appears to be similar to the original entity. In computer systems, the proxy is a program or software, which may be placed in the place of another software or application. The *proxy application gateway* is a program that runs on the gateway or firewall machine. Any request from the internal user has to be routed from the proxy on the firewall. The firewall also works as proxies for a number of applications. For example, if the request for File Transfer protocol (FTP) services is received from the internal user, then proxy receives the request and forwards the request to the FTP server outside.

There are several benefits of proxy servers. Some are listed below:

1. The proxy server may screen the request for application level and forward it to the remote host. All the inbound and outbound packets are screened by the proxy, thereby serving as firewall too.

2. Proxies improve the level of security as all the inbound and outbound packet traffic is routed through proxy servers.
3. It improves the logging-in facility and allows more visibility to the network administrator.

OBJECTIVE TYPE QUESTIONS

Multiple Choice

1. Which of the following are possible security threats?
   (a) Information destruction (b) Information Alteration
   (c) Information Release (d) All of these
2. Which of the following protocol is used for Electronic Payment?
   (a) SET (b) SEPP (c) Both (d) None of these
3. SEPP has been developed by
   (a) Netscape & Master Card (b) Microsoft & VISA
   (c) Both of these (d) None of these
4. Which of the following companies are dealing in credit cards?
   (a) Master Card (b) VISA (c) American Express (d) All of these
5. What payment instruments are used in purchases in electronic medium?
   (a) E Cash (b) Credit Card (c) Debit Cards (d) All of these
6. Encryption is process of converting
   (a) Plain Text to Cipher text (b) Cipher Text to Plain text
   (c) Both of these (d) None of these
7. Decryption is process of converting
   (a) Plain Text to Cipher text (b) Cipher Text to Plain text
   (c) Both of these (d) None of these
8. Which of the following are typical issues in document security?
   (a) Integrity of document (b) authentication of document
   (c) Non Repudiation (d) All of these
9. Public Key of sender is known to
   (a) Sender only (b) Receiver Only (c) Both of these (d) None of these
10. Firewalls are used to
    (a) Restrict the network access (b) serve as fire alarm
    (c) as fire extinguisher (d) None of these

Answers

1-d, 2-c, 3-a, 4-d, 5-d, 6-a, 7-b, 8-d, 9-c, 10-a

State True or False

1. Denial of service is also a security threat to network. [True] [False]
2. SEPP was developed by Microsoft and VISA. [True] [False]
3. Cryptography is science of converting a message into cryptic form. [True] [False]
4. Standardization of public policy is a must to enable E Governance. [True] [False]
5. Public Key of a sender must remain secret with sender. [True] [False]
6. In Asymmetric Key Cryptography both sender and receiver uses a common secret key. [True] [False]
7. Private key of sender can be shared with receiver. [True] [False]
8. Non repudiation must be guaranteed in Digital signatures. [True] [False]
9. Default allow policy of firewall allows the access to network by outside user by default. [True] [False]
10. Multiple encryption is generally slower then single encryption. [True] [False]

Answers

1-True, 2- False, 3-True, 4-True, 5-False, 6-False, 7-False, 8-True, 9-True, 10-True.

SELECTED EXERCISES

1. What is meant by Safe Electronic Commerce? What precautions have to be taken in order to ensure the confidentiality of document sent by the customer?
2. What is meant by electronic payment systems? Compare electronic payment mechanism on the Internet with the conventional payment mechanism.
3. What is meant by message integrity? Discuss the techniques used in electronic commerce to ensure message integrity.
4. Explain the various threats to Electronic Commerce system. How is information release and information alteration on the communication channel harmful to E-commerce?
5. What is meant by Denial of Service? How can a genuine client be denied the service? Is it a threat to safe Electronic commerce?
6. What is meant by payment instruments? List the popular payment instruments in e-commerce transactions.
7. How is online settlement of electronic tokens done?
8. What is the difference between encryption and decryption? Why is the message transmitted over an insecure communication channel in encrypted form?
9. What is the difference between security and protection of a network?
10. What are electronic tokens used in electronic payment system?
11. What are the differences between electronic cash and electronic cheque? How is electronic cash used in purchasing an item on the Internet? How are the electronic cheques issued in an electronic medium by the customer?
12. What do you mean by the term cryptography? How are the cryptographic systems deployed to ensure safe electronic commerce?
13. How is e-cash procured by the customer? Is it possible to store e-cash by the customer?
14. What are Smart cards? How are Smart cards used for shopping on the Web? Draw a diagram showing all the steps involved in purchasing a product by a Smart card in digital medium?
15. What is the difference between Credit card and Debit card? How is a business transaction completed using Debit cards and Credit cards?
16. What is meant by cipher text? How is the cipher text delivered to the recipient over the communication channel? Explain how the cipher text is converted into the original document?
17. What is the difference between plain text and cipher text? How these two forms are converted into each other?
18. What are the differences between the conventional cryptographic system and the modern cryptographic systems?
19. How does the conventional cryptographic system use the method of simple substitution? Explain with the help of an example.
20. What do you mean by Ceasar cipher? Explain the various steps of encryption of the text "MODERN CRYPTOGRAPHY" by shift-by-three substitution method.
21. What is secure electronic payment protocol (SEPP)? Explain the various steps of SEPP using a suitable example.
22. How is the authenticity of a card holder verified in SEPP protocol?
23. How is the final payment realized to the merchant whenever a customer pays for the product using a credit card in SEPP system?
24. Explain the SEPP architecture using a schematic. Explain the role of all the entities involved in SEPP.
25. What is Secure Electronic Transaction (SET) protocol? List the salient features of this protocol. Why this protocol has become a de facto standard for financial transactions on the Internet?
26. How is the authenticity of a card holder verified in SET protocol?

27. How is the final payment realized to the merchant whenever a customer pays for the product using a credit card in SET system?
28. Explain the SET architecture using a schematic. Explain the role of all the entities involved in SEPP.
29. Explain the role and importance of a key in encryption. Is it necessary that the same key be used for the decryption of a document?
30. List and explain the various threats to the cryptographic system. How can an intruder attack the Cipher Text?
31. Explain the various issues related to the security of the documents. How is the integrity of the document ensured?
32. How can the confidentiality of the documents be preserved while sending them over an insecure channel?
33. What is meant by the repudiation of the document?
34. Explain the salient features of secret key cryptography. What are the shortcomings of secret key cryptography?
35. What is meant by Data Encryption Standards? Explain any one of them.
36. What is multiple encryption scheme? Why is multiple encryption scheme considered safer? Explain the shortcomings of the Multiple encryption schemes.
37. What is meant by Public Key Cryptography? What are the differences between Private and Public Keys?
38. What are Digital Signatures? What is the relationship of Digital Signatures with Public Key Cryptography?
39. Explain the basic requirements of a digital signature system. Can digital signature system be implemented using secret key cryptography? If yes, list the shortcomings of this system.
40. Explain the general model of public digital signature model. Explain all the steps, how the document is digitally signed by the sender and how the receiver ensures the authenticity and integrity of the document.
41. How is the problem of Repudiation solved in public digital signature system?
42. What are the differences between Digital Signatures and Finger Prints? Under what circumstances are the finger print more useful?
43. What is RSA algorithm? Explain the salient features of RSA algorithm.
44. What are firewalls? What purpose does the Firewall serve? What are the essential differences between Static and Dynamic firewalls?
45. How can a firewall be used as Proxy? What are the advantages of making a proxy server?

11

DATA MANAGEMENT AND SQL

Contents

11 DATA MANAGEMENT AND SQL

11.1 DATABASE MANAGEMENT

Database is considered one of the most important components of modern day's business applications. A Database may be defined as a collection of interrelated data organized in a systematic way. Database Management System is a collection of data and programs designed to provide efficient storage and retrieval of data. Due to explosive increase in the information available to the society and impact of data and information in decision-making, it has become mandatory to store, retrieve and process data systematically and efficiently. The Database Management System helps the users to store, retrieve and process the data. The Database Management System allows the programmers to write the program without bothering him for implementation details of data files on disk. The data is structured in such a way that it provides a systematic logical view to the programmer. Database Systems are used to define the structure of data and provides the mechanism for manipulation of data. The Database System also provides safety of data in the event of crashes and failures. All computer based information systems provide the information after processing the data. These information systems are designed and developed around the database.

In the early days of programming, the programmer used to write application programs for data handling. The data were stored and maintained in operating system files. Whenever the need arises, application programmer used to write the application program for specific purpose. The data was stored in the files as series of records. Each file used to contain the data for specific function. The application programs for creating a record, modifying contents of a record and deletion of a record were required to be written separately. Increasing volume of data has number of problems in file system. During those days, programmers used the programming language COBOL to store, retrieve and manipulate data. These programs used to contain the intrinsic details as how the data are stored in the file, and specific algorithm to fetch and store the data used to be coded in application program. The structures of the files were also not consistent and used to vary with the skills of the programmer. Program development under such environment was quite complex and often lead to high amount of redundancy in data. This approach results in great amount of data redundancy, Isolation of data, Data Inconsistency and lack of flexibility to use the data.

Major drawbacks of traditional file system may be summarized as following :

1. Data Redundancy
2. Isolation of Data
3. Data Inconsistency

4. Inability to process data due to varying file structures
5. Integrity and Security Problems

The Database Management System is developed around the file system, which accesses, stores and processes the data contained in the files. We may further conclude that DBMS is a collection of program which collectively allows the user to access the data protecting him from the lower level implementation details. It allows the user to define the data, provide storage and retrieval and manipulation of data. The users are provided with higher level perception of data (Logical view of data). Structured Query Language (SQL) is the most common query language used by most of the DBMS. The data definition, querying and application programs are written in SQL. A general structure of database management system is shown in the following figure.

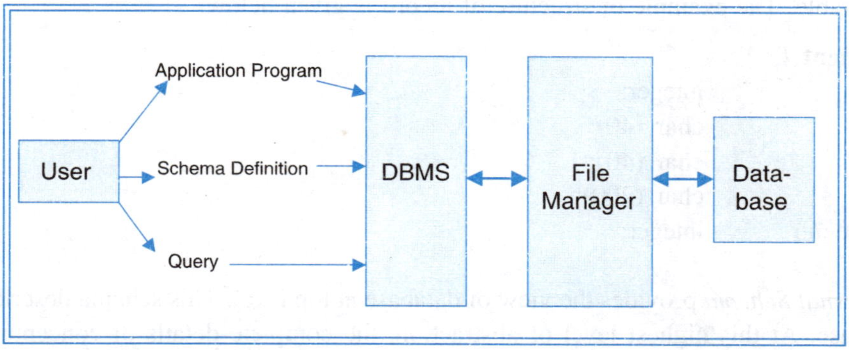

Fig. 11.1: Role of DBMS

As shown in the Figure 11.1, a user who may be application programmer or Database Administrator may submit application program or query to the Database Management System. The DBMS, access the data stored in the database through file manager and processes it.

11.2 LEVELS OF DATA ABSTRACTION

As discussed before, the lower level details of the data files, about their storage are hidden from the database users. However, for efficient data storage and retrieval, it is necessary to incorporate the data structure and algorithm for data representation in the database. A naïve user of database is not required to know the intricate lower level details of data and he is given logical or conceptual view of the data. In this way, different users of the database system perceives the data in different ways. The data in the database may be described at three levels of abstraction. The database description consists of schema. The three schemas corresponding to three levels are given below:

1. Physical Schema
2. Logical or Conceptual Schema
3. External Schema

The *Physical Schema* describes how the data are stored on to the disk and tapes drives. This lowest level of abstraction mainly describes how actually the data has been stored on to the secondary storage devices, algorithm and data structures for storage and retrieval of data, details of index, data structure for efficient and faster access of data from the disk. Design of physical schema is also of great concern in database design.

The *Logical* or *Conceptual Schema* describes the data and its relationship among them. Consider following conceptual schema,

student (roll no, name, fname, address, telephone_no) ;

Various student entities may be defined with their attributes like roll no, name, father's name, address, telephone number. The choice of the attributes and size of attributes are not obvious. We may have to further describe the maximum allowable size of every attribute when a table of records needs to be created. Therefore the conceptual database design provides collection of entities and relationship among them. With this design a user may write SQL statement to create a database according to this conceptual level design. At this level of abstraction, the user is not required to be aware of physical database design. User of this level of abstraction might perceive, as the data is stored in the form of records in a table. The example of structure of record is given below:

```
Record Student {
    rollno          integer;
    name            char (40);
    fname           char (40);
    address         char (200);
    telephone_no    integer;
    }
```

The *External Schema* provides the view of database at top level. This schema describes only a part of the database. At this highest level of abstraction, the complete details of conceptual schema are hidden from different users. Many users of the database are concerned with only a part of the database. These users are not provided with complete conceptual schema, however a part of conceptual scheme called External Schema are made available to them. Therefore, a database has only one physical schema, only one conceptual schema but it may have multiple external schemas. These external schemas are designed to meet the requirement of different users. At this top level of abstraction, the user might have a part view of the database. For example, in student registration might have two components say, fee details and personal details. The database user is allowed to work with personal details will be provided only that view of data which contains only personal details. In this case, the fee details are hidden from this user of database.

Data Independence

One of the most important advantages with the Database Management System is that it provides a high amount of data independence. The data independence refers to the ability to modify the schema at one level without affecting schema at another level. As we have seen in previous section, that physical schema describes the lower level details of data. If we can modify the physical scheme without any modification in conceptual scheme, a ***physical data independence*** is said to have achieved. Therefore, the application programs written on the basis of conceptual schema will remain unaffected if physical schema are changed. This concept is known as Physical Data Independence. The ***logical data independence*** is said to have achieved if we can modify the conceptual schema without affecting the application programs. It is generally easy to have physical data independence because the application programmers are shielded from the lower level details of the data. Logical data independence is difficult to achieve because the application programmer writes the programs using the conceptual schema.

11.3 ARCHITECTURE OF DATABASE MANAGEMENT SYSTEM

The Database Management System (DBMS) is defined as collection of programs/software tools for efficient storage and retrieval of data. The core of any Database Management System is Database. The Database is designed systematically to organize and contain the raw interrelated to real world data. The Database Management System provides the mechanism to define, store, retrieve and manipulate the data. It also allows different users to query the database by writing programs in querying language like SQL. In this section, we will discuss the general architecture of a database management system and its components. DBMS is designed and developed not only to handle the query to database but also they provide the mechanism to ensure the integrity and security of data. In multi programming environment, more than one user may submit their program and queries to database. A simultaneous access to a data object may lead the database into an inconsistent state. DBMS also ensure that a shared data is used in such a way that it does not lead to incorrect result and does not compromise with consistency. One of important role that a DBMS plays is to prevent the database from failures. These failures may be occurred due to logical errors or system crashes. A robust mechanism preventing from failures and recovery from failures are also provided by the DBMS. A general architecture of DBMS is shown in the Figure 11.2.

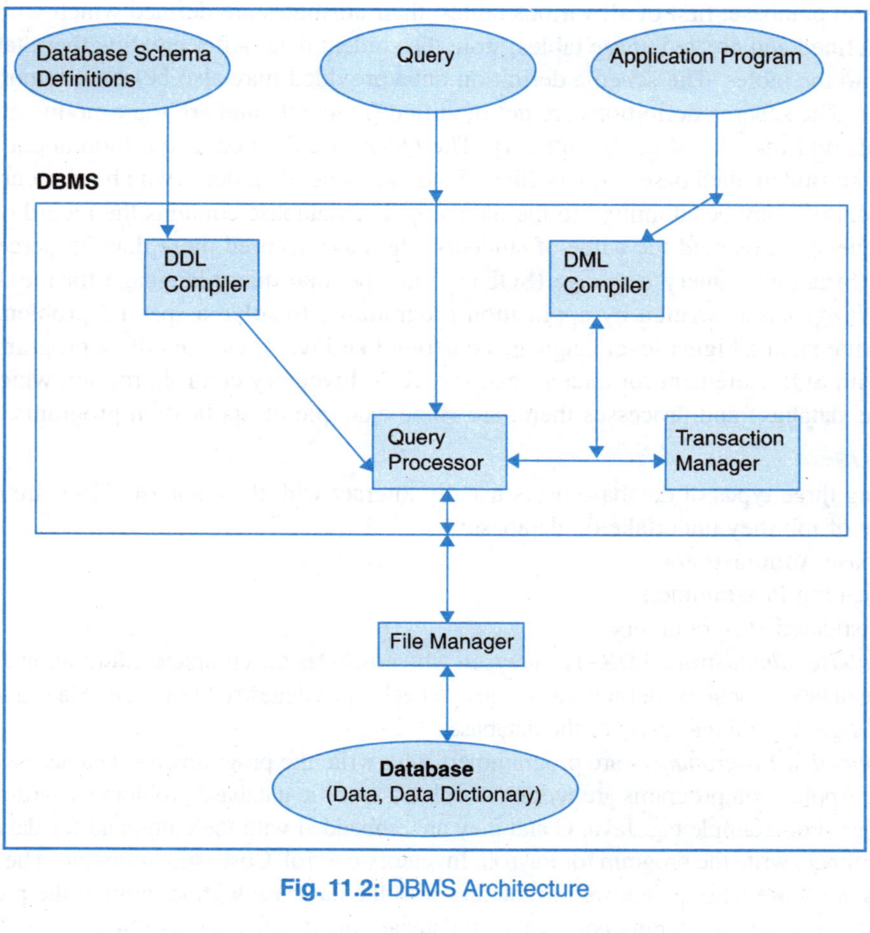

Fig. 11.2: DBMS Architecture

As shown in the Figure 11.2, DBMS accepts three types of input from user. These are database schema, query and application programs. DDL compiler, DML compiler, query processor and transaction manager are important component of DBMS. However, a DBMS also contains the modules for backup, recovery from failures, concurrency control etc. We can view DBMS as an interface between the database and users. The users interact by sending queries and programs to DBMS, which are essentially executed on the data contained in Database.

Database contains not only the raw data but also metadata. The Metadata is defined as definitions of data. It defines the overall structure of the data, which are logically stored in tabular form called Tables. In case of Relational Database, it includes name of relations, name and type of attributes, size of attribute etc. Various constraints on the attribute and tables are also defined.

As shown in the Figure 11.2, following three types input may be given to DBMS:

1. Database Schema Definitions
2. Query
3. Application Program

A database is defined and created on the basis of schema definitions provided by the Database Administrator. The *Schema definitions* define the overall structure of the data. In relational databases, the data are stored in the form of tables. The schema definition contains the information about name of table, name and size of attributes of tables and integrity check on attributes and tables. For example, to create a student database, first of all various tables, their attributes are defined which will hold student data. Once defined and created, these tables, store the student data. After creating these tables, the data is inserted into the tables. The schema definition once provided may also be altered upon the requirement if arises. The schema definitions are not modified frequently and arbitrary modification may lead to loss of data and may sacrifice the integrity. The *Query* are defined as question about the data. For example, in the student data base, a query like " Find the name of students who have secured more than 75 percent Marks" may be submitted to the database. The database contains the record of all students and once a query is executed the name of students who have secured more than 75 percent marks are filtered. The Structured Query language (SQL) is most popular query language for the database. The *Application Programs* is written by application programmer to solve a specific problem. These programs are written using higher level language construct like Java, C etc. and these programs are usually embedded with SQL statement for data access. Pay Roll, Inventory control program which fetches the data from the database and processes them, are some example of application programs.

Database Users

Following three types of database users usually interact with the database. They are distinguished by the nature of job they undertake on database:

1. Database Administrator
2. Application Programmers
3. Sophisticated Programmers

The *Database Administrator (DBA)* is a person who possesses the complete information and centralizes control on the database, schema definitions, integrity checks, privileges/right of users. He is allowed to grant privilege and right to different users of the database.

The *Application Programmers* are programmers who write the programs for data access for a specific environment. Application programs are written to solve a specific database problem by writing program in a host language. For example e.g. Java, C and they are embedded with the command for data access SQL. These programmers write the program for Payroll, Inventory control, Cost estimations etc. The Sophisticated Programmers are those who are allowed to interact with the database without writing the programs. They fetch and update the data by writing commands in database query language like SQL.

Components of DBMS

As shown in the figure 11.2, following are major integral components of a DBMS. There exist other component for backup, recovery, concurrency control, lock manager etc. which are beyond the scope of our discussion.

1. Data Definition Language Compiler
2. Data Manipulation Language Compiler
3. Query Processor
4. Transaction Manager
5. File Manager

The *Data Definition Language* (DDL) describes the database schema definitions. DDL provides the mechanism for converting conceptual schema into database tables. The DDL also provides the construct to define the structures of table, attributes and other integrity checks. The DDL statements are compiled by the DDL compiler and are stored in Data Dictionary in the database. Most of the DBMS supports SQL as Data Definition Language.

The *Data Manipulation Language* (DML) is a language supported by DBMS which allows the manipulation of data. The manipulation of data includes reading data values, insertion, deletion and modification of data. Structured Query Language (SQL) serves the function of both Data Manipulation Language and Data Definition Language in most commercial DBMS. DML compiler compiles queries specified in the DML The Data Manipulation Languages are broadly classified in to two categories:

1. Procedural DML
2. Non Procedural DML

A *procedural DML* requires the user to specify how to get the data, which type of data needs to be accessed. While writing a code for the query in procedural DML, a user specifies the procedure to obtain the data.

A Non Procedural DML does not require the user to specify the procedure to obtain the data. This language construct requires the user to specify what data is required without specifying how to get it.

Most commercial relational database system provides the query language which include the essence of both procedural and non procedural languages. Structured Query Language (SQL), Query By Example (QBE), QUEL, DATALOG are examples of commercial query languages. The Relational Algebra and Relational Calculus are called pure query language as they provide the logical basis for design and development of a commercial query language. Relational Algebra is Procedural Query language and Relational Calculus is Non Procedural.

The *Query Processor* is an important component of DBMS which handle varieties of queries. It not only handles the queries for obtaining the data but also handles the request for insertion, deletion and updation of data. It also handles the request for modification of metadata. Query Processor, after taking the request from the users, finds the optimal solution for query processing.

The *Transaction Manager* is mainly responsible for maintaining the integrity of the system. A transaction is defined as a unit of work, which has to be done in atomicity. In a multiprogramming environment, it has to be ensured that multiple query request does not interfere with other and avoid the conflicting actions. While multiple query are executed simultaneously, they cannot be allowed to proceed in arbitrary order as execution in this manner may lead the database into the inconsistent state. Transaction Manager interacts with the Query manager so that it comes to know what data is being modified by current queries and it delays the execution of some query so that conflicts do not occur. The *File Manager*'s role is to provide and manage the space on the disk. It also maintains various data structures to represent the data stored in the disk.

11.4 DATA MODEL

Data Models are considered a basis for good database design. The data models are used as a tool to capture the data and its relationship in the data. Various data models have been proposed so far, which may be categorized in the following three categories:

1. Object Based Data Models
2. Record Based Data Model
3. Physical Data Models.

The *Object Based Data Models* are being used widely to capture the relationship between the data. These models are more abstract and they provide high level design. These models are highly flexible in the structure and data integrity constraints may also be specified categorically. Entity-Relationship (E R Model) Model, object oriented models are some examples of it. Both of these models are being used extensively in industry.

The *Record Based Data Models* are used to provide the high level description of data and relationship for implementation. These models are used to specify the conceptual structure of database. As the name indicates record based data model uses record as a major component. A record is a collection of values of certain attributes. The Hierarchical Model, Network Model and Relational Model are examples of record based data model. The Relational Model is considered as most popular data model.

The *Physical Data Models* are used to provide the detailed description of data at lower level. These models describe the storage structure of database and elaborate the mechanism to store and retrieve the data. The Physical Models may be used to implement data at lower level. The example of physical data models is unifying model.

11.4.1 Relational Data Model

The Relational Data Models is used to represent the data and relationship among the data through the set of tables. These concepts of tables are similar to the mathematical concept of relation. The relational data models are record based data models. A Table in relational data model is considered as a collection of fixed sized records. The row of the table corresponds to a record, while a column of a table corresponds to the attribute or field. In relational model, a database schema is a collection of relation scheme. A relation scheme is defined by set of fields or attribute.

Consider database schema containing following relation scheme.
student (rollno, name, fname, telephone_no);
hostel (hostel_code, hostel_ name, warden);
allotment (rollno, hostel_code)

Student

roll_no	name	Fname	telephone_no
1	Ravin	Sohail	233837
2	Rajiv	Abhay	765652
3	Manik	Rustam	282837
4	Bharti	Rafiq	452465
5	Shivlal	Anand	232233

Hostel

hostel_code	hostel_name	warden
RH	Radhakrishanan	R K Basu
PT	Patel	G N Pandey

Allotment

Roll_no	Hostel_code
1	RH
2	PT
3	PT
4	RH
5	RH

The tables **student, hostel and allotment,** capture the data about student, hostel and relationship between the entity, student and hostel. A table **'allotment'** defines the relationship between hostel and student. The various student's records and hostel records may be placed in the corresponding table and table **allotment** captures the relationship between these two. The tables of relational model may be implemented by writing a few lines code in structured query language. SQL has been accepted as standard for database query. In the next section, we shall discuss the role of SQL as data definition and data manipulation language.

11.5 QUERYING A DATABASE

11.5.1 System of Keys

The entity relationship model captures the various entities and their relationships. In the relational model, corresponding tables are obtained from entity and relationship. Conceptually all the entities are different from other entity. The differences among the entities are explored using system of keys. Keys correspond to those attributes which uniquely defines the entity. For example, roll number serves as a key to the relation student. The roll number allotted to all students must be unique. We may have three types of keys called Supper Key, Candidate Key and Primary Key.

A *Super Key* is defined as a set of attributes which uniquely identifies an entity in entity set. There may exist more than one super key for the relations. It is also possible that a subset of super key is also a key.

A *Candidate Key* is defined as set of attributes which uniquely identifies an entity in entity set and no proper subset of candidate key is a key. It is also possible to have multiple candidate key for a relation. A *Primary Key* is essentially a candidate key chosen for database design and implementation.

11.5.2 Querying a Database

The Database Management System allows the users to define the structure of data and provides constructs for manipulation of the data stored in the table. These functions are carried by the users through Data Definition Language and Data Manipulation Language.

The Data Definition Language provides the constructs for implementing the data definition as mentioned by database scheme. The DDL compiler compiles code written in the DDL and it generates a set of tables in the database. The execution of DDL statements creates tables which are stored in Data Dictionary. DDL are used to create the basic structure of table in the database. The Data Manipulation Language of the database system provides the constructs to manipulate the data stored in the table. Various operations like Insert, Delete, Modification of record or values stored in the table may be carried out by writing the code in data manipulation language. DML are essentially used to query the database. Structured Query Language (SQL) is a widely used language which provides the constructs for both DDL and DML. Consider the following scheme:

student (rollno, name, fname, marks);
hostel (hostel_code, hostel_ name, warden);
alloment (rollno, hostel_code)

```
create table student
        (rollno                 integer,
        name                    char(30),
        fname                   char(30),
        marks                   integer,
        primary key (rollno)),
create table hostel
        (hostel_code            char(2),
        hostel_name             char(30),
        warden                  char(30),
        primary key (hostel_code)),
create table allotment
        (rollno                 integer,
        hostel_code             char(2),
        primary key (rollno, hostel_code))
```

The above set of statement written in SQL, provides the data definition. These code create the table as per the requirement shown in SQL statements. The same language may be used for Data Manipulation. Code in SQL may be written to insert, delete or update the data values stored in the table. Following are few examples of query which may also be written in SQL:

1. Insert the record of a new student enrolled.
2. List the name of students who secured more than 75 marks.
3. List the name of hostel where the students, who secured more than 75 marks.
4. Add two bonus marks to all the students

Such insertion of new record may be done as follows,

```
insert into student
    values (1,'rahul','vikas',79)
```

These two statements will insert a new record in the table **student** and set the value of fields rollno, name, fname and marks as '1', 'rahul', 'vikas' and 79.

Similarly, to list the name of students who secured more than 75 marks, following code may be written as.

```
select name
from student
where marks > 75
```

Query written above will list the name of those students who have secured more than 75 marks.

11.6 STRUCTURED QUERY LANGUAGE (SQL)

Structured Query Language (SQL) originally developed by IBM at Alamden Research Center for its System-R project. It has become a de facto standard for most commercial DBMS. Majority of commercially available Database Management System has adopted SQL as relational database query language. The SQL language is used for data definition, data manipulation, view maintenance, writing triggers, providing integrity control, security and remote database access. In the previous section, we have presented example of SQL query and in this section we present the basis for formation of an SQL query.

Consider the following schema:

Student-Scheme = (Roll_No, Student_Name, Marks)

Hostel-scheme = (Hostel_Code, Hostel_Name, Warden)

Allot-scheme = (Roll_No, Hostel_Code)

We further denote that STUDENT, HOSTEL and ALLOT are relation based on Student-Scheme, Hostel-Scheme and Allot-Scheme respectively i.e.

STUDENT (Student-Scheme)

HOSTEL (Hostel-Scheme)

ALLOT (Allot-Scheme)

These relations are shown in the following tables. Note that STUDENT relation contain the data about Roll Number, name and the Marks obtained by him. HOSTEL relation contains the data about the Hostel name and Warden name. The relation ALLOT contains the information about student and the hostel allotted.

Student

Roll_No	Student_Name	Marks
1	Ajay	78
2	Rajiv	56
3	Raghu	97
4	Rohil	86
5	Pankaj	55
6	Alok	60
7	Sanjeev	81
8	Arun	74
9	Sudhir	66
10	Sanjay	58

Hostel

Hostel_Code	Hostel_Name	Warden
VA	Vivekanad	B N Misra
RA	Raman	A. Mittal
KA	Krishna	G. Chandra

Allot

Roll_No	Hostel_Code
1	VA
2	KA
3	RA
4	VA
5	RA
6	VA
7	RA
8	KA
9	KA
10	VA

Writing Queries in SQL

Most simple query in SQL uses three keyword SELECT, FROM and WHERE. A SQL query written with these clause '**select**' the tuples '**from**' the defined table '**where**' a condition specified is satisfied. A general from of an SQL query with these clause is given below,

```
SELECT    [List of Attributes]
FROM      [List of Tables]
WHERE     [Condition ]
```

Consider following queries:

Query 1: Find Name of Students who have secured more then 75 marks.

This query requires the name of the student to be selected from the table STUDENT where the condition for the marks is satisfied. Therefore, the SQL statement is,

```
SELECT Student_Name
FROM Student
WHERE Marks > 75
```

Result of this query is given below:

Student_Name
Ajay
Raghu
Rohit
Sanjeev

Query 2: Find Name and Marks of students who secured more than 75 marks.

```
SELECT Student_Name, Marks
FROM Student
WHERE Marks > 75
```

This query will result in as shown below:

Student_Name	Marks
Ajay	78
Raghu	97
Rohit	86
Sanjeev	81

Query 3: Find Roll Number, Name and Marks of all students who secured more than 75 marks.

This query requires all of the attributes to be selected. We may write 'SELECT*', which prints all the attributes. Therefore both the queries written in the box produce the same result as shown below:

```
SELECT Roll_No, Student_Name, Marks
FROM Student
WHERE Marks > 75
```

```
SELECT *
FROM Student
WHERE Marks > 75
```

Roll_No	Student_Name	Marks
1	Ajay	78
3	Raghu	97
4	Rohit	86
7	Sanjeev	81

In the following section we will discuss various operations to be performed on the relations. Understanding of these operation is required to write efficient query in SQL.

11.6.1 Projection and Selection

Projection: Projection operation allows the user to return a relation with certain attribute. We may 'SELECT' the desired attribute to be included in the results of query. Consider the results of Query 1, 2 & 3, where we have projected 'Student_Name', 'Student_Name, Marks' and 'Roll_No, Student_Name, Marks' respectively. In these queries, we projected the desired values of these attributes. Consider table "Student_Info" to understand the power of Projection operation.

Student_Info

Roll_No	Student_Name	CITY	Marks	Tel_Number	Branch
1	Ajay	Lucknow	78	2362384	CS
2	Rajiv	Meerut	56	2732766	CS
3	Raghu	Agra	97	2365335	IT
4	Rohit	Noida	86	2365298	EC
5	Pankaj	Ghaziabad	55	2731431	IT

"SELECT" clause is used to perform Projection operation. This clause tells what attribute(s) of the table should be included in the results of query.

Query 4: Find the Roll_Number, Name, Marks and Branch of all students.

```
SELECT    Roll_No, Student_Name, Marks, Branch
FROM      Student_Info
```

This query produces following result.

Roll_No	Student_Name	Marks	Branch
1	Ajay	78	CS
2	Rajiv	56	CS
3	Raghu	97	IT
4	Rohit	86	EC
5	Pankaj	55	IT

Query 5: A. Find the Name of all students.

B. Find the Name and Telephone Number of all students.

Following are SQL statement for both Queries.

```
SELECT    Student_Name
FROM      Student_Info
```

```
SELECT    Student_Name Tel_Number
FROM      Student_Info
```

These queries will produce following result:

Student_Name
Ajay
Rajiv
Raghu
Rohit
Pankaj

Student_Name	Tel_Number
Ajay	2362384
Rajiv	2732766
Raghu	2365335
Rohit	2365298
Pankaj	2731431

Selection: The selection operation is used to fetch the tuples or record from the table where the condition specified is satisfied. The "WHERE" clause is used to seek the desired records from the table. Let us update the query 4 and find the Roll_Number, Name, Marks of the student whose branch is "CS".

Query 6: Find the Roll_Number, Name, Marks of the student whose branch is "CS".

Note that in the result attribute Roll_Number, Name and Marks has to be projected wherever the student's branch is "CS". Therefore, we have to project Roll_Number, Name, Marks and Branch from the table "Student_Info" where branch='CS'. Following is the SQL statement for this query and result:

```
SELECT Roll_Number Name,
Marks, Branch
FROM Student_Info
WHERE Branch='CS'
```

Roll_No	Student_Name	Marks	Branch
1	Ajay	78	CS
2	Rajiv	56	CS

We can use =, >=, <=, <.>, != operation for comparisons while writing predicate for "WHERE" statement. Two or more conditions may be included using logical "AND", "OR" operators.

Query 7: Find the Roll_No, Name of students who have secured more than 70 marks and their branch is "CS".

The SQL query and result is shown below:

```
SELECT Roll_No, Student_Name
FROM Student_Info
WHERE Marks > 70 AND Branch='CS'
```

Roll_No	Student_Name
1	Ajay

Query 8: Find the Roll_No, Name of students whose branch is either 'CS' or 'IT'.

The SQL query and result is shown below:

```
SELECT Roll_No, Student_Name
FROM Student_Info
WHERE Branch='CS' OR Branch='IT'
```

Roll_No	Student_Name
1	Ajay
2	Rajiv
3	Raghu
5	Pankaj

Query 9: Find all details of students, branch 'CS' and 'IT' who have secured more than 75 marks.

The SQL query and result is shown below:

```
SELECT *
FROM Student_Info
WHERE (Branch='CS' OR Branch='IT') AND Marks >75
```

Roll_No	Student_Name	CITY	Marks	Tel_Number	Branch
1	Ajay	Lucknow	78	2362384	CS
3	Raghu	Agra	97	2365335	IT

11.6.2 Product and Joins

In the previous section, we have considered only those queries, which require the data from only one table. Most of the time a query requires the data to be fetched from two or more tables. The operation **Cartesian Product** and **Join** allows user to write queries combining the data from two tables. The Cartesian product is a binary operation denoted by (X). Consider tables A and B containing students branch and students address information.

A

Roll	Name	Branch
1	Ajay	CS
2	Rajiv	CS
3	Raghu	IT

B

Roll	Name	Address	City	Tel_Number
1	Ajay	2, Malviya Nagar	Lucknow	2362384
2	Rajiv	129/B, Shanati Nagar	Meerut	2732766
3	Raghu	31A Mall Avenue	Agra	2365335

Suppose we have to find out the address, city and telephone number of student who study in the branch "CS" or if we have to find out the branch of the students who live in the city 'Lucknow' then the query can be processed by joining both the table.

Cartesian Product

Cartesian product of the tables A and B is shown below. The Cartesian product of these tables are performed by clubbing all tuples of first table with second's. To distinguish the information from different tables, name of the table is prefixed before the name of attribute. Therefore, A. Name refers to the data under attribute 'Name' from table 'A' and B. Name refers to the data under attribute 'Name' from table 'B'.

A. Roll	A. Name	A. Branch	B. Roll	B. Name	B. Address	B. City	B. Tel_Num.
1	Ajay	CS	1	Ajay	2, Malviya Nagar	Lucknow	2362384
1	Ajay	CS	2	Rajiv	129/B, Shanati Nagar	Meerut	2732766
1	Ajay	CS	3	Raghu	31A Mall Avenue	Agra	2365335
2	Rajiv	CS	1	Ajay	2, Malviya Nagar	Lucknow	2362384
2	Rajiv	CS	2	Rajiv	129/B, Shanati Nagar	Meerut	2732766
2	Rajiv	CS	3	Raghu	31A Mall Avenue	Agra	2365335
3	Raghu	IT	1	Ajay	2, Malviya Nagar	Lucknow	2362384
3	Raghu	IT	2	Rajiv	129/B, Shanati Nagar	Meerut	2732766
3	Raghu	IT	3	Raghu	31A Mall Avenue	Agra	2365335

Notice that the table A and B have 3 tuples each and product AXB contains 9 tuples. Thus, if the table A and B have m_1 and m_2 tuples each then product AXB shall have $m_1 .m_2$ number of tuples. It may also be noted that product of the tables A and B also contains those tuples where the roll number and name of students are different. The product of table, therefore allows to club the tuples from both tables but also contains ambiguous information. Note that only those tuples in product are relevant where the values of common attributes (Roll, Name) are equal. If we perform following query on product AXB,

```
SELECT *
FROM AXB
WHERE A. Roll = B. Roll AND A. Name=B. Name
```

This query produces following result:

A. Roll	A. Name	A. Branch	B. Roll	B. Name	B. Address	B. City	B. Tel_Num.
1	Ajay	CS	1	Ajay	2, Malviya Nagar	Lucknow	2362384
2	Rajiv	CS	2	Rajiv	129/B, Shanati Nagar	Meerut	2732766
3	Raghu	IT	3	Raghu	31A Mall Avenue	Agra	2365335

This table contains relevant tuple but attribute Roll and Name have same values in different columns. The ideal situation is that the common attribute be written only once. Therefore, we must project only one of A. Roll and B. Roll and one from A. Name and B. Name. If we process following query on AXB,

```
SELECT A.Roll, A.Name, A.Branch, B.Address, B.City, B.Tel_Num
FROM AXB
WHERE A.Roll = B.Roll AND A.Name=B.Name
```

Following result is obtained:

A. Roll	A. Name	A. Branch	B. Address	B. City	B. Tel_Num.
1	Ajay	CS	2, Malviya Nagar	Lucknow	2362384
2	Rajiv	CS	129/B, Shanati Nagar	Meerut	2732766
3	Raghu	IT	31A Mall Avenue	Agra	2365335

The final table obtained is called Join of table A and B. The join of tables A and B can be obtained by writing following SQL query:

```
SELECT *
FROM A,B
WHERE A.Roll=B.Roll AND A.Name=B.Name
```

It may be noted that the **product** of two tables contain ambiguous tuples. Therefore, to get unambiguous results, it is necessary to perform **Join**. To perform Join on two tables, only those tuples from the Cartesian product must be fetched where values of common attribute are same.

Query 10 : Find the Name, Branch and Telephone Number of the student studying in branch "CS"

```
SELECT A.Name, A.Branch, B.Tel_Num
FROM A,B
WHERE A.Roll=B.Roll AND A.Name=B.Name AND A.Branch='CS'
```

The result of this query is following:

Name	Branch	Tel_Num
Ajay	CS	2362384
Rajiv	CS	2732766

Query 11 : Find the Name, Address and City of the students who either belong to city "Agra" or studying in the branch "CS".

```
SELECT A.Name, B. Address, B.City
FROM A, B
WHERE (A.Roll=B.Roll AND A.Name=B.Name)
   AND (A.Branch='CS' OR B.City='AGRA')
```

Name	Address	City
Ajay	2, Malviya Nagar	Lucknow
Rajiv	129/B, Shanati Nagar	Meerut
Raghu	31A Mall Avenue	Agra

Query 12: Consider the following schema:

Student =(Roll_No, Student_ Name, Marks)

Hostel = (Hostel_Code, Hostel_ Name, Warden, Roll_No)

a. Find the Hostel Name of the students who have secured more than 75 Marks.
b. List all Students Name and their Hostel.
c. Find the student and their warden of students who secured marks between 60 and 75.
d. Find the name of the warden of hostel "Raman".
e. Find the name of warden where student "Ajay" lives.

a.

```
SELECT Student_Name, Hostel_Name
  FROM Student, Hostel
  WHERE ( Student.Roll_No = Hostel.Roll_No )
        AND Marks >75
```

b.

```
SELECT Student_Name, Hostel_Name
FROM Student, Hostel
WHERE (Student.Roll_No = Hostel.Roll_No)
```

c.

```
SELECT Student_Name, Warden
FROM Student, Hostel
WHERE (Student.Roll_No = Hostel.Roll_No)
    AND (Marks <=75 AND Marks >=60)
```

d.

```
SELECT Warden
FROM Hostel
WHERE (Hostel_Name='Raman')
```

e.

```
SELECT Warden
FROM Student, Hostel
WHERE (Student.Roll_No = Hostel.Roll_No)
    AND (Student_Name='Ajay')
```

11.6.3 Set Operations (Minus, Intersect and Union)

SQL also allows the programmer to use the set operations like Minus, Intersect and Union. These operations have similar meaning to set operations and are applicable to tables also. Consider the following schema. The student relation contains the Roll No, Name and Address of all students of an Institute. Hostel table contains the Roll No and Name of all students who reside in the Hostel. CS_Student and IT_Student table contains the record of students who opted for branch 'CS' and 'IT' respectively.

Student (Roll_No, Student_ Name, Address)
Hostel (Roll_No, Student_Name)
CS_Student (Roll_No, Student_ Name, Address)
IT_Student (Roll_No, Student_ Name, Address)

Union Operation

This operation allows to take union of two tables. Consider following query:

Query 13: List the name of students who have either opted for branch CS or IT.

This query may be written in many ways, however the most convenient way of writing it by taking Union of the set of students from CS_Student and IT_Student. In the union operation it must be remembered that the set of attributes where union operation is being performed must be same, Union is not applicable to different set of attributes. The query is written below:

```
SELECT distinct Student_Name
FROM CS_Student
Union
SELECT distinct Student_Name
FROM IT_Student
```

Note that 'distinct' clause eliminates the occurrences of duplicate values coming in the result of the query. This makes sure that a value will occur only once in the result. We may use the clause 'All' to enforce that duplicate values are not removed from the result.

Query 14: List the Roll No and Name of students who have either opted for branch 'CS' or residing in the hostel.

```
SELECT distinct Student_Name
FROM CS_Student
Union
SELECT distinct Student_Name
FROM Hostel
```

Intersect Operation

This operation allows taking intersection of two tables. This operation is similar to intersection of two sets.

Query 15: Find the name of the students of 'CS' branch who are residing in the Hostel.

```
SELECT distinct Student_Name
FROM CS_Student
Intersect
SELECT distinct Student_Name
FROM Hostel
```

This query is executed by fetching all students name who are from 'CS' branch and student who resides in the hostel. The result is equivalent to intersection of both set of students.

Query 16: List the name of students who opted both CS and IT branch.

```
SELECT distinct Student_Name
FROM CS_Student
Intersect
SELECT distinct Student_Name
FROM IT_Student
```

Minus Operation

This operation is equivalent to the set difference operation in set theory. Consider following query to understand this operation.

Query 17: Find the name of all students who have not opted for 'CS' branch.

This query can be executed by fetching all students name from the table Student and deleting those name who are entered into the table CS_Student.

```
SELECT distinct Student_Name
FROM Student
Minus
SELECT distinct Student_Name
FROM CS_Student
```

Query 18: Find the name of all students of 'IT' branch who have not opted for hostel.

```
SELECT distinct Student_Name
FROM IT_Student
Minus
SELECT distinct Student_Name
FROM Hostel
```

11.6.4 Special Functions

The **'Order By'** clause allows the controls on ordering of values in the result. This causes tuples in the result to appear in sorted order. Similarly, the **'Group By'** function allows the user to list the group of tuples. Tuples with the same values on attribute in 'Group By' clause are placed in single group in the result.

Query 19: List the name of all students of CS branch in order of student name.

```
SELECT Student_Name
FROM CS_Student
ORDER BY student_name
```

By default the SQL prints the values in ascending order. This query will therefore print the values in ascending order. However, if the values needs to be printed in descending order then caluse **'desc'** needs to be included. Following query print the name in descending order.

```
SELECT Student_Name
FROM Student
ORDER BY student_name DESC
```

Query 20: Consider the following scheme.
Student_Branch_Info (Roll_No, Student_ Name, Branch, Address,Marks)
Find the name of the student in the group of branch.

```
SELECT Student_Name
FROM Student_Branch_Info
GROUP BY branch
```

This query will print name of students branch wise.

Following functions further enhance the power to SQL to write queries. These functions are known as aggregate functions.With these functions, we may find Sum, Average, Minimum, Maximum and Count the number of tuples. Aggreagate function and their role is listed below.

Sum	To find additions or Summation
Avg	To take Average value
Max	To find Maximum value
Count	Count the number of tuples
Min	To find Minimum value.

Query 21: Consider the following scheme.

Student_Branch_Info (Roll_No, Student_ Name, Branch, Address, Marks)

(a) Find the average marks obtained by students in their branch.

```
SELECT Branch, Avg (Marks)
FROM Student_Branch_Info
GROUP BY branch
```

This query will print the branch and average marks obtained by students in these branches.

(b) List the branch name and total number of student registered in that branch.

```
SELECT Branch, Count (student_name)
FROM Student_Branch_Info
GROUP BY branch
```

(c) Find the name of branch where average marks obtained is more than 50.

```
SELECT Branch
FROM Student_Branch_Info
GROUP BY branch
Having avg (marks) >50
```

The 'Having' clause are applied after formation of group, therefore it applies to all groups formed.

11.6.5 Defining a Schema in SQL

In this section, we will discuss those construct of SQL which qualifies it as a data definition language. SQL requires the declaration of all attributes on table. First we list major data types which are required to be associated with attribute. The data type defines the type of the data value which may be stored in that attribute/column of the table. Different types are supported by different commercial DBMS. However, we list those which can be supported by major vendors.

1. Character data Types

   Character string can be fixed or variable length. Char(N) data type defines a string to be of fixed length of size N. VARCHAR (N) denotes a variable string which can be up to the size of N character.

2. Integer Type

   INT data type denotes the integer values.

3. Floating Point or Real Number

   Type FLOAT denotes the floating point or real numbers.

4. Date Type

   DATE data type denotes the date format.

Some of the important operations, which can be performed by SQL, are given below:

Creating a Table

Query 22: Create a table for following scheme.

Student_Branch_Info (Roll_No, Student_ Name, Branch, Address, Marks)

Following SQL statement will create a table Student_Branch_Info in the database.

```
CREATE TABLE Student_Branch_Info
(       Roll_No           Int,
        Student_Name      Varchar (30),
        Branch            Char (2)
        Address           Varchar (200)
        Marks             Int
);
```

Query 23: Create a table for following scheme:
Student (Roll_No, Student_ Name, DOB)

```
CREATE TABLE Student
(       Roll_No           Int,
        Student_Name      Varchar (30),
        DOB               Date,
        );
```

Drop a Table

A table can be dropped from the database by DROP TABLE command. This command is different from the Delete command where selected or all tuples may be deleted.

Query 24: Write SQL statement to drop table Student.

```
DROP TABLE Student
```

Note that writing command *DELETE Student* will delete all tuples from the table Student, but *DROP TABLE Student* command have more drastic effect. Drop command not only deletes the tuples from the table but also removes the scheme from the database. After executing DELETE command, it is still possible to insert new data items into the table.

Inserting Values to Table

INSERT command allows user to insert the data values to table. The simple insert command inserts one tuple in to the table.

Query 25: Write SQL DDL statement for creating following table. Write Insert command to insert the data values.

Roll	Name	Branch
1	Ajay	CS
2	Rajiv	CS
3	Raghu	IT

Following SQL DDL statement creates a new table:

```
CREATE TABLE Student
(       Roll_No           Int,
        Student_Name      Varchar (30),
        Branch            Char(2)
        );
```

Following will insert one line/tuple in to the table.

```
INSERT INTO Student
VALUES ( 1, 'Ajay', 'CS' );
```

To insert three line one has to execute following:

```
INSERT INTO Student
VALUES ( 1, 'Ajay', 'CS' );
INSERT INTO Student
VALUES ( 1, 'Rajiv', 'CS' );
INSERT INTO Student
VALUES ( 1, 'Raghu', 'IT' );
```

SQL also allows the data to be inserted from another table.

Query 26: Consider the table Student_Address below and insert the record in to table Student (Roll, Name, City) wherever the student city is 'Lucknow'.

Student_Address

Roll	Name	Address	City	Tel_Num
1	Ajay	2, Malviya Nagar	Lucknow	2362384
2	Rajiv	129/B, Shanati Nagar	Meerut	2732766
3	Raghu	31A Mall Avenue	Agra	2365335

Following SQL statement will insert the data from Student_Address into Student where City='Lucknow'

```
INSERT INTO Student
        SELECT Roll,Name,City
        FROM Student_Address
        WHERE City ='Lucknow'
```

Deleting a Row in the Table

The request of the Delete is executed like an SQL query. It may be noted that Delete Command is executed on one table only. If two or more tables are to be deleted, separate query for each tuple must be written.

Query 27: Write SQL statement for deleting the record of student whose name is 'Rajiv' from the table Student_Address.

```
DELETE Student_Address
WHERE Student_Name='Rajiv'
```

Note that simple DELETE Student_Address command will delete all records from the table.

Updating the Table

The values stored in the table may be updated or modified. UPDATE-SET command update the old values stored in the table and set to new values.

Query 28: Consider the following scheme:

Student_Branch_Info (Roll_No, Student_ Name, Branch, Address, Marks)

Write SQL statement for awarding 5 bonus marks to all students.

```
UPDATE Student_Branch_Info
SET Marks= Marks +5
```

This will increase the marks of all students by 5.

Suppose we want to increase the marks by 5 to all student of branch 'CS', we may write following SQL statement:

```
UPDATE Student_Branch_Info
SET Marks= Marks +5
WHERE Branch='CS'
```

OBJECTIVE TYPE QUESTIONS

Multiple Choice

1. Drawback of earlier file based data processing system are
   (a) Data redundancy (b) Data Isolation (c) Data Inconsistency (d) All of above
2. Database Management provides features for
   (a) Data Consistency (b) Data Security
   (c) Efficient storage and (d) All of above retrieval of data
3. Which of the following exhibits lower level of data abstraction?
   (a) Physical Schema (b) Logical Schema (c) External Schema (d) All of above
4. Which of the following is not a record based data model?
   (a) Relational Model (b) Hierarchical Model (c) E R Model (d) Network Model
5. For student record, which attribute may serve as primary key
   (a) Name (b) Address (c) Roll Number (d) Marks
6. Language used for defining the structure of data are classified as
   (a) DML (b) DDL (c) Both of above (d) None of above
7. Most popular data model of today is
   (a) Relational Model (b) Hierarchical Model (c) Network Model (d) All of above
8. Which of the following are database querying language
   (a) SQL (b) QBE (c) Datalog (d) All of above
9. Which of the following is a procedural query language?
   (a) Relational Algebra (b) Relational calculus (c) Both of above (d) None of Above
10. Which of the operation is SQL is used to write a query involving two relation?
    (a) Join (b) Selection (c) Projection (d) None of above

Answers

1-d, 2-d, 3-a, 4-c, 5-c, 6-b, 7-a, 8-d, 9-a, 10-a

State True or False

1. DBMS is a collection of interrelated data and program for storage and retrieval of data. [True] [False]
2. Super Key uniquely identifies a record in a table. [True] [False]
3. SQL can not be used for implementation of data definition. [True] [False]
4. Logical schema describes the data and relationship among them. [True] [False]

5. At the highest level of data abstraction, external schema provides the top view of database. [True] [False]
6. Relational data model is example of physical data model. [True] [False]
7. Candidate Key is always a subset of Primary key. [True] [False]
8. Seek time for a record is maximum in indexed file. [True] [False]
9. A primary key may contain more than one attribute. [True] [False]
10. Data definitions are contained in Data Dictionary. [True] [False]

Answers

1-True, 2-True, 3-False, 4-True, 5-True, 6-False, 7-False, 8-False, 9-True, 10-True.

REVIEW QUESTIONS

1. Explain the drawback of earlier file system.
2. What do you mean by Database Management? Discuss the components of DBMS.
3. What are data models? Explain the different data model classification.
4. Explain those features of SQL, which make it suitable as data definition language.
5. What are differences in Data Definition language and Data Manipulation Language?
6. What are record based data models? Explain any one of them.
7. Explain the differences in file and database.
8. Explain the classification of users who interact with the database.
9. What are database schema definitions? Explain with a suitable example.
10. What is a Query? How a query is processed?
11. Discuss the general architecture of a Database Management System? What is the role of a File Manager?
12. What are differences in Procedural and Non Procedural Language? Explain with a suitable example.
13. What do you mean by a Transaction? Explain the role of a Transaction Manager.
14. What do you mean by a Key to the relation? What are differences in Super Key, Candidate Key and Primary Key.

12

WEB SITE DEVELOPMENT AND WEB TECHNOLOGY

Contents

- E-Commerce Application Development Life Cycle
- Characteristics of E-Commerce Projects
- Introduction to Java
- Java Applets
- Hyper Text Markup Language (HTML)
- Wireless Application Protocol (WAP)
- Wireless Markup Language (WML)
- Introduction to VBScript
- Introduction to JavaScript
- Java Server Pages (JSP)
- Enterprise Java Beans (EJB)
- Extensible Markup Language (XML)

12 WEB SITE DEVELOPMENT AND WEB TECHNOLOGY

12.1 E-COMMERCE APPLICATION DEVELOPMENT LIFE CYCLE

We have seen that conventional software development has several stages from early planning to implementation. The E-commerce projects are also developed in almost the same way, but more attention is paid to the selection of the technology for implementation. The various requirement in the development of web project are subject to change more frequently as compared to traditional software projects. Proper implementation of a web project may have the following stages of development. This is known as E-commerce application development life cycle.

Awareness Training

This is the first phase of an E-commerce or web project development. An awareness training is required to understand the scope of available technologies and their complexities. While selecting a technology, the web team must know as to what it can do for the improvement of business is compared to the conventional practices in business. Before the project actually starts the scope of all the technologies to be used must be defined and a compensatory plan be evolved to center for technological advances or obsolesce.

Business Analysis

This is concerned with determining the impact of technology on business avenues and opportunities. After all, the sole purpose of adopting new technologies is to improve the business of a company. To assure maximum value from electronic commerce or web project, there must be a thorough understanding of how the new technology can help the business. Business analysis requires that a cost/benefit analysis is performed in order to find which option is vaild and can provide more value to the new system.

Requirement Analysis

This analysis is done to decide what features are to be implemented in the web project as well as to decide which functions are to be implemented in the E-commerce site or web site. The development of a web site should not only include the features to receive the requests from customers, but also the features which enable the organisation to keep customers informed of changes and modifications in the product. In this phase, business related data and facts are collected to understand the role of web site in the future, how the web site will cater to the requirements of various customers and how the organization will be benefited. Any inconsistent and incomplete requirement must be omitted as inconsistent requirement will contradict the other requirement and incomplete requirement will lead to poor design.

Design Phase

In this phase a detailed design of the project is created. Various factors like mode of payment, involvement of third parties in electronic payment, design of robust mechanism for payment instrument etc. are given more focus in this phase. The role of other participating vendors clearly defined. This phase also includes the layout design of the web site and database server. The web technologies which are to be involved and implemented are also clearly explained.

Testing and Implementation

In this phase the system becomes real and fully functional. It requires the new business process to start operating this phase also includes the testing of the product developed against several conditions. The system is then implemented and training is conducted for system management. The new business process begins to function by using the system thus developed.

Maintenance

E-commerce web sites require constant maintenance and therefore this phase is of at most importance. It also lasts for a longer time as compared to the other phases. With new practices being regularly implemented and introduced it is a great challenge to maintain the site. The information contents have to be consistently updated, new information added and the irrelevant information deleted. It also deals with the unforseen circumstances, and plans for improvement.

These various stages must be properly deployed in order to develop a good robust E-commerce web site. It will help to reduce development time, effort and money. Not only should the various stages be invoked and executed but also the effort required in each stage be computed according to the need. In many cases, more emphasis is required in the Design phase while in other cases more emphasis is given to business and requirement analysis phases. All this depends upon the specific needs of the business organization.

In the following section, we will introduce various web technologies and will see how these technologies may be used to develop a commercial web site.

12.2 CHARACTERISTICS OF E-COMMERCE PROJECTS

The commerical web development projects are subject to change because of unforeseen reasons as well as their own characteristics. These characteristics are listed below.

1. Development schedules in web projects are short. The reason is that web is relatively a new concept and with introduction of new technologies, it is always possible for both client and developer to underestimate the web project.
2. It becomes most of the time inevitable to use the current web technology because of several requirements. It has been observed that web projects are developed using the technologies for which no final software products have been launched. Using trial or beta versions of software to implement web sites may prove to be problematic, if the final software product contains major changes.
3. The costing part in web projects is most critical as there does not exist any model by which the costs to be incurred in the various phases of the web project can be estimated. This happens because of changes in the scope of the project while the web project is still in its development phase.

4. There are several standard models available for various product development projects but there does not exist any standard model for the web development. That is probably the reason why most of the time adhoc styles are used in web development.
5. Most of the time, the requirements of a web project are either ill defined or not completely defined. This eventually triggers various changes and alterations in the final product or in design, unlike any other conventional product development.

12.3 INTRODUCTION TO JAVA

12.3.1 Introduction

JAVA, introduced as an object Oriented Language, was initially considered to be simply the "Internet version of C++". Java is related to C++, which is a direct descendent of C. Because of the similarities between Java and C, the initially impetus for Java was not the Internet. Instead the primary motivation was the need for an architecture neutral or platform independent language that could be used to create software for embedded application in various consumer electronic devices, such as microwave ovens and remote controls. We should also note that Java was not designed to replace C++, it was simply designed to solve a certain set of problems while C++ was designed for different requirements.

12.3.2 Java Byte Code

The feature that makes Java secure and portable is that the output of a Java compiler is not an executable code, rather it is a bytecode. Bytecode is a highly optimized set of instructions designed to be executed by a virtual machine that the Java runtime system emulates.

Because Java programmes are interpreted rather than compiled, it is much easier to run them in a wide variety of environments. The fact that Java is interpreted also helps to make it secure. The execution of every Java program is under the control of the runtime system. Which can contain the program and prevent it from generating side effects.

12.3.3 Advantages with Java

OOP organizes a program around its objects and a set of well defined interfaces to that. OOP is at the core of Java. In fact, all Java programs are object oriented. An essential element of object oriented programming is abstraction. Object oriented concepts form the heart of Java just as they form the basis for human understanding. All object oriented programming languages provide mechanisms which help to implement the object-oriented model. Following are the JAVA advantages. The popularity and general acceptability of JAVA code lies behind the following characteristics.

➢ **Java is simple**

Java system was built as closely to C++ as possible in order to make the system more comprehensible. Java omits many rarely used, poorly understood, confusing features of C++ that bring more grief than benefit.

➢ **Java is secure**

Java is intended to be used in networked/distributed environments. So, keeping that view in mind, a lot of emphasis is given on security. It enables the construction of virus free tamper-free systems.

➢ **Java is portable**

As already discussed, Java is compiled to bytecode which is platform independent this provides portability to Java. The sizes of primitive data types are specified, as is the behavior of arithmetic on them.

➢ Java is object-oriented

The object-oriented features are as essential to Java as they are to C++. Object-oriented design is a technique of programming that focuses on the data and on the interfaces to that object. To make an analogy with carpentry, an ''object-oriented'' carpenter would be mostly concerned with the table he was making, and secondarily with the tools used to make it; a "non object-oriented'' carpenter would think primarily of his tools.

➢ Java is robust

Java is intended for writing programs that must be reliable in a variety of ways. This feature is also very useful. The Java compiler detects many problems that in other languages would only show up only at run time. A programmer chasing memory corruption caused by a pointer bug will be very happy with this feature of Java.

➢ Java is multithreaded

Java provides an easier way of multithreading than any other language. Mulithreaded programming allows writing programs that can do many things at once. Threads in Java also have the capacity to take the advantage of multiprocessor systems if the base operating system does so. Nonetheless, the ease in multi-threading is one of the main reasons why Java is such an appealing language for server side development.

➢ Java is architecture-neutral

A cental issue for Java designers was "write once, run anywhere, any time, forever''. Due to operating system upgrades, processor upgrades, and changes in core system resources, there was no guarantee that if you write a program today, it will run tomorrow even on the same machine. The Java designers made many hard decisions to provide platform independence, and to a great extent, this goal was accomplished.

➢ Java is interpreted

The Java interpreter can execute Java bytecode directly on any machine to which the interpreter has been ported. But on the other hand, it provides disappointment by being quite slow.

➢ Java provides high performance

While the performance of interpreted bytecode is usually more than adequate, there are situations where high performance is required. The bytecode can be translated on the fly (at run time) into machine codes for the particular CPU the application is running on.

➢ Java is distributed

Java has extensive library routines for copying with TCP/IP protocols like HTTP and FTP. Java applications can open and access objects across the net via URLs with the same ease as accessing a local file system.

➢ Java is dynamic

Java was designed to adapt to an evolving environment. Libraries can add freely new methods and instance variables without any affect on their clients. So in that way, Java is more dynamic than C++.

12.3.4 Java Code

```
public class Sample
{
public static void main (String args [ ])
{
System.out.println (''Its easy to use JAVA'');
}
}
```

The file name of the source code is named the same as the name of the public class itself with the extension 'Java'. So the name of the above file should be Sample.java. Keep in mind that it is case sensitive. Now the program is compiled on DOS prompt as follows:

C:/java Sample.java

After the compilation is over and no error is present, it creates class file. It is executed on DOS prompt as follows:

C./java Sample

This produces the desired output as follows:

'It easy to use JAVA'

12.3.5 Java for Internet Applications

Java being a platform of independent language, is considered to be the best suited language for Internet application. It provides flexibility in writing the Java code and distributing it over the network. This code does not require any specific platform to run as the Java byte code is not an executable code. On the distribution of Java code, various users may down load the Java bytecode and may run them on their machines. Actually the web pages where the Java program runs is called Java Applet. To run the Java bytecode, a Java enabled web browser is required to interpret the bytecode. These web browsers may be used on various platforms such as Unix, Linux or Windows. Therefore, the same Java bytecode may be executed on any platform. This feature of Java makes it most suitable for Internet applications.

There are some misconeptions about Java and its functionality. Following are the general misconception about Java.

12.3.6 Misconception about Java

1. People think Java is an extension to HTML. This is not ture. Java is a programming language in which programs are written and executed. HTML is truly not a programming language as the name indicates; rather it is used to describe the information contents appearing on the web page.
2. Java will soon become the Universal Programming Language. This is not true because people have been using programming languages such as C and C++ since many years. Several applications have already been developed using C and C++. For example, word processor and web browsers were developed and written in these languages and since these application programs have already became popular, therefore there is no point in rewriting these programs in Java. However, because of excellent constructs provided in Java, it soon became a language for Internet applications.
3. All Java programs run in the Web Pages. This is not true. Java programs may be written and independently executed outside the web browers. It is only Java applets which run under web browsers. Java may be used as a programming language like any other language such as C, C++ or VB to develop an application.
4. JavaScript is another version of Java. This is not true. JavaScript is a scripting language and Java is a fully functional programming language. Typically there is nothing common between JavaScript and Java except the word Java.

12.4 JAVA APPLETS

12.4.1 Introduction

JAVA programs that work on Web pages are called Applets. They are embedded in HTML files. To use an applet, one needs to have a JAVA enabled web browser, which interprets the bytecode. Applets can also be used to add buttons and input fields to a web page. In general, when the user downloads an applet, it works much like embedding an image in a web page. The applets become part of the page and the text flows around the space used for the applet. Here the striking feature is that the image is live. It reacts to user command, changes its appearance and sends the data between the computer and the computer serving it.

Applets like, application programs can do many things. They can perform arithmetic operations, display graphics, playgrounds etc. In order to locate and load applets on the Web, we must know their address on the Web. This address is known as URL (Uniform Resource Locator) and must be supplied in the applet's HTML document.

12.4.2 Application vs Applet

- Applets don't use the main method to initiate execution.
- Applets can't be run independently. They can only be run in a Web page.
- Applets can neither read nor write to files of the local computer.
- Applets can't communicate with other servers on the network.
- Applets can't run any program from the local computer.
- Applets are not allowed to use libraries from other languages such as C/C++.

All this is possible because applets are interpreted by Java Virtual Machine and not directly execute by the CPU on the user's computer. Actually, applets are generally used to add something dynamic in the display of web pages and to have some flash output. Following are the steps taken to write and embed an applet in a web page;

- Building an applet source file (.java file)
- Creating an executable applet (.class file)
- Preparing an <APPLET> tag.
- Incorporating <APPLET> tag into Web page.
- Creating HTML file.
- Testing the applet inside the browser.

12.4.3 Life Cycle of Java Applet

In applet life cycle an applet contains a set of default behavior from the Applet class. When the applet is loaded, it runs through different states. The different states are discussed below:

1. Born or Initialization state
2. Running state
3. Idle state
4. Dead or destroyed state

Initialization State

Applet enter the initialization state when it is first loaded. This is achieved by calling the init() method of Applet class. The applet is born. At this stage, we may do the following if required:

- Create Objects needed by the applet.
- Set up initial values.
- Load images or fonts.
- Set up colors.

We can initialize the applet using into(), as given below:

```
Public void init()
{
..........................
```

(actions)

....

}

Running State

Applet enters the running state when the system calls the start() method of Applet class. This occurs automatically after the applet is initialized. Starting can also occur if the applet is already in "stopped" (idle) state.

For example, we may leave the web page containing the applet temporarily so to another page and return back-like as.

```
Public void start()
{
.........................
.........................(action)
.........................
}
```

Idle or Stopped State

An applet becomes idle when it is stopped from running. Stopping occurs automatically when we leave the page containing the currently running applet. We can also do so by calling the stop() method explicitly. Like as,

```
Public void stop()
{
.........................
.........................(action)
.........................
}
```

Dead State

An applet is said to be dead when it is removed from memory. The dead state can be invoked by using destroy(). This stage occurs only in the applet's life cycle.

```
Public void stop()
{
.........................
.........................(action)
.........................
}
```

12.4.4 Writing Code for Applet: An Example

Now we see the code of a typical applet.

```
// Creation of an applet
import java.awt*;
import java.applet*;
public class pise_muk extends Applet
{
        public void paint (Graphics g)
        {
```

```
        g.drawstring (''PISE & MUKHERJEE'', 20, 150);
    }
}
```

This was the code of an applet. Now we'll incorporate this code into a Web page that is HTML file.

```
<HTML>
<!THIS FILE EMBEDS APPLET>
<HEAD>
<TITLE>
THIS IS APPLET EXAMPLE
</TITLE>
</HEAD>
<BODY>
<CENTER>
WELCOME TO APPLET
</CENTER>
<CENTRE>
<APPLET>
CODE=Pise_muk.class
width=200
height=20>
</center>
</body>
</Html>
```

12.5 HYPER TEXT MARKUP LANGUAGE (HTML)

12.5.1 Introduction

HTML and the web were first conceived in 1989 by a researcher named Tim Berners Le who worked for CERN, the European laboratory for practical physics in Geneva, Switzerland. CERN researchers developed the initial World Wide Web programs in 1990 and began releasing programs and specification to Internet users in 1991. Contrary to its name, HTML does not qualify as a language. It actually follows a script pattern where you may enter text, table, links, image, graphics etc. and may be produced on the web browser in a desired format.

Now we will explain what each word means in the name Hypertext Markup Language.

Hypertext

It is ordinary text that has been dressed with extra features, such as formatting, images, multimedia, and links to other documents. Thus it is more than a simple text. Usually, those who have visited the net know that clicking on certain text or line or work, opens a new page of information relating to the text. Thus it is called Hyper Text.

Markup

It can be termed as the process of taking ordinary text and adding extra symbols. Each symbol used for markup in HTML is a command that tells a browser how to display the text.

Language

This is actually a key point to remember about HTML. Markup languages are a special type of computer language because they are solely concerned with classifying various parts of a document according to their functions. In other words, HTML is used to define the different parts of your document.

Thus HTML is not really a programming language. Instead, HTML is markup language that has different goals. The important thing to remember is that HTML is designed to work on a wide variety of platforms, such that you should be able to trust that your document will be attractively and correctly displayed by any browser on any computer any where in the world. HTML has several inherent advantages including flexibility, affordable price and independence of machine of platform. At present many versions of HTML, e.g. HTML, HTML+, HTML 2.0, HTML 3.0, HTML 3.2, HTML 4.0 are available.

12.5.2 HTML Tags

The basic element in HTML is the 'tag'. You may write text, include table, image, audio, graphic etc. within the tag. Tag defines the way of presentation or combination of all components on the web browser. Following is a simple code written in HTML which displays information (few text lines) about Computer Science Department of Institute of Engineering and Technology.

```
<html>
<head>
<title> INSTITUTE OF ENGINEERING & TECHNOLOGY </title>
</head>
<body>
<h1> <b> Welcome To The Department of Computer Science and Engineering
</b><h1>
<h2><b> COURSES UNDERTAKEN</b><h2>
<01>
<li>B.Tech. (Computer Science and Engg.)</li>
<li>B.Tech (Information Technology.)</li>
<li>MCA.</li>
</ol>
<h4> To view the course structures click <a href=''syllabus.html''>here</a>
</body>
</html>
```

It may be observed from the code written above that a general html document contains two parts, namely, Head and Body.

Head describes the elements that define certain information about an HTML document, for example, what is the title of a page. In the above example, the title is defined using <title> </title> tags which is "Institute of Engineering and Technology".

Body describes the real code for the display of the web page to be developed. Whole of the html document is wrapped within the <body> and </body>tags.

The following section explains the main building block called the HTML Tags. The tags are used in the Body section and belong to two categories called Block Level Tags and Text Level Tags.

Block-Level Tags

They include tags that position the text on the page, set heading levels and create lists. Commonly used block-level elements and their tags are listed below:

- Paragraph <p> and </p>
- Headinglevels: <h1> and </h1> and </h2>..........<h7>and </h7>
- Horizontalrule: <hr>
- Centering: <center> </center>.

Text Level Tags

They are used to markup bits of texts, including changing text appearance or creating hyperlinks. Some commonly used text-level elements are:

- bold <b> and </b>
- italic <I> and </I>
- line break-
- line-anchor <a href="url"> and </a>
- image <img src="url">

12.6 WIRELESS APPLICATION PROTOCOL (WAP)

12.6.1 Introduction

WAP or Wireless Application Protocol is the latest buzzword in IT industry. WAP is said to have started when Ericsson began work on a protocol known as ITTP or Intelligent Terminal Transfer protocol, with the intent of making it easy to add services to mobile telephony platforms. During 1996 and 1997, Nokia began work on a concept called Smart Messaging, and Unwired Planet created HTML. The Handheld Device Markup Language was a markup language similar to HTML, but optimized for devices with small screens such as phones and PDAs. Realizing that these competing protocols could fragment and possibly destroy the potential market, in December or 1997, Ericsson, Motorola, Nokia and Unwired Planet (now known as Phone.com) joined forces to launch the WAP Forum.

Wireless Application Protocol is a new set of standards designed to extend Internet services to the mobile telephony environment that includes, mobile phones, pagers and Personal Digital Assistants (PDAs). WAP is a method of letting a wireless device, usually a mobile phone where WAP is enabled, to view very simple Internet pages, through the existing wireless networks. The web site has to be specially designed for the WAP phone, and the pages have to be fairly small as the data speed on mobile phones is a lot slower than a domestic modem. Also all the phones will have different shape and size screens, so pages will look different depending on the phone you are using.

12.6.2 Motivation for WAP

WAP was designed to meet the constraints of a wireless environment. Both limitations in the network and client are taken into consideration. WAP was created to address three main issues related to data communications across wireless networks:

- Low Bandwidth
- High Latency
- Connectivity

12.6.3 WAP Adaptation to Wireless Devices

WAP is targeted at handheld devices of various kinds. Services should be accessible from a handheld PC as well as from a small phone. WAP address this requirement by taking into consideration the following:

- Small displays
- Limited input facilities
- Limited memory and slow CPU
- Limited battery power

12.6.4 WAP Advantages

Using WAP technology to deliver Internet content and applications to mobile phones offers great potential benefits to both organizations and the endusers. In the near future, it is likely that a well-written and maintained WAP site will be as important for a company's profile as its current web site. Their relatively low cost, ease of use and small size means that WAP enabled phones offer some distinct advantages over portable computers. At present, limited screen size and resolution mean that WAP phones may not be used to surf the Internet in the same way that people use the standard PC web browsers. As the technology grows, so will the scope of the applications offered.

WAP must provide independence across air interfaces and devices. The majority of WAP solutions that have already surfaced in the marketplace must support several forms of independence. These forms of independence are air interface independence, device independence, and full interoperability. The term *air interface independence* means that WAP solutions are to be designed to work optimally with all air interfaces. This allows the largest number of mobile service providers, software developers and handset manufacturers to create solutions for a unified specification. *Device independence* suggest that WAP solutions must also be independent of any particular wireless device. *Interoperability* enforces that any solution component built to be compliant with the WAP specification can interoperate with any other WAP-compliant component.

12.6.5 WAP Specification

WAP specification defines an open, standard architecture and a set of protocols for implementing wireless Internet access. The key elements of WAP specification are:

- A programming model based heavily on the existing WWW programming model. Much like a web browser, a WAP device engages in a series of request/response transactions with content servers that delivers both static and dynamic content.
- A markup language adhering to XML standards. The language used to write applications, the Wireless Markup Language (WML), has a limited number of XML elements (called tags in HTML) and is designed to work with small screen displays. Much like HTML, WML focuses on presenting formatted content and limited execution options for users.
- The WML Script scripting language designed to add computational capabilities to WML.
- A specification for a micro browser to control the user interface. An analysis can be made with a standard web browser. This specification defines how WML and WML Script be interpreted in the handset and presented to the user. It also defines the minimum functionality and the basic user interface a WAP device must have.

12.7 WIRELESS MARKUP LANGUAGE (WML)

12.7.1 Introduction

WAP, similar to HTML, is a tag-based decument language. In particular, it is an application of a generalized markup language, WML shares its heritage with the World Wide Web's HTML and handheld device markup language HDML2. WML is specified as an XML document type it is optimized for specifying presentation and user interaction on limited capability devices such as telephones and other wireles mobile terminals.

Given the wide and varying range of terminals targeted by WAP, WML and its supporting environment were designed with certain small narrow band device constraints in mind including small displays, limited user input facilities, narrow band netword connections, limited memory resources and limited computational resources.

12.7.2 Salient Features of WMI

Support for user input

WML includes a small set of input controls to receive the users input. WML includes a text entry control that supports text and password entry. Text entry fields can be masked to prevent the end user from entering incorrect character types. WML includes an option selection control that allows the author to present the user with a list of options that can set data, navigate cards. WML also includes task invocation controls.

Support for navigation and history stack

WML allows several navigation mechanisms using URLs. It also reveals a first class history mechanism. Navigation includes HTML style hyperlink, inter card navigation well as history navigation elements.

Support for text and images

WML provides the authors with the means to specify text and images to be presented to the user. This may include layout and presentation similar to other markup languages. WML requires the author to specify the Presentation in very general terms and gives the user agents a great deal of freedom to determine exactly how the information is to be presented to the end user. WML also provides a set of text-up elements including various emphasis elements. Another WML advantage is that its character set is UNICODE and this allows presentation of most languages and dialects.

12.8 INTRODUCTION TO VBSCRIPT

12.8.1 Introduction

VBScript or the Microsoft Visual Basic Scripting Edition Language, is a simplified version of the Visual Basic programming language. It is a powerful and easy to learn tool that can be used to add interaction to the web pages. VBScript is a powerful, light-weight scripting language for creating interactive, multimedia-rich, and ActiveX-enhanced Web applications. Before scripting languages such as VBScript, dynamic web pages were created by server-side CGI applications. In some cases, the execution of server-side CGI application is unnecessarily resource intensive. VBScript can be used in such cases to create dynamic content without any interaction with the Web server. If you are using Internet Information Server 3.0 or later, VBScript can also be used to develop server-side web application in the form of Active Server Web. Basically scripts make a web page come alive. A script tells the elements on a page, how to behave and interact with one another. VBScript is more precisely a "scripting environment", which can enhance HTML web pages by making them active, as compared to a simple static display. A script is a series of commands that are executed by the host environment, which is either the client or the server, VBScript can be written to run at either end.

12.8.2 Tools Required to Write VBScript

1. A Text-Editor : Any word-processor or Notepad, Word pad or any HTML editior.
2. An Internet browser that supports VBScript like IE 3.0 or above.
3. VBScript is a scripting language. This means that it does not really do anything on its own and it is dependent on the web page.

12.8.3 VBScript Advantages

1. VBScript is powerful.
2. Lightweight, easy-to-use.
3. Freely available.
4. Crosss-platform.
5. Cross-language scripting language for the Internet.

12.8.4 Sample VBScript Code

All web page editors provide the mechanism to include the VBScript with HTML. However, the embedding of VBScript into HTML document may be done using any editor such as Notepad etc. In an ASP page, VBScript code is included within <% and %>. Following is an example:

```
<HTML>
<HEAD><TITLE>ASP with VBScript </TITLE></HEAD>
<body>
This is a
<% For I=1 To 10%>
Very,
<% Next %>
simple example of VBScript. The current time is <%= NOW() %>
</BODY>
</HTML>
```

When a Web browser displays this ASP, output is:
This is a Very, Very, Very, Very, Very, Very, Very, Very, Very, Very simple example of VBScript.

12.9 INTRODUCTION TO JAVASCRIPT

12.9.1 Introduction

JavaScript was developed by Netscape Communications Corporation, the makers of the popular Netscape Navigator web browser. JavaScript was the first web scripting language to be introduced, and it is by far the most popular. JavaScript is almost as easy to learn as HTML, and it can be included directly in HTML documents. Here are a few of things you can do with JavaScript:

- Add scrolling or changing messages to the brower's status line.
- Validate the contents of a form and make calculations.
- Display message to the user, either as a part of a web page or in alert boxes.
- Animate images or create images that change when you move the mouse over them.
- Detect the browser in use and display different content for different browsers.
- Detect installed plug-ins and notify the user if a plug-in is require.

JavaScript is a kind of script which provides a set of instructions for the browser to perform. Web script provides the same type of instructions for the browser. HTML is one of the computer languages that browens understand. Since HTML is a simple text markup language, it can't respond to the user, make decisions or automate repetitive tasks. Interactive tasks like these require different languages, a programming language or a scripting language. While many programming languages are complex, scripting languages are generally simple. They have simple syntax, can perform tasks with a minimum of commands, and are easy to learn. Web scripting language allows you to combine scripting with HTML to create interactive web pages.

12.9.2 JavaScript vs Java

It's a matter of common misunderstanding that JavaScript and Java are the same or one is the extension of another. In fact, Java and JavaScript share the name only. Both of them are entirely different languages. Java is a programming language development by Sun Microsystems that can be used to create applets, or programs that excute within a web page. Java is a compiled language, but the compiler produces code for virtual machines rather than a real computer. The virtual code is then interpreted by a web browser. This allows a particular Java applet to execute the same way on PCs, Macintoshes, and UNIX machines, and on different browsers—at least in theory.

Here are a few of the differences between JavaScript and Java.

- Java uses simple text commands, which can be included in Java applets, and compiled into clas files to be used on a Web page, but JavaScript is in HTML document itself.
- Java applets are generally displayed in a box within the Web document; JavaScript scripts can affect any part of the web document itself.
- While JavaScript is best suited for simple application and adding interactive features to web pages, Java can be used for incredibly complex applications.

There are many differences between the two but the important thing to remember is that JavaScript and Java are separate languages. They are both useful for different things; in fact, they can be used together to combine their advantages.

12.9.3 Platform to Create JavaScript

JavaScript scripts are stored in simple text files, usually as part of HTML documents. Any editor that can store ASCII text files will work. For Windows computers, some of the recommended editors are:

- Microsoft FrontPage 2000
- NetObjects Script Builder
- Editpad

12.9.4 How JavaScript Fits Into A Web Page

HTML is the language we use to create web documents. These documents consist of a header within the <head> tag and the body of the page within the <body> tags. To add JavaScript to a page, we use a similar tag <script>. The script tag tells the browser to start treating the text as a script and the </script tag returns to the regularly scheduled HTML. There are actually four different places where we might use scripts in a HTML document:

- In the body of the pages. In this case, the output of the script is displayed as a part of the HTML document when the browser loads the page.
- In the header of the page between the <head> tags. Scripts in the header are not executed immediately, but can be referred to by other scripts.
- Within an HTML tag. Thus is called an event handler and allows the script to work with HTML elements.
- In a separate file entirely. JavaScript supports the use of files with the . is extension containing scripts: these can be included by specifying a file in the <script> tag.

12.9.5 Displaying the JavaScript on Web Browser

Like HTML, JavaScript requires a web browser to be displayed, and different browsers may display it differently. Unlike HTML, the results or browser incompatibility the Java Script are more drastic rather than simply displaying your text incorrectly, the script may not execute at all, may display an error message, or may even crash the browser. However, since the JavaScript language was developed by

Netscape, the newest features of the language are supported only under Netscape Navigator. Internet Explorer does support the basic JavaScript commands, and newer versions may implement all of the new features.

12.10 JAVA SERVER PAGES (JSP)

Introduction

Java Server Pages technology allows web developers and designers to rapidly develop and easily maintain, information-rich, dynamic web pages that leverage existing business systems. JSP technology enables rapid development of web-based applications that are platform independent. JavaServer Pages technology separates the user interface from content generation enabling designers to change the overall page layout without altering the underlying dynamic content. JSP is a server-side technology that allows developers to create web-based applications that can make use of components that are developed in the Java programming language, according to the JavaBeans specification. In some respects, it can be compared to server-side scripting languages such as ASP and PHP. JSP is similar to PHP in the C-styly syntax of the Java language, but JSP was also designed to be extendable using components like ASP.

Java Server Pages allows you to mix regular, static HTML with dynamically-generated HTML. Many web pages that are built by CGI programs are mostly static, with the dynamic part limited to a few small locations. But most CGI variations, including servlets, make you generate the entire page via your program, even though most of it is always the same. JSP lets you create the two parts separately. You normally give your file a JSP extension. The JSP page just get converted to a normal servlet, with the static HTML simply being printed to the output stream associated with the servlet's service method.

JSP Building Blocks

Following are the main JSP constructs to create JSP documents. These are:

1. Scripting elements.
2. Directives.
3. Actions.

Scripting elements let you specify Java codes that will become a part of the resultant servlet. Directives let you control the overall structure of the servlet, and *actions* let you specify existing components that should be used, and otherwise control the behavior of the JSP engine. JavaServer Pages technology uses XML-like tags and scriptlets written in the Java programming language to encapsulate the logic that generates the content for the page. Java Serve Pages technology is an extension of the Java Servlet technology. JSP technology and servlets provide an attractive alternative to other types of dynamic web scripting/programming that offers platform independence, enhanced performance, separation of logic from display, ease of administration, extensibility into the enterprise and most importantly, ease of use.

JSP pages share the "Write Once, Run Anywhere" characteristic of Java technology, JSP technology is a key component in the Java 2 Platform, Enterprise Edition, Sun's highly scaleable architecture for enterprise applications.

Benefits and Demerits of JSP

JSP Advantages

1. Extremely fast.
2. Platform independent.

3. Highly scaleable with built-in support for distributed processing.
4. Compatible with all major web servers.
5. Portable to non-Microsoft web servers.
6. It is more poweful and easier to use.
7. Extensibility into the enterprise.

Demerits of JSP

1. Java Code is required.
2. JSP actually demands putting Java code in the page.
3. JSP technology is far more complex than the counterpart to learn.
4. Lousy looping.
5. JSP page syntax errors can cause surprisingly odd useless error messages. This is due to the fact the page is transformed into a servlet and then compiled.
6. Needs a compiler.
7 Requires more space.
8. JSP consumes extra hard drive space and extra memory space.

12.11 ENTERPRISE JAVA BEANS

Introduction

Enterprise Java Beans (EJB) is a specification model for server side computing which is used in the distributed application environment. The Enterprise JavaBeans specification is a dramatic step forward in the standardization and simplification of distributed object computing. It is a major piece of the Java 2 Enterprise Edition (J2EE) platform and is receiving much support from the distributed object community. Many tools are currently available or will be available in the near future to help accelerate the development of EJB components.

Suppose you need to develop a multi-tiered application to view and update records in a database through a web interface. You can write a database application using JDBC, a web interface using JSP/ servlets, and distributed system using CORBA/RMI. But what extra factors must you consider while developing a distributed object system rather than just knowing API's? Here are the issues:

Performance

The distributed objects you create must perform well, as they could potentially serivce many clients at a time. You'll need to use optimization techniques such as caching as well as pooling resources like database connections. You'll also have to manage the lifecycle of your distributed objects.

Scalability

The distributed objects must also be scaleable. Scalability in a distrubuted application means that the number of instances of your distributed objects can be increased and moved into additional machines without modifying any code.

Security

A distributed object must often manage the authorization of the clients that access it. Ideally, you can add new users and roles to it without recompilation.

Distributed Transactions

A distributed object should be able to reference distributed transactions. For example, if you are working with two separate databases, you should be able to update them simultaneously within the same transaction and roll them both back if a certain criteria is not met.

Reusability

The ideal distributed object can be effortlessly moved onto another vendor's appolication server. It would be nice if you could resell a distributed object component without making special modifications, or buy someone else's component and use it without having to recompile or rewrite it.

Availability

If one of the machines in the system goes down, clients should automatically fall-over to backup copies of the objects running on other machines.

These considerations, in addition to the business problems that you set out to solve, can make for a daunting development project. However, all the issues except for your business problem are redundant-solutions must be reinvented for every distributed business application. Sun along with other leading distributed object vendors, realized that sooner or later every development team would be reinventing these particular solutions, so they created the Enterprise JavaBeans specification (EJB). EJB describes a server-side component model that tackles all of the considerations mentioned above using a standard approach. This approach allows developers to create business components called EJBs that are isolated from low-level "plumbing" code and that focus solely on providing business logic. Because EJB's are defined in a standard way, they can be vendor independent.

12.11.1 JavaBeans vs EJBs

Because of the similarity in names, there is much confusion about the relationship between the JavaBeans component model and the Enterprise JavaBeans specification. While both the JavaBeans and Enterprise JavaBeans specifications share the same objectives in promoting reuse and portability of Java code between development and deployment tools with the use of standard design patterns, the motives behind each specification are geared to solve different problems. The standards defined in the JavaBeans component model are designed for creating reusable components that are typically used in IDE development tools and are commonly, although not exclusively, visual components. The Enterprise JavaBeans specification defines a component model for developing server side Java code. Because EJBs can potentially run on many different server-side platforms-including mainframes that do not have visual displays—an EJB cannot make use of graphical libraries such as AWT of Swing.

The EJB specification describes a server-side component model. It defines six roles that are used to perform the tasks in development and deployment as well as defining the components of the system. These roles are used in the development, deployment and running of a distributed system. Vendors, administrators and developers play the various roles, to allow the partitioning of technical and domain knowledge. The vendor provides a technically sound framework and the developers create domain-specific components; for example, an "accounting" component. The same party can perform one or many roles. The roles defined in the EJB specification are summarized as follows.

12.11.2 Types of EJB

The Enterprise JavaBeans specification defines different types of EJBs that have different characteristics and behaviors. Two categories of EJBs have been defined in the specification. Session Beans and Entity Beans, and each category has variations.

Session Beans

Session Beans are used to represent Use-Cases or Workflow on behalf of a client. They represent operations on persistent data, but not the persistent data itself. There are two types of Session Beans, Stateless and Stateful. All Session Beans must implement the *javax.ejb.SessionBean* interface. The EJB Container governs the life of a Session Bean.

Stateless Session Beans are the simplest type of EJB component to implement. They do not maintain any conversational state with clients between method invocations so they are easily reusable on the server side and because they can be cached, they scale well on demand. When using Stateless Session Beans, all states must be stored outside of the EJB.

Stateful Session Beans maintain state between invocations. They have a one-to-one logical mapping to a client and can maintain state within themselves. The EJB Container is responsible for pooling and caching of Stateful Session Beans, which is achieved through Passivation and Activation. If the EJB Container crashes, data for all Stateful Session Beans could be lost. Some high-end EJB Containers provide recovery for Stateful Session Beans.

Entity Beans

Entity Beans are components that represent presistent data and behavior of this data. Entity Beans can be shared among multiple clients, the same way that data in a database can be shared. The EJB Container is responsible for caching Entity Beans and for maintaining the integrity of the Entity Beans. The life of an Entity Bean outlives the EJB Container, so if an EJB Container crashes, the Entity Bean is still expected to be available when the EJB Container again becomes available.

There are two types of Entity Beans: those with Container Managed persistence and those with Bean-Managed persistence. A *Container Managed Persistence* (CMP) Entity Bean has its persistence implemented on its behalf by the EJB Container. Through attributes specified in the deployment descriptor, the EJB Container will map the Entity Bean's attributes to some persistent store (usually, but not always, a database). CMP reduces the development time for the EJB, as well as dramatically reducing the amount of code required.

A Bean Managed Persistence (BMP) Entity Bean has its persistence implemented by the Enterprise Bean Provider. The Enterprise Bean Provider is responsible for implementing the logic required to create a new EJB, update some attributes of the EJBs, delete and EJB and find an EJB from persistent store. This usually involves writing JDBC code to interact with a database or other persistent store. With BMP, the developer is in full control of how the Entity Bean persistence is managed. BMP also provides flexibility where a CMP implementation may not be available. For example, if you want to create an EJB that wrapped some code on an existing mainframe system, you could write your persistence using CORBA.

12.12 EXTENSIBLE MARKUP LANGUAGE (XML)

Introduction

HTML is still considered to be most favorite markup language and millions of web pages have been written using HTML. Now people have started realizing the inherent limitations with HTML and a swing towards XML is being felt. Following are some of the limitations of HTML which have been reported.

- HTML lacks syntactic checking i.e. validation of HTML code.
- HTML is not content aware.
- HTML is not suitable for data interchange.
- HTML lacks a robust linking mechanism
- HTML is not extensible.
- Above all, HTML defines and uses its fixed set of tags. XML solves this problems with limited flexibility.

XML is derived from SGML. SGML (Standard Generalized Markup Language) is a meta language or a language for describing markup languages. HTML is one such markup language and is therefore called an SGML application. XML uses the features of SGML that it needs and tries to incorporate the lessons learned from HTML. XML is a set of rules for defining the semantic tags that breaks the documents into parts. The tags in XML may be used in such a way that XML makes easy various web development tasks which were quite painful in doing with HTML. Various features of XML are listed below. These feature make XML a programmers choice for web development.

- XML can use existing web protocols (such as HTTP and MIME) and mechanisms (such as URLs) and it does not impose any additional requirements.
- XML supports a wide variety of applications. It is difficult to support a lot of applications with just HTML; hence, the growth of scripting language.
- It is easy to write programs that process XML documents.
- The number of optional features in XML has been kept to an absolute minimum.
- XML documents are reasonably clear to the lay person.
- The design of XML is formal and concise.
- XML documents are easy to create.

XML is commonly called a subset of SGML but actually it is an application profile of SGML; whereas HTML uses SGML and is an application of SGML, XML is just SGML on a smaller scale. From HTML, XML inherits the use of web address (URLs) to point to other objects.

Application areas of XML

XML is being considered so powerful and flexible that many people are considering it for several purposes other than just a markup language. XML is best suited for the applications shown below:

- XML may be used to describe meta content regarding documents or online resources.
- To publish and exchange database contents.
- As a messaging format for communication between application programs.

12.12.1 XML Advantages

Following are the major advantages with XML:

1. Modularity

HTML possesses an implied DTD (Document Type Definition), hard-wired into web browsers. SGML has a limitless number of DTDs, but only one can be used for one document. XML enables you to leave out the DTD altogether or combine separate DTD into one compound instance.

2. Extensibility

XML's powerful linking mechanism allows you to link to the material without requiring the link target to be physically present in the object.

3. Distribution

XML introduces composite documents, i.e. documents composed of fragments of other documents that are automatically assembled to form what is displayed at a particular moment.

4. International character dealing

Both HTML and SGML rely heavily on ASCII, which makes using foreign characters very difficult. XML is based on Unicode and requires all XML software to support Unicode as well.

5. Data orientation

XML operates on data orientation rather than readability by humans.

OBJECTIVE TYPE QUESTIONS

Multiple Choice

1. Which of the following is true for Java?
   (a) Java is object oriented (b) Java is portable
   (c) Java is multithreaded (d) All of these
2. A Java Byte Code is
   (a) Interpreted (b) Compiled (c) Both of these (d) None of these
3. Which of the following is true for Java?
   (a) Java is a Universal (b) Java is extension of HTML Programming language
   (c) Java Script is a variant (d) Java support Multithreading of Java
4. Which of the following are programming language?
   (a) Java (b) HTML (c) Java Script (d) None of these
5. Which language is mostly used for WAP applications?
   (a) HTML (b) C++ (c) COBOL (d) WML
6. Which of the following are called scripting language?
   (a) VB Script (b) Java script (c) Both of these (d) None of these
7. Which of the following are basic building block of Java Server Pages?
   (a) Scripting Elements (b) Directives (c) Actions (d) All of these
8. Which of the following are true?
   (a) HTML is not content aware (b) HTML is not extensible
   (c) HTML lacks syntactic (d) All of above checking
9. A java Applet can be in following state
   (a) Idle State (b) Dead State (c) Initialization State (d) All of these
10. RMI stands for
    (a) Remote Method Invocation (b) Revised Module Invocation
    (c) Retail Method Invocation (d) None of these

Answers

1- d, 2-a, 3-d, 4-a, 5-d, 6-c, 7-d, 8-d, 9-d, 10-a

State True or False

1. Nature of E Commerce projects are different from traditional IT projects. [True] [False]
2. E Commerce project may fail due to technological development. [True] [False]
3. Java can not be used for purpose other than internet application. [True] [False]
4. Java program can be executed in web pages only. [True] [False]
5. Java Script is another version of Java. [True] [False]
6. HTML is a true programming language. [True] [False]
7. WML is used for wireless application. [True] [False]
8. VB script is extension of Visual Basic. [True] [False]
9. XML is content aware. [True] [False]
10. HTML is not suitable for data interchange. [True] [False]

Answers

1-True, 2-True, 3-False, 4-False, 5-False, 6-False, 7-True, 8-False, 9-True, 10-True.

SELECTED EXERCISES

1. What is meant by E-commerce application development cycles? Explain the various stages of E-commerce application development.

2. What are the activities to be undertaken in Business requirement stages of E-commerce application development?
3. Why is the maintenance stage supposed to be longest stage in terms of time?
4. What are the reason for which the changes in the scope of E-commerce project are so frequent? Why E-commerce projects are subjected to the modifications?
5. Development schedules in the web site development project are dramatically short but all later stages require more time to complete the project. Explain why?
6. What are the short comings in the development phase of web project in comparison to traditional software projects?
7. Why Beta version of technologies and software are frequently used in web site development project? What are the disadvantages of using beta technologies?
8. Why is the costing part in a web project so critical? Explain the reason why costing of the web projects are not usually so accurate?
9. Compare the traditional software development life cycle and E-commerce application development life cycles. What are the basic differences in handling these software projects?
10. Explain the reasons why Java is considered as the best language for Internet applications?
11. What are the advantages of Java over other programming languages?
12. What is Java Bytecode? How this feature of Java makes the language platform independent?
13. Explain how a Java program is written and executed. What is meant by JDK (Java Development Kit)?
14. What are Java Applets? How the Java applet executed? Explain with an example.
15. What are the common misconceptions about Java.
16. Do you think that very soon Java will replace all other programming languages? Justify your answer.
17. What is the relationship between Java and HTML. Is it true that Java is another form of HTML? If no, then why?
18. What is the relationship between the JavaScript and Java programming language? Do they have anything common?
19. What are the differences between a Java application and Java applet?
20. Explain the various stages of Java Applet life cycle.
21. Explain with a suitable example how Java applets are included into web pages (HTML code).
22. What is meant by HTML? Why is HTML not considered as a programming language?
23. What does the term Hypertext mean in Hyper Text Markup Language? How Hypertext is related with Hyper Media?
24. What are HTML tags? What is the role of HTML tags in HTML code? Explain any two tags in brief.
25. List any five text level tags in HTML.
26. List and explain any two Body level tags of HTML.
27. What is Wireless Application Protocol? What are basic requirements for WAP application?
28. What are the advantages of WAP? List and explain any two areas where WAP can be used.
29. What is the language used for WAP application?
30. List the salient features of Wireless Markup Language (WML). How WML is different from HTML?
31. What are WAP sites? How are they different from traditional web sites?
32. What is VBScript? Is there any relationship between VBScript and Visual Basic? What are the application areas of VBScript?
33. What is JavaScript? What is common between JavaScript and Java programming languages.
34. What are the application areas of JavaScript? How is JavaScript different from VBScript?
35. How does a JavaScript code fit into a web page? Explain with an example.
36. What are Java Server Pages? What are the advantages of using Java Server Pages? List any two demerits of using Java Server Pages.
37. What are Enterprise Java Beans (EJB)? What are the advantages of EJBs.
38. What are the types of Enterprise Java Beans? What are the essential differences between Session beans and Entity beans?
39. What is XML? Discuss various areas where XML may be used.
40. Compare XML with HTML. What are the shortcomings of HTML and how they are solved in XML?

13

INFORMATION TECHNOLOGY APPLICATIONS

Contents

- Introduction
- Educational & Research Network (ERNET)
- National Informatics Center Network (NICNET)
- Other Important Dedicated Networks
- Developments in India
- Application of Information Technology

13 INFORMATION TECHNOLOGY APPLICATIONS

13.1 INTRODUCTION

The then chairman of NASSCOM, Late Mr. Dewang Mehta, had once given a slogan "*Roti Kapda Makan Aur Bandwidth*". A man of vision could realize that apart from the three basic necessities, a good communication infrastructure is essential for the development of any country in the modern perspective. In the current Information Technology scenario, various organizations and companies all over the world are relying heavily on access to information in the electronic medium. The Internet is the major source of information in knowledge based societies. There has been a major thrust in both the developed and developing countries to establish a robust and sufficient communication infrastructure. The early lead in infrastructure development by the different government organizations has witnessed considerable economic growth. In a noteworthy statement, the Prime Minister of Malaysia said: "it can be no accident that there is today no wealthy developed country that is information poor, and no information rich country that is poor and underdeveloped". No wonder that among the Asian countries, Malaysia was among the pioneers to reap the maximum benefit of Information Technology revolution and it is among the few countries along with India to have passed an Information Technology Act. Trading through the electronic medium in this country has become a reality. More and more people are taking advantage of IT. In any knowledge based society, early access to relevant information is the key to success. Information explosion through Internet has been tapped well by western countries and they have profitably utilized the Information Technology in different sectors like Banking, Agriculture, Transportation, Environment, Business and Entertainment and Education etc. After penetrating the western countries, the Information Technology has started making an impact in India also. The Central and State Governments have taken several initiatives for a wide propagation and utilization of Information Technology. The last decade in India has witnessed a major Information technology revolution. An example is the growing use of Internet. In a very short span of time, the use of computers at offices and homes has become a reality. Use of Internet at office and home is increasing day by day at an exponential rate. Inspite of this, studies show that out of the total population of Internet Users, USA contributes more than 50%, followed by the European countries. The Asian countries contribute merely 10-15%. Thus, there is a lot of scope for improvement and growth. The government of India has started several projects in this regard. ERNET and NICNET are good examples of these project.

13.2 EDUCATIONAL AND RESEARCH NETWORK (ERNET)

The Educational and Research Network (ERNET) was initiated in 1987 by the Department of Electronics (DoE) to provide computer communication for the academic and research community in India. ERNET is a joint project of the Department of Electronics (DoE), Government of India and United Nations Development Program (UNDP). It is India's first TCP/IP network set up for fostering educational and research activities in the premier institution and research laboratories. The main focus of ERNET project was to provide the Internet access to software developers, students, research scholars and academician at the premier research institutes and laboratories. Full fledged Internet connectivity was started few years later by another government agency VSNL (Videsh Sanchar Nigam Limited). It is an organization which has opened India's long distance communication services to the public. It is providing services such as E-mail, file transfer, remote login and database access. Another government agency, the National Informatics Center (NIC) was set up in the late 1980s to provide computer support to the government and public sector undertakings. It also provides limited Internet access to exporters and educational and research institutions.

ERNET involved the participation of eight educational and research institutions in the country. The five Indian Institutes of Technology at Mumbai, Kharagpur, Kanpur, Chennai and New Delhi, the Indian Institute of Science, Bangalore, the National Center for Software Technology, Mumbai and the Department of Electronics (DE) New Delhi are serving as nodal centers for the ERNET project. The main objectives of this project are given below:

1. To establish a countrywide computer network involving premier educational and research institutions in the country in order to foster academic and industrial research. One of the objectives of this network is to provide connectivity to the educational and research institutions abroad.
2. To develop Informatics infrastructure in the country.
3. Human resource development by providing education and training to increase the awareness of information resources available through the Internet.
4. To open the gateway to the world to provide an information base to the servers located abroad.

ERNET uses the network infrastructure in two folds. It uses at terrestrial wide area network that interconnects the backbone nodes as well as a VSAT based link that interconnects the backbone nodes and other remote VSAT sites. There are few other service providers that have also started providing the Internet services under the government setup. These are 'SOFTNET' by Software Technology Park of India, NICNET by National Information Center and Gateway Internet Access Services (GIAS) by the Department of Telecommunication and VSNL.

ERNET Nodal Centers

As mentioned earlier, there are eight nodal centers set up by the government for the successful conclusion of ERNET project. These centers have been established at premier education and research institutes. These nodes of ERNET are connected to each through leased lines. Approximately two hundred academic and research institutions are connected to each other through ERNET in the country. Thousands of academicians and researchers are being benefitted by sharing the information across these institutions through ERNET. ERNET also provides international access by using a 64 Kbps leased line at the National Center for Software Technology, Mumbai and it is also planning to establish a satellite communication to provide its services to centers located in remote places which do not have good data communication links.

13.3 NATIONAL INFORMATICS CENTER NETWORK (NICNET)

The establishment and growth of a good network infrastructure has been relatively slow in India due to its poor telecommunications infrastructure. National Informatics Center (NIC) was set up in the late 1980s to provide computer support to the government and public sector undertakings. NICNET (National Informatics Center Network) is one of the most important networks connecting several government departments and organizations in the country. The objective of this project is to provide the network and communication infrastructure for fast information storage and data transfer across various government organizations. This network provides both ways data communication for government agencies. It is also serving as a backbone for fostering the development planning and administrative monitoring by the government. NICNET is a satellite-based communication network using approximately five hundred earth stations and connecting government agencies at the central, state and district levels. The NIC is also developing the software for facilitating the government activities, project monitoring and economic planning. Although a government agency, the NIC is increasingly functioning like a commercial entity by distributing a variety of third party software products as well as its own applications.

NICNET now-a-days is providing limited V-SAT and dial-up Internet access to Government departments and Software Export Groups. It started its shell access initially at 2 Kbps, at 2400 bps and now-a-days it is providing high speed TCP-IP access through 64 Kbps V-SAT links.

ERNET and NICNET are considered as India's first ISPs that have provided internet access. However, several other government agencies like Department of Telecom (DoT) and VSNL (Videsh Sanchar Nigam Limited) are offering Internet services to a variety of subscribers on commercial basis. Several private organizations have also been given permission to provide internet services. Some of the important Internet service providers in the private sector are Satyam, BPL, HCL Avadh on Line etc.

13.4 OTHER IMPORTANT DEDICATED NETWORKS

CMC Ltd (Formerly Computer Maintenance Corporation), a government company has established it's own network called INDONET for the computer users community in the country. The network provides distributed data processing facilities on an all-India basis to large organizations using CMC's computers for their data processing operations. CMC has also taken up large software projects for the automation of Railways and other government departments. Other important networks already under operation under the aegis of the government are SIRNET (Scientific and Industrial Network), BTISNET (Biotechnology Information System Network), and SOFTNET by Software Technology Park. All these networks are self sufficient and are being used for file transfers. E-mails, video telephony and other Internet services.

13.5 DEVELOPMENTS IN INDIA

India being one of the largest nations in the world, with a rich heritage of education and training, possesses tremendous potential for economic growth through information technology. This is evident from the phenomenal growth of IT companies in India. The IT industry in the past decade has shown an exponential growth. In comparison to other developing countries, India has shown a significant growth in the utilization of information technologies and in managing information. One study shows that the sales of Personal Computers in India have been growing at more than 20% per year. A contributing factor in this growth was the intense competition between various hardware companies which led to a sharp decline in the prices of PCs, networking equipment and other peripherals. There are three areas related to Information technology which are significant for industrial growth. These are (i) a National Information Technology Policy, (ii) guidelines for establishing a communication and information infrastructure and focus on education and, (iii) training in IT. National information policy is required to facilitate the commercial activities on the internet. India has already passed and implemented an Information Technology Bill, which has formed a basis for Electronic Governance. Various tasks like lodging an FIR by E-mails, communication and meeting on the Internet, seeking the desired information on the internet about government organization can now be done. Similarly, payments by the customers on the net have a legal status. A national policy is very much required to remove the legal and administrative hassles by adopting novel ways to strengthen the business using Information technology. National information policy in developing countries is concentrated on trade, international relations, national security and technology. The regulatory framework in developed countries is enforced to protect investment, intellectual property and individual privacy in the information market. The legal framework addresses the private sector involvement, skilled human resources, standards and implementation aspects. In most developing countries, a regulatory framework hardly exists for the information work in the country. This is urgently required as the rapid growth of information technology is changing the mode of business. The virtual corporation, electronic market and Electronic Business, customer relationship, product assessment activities have changed the modes of business considerably after adopting the innovative applications of Information Technology. While the information technology including telecommunication has penetrated every market in the developed world, the developing countries still largely view information technology as only a means to support MIS, finance and accounting facilities and data processing.

The work force in developing countries is changing from the labor-intensive to knowledge-based activities. In developed countries, surveys have shown that the usage of Internet is closely associated with higher education. The same concept applies to a developing nation like India. An Education and Training policy is required to improve the literacy rate. There is a difference between computer literacy and conventional literacy. A computer literate person is one who possesses the experience of handling personal computers, is capable of preparing the documents, writing the E-mail etc. It is the responsibility of the government departments to work together to increase literacy in developing countries. Only through this, can people in the country better themselves and compete globally to access and disseminate information using the Internet. In this context, the training of information professionals should be given priority. The trained information professionals would be able to utilize the Internet more efficiently and will be more effective in acquiring, organizing and disseminating information.

To cater to the growing demand of taking full benefit of Information technology revolution, the government has taken several initiatives like forming a Information Technology ministry at the Central level. Several state governments have also formed separate IT ministries. Several initiatives for improving the problem of bandwidth for data transfer and communication have also been taken by the government agencies.

13.6 APPLICATION OF INFORMATION TECHNOLOGY

13.6.1 Multimedia Applications

Multimedia is the term used to denote the combination of multiple mediums. The term Multi indicates many and Media indicates the means adopted for communication. We can define a multimedia system as a computer controlled environment which is used to process individual images, sound and text. Multimedia includes the combination of text, audio, video, graphics and animation. It has become a popular technology in the last decade and widely used in advertisement, cinematography and fashion design. Multimedia is closely related with interactive videos that produce information represented as animation, audio, video, graphics text etc. on demand. It is a powerful media to provide effective interaction between the users and information. Interactive multimedia is finding application in geographical information system, business and corporate presentations, education and training. Several software products for manipulating and editing the information represented in audio, video, graphics and animation have already arrived in the market. Some of these are Corel Draw, Sound Blaster, Macromedia Flash and MS Office tools. A typical multimedia presentation comprises an effective use of textual matter, images, digital audio and digital videos etc. The combination of all these mediums can be profitably used in entertainment, business communication and knowledge transfer. It also finds a valuable application in the medical field with the use of communication technology. Telemedicine is the area where doctors can be consulted by patients located in remote places. The patient can submit his diagnosis reports online to the doctor in the form of images, sound and videos. This technique uses video conferencing sessions where both doctor and patient can consult each other. Various components of multimedia are discussed below:

Textual Contents

Text, in its most simple form, is the collection of alphabets, numerals and special characters. Text may be composed using alphabets, numerals and special characters like,"@ # $ etc. Text is considered to be the most dominating component in any Multimedia Presentation.

Audio

Audio or sound is produced by vibration of waves and it is a physical characteristic of matter or substance. Its outcome is the waveform produced through oscillation. Audio may be analysed in terms of parameters like amplitude, frequency, bass etc. Several methods have been developed for storage and retrieval of sound using the digital computer. There are several software programs which may be used to store, produce and process the information contained in the audio. Audio editing, which is modifying the sound quality by changing the parameters through the software, is quite common now-a-days. The quality of audio can be interpreted by hearing only. Audio serves as an important data type and it helps various experts in taking decisions. The audio may be stored in a database in the form of files and audio data may be processed by the digital computer. For example, mixing of sound or modifying the sound parameters like frequency, pitch, amplitude, bass etc. is done frequently to enhance the impact of presentations. The inclusion of sound or audio makes any multimedia presentation much more effective.

Images and Graphics

Image is the spatial representation of an object or entity. It contains lot of information value in the sense that many times an image itself is sufficient to trigger a decision making process. There are several ways to represent an image in the digital medium. Bit Map Images are the basic mechanism to store any image in digital form. The image parameters like color, intensity, hue etc. are stored in the form of numbers and the same may be used to generate the images. GIF, JPEG, TIFF are other formats used to represent images on digital computers. Using images in multimedia presentation, adds enormous value to the effectiveness of the presentation.

Digital Video

Video is the collection of synchronized images and sounds. When several continuous images are produced before the eye at a regular interval with sound the effect of motion is produced. Video is also sometimes called Motion Video. Since a video contains many images and sound, it requires a huge space for storage. MPEG is the group accredited by ISO for the production and representation of video. The video camera may be used to capture the video and it may be stored in the digital computer. There are several software programs by which the video may be played and even edited. The video is perhaps the most powerful medium to detail out any event.

Interactive Multimedia is being used in many domains like advertisement, fashion design, textile design, corporate training, education, games etc.

13.6.2 Office Applications and Desk Top Publishing

Computers are also finding applications in solving day-to-day office problems. In any office, be it government or private organization, the processing of several types of documents e.g. reports, orders, contract, form, letters etc. is required. The computers can be used to create, store and retrieve as well as, edit and print the document. An electronic office uses computers for procurements of files, office communication, assisting in decision making and administrative work. Several software products are available for assisting office and secretarial work. These are word processing tools like MS Word, Word Star, Chi Writer etc, spread sheets using Lotus 123, Excel etc. and for database application, FoxPro, Fox Base etc are used. MS Access is also used in offices for day-to-day database application. Computers are being used for Desk Top Publishing. The DTP work includes the production of documents with text, images and graphics. Ordinary word processors like Word, Chi may not take up the job of desk top publishing. There are several softwares dedicated for desk top publishing like Page Maker, Ventura etc. DTP software uses a page layout and allows the user to enter the text and place the images and other graphic objects on to it. All these objects can be adjusted by modifying the size and other parameter to fit on to the page. These software programs are being used in the publishing industry for the production of newspaper, books and magazines.

13.6.3 Education

Information technology has proved to be extremely useful for education and research. It is not too far from now, when people used to collect the relevant information in the library journals and books. A lot of time used to be wasted in finding the relevant information source. With the popularity of the World Wide Web and easy accessibility to the Internet, it now takes a few seconds to find any desired information. Information Technology is considered as the convergence of several fields of science, technology and communication. It can be profitably used in education as it supports the thinking process by providing a set of examples to solve a problem with the use of Instructional Software. The Instructional Software has a complete range, starting from school kids to professionals. It is not uncommon to keep important lectures and presentations in digital forms like CDs. In several schools/ institutions, computers are being used as teaching aids. Computer Assisted Instruction (CAI) softwares are being written by professionals for school children. These software present the problems and solutions in a systematic manner which help the students to logically understand the subject. In colleges and universities, the lecture series of various professors are recorded and may be referred later on. Virtual Classrooms and teaching are gaining momentum day by day.

Computers may be used for individual and collaborative learning in schools. There are several softwares, which explain the concepts of mathematics, logical reasoning, basic science by repetitive presentations. A student may keep interacting with the problems and these problems are designed in such a way that the student gets thorough understanding of the subject. Computers may be used for classroom teaching and instruction by providing a full and effective multimedia presentation on the topics. Collaborative software for education are used where groups of students take up the problem collectively and this provide ample scope for group learning.

13.6.4 Banking and Financial Institutions

Information technology has helped the banking and financial institutions to automate their business process and minimize the transactional delays. In the banking and financial institutions, the performance is measured in terms of processing speed and customer satisfaction. With the application of computers, it has become possible to clear the recurring dues like payment for electricity, telephone bill, shopping bill by instructing the bank for payment from customers account. Telebanking is a good example of this. After the introduction of computer in banks, online funds transfer from one account to another has also become possible. The customer may instruct the bank's computer for payment to a third party, account transfer after providing the authentication detail. Authentication of credit card, debit card and other electronic payment instrument by the bank has also facilitated shopping, purchasing and minimized the transaction delays. Internet banking offers both bank and customers a huge opportunity by convenience. With the introduction of ATM (Automatic Teller Machine), it has become possible for customers to withdraw cash from the bank round the hour. Now it is not necessary for the customer to move down to the bank premises for collecting the cash. The ATMs are installed or are being installed at several places in most towns.

13.6.5 Weather Forecasting

Weather Forecasting is one of the important areas of application of information technology. Traditional weather forecasting methods were based upon the analysis and prediction through experiences. It was a combination of both science and art. In modern days, after utilizing the enormous processing capabilities of digital computers, several scientific methods for weather forecasting have been developed. These methods employ numerous factors such as availability of data, previous experiences and the level of difficulty that the forecast situation presents. In the modern and scientific techniques, it is possible to read the weather maps in digital medium and these maps may be processed in such a way, that a pattern for the next few days is obtained. Based on the forecaster experience and projected weather maps, the forecasting is done. Use of computer has facilitated the job of data processing related with weather. The size of data used for weather forecasting is normally huge, therefore use of computers for processing these data is essential. Following are the techniques used in weather forecasting:

Conventional Weather Forecasting

Conventional methods of weather forecasting used the most simple method of prediction based on yesterday's weather and the experience of the forecaster. This method is called Persistence method. It is perhaps the most simple way of weather forecasting. In this method, the weather forecaster uses the present day weather as a basis for declaration of the next day's weather. It is assumed that the weather conditions do not normally change drastically. The persistence method works for the geographical region where the weather conditions do not change very fast and the weather maps are changed slowly. For the geographical regions where the weather conditions change very frequently, these forecasting methods do not work.

Another important technique for making a forecast is through weather maps. The weather forecasting methods which employ the prediction based on the weather maps and experience of the forecaster are called Trend Methods. These methods involve determining the speed and direction of the movement of elements, air masses, fronts, pressure systems, and areas of clouds and precipitation. Using this information, the forecaster can predict the location of these elements in the future. Differences in latitude, possible acceleration/deceleration of storm systems, local effects such as topography, bodies of water etc. are some of the important parameters used for weather forecasting using trend methods.

Analog Methods for Weather Forecasting

The Analog Method works on a very simple principle. This method compares the weather condition of the day with the weather condition in the past when the weather scenario looked very similar. Based on the past record, the weather for the coming days is predicted. It is assumed that the previous effects on the weather will continue because similar causes have similar effects once again. This approach works well for the region where the climatic variables do not change dramatically. A similar weather conditions can be examined from the past weather data for that particular area and depending upon the past experiences or data, a forecasting may be done. The use of analog method is difficult and complex because it is very difficult to find a perfect match of similar weather conditions in the past. Various weather features rarely line up in the same location and in the same manner as they did on the previous occasion. Even small differences between the current time data and the comparing past data can lead to very different results.

Computer based Numerical Methods for Weather Forecasting

The numerical methods for weather forecasting use the processing capability of digital computers. Numerical Weather Prediction is another technique based on numerical methods, where data are processed by a digital computer according to forecasting algorithms. The weather maps in digitized form take huge space and multiple maps for different conditions are processed in order to predict the weather of tomorrow. Several Forecast Models have been developed for weather forecasting and are executed on the supercomputers. They provide predictions based on many atmospheric variables such as temperature, pressure, wind speed, direction and rainfall. A forecaster examines how the features predicted by the computer will interact to produce the day's weather. The numerical weather prediction methods are also not accurate because of the complex nature of atmospheric conditions, therefore, the equations used by these models to simulate the atmosphere are not always correct. Despite these shortcomings, the numerical weather forecasting methods are still considered as the most accurate forecasting methods.

There is another similar method for Weather Forecasting through Textual Examinations.

This technique uses the data providing a clear picture of the weather in the previous days and the current data is analyzed for the weather prediction based on previous data. For example, a previous day climatic data is analyzed which gives the precipitation, temperatures, humidity and other parameters. Maps are then plotted at regular intervals to get the trend of weather changes. These maps are analyzed and weather for future is predicted.

Computers are very much required to develop weather forecasting models. Weather forecasting requires enormous data to be processed, therefore usage of computer for this application not only saves time but also a high degree of precision in the forecasting is obtained.

13.6.6 Graphics and Image Processing

Image processing and publishing is being used in almost all areas of life. Processing an image without a computer is a complex and tedious job. It takes many hours to conceptualize the image and edit it conventionally. With the introduction of computers, processing an image has become quite simple.

There are areas like Geographic Information System, Path Finder etc. which are based on image processing. Image processing is being used in weather forecasting where the images captured by satellites are analyzed and processed to study the environmental changes.

Graphics is a powerful medium which may replace a thousands of words. Now-a-days, with the introduction of information technology editing and processing of images has found new dimensions. All the publication media like newspapers, books, magazines, film production, television use information technology concepts for processing, editing, reproducing, storage and retrieval of images and graphics. There are several software products available for these jobs. It has also become possible to minimize the cost of processing the images in digital formats and communicate the images to other users instantly. The images broadly may be classified into two categories called Vector Images and Raster images.

Vector images are described by their geometric parameters. An image containing several objects having similarities to lines, circles, square, cube, parallelogram or may be captured using their geometric parameters like radius, length, thickness etc. and location. The colors are also captured by their parameter like combination, hue and saturation. A vector image is resolution independent. A Vector image may be scaled to any size and printed on any output device at any resolution. This process does not allow the image to sacrifice its details and clarity. The vector image is a good option for storing and representing small sized images where the object may be scaled to any size.

Raster images are captured by a grid of small points called pixel. The collection of pixels constitute the raster image. Every pixel denotes a position and color contents. The position of pixel and color values for every pixel are used to represent a raster image.

13.6.7 Science, Technology Problems and Industry Automation

Scientific and industrial design requires the solution of several complex problems. These problems generally involve bulk of data to be processed. Use of digital computers to solve the most intricate scientific and industrial problems is increasing day by day because of their fast computational speed and time saving. Design of electrical appliance, transformers, simulations of power generation and distributions, mechanical and nuclear reactor designs, civil structures, beams, building and bridge design need complex computations. Several software for handling these complex and specialized applications are available. Computer Aided Design (CAD) tools are examples of this. Computers are also being used intensively for the Process Control in an automated plant. Microprocessor based controllers in the process plant are programmable, and once programmed they perform specialized tasks effectively and accurately. On several occasions, the humans are not employed in hazardous working conditions such as gas chambers, working under high temperatures, or in high current zones etc. In these areas, computers are being deployed. The computers are also playing a very important role in military communications. Radar system employs computers for processing the image data and computer controlled radar system predicts the speed and direction of the flying objects. Several customized software have been developed and deployed for specialized application areas.

OBJECTIVE TYPE QUESTIONS

Multiple Choice

1. Which of the following are true for ERNET?
   (a) It was established by DOE
   (b) It has objective of providing Informatics Infrastructure
   (c) Provides connectivity to Academic Institutions
   (d) All of above

2. VSNL has been taken over by
   (a) Tata (b) Reliance (c) JK (d) None of these
3. Web pages are created in language
   (a) HTML (b) C++ (c) COBOL (d) None of these
4. Which of the following Indian organization has developed super computer "PARAM"?
   (a) C DAC (b) DOE (c) Tata (d) Reliance
5. Which of the following are methods for weather forecasting?
   (a) Analog methods (b) Computer based (c) Both of these (d) None of these

Answers

1-d, 2-a, 3-a, 4-a, 5-c

State True or False

1. ERNET project was started to link academic and research institutions. [True] [False]
2. VSNL provides long distance communication services. [True] [False]
3. India has passed Information Technology Act. [True] [False]
4. Tele Banking in India has started and many banks are providing Tele Banking services. [True] [False]
5. JavaScript is another version of Java. [True] [False]

Answers

1-True, 2- True , 3-True, 4- True, 5- False

SELECTED EXERCISES

1. Explain the impact that Information Technology revolution has on our daily working life. Explain with suitable examples how IT revolution has affected our nation in the past five years.
2. What is ERNET project? When was this project started and what were the objectives of this project? Explain the significant achievement of this project.
3. Explain why the problem of bandwidth is being considered as a basic issue for the overall development of the nation? List the major steps taken by various government and public sector companies to improve the bandwidth.
4. List the nodal centers of ERNET project. What role these centers are playing in the implementation of this project? Which agency is responsible for providing access to servers abroad?
5. What is NICNET? What were the objectives of establishing this network? What role is NIC playing for automation of government departments?
6. Explain the salient features of NICNET. List other specialized and dedicated networks existing in the country.
7. Why a National Information Policy is required? What steps have been taken in this direction.
8. What is multimedia? Explain the importance of multimedia in our day to day life. List and explain various components of multimedia.
9. What is meant by Desk Top Publishing? Explain what role computers are playing in DeskTop Publishing?
10. Explain the role of computers in education and research.
11. Explain how computers are being used in banking and financial institutions? How are the banks and customers benefited by the Information Technology revolution?
12. What is weather forecasting? Explain various methods for weather forecasting. Explain in brief why computers are used in weather forecasting.
13. What do you understand by scientific and industrial problems? How well may they be tackled with computers?
14. What is meant by Image Processing? List and explain various image formats.

APPENDICES

QUICK REFERENCE TO PROGRAMMING IN C

A.1 PROGRAMMING LANGUAGES

A Program is a set of well-defined instructions written in the programming language, which a computer understands. These instructions are executed sequentially i.e. one after another. A Programming Language is essentially the neat and clean description of set of rules in which real world problems may be submitted to computer. Till date many programming languages has been developed for various specific and general-purpose problem domains. Essentially we may classify the programming language into three sets called Machine Languages, Assembly Language and Higher Level Programming Languages. In early days, a programmer used to write the program in the machine language which was hardware dependent and programming in that language was a tough and complex job. In assembly language, programs are written in mnemonic and writing programs in assembly language are convenient to programmers. Program written in the assembly language is converted/translated into machine level program by a translator is called Assembler. Writing programs in the higher level language are most convenient to the programmers.

Programs written in Higher Level Languages are translated by a translator called Compiler. Till date many general purpose programming languages have been developed. FORTRAN, BASIC, PASCAL, LISP, ADA, PROLOG, COBOL, APL and PL/1 are the popular examples. C programming languages is a distinguished programming language, which is being widely used by the scientific community. C is a versatile programming language in the sense that you may write program from any problem domain. Program written in C is portable in the sense that it may be executed on different computing environment.

A.2 GENERAL PROGRAM STRUCTURE

Program written in C contains one or more functions. The program must contain a function called main and program begins with main function. Every function contains, a function heading, a list of argument declaration and a set of statements. You may also put the comments for your ready reference or for any other purpose in the C Program. A compiler omit the comments when it translate the program. The comment must be bounded by /* comments */.

Let us write the first program, which will display a statement "Welcome to C World".

Program 1

```
*****************************************************************************
/* This is the first program in C */
# include <stdio.h>
main ( )
{
printf("Welcome to C World");
}
*****************************************************************************
```

In the program 1, first line contains the remark "This is first program in C". Second line #include <stdio.h> is preprocessor directive which ensures reading a header file stdio.h. A preprocessor directive is a command to the preprocessor pass of compilation to perform a specific task. Third line contains the beginning of the main function. Immediately after this within curly parenthesis, the statement of the C program are included. This statement prints a line on the standard output (your monitor). Basic block structure of the C program is as follows. It may contain one or more section as defined below:

⇒ Comment Lines
⇒ Link section
⇒ Definition section
⇒ Global declaration section
⇒ Main()
⇒ {
⇒ declarative statements;
⇒ executable statements;
⇒ }

Here comment lines consists of set of comment lines containing the name of author, date of program, purpose of program etc. or any other thing which a programmer wish to attach with the program. Link section contains instructions to compiler to include the system function from the C library. In the definition section defines all symbolic constants and global declaration section contains the declaration of variable which will be used in the program. Main body of program contains declaration of variables etc. and executable statements of the program.

A.3 DATA TYPES

A.3.1 Character Set

The number of characters which may be used in the C programming language may be grouped in the following four categories namely letters, digits, special character, white spaces. Any variable, statement, constant may consist of the character from the character set.

⇒ Letters	
Lowercase Letter	a to z
Uppercase Letter	A to Z
⇒ Digit	0 to 9
⇒ Special Character	!,@,#,$,%,^,&,*,(,),+ etc.
⇒ White Spaces	Blank space, Tabs, Return, New line

A.3.2 Identifiers

Identifiers are the word or names used to refer to the variable, constant, function name etc. These are user-defined name which consist as a string of character from character set. There are also a list of key word which have a fixed meaning in the C. const, case, if, then, else, while, do etc. are the key words. Programmer to define any variable or constant cannot use the key word.

A.3.3 Constant

Constant in the C may be classified in to four categories namely Integer constant, real constant, character constant and string constants.

Integer Constant: Integer constant refer to the sequence of digit. It must not have any character except digit, however an integer constant may be preceded by '+' or '–'.

Example :

153, –876, 3543, 0, 2, –998, +118 are the valid integer constant.

11,435, $ 4000, Rs 5000, 7500/- are invalid constant.

Real Constant: A real constant in the C is numeric constant with a sign of decimal point or exponent or a combination. Following is an example showing the list of invalid and valid real constant.

Example :

34.789, 0.0001, 9.0, 3e–9, +247.0, 4e–3, 2.58e+3, 315. are the valid real constant.

2, 2,000.00, .34e+12.67, are invalid real constants.

Character Constant: A character constant is any symbol or value that is the part of valid character set. A valid character constant must be enclosed within the single quotes.

Example :

```
Char c;      /* define the character c */
c= ' B' ;    /* assigns character 'B' to the variable c of character type. */
```

String Constant: String constant is the sequence of the one or more characters from the defined character set i.e. Following are the example of valid string constants:

"Fine", "27863", " @#$%&* ", "b" are the valid string constants.

A.3.4 Variables

A variable is the meaningful name assigned represent a data object. The value of the variable may change during the execution of the program. There are few rules for declaring the variable name. They are as follows:

- Variable name must start with a letter (a-z or A to Z)
- Variable name can not begin with the digit.
- Variable name can not contain punctuation mark, math symbol or other special symbols.
- ANSI (American National Standard Institute) restrict variable to be of 32 characters.
- Reserved words name can not be used as variable name.

'tax', 'value', 'intrate' 'a123' are the valid variable name. '-vi', 'static', '+value' are the example of invalid variable names.

Assigning Value to Variable

Variables are created to store the value of data object in the program. Result of an computational statement may be assigned to a variable.

Program 2

```
**************************************************************************
/* This program prints result of addition of two numbers */
#include <stdio.h>
main ( )
{
int  number1;
int number2;
int result;
number1=50;
number2=100;
result= number1+number2;
printf("Result of addition is", result);
}
**************************************************************************
```

Output of the program is as follows:

Result of addition is 150

In the Program 2, addition to number 1 and number 2 is assigned to variable result.

A.3.5 Relational Operator

Relational operators are used to compare the value of two variable for various conditions such as greater, less than or equal etc. All relational operator returns the result in either 'True' or 'False'. Following are some widely used relational operator in C:

- < less than
- <= less than or equal to
- > greater than
- >= greater than or equal to
- == equal to
- != not equal to

Following is the example showing result of some relational expressions:

12 !=15	True
12==12	True
46 >= 47	False
2.88 <= 3.10	True

A.3.6 Logical Operator

An expression, which combines two or more relational expression, is called logical expression. Just similar to the relational expression, a logical expression results in either true or false. Following are the logical operators used in the C program:

&& Logical AND
|| Logical OR
! Logical NOT

A table showing the result of two relational expression A and B is shown below:

A	B	A &&B	A‖B
True	True	True	True
True	False	False	True
False	True	False	True
False	False	False	False

Example:

Suppose

Int a=10

Float b = 2.5

Char c = 'a'

Then the following relational expression yields true or false as follows:

Expression	**Boolean Value**
a < 15	true
((a > 5)&&(c=='a'))	true
((a< 5)&& (c=='a'))	false
(c != 'd')‖ ((a+b)< 15)	true
(c =='d')‖ ((a -b)== 6)	false
! ((a > (b+2))	false
c >= 100 * (a+b)	false

A.3.7 Conditional Operator

Conditional operators are used in place of inf-then-else construct. An expression, which uses the conditional operator, is called conditional expression. This type of expression is used in place of if-then-else statement. General format of this expression is as follows:

E1 ? E2 : E3, here E1, E2, E3 are expressions.

In such cases the E1 is evaluated first. If its value is found to be true then E2 is evaluated. If the E1 is evaluated to be false then expression E3 is evaluated. For example consider the following statements:

I= 5 ;

J= 10

Val = (I > J)? I : J ;

In this example the, Val is evaluated as follows:

If (I > J) then Val = I

Else Val = J

A.3.8 Library Functions

C allows some mathematical functions also. These functions are called mathematical functions. The compiler evaluates these functions. Following table presents some widely used library functions:

FUNCTION	EXPLANATION
Sqrt (x)	Square root of x
Exp(x)	'e' to the power 'x'
Pow(X,Y)	X to power Y
Log (x)	Log of x with base e
Abs(x)	Absolute value of x
Rand()	Generate positive random number
Ceil(x)	Rounds the value of x to nearest integer
Sin(x)	Sin x
Cos(x)	Cos x
Tan(x)	Tan x
Tolower(x)	Return lower case value of character
Toupper	Converts to uppercase
Toascii(x)	Returns ASCII value of character x
Getchar ()	Enters a character from the keyboard
Putchar(c)	Prints a character to output device
Rand(0	Returns a positive random number

These library functions are not the part of the language but these are supplied with the C. In order to use these library function it is necessary to use header file. The header files are the logical collection of various functions. For example the functions which are used to carry out standard input/output operation, functions for character handling, mathematical functions are bundled in the appropriate header file. If you do not include the appropriate header file in the program, these functions will not be available for use. The vendor as a part of C compiler supplies these library or header files. The name of these header files are supplied by individual C compiler vendor, but some of the common header files are stdio.h, conio.h, math.h etc. These gheader files are included to your program using preprocessor directive as given below:

```
# include <stdio.h>
#include <conio.h>
#include <math.h>
```

A.3.9 Basic Input and Output instructions

♦ **Scanf:** This function is used to input a set of values. The general format of the scanf function is as follows:

Scanf (FS, List of arguments)

Here FS is known as format string and list of argument contains the variable in to which the value or data from standard input will be stored. Format string is a string with characters indicating the format of the variables. Each format must start with % sign. Each numeric variable must be preceded by & sign.

Example:

Scanf ("%d", & number);

This statement will store a decimal type of integer data into the variable number from the input.

Scanf ("%s %d %f ", code, & quantity, & rate)

This statement will store a string to variable code, decimal type integer data to quantity and floating point value to rate from the standard input.

◆ **Printf:** This function is used to print any combination of string, number or character to the standard output (monitor of your computer). The format of the printf statement is given below:
Printf ("FS", List of arguments) ;
Here format string contains the format characters for the corresponding variables. It must be preceded by the % sign.

Example:

Printf ("sum = %f Number 1 = %d Number 2= %d \n", sum, number 1, number 2);

This statement prints the value of floating variable sum and integer value of number 1 and number 2 variables.

A.3.10 Single Character Input/Output Statement

Single character may be entered from the standard input using the standard I/O library function getchar(). It when executed, expects a character from the standard input e.g. keyboard. Single character may be displayed to the standard output e.g. monitor using standard input/output library function putchar ().

Example:

Char I ;	declares I as character variable
I= getchar() ;	assign input from keyboard to I
Putchar (I)	displays or send the value of I to monitor.

Program 3

```
**************************************************************************
/*THIS PROGRAM CONVERTS A BINARY NUMBER TO DECIMAL*/
#include <conio.h>
#include <stdio.h>
#include <math.h>
#define M 15
main()
{
int n,a[M],count=0,p,i,sum=0,temp;
clrscr();
printf ("\n GIVE THE NUMBER IN THE BINARY FORM (only 1 & 0 are allowed)\n");
scanf("%d",&n);
p=n;
do
{
 a[count]=n%10;
 count++;
 n=n/10;
}while(n>0);
for(i=0;i<count;i++)
  {
  temp=a[i]*pow(2,i);
  sum=sum+temp;
  }
printf("\n\nTHE DECIMAL EQUIVELENT OF %d IS : %d",p,sum);
getch();
}
**************************************************************************
```

A.3.11 Assignment Statement and shorthand operator

Assignment operators are used to assign the result of computational statements. C also provides the use of short hand operators for the purpose of assignments.

The assignment statement A O = E ; where A is the variable and O is the operator and E is the expression.

This statement is equivalent to

A= A O E;

Example :

X+=3; is equivalent to x=x+3;

A-=3; is equivalent to A=A-3;

A/=B+C; is equivalent to A=A/(B+C);

A*=A is equivalent to A=A*A

Increment and Decrement Operators:

C provides to operator for the purpose of increment and decrement. These operators are ++ and – –. First operator adds one to the value of variable and other decrement the value of variable by one. These operator may be used in two way i.e. it may precede or succeed the variable name.

Example:

++a, a++, a– –, – –a are the valid statements. ++a and a++ increase the value of a by one and a– –, – –a decrement the value of a by 1. The difference in the mode is given in the following example. A prefix operator first adds one to the operand and then result is assigned to the variable on the left hand side. A post fix operator first assign the value to the variable on left then increment the operand.

Example:

Consider following statements:

A=1;

B=++A ;

After the execution of the second statement value of A and B would be 2.

Consider following statements,

A=1;

B=A++;

In this case value of B would be 1 and value of A would be 2.

Program 4

```
****************************************************************************
/* This program illustrate the usage of short hand operator */
# include <stdio.h>
main( )
{
int a,b,c;
a=2;b=3;c=4;
a*=b+c;
printf ("%d %d %d ", a,b,c);
c++;
printf ("%d %d %d ", a,b,c);
}
****************************************************************************
```

```
Output of this program after first print statement
A=14,b=3,c=4
Output of this program after first print statement
A=14,b=3,c=5
```

Program 5

```
*************************************************************************************
/* This program computes the gross pay
gross pay= basic pay + basic pay * Dearness Allowance */
#include <stdio.h>
main ( )
{
int basic_pay, da;
float gross_pay;
printf ("enter the basic pay & dearness allowance);
scanf("%d %d", & basic_pay, & da);
gross_pay= basic_pay + (basic_pay * da);
printf("Gross pay =  %f\n", gross_pay)
}
*************************************************************************************
```

A.4 CONTROL STRUCTURES IN C

Decision making and looping is one of the basic construct of any programming language. These constructs are also provided in the C Programming language.

A.4.1 If Then Else Statement

Decision making in the C programming language is provided through if -then -else statements. There are several instances when a decision is required subject to the fulfillment of a specified condition. The syntax of this statement is given below:

```
If (Condition Expression)
{
statement set1;
}
else
{
statement set2;
}
```

In this statement, the expression given as condition expression is evaluated as true or false. If the condition expression is evaluated to true, the statements given in the statement set1 are executed. if the condition expression is evaluated to be false, then the statements given in the statement set 2 are executed. For example, in the given program, if the value of "a" is greater than "b", first printf() is executed. This will print the statement "A is greater than B" otherwise if the value of a is less than or equal, the second printf() statement is printed. This will print that "A is less than or equal to B".

```
If (a>b)
Printf ("A is greater than B");
```

Else
Printf ("A is less than or equal to B);

Program 6

```
*********************************************************************************
/* This program finds the Largest of the three numbers */
#include <stdio.h>
main ( )
{
int p,q,r;
printf("enter all the three number\n");
scanf ("%d %d %d", &p,&q, &r);
if (p>q)
{
if (p<r)
{
printf ("Largest  number is %d\n", p);
}
else
{
printf("Largest Number is %d \n", r);
}
}
else
{
      if (r>q)
            {
                  printf("Largest Number is %d \n",r);
            }
      else
            {
                  printf ("Largest Number is %d \n",q);
            }
}
}
*********************************************************************************
```

A.4.2 While Statement

One of the mostly used control structure for repeated execution of statement is while statement. When a large number of statements are to be executed sequentially for number of time or subject to the fulfillment of certain condition the WHILE statement is frequently used. Syntax of this statement is given below:

```
While (condition expression)
{
statement1;
statement2;
```

statement n;
}

In this statement, the condition expression is evaluated before the execution of the statements. If the condition is found to be true, then statements given in the statement set are executed. These statement are executed in the sequential manner till the condition is evaluated to be true.

Program 7

```
**********************************************************************************
/* This program calculate m to the power n */
#include<stdio.h>
main ()
{
int m,n,count;
printf ("enter the value of m & n");
count=1;
while (count < n)
{
m*=m;
count++;
}
}
**********************************************************************************
```

Program 8

```
**********************************************************************************
/* This program reverses a string*/
#include<conio.h>
#include<stdio.h>
#include<string.h>

main()
{
    int i,counter=0;
    char str[20],str2[20];
    clrscr();
    printf("THIS IS A PROGRAM OF REVERSING THE STRING ORDER");
    printf("\nenter your desire string");
    scanf("%s",str);
 /counter= strlen(str);
    for(i=0;str[i]!='\0';i++)
       counter++;
    for(i=0;i<=counter;i++)
    str2[i]=str[i];
  printf("\nthe reverse string-\n");
  for(i=counter;i>=0;i–)
    printf("%c",str2[i]);
```

```
printf("\nthe length of string= %d",counter);
getch();
}
```

****

A.4.3 Do Statement

This statement is similar to while statement with little difference. Syntax of this statement is given below:

```
Do
{
statement 1;
statement 2;

statement n ;
}
while (condition expression)
```

In this statement the while condition is tested after the statements execution. Next time the statement will be executed if the condition is evaluated to be true again.

Program 9

****

/* This program print a table Fahrenheit, Celsius for the temperature given from 1 F to 100 F in a step of 2 */

```
#include <stdio.h)
main()
(
float fahr, celc;
fahr=1.0;
do
{
celc= (fahr-32.0)/1.8;
printf ("%f %f \n",fahr,celc)
fahr=fahr+2.0;
}
while (fahr<=100.0);
)
```

****

Program 10

****

/*THIS PROGRAM CONVERT A DECIMAL NUMBER INTO BINARY*/

```
#include<conio.h>
#include<stdio.h>
#define M 15
void main()
{ int n, a[M],i=0,j,p;
```

```
clrscr();
printf("Enter the decimal number\n");
scanf("%d",&n);
p=n;
do
{
a[i]=n%2;
i++;
n=n/2;
//i++;
}while(n>0);
printf("\nTHE BINARY EQUIVELENT OF  %d IS :: ",p);
for(j=i-1;j>=0;j-)
printf("%d",a[j]);
getch();
}
```

****

Program 11

****

/*THIS PROGRAM IS FOR FIBONACCI SERIES */

```
#include <conio.h>
#include <stdio.h>
#define M 20
main()
{
int i,n,a[M],sum=0;
char ch;

clrscr();
printf("\n Enter a number of term you wants in your series ?(less than
%d)\n",M);
scanf("%d",&n);
a[0]=0;
a[1]=1;
for(i=2;i<n;i++)
    a[i]=a[i-1]+a[i-2];
printf("\nTHE FABONACCI SERIES OF  %d  TERM",n);
for(i=0;i<n;i++)
    printf("%d",a[i]);
printf("\n\nDO YOU WANT THE SUMMATION OF THIS SERIES (y/n)");
ch=getch();
if(ch=='Y'||ch=='y')
{
for (i=0;i<n;i++)
    sum=sum+a[i];
printf("\n\n THE SUM OF FIBONACCI SERIES IS %d",sum);
}
```

```
else
   exit(1);
getch();
}
```

****

A.4.4 For Statement

For statement is also a widely used statement in the C programming language. Syntax of the for statement is given below:

For (expression1 ; expression2 ; expression3)
{
statements;
}

In this statement, expresssion1 is normally used to initialize the variables that controls th e loop. The expression2 is the test condition that determines whether the next round of execution of the statement is possible. Expression 3 provides the steps under which the value of the variable should change.

Program 12

****

```
/* This program prints the number from 1 to 10 */
#include <stdio.h>
main ( )
{
int a;
for (a=1;a<=10;a++)
{
printf ("%d\n",a)
}
}
```

****

Program 13

****

```
/*This program generate table for any given number */
#include<conio.h>
#include<stdio.h>
void main()
{
int n,i;
clrscr();
/*printf("\n ENTER THE NUMBER WHOSE TABLE IS REQUIRED:");
scanf("%d",&n);*/
printf("\n\nTHE TABLE UPTO 10 IS AS \n\n");
for (i=1;i<=10;i++)
{
for(n=1;n<=10;n++)
{
printf("%5d", n*i);
```

```
}
printf("\n");
}
getch();
}
```

****

Program 14

****

```
/*THE PROGRAM FOR FINDING THE FACTORIAL OF ANY GIVEN NUMBER GREATER THAN
1*/
#include<conio.h>
#include<stdio.h>
main()
{
int i,n;
long  f=1;
clrscr();
printf(" /*THE PROGRAM FOR FINDING THE FACTORIAL OF ANY GIVEN NUMBER
GREATER THAN 1*/");
printf("\n\n GIVE THE NUMBER WHOSE FACTORIAL IS REQUIRED (LESS THAN
16)");
scanf("%d",&n);
if(n==0)
f=1;
else if(n==1)
f=1;
else{
for(i=1;i<=n;i++)
f=f*i;
}
printf("\nTHE FACTORIAL OF %d IS :: %ld",n,f);
getch();
}
```

****

A.4.5 Switch Statement

If then else statement is a nice construct to when one of many alternatives are to be selected. Use of nested IF construct become little complex when the selection is to be made out of many alternatives. Switch - Case statement is a feature of C programming language, which provide multiple branch selection. It checks for the value of an expression against a list of integer or character constant. If the match is successful, the group of statement associated with that constant are executed. The SWITCH statement test for the value of a given expression against a list of CASE values. When the match is found, group of statement associated with that CASE statement are executed. The general form of SWITCH CASE statement is given below:

```
Switch (Expression)
{
```

```
case  constant 1:
      group of statement 1;
      break;

case  constant 2:
      group of statement 2;
      break;
..........
..........

default:
      group of statement 3;
}
```

The switch statement check for the equality with the constant, whereas as IF THEN ELSE statement may evaluate the relational or logical expression. It is also not possible for the two case statements to have same value. These are some of the restrictions with the Switch-Case statements.
Following program calculate the final velocity (v) using different Newton's Law of motion.

Program 15

```
****************************************************************************
/* THIS PROGRAM IS TO CALCULATE FINAL VELOCITY, DISTANCE USING DIFFERENT
NEWTON'S LAW */

#include <conio.h>
#include <stdio.h>
#include <math.h>
main()
{
int n;
float u,v,a,t,s;
clrscr();
printf("\n   THE THREE FUNDAMENTAL NEWTON'S EQUATIONS ARE\n\n");
printf("\n 1.  v = u + a*t \n 2.  s = u*t + (1/2) a*t*t");
printf("\n 3.  v = sqrt(u*u + 2*a*s)");
printf("\n\n\n WHERE    u = intial velocity\t v = final velocity");
printf("\t a = accelartion\t\t  s = displacement\t t= time");
printf("\n\n\n THE EQUATION WHICH YOU REQUIRE TO USE :  ");
scanf ("%d",&n);
switch(n){
    case 1:
          printf ("\n\n Enter the value of intial velocity(u)");
          scanf ("%f ",&u);
          printf ("\n\n Enter the value of accelartion(a)");
          scanf ("%f ",&a);
          printf ("\n\n Enter the value of time(t)");
          scanf ("%f ",&t);
          v=u+a*t;
```

```
            printf("\n\n THE FINAL VELOCITY IS  v = %f m/sec",v);break;
        case 2:
            printf ("\n\n Enter the value of initial velocity(u),
        accelaration(a),time(t)");
            scanf ("%f %f %f",&u,&a,&t);
            s=u*t+(1/2)*a*t*t;
            printf("\n\n THE TOTAL DISPLACEMENT IS s = %f m",s);
            break;
        case 3:
printf ("\n\n Enter the value of initial velocity(u),
accelaration(a),displacement(s)");
            scanf ("%f %f %f",&u,&a,&s);
            v=sqrt(u*u+2*a*s);
            printf("\n\n THE FINAL VELOCITY IS v = %f m/sec",v);
            break;
        default:
             printf("\n\n !!!  SORRY YOU HAVE ENTERED THE WRONG CHOICE");
             break;
             }
getch();
}
```

****

Program 16

****

/*THIS PROGRAM IS TO FIND THE ROOTS OF A QUADRATIC EQUATION */

```
#include<conio.h>
#include<stdio.h>
#include<math.h>
void main()
{
float a,b,c,d,r1,r2;
float real,img,p;
clrscr();
printf("\n\n PROGRAM TO FIND THE ROOTS OF A QUADRATIC EQUATION");
printf("\n\n THE GENERAL FORM OF QUADRATIC EQUATION IS :  ");
printf("\n\n\t ax^2 + bx + c ");
printf("\n\n Enter the values of  'a',  'b',  'c'  of your equation\n");
scanf("%f %f %f",&a,&b,&c);
d=b*b-4*a*c;

if(d==0)
   {
   printf("\n\n THE ROOTS ARE EQUAL");
   r1=(-b)/(2*a);
   r2=r1;
   printf("\n\n THE ROOTS ARE r1 = r2 = %f ",r1);
```

```
   }
if(d>0)
   {
    printf("\n\n THE ROOTS ARE DISTINCT");
    r1=((-b)+sqrt(d))/(2*a);
    r2=((-b)-sqrt(d))/(2*a);
    printf("\n\n THE ROOTS ARE \n\tr1 = %f \n\tr2 = %f ",r1,r2);
    }
if(d<0)
   {
   p=sqrt(-d);
   real=((-b)/(2*a));
   img=p/2;
   printf("\n\nTHE ROOTS ARE IMAGINARY");
   printf("\n\n THE ROOTS ARE:");
   printf("\n\n\tr1  = %f +  %f i ",real,img);
   printf("\n\tr1  = %f - %f i ",real,img);
   }
getch();
   }
```

****

A.4.6 Break and Goto statements

The Break and Goto statements are used to change the flow of execution. The goto statement is considered to be hazardous statement and is not preferred by rich programmers. Goto statement is rarely used but still it may be useful in certain circumstances. This statement requires a label and control is transferred to that label whenever goto statement is executed. Following is the genera syntax of this statement:

Goto LABEL;

Statements;

Label: Statement;

The break statement is used in conjunction with SWITCH-CASE statement. However this statement may be used to discontinue the loop e.g. for loop, while loop. Whenever, the break statement is encountered within the loop, execution of further statements of that loop is abandoned and program control comes out of the loop. For example,

```
# include <stdio.h>
main( )
{
int I=1 ;
while (I< 100)
{
printf ("Number = %d \n", I);
I++
```

```
If (I==20)  break;
}
```

The above program segment will print the number up to 20 and when ever value of I becomes 20 the loop will be forced to terminated without reaching the while condition.

Program 17

```
**************************************************************************
/* PROGRAM TO CHECK WHEATHER THE GIVEN NUMBER IS PRIME OR NOT*/

#include<conio.h>
#include<stdio.h>
#include<math.h>
void main()
{
int n,p,i;
clrscr();
printf("\nENTER THE NUMBER TO BE CHECKED");
scanf("%d",&n);
p=sqrt(n)+1;
i=2;
while(i<=p)
{
if(n%i==0)
{
printf("\n\n THE GIVE NUMBER %d IS NOT PRIME",n);
break;
}
i++;
}
if(i==p+1)
printf("\n\nTHE GIVEN NUMBER %d IS PRIME",n);
getch();
}
**************************************************************************
```

A.5 INTRODUCTION TO ARRAYS

An ARRAY is a collection of variables of same type that are represented by a common name. A specific element of an array is accessed by an index. For example, in a class of 50 students, an array 'height' may be defined to represent the height of all 50 students. Thus array 'height' may be used to access on or more values pertaining to get the height of a student. Each array element is accessed by specifying a array name followed by subscript. Each subscript must be a non negative number. Following figure shows the logical representation of array of height of 50 students:

Student

191	152	———	———	———	178

student[0] **student[1]** **student[49]**

Here in this example, **student[1]** represent the value stored in the array student at the index 1. Similarly **student [n]** refers to the nth element in the array students. It must be remembered that size of an array must be specified at the time of declaration of an array. For an array of size n, the indexes begins with 0 to n-1.

The number of the subscripts defines the dimension of the array. In the previous example, the student array is one dimensional array because this uses one sub script. In the similar way, A [I] [j] refers to an element in a two dimensional array. This item exist at j^{th} element of Ith row. Following is the representation of a two dimensional array:

A[M][N] **: Array of Size M X N**

A[1][1]	A[1][2]	A[1][3]	A[1][N]
A[2][1]	A[2][2]	A[2][3]	A[2][N]
- -	- -	- - - - - -	- -
- -	- -	- - - - -	
- -	- -	- - - - - -	- -
A[M][1]	A[M][2]	A[M][3]	A[M][N]

Thus increasing number of subscripts means increasing the dimension of an array. A[I][j][k] indicate that array A is a three dimensional array. An n dimensional array will use n subscript to represent an item. Array having n subscript. It must be remembered that array is collection of homogeneous items. The values stored in an array must be of same type. Every array has a base type and all the entries to an array must be of the base type.

A.5.1 Declaration of Array

Arrays are defined in the way similar to that of defining other variable. It can be thought of declaring another variable with an index or sub-script. A one dimensional array is defined by defining its type followed by an identifier with a expression in the bracket. This expression must be evaluated to positive integer value. This is called the size of an array. For example, declaring a array to store the height of the students for a class of 50 students:

Int student[50];

This statement will define a array student, whose base type is integer and size of array is 50. Index of this array start with 0 and last index, which may be accessed, is 49. It is always a good strategy to define the size of an array as a symbolic constant. For example,

```
# define M      50
int student[M];
```

Following are the example of array definitions:

```
Int  Salary [10] ;
Char    name[25] ;
Float   amount[100] ;
Float    Matrix [10][10];
Char   Value [5][10][10];
```

A.5.2 Initialization of Array

As indicated above the elements of an array can be initialized as the other variables at the time of declaration. Base type of an array can be of Int, Char, float etc. The syntax of the initialization of array can be defined as below:

Static data_ type array_name[size] = { list of elements };

Here 'static' is a keyword, data_type is the base type of the elements, array_name is the identifier which requires a meaningful name to an array, size is the size of an array which represents the number of elements to be stored in an array, list of elements is the actual list of elements which requires to be stored in an array.

Following are the examples of the array initialization:

Static int height[5] = {178, 162, 153, 169, 171};

Static char name [7] = {'S', 'U', 'R', 'A', 'B', 'H', 'I'};

Static float price[4] ={2.50, 5.30, 4.10, 0.45};

First statement declares the one-dimensional array of size 5 and initializes the values as follows. This statement declares the array of size five and its entries are represented as height[0], height[1] ....height[4].

Height[0]	178
Height[1]	162
Height[2]	153
Height[3]	169
Height[4]	171

Similarly second and third statement declares the one-dimensional array as follows:

Second statement declares its entries to be represented as name[0], name[1] ....name[6] and third statement declares its entries to be declared as price[0], price[1].. price[4].

Name[0]	S
Name[1]	U
Name[2]	R
Name[3]	A
Name[4]	B
Name[5]	H
Name[6]	I

Price[0]	2.50
Price[1]	5.30
Price[2]	4.10
Price[3]	0.45

A.5.3 Dynamic Arrays

All the arrays declaration define the maximum size of an array thus they are called static arrays. 'C' also provide a flexibility not to define the size of an array explicitly. A programmer may leave the size of an array unspecified. The total number of the entries specified in the list of values define the maximum size of an array. This type of an arrays are called dynamic arrays. Following are the examples of dynamic arrays:

Int student_age [ ] = {12, 8, 9, 10,14};
Float price [ ] = {2.50, 4.20, 3.0};
Char name [ ] = {'A', 'K', 'K', 'U'};

In the above three examples the size of an array is determined by the 'C' compiler itself. First declaration defines the size of an array to be five as there are five entries in the list of values. Similarly second and third array declaration defines the array size to be fixed at three and four respectively.

A.5.4 Initialization of Multi Dimensional Array

In the one-dimensional arrays the value to be stored are simple. Multidimensional array may have multiple size indices. Following are the examples of declaration of multidimensional array.

Int marks [3][5] ; /* Two dimensional Array */
Float values [5][5][5] /* Declaration of three dimensional array */

Similar to previous examples, it is also possible to mention the list of entries in the multidimensional arrays. Following are the examples:

Static int marks [3][4] ={34, 56, 56, 57, 12, 34, 23, 23, 45, 43, 24, 23};
Static int value[2][3] ={2, 4, 3, 4, 5, 3};

This example initializes the elements of the first row as (2,4,3) and second row as (4,5,3). The same initialization may be done as under where the braces surround elements of rows.

Static int value [2][3] ={{2, 4, 3}, {4, 5, 3}};

There may exist situation that one may require putting the table in an array. For example the marks obtained in four subjects in a class of five students. Following table shows this situations.

Student	Subject 1	Subject 2	Subject 3	Subject 4
1	54	76	67	76
2	56	87	65	71
3	56	76	86	87
4	76	78	55	76
5	65	76	55	56

All of the entries in this table are contained in the five rows and four columns. Each rows represents the students number and each column represents the subject number. If we represent above table as matrix, then element '54' in first row and first column represents the marks obtained by the first student in the first subject. Thus if this matrix is represented by A, then A[I][j] represents Ith row and jth column.

This array may be declared and initialized by putting the values inside the array declaration. But a good strategy is to read the values from the standard input using 'scanf' statements.

Program 18

```
*************************************************************************
/* This program reads the height of ten students and print their average */
#Include <stdio.h>
main ( )
```

```
{
      int I
float  sum, height [10] ;
for (I=0;I<10;I++)/* This statement reads height of 10 students to,array */
      {
printf ("Enter the height of the  student No=%d\n", I+1);
scanf ("%d", height[I]);
}
for  (I=0;I<10;I++)/*  This  statement  computes  the  sum  of  height  of  10
students */
{
sum= sum + height[I] ;
}

printf (" Average Height of the Class =  %d \n", sum/10.0)
}
```

****

A.5.5 Processing an Array

As shown in the previous example that it is not possible to process an array in a single shot. If an operation is to be carried out on array, it must be done on element basis. This is usually done using a control structure like For Loop, Do While Loop etc on element basis until end of array is achieved. Suppose the element or the values stored in the two array has to be processed (e.g. addition, multiplication etc.), then element of both the arrays are read from the respective indices and in each pass of the loop the appropriate action is carried out. This process is done until the computation is completed. Following is the program which read the element of two one-dimensional array and storing the sum and multiplication of elements in another array.

Program 19

****

/* This program read the values to two arrays (A & B) and stores addition and multiplication of elements in to array C & D.   */

```
# include <stdio.h>
main ( )
{
int I, j, a[5], b[5], c[5], d[5];

printf ("Enter the elements of array A\n");
for (I=0 ; I<5; I++)
{
scanf  ("%d", & a[I]);
}
printf ("Enter the elements of array B\n");
for (I=0; I<5; I++)
{
```

```
scanf ("%d", & b[I]);
}
/* This segment computes addition & multiplication */
for (I=0; I<5; I++)
{
c[I]= a[I] +b[I];
d[I]=a[I] * b[I];
}
/* This segment prints the elements of array C & D  */
for (I=0; I<5; I++)
{
printf ("%d %d\n", c[I],d[I]);
}
*****************************************************************************
```

The two and multidimensional arrays can be processed in the same way. Following is the program for addition of two matrices. Each matrix is represented as a two dimensional array. Addition of the receptive elements is done in almost the same way as in one dimensional array.

Program 20

```
*****************************************************************************
/*THE PROGRAM  FOR ADDITION OF TWO MATRIX */
#include<conio.h>
#include<stdio.h>
#define M 5
main()
{
int i,j,p,q;
int a[M][M],b[M][M],sum[M][M];
clrscr();
printf("FOR ADDITION OF TWO MATRIX THEIR ORDER SHOULD BE SAME");
printf ("\n\n Give the order of first & second matrix");
printf("\n\n   ENTER THE NUMBER  OF ROWS");
scanf("%d",&p);
printf("\n\n ENTER THE  NUMBER  OF COLUMN");
scanf("%d",&q);

/* THIS SEGMENT  ENTER  THE ELEMENTS OF FIRST MATRIX */
for(i=0;i<p;i++)
  {
  for(j=0;j<q;j++)
     {
  // printf("\n ENTER THE ROW NO %d COLUMN NO %d's ELEMENT :: ",i+1,j+1);
     scanf("%d",&a[i][j]);
     }
  }
/* THIS SEGMENT READS THE  ELEMENTS OF SECOND MATRIX */
for(i=0;i<p;i++)
```

```
      {
      for(j=0;j<q;j++)
         {
      // printf("\n ENTER THE ROW NO %d COLUMN NO %d's ELEMENT :: ",i+1,j+1);
         scanf("%d",&b[i][j]);
         }
      }

for(i=0;i<p;i++)
      {
      for(j=0;j<q;j++)
         {
         sum[i][j]=a[i][j]+b[i][j];
         }
      }
printf("\n THE FIRST MATRICES IS AS ::\n\n");
for(i=0;i<p;i++)
      {
      for(j=0;j<q;j++)
         {
         printf("%5d",a[i][j]);
         }
         printf("\n");
       }
printf("\n THE SECOND MATRICES IS AS ::\n\n");
for(i=0;i<p;i++)
      {
      for(j=0;j<q;j++)
         {
         printf("%5d",b[i][j]);
         }
         printf("\n");
       }
printf("\n THE SUM OF TWO MATRICES IS THE GIVEN MATRIX\n\n");
for(i=0;i<p;i++)
      {
      for(j=0;j<q;j++)
         {
         printf("%5d",sum[i][j]);
         }
         printf("\n");
       }
getch();
}
```

****

Following program computes the exponential series

.e^ x = ? x^n / n ! where 0<x<1.

Program 21

```
**********************************************************************************
/*To compute exponential series    e^x (e to power x)*/
#include <conio.h>
#include <stdio.h>
#define M 30
main()
{
float x, t[M],sum=0;
int n=5,i;
clrscr();
printf("THE GENERAL FORM OF SERIES IS AS  ::");
printf("\n\n Enter the value of x :");
scanf("%f",&x);
t[0]=1;
t[1]=x;
for (i=2;i<=n;i++)
t[i]=t[i-1]*(x/n);
for (i=0;i<=n;i++)
sum=sum+t[i];
printf("\n\n THE SUMMATION OF e^x  i.e. e^%f IS :: %f",x,sum)·
getch();
}
**********************************************************************************
```

Program 22

```
**********************************************************************************
/*THE PROGRAM FOR FINDING THE FACTORIAL OF ANY GIVEN NUMBER GREATER THAN
1*/
#include<conio.h>
#include<stdio.h>
void main()
{
int i,f=1,n,a;
int facto(int p);
clrscr();

printf("/*THE PROGRAM FOR FINDING THE FACTORIAL OF ANY GIVEN NUMBER
GREATER THAN 1*/");
printf("\n\n GIVE THE NUMBER WHOSE FACTORIAL IS REQUIRED");
scanf("%d",&n);
a=n;
if(n==0)
f=1;
```

```
else
f=facto(n);

printf("\n\n THE FACTORIAL OF %d! IS %d ",a,f);
getch();
}

int facto(int p)
{
 int s;
if(p==1)
  return(1);
else
s=p*facto(p-1);
return s;
}
```

****

B.1 INTRODUCTION TO FUNCTIONS

We have discussed the Library functions in the previous chapter. The C vendor as a package supplies these functions. These functions when used require the programmer to include appropriate header file or package that contains the function definition. C provides the facility to create the function of your requirement, which may be used repeatedly whenever required. These functions are called user-defined function. Normally these functions are created and defined when set of instruction is to be used repeatedly. User defined function are called from the main program. The use of these functions allows a great flexibility to the programmer as a programmer may write code for different modules and may call it to the main program as and when required. This programming approach is called Modular Programming. In this programming methodology, the whole program is broken into the pieces that are smaller and self contained. There are number of advantages of modular programming over writing a large monolithic program. At many times programmer wants that a group of statements be executed at different places in the main program. These statements may be grouped and defined under single function. At every place, where the group of statement needs to be executed then appropriate function is accessed. At the time of decomposition of large program in to a collection of small programs, logical clarity and self sufficiency should not be sacrificed. If functions has been written keeping this constraint in the mind, then debugging of that programs becomes easier. Programmer or user may also create a library of his own defined functions. Each routine or module may be programmed as special function and may be stored in a header file. This avoids repetitive programming and makes the program more portable.

Consider a case of evaluation of power series where a factorial of numbers is to be used repeatedly. It will be very cumbersome for the programmer to write a group of statement that calculates the factorial of that numbers and using it again and again. It would be better strategy, if programmer write a function that returns the value of factorial whenever the value for factorial is needed. Consider the following syntax,

```
# include <stdio.h>
main ( )
{
..................
..................                  Main Program
..................
Value = Factorial (n);  <----       Call for Function
..................
}
int Factorial (n)
{
............
............
............                        User Defined Function
............
}
```

In this example, Factorial (n) invoke the function. It then computes the factorial of n written separately. After the computation, the function passes the value of factorial of n to main program which is then assigned to the variable Value.

B.2 SCOPE OF THE USER DEFINED FUNCTION

C programming language recognizes 'main' as a very special function. Every program written in C ought to have 'main' function. It is the function, code pertaining to that is executed first. As discussed before, modular programming approach require dividing the main program logic in to various modules. These modules may be written independently leading to multiple functions. Each function complete the task (sub task) associated with it and passes the value to the calling environment. The function may be invoked from the 'main' function or from another function. Thus a function may call another function. The function is also called black box as once it is written it does the specific task by receiving the argument list from the calling environment and return the value (result) to the calling environment. The calling environment does not know details written inside the functions. It is also possible to write the whole code within the 'main' function but it leads to several problem like debugging, testing and program becomes complex. Let us try to understand how the functions are called.

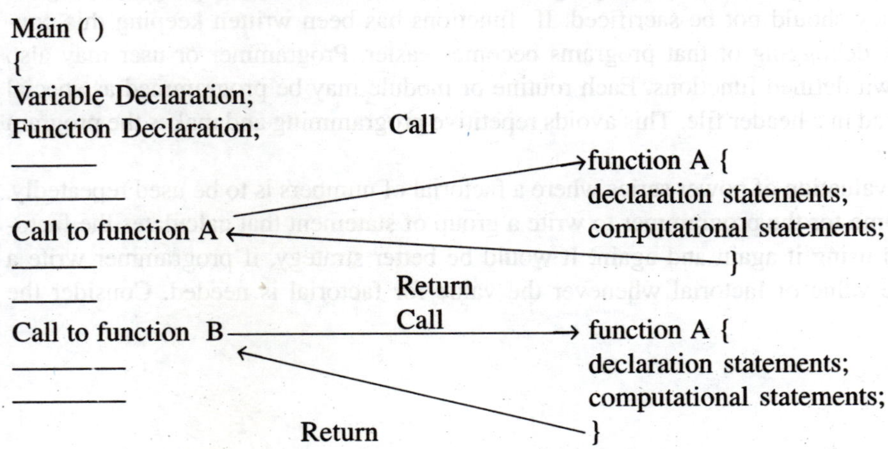

}

Main Program	Function
(Calling Environment)	(Called Environment)

B.3 GENERAL STRUCTURE OF THE USER DEFINED FUNCTION

The general syntax of the function is given below:

```
Base_Type  Function_ Identifier (Parameter List)
{
Body of the function;
}
```

The base type denotes the type of the data or value that a function returns. A function may return any type of the data except the array. Function identifier is the meaningful name given to the function. For example, the function doing multiplication may be given the name 'mult'. The parameter list contains the list of variables and their types. Variable included in the list of parameter are used to receive the values when a function is called. It is not mandatory to have parameter list i.e. parameter list may be blank. A blank parameter list indicates that there is no values to be passed from the calling environment but it must be specified. Following are the example of function parameter declaration.

```
Mult (int a, int b, int c);
Power (int a, float b);
Max (int a, int b);
```

A function may be viewed has either function declaration and function definition statements. Usually these words are considered to be same but there is a difference in it. A function definition statement declares the function type, function name and list of parameter or argument list. In the function declaration statement, function is only declared thus there is no code allotted to it. This considered as information by the compiler and it places the function information in the symbol table. A function definition contains the function declaration as well as the code pertaining to the function. This is called as function body.

B.3.1 General Program Structure

Writing a function in C to solve any complex or intricate problem is a necessity. It is very common and advisable to break the logic of main program into pieces and code them independently. In such cases a 'C' program may be considered to have a collection of various functions. Each function is designed to do a specific task. The 'C' program is developed by creating different function and then put them together. The General structure of a 'C' program would be as follows,

```
Documentation statement
Link Statement
Definition statement
Global variable declaration statement
Main ( )
{
local declaration;
```

```
computational statements;
}
Function Definitions
```

As described earlier, documentation statement are normally the comment line which describe the program written. It may contain the other detail pertaining to the program. The Link statement is a set of statement which link to the library functions. Definition statement includes the constant declarations. Every program written in C must have 'main' function. The main function can be instantiated only once. It consists of local declaration and computational statements that do the main computational work as per the logic. At the last function code is written. It is also known as sub-program. It contains all the computational statement which does the sub-task in totality. This sub-program returns the value to the main program whenever they are invoked. The values or arguments for which the function is to be executed receives it from the main program or from the function they are called.

B.3.2 Global and Local Variable

In C, you may declare the variable whose presence is global i.e. they need not be declared in the sub-program or function separately. Consider the following example,

```
#include <stdio.h>
Int I;
Float j;
Main ( )
{
int k;
int l;
___
___
l= max ( )
}
max ( )
{
int k;
___
___
}
```

In the above example, the variable declared outside the scope of any function are i and j. These variables are recognized by all the function of the program without their further declaration in the function where they will be used. Thus these variable have their global presence and recognition. These variables are called Global Variable or External Variable.

Consider the variable k and l, which are declared in the main function. These variable are not known to other functions as they are visible to the function, in which they have been declared. These variables are called Local Variables. Similarly, the variables declared inside the max () function is 'k'. It may be noted that 'k' has been declared in the main also. Value of 'k' does not conflict as they are considered as different entity by the compiler. The value of 'k' keeps modified independently, therefore changing the value of 'k' in one function will not affect the value of 'k' in another function.

Consider the following example to understand global and local variable:

Program 23

/* Illustration of Local and Global Variable */

```
*****************************************************************************
#include <stdio.h>
int  a= 4;                                          Global Variable
int b= 6;
main ()
{
a=10;
multiply ( );
}
void multiply ( )
{
int mult;                                           Local Variable
mult = a*b;
printf ("multiplication of a and b = %d \n",mult);
}
*****************************************************************************
```

B.4 STORAGE CLASSES

Every variable in the 'C' programming language is defined by two characteristics, namely, Type and Storage Class. Type of variable defines the basic type of variable e.g. int, float, Char etc. Its storage class indicates the acceptability or recognition of the variable inside or outside the function where they have been declared. In particular, the storage class specifies the life and scope of the variables in the function or program. There are four type of storage class in 'C'. These are listed below:

1. Auto
2. Static
3. Extern
4. Register

B.4.1 Automatic (Auto) Variable

It is not mandatory to mention the storage class of a variable. If the storage class of a variable is not specified then it is taken as 'auto' storage class variable. Declaration of the variable inside the function is 'auto' and remain confined to the function. Inside the function these variables are considered to be local to that function. Whenever that function is invoked, memory space for that block is kept reserved. Whenever, the function call is over, the computer releases the memory that was kept reserved for that variable. Thus after the exit, these variables are not available to any other function. Whenever the function is again invoked, the system does the memory allocation again and the values stored to variable earlier are lost. To understand the scope of 'auto' variable, consider the following example:

Program 24

```
*****************************************************************************
```

/* Understanding Automatic Variables */

```
#include <stdio.h>
```

```
main ( )
{
auto int a;
fun_call (a);
printf ("b=%d\n",b);
}
void fun_call(a)
int a;
{
int b;
b=a*a;
}
```

****

In the above program, the 'a' is declared as 'auto' integer variable. Note that 'b' is declared in the function 'fun_call'. This program, when compiled, will give an error that undeclared/unrecognized variable in function 'main'. This happens because, variable 'b' is defined in the function and the scope is limited to function. The memory space for the 'b' will be allotted when the function is called. When the function call is completed, the space reserved for the 'b' is released. Therefore the 'b' will not be available to the 'main' function.

B.4.2 Static Variable

Static variables are permanent within the function they are declared. They work in the similar way as 'auto' variable but they retain the latest value in such a way that whenever the function is invoked again, previous value allotted is available. This all happens because system does not release the memory space allotted to static variable whenever the call to the function is completed. In the case of re-invocation of that function, the previous value of that variable is made amiable. There are two type of static variable available in 'C' namely, internal static and external static. Internal static variables are defined inside the function and there scope is limited to the function where they have been declared. Whereas, the external static variables are declared outside the function and their scope are lies in the remainder of the program.

B.4.3 External Variables

Variables declared as external are similar to the global variable. The variables declared before the 'main' function are available to the rest of program and all the functions.The variable declared as 'extern' are similar to the global variables. By vitue of being declared as 'extern', these variables scope lies with entire program and all the functions, although they are declared in the function.

Example: extern int salary;

B.4.4 Register Variables

The registers are considered as the fastest storage. Thus keeping a value in the register will be accessed with minimum time. The variables, which are used and accessed frequently, are kept in the register, provided they have been declared as of 'register' type. Advantage of declaring a variable as 'register' that it will improve the performance and program will be executed in lesser amount of time i.e. faster execution. There are certain rule to be followed when a variable is declared as 'register' type. Only a limited number of variable can be declared as 'register'. It is not possible to access the address of register because they are not kept in the memory. Type of 'register' must be of int, float or pointer type.

Example: register int salary;

B.5 Passing Parameter to Function

As explained in the previous section that a function body is executed only when it is called from the calling environment. At the invocation of the function, a list of arguments is passed to the function, which receives the values of parameter or argument and does the computation based on it. This process is called parameter passing. There could be several ways the parameter may be passed. When a single value is passed to the function using argument, value of actual parameter is copied to the function. This procedure of coping the value is called as passing by value. In this case the value of the argument from the calling environment is passed to the function by copying the argument. The function may change or modify or alter the value of the argument but the value of argument the main function will remain same. Let us consider following program segment,

Program 25

```
****************************************************************************
/* This program computes the square of integer by calling a function */
# include < stdio.h>
main ()
{
int x, y;
void  square (int x);
x=  5;
Printf ("At first print statement value of X=%d\n", x);
square (x);
Printf ("At second  print statement value of X=%d\n", x);
}
void  square (int x)
{
x= x*x;
Printf ("At third  print statement value of X=%d\n", x);
Return;
}
****************************************************************************
```

In this program, it is important to note that in the calling environment (Main function) when 'square (x)' is executed, function square (X) is invoked. The value of argument x (x=5) is passed to function by copying. The function square(x) computes the square of 5. In the first print statement, value of x will be printed as '5'. After a call to function, print statement (third print statement) written in the function will print the value of x as '25' i.e. after computing square of 'x'. When the program control is returned back to calling environment after the 'return' statement , the second print statement will print the value of x as '5'. Thus the program shows the output as follows,

At first print statement value of X= 5
At third print statement value of X= 25
At second print statement value of X= 5

Thus it is evident that the function may modify or alter the value of argument but value of actual argument (declared in main) within the calling environment will not change.

Consider following program, which has a function to compute the square and the computed value may be returned to the calling environment. This value may be used for further computation in the calling environment. Following is the program, which computes the area of a circle.

Program 26

```
*************************************************************************
/* writing a function to compute the area of circle */

# define PI 3.14
main( )
{
float radius;
float area (float radius);/* Protoype declaration */

radius = 5.0;
m= area (radius);
printf ("First time —area of circle is = %f \n", m);
}
float   area (float r)/* Prototype Definition */
{
float a;

a = PI * r * r;/* Area of circle */

printf ("Second time —area of circle is = %f \n", a);
return (a);
}

*************************************************************************
```

In this program, a prototype declaration and prototype definition of a function 'area' is used. When a function is called from the calling environment, it is not mandatory to have the same names of arguments given in the declaration that of actual arguments. It is also not mandatory to have the same data type in actual argument and name given in the declaration.

The variable 'a' has been defined as a local variable in the function definition. 'radius' has been defined in the main program, when a call to function is invoked at statement 'm=area(radius)' the value of radius (= 5.0) is passed to function and variable 'r' in the function definition is initialized at '5.0'. Function thus computes the area of circle and assigns this value to variable 'a'. Finally at the last statement 'return(a)' statement return this value to calling environment and variable 'm' get the value equal to area of circle. Thus both the print statement print the area as 94.985.

Thus the above example present both the type of function, one which returns a value, secondly which returns nothing. It must be remembered that A function may or may not return a value. If at all it returns a value, it is always single. 'Actual' argument list should be contained in the function call. Actual and format argument must have the same data types. By default, the functions return integer value. If function return the value other than the integer ten its type must be defined in the function header. A function without the return statement will not return any value but a global variable will retain (if modified) its value for the future use.

B.6 CALL BY VALUE AND CALL BY REFERENCE

The functions are invoked by their name and passing the list of parameter to the function. These parameters or arguments must be of same type and number in the function definitions. All the arguments passes the value to the function when the function is invoked. This mechanism is called Call by Value. Here it must be noted that the value is passed to function not the parameter itself. In such cases, the value of variable in the calling environment will not be changed, however the called environment or function may change the value of variable. The value passed must be assigned to a local variable declared inside the function. Consider the following example,

Program 27

/* illustration of concept of *Call by Value* parameter passing */

```
******************************************************************************
# include <stdio.h>
int mult (int m,int n);
main ()
{
int m,n, result;
printf ("Enter the value of M  & N \n");
scanf("%d %d", &m,&n);
printf ("Value of M & N before the call to function = %d   %d\n", m, n);
result = mult (m,n);
printf ("Value of Multiplication  = %d \n", result);
printf ("Value of M & N after  the call to function = %d   %d\n", m, n);
}
int mult (int m, int n)
{
int result=0; temp;
/* swaping the values of m & n */
temp= m;
m=n;
n= temp;
result= m * n;
return (result);
}
******************************************************************************
```

In the above program, suppose you enter following values to m and n

m = 4, n = 2

The value of m and n before the function call : m = 4, n = 2

At the function call mult (m,n), the values of m & n will be copied to function.

Function swaps the values of m and n: thus m = 2, n = 4

Function passes the result of product : result = 8

In the Main function, value of result will be printed as : result = 8;

Next print statement will print the values of m and n as : m = 4, n = 2

Thus you may see that although the values of m and n has been altered in the function call, but it remained unchanged in the main function. This happened because the variable itself has not been passed but the values has been passed. This "Call by Value" parameter mechanism is strictly followed in 'C'.

"***Call by Reference***" is another mechanism of parameter passing. Several other language provides this mechanism. As you have seen in previous example that in the case of "Call by Value" mechanism, the values of the parameters in the calling environment remains unchanged. "Call by Reference" is the mechanism in which the values of variables are changed in the calling environment as per the changes in the functions. This mechanism may be accomplished in the 'C' using pointers. When the function is called the addresses of variables (through pointers) must be passed as argument. Since the address of the variable is passed as value, then changes in the variable value takes into effect. Following example show this mechanism:

Program 28

```
*******************************************************************************
/* Illustration of concept of Call by Reference parameter passing. This
example swaps the value of two variables */
#include <stdio.h>
swap (int *, int *);
main( )
{
 int m,n;
printf (" Enter the value of M  & N \n");
scanf("%d %d ", &m,&n);
printf("Values of M & N before  the swap m=%d  n=%d\n",m,n);
swap (&m,&n);
printf("Values of M & N after the swap m=%d  n=%d\n",m,n);
}

void  swap (int  *a, int *b)
{
int temp;
temp = *a;
*a=*b;
*q = temp;
}
*******************************************************************************
```

The above example swaps the values of m and n. supose you enter following values for m and n,

M = 1, N = 2

The values of m and n before the call to swap( ) function are : M = 1, N = 2

The values of m and n after the call to swap () function are : M = 2, N = 1

Thus it may be noted that using pointers, it is possible to change the values of variable in the calling environment in accordance with the changes made by the function. This process of parameter passing is defined as "Call by Reference".

Program 29

```
*******************************************************************************
/*THE RECURSIVE PROGRAM FOR FINDING THE FACTORIAL */
#include<conio.h>
#include<stdio.h>
```

```
void main()
{
int i,f=1,n,a;
int facto(int p);
clrscr();
printf(" /*THE PROGRAM FOR FINDING THE FACTORIAL OF ANY GIVEN NUMBER
GREATER THAN 1*/ ");
printf("\n\n GIVE THE NUMBER WHOSE FACTORIAL IS REQUIRED");
scanf("%d",&n);
a=n;
if(n==0)
f=1;

else
f=facto(n);

printf("\n\n THE FACTORIAL OF  %d!  IS %d ",a,f);
getch();
}

int facto(int p)
{
 int s;
if(p==1)
  return(1);
else
s=p*facto(p-1);
return s;
}
```

****

B.7 RECURSION

The process of calling a function by itself is called Recursion. This process is continued until a particular condition is satisfied. This process is used for the repetitive computations in which each function call return a value, for which the function needs be invoked again. As shown in the previous program, the function 'Fact' is called until the condition for call is satisfied. Logic for the factorial computation by recursion may be understood as given below:

n! = n * (n-1)!   And 1!=1

To calculate 5! Following steps are taken:

Step 1	5! = 5 * 4!	Compute 4!
Step 2	4! = 4 * 3!	Compute 3!
Step 3	3! =3 * 2!	Compute 2!
Step 4	2! = 2 * 1!	1!=1

In this case the function 'fact' must be called four times, one each for 4!, 3!,2!, and 1!. Thereafter the values from each function called are passed back to previous one. Thus after four returns the value of !5 is computed. This is made possible by using the stack (First in Last out) structure. When the function calls are made, the recursive function calls are not executed immediately. These calls are placed on the stack until the termination condition is achieved.

There are several function which needs be represented recursively. For example, the each term in Fibnocci Series may be defined as follows,

F(1)= 1;
F(2)=1;
F(n) = F(n-1) + F(n-2);

Where the F(n) denotes the nth term of Fibnocci Series. Few of the terms of Fibnocci Series are as under.

1, 1, 2, 3, 5, 8, 13, 21, 34

Program 30

```
*****************************************************************************
/* Write a Recursive Program / Function to compute nth term of Fibonaci Series */

#include <stdio.h>
int term (int n)
int sum (int  m)
main( )
{
int n;
printf ("\n Enter the term\n");
scanf ("%d", &n);
Printf ("\n Enter the Term number to which the sum is to be computed\n");
Scanf ("%d", & m);
printf (" n th term of Fibonacci series is  = %d\n", term (n));
printf (" Summation of all terms up to n th term is  = %d\n", sum (m));
}

int term (int n)
{
if (n<=2)
return (1);
else
return (term(n-1) + term(n-2))
}
int sum (int  m)
{
int I;
int result =0;
for (I=1; I<=m;I++)
{
result= result + term (1);
}
return(result);
}
*****************************************************************************
```

Program 31

```
*************************************************************************************
/* Write a function to compute the x to power n */
#include<stdio.h>
#include<conio.h>
void main()
{
 int n;
 float x,y;
 char ch;
 float power(float, int);
 clrscr();
 do{
  printf("\nEnter the number(in fraction) of which power is to be
calculated\n");
  scanf("%f",&x);
 printf("\nEnter the power upto which the value is to be calculated\n");
  scanf("%d",&n);
 y=power(x,n);
 printf("\n The computed value is: %f",y);
 getch();
 printf("\n Do you wish to calculate for another(y/n):");
  fflush(stdin);
  scanf("%c",&ch);
  }while(ch=='y');
}
//********************************
float power(float a, int b)
{ int i;
  float c=1.0;
  float d;
  d=a;
  for(i=1;i<=b;i++)
  c=c*d;
  return(c);
  }
*************************************************************************************
```

Program 32

```
*************************************************************************************
/* Write function to compute the GCD of two numbers */
#include<stdio.h>
#include<conio.h>
#include<process.h>
int a,b;
void main()
{
printf("\nEnter the two numbers of which gcd is to be calculated\n");
```

```
scanf("%d\n %d",&a,&b);
gcd();
}
void gcd()
{
if(a==b)
{
printf("\ngcd of the two no. is %d",a);
getch();
exit(0);
}
else if(a<b)
{
b=b-a;
gcd();
}
else{
a=a-b;
gcd();
}
}
```

****

C.1 INTRODUCTION TO STRUCTURE

Structure is a collection of variables defined under single name. These variables need not be of same type. Thus, Structure provides the convenient way of bundling the related information. The Structure is convenient tool for handling a group of logically related data items. The variables that contribute to make a Structure are called members. Consider a database of student of a class where the individual record of their Roll No, Name, Father Name, Marks etc has to be maintained. All of this information may be put and used as Structure. We may define following structure,

```
Struct Student
{
Int          Roll_Number ;
Char         name[25];
Char         Fname [25];
Int          Marks;
Float        Weight;
};
```

In the above example, the structure Student have been declared to hold a group of five data items. These data item and their type are defined within the braces separated by semi colon. Here the data items are Roll Number, Name, Father Name, Marks and Weight of the student. These data items are called the structure element or the members. There is no restriction on any members for data type. Every member may have different data type. Student is the name of the structure and is called Structure Tag. Structure help to organize the complex data in more meaningful way. It gives lot of freedom and flexibility to the programmer to write a code in C.

C.2 DECLARATION OF STRUCTURE

The structure provides the mechanism to group the data of different type, which grouped together presents a information. We may declare a structure 'employee' with the attributes employee name, Department, Designation, Basic Pay, Gross Pay, DA, HRA. Following is the 'C' program segment, which declare the structure:

```
Struct Employee
{
Char  emp_Code[5];
Char  emp_name[50];
Char  department[50];
Char  designation[30];
Float basic_pay;
Float gross_pay;
Float da;
Float hra;
};
```

Following is the template, which will be used to describe information.

Emp_code	Array of Five Character
Emp_name	Array of fifty Character
Department	Array of fifty Character
Designation	Array of thirty Character
Basic_Pay	Float
Gross_pay	Float
DA	Float
HRA	Float

Consider the structure 'student' defined above, we may declare the structure variable using the tag name. 'C' segment to declare the structure variable student1, student2 is as follows.

```
Struct Student
{
Int   Roll_Number;
Char  name[25];
Char  Fname [25];
Int   Marks;
Float Weight;
};
Struct student student1,student2;
```

It must be noted that use of tag name is not mandatory. The above declaration along with the structure variable as shown below is also valid.

```
Struct
{
Int   Roll_Number;
Char  name[25];
Char  Fname [25];
Int   Marks;
Float Weight;
} student1, student2;
```

The structure definition appears at the beginning of the program, normally before declaration of any other variable. They may also appear before the 'main', in such cases the definition is global and may be used by any function.

C.3 INITIALIZATION OF VALUES TO MEMBERS OF STRUCTURE

The following program segment assign the values to members of structure variable student:

```
Main()
{
Static Struct
{
Int    Roll_Number;
Char         name[25];
Char         Fname [25];
Int          Marks;
Float        Weight;
};
student = {111, "Ansuman Yadav", "V S  Yadav", 29, 51.8};
```

This assigns the values as

Student. Roll_number	= 111
Student. Name	= "Anshuman Yadav"
Student. Fname	= "V S Yadav"
Stdent.Marks	= 29
Student.weight	= 51.8

The link between the variable and member is established by a dot '.'.

Another way of assigning values to members of structure is as follows:

```
Struct Student
{
Int   Roll_Number;
Char        name[25];
Char        Fname [25];
```

```
Int    Marks;
Float       Weight;
} student1;
```

we may assign the values to the members of structure variable Student1 as shown below:

Student1.roll_number = 111;
Strcpy(student1.name, " Anshuman Yadav");
Strcpy (student1.fname," V S Yadav");
Student1.marks = 29
Student1.weight =51.8;

It is also possible to use the 'scanf' statement to input the record from the standard input e.g Key board. Following program reads the values from the input and assign it to the members of structure variable.

Program 33

```
*****************************************************************************
/* Program to read value using 'Scanf' assiging it to member of structure */

Struct Student
{
Int         Roll_Number ;
Char        name[25];
Char        Fname [25];
Int         Marks;
Float       Weight;
} ;
main ()
{
struct student student1;
Printf(" Enter the values \n");
Scanf (" %d   %s   %s   %d    %f",& student1.roll_number, student1.name,
student1.fname, &student1.marks, &student1.weight);

Printf (" Printing the record \n");
Printf (" %d   %s   %s   %d    %f\n", student1.roll_number, student1.name,
student1.fname, student1.marks, student1.weight);
}
*****************************************************************************
```

C.4 ARRAYS OF STRUCTURE

Use of structure is not limited to just a collection of heterogeneous type variable. As we have seen that a student entity may be represented as structure and its attributes may be represented as members. It is also possible to create an array of structure. For example, if we have to represent the class of fifty students, each student's attribute may be stored and processed by declaring the class as an array of structure. This is done by doing following:

Struct Class student[50];

This statement defines an array of structure called Class. Each element of this array is an struct type. We can initialize the members of all the fifty student by doing following. Following is the example, which initialize the members of only three students.

```
Struct Student
{
Int        Roll_Number;
Char       name[25];
Char       Fname [25];
Int        Marks;
Float      Weight;
};
main( )
{
static struct student class[4] = {{111, "Ritendra Goel", " P P Yadav", 29,
51.8}, {112, "S S Soam", "O S Soam", 55, 71.8}, {113, "Tanvir Tahir", "Y
M Tahir", 53, 99.9},{114,"Ankita Singh", "D S yadav",33,23.6}};
}
```

This program segment declares class as an array of four element class[0], class[1], class[2], class[3] and initializes the values as following.

Class[0].roll_number = 111;
Class[0].name = "Ritendra Goel"
Class[0]. Fname = "P P Yadav"
——

———

class[3].rollnumber =114
class[3].name = "Ankita Singh"
Class[3].fname = "D S Yadav"
Class[3].marks = 33
Class[3].weight = 23.6

In case of large data required to initialize the member, it is advisable to read the data from standard input. This can be done using 'scanf' statement. Following program read the student data from the input. This program prints the complete record of student who have obtained maximum marks.

Program 34

```
*********************************************************************************
/* Program to find the student who have obtained maximum marks */
Struct Student
{
Int    Roll_Number;
Char        name[25];
Char        Fname [25];
```

```
Int   Marks;
Float       Weight;
};
main ()
{
int n,index, max
Struct student class[50];

For (n=0; n<50; n++)
{
Printf(" Enter the record of %d student\n", n+1);
Scanf (" %d   %s   %s   %d    %f",& class[n].roll_number, class[n].name,
class[n].fname, & class[n].marks, &class[n].weight);
}
Max= 0;
for (n=0; n<50; n++)
{
if (Max <  class[n].marks)
index =n;
}

Printf (" Printing the record of student obtained maximum marks\n");
Printf (" %d   %s   %s   %d     %f\n", class[index].roll_number,class
index].name, class[index].fname, class[index].marks, class[index].weight);
}
```

****

D.1 INTRODUCTION TO POINTERS

Pointers are probably the most important feature of C programming language. Pointer is a powerful tool to efficiently access the data by indirect reference because it holds the address of data item in question. Pointer are very efficient in writing the program which requires handling with the table. Real power of C lies with efficiently using the pointers. Typically the pointer is integer variable which holds the address of the another variable. The pointer always contains the memory address. Here memory address refers to the memory location where a variable has been allotted space to hold the value. If out of two variable, one variable holds or contain the address of another variable, the first is said to point to second variable.

For example the following statement declares and initialize the variable amount,

Int amount = 100;

This statement prompt the system to allot the space for this variable in the memory. The Value 100 is stored in that memory location and is called the content of that memory location. Suppose the system has allotted the memory location 1000 to the variable amount.

Memory Address	**Content of Memory**	**Logical Name**
0		
1		
____		
____		
____		
999		
1000	100	amount
1001		
1002		
____		
____		

In the above figure, you may observe the continuos memory location. System may allot any memory location to the variable. Every memory location may be thought to be composed of its address and contents. This memory location may be addressed by giving the logical name as declared in the program. Here 'amount' is allotted memory location whose address is '1000' and value of amount '100' is pushed to memory location. Now, the value '100' may be accessed in two ways, one by logical name 'amount', seconuly by address '1000'. Memory address are always integer and they may be assigned to any integer variable which can also be stored in the memory just like any other variable. These variable are called pointer, because they hold the memory address of another variable.

Suppose the variable 'ptr' holds the memory address of variable 'amount' i.e. '1000'. The 'ptr' is called the pointer (variable) and it points to 'amount'. It may be represented as following:

Name of variable	amount	ptr
Content of Memory Location	100	**1000**
Memory Address	**1000**	2000

Here you may note that 'ptr' is a pointer to 'amount' as contents of 'ptr' are the memory address of 'amount'. However, the memory address of 'ptr' variable is '2000'.

The memory allocation for a variable is done on 'run time', therefore the address of the variable is not known immediately. However, the address of the variable may be determined using '&' operator. For example,

ptr = & amount;

this statement returns the address of variable 'amount' and initialize to 'ptr'. The '&' operator may be used in conjunction with any variable or array element. Consider the following array declaration:

Int Marks[10];

This statement initializes an array 'Marks'.

I = & Marks[1]; statement returns the address of 1st element of 'Marks' array and assigns to 'I'.

D.2 DECLARATION AND INITIALIZATION OF POINTERS

The pointer contains the address of variable and variable may be of any data type. The general declaration syntax of pointer is as shown below:

Data Type * name;

Here the Data Type indicate the type of variable to which this pointer points. "*" shows that the variable 'name' is pointer. 'Name' is the name of pointer variable. Following are some example of pointer declaration:

```
Int *amt_ptr;
Float *q;
```

First declaration declares 'amt_ptr' as pointer variable which points to variable of 'int' datatype. Second statement shows that 'q' is pointer variable which point to variable of 'float' data type. After the declaration of pointer variable, it can be initialised to point to a particular variable. For example,

```
    amt_ptr  = & amount;
or  q        = & v;
```

These statements initialises the pointer, as shown, first statement state that 'amt_ptr' pointer points to variable 'amount' and second shows that 'q' points to variable 'v'. It must be remembered that pointer must point to the variable whose datatype is same as of pointer declaration. For example,

```
Int *amt_ptr;
Float amount;
Amt_ptr = & amount;
```

These statement are incorrect, as 'amt_ptr' has been declared to point to the variable of type 'int'. But the variable 'amount' has been declared as 'float'. Thus these statement will result in to incorrect.

D.3 POINTER ARITHMETIC

It would be advisable initially to understand the meaning of "*" and "&" as following:

'*' Contents of Memory Location

'&' Address of memory location.

For example consider the following set of statement:

```
Int *amt_ptr;
Int next, amount        =100;
amt_ptr                 = & amount;
next                    = *amt_ptr;
```

First statement declares 'amt_ptr' as a pointer, second declares 'next' and 'amount' variable of 'int' data type. Third statement declares the 'amt_ptr' as pointer to variable 'amount' by putting the address of variable 'amount' in to 'amt_ptr'. Fourth statement, returns the contents of memory location whose address is stored at 'amt_ptr', which is equal to '100'. Thus 'next' would be initialized as '100'. Thus it may be noted that following two statements:

```
amt_ptr = & amount;
next    = *amt_ptr;
```

may be written as

```
next = *& amount;
```

which is equivalent to following statement:

```
next = amount;
```

The pointer may be used in the expression just like any other variable. The 'a', 'b' and 'c' are the pointers then following expression are valid:

```
Interest = amount  * (*b);
*a = *b * *c;
amount =  *b / *c +   *a * *b;
a++;
amount *=  *c;
- -  c;
```

D.4 ACCESSING AN ARRAY USING POINTER

At the time of declaration of array, the contiguous memory locations are allotted to each element of an array. Consider following array declaration statement:

Int Marks [3];

This will allot the contiguous memory location for each element of array 'Marks' as shown below:

Element of array	Marks[0]	Marks[1]	Marks[2]
Address	2500	2502	2504

It may be noted that each integer takes two bytes to store an integer, therefore every element of array will take two byte to store single value. We may declare 'ptr' pointer to pint the array 'marks' as shown below:

```
Int *ptr;
ptr = marks;
```

First statement declare the 'ptr' as pointer and second makes the pointer to point to array 'marks'. Immediately after second statement 'ptr' will contain the address of memory location marks[0] i.e. ptr = & marks[0]. Now to access other element of array 'ptr' may be incremented by one each time. Following program uses pointers to access an array:

Program 35

****

/* This program finds largest number in the array using pointer */

```
# include <stdio.h>
main( )
{
int *ptr, max, n;
int  Marks[50];
max=0;
ptr=marks;
Printf("Enter the numbers\n");
For (n=0; n<50; n++)
{
scanf(" Enter number ::  %d \n",&Marks[n];
}
n=0;
while (n<50)
{
if  (max > *ptr)
max= *ptr;
n++; ptr ++
}
printf ("Largest number = %d\n", max);
}
```

****

D. 5 DYNAMIC MEMORY ALLOCATION

When a program written in 'C' is executed the various structures like Variables, Array etc are allotted memory space as per the requirement. This memory allocation requirement is normally 'static' in nature. For example, following array declaration:

Int amount[50];

Reserves the memory location required to store '50' integer values. In many cases, the array requirement is over estimated by the programmer. This allocation is done as per the programmer wish and a whole lot of memory is reserved before the start of execution of program. This type of memory allocation is called static memory allocation. In short, in the case of static memory allocation, size of memory may be required for the computation work before the execution. In the case of Dynamic Memory Allocation, the size of memory is determined and allotted at the time of execution. The Dynamic Memory allocation has many advantages over static memory allocation.

Consider a case of array of structures, whose declaration is given below:

```
Struct Student
{
Int  Roll_Number;
Char        name[25];
```

```
Char          Fname [25];
Int    Marks;
Float         Weight;
};
Struct student class[1000];
```

In the above declaration, the memory space for storing the '1000' element of 'struct' type is allotted statically. But at the run time, it might be the case that only '400' students record is to be entered. In such cases, the memory worth storing '600' such record is wasted. Secondly, if it is required to change the size of memory (e.g. entering '2000' student record in this case) will lead to an error. This is because the size reserved for the array is lower than the actual requirement. In this case, you have to change the code of your program. Both of the cases are not desirable. Thus the preferred strategy is to allot the memory whenever required at the run. This concept is known as Dynamic Memory Allocation and supported by the 'C' Programming Language.

Allocating the Memory

Malloc() function is used in 'C' programming language to allocate the memory dynamically. This function reserves the memory and returns a pointer which point to the memory where it has been reserved. Consider the following statement:

ptr = (int *) malloc (10 * sizeof (int));

This function (malloc) reserves the block of memory location whose size is 10 times the size required to store one integer. This function returns a pointer to an integer ('ptr') which points to the beginning of the memory block.

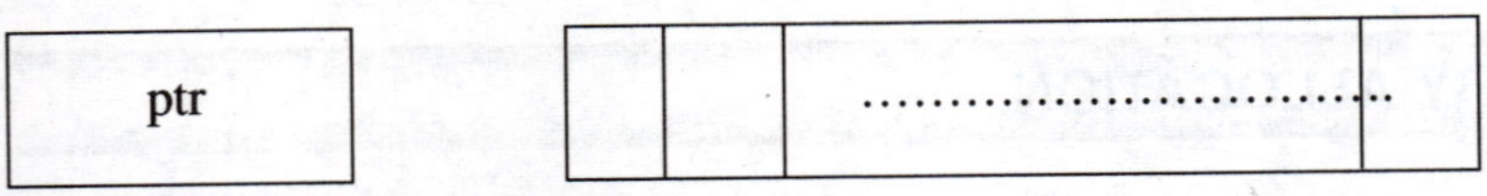

Address of First Memory Location   *memory to store 10 integer.*

Similarly the statement,

ptr = (char *) malloc(100);

reserves the memory to store 100 character and return a pointer to character ('ptr') which points to the first memory location, in other words, the address of the first memory location is assigned to ptr.

Similarly it is also possible to allocate the memory block for 'structure'. For example,

ptr = (struct student *) malloc (size of (struct student));

reserves the memory location to store the record of student (struct 'student' has been defined in structure section) and return a pointer. If the system fails to allocate the memory then it returns 'NULL'.

Consider following program, which uses Dynamic Memory Allocation to create an array of integer and sort the numbers entered in increasing order.

Program 36

****

/* This program create a table of numbers using dynamic memory allocation and sorts the number in increasing order */

```
#include <stdio.h>
#include <stdlib.h>
# define NULL 0
void sort (int size, int * q);
main ( )
{
int  *q;
int I, size;

Printf ("Enter the number of entries to be  entered\n");
Scanf ("%d", &size);

/*Allocate the memory to store the integer whose number is 'size'*/
q= (int *) malloc (size * sizeof (int));

/* Read the entries */
printf ("please enter total %d  entries", size);
for (I= 0; I < size; I++)
{
printf ("Enter   %d  number", I+1);
scanf ("%d", q + I);
}

/* Function to sort the number */
sort (size, q);

/* Print the sorted numbers */
for (I=0; I< size; I++)
{
printf("position = %d value = %d \n", I+1, *(size + I));
}
}

void sort  (int size, int *q)
{
int I, item, temp;
for  (item=0; item < size; item ++)
{
for (I= item + 1;I < size; I++)
{
```

```
if (*(q+I) < *(q+item))
{
temp = *(q+item);
*(q+item) = *(q+I);
*(q+I) = temp;
}}}
return;
}
```

****

Program 37

****

/* Write a program to find number of character in a line */

```
#include<stdio.h>
#include<conio.h>
void main()
{
 char ch;
 int count=0;
 clrscr();
 printf("\n\t\tProgram to find number of characters in a line\n");
 printf("\t\t**********************************************\n");
 printf("Enter the character string\n");
 do{
 ch=getc(stdin);
 count++;
} while(ch!='\n');
 count-;
 printf("\n Number of characters in the line are\n");
 printf(":%d",count);
 getch();
 }
```

****

Program 38

****

/* Write a program using pointer to concatenate two strings */

```
#include<stdio.h>
#include<conio.h>
void main()
{
 char *str1,*str2,*str3;
 int i,j;
 clrscr();
 printf("\n\t\tProgram to concatenate two strings");
 printf("\n\t\t*********************************\n");
 printf("\n Enter string1:");
```

```
 gets(str1);
 printf("\n Enter string2:");
 gets(str2);
 for(i=0;str1[i]!='\0';i++)
 str3[i]=str1[i];
 str3[i]=' ';
 for(j=0;str2[j]!='\0';j++)
 str3[i+j+1]=str2[j];
 str3[i+j+1]='\0';
 printf("\n The concatenated string is:\n %s",str3);
 getch();
 }
```

****

Program 39

****

```
/* Write a program to  find number of words in a statement.      */
#include<stdio.h>
#include<conio.h>

void main()
{
 char *str,ch;
 int count=0;
 clrscr();
 printf("\n\t\tProgram to find number of words in a statment");
 printf("\n\t\t****************************************\n");
 printf("\n Enter the character string:\n");
 fflush(stdin);
 //gets(str);
 do{
 ch= getc(stdin);
 if(ch==' ')
 count++;
 }while(ch!='\n');
 count++;
 printf("\n The number of words in the string are: %d",count);
 getch();
 }
```

****

Program 40

****

```
/* Write a program to sort the name in Alphabetical Order using Pointers */
#include<stdio.h>
#include<conio.h>
#include<string.h>
```

```
void main()
{
 char *str[10];
 char *temp;
 int i,n;
 clrscr();
 printf("\n\t\tProgram to sort names in alphabetical order");
 printf("\n\t\t***************************************\n");
 printf("\n Enter how many names do u want to sort:");
 scanf("%d",&n);
 printf("\n Enter %d names one by one:",n);
 for(i=0;i<n;i++)
 {
 printf("\n Name[%d]:",i);
 gets(str[i]);
 }
 for(i=1;i<n;i++)
 {
 for(j=1;j<=n-i;j++)
 {

  if(strcmp(str[j-1], str[j])>0)
  {
  strcpy(temp,str[j-1]);
  strcpy(str[j-1],str[j]);
  strcpy(str[j],temp);
   }
   }
   printf("\n The names in sorted order are:\n");
  for(i=0;i<n;i++)
  {
   printf("%s",str[i]);
  }
  getch();
  }
Example Programs
*********************************************************************************
```

Program 41

****

/* Write functions to compute the multiplication and summation of terms of series x,x**2,x**3,.... for x<1 */

```
#include<stdio.h>
#include<conio.h>
#include<stdlib.h>
void main()
{
```

```
 int n,i,j,m;
 float x;
 char ch;
 void multi(float, int);
 void addition(float, int);

 clrscr();
 printf("\n Program to compute the multiplication and addition of series
x,x**2,x**3,....for x<1");
 do{
 printf("\n\n Enter the power upto which manipulations are to be taken
into account\n");
 scanf("%d",& n);
 printf("\n Enter the value of which power is to be calculated\n");
 scanf("%f",& x);
 if(x>=1)
 {
 printf("\n Program terminated\nx should be less than 1");
 getch();
 exit(0);
 }
 printf("\n Main Menu");
 printf("\n1. Multiplication of Series");
 printf("\n2. Addition of Series");
 printf("\n3. exit");
 printf("\n\nEnter your choice");
 scanf("%d",&m);
 switch(m)
 {
 case 1:multi(x,n);
      break;
 case 2:addition(x,n);
      break;
 case 3:printf("\nexiting from the program");
      exit(0);
  }
printf("\nDo u wish to calculate for another(y/n):");
fflush(stdin);
scanf("%c",&ch);
}while(ch=='y');
 }

// ************************************
 void multi(float a, int b)
 {
 int c;
 float mul=1;
```

```
int i,j=0;
float d,arr[10];
d=a;
for(c=1;c<=b;c++)
{
 arr[j]=d;
 d=d*a;
 j+=1;
 }
 for(i=0;i<b;i++)
 {
  mul  =mul * arr[i];
  }
  printf("\n The multiplicated value of series is\n");
  printf("%f",mul);
  return;
  }

//*********************************************
 void addition(float a, int b)
 {
  int i,c;
  float arr[10],d;
  float add=0;
 int j=0;
 d=a;
  for(c=1;c<=b;c++)
{
 arr[j]=d;
 d=d*a;
 j+=1;
 }
 for(i=0;i<b;i++)
 {
  add = add + arr[i];
  }
  printf("\n The calculated value of series after addition is\n");
  printf("%f",add);
  return;
  }
```

****

Program 42

****

/* Write a function to check if a number is prime or not */

```
#include<stdio.h>
```

```
#include<math.h>

void main()
{
int n;
char ch;
void prime(int);

clrscr();
do
{
printf("Program to check the given no. for prime\n");
printf("Enter the no.\n");
scanf("%d",&n);
prime(n);
printf("\nDo you wish to check another number(y/n)\n");
fflush(stdin);
scanf("%c",&ch);
}while(ch=='y');
}

void prime(int n)
{
 int a,b,c;
  a =(int) sqrt(n);
  for(b=2;b<=a+1;b++)
   {
    c = n % b;
    if(c==0)
    {
      printf("\nGiven no. is not prime\n");
      break;
    }
    else if(c!=0 && b<(a+1))
      continue;
    else if(c!=0 && b==(a+1))
    {
      printf("\nGiven no. is prime number");
      break;
    }
  }
}
```

****

Program 43

****

/* Write a recursive call to evaluate the following series.

F(x) = x - x^3/3! + x^5/ 5! - x^7/7! + ...

```
*/

# include <stdio.h>
# include <conio.h>
# include <math.h>

void main()
{ float power(float,int);
  long int fact(int);
  float x,sig,term,sum=0,sine;
  int i,n,j;
  clrscr();
  printf("Enter the value of x:");
  scanf("%f",&x);
  printf("Enter the number of terms:");
  scanf("%d",&n);
  for(i=0;i<n;i++)
  { j=2*i+1;
    sig=power(-1,i);
    term=sig*(power(x,j)/fact(j));
    sum=sum+term;
  }
  sine=sin(x);
  printf("\nThe sine of %f is %f",x,sine);
  printf("\nThe value of sum is %f",sum);
  getch();
}

float power(float a,int b)
{ int m;
  float val=1;
  for(m=1;m<=b;m++)
  { val=val*a;
  }
  return(val);
}

long int fact(int num)
{ int p;
  long int f=1;
  for(p=1;p<=num;p++)
  { f=f*p;
  }
  return(f);
}
*******************************************************************************
```

Program 44

****

```
/*
#include<conio.h>
#include<stdio.h>
#include<string.h>

void main()
{
    int i,counter=0;
    char str[20],str2[20];
    clrscr();
    printf("THIS IS A PROGRAM OF REVERSING THE STRING ORDER");
    printf("\nenter your desire string");
    scanf("%s",str);
 //  counter= strlen(str);
    for(i=0;str[i]!='\0';i++)
       counter++;
    for(i=0;i<=counter;i++)
    str2[i]=str[i];
  printf("\nthe reverse string-\n");
  for(i=counter;i>=0;i–)
    printf("%c",str2[i]);
  printf("\nthe length of string=   %d",counter);
  getch();
  }
```

****

Program 45

****

/* This program adds the digits of a given number */

```
#include<stdio.h>
#include<conio.h>
#define  max  12
void main()
{
   int i=0,num,sum=0;
    int rem[max];
 clrscr();
 printf("\nTHIS IS A PROGRAM OF ADDITION OF DIGITS OF A NUMBER\n");
 printf("\nenter the number which u want\n");
 scanf("%d",&num);
 do
    { rem[i]=num%10;
      sum=sum+rem[i];
```

```
   }
  while(num>0);
  printf("the sum of digit your desire number=%d",sum);
  getch();
 }
```

****

Program 50

****

/* Program to accept two string at input & find length of greatest common substring */

```
#include<conio.h>
#include<stdio.h>
#include<string.h>
void main()
{
char  str1[10],str2[10],str3[10];
int  i,j,len1,len2,count=0;
clrscr();
printf("\n Enter the first string ");
scanf("%s",str1);
printf("\n Enter the second string ");
scanf("%s",str2);
len1=strlen(str1);
len2=strlen(str2);
for(i=0;i<=len1;i++)
   {
    for(j=0;j<=len2;j++)
        {
        if(str1[i]==str2[j])
        {
        str3[count]=str1[i];
        count++;
        //   break;
        delete str1[i];
         }
       //break;
       }
    }
printf("%d  %d \n ", len1,len2);
printf("%s   %s   %s",str1,str2,str3);
getch();
}
```

****

Program 51

****

/* THE PROGRAM IN C TO FIND THE SUM OF ODD & EVEN NUMBER FROM 1 TO 100*/

```
#include<conio.h>
#include<stdio.h>
```

```
void main()
{
int num,i,j;
int evensum=0,sumodd=0;
clrscr();
printf("\n The sum of odd numbers is\n");
printf("0");
for(i=1;i<=99;i=i+2)
{
sumodd=sumodd+i;
printf("+ %d",i);
}
printf("= %d\n\n\n",sumodd);
printf("The sum of even number\n\n");
printf("0");
for(i=2;i<=100;i=i+2)
{
evensum=evensum+i;
printf("+ %d",i);
}
printf("= %d",evensum);

getch();
}
```

****

Program 52

****

/* Program to calculate the compound interest for a given principal amonut */

```
#include<conio.h>
#include<stdio.h>
void main()
{
float principal_amount,original_amount;
float rate_interest;
int i, no_of_year;
float simple_interest,compound_interest;
clrscr();
printf("\nEnter the principal amount");
scanf("%f",&principal_amount);
original_amount=principal_amount;
printf("\nEnter the rate of interest");
scanf("%f",&rate_interest);
printf("\nEnter the number of year");
scanf("%d",&no_of_year);
simple_interest=principal_amount * rate_interest * no_of_year/100;
printf("\n Simple interest =  %f",simple_interest);
for(i=1;i<=no_of_year;i++);
```

```
{
 simple_interest=principal_amount * rate_interest * i/100;
 principal_amount=principal_amount+simple_interest;
 }
compound_interest=principal_amount-original_amount;
printf("\n compound interest = %f ",compound_interest);

getch();
}
```

****

Program 53

****

```
/* Program to print 'a' ...'z' and digit '0'...'9' and their ASCII integer value in Decimal */
#include <conio.h>
#include <stdio.h>
void main()
{
char ch='a';
int i;
 clrscr();
printf("\n The ASCII value of \n");
for(i=0;i<26;i++)
{
printf("\n%c = %d",ch,ch);
ch=ch+1;
}
ch='0';
printf("\n");
for(i=0;i<=9;++i)
{
printf("\n%c = %d",ch,ch);
ch=ch+1;
}

getch();
}
```

****

Program 54

****

```
/* Program to convert upper case to Lower case letter */
#include<conio.h>
#include<stdio.h>
void main()
{
char ch;
```

```
printf("\nEnter a letter");
scanf("%c",&ch);
printf("\n%c\t%c",ch,ch+32);
getch();
}
```

****

Program 55

****

/* Write a program to Evaluate the Polynomial 3*x*x*x - 5*x*x +6 for x=2.25 */

```
#include<conio.h>
#include<stdio.h>
#include<string.h>
void main()
{
float x,Z;
clrscr();
printf("Z= 3*x*x*x -5*x*x+6");
printf("\n Enter the value of x ");
scanf("%f",&x);
Z= 3*x*x*x -5*x*x+6;
printf("\nZ= %f",Z);
getch();
}
```

****

Program 56

****

/* Program to Convert millimeter to meters, centimeters */

```
#include<conio.h>
#include<stdio.h>
#include<string.h>
void main()
{
float mtr,mm,cm;
clrscr();
printf("\n Enter a Quantity in Millimeters ");
scanf("%f",&mm);
cm=mm/10;
mtr=mm/1000;
printf("\n%7.3f  millimeter = %7.3f cm\n\n %7.3f millimeter = %7.3f
mtr",mm,cm,mm,mtr);
getch();
}
```

****

Program 57

```
*****************************************************************************
/* Write program to evaluate Z for values of x & y varying from -2 to 2 step 1 */
#include<conio.h>
#include<stdio.h>
void main()
{
int Z,x,y;
clrscr();
printf("\n\n The required expression is");
printf("\n\nZ=x*x*x - 2*x*y*y + 3*x*y + y - 2*y*y*y");
for(x=-2;x<=2;x++)
{
    for(y=-2;y<=2;y++)
    {
     Z=x*x*x - 2*x*y*y + 3*x*y + y - 2*y*y*y;
     printf("\nfor x= %3d and y=%3d value of Z is : %3d  ",x,y,Z);
     }
   printf("\n");
   }
getch();
}
*****************************************************************************
```

Program 58

```
*****************************************************************************
/* Write program to calculate Cosine values for angle 0 to 180 */
#include<conio.h>
#include<stdio.h>
#include<math.h>
#define PI 3.1416
void main()
{
int i;
float angle;
clrscr();
printf("\n The cosine of different angle");
printf("\n\n angle \t COS(angle)\n\n");
for(i=0;i<=180;i=i+10)
{
angle=(PI/180) *i;
printf("\n %3d\t %7.5f",i,cos(angle));
}
getch();
}
*****************************************************************************
```

Program 59

****

57

```
/* Program to find numbers of integers & sum of integers greater than 100
and less then 200 that are divisible by 7 */
#include<conio.h>
#include<stdio.h>
void main()
{
int  num[20],sum=0,count=0,i;
clrscr();
for(i=100;i<=200;i++)
{
if(i%7==0)
{
  num[count]=i;
  count++;
  sum=sum+i;
  }}
  printf("\n The numbers are :-\n");
  for(i=0;i<count;i++)
  {
  printf("\t%d",num[i]);
  }
   printf("\nThe total number is    %d\n The sum of these numbers are
%d",count,sum);
  getch();
  }
```

****

Program 60

****

/* Program to process the application of students and list eligible candidate subject to following eligibility criteria

```
Maths Marks >=60,  Physics Marks >= 50, Chemistry Marks >=10, Total >= 200  */
#include<conio.h>
#include<stdio.h>
void main()
{
int maths,phy,che,total;
clrscr();
printf("\nEnter the marks of Maths");
scanf("%d",&maths);
printf("\nEnter the marks of physics");
scanf("%d",&phy);
printf("\nEnter the marks of Chemistry");
scanf("%d",&che);
```

```
total=maths+phy+che;
if((maths>=60 && phy>=50 &&che>=10&&total>=200)||((maths+phy)>=150))
      printf("\n Your are  an eligible Candidate");
else
printf("\nSORRY !! SORRY !!");
getch();
}
```

****

Program 61

****

/*Cost of operation of unit consisting of two components C1 & C2 can be expresed as function of a parameter p as follows
C1=30-8P ; C2= 10 + P*P ; The parameter ranges from 0 to 10. Write program in C which determine C1 & C2 with different values of I */

```
#include<stdio.h>
#include<conio.h>
void main()
{
float C1,C2,p;
int i;
clrscr();
printf("\nThe Expressions are \n C1= 30 - 8*p \nC2 =10+p*p\n");
/*printf("Enter the value of p:");
C1 =30 - 8*p;
C2 =10+p*p;      */
printf("\nThe value of C1 and C2 for different range of values of p from
0 to 10");
for(i=0;i<=10;I=i++)
{
C1= 30 - 8*i;
C2 =10+i*i;
printf("\nfor i=%2d the C1 = %7.2f and C2 = %7.2f",i,C1,C2);
}
getch();
}
```

****

Program 62

***/

* Write program to evaluate equation V=P(1+r)n for various combination of P, r and n
P=1000, 2000,…….10000; r=.10,.11,.12……….. .20 ; n=1, 2, 3, 10;

```
#include<conio.h>
#include<stdio.h>
#include<math.h>
```

```
int i,j,k, count=0;
float v[30],p,r,n;
clrscr();
printf("\n ");

for(i=1;i<=3;i++)
  {
   p=1000*i;
     for(j=1;j<=3;j++)
      {
       r=0.10+i*0.01;
       for(k=1;k<=3;k++)
       {
       n=k;
       v[count]=p*pow((1+r),n);
       count++;
       }
      }
    }
    for(i=0;i<count;i++)
printf("\n %f ",v[i]);
getch();
}
```

****

Program 63

****

/*THIS PROGRAM IS TO FIND THE ROOTS OF A QUADRATIC EQUATION */

```
#include<conio.h>
#include<stdio.h>
#include<math.h>
void main()
{
float a,b,c,d,r1,r2;
float real,img,p;
clrscr();
printf("\n\n PROGRAM TO FIND THE ROOTS OF A QUADRATIC EQUATION");
printf("\n\n THE GENERAL FORM OF QUADRATIC EQUATION IS :  ");
printf("\n\n\t ax^2 + bx + c ");
printf("\n\n Enter the values of  'a',  'b',  'c'  of your equation\n ");
scanf("%f %f %f",&a,&b,&c);
d=b*b-4*a*c;

if(d==0)
   {
   printf("\n\n THE ROOTS ARE EQUAL");
   r1=(-b)/(2*a),
   r2=r1;
```

```
    printf("\n\n THE ROOTS ARE r1 = r2 = %f ",r1);
    }
if(d>0)
  {
    printf("\n\n THE ROOTS ARE DISTINCT");
    r1=((-b)+sqrt(d))/(2*a);
    r2=((-b)-sqrt(d))/(2*a);
    printf("\n\n THE ROOTS ARE \n\tr1 = %f \n\tr2 = %f ",r1,r2);
    }
if(d<0)
  {
   p=sqrt(-d);
   real=((-b)/(2*a));
   img=p/2;
   printf("\n\nTHE ROOTS ARE IMAGINARY");
   printf("\n\n THE ROOTS ARE  :");
   printf("\n\n\tr1  = %f +  %f i ",real,img);
   printf("\n\tr1  = %f -  %f i ",real,img);
   }
getch();
  }
```

****

Program 64

****

/* Write a program using pointers to prepare salary slip of the employee. The program is written with Dynamic Memory Allocation. An employee record contain Employee Code, Employee Name, Designation, Basic Pay, DA, HRA, PPF, GPF, Net Pay. DA is computed as 45% of Basic pay, HRA is 10, PPF is 5% and GPF is 10% of basic Pay. Gross Pay is computed as sum of Basic Pay,DA, HRA and Net Pay is computed by deducting PPF & GPF contribution from Gross Pay*/

```
#include<stdio.h>
#include<conio.h>
#include<string.h>
#include<alloc.h>
struct employee
{
 char emp_code[10];
 char emp_name[20];
 char designation[20];
 float basic_pay;
 float da;
 float hra;
 float ppf;
 float gpf;
 float netpay;
 struct employee *next;
 };
```

```
void get_data(struct employee **);
void net_pay(struct employee **);
void main()
{
struct employee *p=NULL;
int choice;
while(1)
{
clrscr();
printf("\n\t Main Menu");
printf("\n\t1. Enter the record of employee:");
printf("\n\t2. Salary slip of employee");
printf("\n\t3. Exit");
printf("\n\n Enter your choice:(1,2,3)");
scanf("%c",&choice);
switch(choice)
{
case 1:get_data(&p);
      break;
case 2:net_pay(&p);
      break;
case 3:exit(1);
      break;
default:printf("\nError!!!!");
       printf("\nWrong choice entered.....");
       getch();
       break;
}
}
}
//*************************
void get_data(struct employee **p)
{
struct employee *q=*p;
struct employee *r,*s;
char choice;
char emp_code[10];
char emp_name[20];
char designation[20];
float basic_pay;
do{
q=*p;
r=(struct employee *) malloc (sizeof(struct employee));
printf("\n\t\tEmployee Record");
printf("\n\t Employee id: ");
fflush(stdin);
gets(emp_code);
```

```
strcpy(r->emp_code,emp_code);
printf("\n\t Employee Name: ");
fflush(stdin);
gets(emp_name);
strcpy(r->emp_name,emp_name);
printf("\n\t Designation: ");
fflush(stdin);
gets(designation);
strcpy(r->designation,designation);
printf("\n\t Employee's basic pay: ");
scanf("%f",&basic_pay);
r->basic_pay=basic_pay;
r->next=NULL;
if(*p=NULL)
*p=r;
else
{
while(q!=NULL)
{
s=q;
q=q->next;
}
if(q==*p)
{
r->next=q;
*p=r;
}
else
{
r->next=q;
s->next=r;
}
}
printf("\n Do you want to add more employee records(y/n): ");
fflush(stdin);
scanf("%c",&choice);
}while(choice=='y'||choice=='Y');
}
//*******************************************
void net_pay(struct employee **p)
{
struct employee *q = *p;
if(q==NULL)
printf("\n No data currently stored");
else
{
q->da =.45 * q->basic_pay;
```

```
q->hra =.10 * q->basic_pay;
q->ppf =.05 * q->basic_pay;
q->gpf =.10 * q->basic_pay;
q->netpay = (q->basic_pay + q->da + q->hra) -(q->ppf + q->gpf);
printf("\n The employee's salary is: %d",q->netpay);
}
}
```

****

EXERCISE

Write a program in C using structures which maintains the records of students (roll_no, name, hostel_no, physics marks, chemistry marks, math marks). Write functions which computes the following.

1. Find the student who scored the maximum marks (Topper)
2. Find average marks in Physics.
3. Find Averge marks in Chemistry.
4. Find Average Marks in Mathematics.
5. Find students who lives in a particular Hostel.
6. To add 10% bouus marks to all the students in individual subject.

Program 65

****

```
#include<stdio.h>
#include<conio.h>
#include<alloc.h>
#include<process.h>
#include<string.h>
#define NULL 0

struct student
 {
 int roll_number;
 char name[30];
 int hostel_no;
 float physics;
 float chemistry;
 float maths;
 struct student *next;
 };
void get_data(struct student **);
void maximum(struct student **);
void average(struct student **,char *);
void hostel(struct student **);
void bonus(struct student **);

void main()
 {
```

```
struct student *p=NULL;
int choice;
while(1)
 {
  clrscr();
 printf("\n\t1. ENTER RECORD OF STUDENT");
 printf("\n\t2. MAX MARKS OF TOPPER");
 printf("\n\t3. AV_MARKS_PHYSICS");
 printf("\n\t4. AV_MARKS_MATHS");
 printf("\n\t5. AV_MARKS_CHEMISTRY");
 printf("\n\t6. DISPLAY RECORD OF STUDENT ACCORDING TO HOSTEL NO.");
 printf("\n\t7 ADD BONUS MARKS");
 printf("\n\t8. EXIT");
 printf("\n\tENTER YOUR CHOICE(1,2,3,4,5,6,7,8): ");
  scanf("%d",&choice);
   switch(choice)
   {
   case 1:get_data(&p);
          break;
   case 2:maximum(&p);
          break;
   case 3:average(&p,"PHYSICS");
          break;
   case 4:average(&p,"MATHS");
          break;
   case 5:average(&p,"CHEMISTRY");
          break;
   case 6:hostel(&p);
          break;
   case 7:bonus(&p);
          break;
   case 8:exit(1);
          break;
      default:printf("\n\tERROR!!!!!");
            printf("\n\tWRONG CHOICE ENTERED....");
            getch();
            break;
     }/*end of switch-case*/
   }/*end of while*/
 }/*end of main*/

void get_data(struct student **p)
 {
   struct student *q = *p;
   struct student *r,*s;
   char choice;
   int roll_number;
   char name[30];
```

```
    int hostel_no;
    float physics;
    float chemistry;
    float maths;
    do
    {
    q=*p;
    r = (struct student*)malloc(sizeof(struct student));
    printf("\n\t******STUDENT RECORD*****");
    printf("\n\tNAME : ");
    fflush(stdin);
    gets(name);
    strcpy(r->name,name);
    printf("\n\tROLL NUMBER : ");
    scanf("%d",&roll_number);
    r->roll_number = roll_number;
    printf("\n\tHOSTEL NO. : ");
    scanf("%d",&hostel_no);
    r->hostel_no = hostel_no;
    printf("\n\tPHYSICS MARKS : ");
    scanf("%f",&physics);
    r->physics = physics;
    printf("\n\tCHEMISTRY MARKS : ");
    scanf("%f",&chemistry);
    r->chemistry = chemistry;
    printf("\n\tMATHS MARKS : ");
    scanf("%f",&maths);
    r->maths = maths;
    r->next = NULL;
    if(*p==NULL)
     *p=r;
    else
     {
     while(((r->physics + r->maths + r->chemistry)<=(q->physics + q->maths
+  q->chemistry))&&q!=NULL)
       {
        s=q;
        q=q->next;
       }
      if(q==*p)
       {
        r->next=q;
        *p=r;
       }
      else
       {
        r->next=q;
        s->next=r;
```

```
      }
    }
   printf("\n\tDO YOU WANT TO ADD MORE RECORDS(Y/N): ");
   fflush(stdin);
   scanf("%c",&choice);
   }while(choice=='y' || choice=='Y');
 }

void maximum(struct student **p)
 {
   struct student *q = *p;
   if(q==NULL)
    printf("\n\tNO RECORDS CURRENTLY STORED");
   else
    {
     printf("\n\t******MAXIMUM MARKS OF TOPPER********");
     printf("\n\tPHYSICS : %f",q->physics);
     printf("\n\tCHEMISTRY : %f",q->chemistry);
     printf("\n\tMATHS : %f",q->maths);
     printf("\n\tTOTAL : %f",(q->physics + q->chemistry + q->maths));
    }
   getch();
 }

void average(struct student **p,char *c)
 {
   struct student *q=*p;
   int i=0;
   float total = 0;
   if(q==NULL)
    printf("\n\tNO RECORDS CURRENTLY STORED");
   if(strcmpi("physics",c))
    {
     while(q!=NULL)
      {
       total = total + q->physics;
       i++;
       q = q->next;
      }
    }
   else
    {
     if(strcmpi("chemistry",c))
      {
       while(q!=NULL)
      {
       total = total + q->physics;
       i++;
```

```
        q = q->next;
       }
       }
      else
       {
        if(strcmpi("physics",c))
       {
        while(q!=NULL)
         {
          total = total + q->physics;
          i++;
          q = q->next;
         }
       }
       }
     }
    printf("\n\tAVERAGE MARKS IN %s : %f",c,(total/i));
    getch();
 }

void hostel(struct student **p)
 {
    struct student *r=*p;
    int n;
    if(r==NULL)
     printf("\n\tNO RECORDS CURRENTLY STORED");
    else
     {
      printf("\n\tENTER THE HOSTEL NO. : ");
      scanf("%d",&n);
      printf("\n\t******STUDENT RECORD*****");
      while(r!=NULL)
       {
        if(r->hostel_no==n)
       {
        printf("\n\tNAME : %s",r->name);
        printf("\n\tROLL NUMBER : %d",r->roll_number);
        printf("\n\tPHYSICS MARKS : %f",r->physics);
        printf("\n\tCHEMISTRY MARKS : %f",r->chemistry);
        printf("\n\tMATHS MARKS : %f\n",r->maths);
       }
        r=r->next;
       }
     }
    getch();
 }

void bonus(struct student **p)
```

```
{
  struct student *q = *p;
  int n;
  if(q==NULL)
   printf("\n\tNO RECORDS CURRENTLY STORED");
  else
   {
    printf("\n\tENTER THE STUDENT ROLL NUMBER :");
    scanf("%d",&n);
    while(q!=NULL && q->roll_number!=n)
     q=q->next;
    if(q->roll_number==n)
     {
      q->physics = q->physics + (0.10 * q->physics);
      q->chemistry = q->chemistry + (0.10 * q->chemistry);
      q->maths = q->maths + (0.10 * q->maths);
     }
    else
     {
      printf("\n\tNO RECORD CORRESPONDING TO THIS ROLL NUMBER EXISTS");
      getch();
     }
   }
}
```

****

OUPUT

****

1. ENTER RECORD OF STUDENT
2. MAX MARKS OF TOPPER
3. AV_MARKS_PHYSICS
4. AV_MARKS_MATHS
5. AV_MARKS_CHEMISTRY
6. DISPLAY RECORD OF STUDENT ACCORDING TO HOSTEL NO.
7. ADD BONUS MARKS
8. EXIT

ENTER YOUR CHOICE(1,2,3,4,5,6,7,8): 1
******STUDENT RECORD*****
NAME : Shyam
ROLL NUMBER : 1
HOSTEL NO. : 5
PHYSICS MARKS : 97
CHEMISTRY MARKS : 95
MATHS MARKS : 98

```
DO YOU WANT TO ADD MORE RECORDS(Y/N): y
******STUDENT RECORD*****
NAME : Gaurav
ROLL NUMBER : 3
HOSTEL NO. : 3
PHYSICS MARKS : 96
CHEMISTRY MARKS : 86
MATHS MARKS : 92

DO YOU WANT TO ADD MORE RECORDS(Y/N): n
```

MAXIMUM MARKS OF THE TOPPER

```
1. ENTER RECORD OF STUDENT
2. MAX MARKS OF TOPPER
3. AV_MARKS_PHYSICS
4. AV_MARKS_MATHS
5. AV_MARKS_CHEMISTRY
6. DISPLAY RECORD OF STUDENT ACCORDING TO HOSTEL NO.
7. ADD BONUS MARKS
8. EXIT
ENTER YOUR CHOICE(1,2,3,4,5,6,7,8): 2

******MAXIMUM MARKS OF TOPPER********
PHYSICS : 97.000000
CHEMISTRY : 95.000000
MATHS : 98.000000
TOTAL : 290.000000
```

AVERAGE MARKS IN VARIOUS SUBJECTS

```
1. ENTER RECORD OF STUDENT
2. MAX MARKS OF TOPPER
3. AV_MARKS_PHYSICS
4. AV_MARKS_MATHS
5. AV_MARKS_CHEMISTRY
6. DISPLAY RECORD OF STUDENT ACCORDING TO HOSTEL NO.
7. ADD BONUS MARKS
8. EXIT
ENTER YOUR CHOICE(1,2,3,4,5,6,7,8): 3
AVERAGE MARKS IN PHYSICS : 96.000000
*****************************************************************************
```

SELECTED EXERCISES

1. Define the overall structure of a C program. Explain in brief the role of the comment lines.
2. What are the Data Type? List the various categories from which the Character Set of C is formed.
3. What are Constants? How they are declared in the Program. Discuss various types of constant declared in C.
4. What are variables? How the value are assigned to variables.
5. Which of the following are invalid constant and why?
   0.234 4 * 566 "2xbnbf%" -12.34 0.00001
6. What do you mean by Static Memory Allocation? What are the disadvantages of it?
7. What is Dynamic Memory Allocation? Discuss the main advantage of Dynamic Memory Allocation.
8. What are the difference between an array & structure?
9. Give the general syntax for the declaration of structure? Is it possible to define a member of structure as a structure itself?
10. What are structure variable? How are the they initialized?
11. What do you understand by array of structure? How the array of structures are declared and initialized?
12. Define a structure that contain following three members:
    (i) Character array with length of 50. (Name)
    (ii) Floating point quantity (Age)
    (iii) Structure containing two integer (phone numbers)
13. Is it possible to pass entire structure to a function? If yes then How?
14. How can an individual member of a structure be accessed by pointer.
15. What are pointers and how are they initialized?
16. List the different kind of object that can be associated with pointer variable?
17. Is it possible to pass a part of an array to function? If yes then how?
18. Describe the two different ways to specify the address of array element?
19. How can a multidimensional array defined in terms of a pointer to collection of contiguous array?
20. Give different ways to initialize the values to member of a structure.
21. What are memory locations? Who determines the memory requirement after the declaration of an array?
22. What do you mean by pointer arithmetic?
23. How the memory is allocated using 'malloc' statement?
24. Discuss various preprocessor directives?
25. While declaring an array of integers, how the address of all the memory locations are determined to be used by pointers?
26. What are Function? Why dividing the main logic of a problem in to the pieces is considered to be good programming strategy.
27. What is the difference between standard library function and user defined function? State with suitable example.
28. Give the general syntax of User Defined Functions.
29. What do you mean by a Call to a function? Can a function call another function in C?
30. What are Global variable? State the scope of Global Variables? How are they declared?
31. What are Local Variable? state the scope fo local variables.
32. What do you mean by the Storage Class?
33. Explain the key difference between Auto, Static, External & Register Variable.
34. How and When Register Variable are declared and used.
35. What to you mean by Parameter Passing?
36. Explain the "Call by Value" parameter passing.
37. Is it possible to have "Call by Reference" parameter passing mechanism in C?
38. What do you mean by Recursion? How it is different than Iteration?
39. Write a function which return a maximum of three integers.
40. Write a program in C that prints the lower case letter and digit "0....9" and returns their ASCII value.

41. What is the purpose of return statement?
42. What are function prototypes? What is the purpose of function prototypes?
43. What are the differences between actual argument & formal argument?
44. How the local variable declared inside a function are interpreted when there is a recursive call?
45. List some of the advantages of using recursion.
46. What is the difference between Relational operator & Logical operator? Explain with a suitable example.
47. What are Library function? How are they used?
48. What is a String? Write statement in C to read five names from the input.
49. What are Short Hand operator?
50. State with the example, the difference between postfix operator & prefix operators.
51. Write a program in C to evaluate following expressions:
    (i) V= U + A*T
    (ii) S= U*T + 1/2 **A*** T^2
52. Write a program in C to find the root of Quadratic Equation.
53. Write a prgram to convert Pounds & Ounces to Kilogram & Grams.
54. Consider following code
    (i) Int I=10, J=11,K=13;
    (ii) I += J += K += 7;
55. Write a equivalent statement that is fully parenthesized.
56. What are control structure? What is a nested IF Statement?
57. What is advantage of CASE Statement? Can it be a replacement for IF statement? If not, Justify your answer.
58. What is the use of Continue statement in C language?
59. Why the use of GOTO statement is discouraged? Give reason why break statement is considered Harmful.
60. Give the syntax of following control structure:
    (i) For statement
    (ii) While Statement
    (iii) Do While Statement
61. What do you mean by formatted output? Give the frequently used format symbol to ouput a floating number.
62. Distinguish between the Local & Global Variables.
63. What are Identifiers? How a user defined identifier different from a keyword ?
64. Why is C called a Structured Programming Language ?
65. Discuss the role of qualifiers, Constant and Volatile.
66. Write a formatted input statement for following input data:
    (i) “s52”
    (ii) 12.345
    (iii) 101
67. Write a C program to read a string and print it in a reverse order.
68. Write a iterative program to compute the factorial of a number.
69. Write a program to read a statement and print the total number of character in it.
70. Write program in C to convert all lower case letter to upper case.
71. What is the condition to be satisfied by the all element of an array?
72. What are subscripts? How they are written?
73. What is the advantage of declaring an array size in terms of symbolic constant over fixed integer quantity?
74. How are arrays processed in C? Can entire array be processed with single instruction without repetition?
75. How are multidimensional arrays defined? How is the values to the multidimensional arrays are assigned?
76. What values are assigned to array when they are not initialized?

INDEX

E

F

G

H

I

J

K

L

M

N

O

P

Q

R

S

T

U

V

W